LOOK AT
STONY STRATFORD

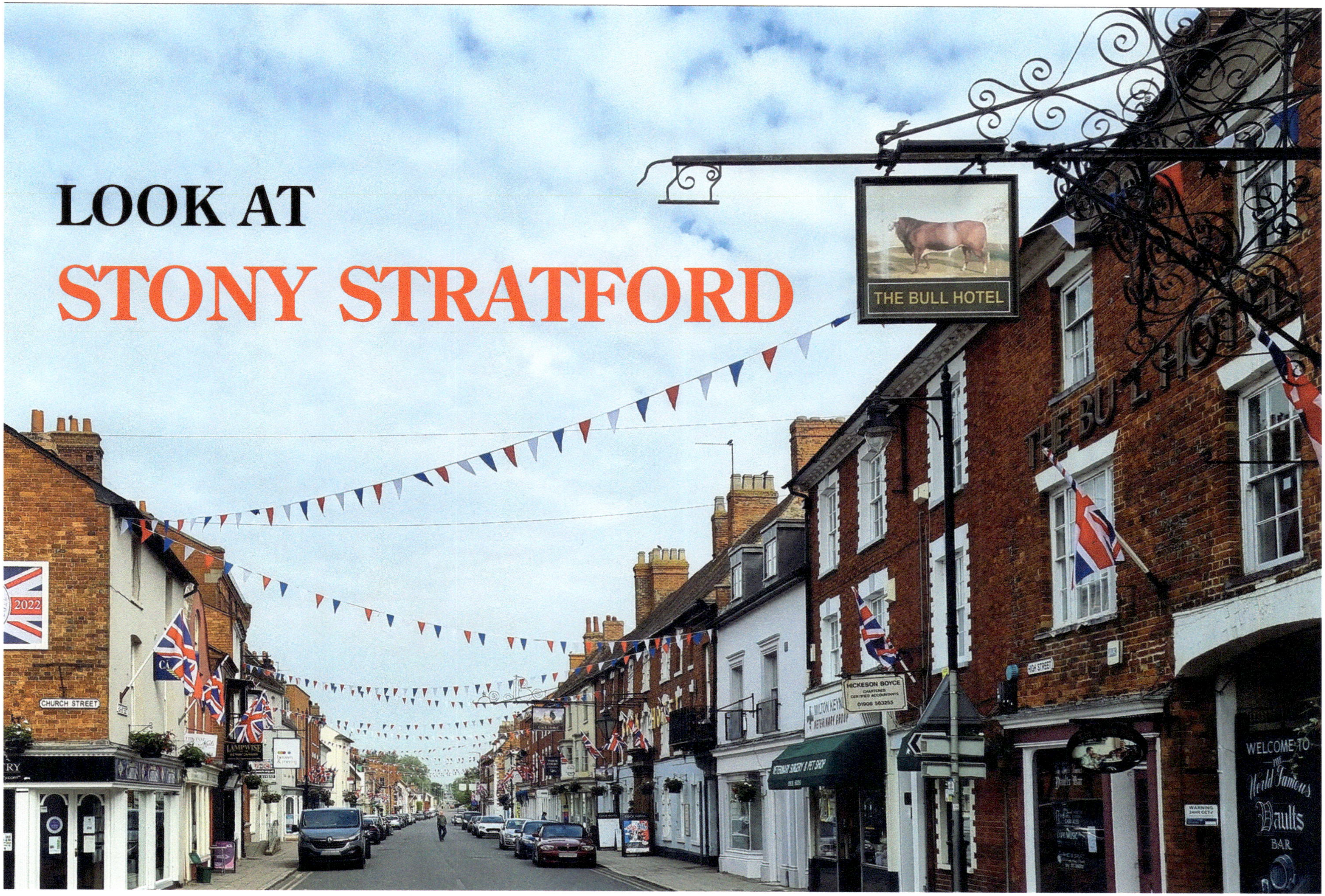

LOOK AT STONY STRATFORD

Published by Magic Flute Publishing Ltd. 2023
ISBN 978-1-915166-15-9

Magic Flute Publishing Limited

231 Swanwick Lane

Southampton SO31 7GT

www.magicflutepublishing.com

A catalogue description of this book is available from the British Library

MAGIC FLUTE
PUBLISHING

Contents

To Begin at the Beginning

Unlike the majority of old towns and villages in England, we do have some idea when Stony Stratford started. In the 12th century there were fields and meadows on either side of the highway known as Watling Street. The villagers of Wolverton and Calverton mostly clustered around the manor houses and the churches and we can imagine that nobody saw much point in living beside the road, but at some time after 1180 some saw the potential of serving the limited traffic on the Watling Street. From archaeological and some documentary evidence we know that three roadside strip lots were granted by Lord Hamon of Wolverton. These lots were exactly on the land now occupied by the *Cock* and the *Bull*. Each fronted the road on the Wolverton side and stretched back to the east to occupy about one acre each. It is assumed that they provided services to travellers, offering at least one inn, pasture, stabling and farrier services.

Up to the 19th century it was believed that Stony Stratford was a Roman settlement. Documentary evidence recorded a camp at *Magiovintum*, beside the River Ouzel at Fenny Stratford and *Lactodorum*. It seemed obvious that *Lactodorum* would be beside the River Ouse crossing, but it would appear not. No archaeological evidence of Roman settlement has been discovered either side of the river and it was later realised that *Lactodorum* was a camp at Towcester.

From these medieval beginnings the settlement grew rapidly. The commercial success of these pioneers led to further grants along the street, to the north of the *Cock*, and, not to be outdone, similar lots were portioned off on the Calverton side. The best illustration of the power of this commercial activity was that Gilbert de Basset, who owned the Calverton manor, secured a warrant from King Richard I to establish a market in 1184. This of course became the basis of what we know now as the market square.

In 1215 King John stayed here for three days, and given that the king's party was bound to be large, some 200 people, beasts of burden, wagons and horses, this was a good indication of how quickly the town had grown. In 1290, when Queen Eleanor's cortege made its journey from Lincoln to London, Stony Stratford was one of the stopping places, a sure sign of its ability to accommodate large parties. The night before the cortege had stayed at Delapré Abbey in Northampton and after leaving Stony Stratford proceeded to Woburn Abbey. During the Middle Ages, only abbeys had the facilities to accommodate travellers and this marks out Stony Stratford as unique. Had it not come into existence travellers would have to make their way to Bradwell Priory.

By the end of the 13th century, the chapelries of St Mary Magdalen on the Wolverton side, and St Giles on the Calverton side of the street, became churches, so within a space about 100 years Stony Stratford had become an important roadside town.

So as we start our journey through Stony Stratford, we can stand at the corner of the High Street and Church Street, knowing that over 850 years ago there was nothing but open fields on either side of the Watling Street.

Several major inns had become well established on the east side by 1500. The *Cock* is mentioned in a deed in 1529 and rival establishments such as the *Swan* and the *Red Lion* were situated to the north. There was also an inn for carters, known as the *Horseshoe*. The *Bull* does not make an appearance in any document until 1609, although it is fair to assume that it was operating many years before that. The west side inns tended to be smaller establishments. It is not altogether clear why this was the case but it may be due to the amount of land available. The course of the River Ouse limited the amount of land for growing crops and for grazing pasture. Inns had to be self-sufficient enterprises in medieval times.

The story of Stony Stratford, up to the creation of the railway in 1838, was that of an important roadside town.

LOOK AT THE BEGINNING

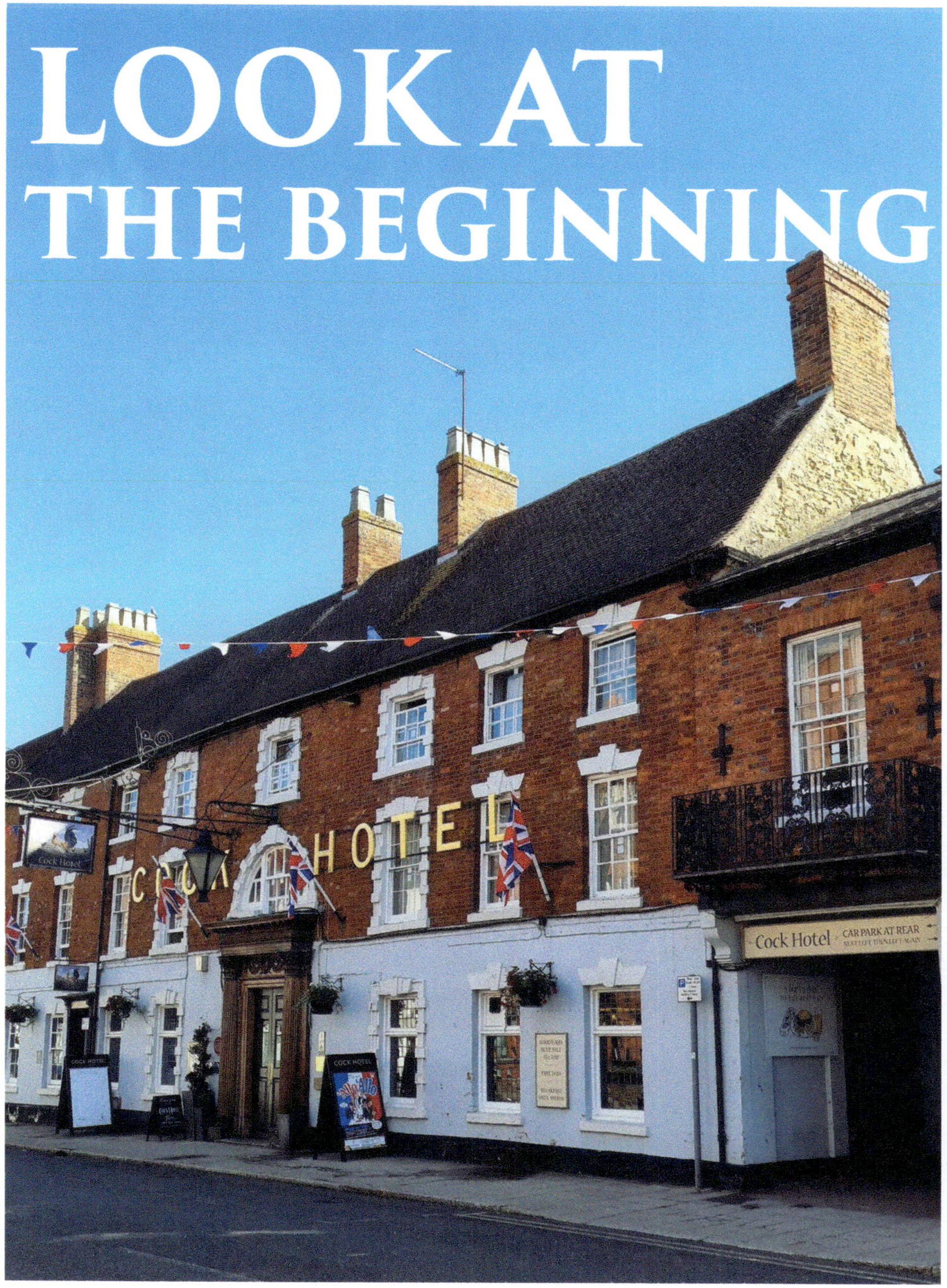

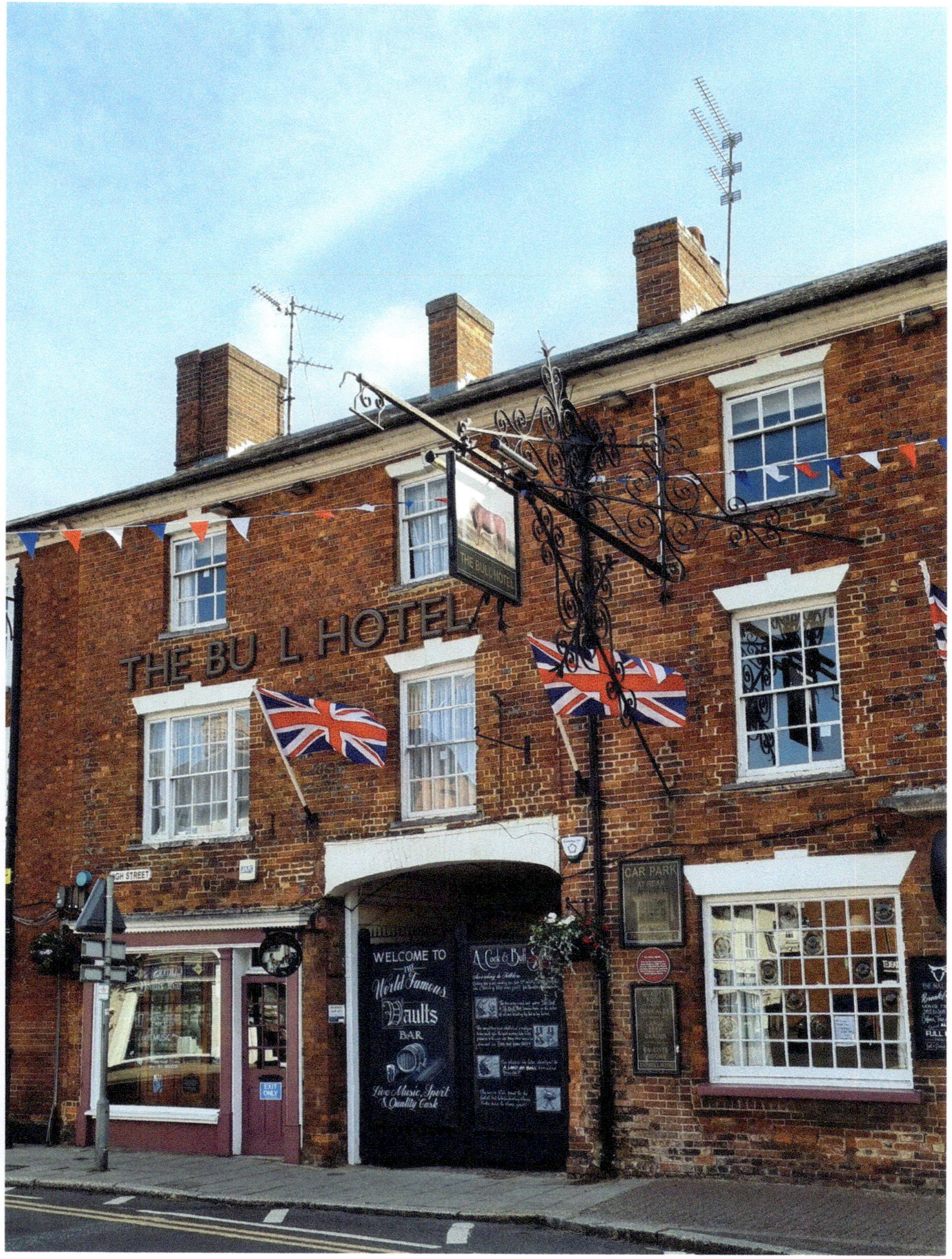

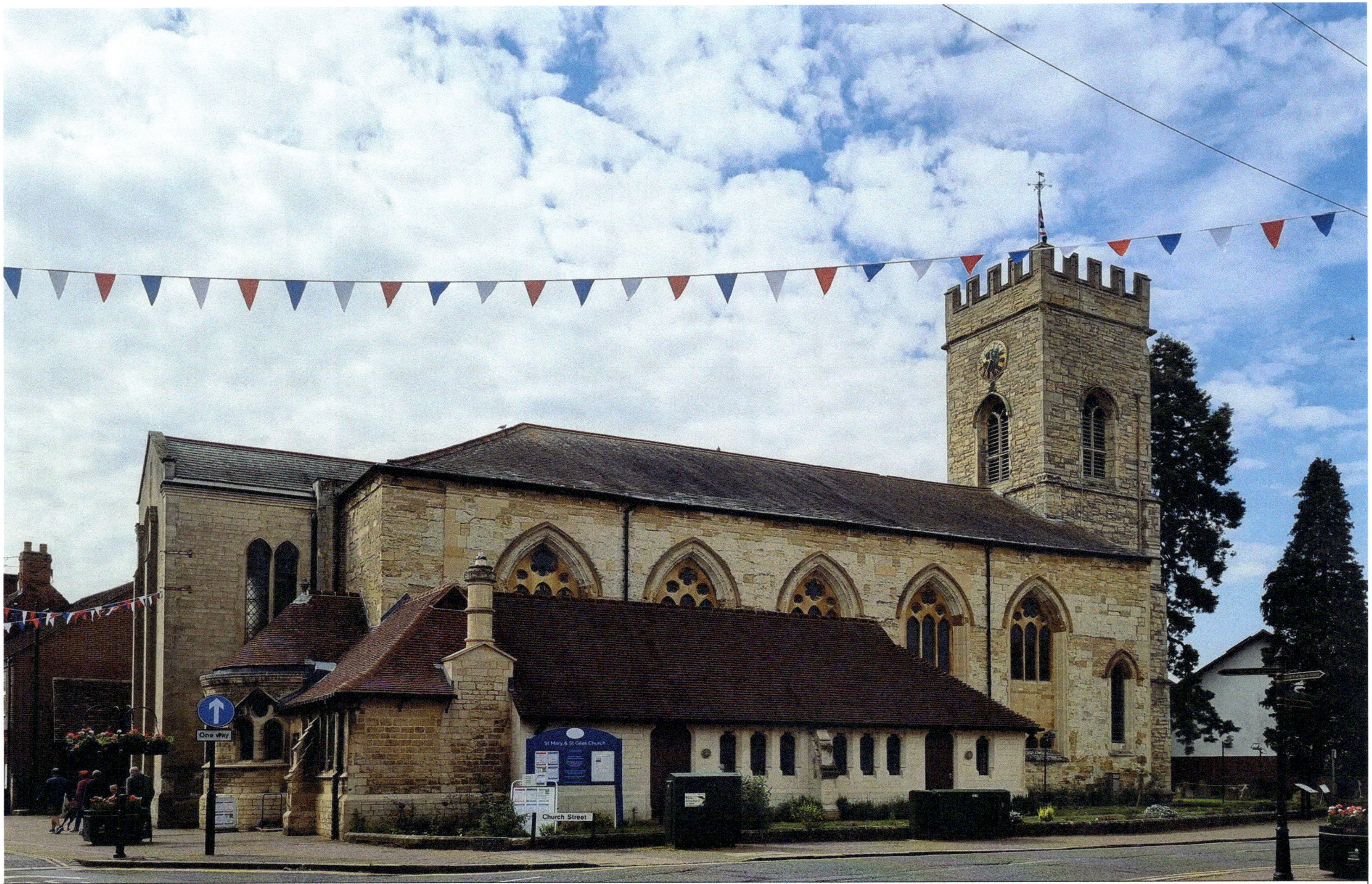

St. Giles Church sits on the Calverton side of the street at the centre of Stony Stratford. The building dates from the late 19th century, although it has been much changed over the centuries.

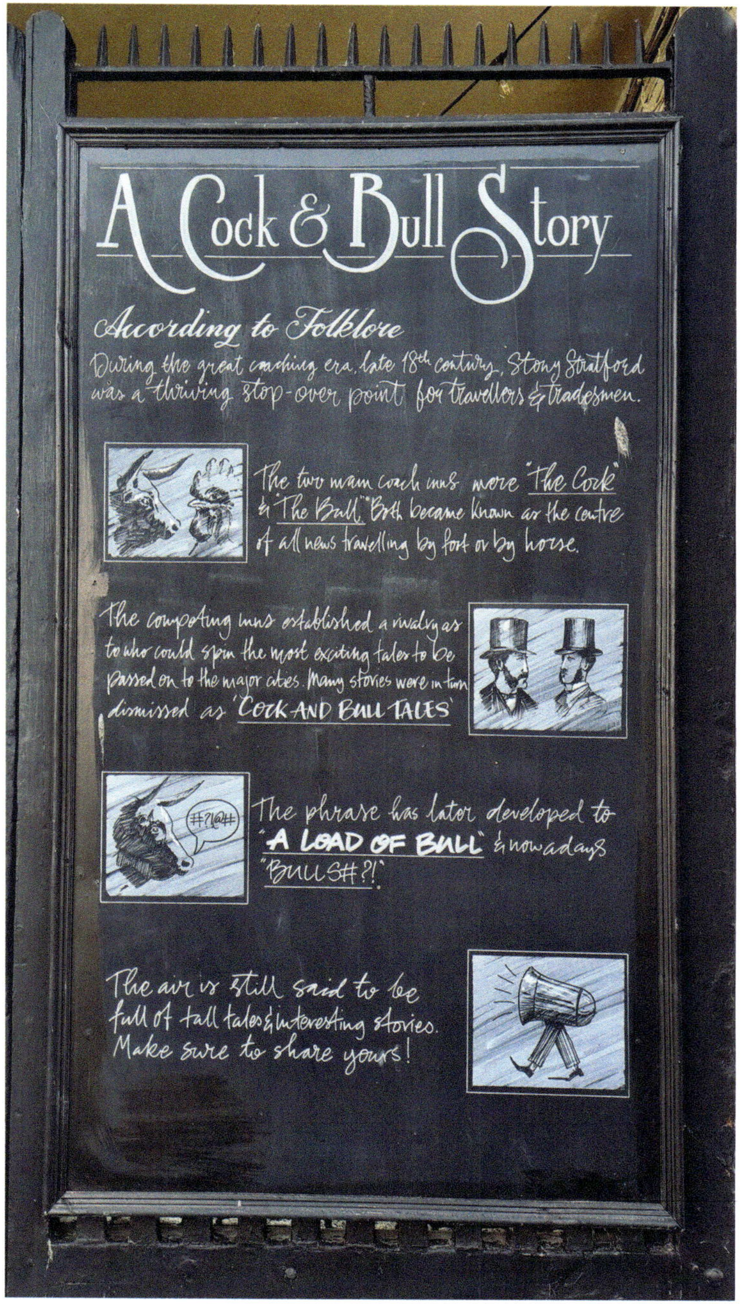

A Cock and Bull Story

Almost side by side in the centre of Stony Stratford and almost the same in size and appearance, *The Cock and The Bull* are prominent features of the town. Whatever their origins, by the 17th century they were, with the exception of the *Swan* and the *Horseshoe*, the two largest inns in the town, and since the *Horseshoe* was mainly an inn for wagoners, the *Cock*, the *Bull* and the *Swan* had the quality trade between them.

The phrase "a cock and bull story" is usually applied to a story which is slightly preposterous or fanciful - a bit of a tall tale. It has certainly slipped into common language. Where did it come from? The truth is that nobody knows how the phrase came into being. Local legend certainly has it that the rivalry between the two High Street inns extended to the telling of traveller's tales, bragging rights going to the inn that could boast the most entertaining tales. Thus the phrase "Cock and Bull story" came to be applied to any story that you might doubt the truth of - "That's a bit of a Cock and Bull Story!"

The Cock, as a figure in story telling, has a very old tradition. It features in Chaucer and other medieval writers. Usually the tales were told in a comic tradition so the cock is never a serious figure. The Bull scarcely has a literary pedigree other than perhaps the minotaur of myth and tends to be seen as a dangerous and threatening animal - not material for comedy.

Therefore, the first written reference to a cock and a bull in the same sentence is found in a book entitled *The Anatomy of Melancholy* by Robert Burton written in 1621:

> Some men's whole delight is to take tobacco, and drink all day long in a tavern or alehouse, to discourse, sing, jest, roar, talk of a Cock and Bull over a pot.

This does not take us very far. However, the habit of talking rubbish over a pint in a bar dies hard, and it may be that "a cock and bull story" was associated with such talk. In the great coaching age the *Cock* and the *Bull* in Stony Stratford became famous and the phrase may have become associated with these two inns.

There are those who argue that the phrase does not have its origin in Stony Stratford. They may be right, but why spoil a good story?

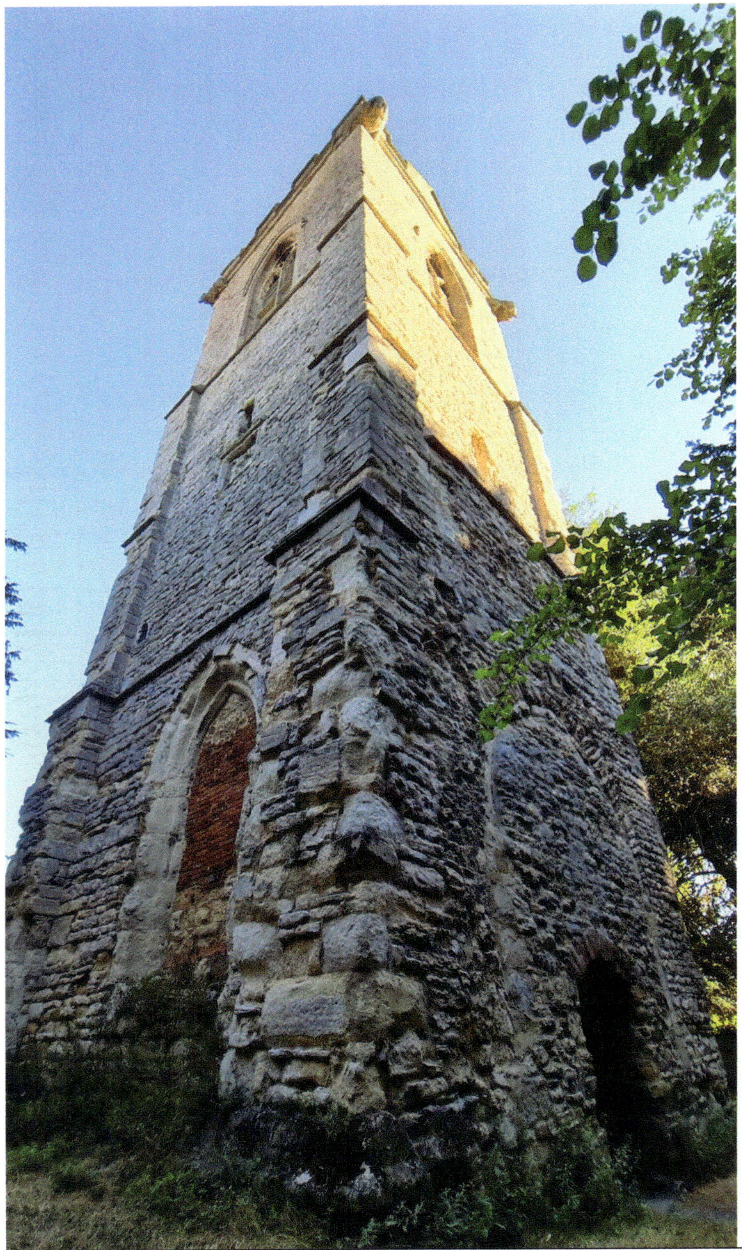

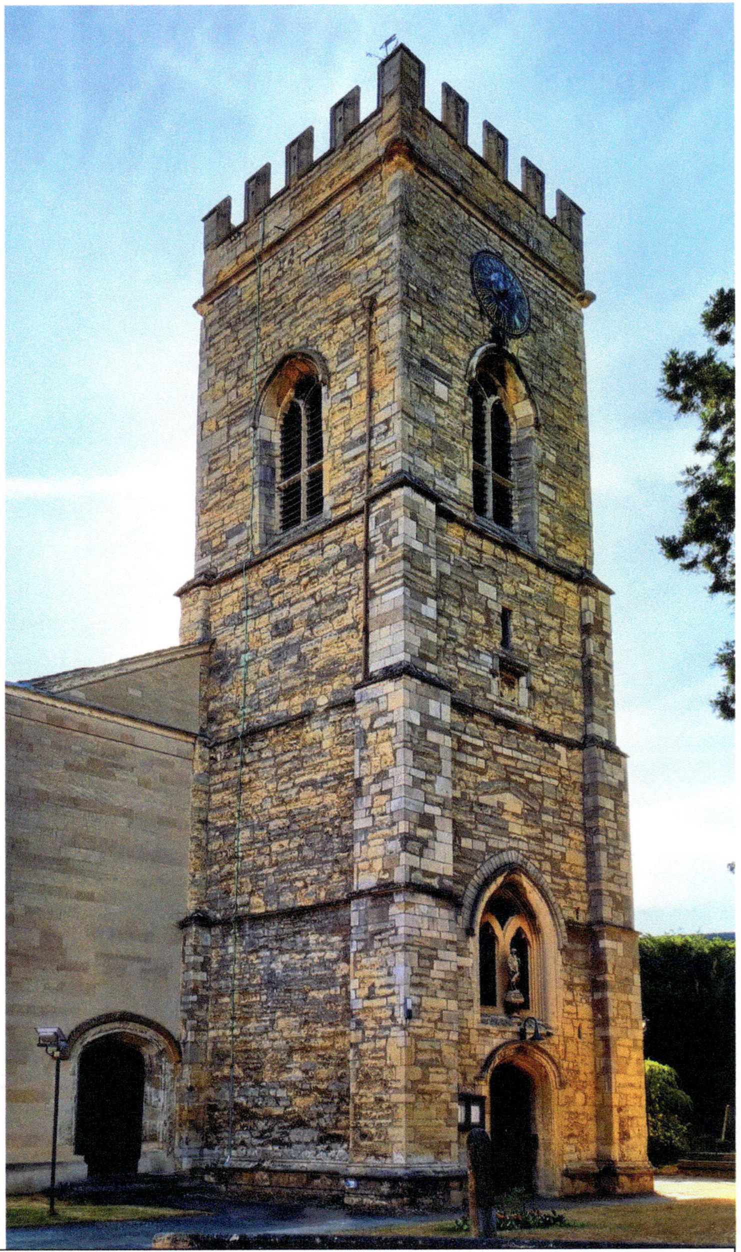

Left: The abandoned tower of St Mary Magdalen. Right: St Giles.

ONE STREET, TWO PARISHES

The Watling Street marked the boundary between the Wolverton and Calverton manors. Thus, Stony Stratford grew under two jurisdictions, which became two parishes. One served the Wolverton side, St Mary Magdalene; the Calverton side was served by St Giles. Both survived to the 20th century. The churches were founded near the end of the 13th century. St Mary Magdalene was destroyed by fire in 1742.

There were attempts to restore it, but the drive for money got no further than a contribution from Browne Willis of Whaddon Hall to rebuid the tower.

The townspeople then concluded that St Giles would meet the needs of both parishes and there was no need to rebuild the church. Parish records were still kept separately, so that births, marrriages and burials, although conducted in the St Giles Church, were still entered in the St Mary register - a practice that continued to 1837.

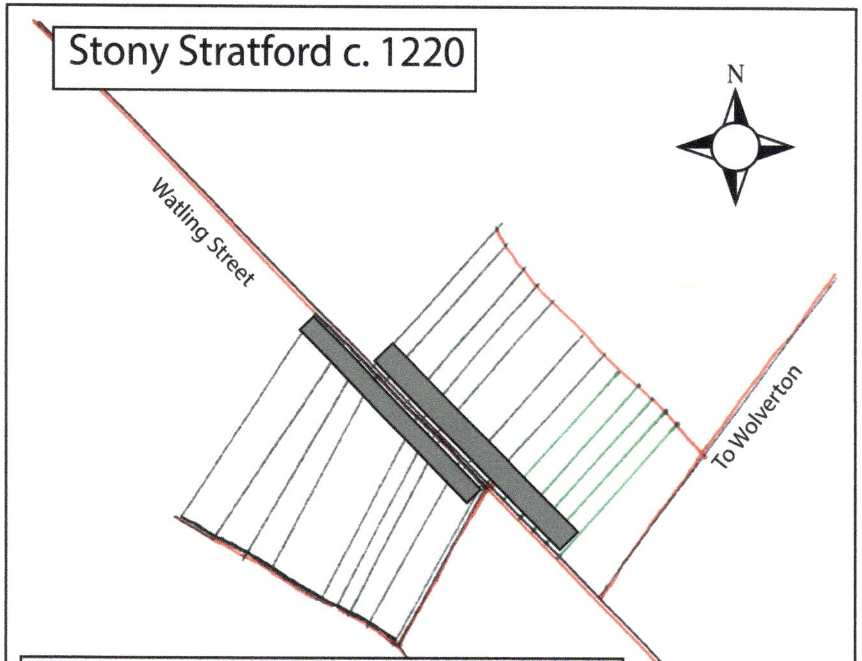

There were 19 houses on burgage plots during the years 1200-1230. Archaeological work suggests that this might be a possible plan. The churches had not been built or were at best chapels of ease.

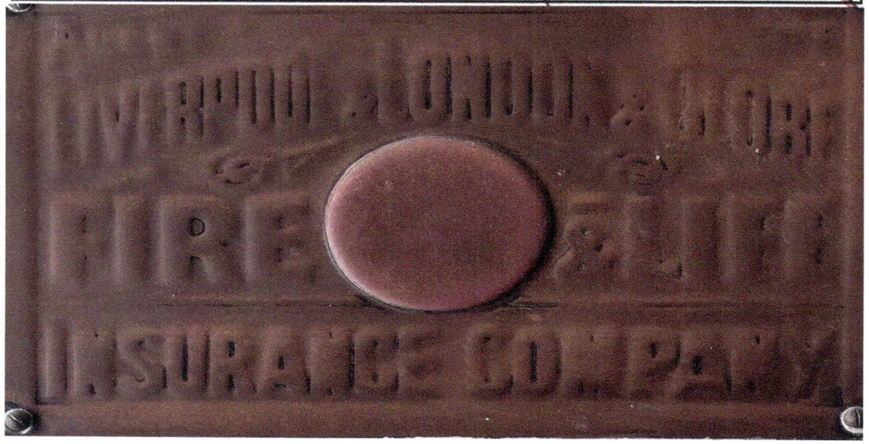

The Great Fire of 1742

It will not escape anyone's notice that all of the buildings north of the *Bull* are either 18th or 19th century buildings.

Very little of medieval Stony Stratford survives. An accidental fire started in *The Bull* in 1742. It got out of control and was driven by a strong wind up that side of the High Street and, as everyone still had thatched roofs, all buildings were destroyed.

The fire was caused by a chambermaid who was drying sheets before an open fire. One of them singed, and fearful of getting into trouble, the girl stuffed the sheet up the chimney. The consequences were dire and much of medieval Stony Stratford was destroyed. Fortunately, almost everyone had insurance - an earlier fire in 1736 that started in Church Lane, also devoured much of the west side of the High Street, so many property owners had taken out fire insurance. The great inns on the east side - *The Cock*, *The Bull*, *The Three Swans*, *The Red Lion* and *The Horseshoe*, were quickly rebuilt.

Today the frontages of the *Bull* and the *Cock* are classic 18th century buildings. This was also the age of the stage coach, so each establishment has a high arched entrance to allow the coaches to enter the yard.

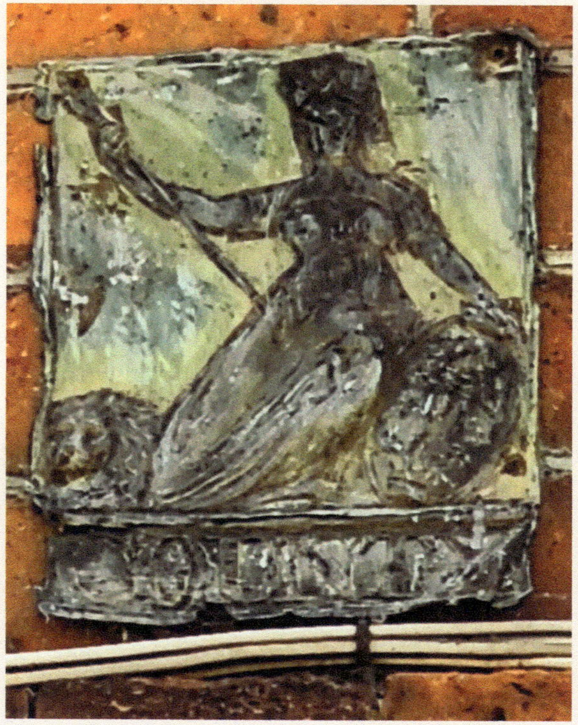

Two Fire Insurance signs.
It was customary to display these signs on the outside walls to reassure the general public that the building was insured.

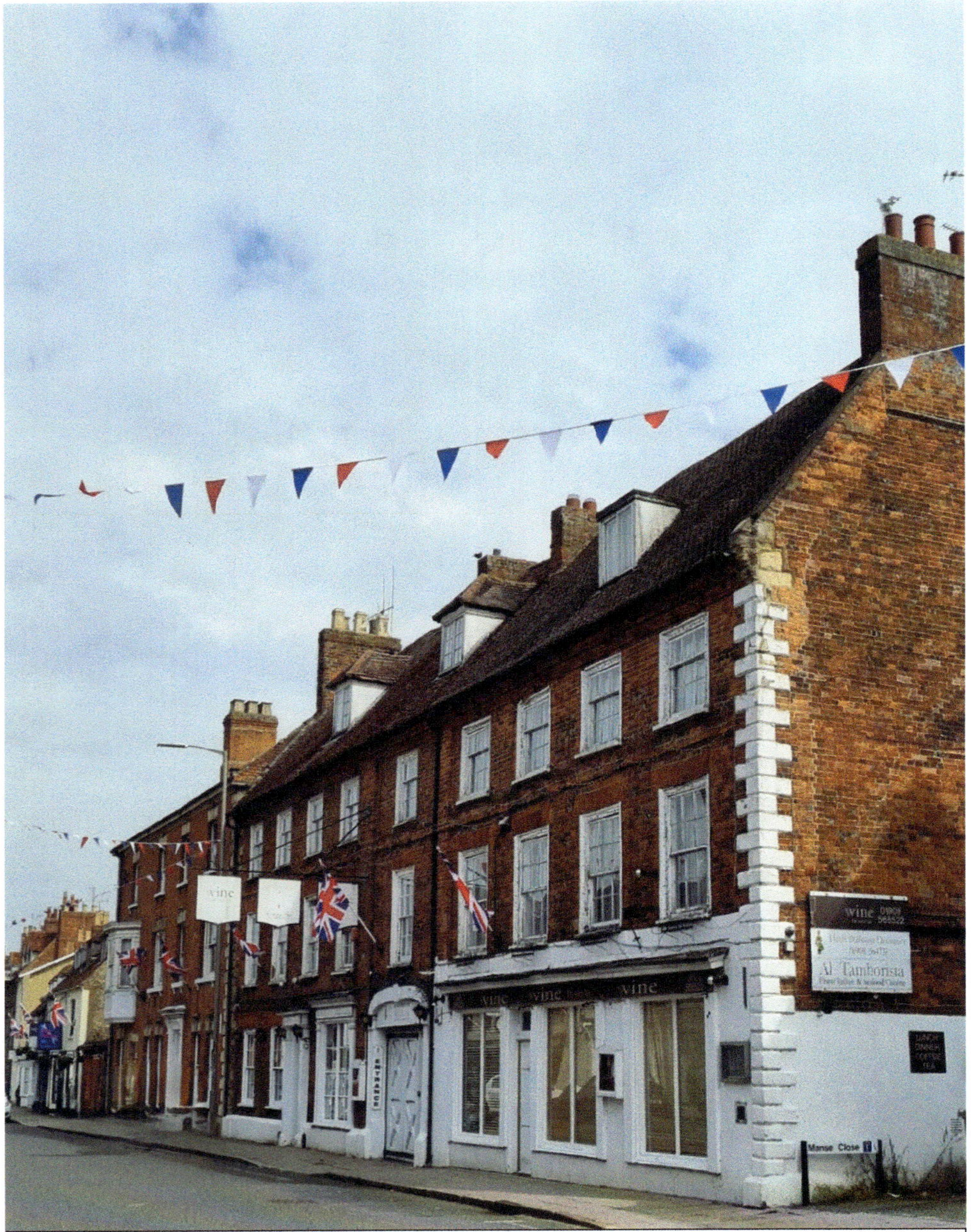

The former Three Swans hotel, re-built after 1742.

THE THREE SWANS

This building was once known as the *Three Swans*. It had been the site of the *Swan* since medieval times, but it was rebuilt in 1687 and given its new name. As with all other buildings on this side of the street it was destroyed by the great fire of 1742 and rebuilt in its present form.

The central arch is the tell tale sign that this was once an inn.

The size of the buildings show us that it would rival the *Cock* and the *Bull* in its size and amenities, but toward the end of the 18th century, the hotel was evidently no longer viable. The owner, a widow called Mrs Ann Whittaker, decided to sell up and retire and it took three days for the auctioneer to sell the contents. She could not sell the property as the land was still owned by the Radcliffe Trust, which therefore owned all the buildings on this land. There was no interest in taking it on as an inn, so in 1802 it was sold to Thomas Harrison, who probably converted the building to apartments.

At 10 o'clock on the morning of Monday 25th November 1782, the auctioneer John Day opened the sale of all of the property of the aged and ailing Mrs. Ann Whittaker. She and her husband had been tenants of the Three Swans since 1759. William Whittaker had died in 1763 and for almost 20 years she had gamely ran the business of one of Stony Stratford's larger inns. This marked the end of an era.

The sale took three days so there was a large inventory. The amount of money the sale realised was unreported.

This was still the 'golden age of coaching.' Improvements in the quality of roads and the efficiency of the stage system raised the average speed of a fast coach to 12 miles per hour. This meant that Stony Stratford, which may have been a day's journey from London at the beginning of the century, could now be accomplished in half a day.

Overnight stops must have been much reduced as travellers could speed on a further 50 miles before bedding down for the night.

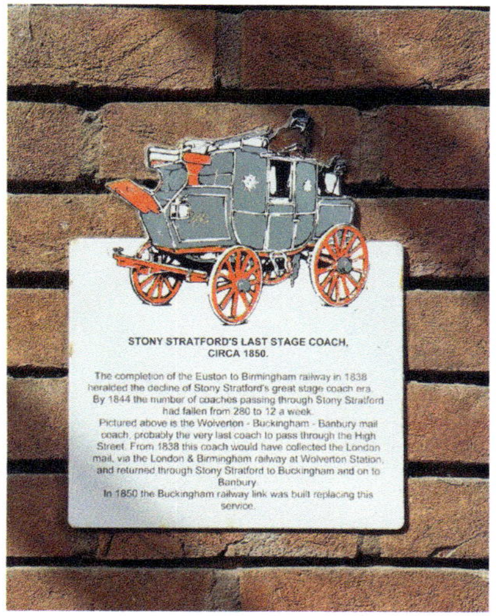

The next revolution was to come in 1838, when the steam train halved the journey time yet again. A full day travelling from London to Birmingham by express coach was cut to a mere morning's travel.

This led to a serious downturn in Stony Stratford's economy. The *Bull* struggled but the *Cock*, possibly because they had the freehold, managed better in the mid-19th century.

Around 1600 a play called *Sir John Oldcastle* appeared on the London stage. It was a collaborative effort between Michael Drayton, Anthony Munday, Robert Wilson and Robert Hathaway. It is not a great piece of literature, but Stony Stratford (probably thinking of the Horseshoe Inn), does get a mention.

The lines come from Act V Scene II:
A high road near St Albans

[Enter Hostler.]
HOSTLER. What, gaffer Club? Welcome to Saint Albans. How does all our friends in Lancashire?
CLUB. Well, God have mercy, John; how does Tom; where's he?
HOSTLER. O, Tom is gone from hence; he's at the three horse-loaves at Stony-stratford. How does old Dick Dunne?

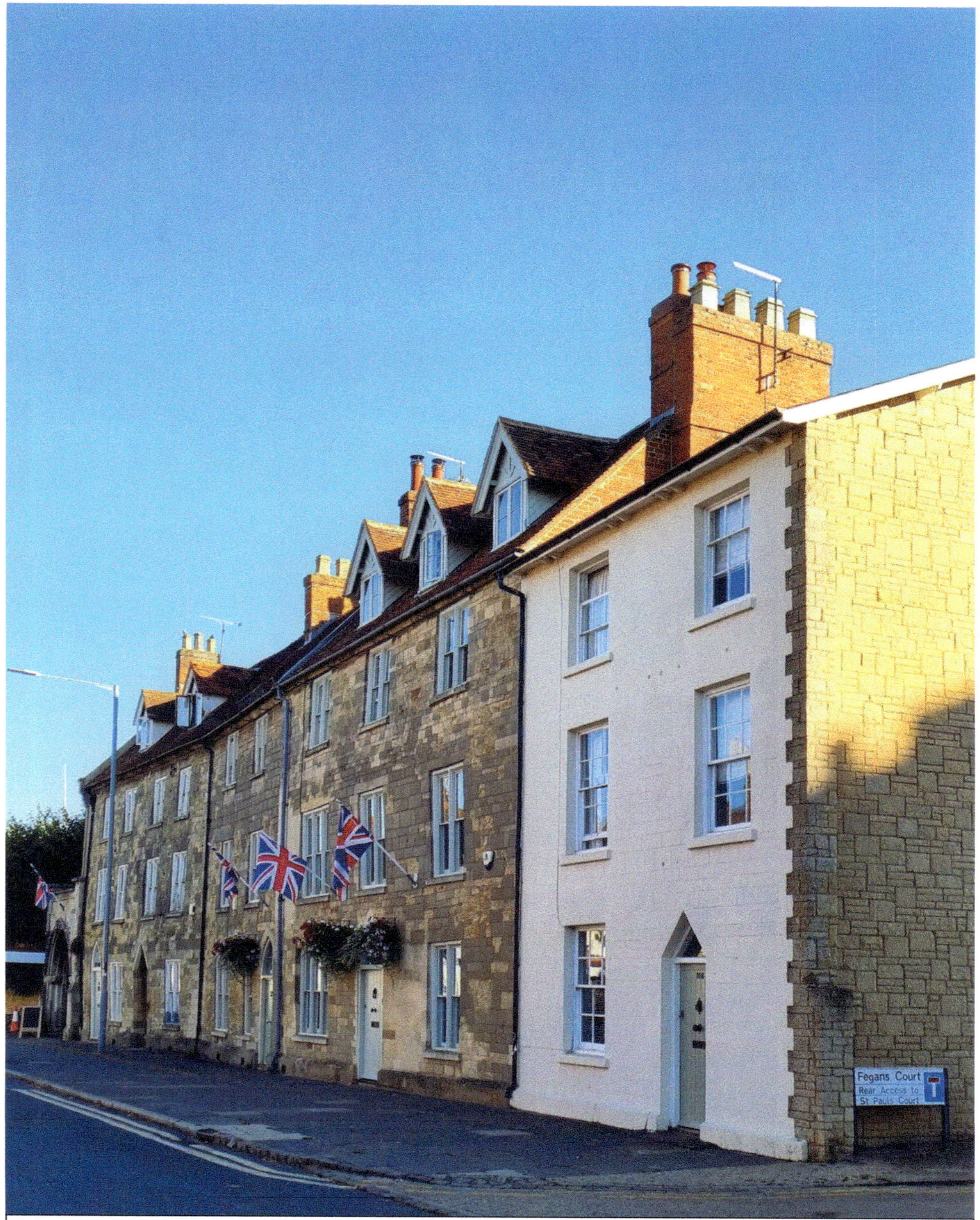

These 19th century houses replaced older buildings, including the former Red Lion and Horseshoe Inns.

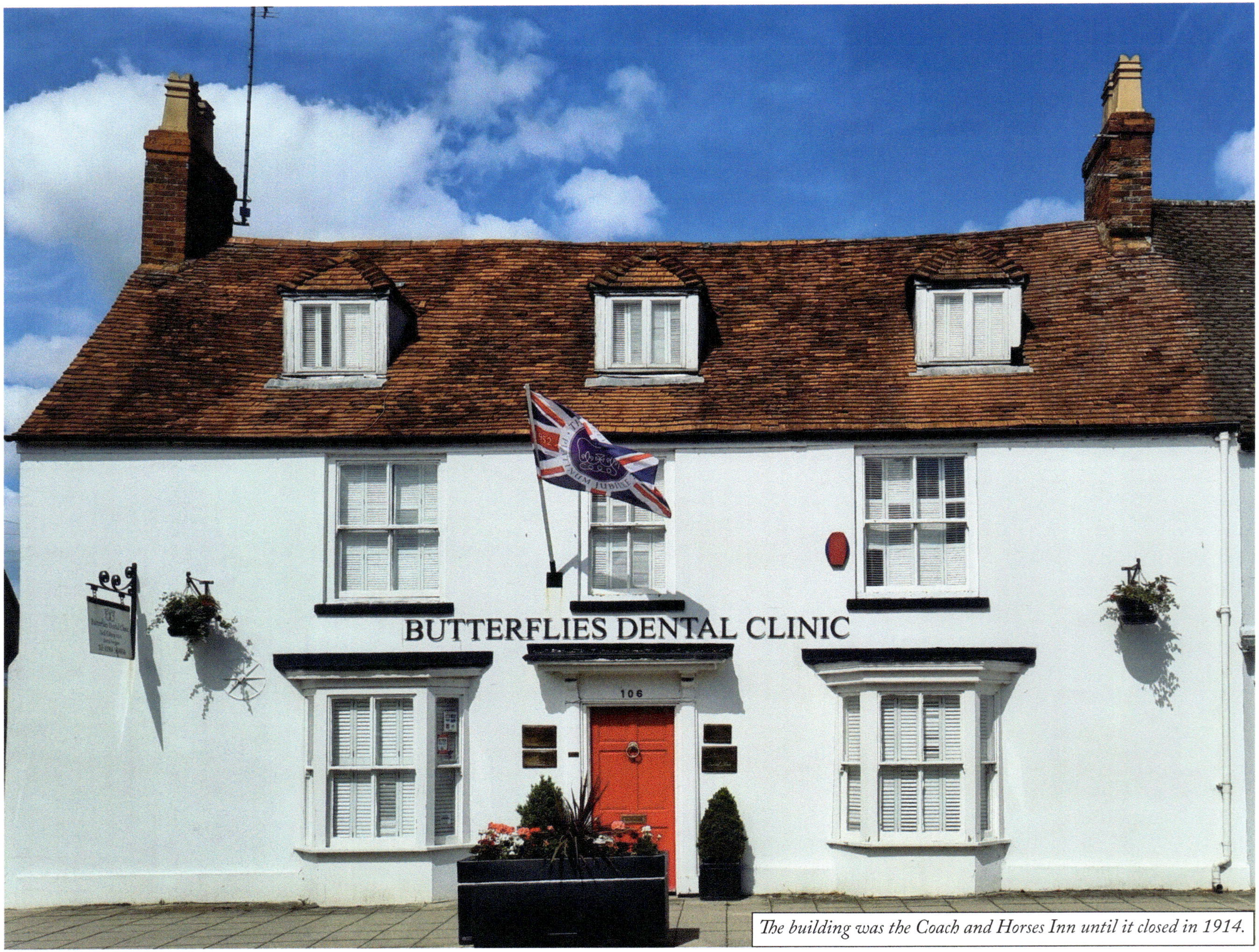

The building was the Coach and Horses Inn until it closed in 1914.

The Coach and Horses

The side street presently named *Fegan's Court* was known as *Coach and Horses Lane* in the 19th century. The reason was obvious, as the building now known as the *Butterflies Dental Clinic* was an old inn which traded under the sign of the *Coach and Horses*. It would have been rebuilt after the great fire of 1742, but it may have been an earlier foundation.

The *Coach and Horses* began its life under that name in 1792 and continued trading as such until it closed just before 1914. The rebuilt house dates from the first half of the 18th century according to the listed buildings survey. There was a house on this site in 1487 and therefore clearly a medieval establishment. Whether or not it was an inn we do not know.

It appears in a lease to Robert Edge, who is named in the deed. He was a gardener by trade and his alehouse provided him with an additional source of income. What he gets in this deed is "all that messuage, or tenement, with the appurtenances situate on the east side" and "a pyghtle of pasture" - meaning a small plot of land. A "messuage" is Norman French, still in use in the 17th century, for a house, any outbuildings and the yard. It may have been known as the *Blue Anchor* in 1678.

We find it as the *Drum and Anchor* in 1753 under licence to Francis Lambert and thereafter. Lambert, whose name is sometimes written as Lambourn, may possibly be a descendant of Michael Lambourn who was prominent in the early 17th century. It should be added that the Lambourns were related to Michael Hipwell who founded the *Rose and Crown Charity*.

Fortunately the house has some continuity and held this name (apart from one bizarre record in 1789 when it is recorded as the "*Tong and Ancre*" under the management of one Charles Wasse) until 1792 when John Marshall, who had taken over the previous year, changed the name to the *Coach and Horses*.

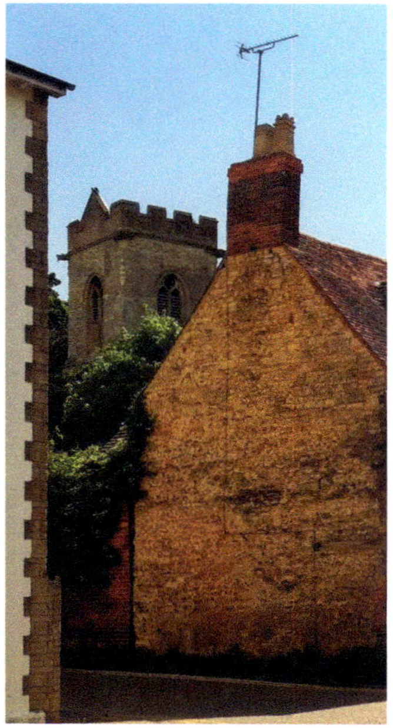

Here is an interesting report from the *Northampton Mercury* Saturday 19th May 1792.

On Saturday last, another inquisition was taken at Stony Stratford before the same Coroner, on view the body of William Pearson, a traveller, who died suddenly as he was sitting in the chimney-corner at the coach-and-horses public house in that town. - Verdict, That he died by the visitation of God.

For this reason we can identify the location of the *Coach and Horses* and its former namesake the *Drum and Anchor*, at least from 1753, and the building is still there at 106 High Street. As we have mentioned, the house will have an older tradition but there is no evidence to attach it to any other name. There was a 17th century house called the *Blue Anchor* that may possibly have a connection with the later name. The *Blue Anchor* was certainly on the east side.

The *Coach and Horses* continued in business until the early part of the First World War, possibly a casualty of restricted opening hours. Since that time it has either been residential or other commercial premises.

It appears that this building, as an inn, alehouse and a public house, had a history of about 250 years.

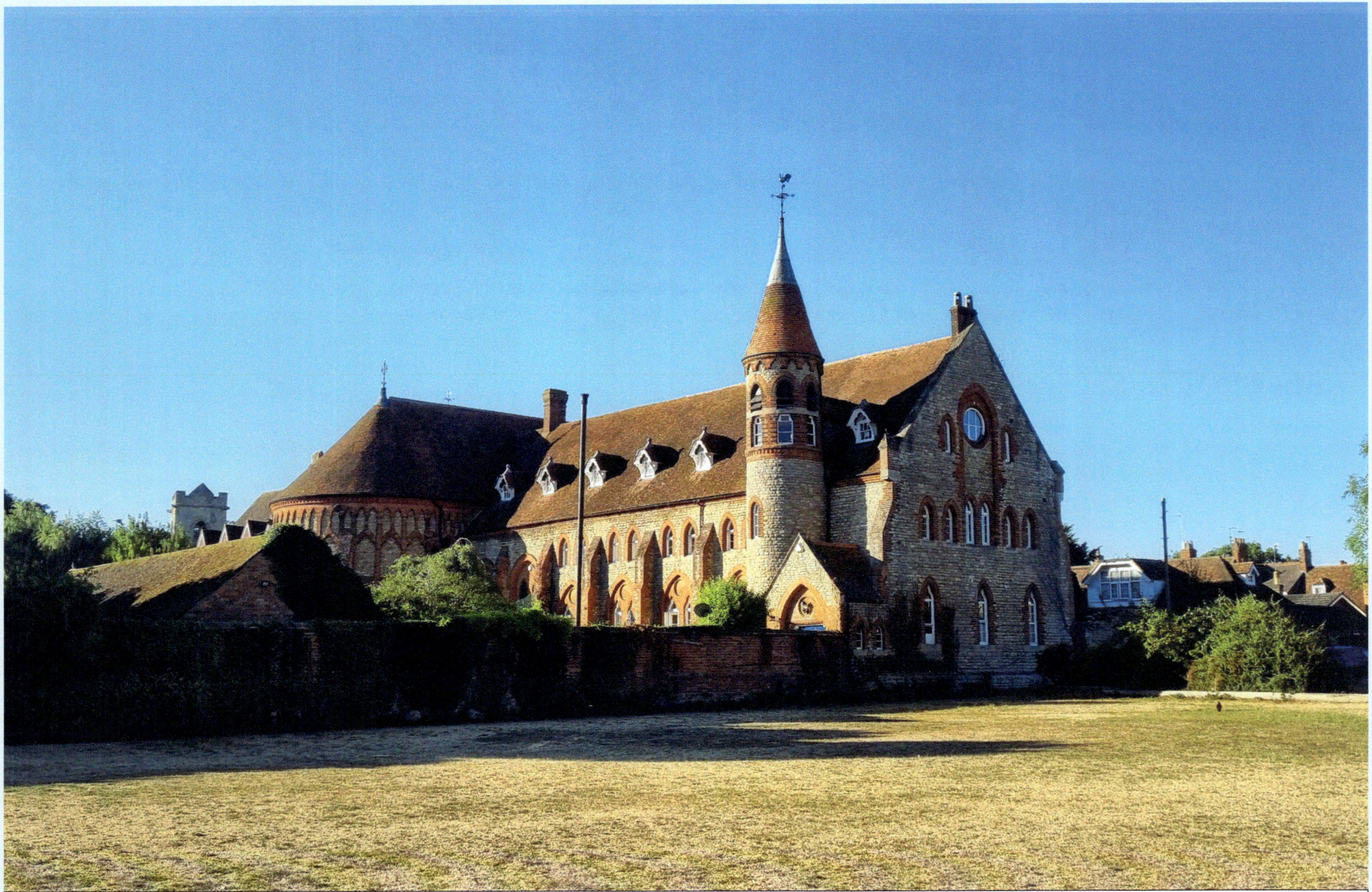

St. Paul's School and Chapel was built in 1863 and operated as a private school for about 20 years. It became an orphanage in 1904.

Of inns, Schools, Tobacco Factories and Orphanages.

The northern, less busy end of the High Street, was once the location of an inn for carters or waggoners. It was, if you like, the equivalent of a truck stop today. In medieval times goods were hauled by carters, usually with a team of six oxen. They plodded along the road at not much more than 3 miles an hour. After the more complex harness for horses had been invented, oxen were usually replaced by horses. Either way, these animals needed to be fed and inns catering for waggoners had to have a lot of pasture. Thus the *Horseshoe,* as we know it, was leasing 74 acres in the 18th century.

In 1859 Stony Stratford acquired a new vicar, William Thompson Sankey, who was the second son of William Sankey and Elizabeth Thompson. William Sankey senior was vicar of St James in Dover. Young William went to Oxford and followed in his father's footsteps. This was an unremarkable career pattern for many 19th century vicars, but in his case it is fair to say that he left a lasting impact on the town.

Sankey became a buiding vicar and could afford to do so because he had recently married into money. His new bride in 1858 was Jane Royds, formerly Jane Oddie, who, at the age of 40, was recently widowed from her first husband George. They had lived in some comfort at Portland Place in London and latterly near St Albans. When her first husband died she had four children and Sankey, ten years her junior, was willing to take them on. George Royds figures in the 1851 census as a "Landed proprietor and fundholder" and his father was also living in London as a man "of independent means." One can only assume that Jane Royds came into her new marriage with a substantial inheritance from her former husband. So while W T Sankey gets all the credit for his building program, it is as well to bear in mind that the money came from his wife.

On their arrival in Stony Stratford they rented Wolverton House until a new vicarage was built. The existing vicarage on the High Street was deemed to be too small. The Sankeys then built a new vicarage to the east, an impressive house which was later destroyed by fire. They lived well with four servants to cater to their needs.

The Sankeys were wealthy and the new vicar did not hesitate to spend it on some very ambitious building projects.

He initiated what can only be described as a slum clearance by pulling down some old hovels and buildings in *Ram Alley* to create *New Street,* which survives today with some unique features. At the end of the street he built a primary school. He became even more ambitious and created *St Paul's School.* This was Sankey's brainchild and he apparently had the ambition to create a school to rival some of the best residential schools in England. Land and buildings at the north end of town beside the evocatively named *Pudding Bag Lane* were purchased. These buildings, including the ancient *Horseshoe Inn* and *Red Lion*, were acquired, part demolished, and the new College and Chapel were built at a cost of £40,000, a very large investment in 1863. The school could accommodate up to 200 boys and under Sankey's leadership appeared to have a good reputation. Unfortunately that reputation did not survive Sankey's death in 1875 and under the headship of Walter Short, it appears to have degenerated into a kind of "Dotheboys Hall" where, according to the historian Oliver Ratcliff, "The management having changed hands to men who ruled as tyrants, and wielded the birch incessantly, its reputation as a school soon became ruined." Even in Victorian times, parents were not willing to pay 30 guineas a year to have their sons repeatedly flogged!

Very, very quickly the school was drained of pupils and the school closed in 1882. An attempt to revive it was made in 1888 but the harm to its reputation was such that it did not attract sufficient numbers to maintain the school. After closure it remained empty for a while until is was used as a tobacco factory. This venture did not last and the whole property was acquired in 1900 at a knockdown price by Mr Fegan, a successful London businessman who wished to use his fortune to provide orphanages. The property was sold to a commercial developer in 1972.

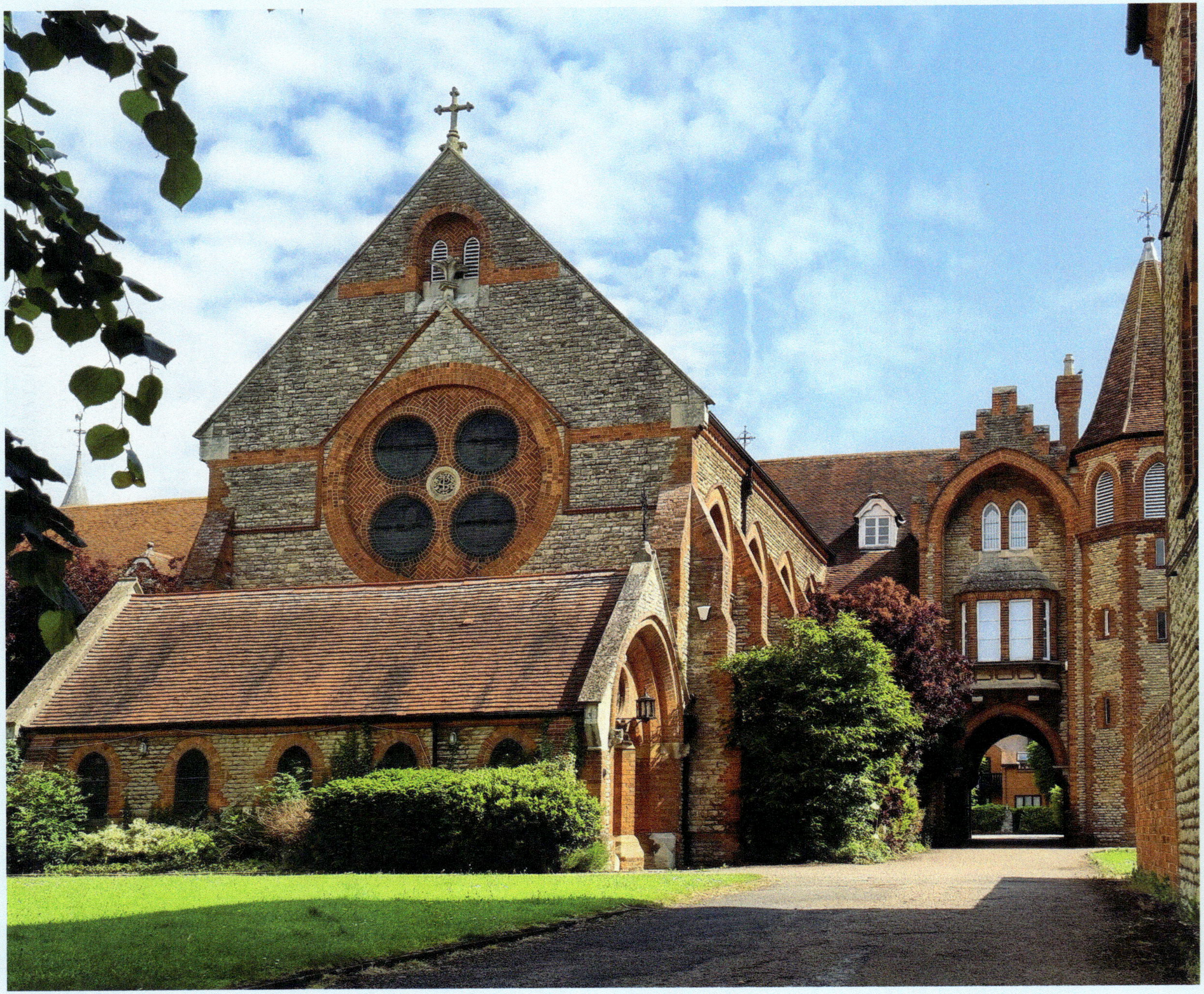
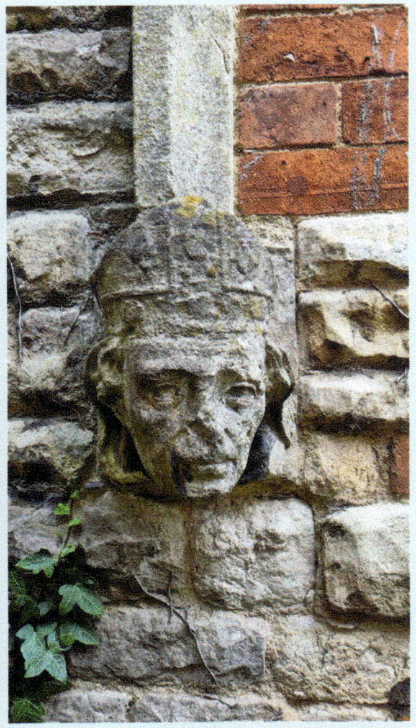
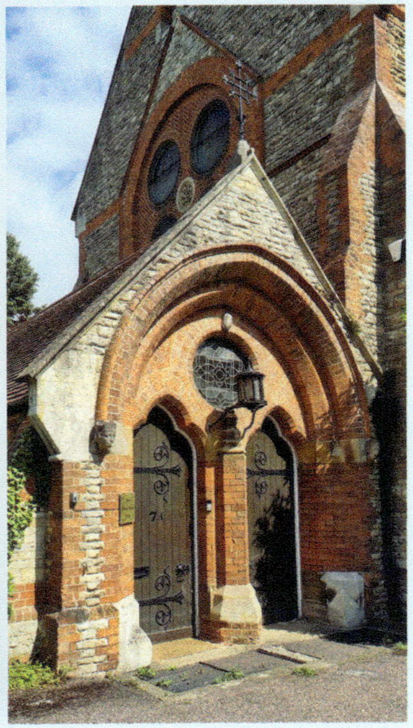

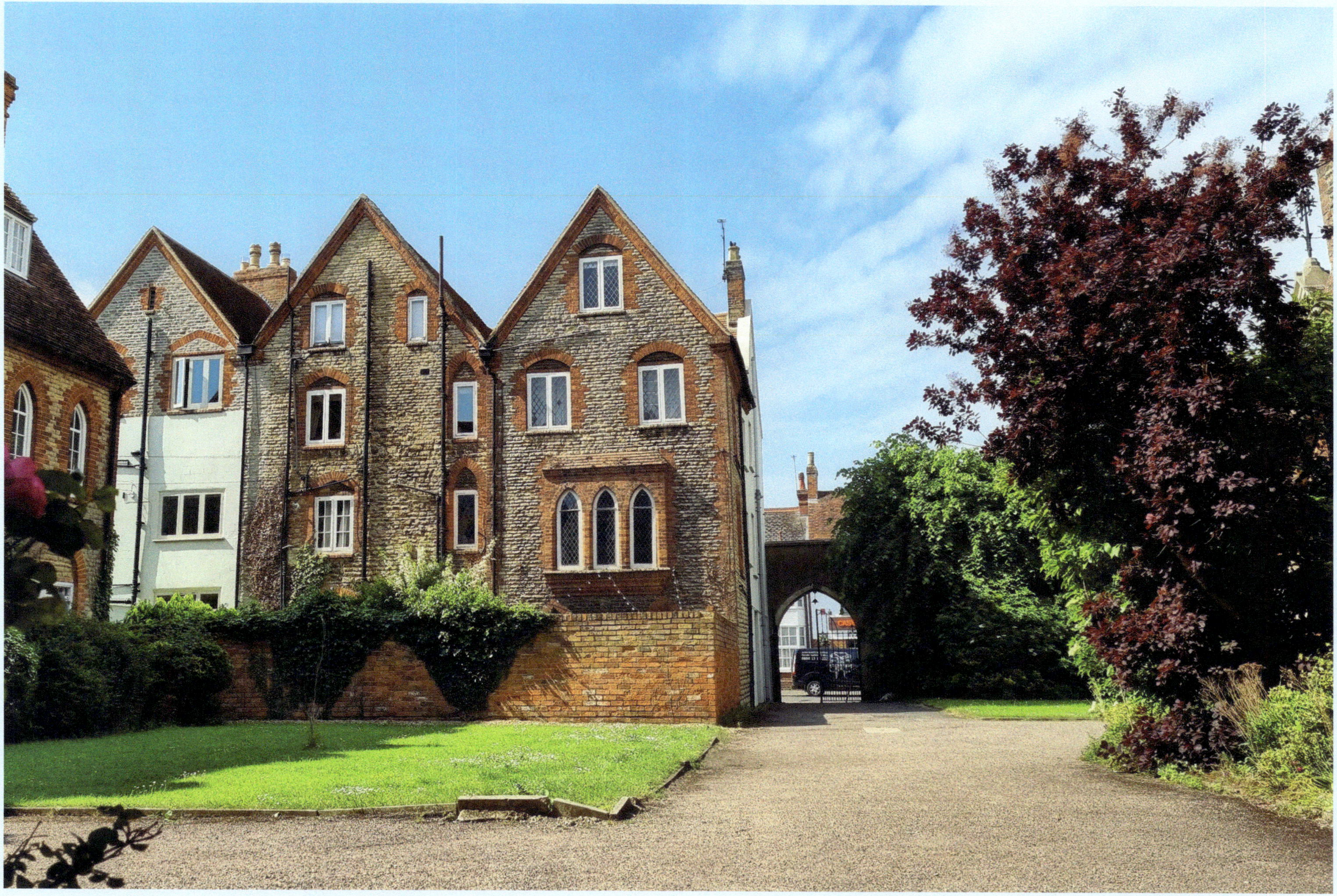

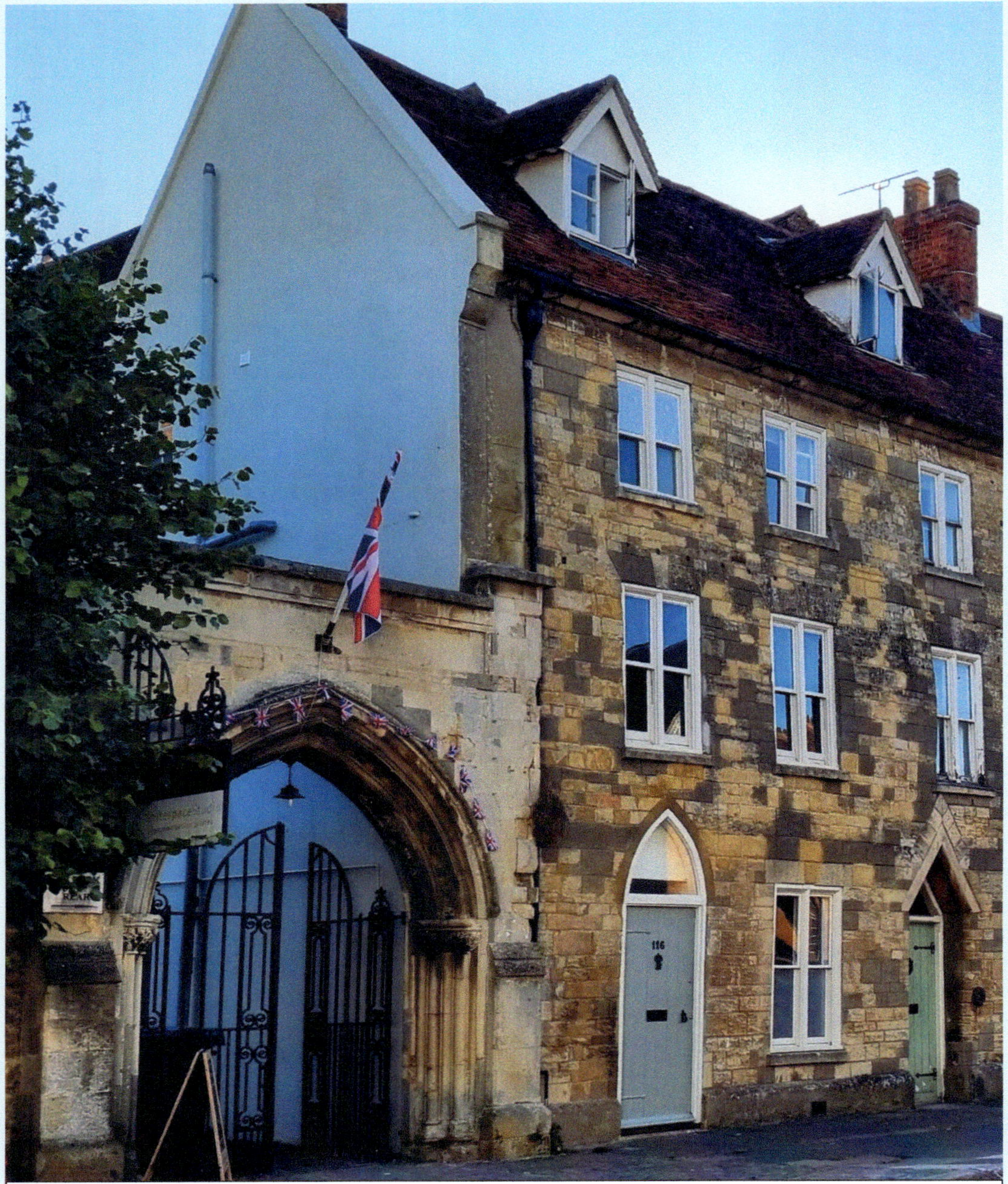

The entrance to St. Paul's School.

Horseshoe and Red Lion

The Horseshoe Inn in Stony Stratford had catered to the waggon trade since medieval times. The inn accommodated the carters, their oxen and later their horses, who could be fed, pastured and rested before the next stage of the journey. One indicator of the scale and nature of this operation was the large amount of land they leased early in the 18th century.

The new network of canals had finished off much of the long distance carting trade. Even though the Grand Junction canal through the district was still under construction when the *Horseshoe* closed its doors, a great portion of the carting business up the Watling Street had been siphoned off by the canals. Longboats could carry more at less cost; a single horse could tow a heavily laden barge on water, whereas a cart required a team of six to eight horses and even then could only progress at three miles an hour on average. Canals now had a clear competitive advantage. At the end of the 18th century, road traffic was the preserve of passenger and the mail service; goods were moved by water, where possible.

The owners of the inn probably watched helplessly as its business declined and they closed its doors for good in 1796, after several hundred years of successful operation.

The *Red Lion,* a neighbouring property, was certainly active in the 17th and 18th centuries, and may have been in existence earlier, as there is a reference to a *Red Lyon* in 1529.

In 1769, it was taken over by its neighbour the *Horseshoe*, which itself went out of businerss 30 years later. The buildings were demolished around 1860 for the creation of St Paul's School.

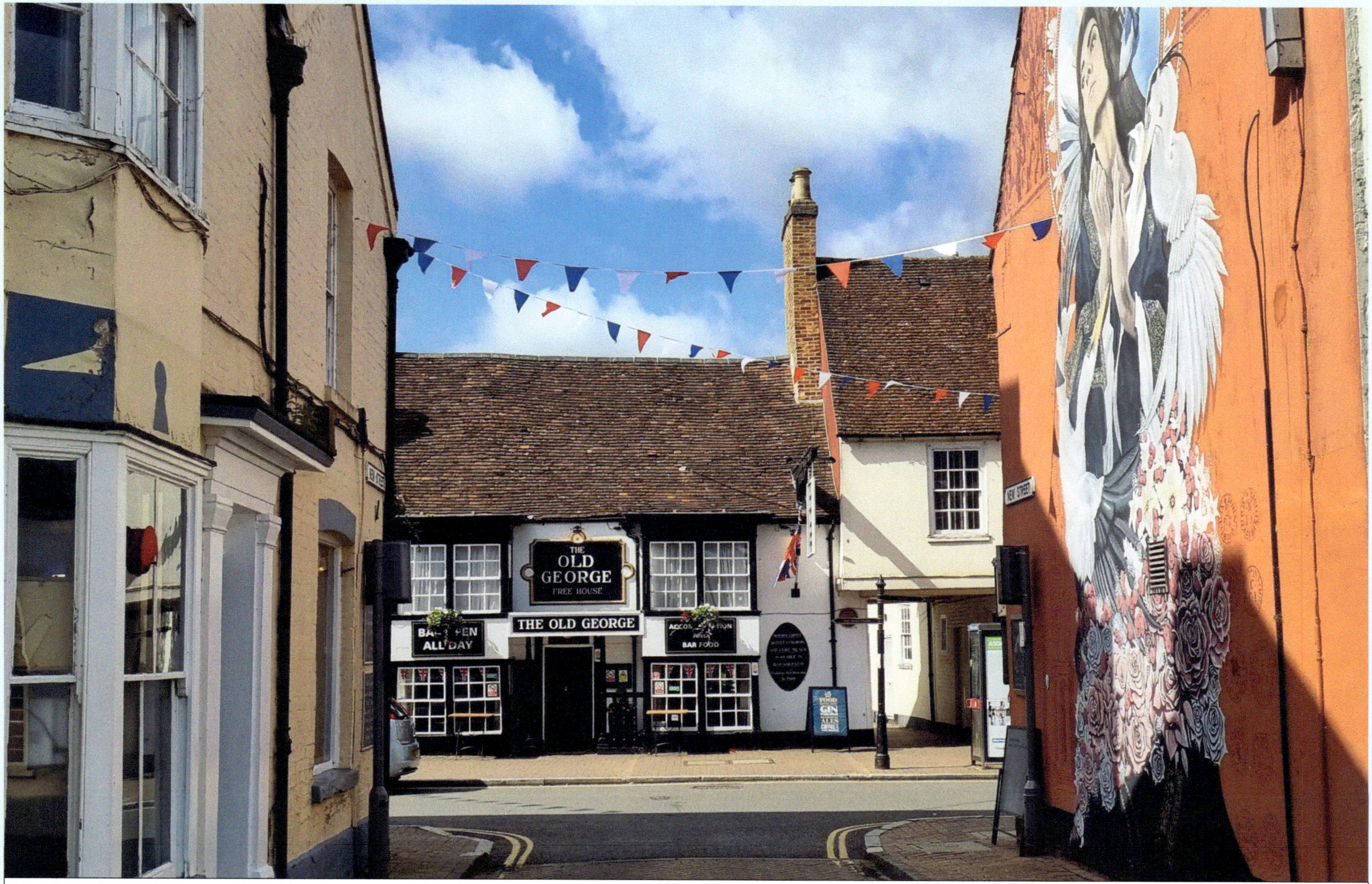

New Street forms a junction with the High Street opposite The George. This was the first of Reverend W T Sankey's building projects in 1860 - shown on pages 15-19.

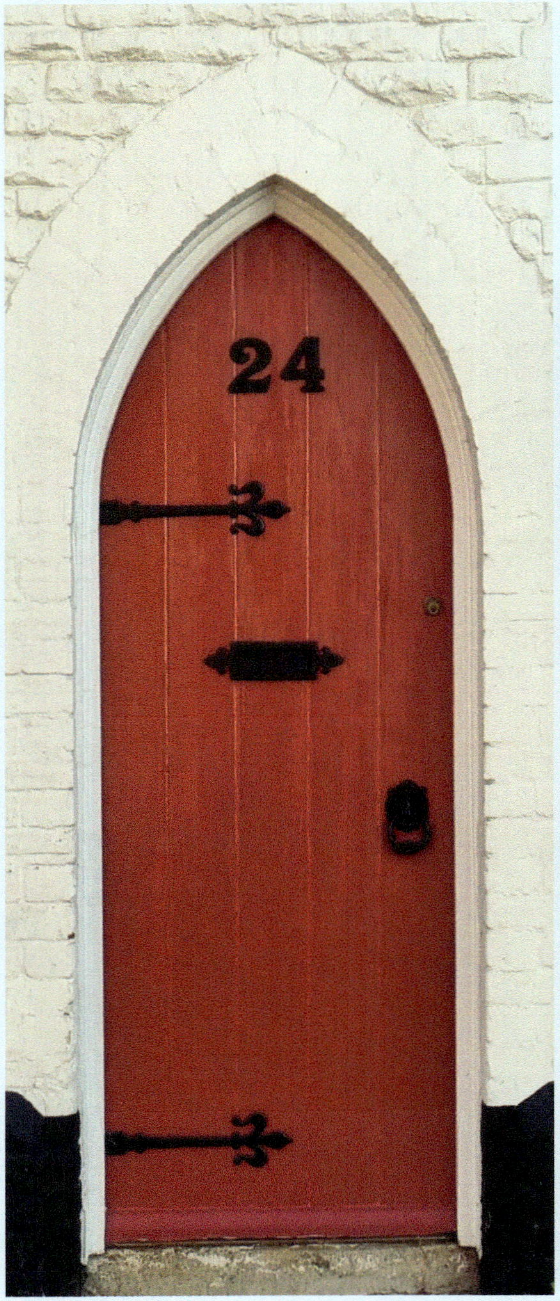
24

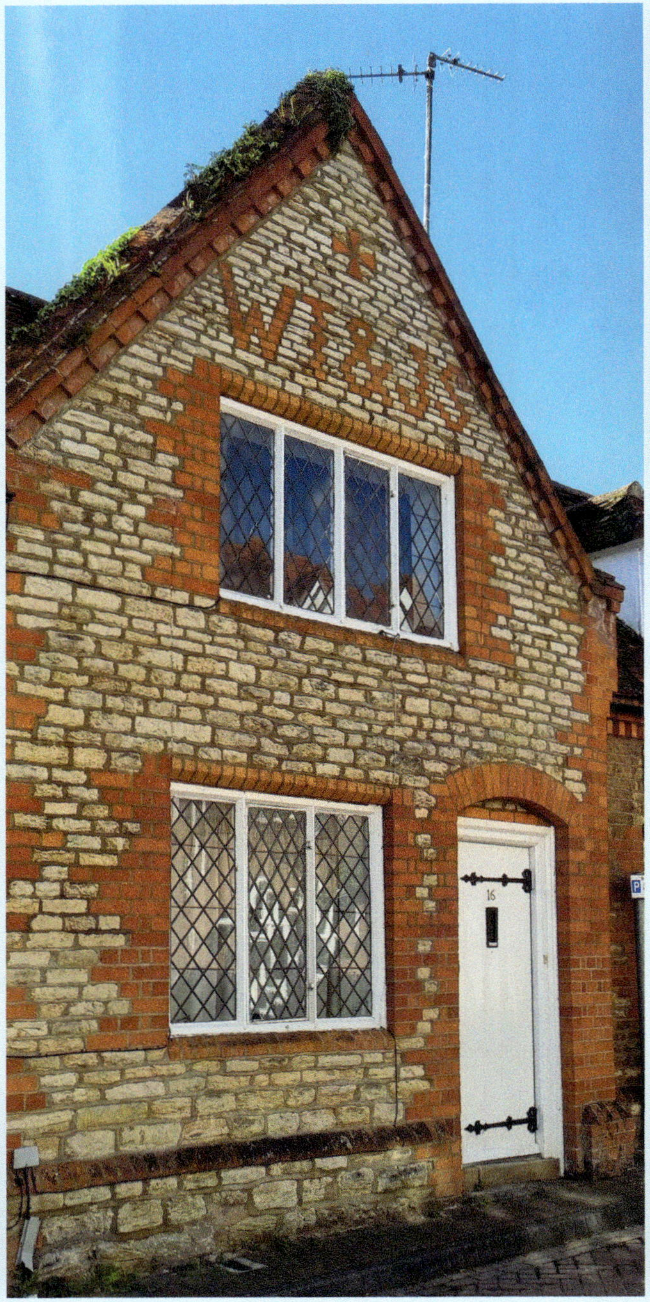

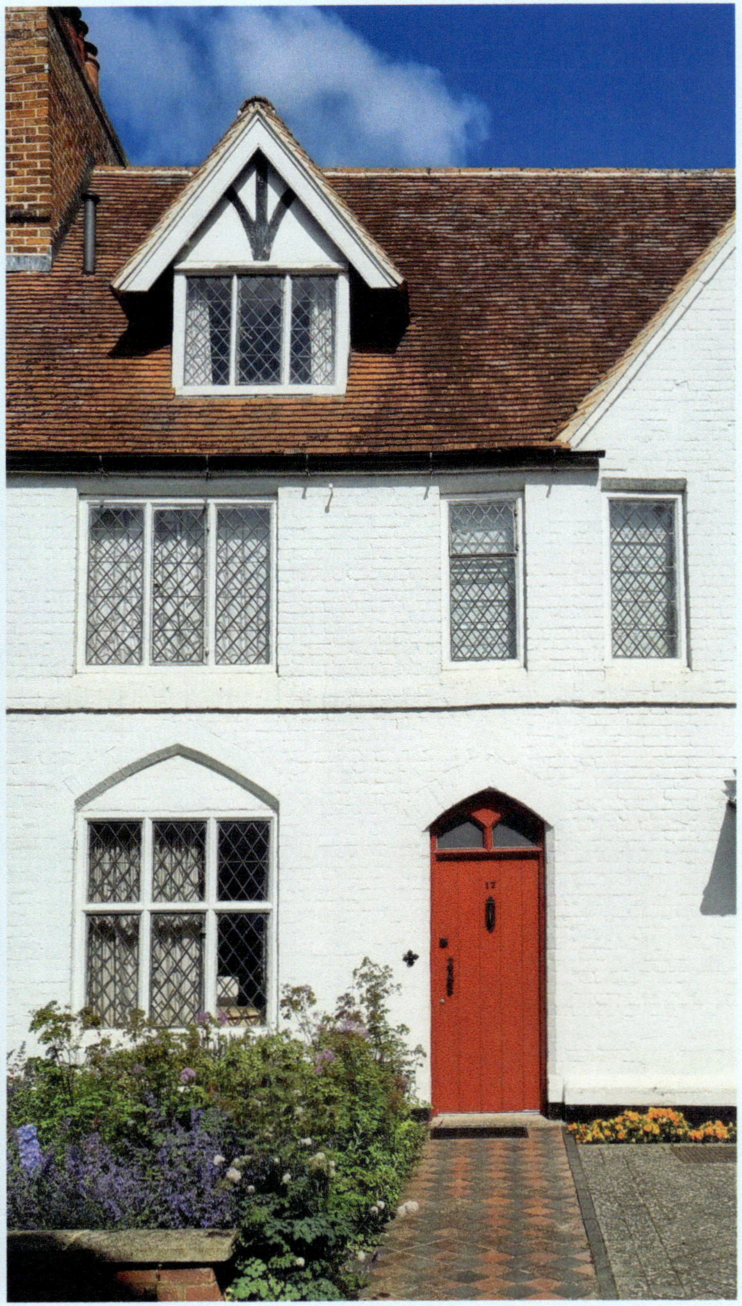

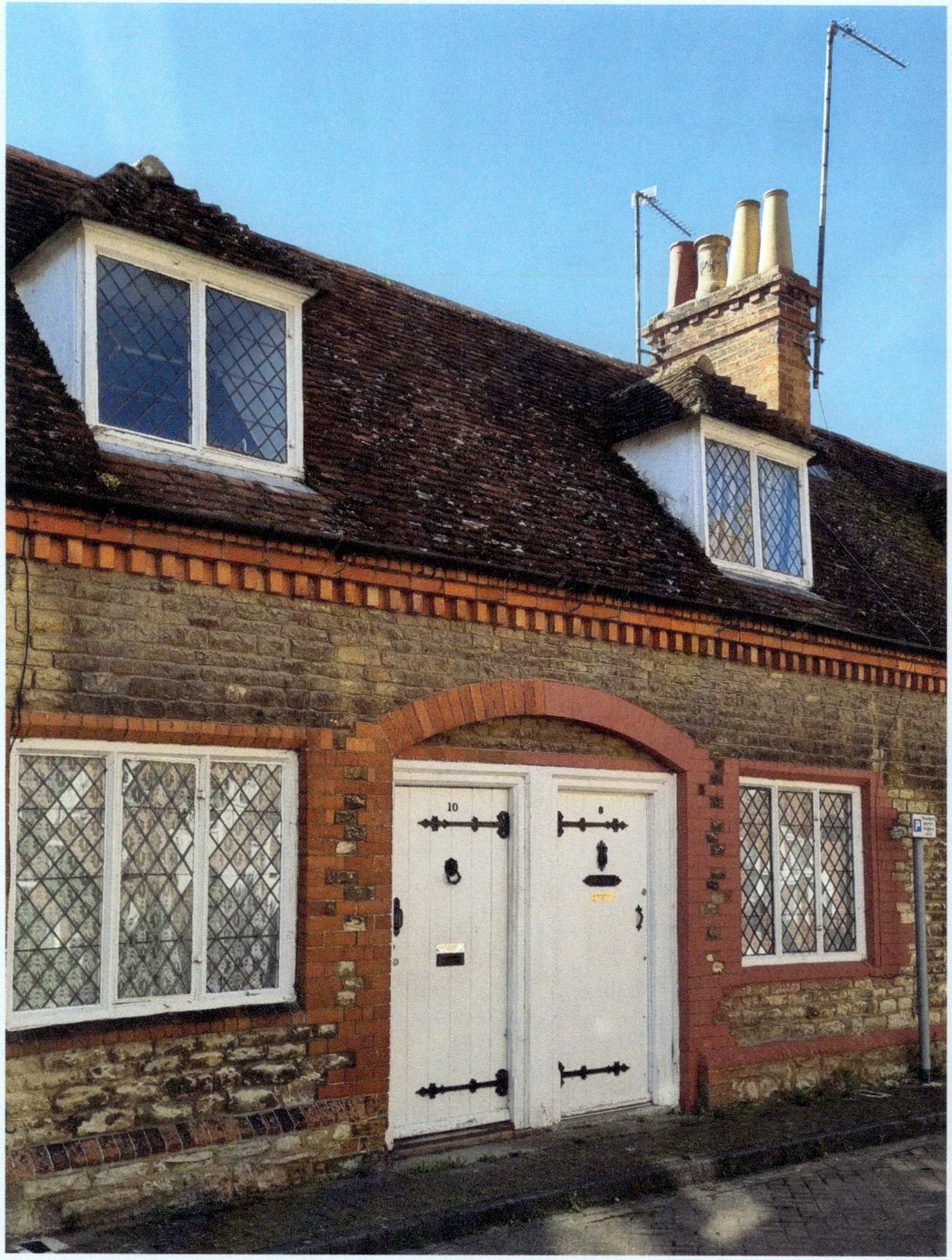

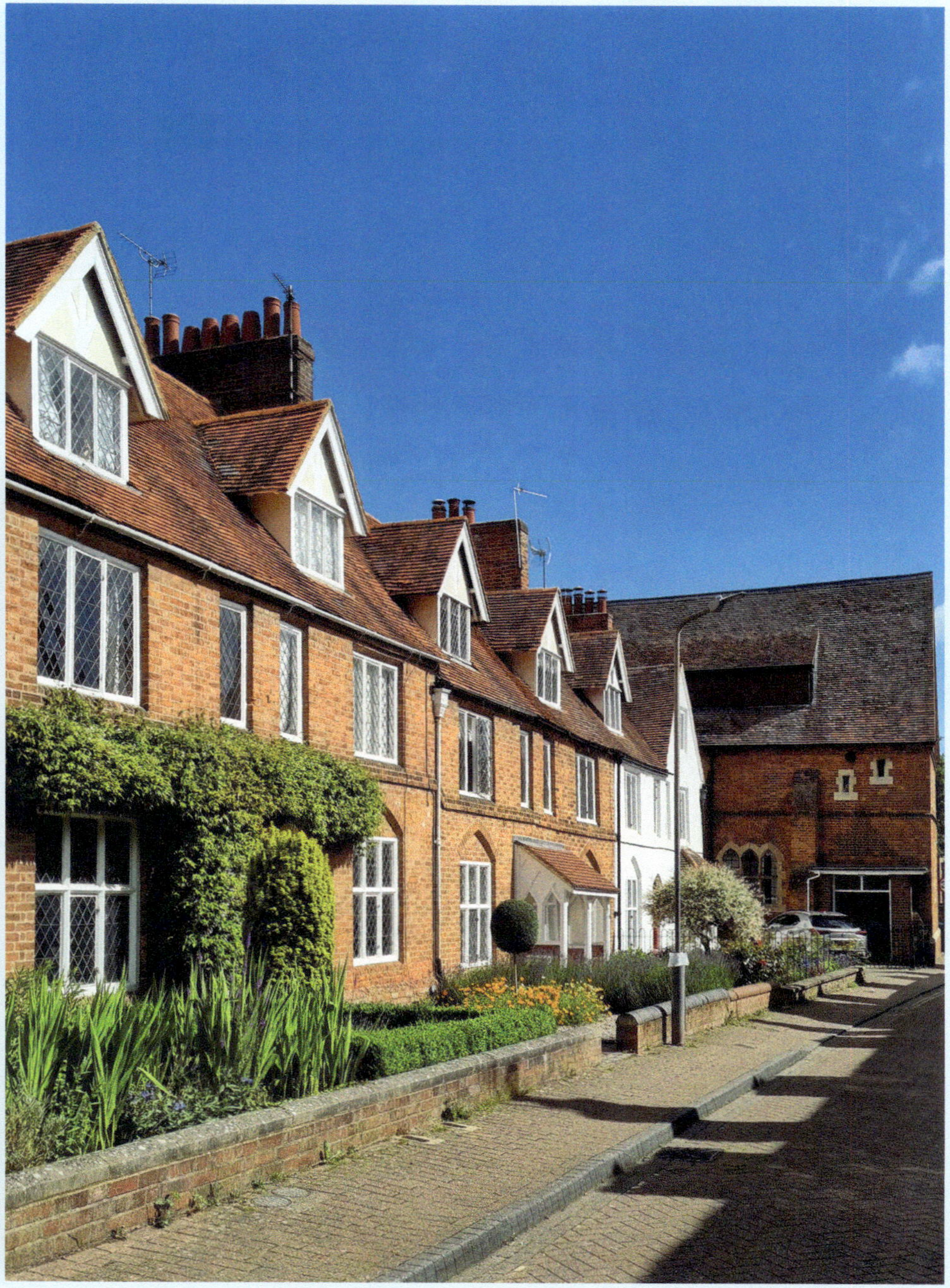

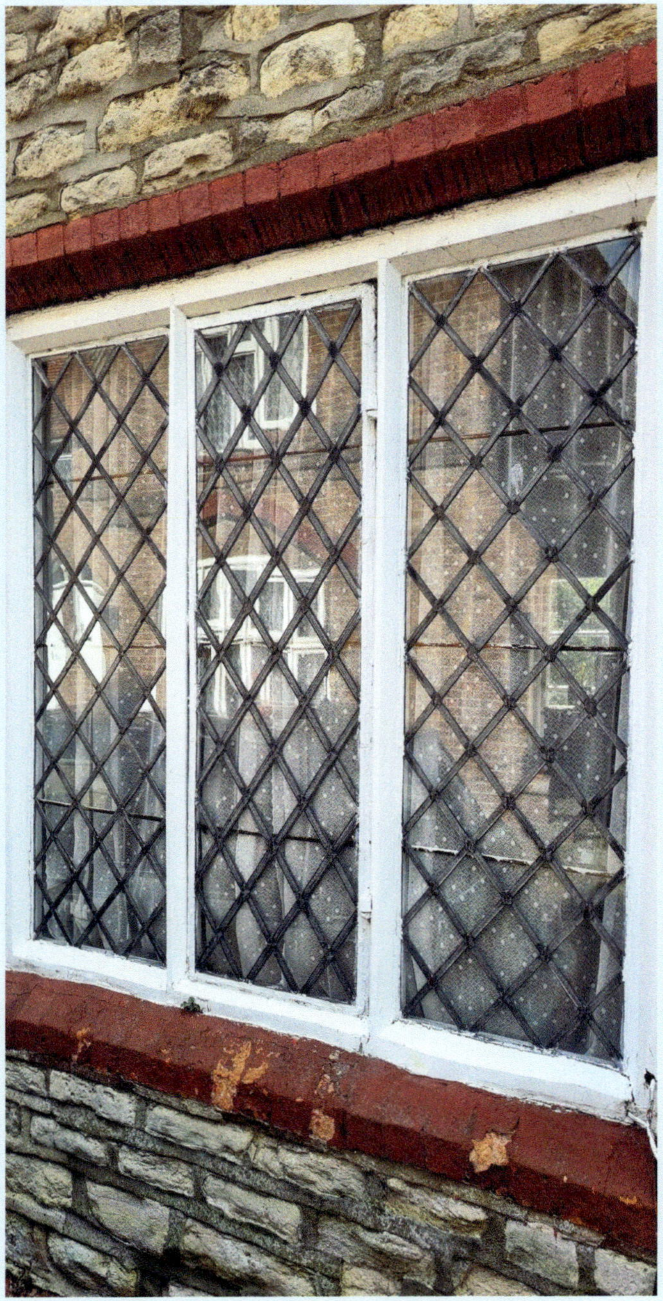

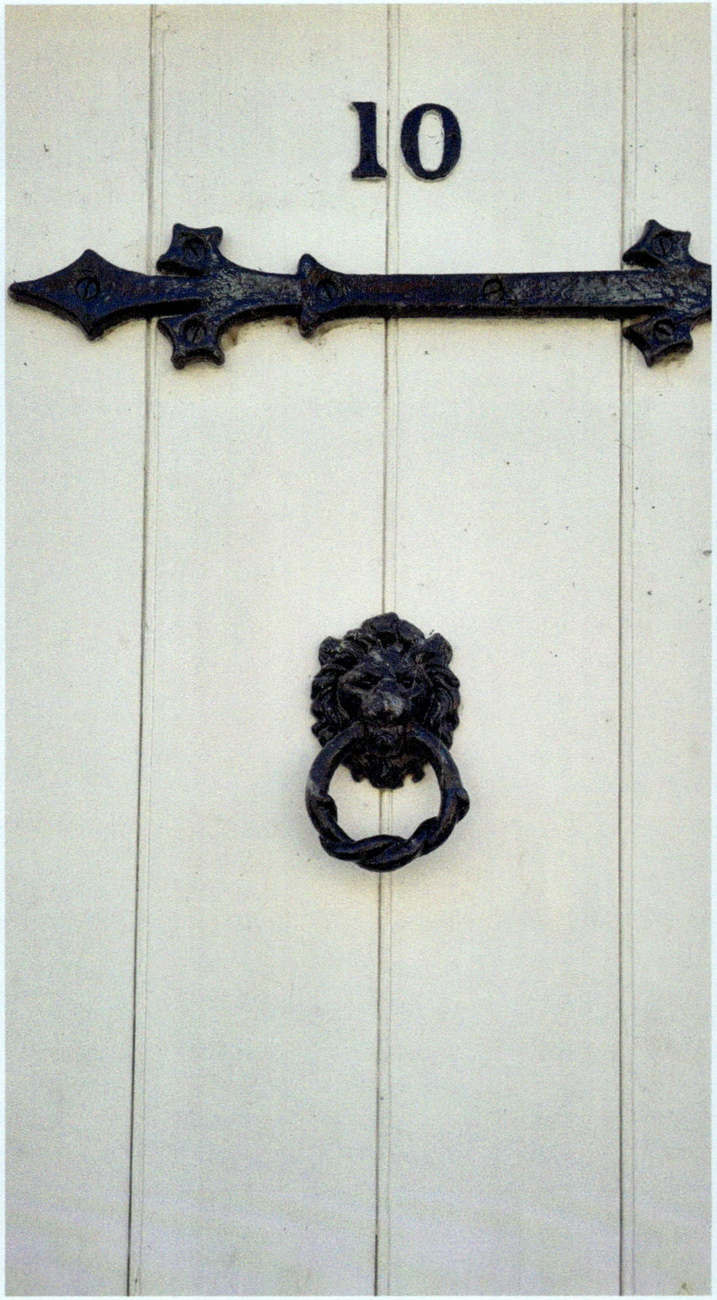
10

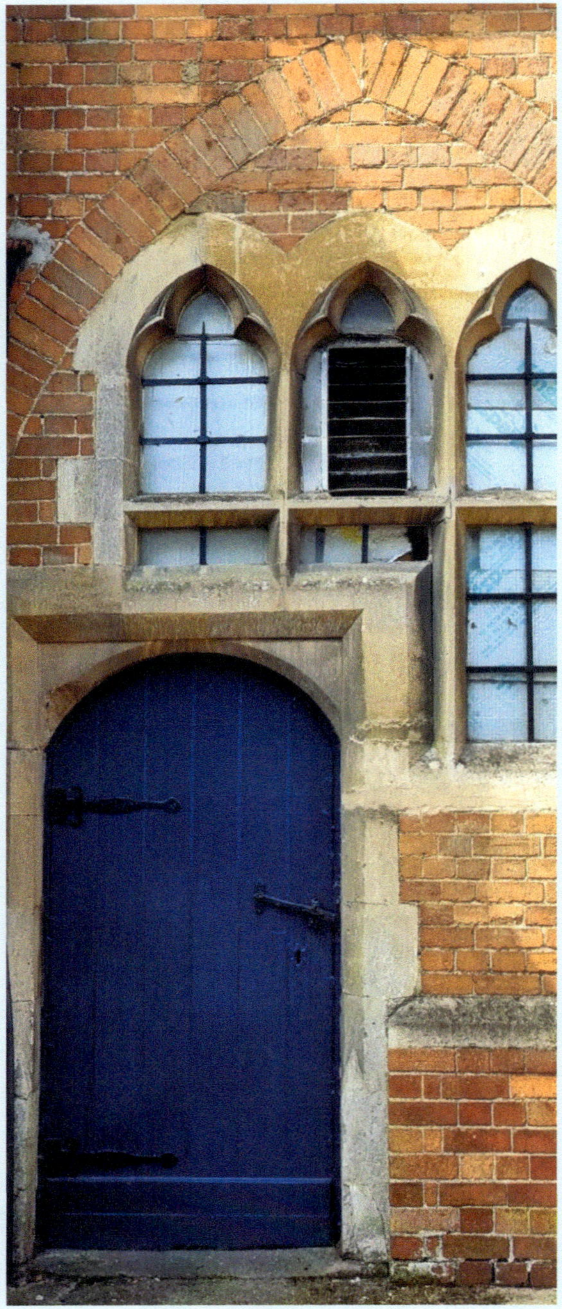

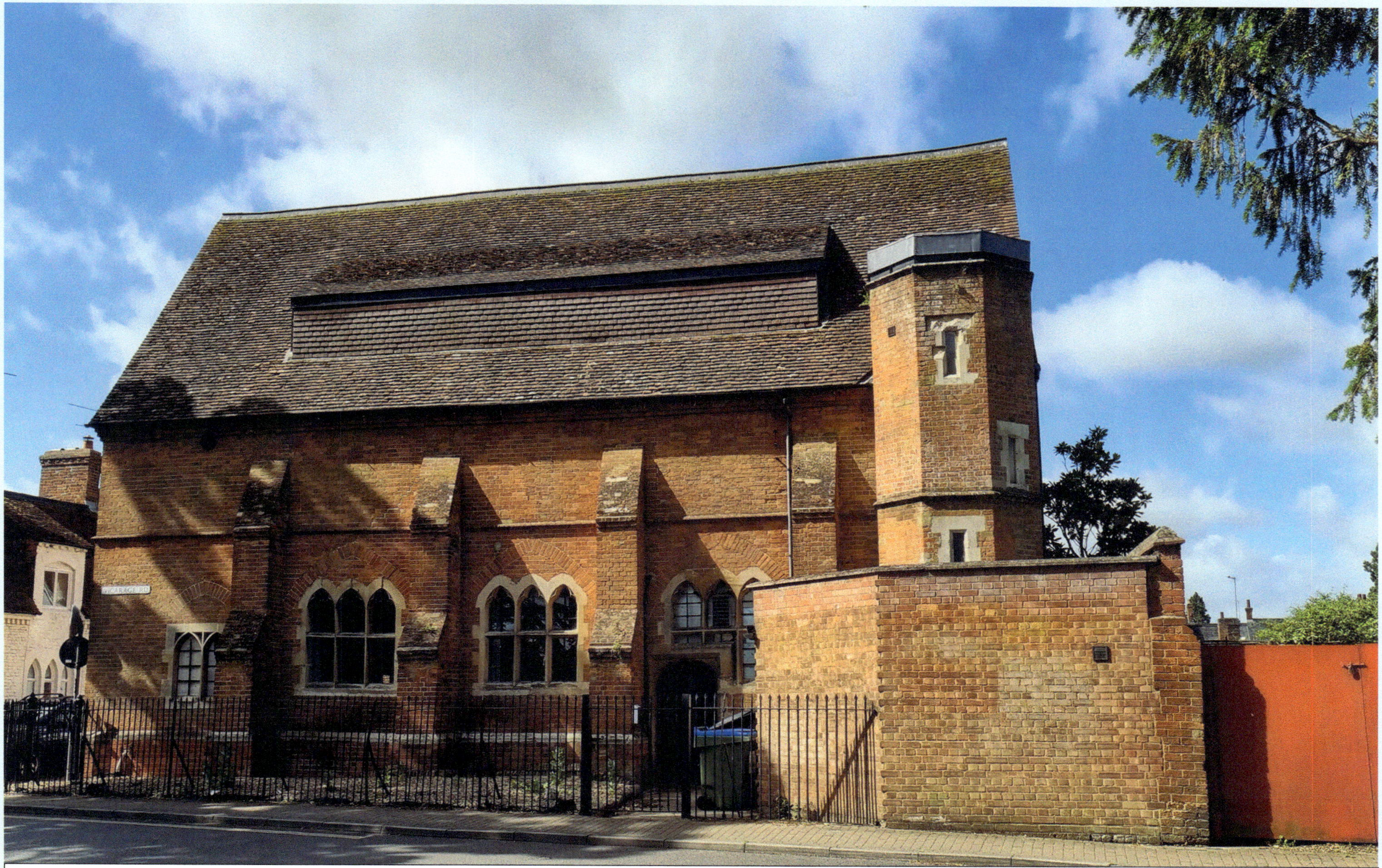

New Street (shown on pages 15 to 19) was a lane of ramshackle cottages with the local name of Ram Alley. In 1860, the new vicar William Thompson Sankey, purchased the land and developed what were then modern cottages. At the end of the street he also built a new school.

Entering Stony Stratford

For many years there was a toll bar at the northern entrance to the town. In medieval times, the toll bar's purpose was to charge for admission to the markets; in the 18th and 19th centuries tolls were charged for the upkeep of the road.

The house pictured on the right was a pub. It is an 18th century building and first opened for business under the sign of *The Angel.* It was later changed to the *Barley Mow.*

The document is in Latin. The deed relates to the transfer of rights to the fish ponds between the Stony Stratford bridge and "Grilkes Herber" from John le Forester to Sir John de Wolverton. It is dated in the tenth year of the reign of Edward II, which makes it 1317. The fish ponds were on the west side of the High Street and Sir John was keen to get some control of land on that side. Grilkes Herber was named in the deed to help locate that land in question, and it was not part of the sale. However, either the de Wolvertons or the Longuevilles must have acquired Grilkes Herber because it does appear in the particular of the Wolverton manor in 1713 under the name of "Gregg's Arbour."

From this casual reference we can infer that there was an inn near to the river, probably on the very north edge of the town. The word herber probably derives from the French word to mean an inn - now *auberge*. "Grilke" is probably Grik or Gryk (Greek) and about this time there is a Thomas le Gryk who appears as a witness to documents dated 1296 and 1304.

There is a consensus that this inn was most likely on the site of that strip of land between the river and the beginning of Stony Stratford. It has been suggested that it was where the house that used to be *The Barley Mow* now stands. Some partial excavation has revealed some medieval foundations, although a full excavation has not been undertaken. A 1713 document, which records this a piece of land as Gregg's Arbour, details a lease to William Perry, the miller, with rights to moor boats. There is no indication that this included any buildings, so if there still was an inn here, it must have been separated from the land at some point.

We should also take into account that when the *Barley Mow* was sold in 1807, it was still part of the manor of Calverton, then in the possession of the Marquess of Salisbury. If it never left the manor then any building on the "Grilkes Herber" site may have been closer to the riverbank. In the 13th or 14th century the "herber" was probably an outgrowth of a toll bar that would have been placed here to charge merchants coming to sell at the Stony Stratford markets. The relative prominence of the le Gryk family in this period, judging from their inclusion in deeds, may suggest that they were of sufficient status for the lord to allow them to operate the toll bar.

There is not sufficient evidence to say that there has been an inn continuously on or near this site since the middle ages, and knowing that it is part of the flood plain of the Ouse, it would be a brave soul who built near the riverbank.

Today, and since the 18th century, the furthest reach of Stony Stratford is the house at 185 High Street that used to be the *Barley Mow*, formerly *The Angel.*

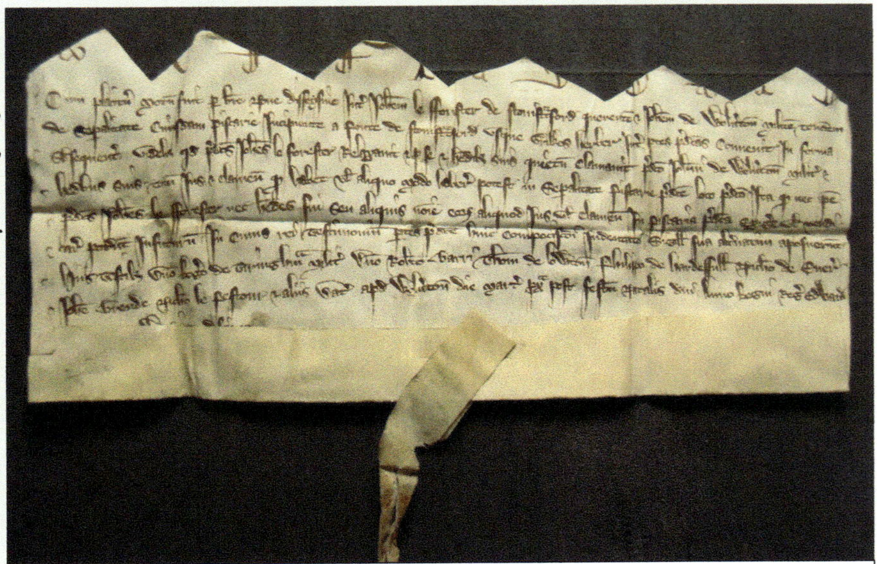

The 14th century deed that referenced an inn at this location.

LOOK AT THE ENTRANCE TO THE TOWN

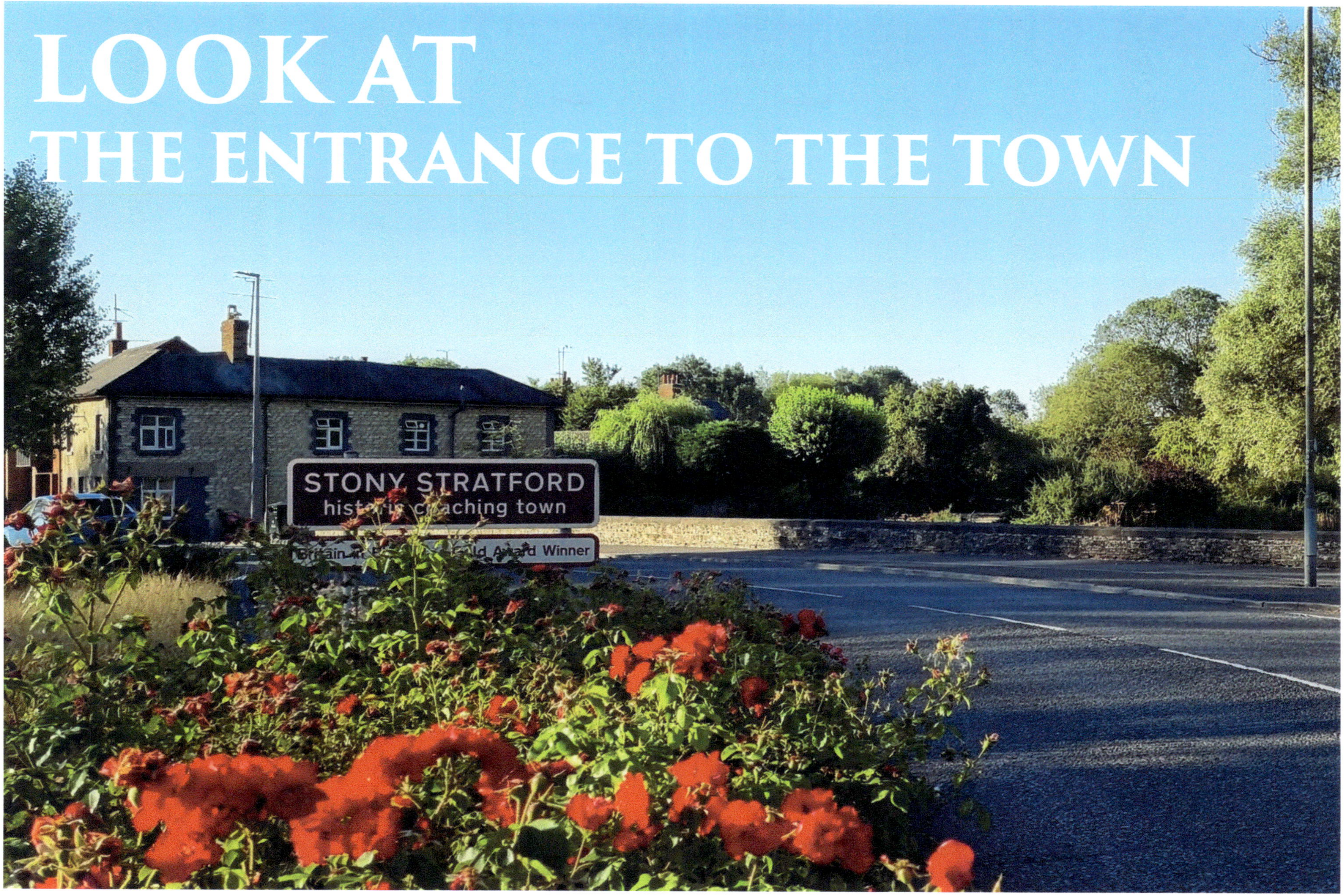

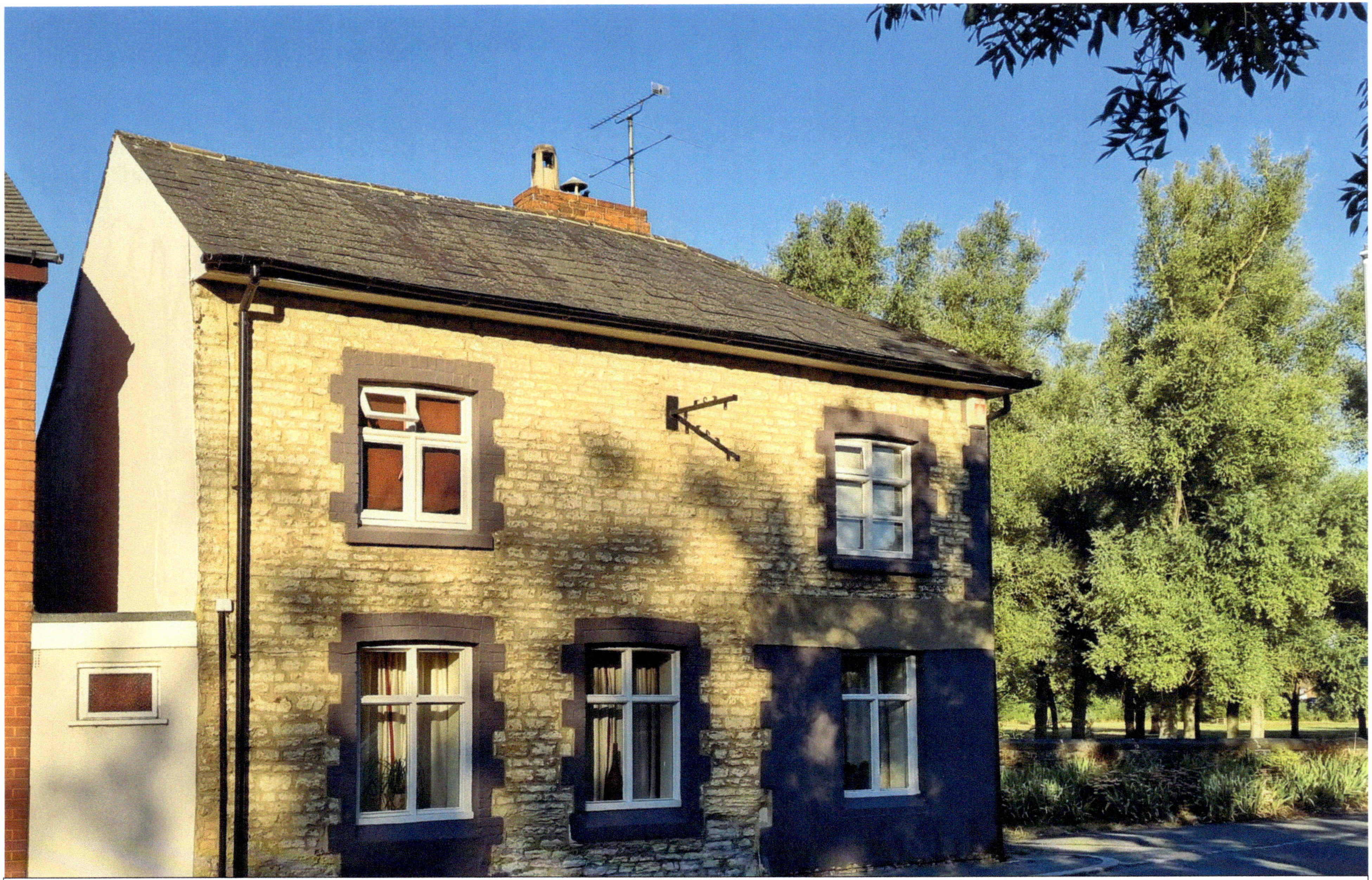

The house that started as The Angel and then became The Barley Mow.

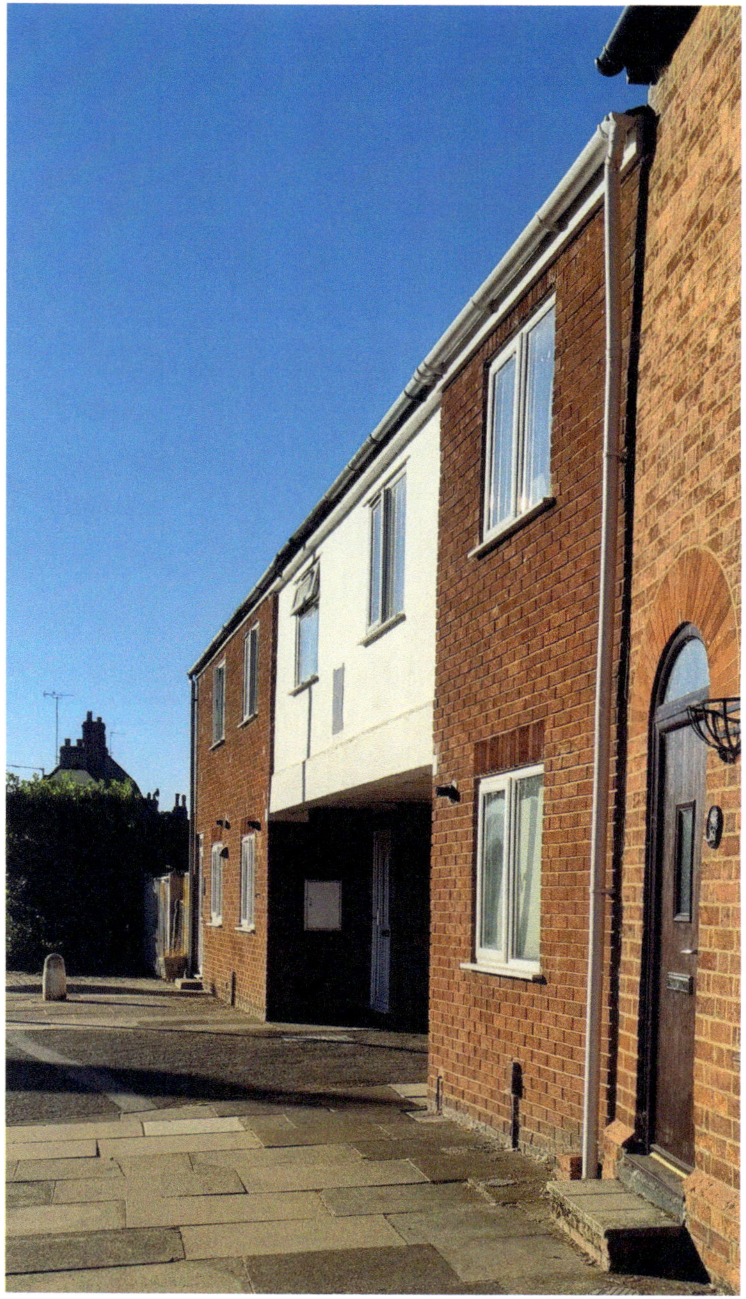

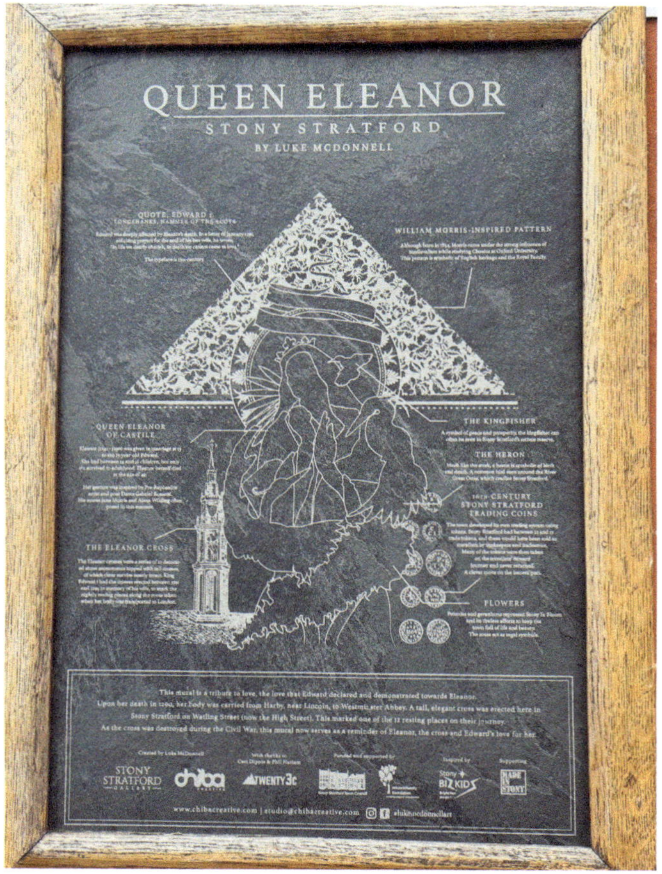

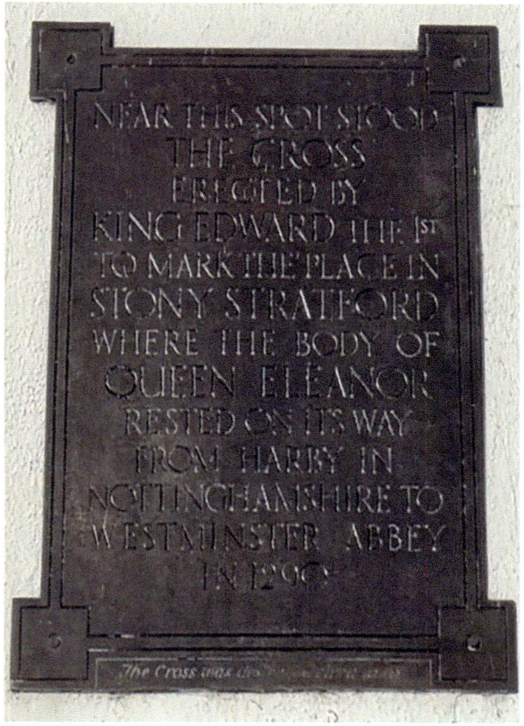

Towards the north end of the High Street, the road unaccountably widens and it is believed that this was the site of the Eleanor Cross that was erected here after 1290.

This is the story. In 1290 Queen Eleanor died near Lincoln. Although she was not a popular queen she was much loved by her husband, King Edward I, and he chose to mark her passing by erecting a stone cross at every place where the funeral cortege stopped on its way to London. One of these places was Stony Stratford. The cross stood for several centuries until 1646, when Parliamentary soldiers, camped nearby, decided that the stone cross was idolatrous and one evening, probably after a good night's drinking, proceeded to demolish the cross. The base lay there for some years after and was eventually removed. Thus the road was widened at this point.

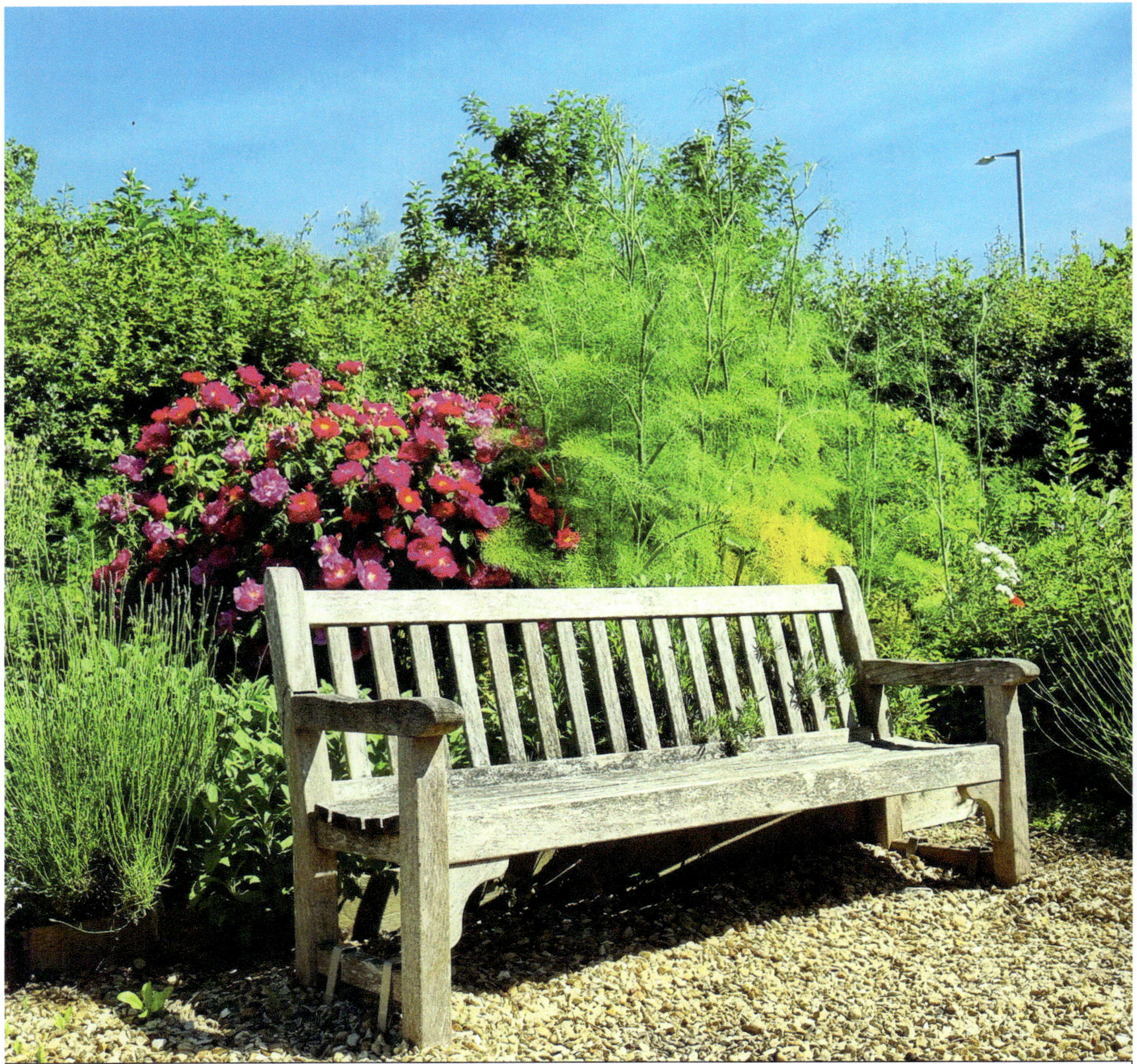

"Queen Eleanor's Garden and Orchard" at the north end of the town.

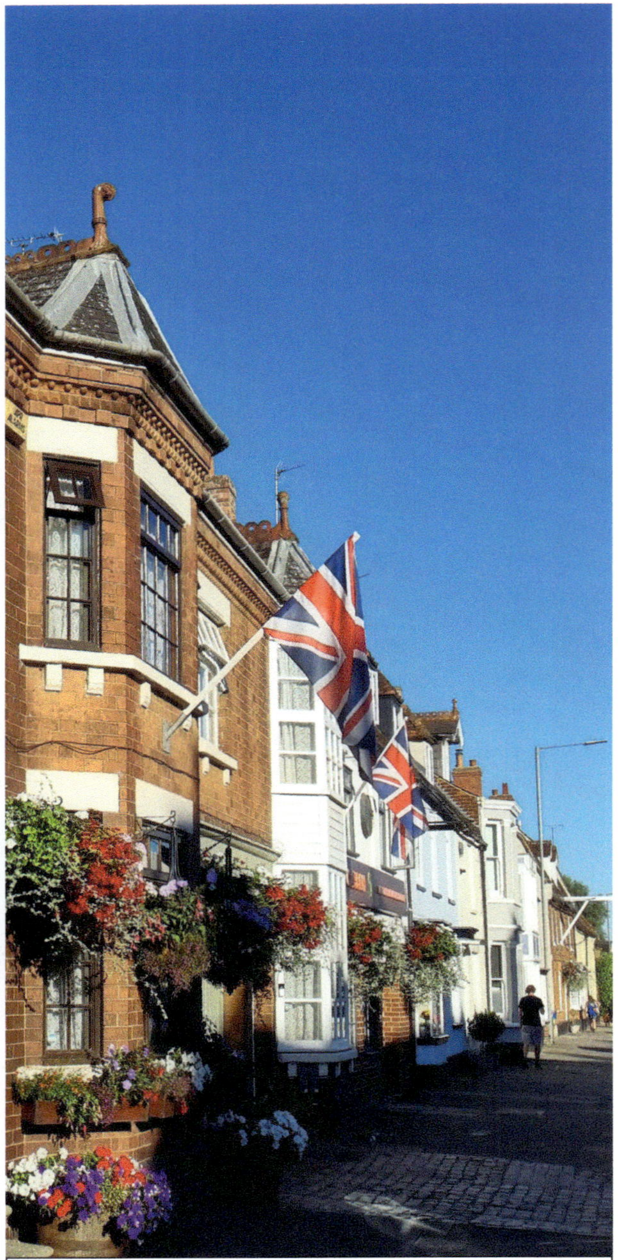

Newer houses on the upper High Street.

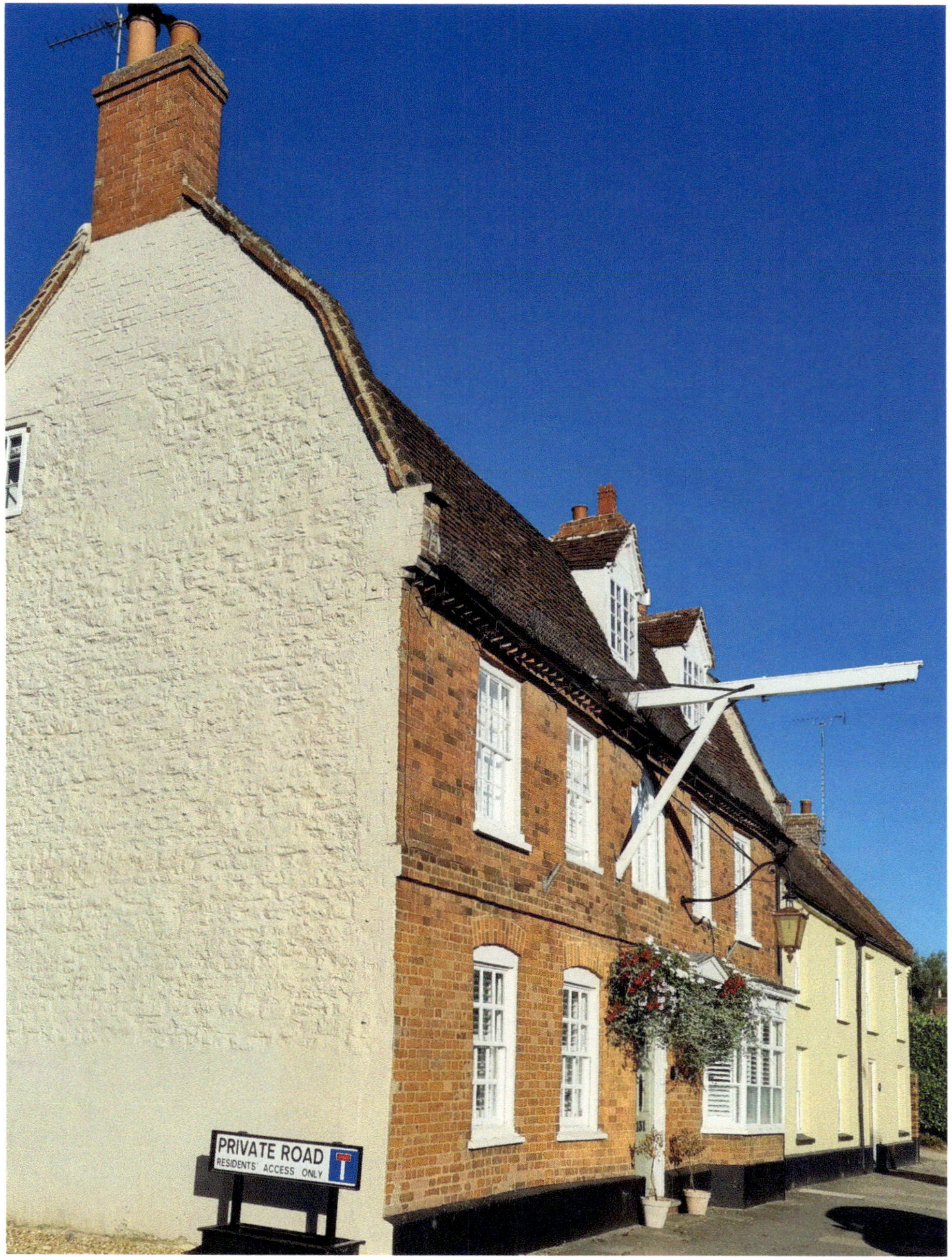

The Rising Sun

The Rising Sun, at 131 High Street, has a continuous history from 1753 (and probably before that date) to the late 1970s, when it closed for good. The building has been standing for almost 300 years, although the precise date of its construction is unknown. Archaeological surveys infer a date in the 1740s, based upon construction techniques and written documentation, which starts to appear in 1753. The house is stone built but was faced with brick at a later date, which gives it its present appearance.

The first owner of record was a man called Solomon Barley, whose principal occupation was a carrier. The running of an inn or alehouse may have been a sideline and was possibly only undertaken after he married Ann Willcocks in 1748. At any rate, their interest in the property did not last long because they sold the property to John Fletcher, a shopkeeper on February 13-14 1753, who quickly passed it on to William Hutson or Hudson on 16/17 November of that same year.

William Hudson's time as landlord of the *Rising Sun* was short lived. On 2/3 April 1755, he sold the property to Joseph Mycock, an inn holder from Daventry. Mycock was a more durable proposition and continued as the licensee until 1779. He was succeeded by Daniel Adkins, a tenant licensee in 1780 for two years and then the property was acquired by Henry Harris in 1780. He sold the property in 1807 to John Williams of Greens Norton, who quickly re-sold it to Thomas Green of Stony Stratford in 1809, although Williams continued as tenant until 1812.

It continued throughout the 19th and most of the 20th century as an established public house. It is now a private residence.

It may have had an earlier history as an inn. The field behind it was once known as Lyon Close, and we do know of a *Golden Lion* from a 1619 record.

Left: The former Rising Sun.

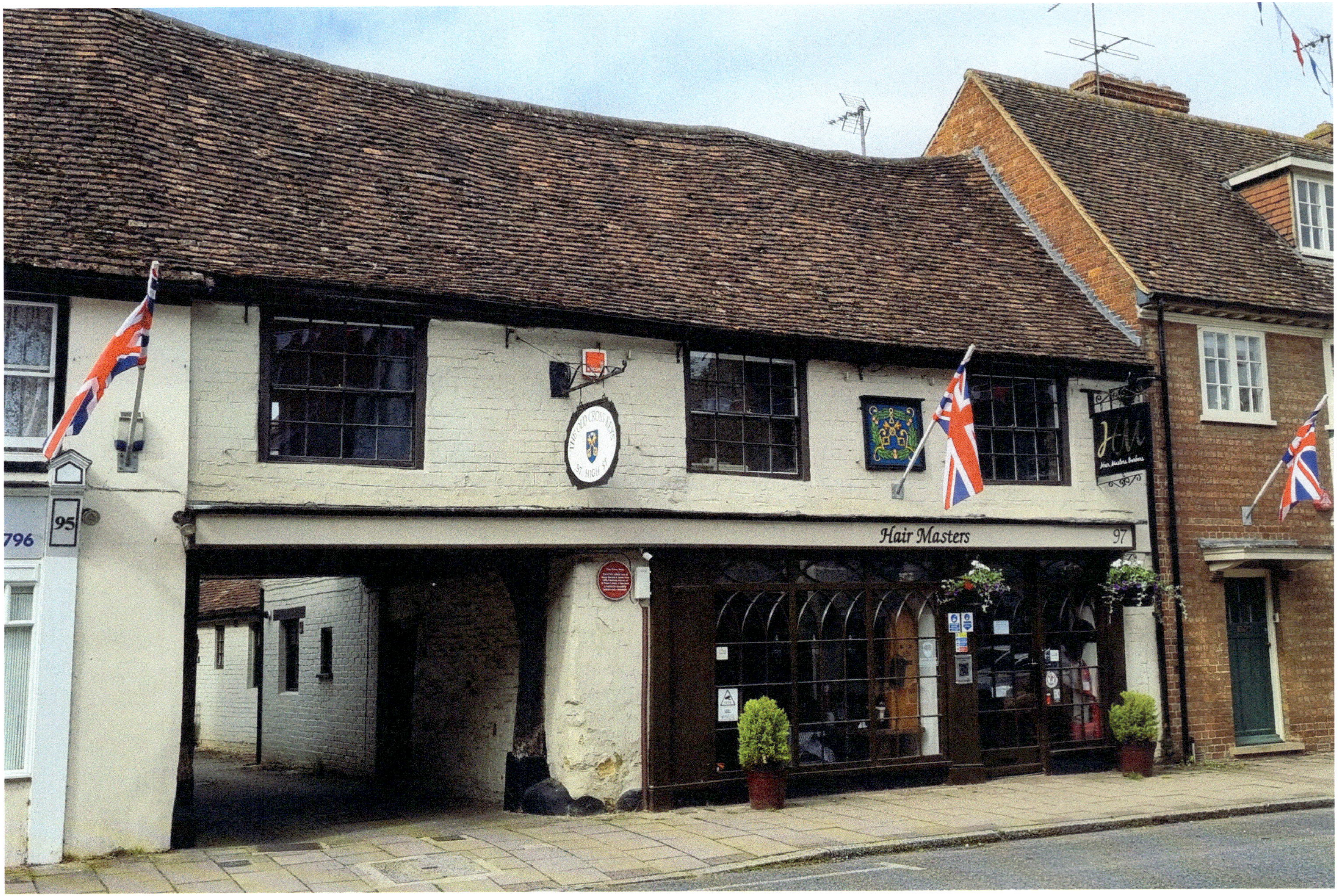
796
95
Hair Masters
97

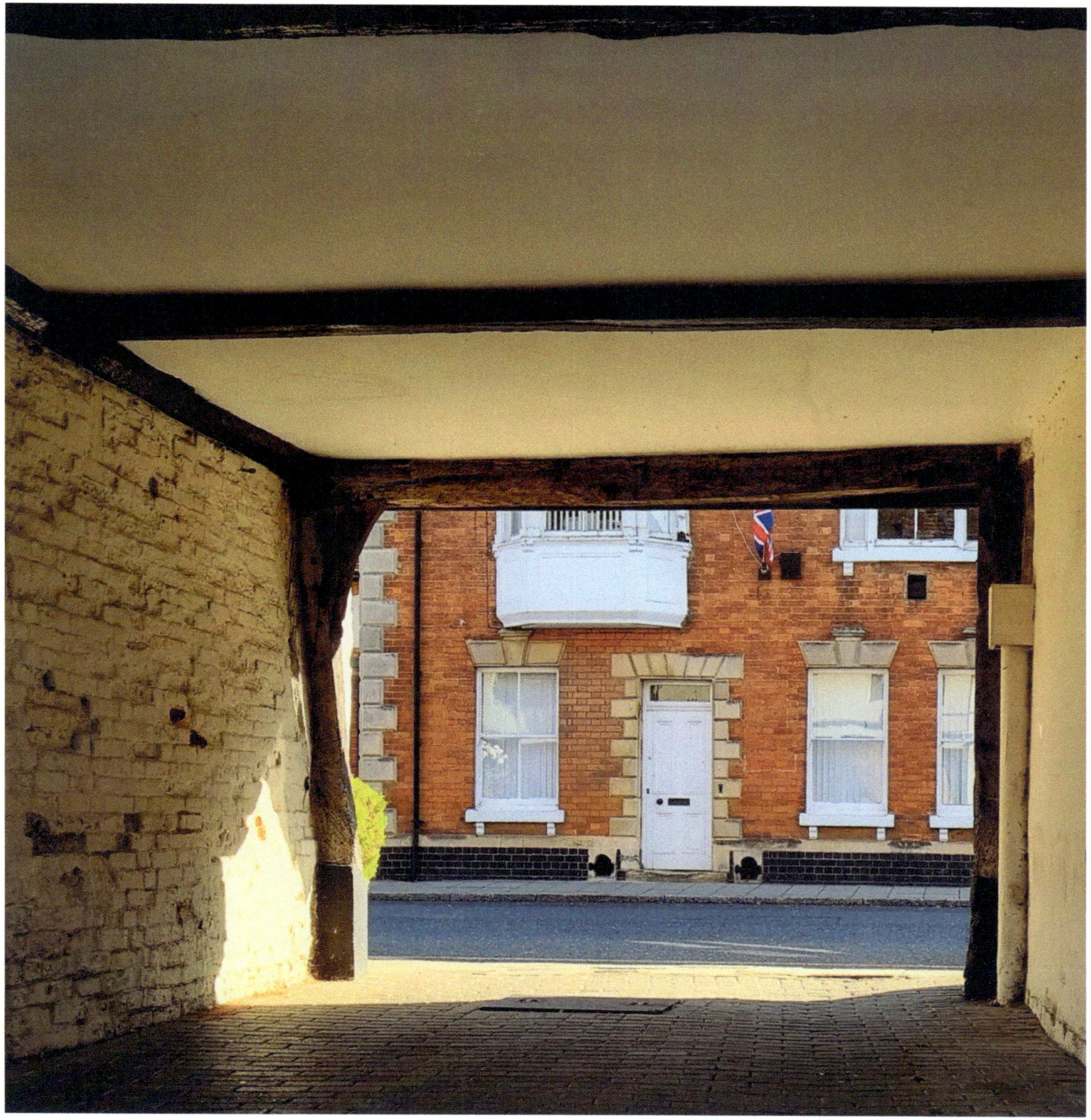

The Cross Keys

This late medieval building was once known as the *Cross Keys*.

This building is undoubtedly medieval in origin and may be one of the oldest surviving buildings in Stony Stratford. The configuration of its buildings strongly suggest that it was an inn. The low arch was constructed before the invention of sprung carriages, which raised the height of the vehicle. Clearly this building escaped the fire of 1736.

The buildings, now separate properties, have been rebuilt, repaired and modernised over the centuries, but they still retain some 15th century timbers. Excavations in 1936, as a by-product of building work, revealed the medieval inn yard some 2 feet below the present road surface. At the same time, evidence of a banqueting hall was exposed.

The name *Cross Keys* is not so ancient. It first appears in a license register in 1773 and it ceased to trade as a public house in 1870. For some years in the 20th century, half of the building was a tea room, trading under *Ye Olde Cross Keys*.

On page 26, the late medieval building that once traded as the Cross Keys.
On this page the low arch - wide enough for carts and waggons but not high enough for sprung stage coaches.

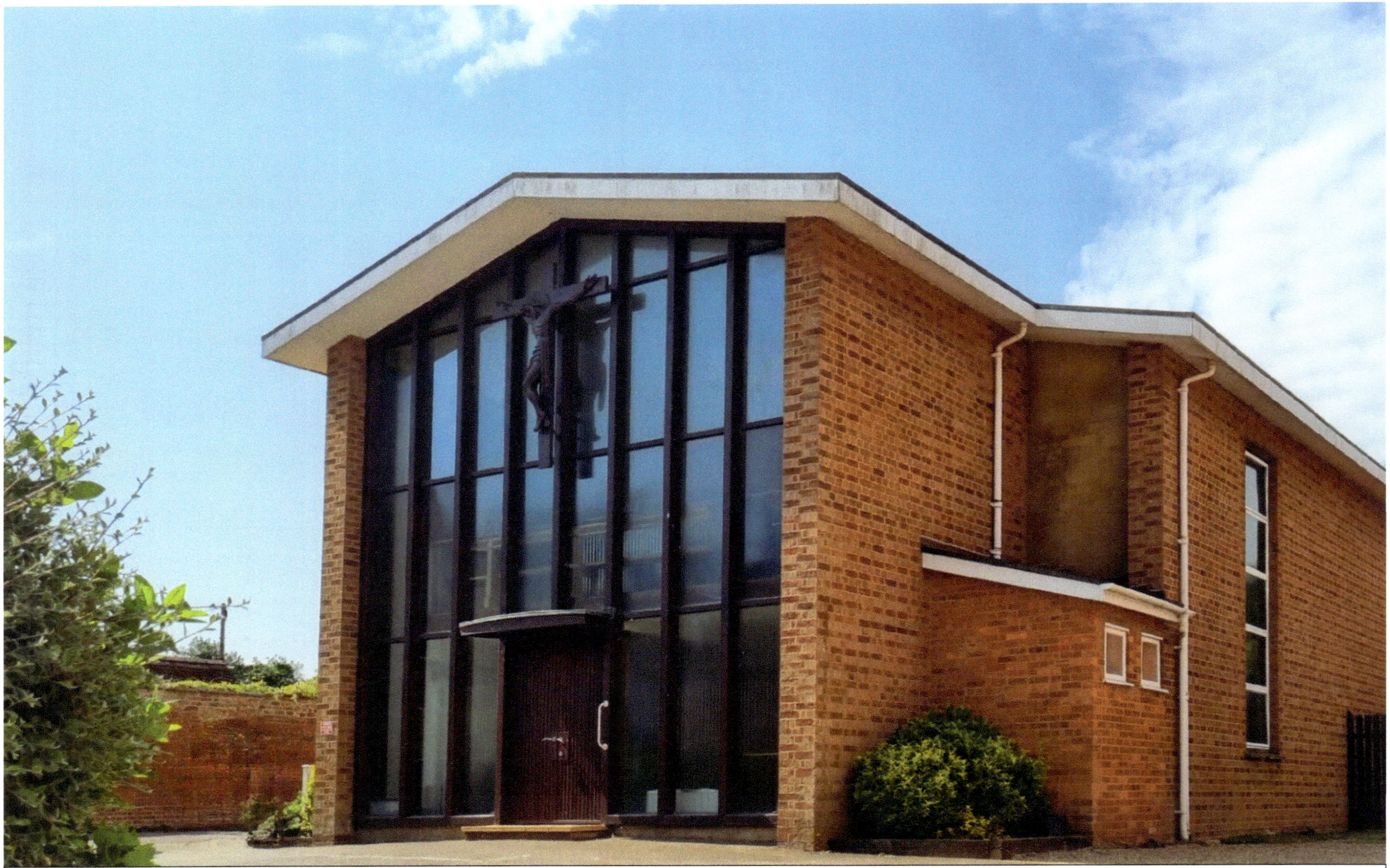

Roman Catholics were very thin on the ground before 1840 and until St Francis de Sales was built in Wolverton after 1860 the nearest places of worship were Weston Underwood (12 miles) and Northampton (14 miles). This church, dedicated to St Mary Magdalene was blessed in 1958.

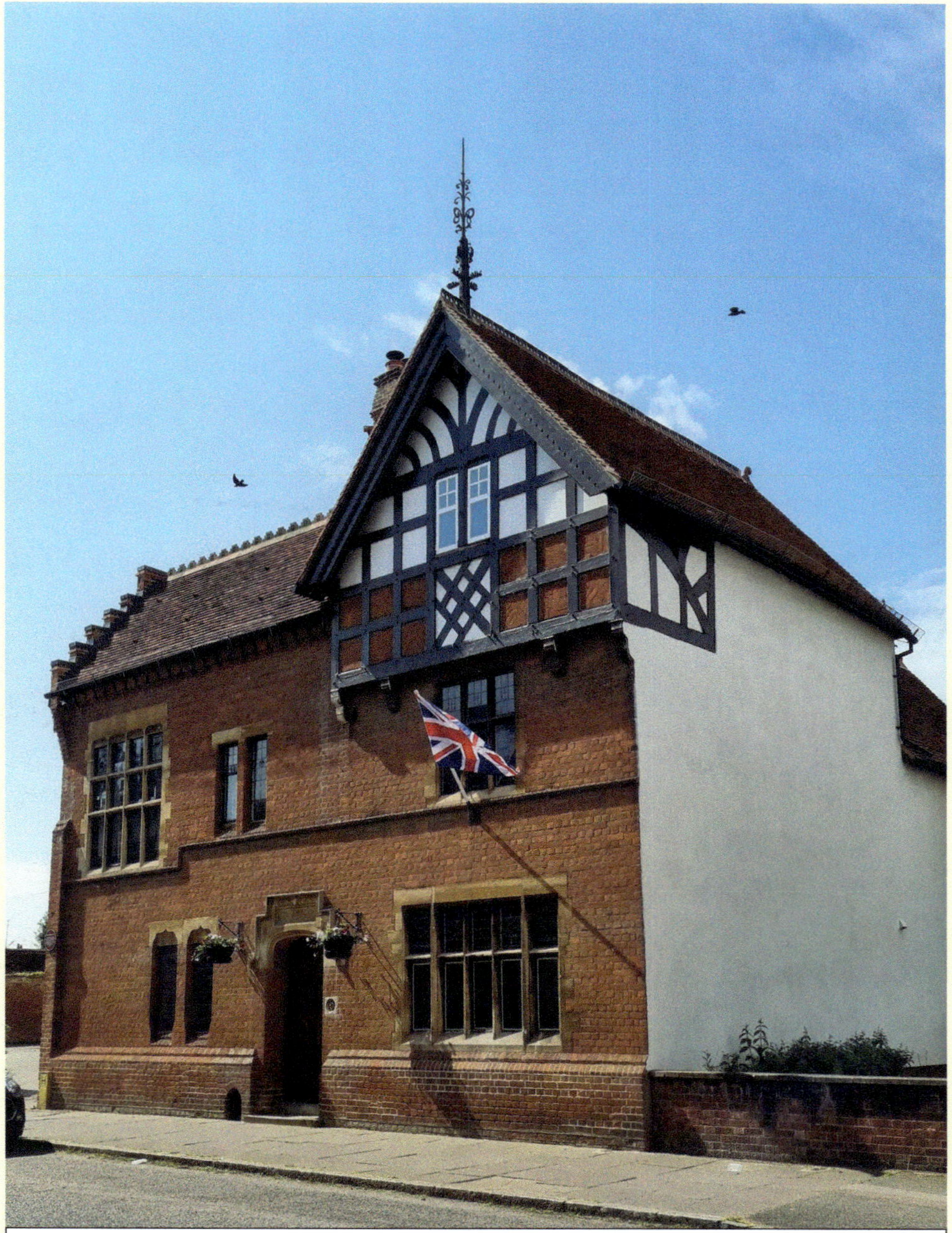

The 'Rothenburg House', built by the celebrated architect, Edward Swinfen Harris.

EDWARD SWINFEN HARRIS

Edward Swinfen Harris, born in Stony Stratford in 1841, was a distinguished architect with a national reputation. Nicholas Pevsner described him as "the only outstanding local architect working in the north of the county." He worked in London, as well as Stony Stratford, and although his legacy is predominantly local there are surviving buildings in London, Dorset and Northamptonshire. The house shown here, known as the Rothenburg House, was designed and built for himself after 1887.

He was born on July 30th 1841 at 36 High Street, Stony Stratford. His father was the clerk to the town bench of magistrates, the Board of Guardians and other bodies, and Edward was the eldest son. The family later moved to Back Lane (later Russell Street). He began his formal education when he was 11 at the Belvedere Academy, at Old Stratford. He was then sent to Ullathorpe House School in Leicestershire, where he boarded.

Around 1858 he was apprenticed to the book trade. He didn't stay long and rather like his contemporary, Thomas Hardy, the poet and novelist, became articled to an architect in London. On completion of his apprenticeship he then shared an office in London with two friends, but in 1868, he returned to Stony Stratford to make additions to the vicarage of Wolverton St. Mary.

In the following years he was greatly involved in ecclesiastical architecture, restoring many churches. The vestry added to St Giles is his design and he was commissioned to work on London churches. He became a Fellow of the Royal Institute of British Architects and travelled extensively in Europe to study architecture.

After marriage in 1870, he settled in Stony Stratford at a new house at 15 Wolverton Road. In this period he designed the house at 19 Wolverton Road for Dr McGuire.

In his professional life he was the county surveyor of North Bucks and

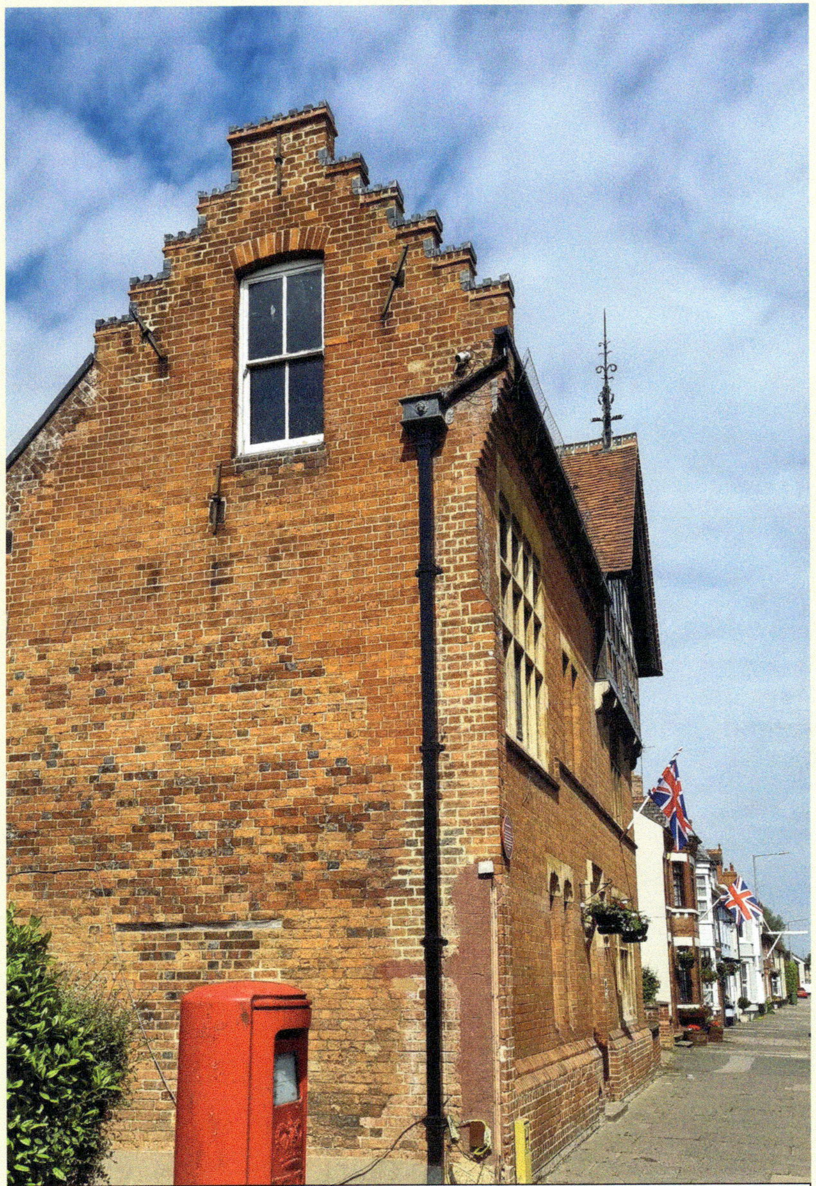

Above: Another view of the 'Rothenburg House.'
Right: 36 High Street, to the left of the Kardamom Lounge, where Harris was born in 1841. His father was a clerk to the magistrates.

after the passing of the Education Act built a number of local schools, including that of St. Mary's in the town.

Many local examples of the architect's work can still be seen in the local area. Among them are the pub on the corner of the Wolverton and London Road (formerly a school), the house at 15 Wolverton Road, The Elms at Wolverton, Lovat Bank at Newport Pagnell, the Maids Moreton Rectory and the stables at Bletchley Park.

He retired in 1914 and lived to May 30th 1924. His architectural legacy is an important one. Many of his buildings have been adapted and in some cases demolished.

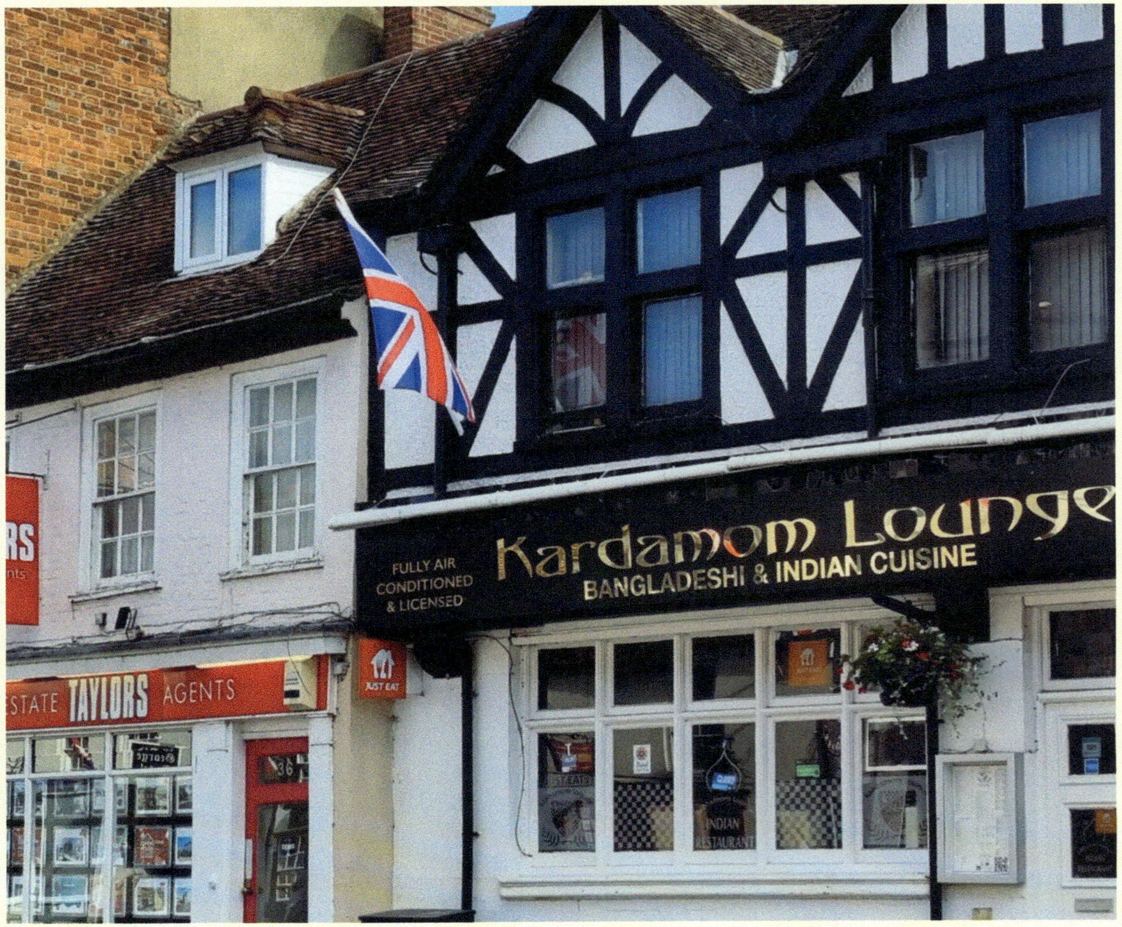

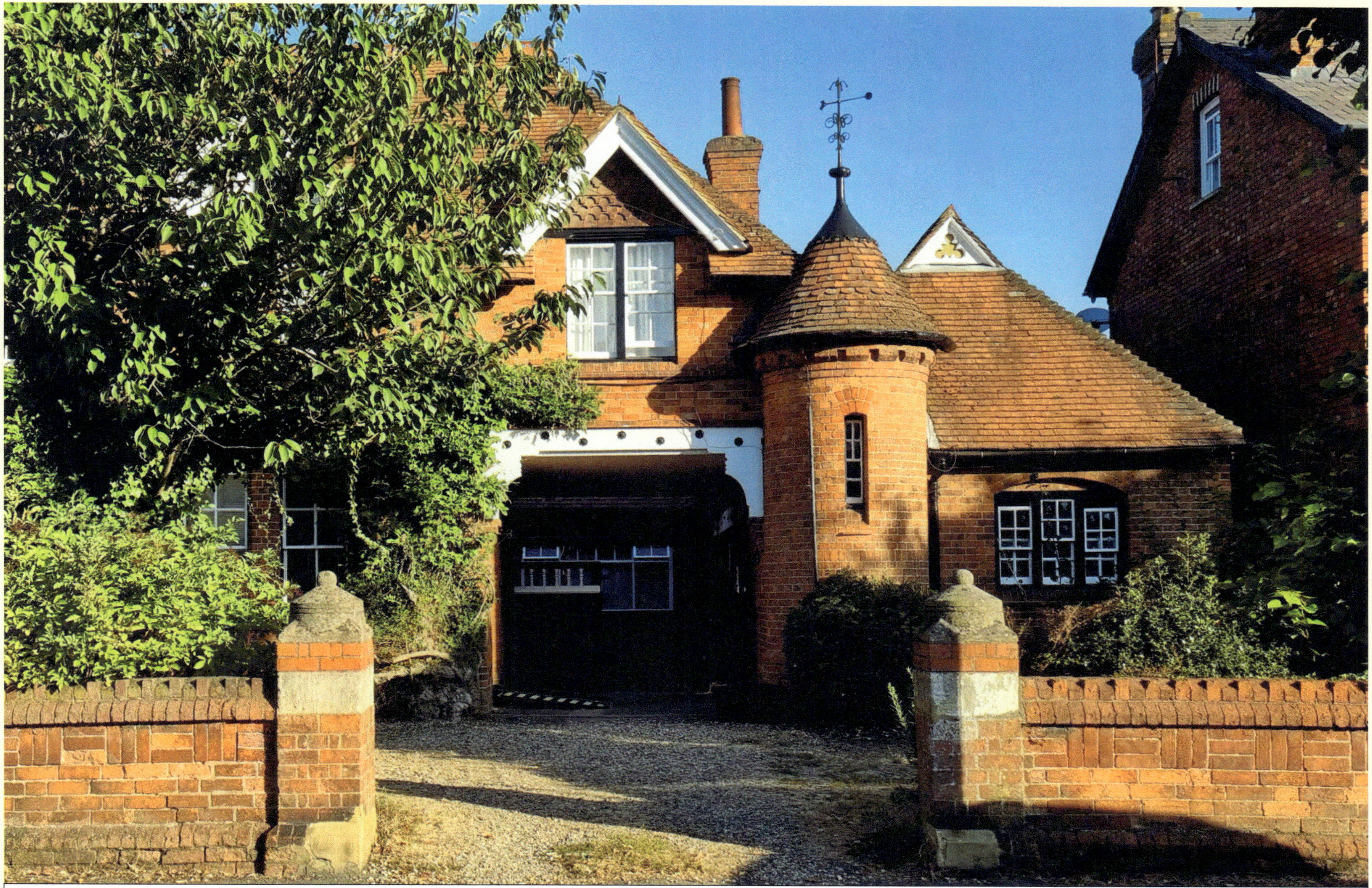

A substantial house on the Wolverton Road designed by Edward Swinfen Harris.

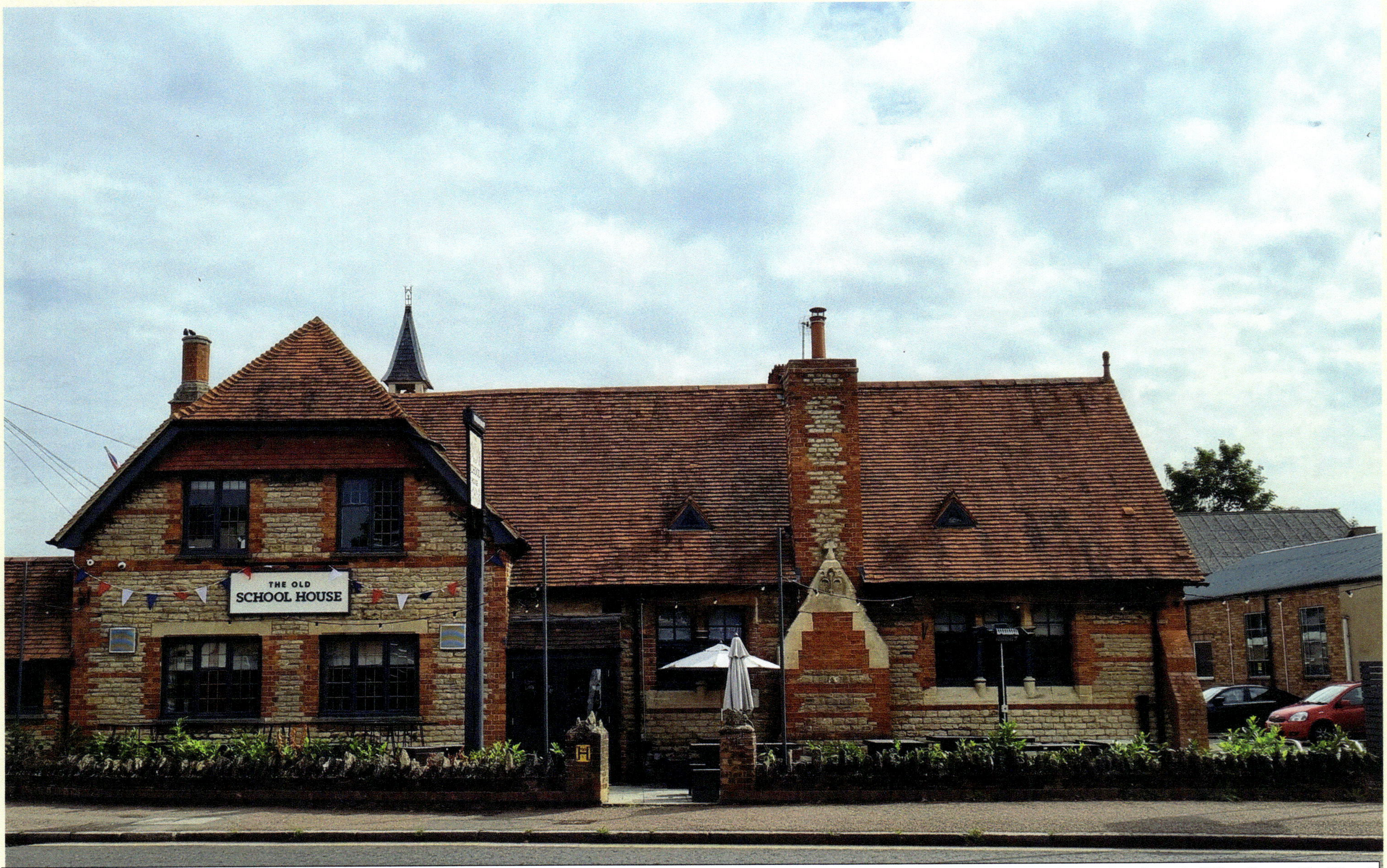

The collection of buildings on this corner replaced some tumbledown cottages as a new school. It was used for this purpose until 1936 when a new school opened at the end of King Street. The Plough Inn, which had been next door for at least 200 years, took the opportunity to move in. The pub has recently changed its name to reflect its original purpose.

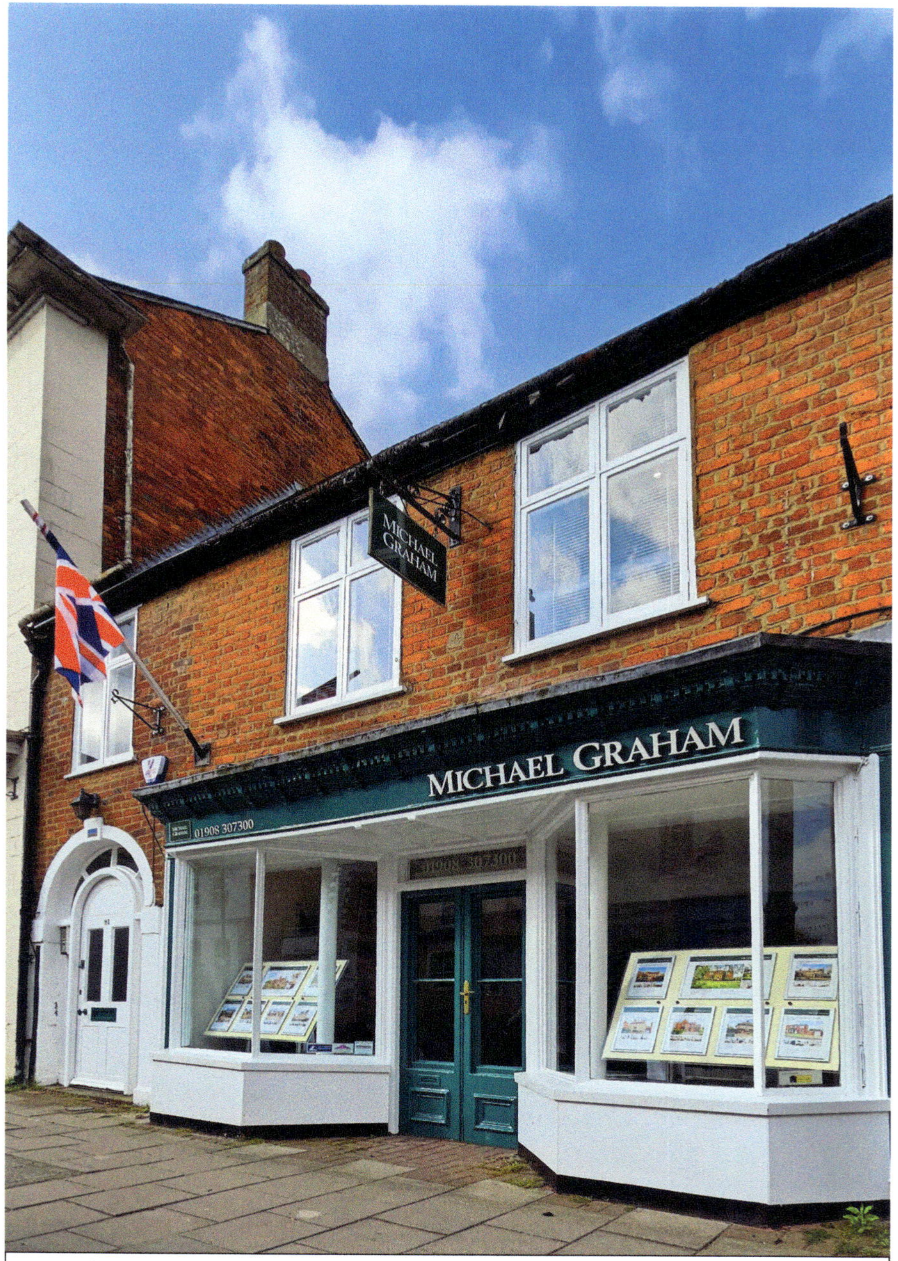

81-83 High Street, at one time the site of the Talbot Inn.

THE TALBOT

The only clue that these houses and shops were once an inn, lies in the arched door way to the left which was likely the entrance to the inn yard.

The Talbot had a recorded life of just over a century. On record it makes its first appearance in 1680 in the Overseer's Papers. It is in the licensing records under Richard Whitmay from 1753 to 1761. He may have been succeeded by George Dodson, who was a licensee from 1761 to 1772. Unfortunately, in his case, no inn sign is recorded, so it is speculation on my part and is based solely on the dates. However, when names are once again recorded against licensees names in the register in 1776, *The Talbot* has disappeared. There are two possible explanations: either it closed down for good after the death of Richard Whitmay, (his burial was recorded in the St Giles parish register as 21st April 1762) or it continued its functions under another name. If the latter, the only one that might fit the circumstances was the *White Lyon,* which had business from 1765 until 1783.

Like most buildings in Stony Stratford that may have survived from earlier times, the *Talbot* has been substantially rebuilt in the 18th and 19th centuries, although some medieval timbers survive in the roof. The name *Talbot* itself is certainly an old medieval name. It was a name for a white hunting dog and this may have been the origin of the surname of Sir John Talbot, who became the first earl of Shrewsbury. Talbot was a very famous warrior in the 15th century and many inns were named in his honour. Either way the name has medieval origins and it is possible that the *Talbot* in Stony Stratford is much older than its recorded history suggests.

The presence or absence of any written records is not a great deal of help. Most affairs were conducted without much paperwork and even in 18th century Wolverton you can find substantial farmers who were illiterate. When we do find records, it is usually for some incidental purpose to the activities of an inn.

It would certainly make sense for an inm to be established in that location. It was central to the town and on the High Street. So the *Talbot* may have had a longer life than appears at first glance but certainly no life as an inn after the third quarter of the 18th century. The building itself survives and is now separated into two premises, numbered 81-83 High Street.

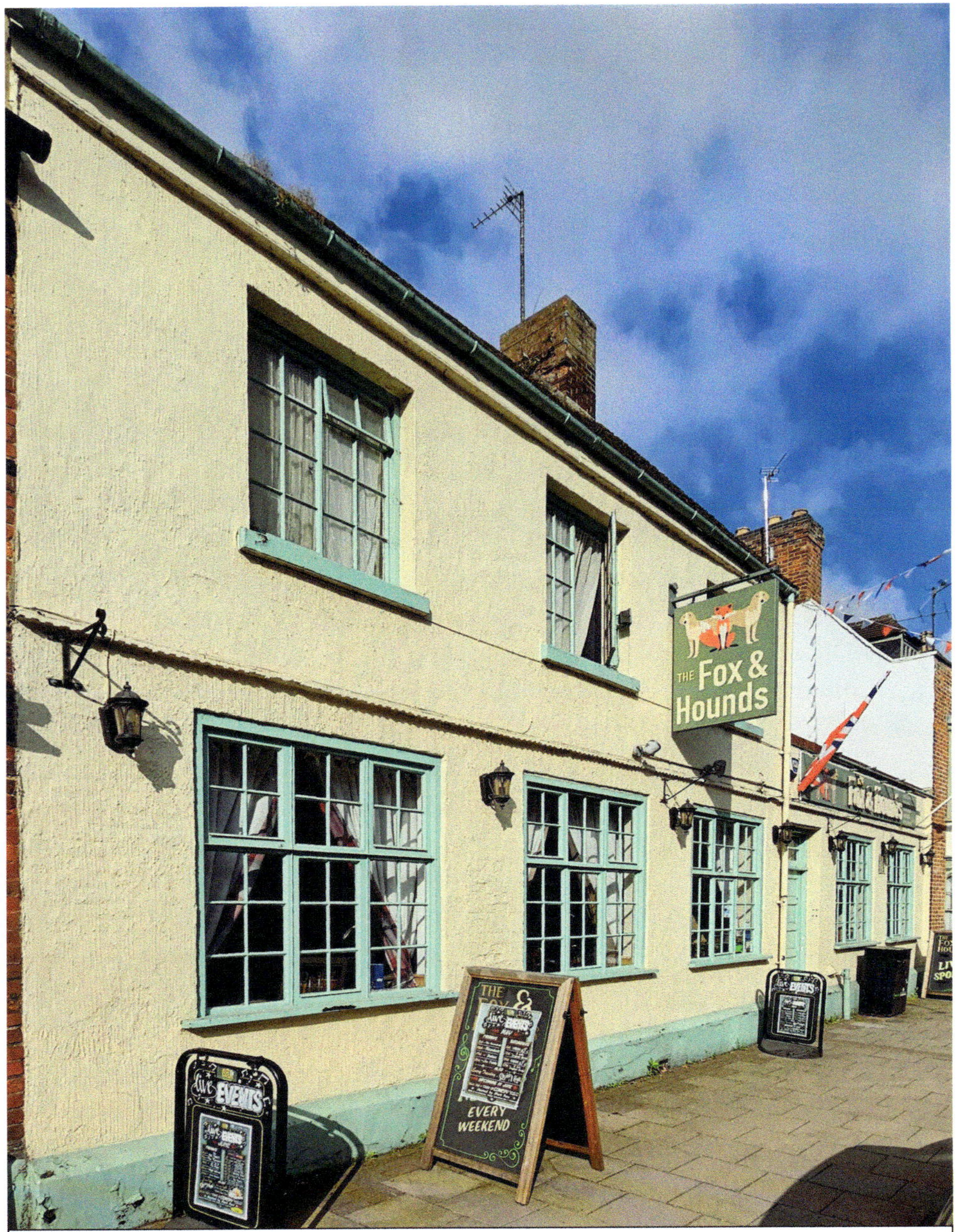

The Fox and Hounds.

THE FOX AND HOUNDS

The *Fox and Hounds* now occupies two houses, although it appears to have started as a beer shop in the middle of the 19th century. A 20th century fire in one of the houses caused great damage and the upper storey was never replaced.

THE YORK HOUSE STORY

York House School was a private school of some distinction and operated from a house on the London Road, which today bears the name. However, the original York House was this building at the corner of York Road, presently the Conservative Club.

Ann Slade, the wife of Edward Slade, an engineer, had started a school for girls in Hanslope as far back as 1853. They later found premises in Great Linford. Their son, Edward Adams Slade, married Adeline Agnes Wheeler in 1876, and she took over the school business. In 1892 they came to Stony Stratford, where they rented a house at 77 High Street, a house built in 1840 by John York, and was known as York House.

The arrangement with the landlord proved less than satisfactory for Mrs Slade, and she made complaints about maintenance that were never addressed to her satisfaction and in 1902 she rented Clarence House on the London Road for £50 a year. The house had been built by John Oliver, the son of John York's former banking partner. She decided to keep the name York House and her new premises were so-named. The school enjoyed a good reputation, which continued into the next generation after Mrs Slade died in 1931 and her daughters took over. They retired in 1957 and the school business, but not the premises, was sold. The premises were auctioned and purchased by a Mrs Ogilvie, who sold them on the following year to Mr Littleden, who owned the London Road Garage. He had some intention of expanding his car showroom but this did not come to pass and he was approached by the St Giles Youth Club about a possible sale. He agreed and York House was sold in 1963. And so a name which originated with an obscure Stony Stratford banker in the 19th century is still preserved today in the 20th.

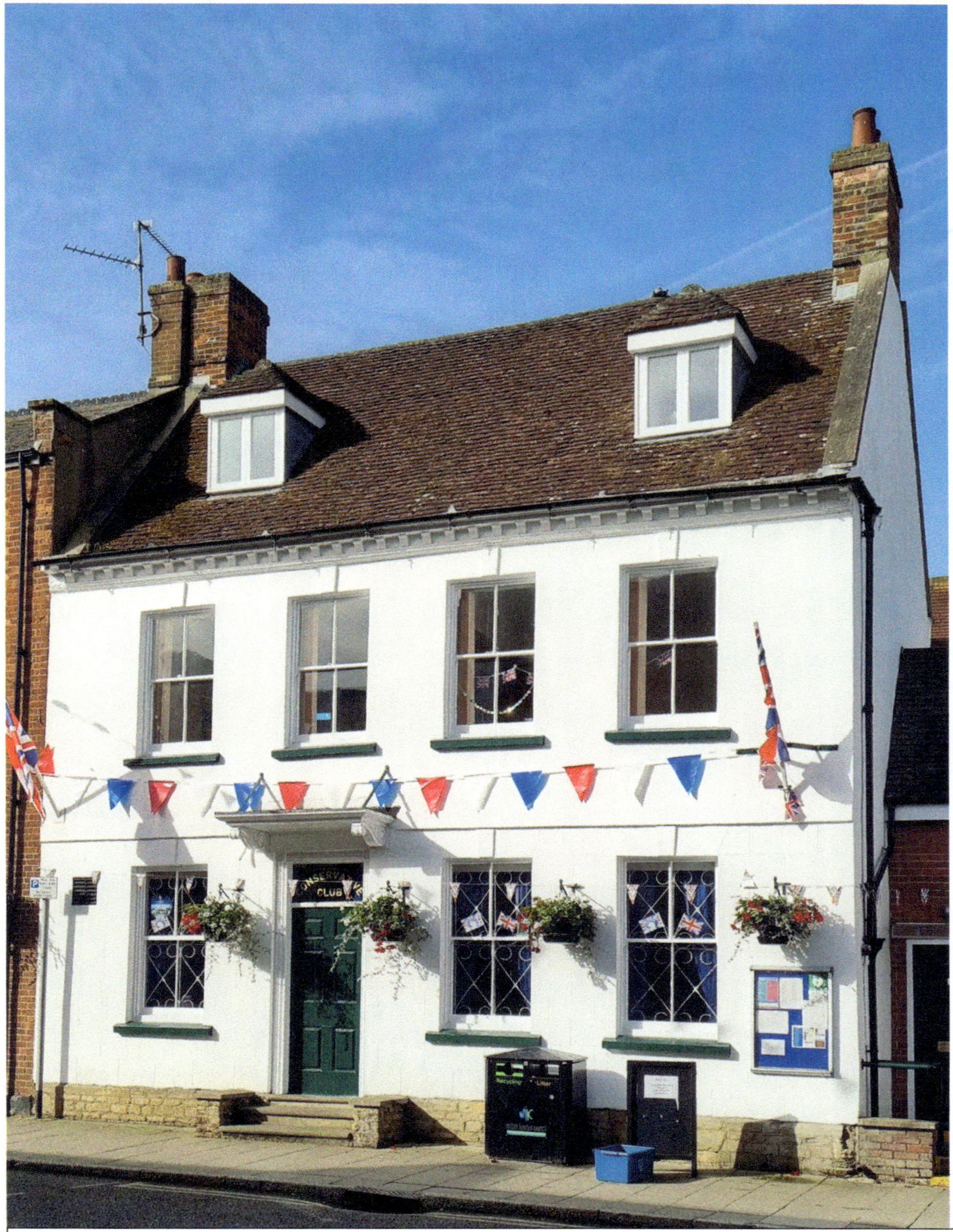

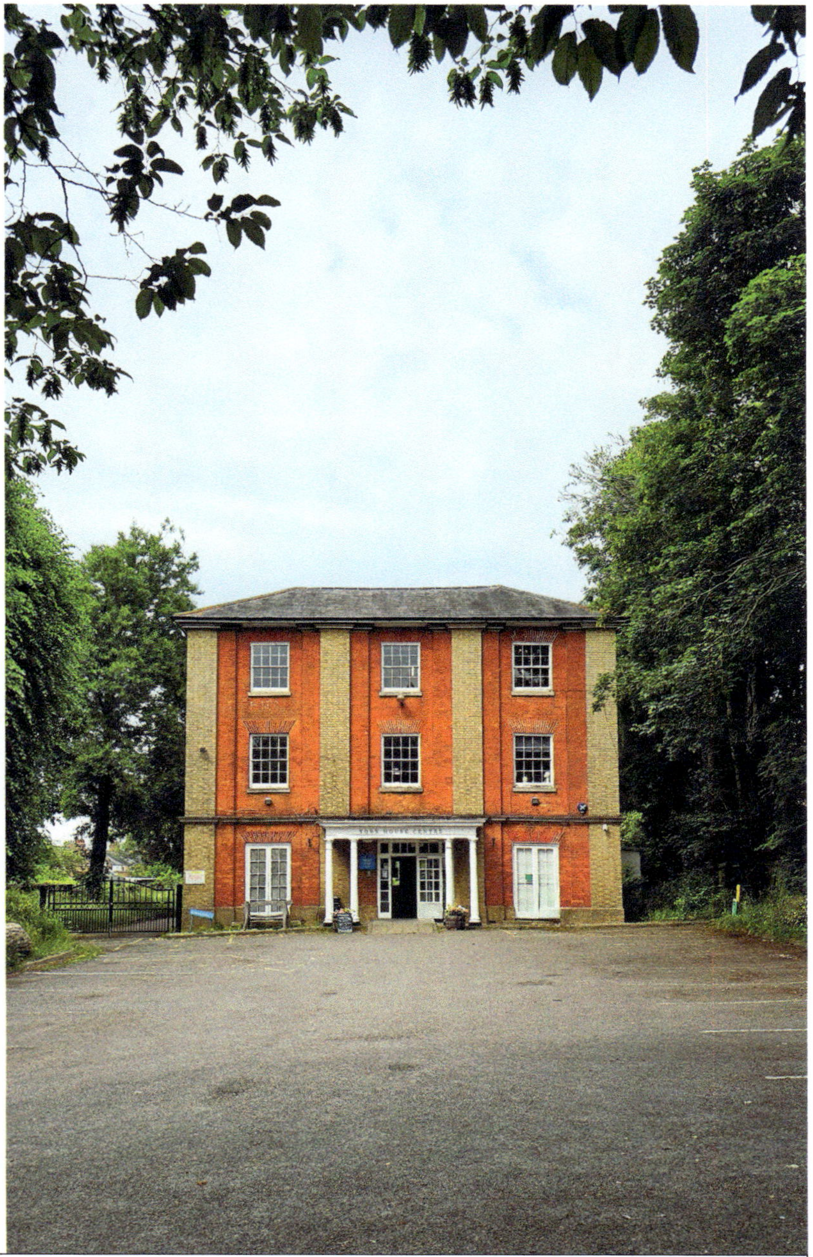

The original York House, now the Conservative Club. Right: York House today.

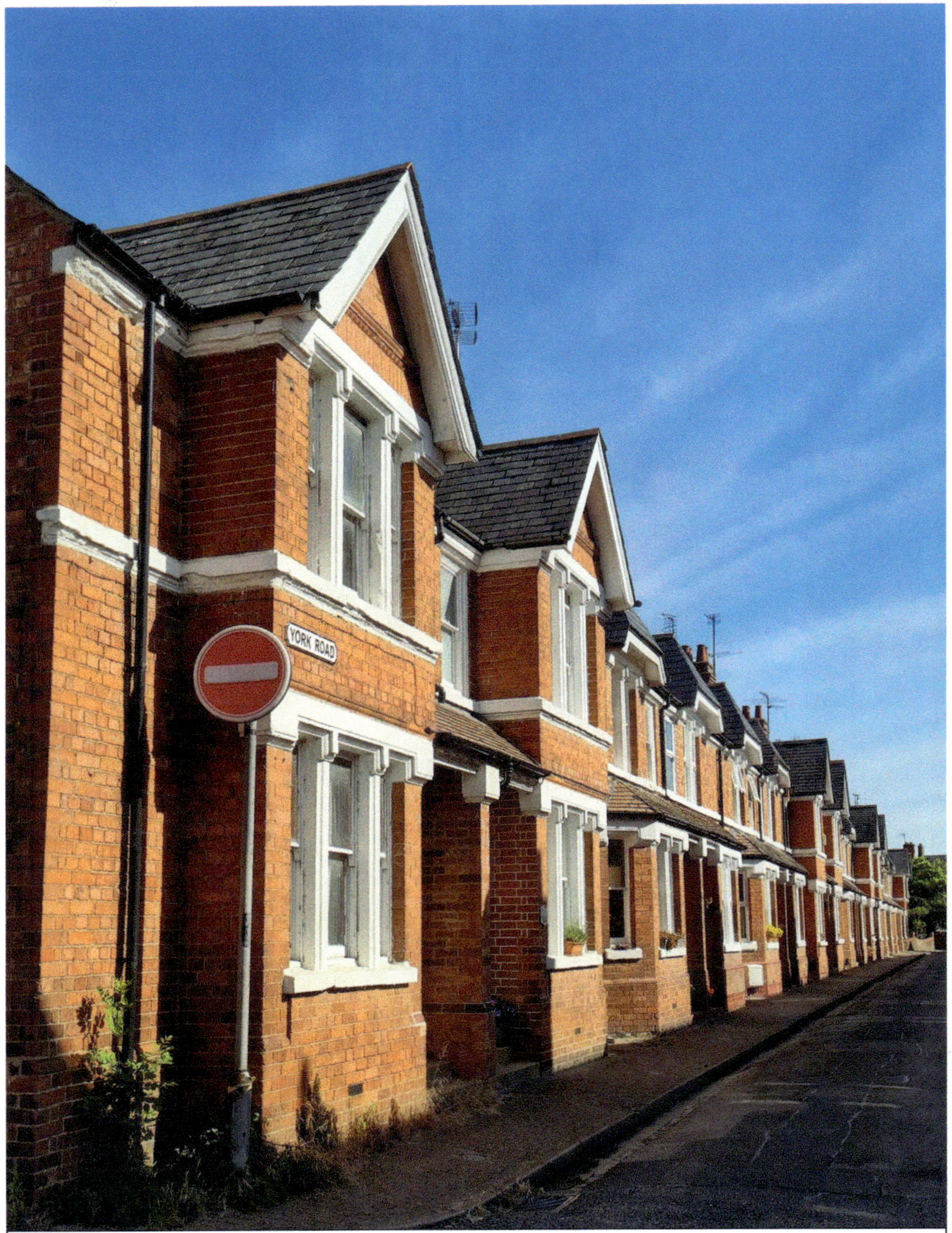

The 20th century terrace of York Road, named after York House at the corner.

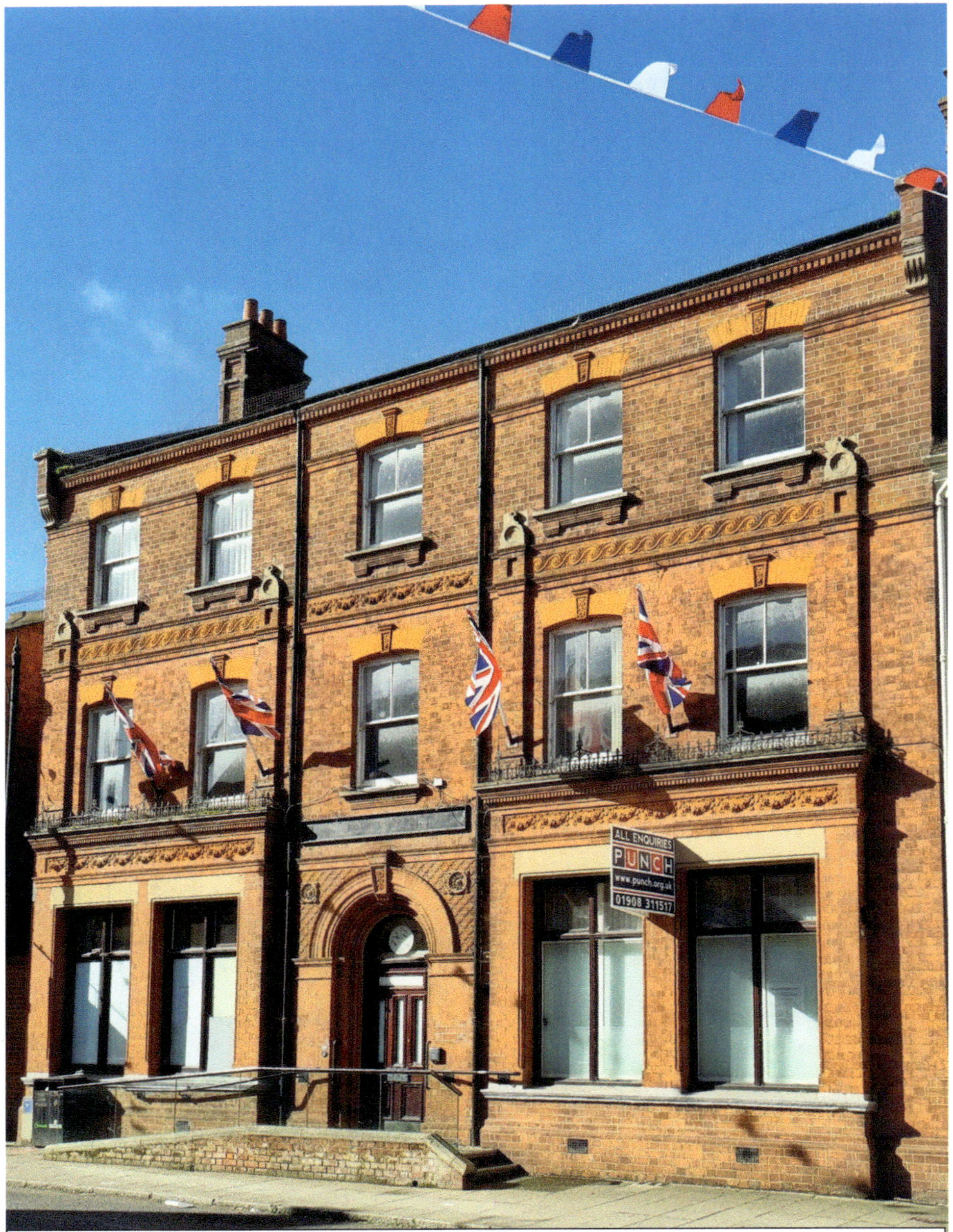

The former Lloyds Bank building.

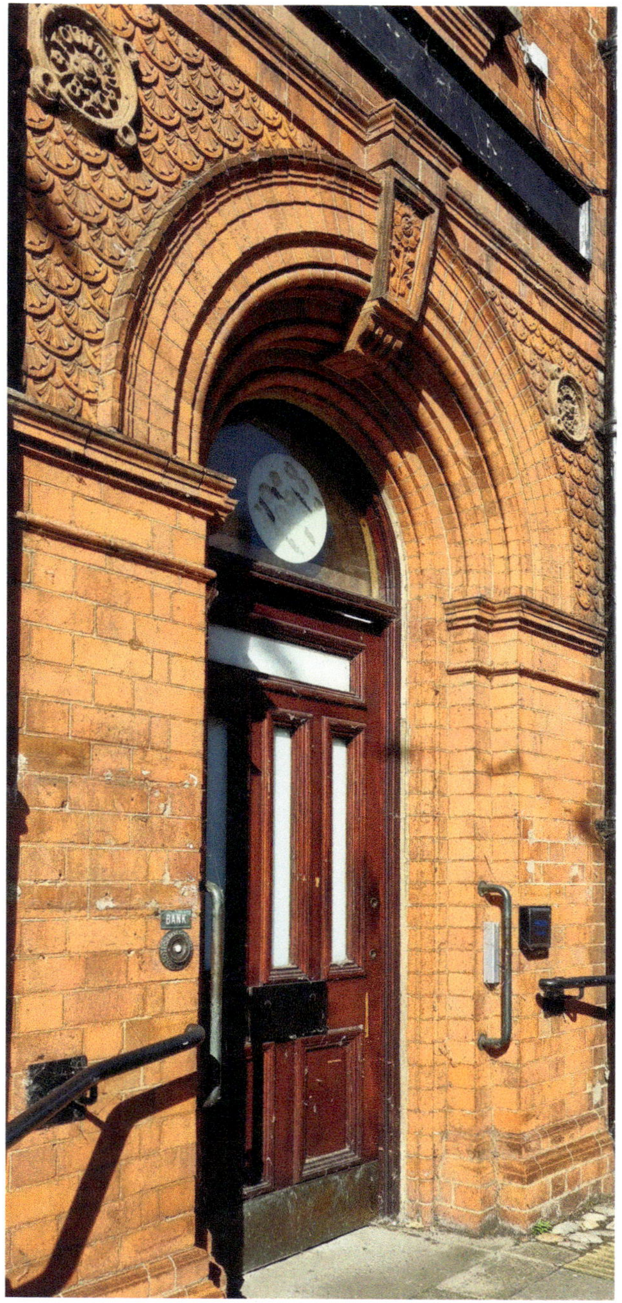

Banking

Banking services started to spread into the provinces in the early 19th century. Richard Harrison, of Wolverton House, set up a bank in Stony Stratford in the 1820s. Unfortunately, it soon failed, and Harrison had to pay off all his creditors. Nevertheless, he had the resources to do so without facing the ignominy of bankruptcy.

The demand for banking services was still strong and by 1830 there were two bankers in Stony Stratford, both supported by stronger financial institutions. One was a branch of a Buckingham bank, Bartlett, Nelson and Co, who were underwritten by Praeds and Co of London; the second was run by two Stony Stratford businessmen, William Oliver and John York and drew upon Jones, Lloyd and Co of London. By 1847, there was one bank in Stony Stratford, operating under the name of Bartlett, Parrot, Hearn and Parrott. In 1895 the London and County Banking Company, with a head office in Lombard Street had a branch at Stony Stratford, open only on Tuesday and Friday.

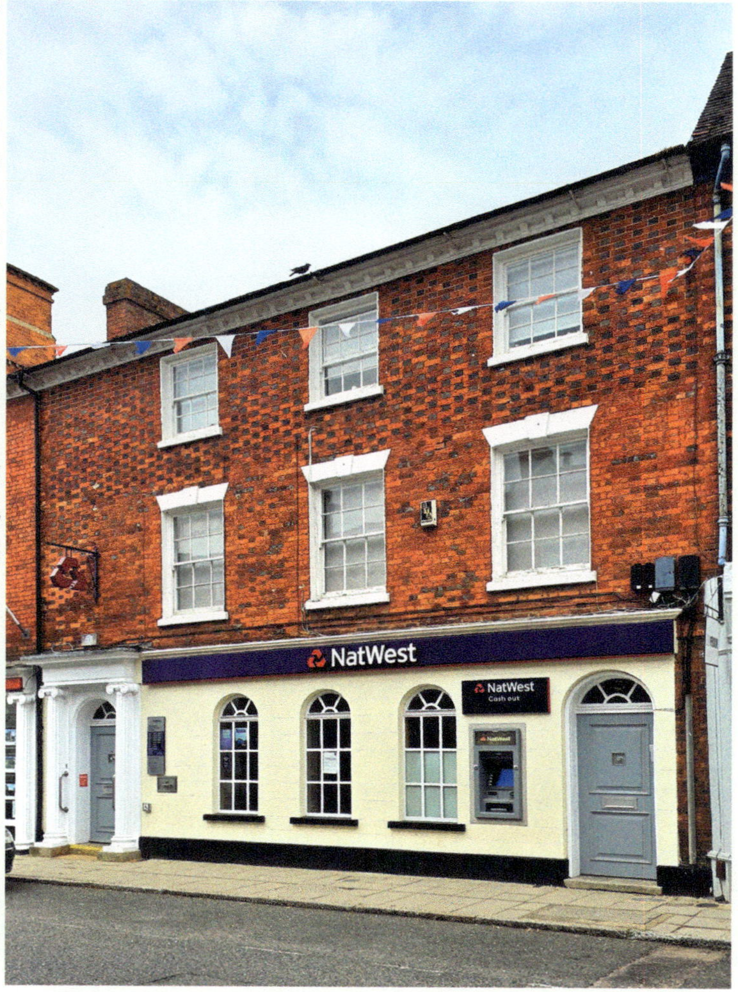

By this time banking was becoming more secure and professionalised. Larger, mostly London based banks, were beginning to replace the small private enterprise operations established earlier in the century.

In the 20th century bank consolidation led to two branches of national banks in Stony Stratford - Lloyds Bank at 69 High Street and the Westminster Bank at 80 High Street. The latter is now the National Westminster Bank.

As we write this, High Street banking is slowly disappearing as internet services take over.

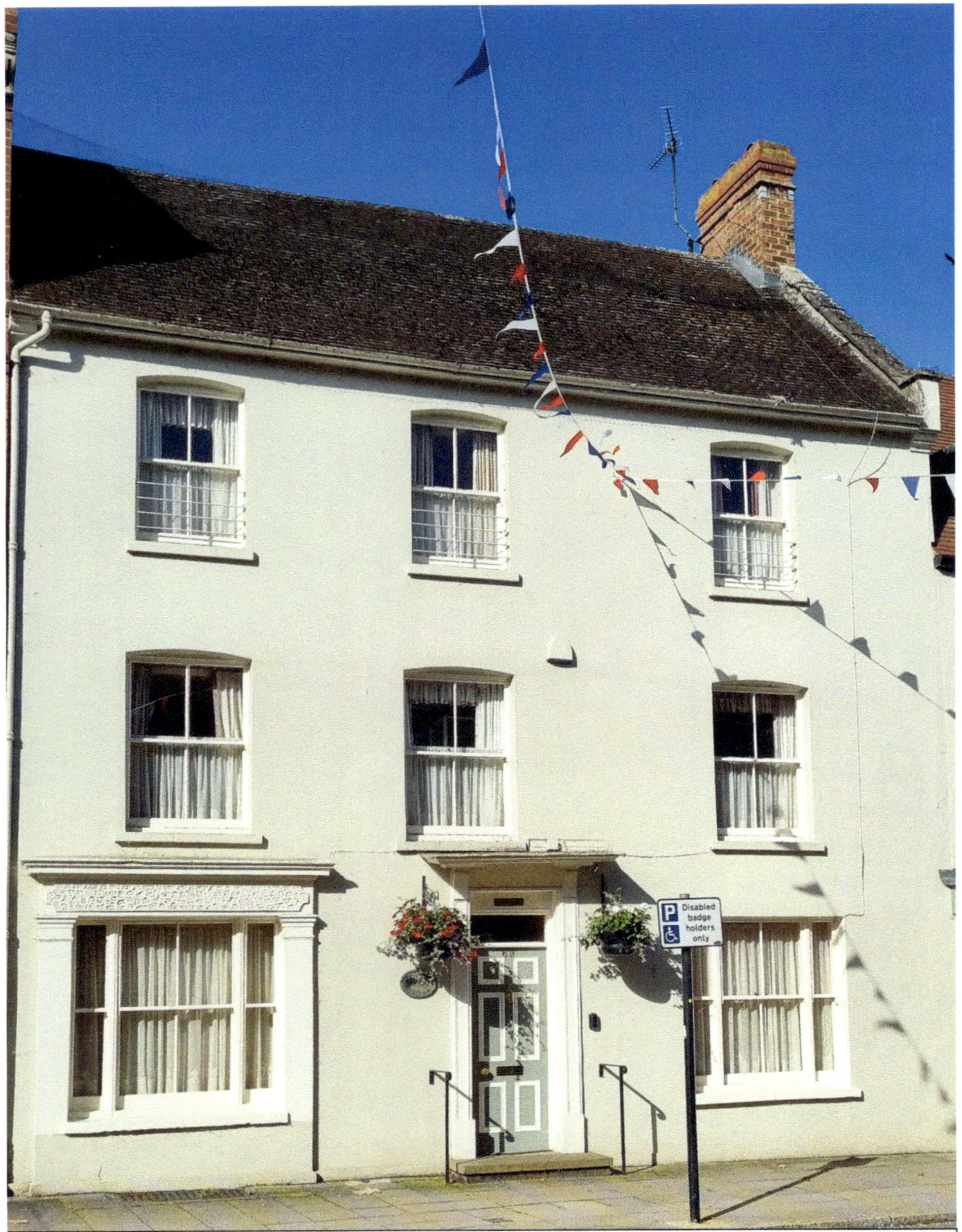

Late 18th century or early 19th century houses usually had a top floor for servants.

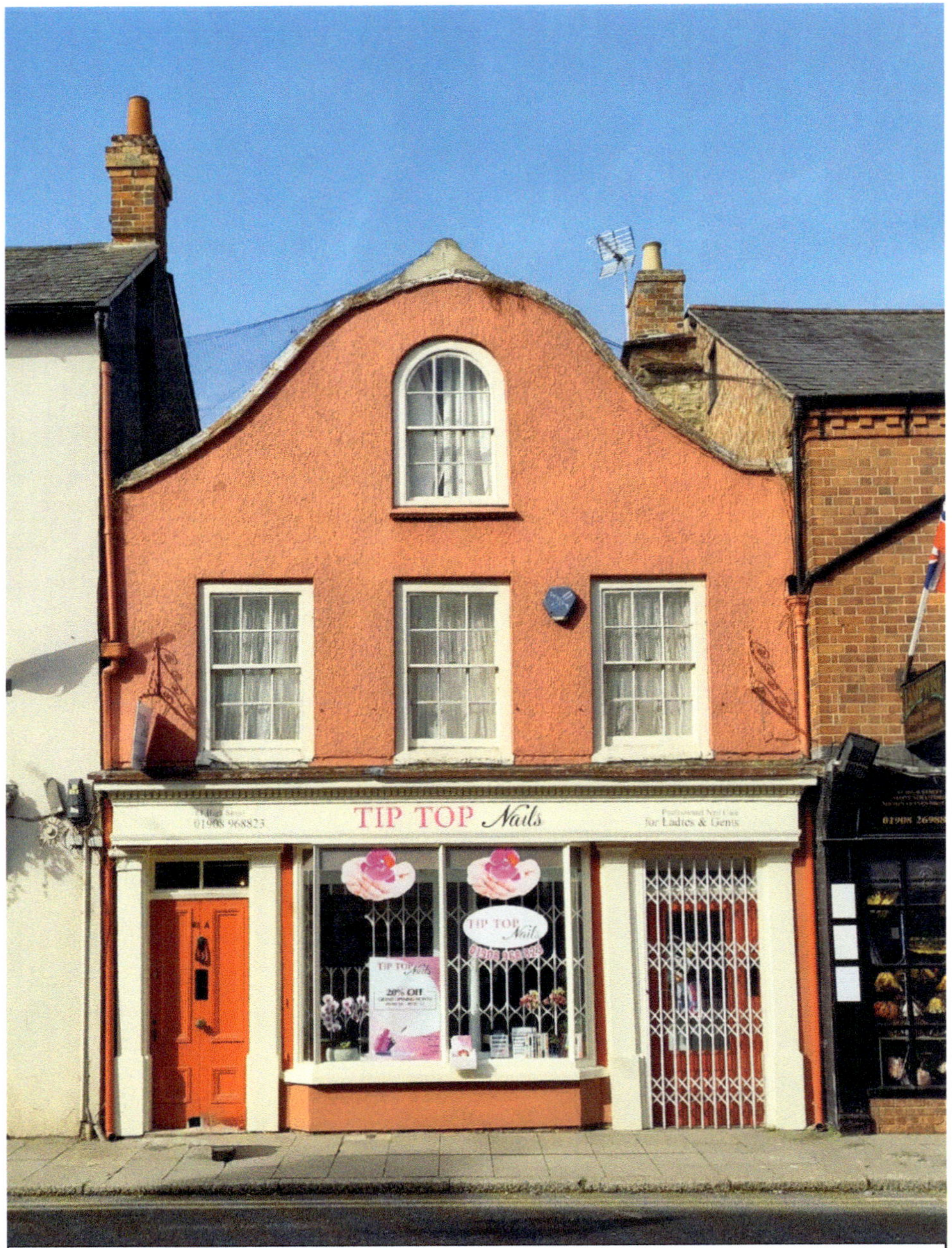

An unusual Dutch gable in the design of this house.

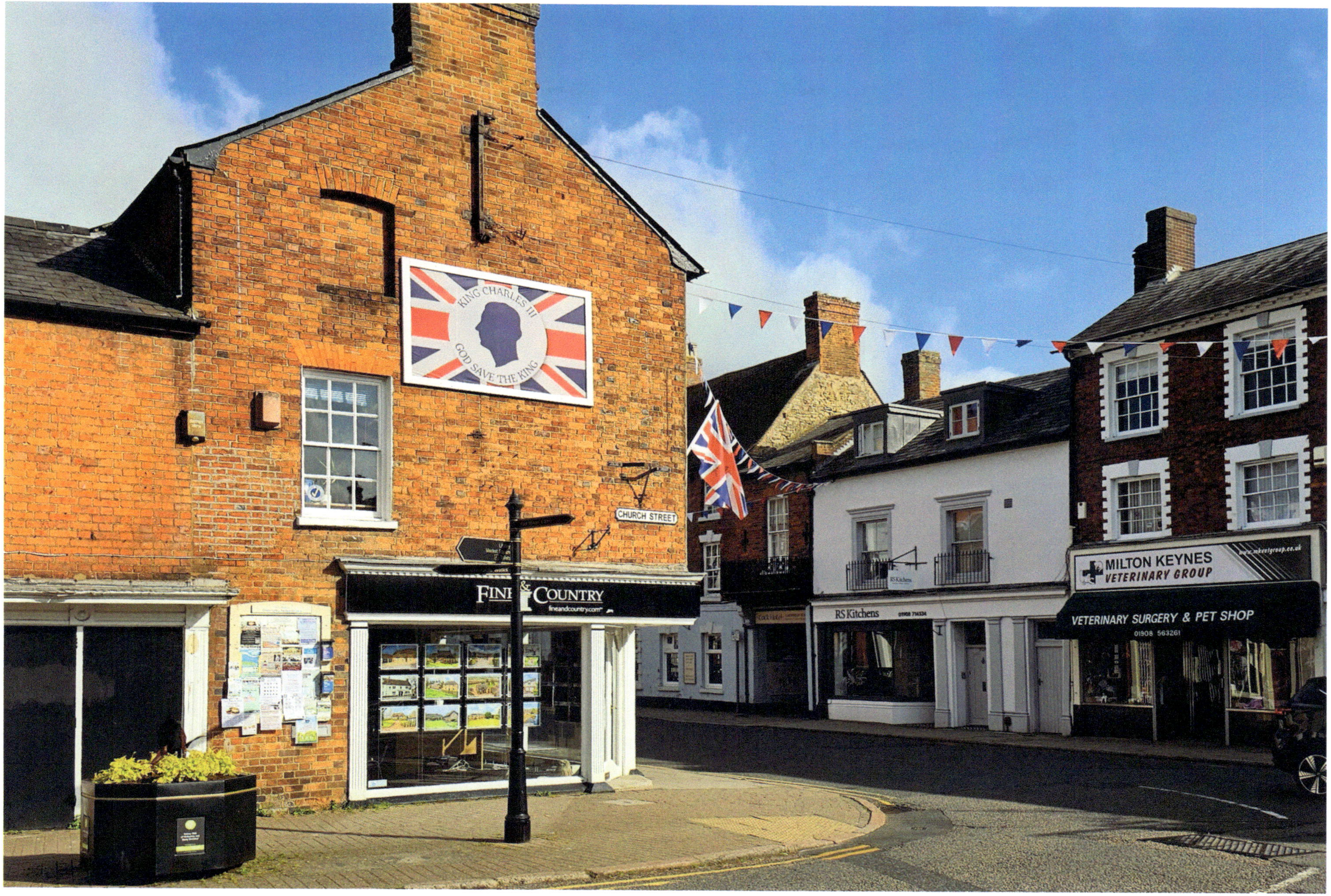
KING CHARLES III
GOD SAVE THE KING
CHURCH STREET
FINE & COUNTRY
fineandcountry.com
RS Kitchens
MILTON KEYNES
VETERINARY GROUP
VETERINARY SURGERY & PET SHOP
01908 563261

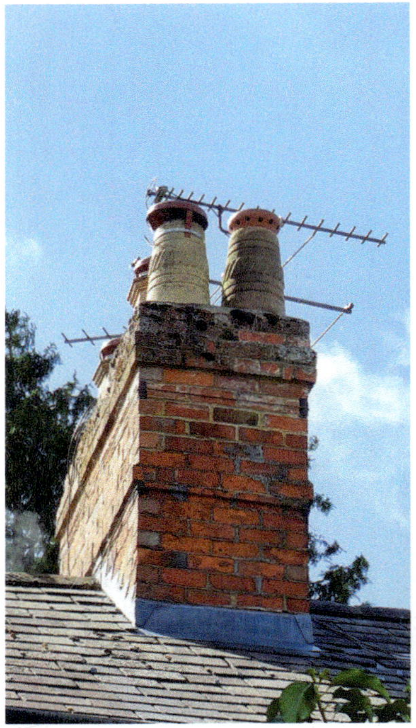
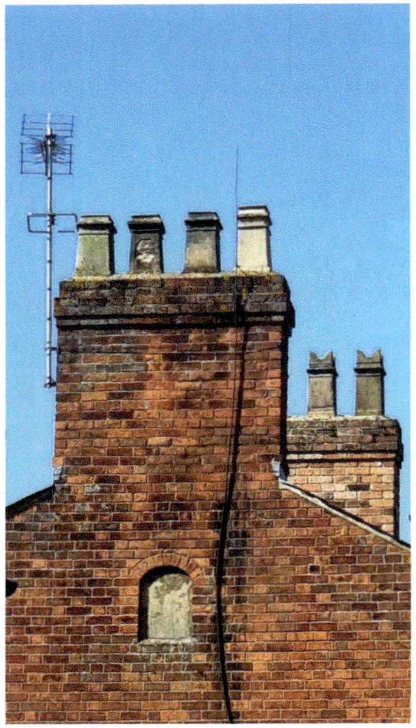
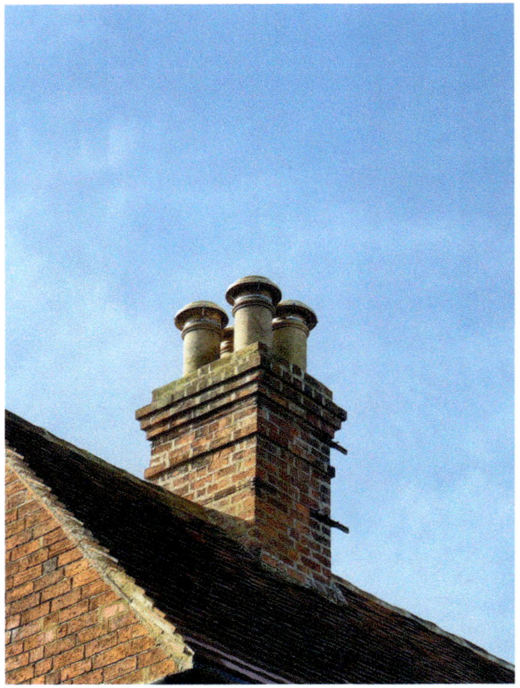
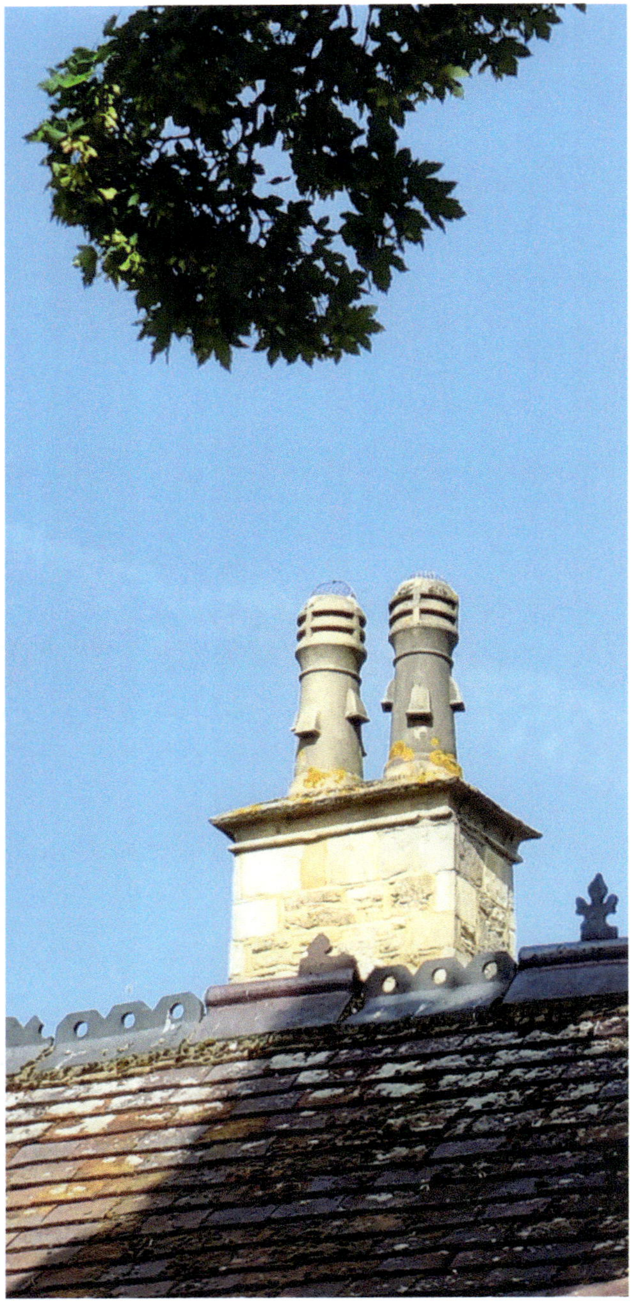
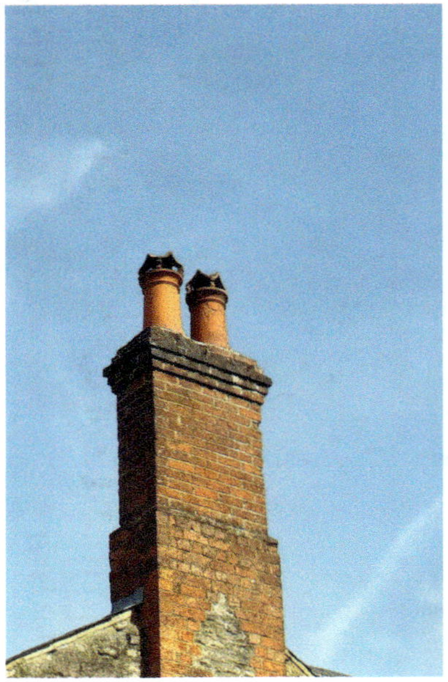
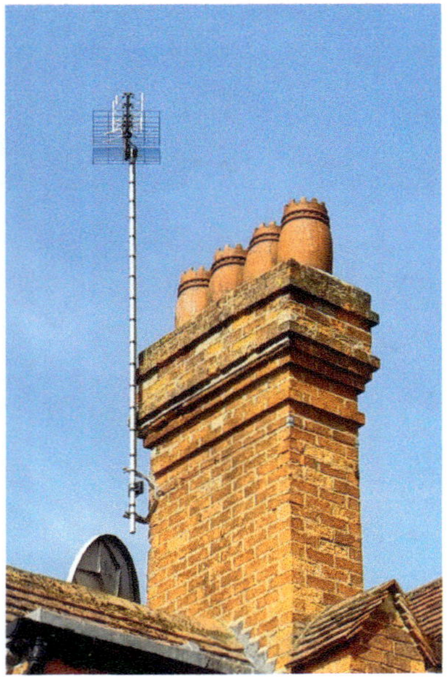
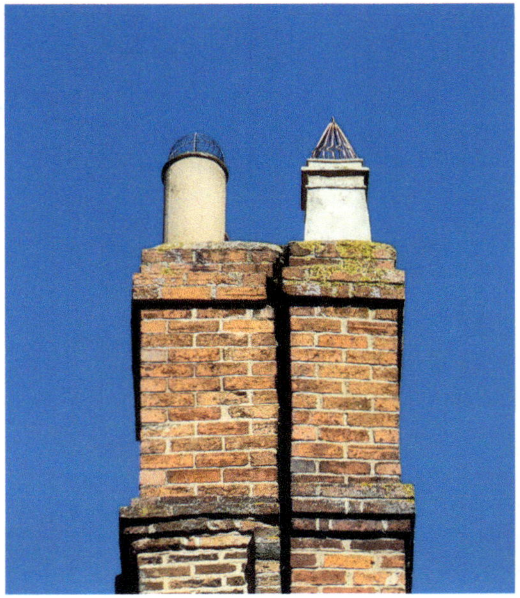

LOOK UP

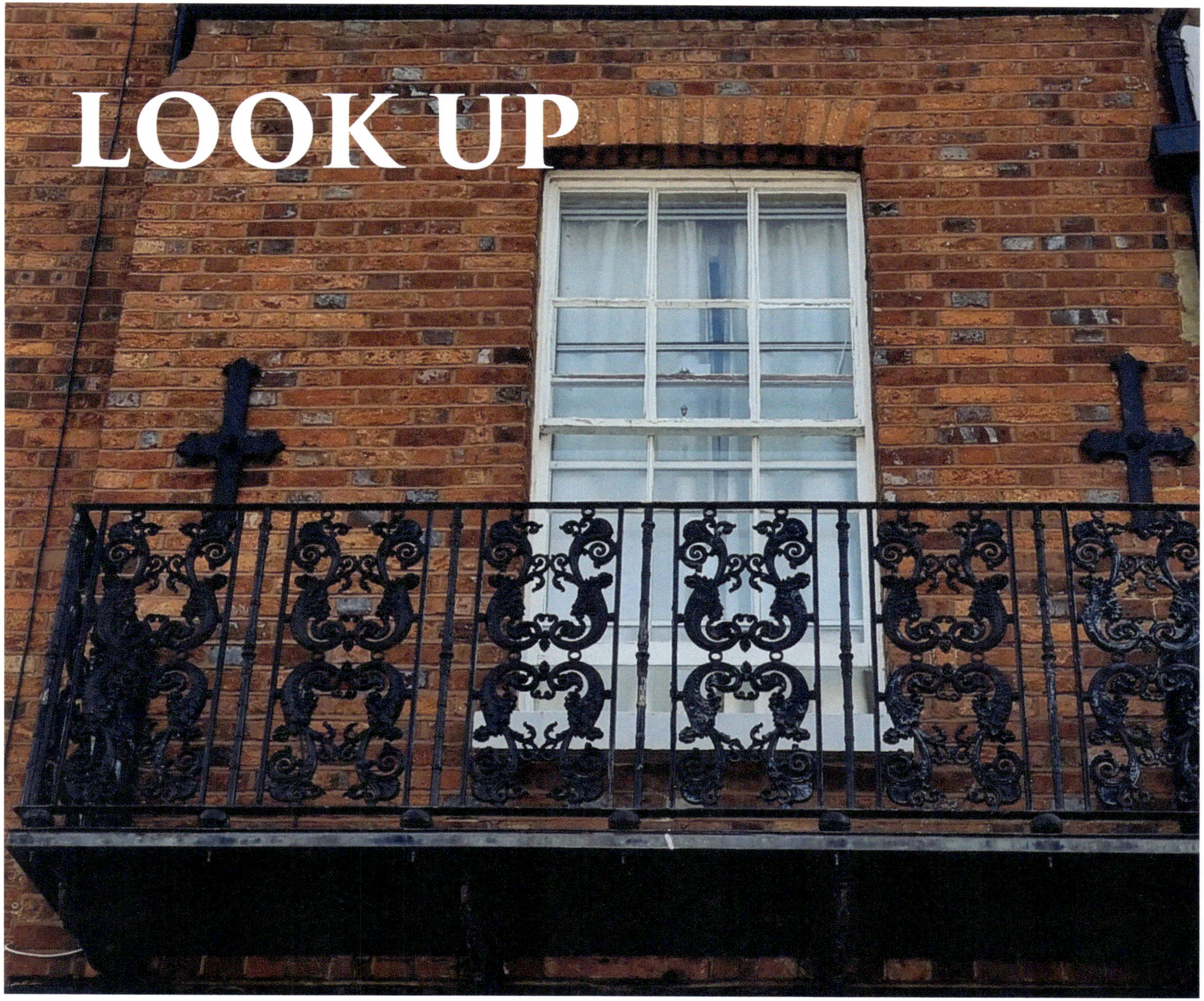

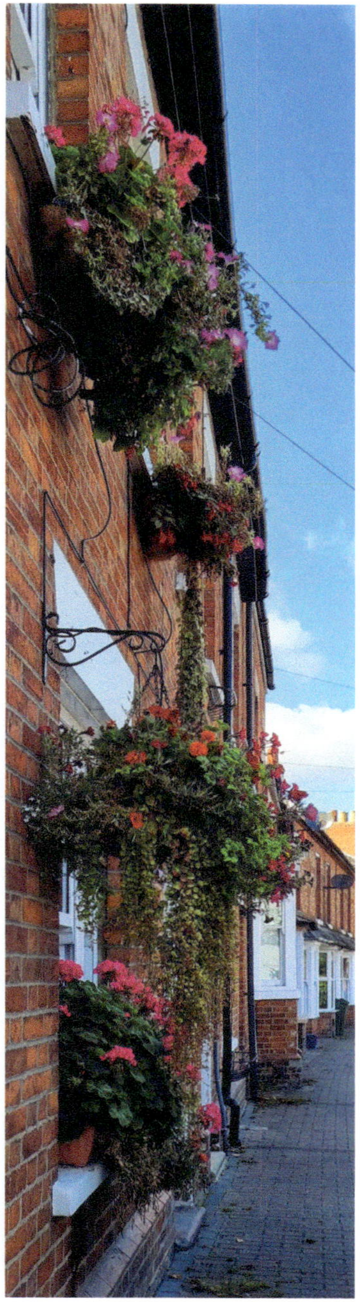

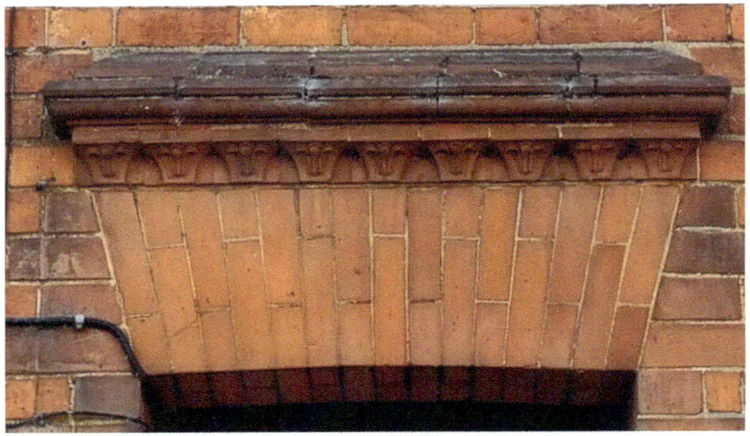
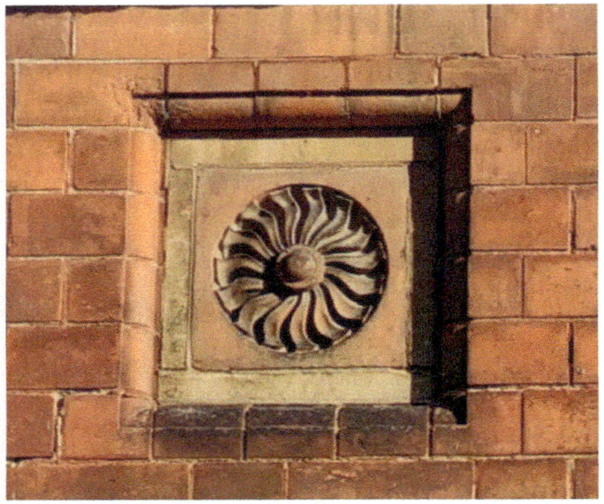
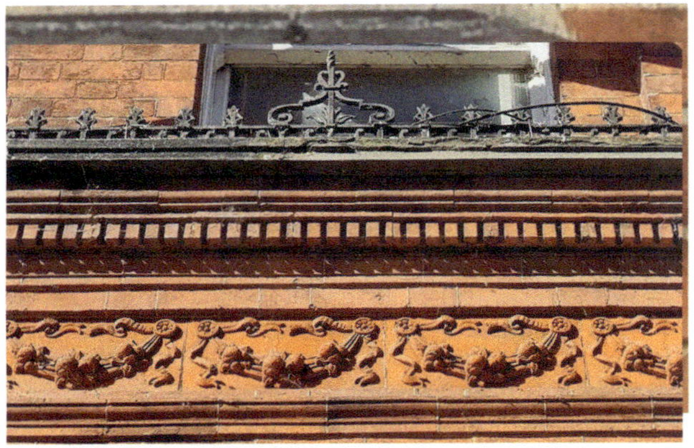
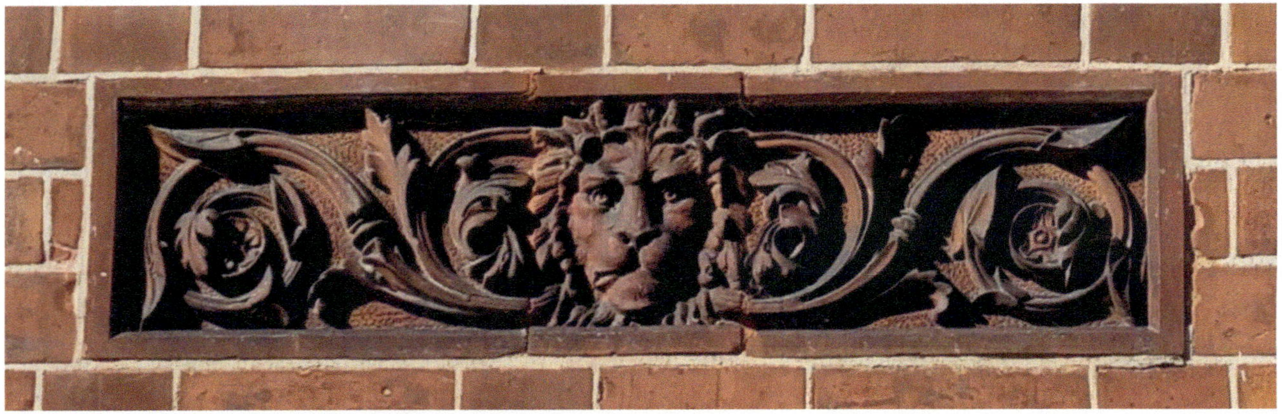
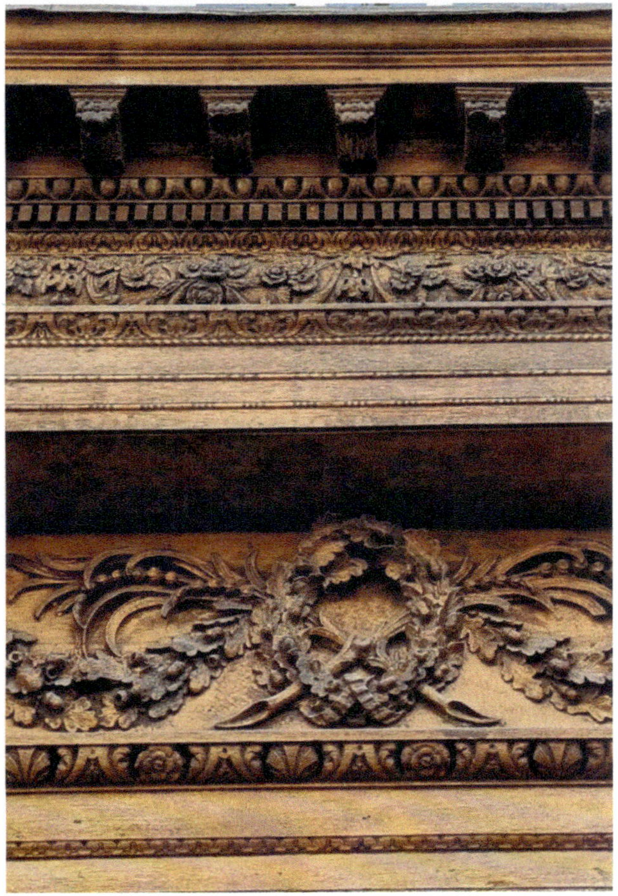
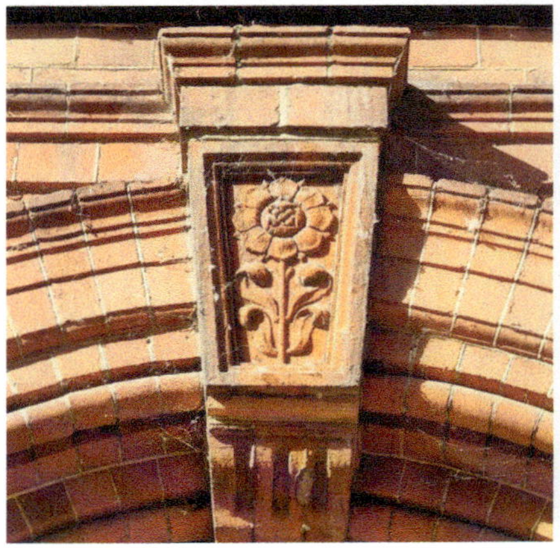
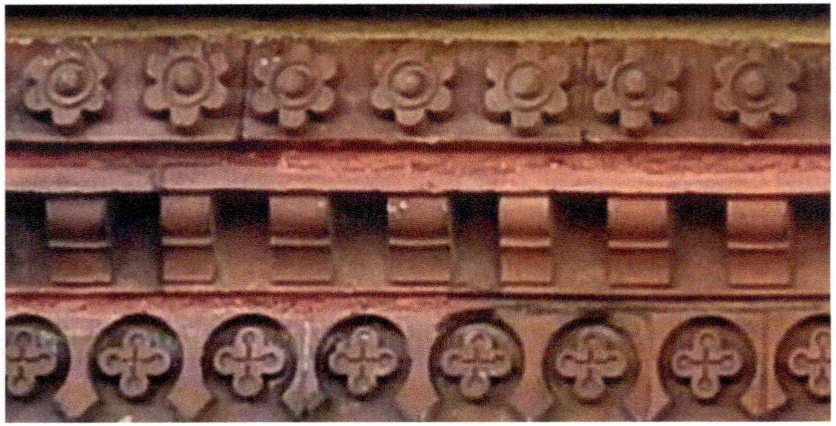

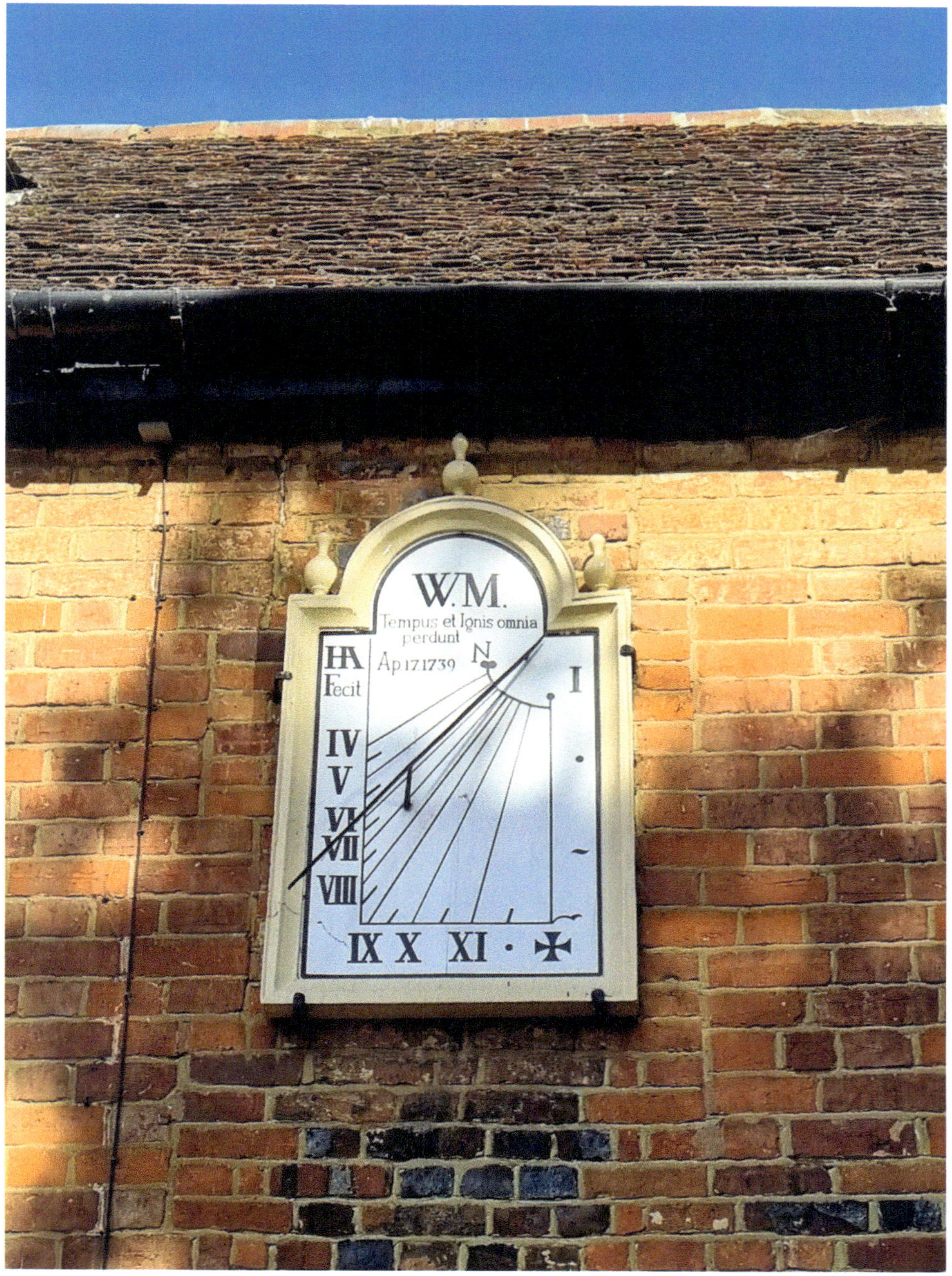
W.M.
Tempus et Ignis omnia perdunt
HA Fecit
Ap 17 1739
N
I
IV
V
VI
VII
VIII
IX X XI

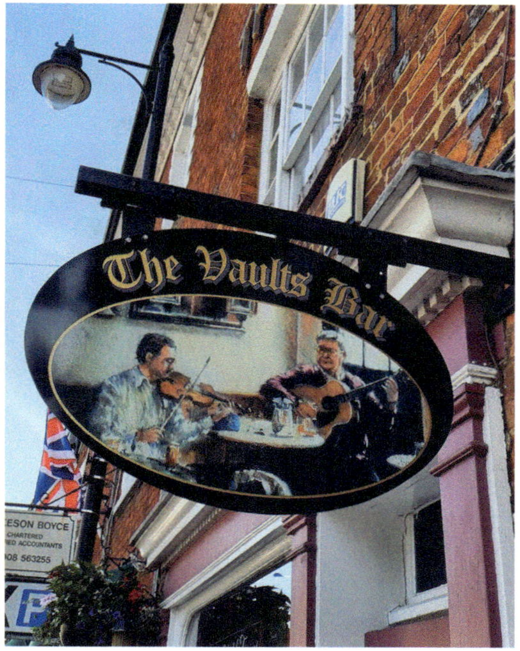
The Vaults Bar

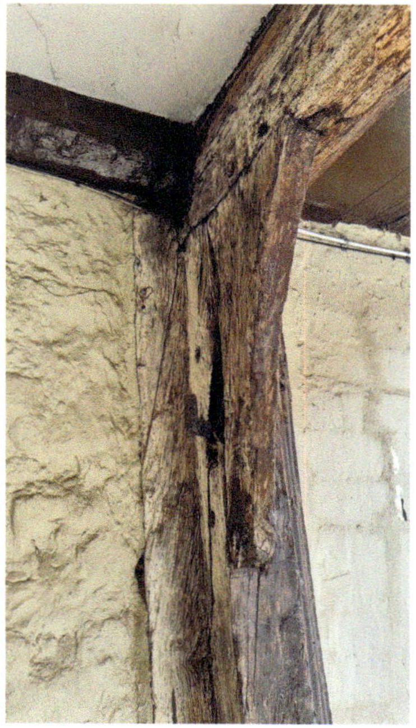

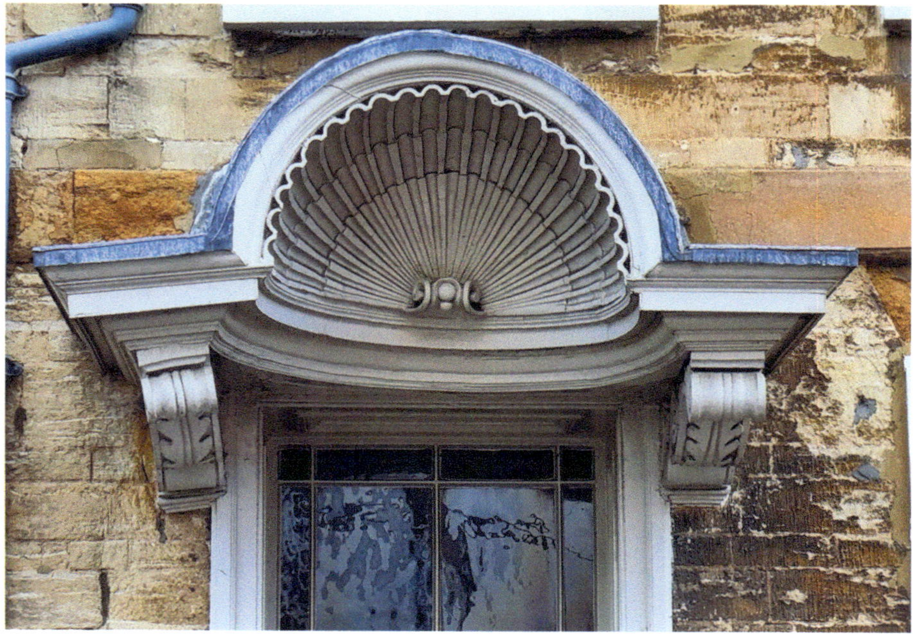

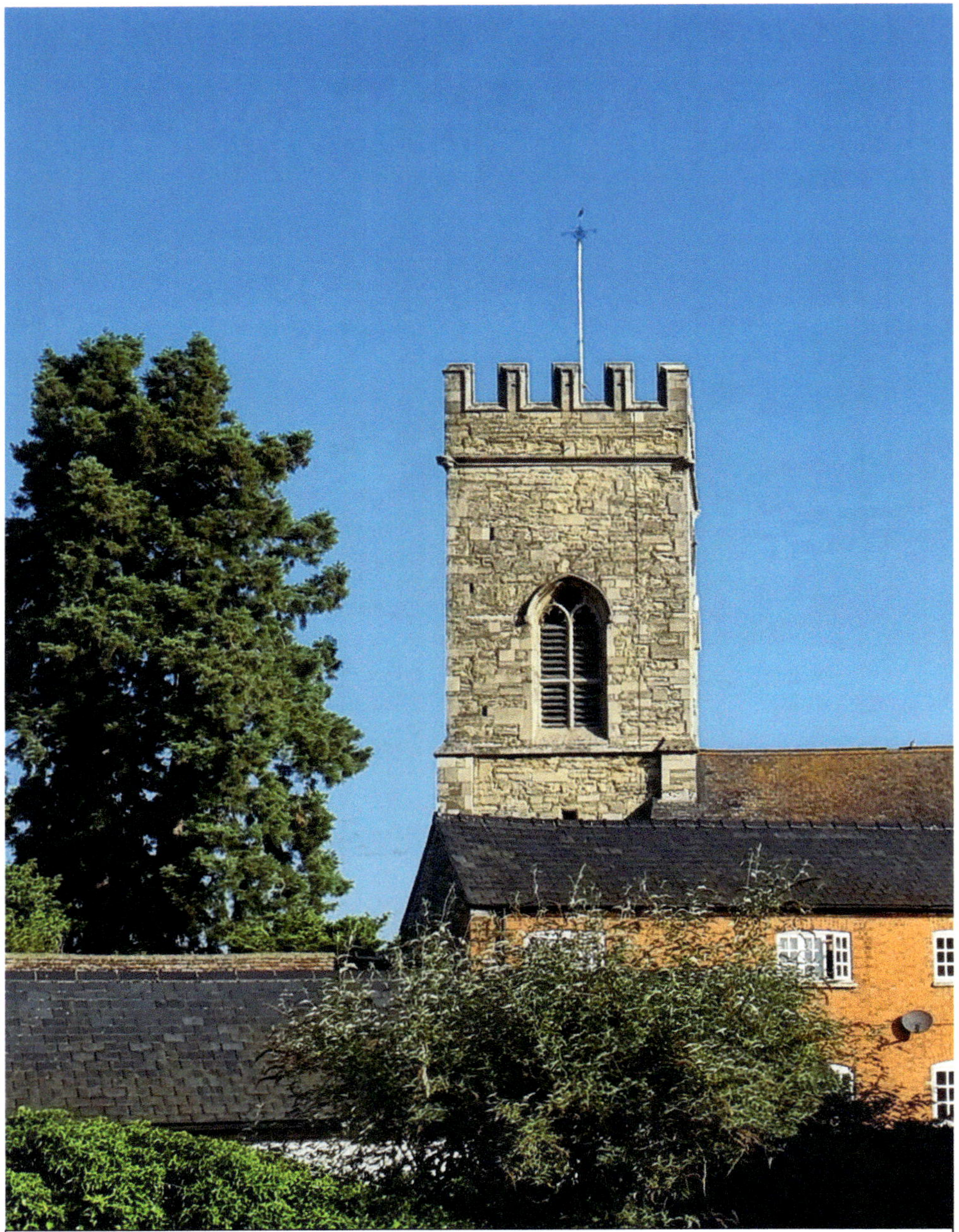

A view of St Giles tower.

The Market Square

A field was reserved for a market on the west side of the Watling Street. Gilbert de Basset, who owned the land, went to great lengths to secure a licence from King Richard I in 1194. Thus, its use as a market can date from this time.

The church of St Giles took up part of the land in the 13th century, but it was probably only in the 17th century that buildings started to surround the field, which then became a square.

There were several inns. On the Square's west side there were establishments known as the *Bell,* the *Fighting Cocks,* and the *King's Head.*

On the south side, the *Barley Mow,* the *Crown,* the *White Hart,* the *White Lion* and the *Plough* could be found. Church Lane was the address for the *Crooked Billet* and the *Sun and Moon.*

Before the age of High Street shops, markets and fairs were the principal methods of trading. Stony Stratford had its main market on this square, but a little further south was Cow Fair (re-named Silver Street) and Horse Fair.

By the early 19th century, the south side of Church Lane was occupied by some shambles and a lock-up known as the 'cage.' This was replaced by a police station, court rooms and a secure jail in 1864.

One feature of the square, for many years, was a large tree known as "Wesley's Tree" - so-named because the famous 18th century preacher spoke at this spot on at least two occasions.

Many years have passed since a market was held in the Square.

Mill Lane and the Mill

There was a mill on this site in 1086 and was rebuilt many times over the centuries. The large 19th century corn mill became disused in the 20th century and has now been converted into flats.

Mill Lane never attracted too much development until recent times.

Ousebank is a large 19th century house at the beginning of the lane.

LOOK AT THE MARKET SQUARE

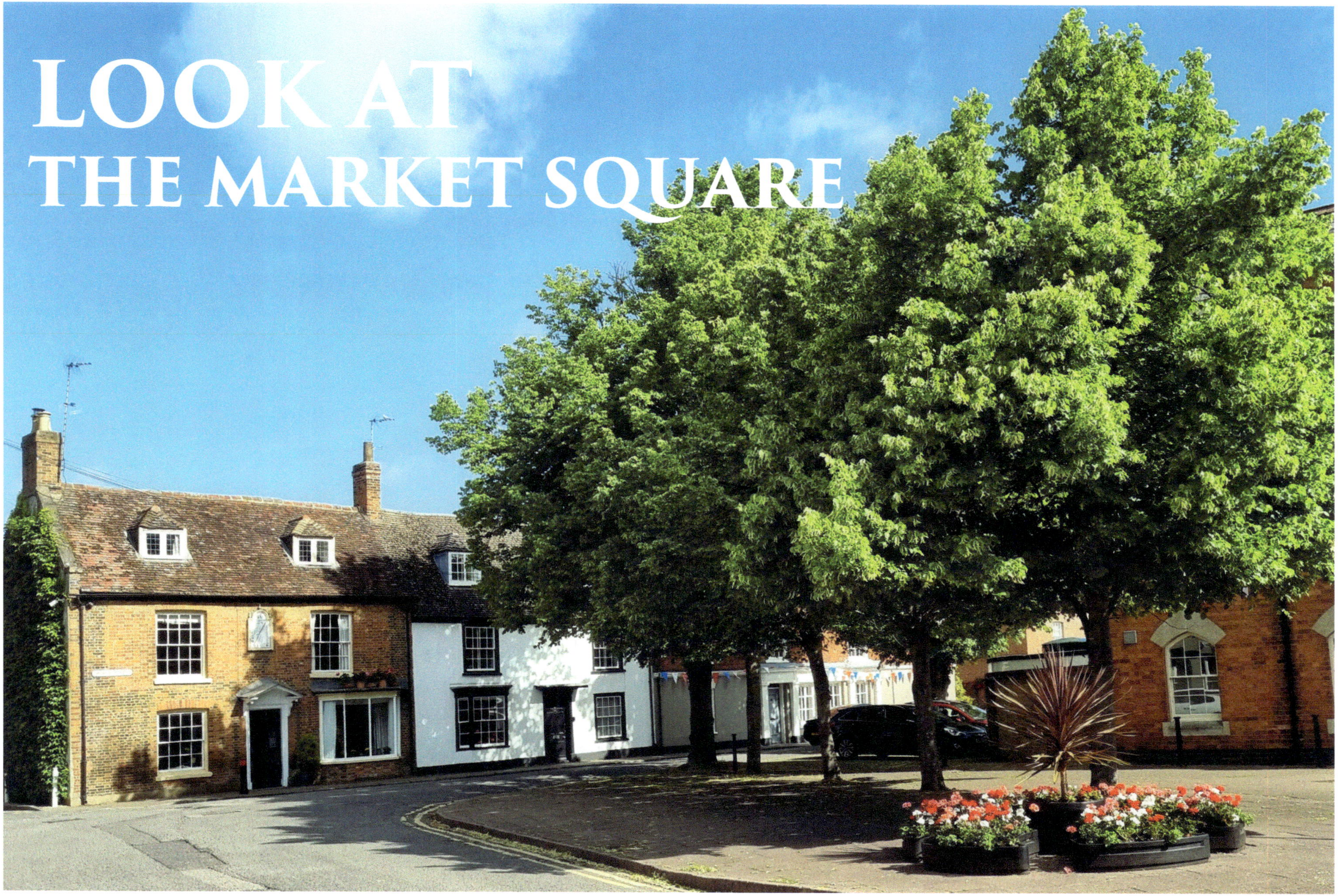

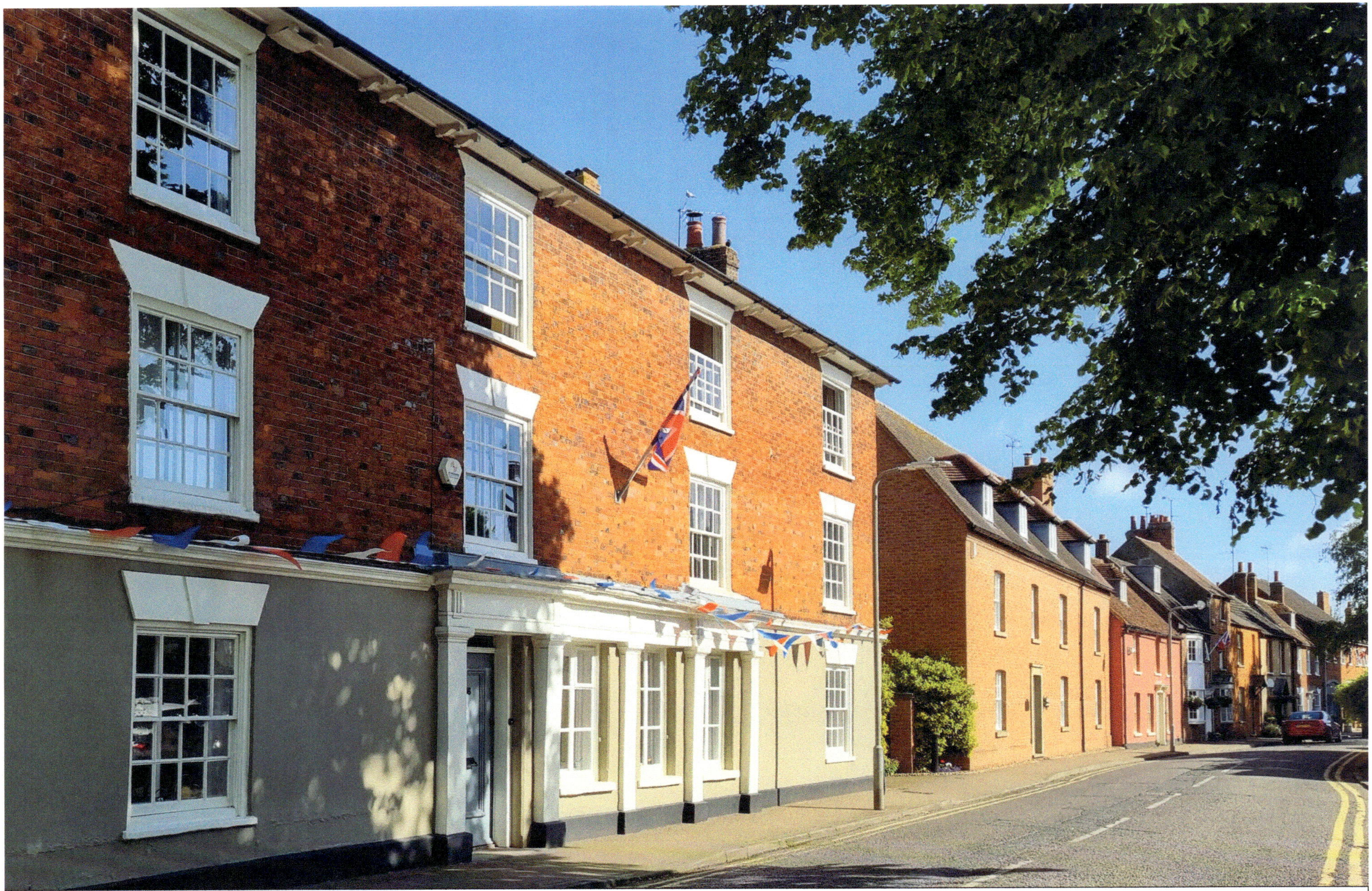

Church Street.

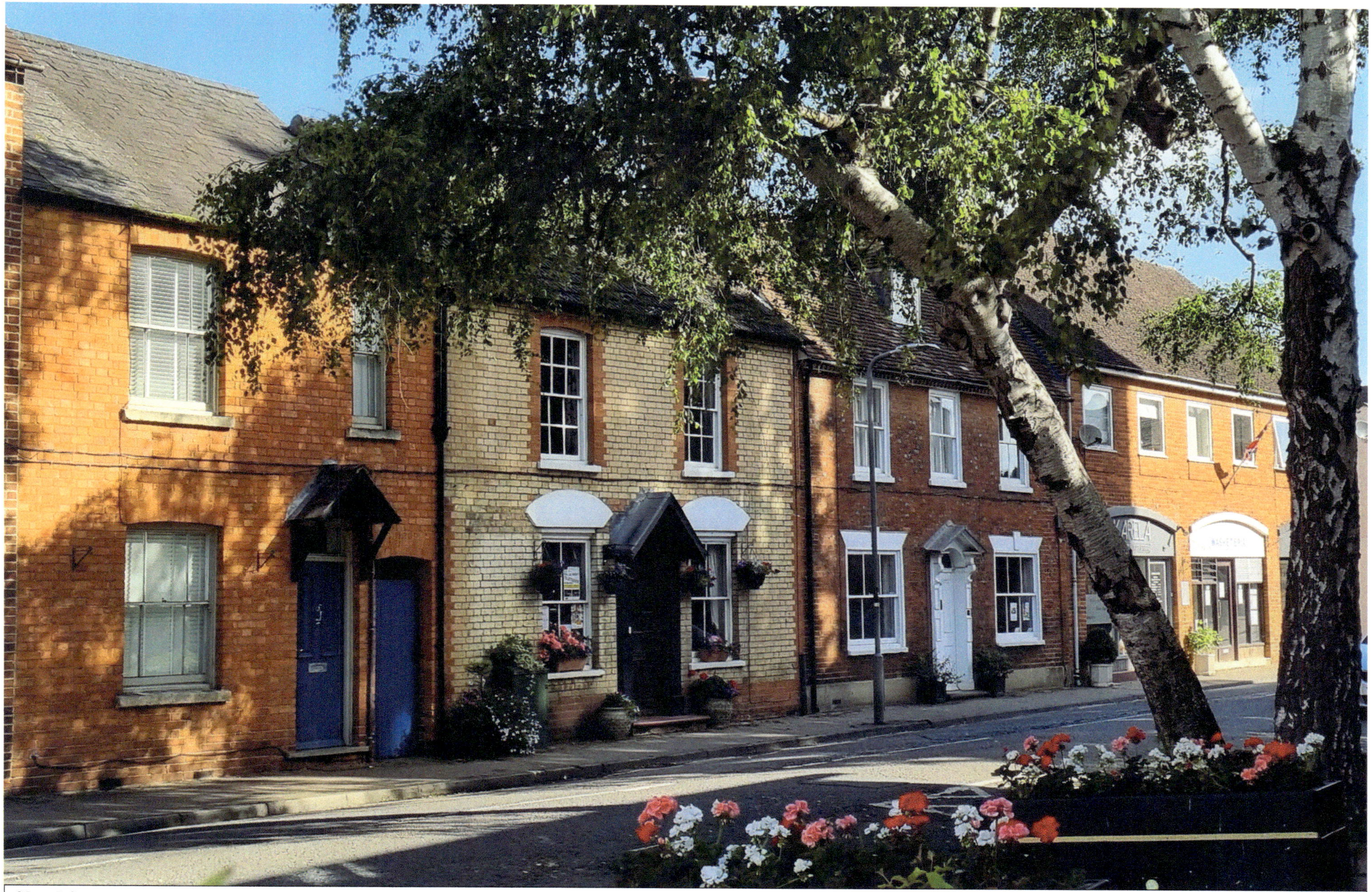

Church Street.

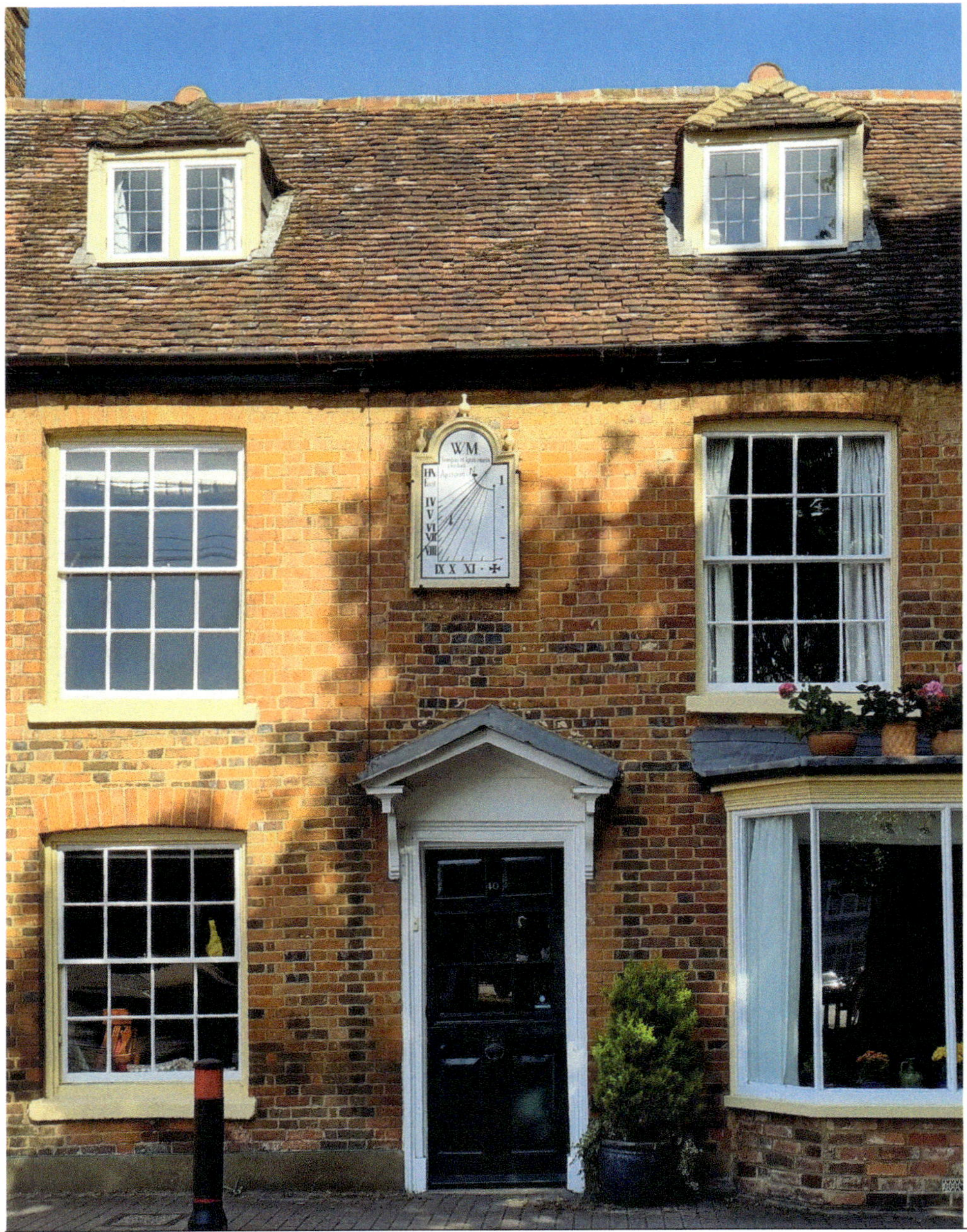

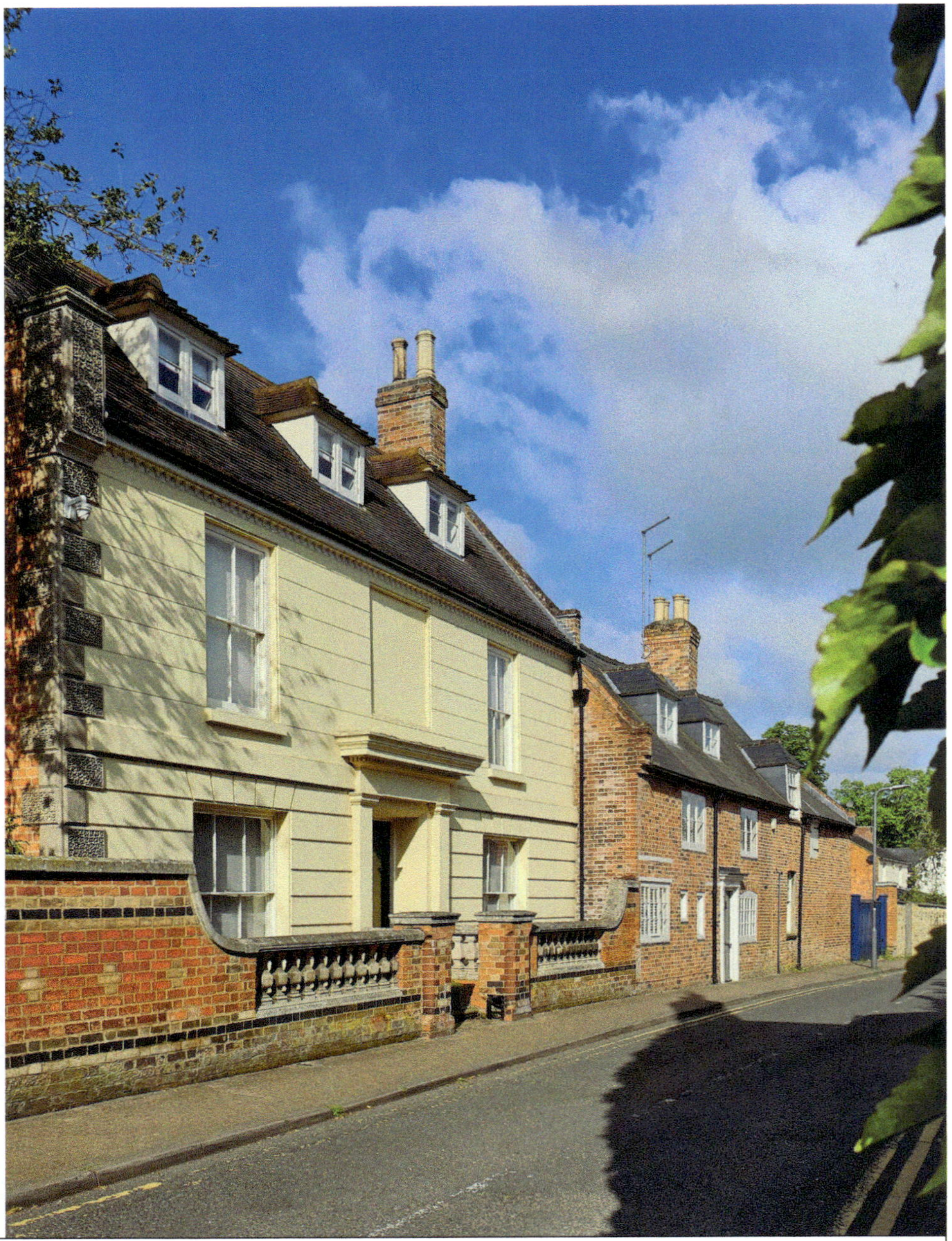

The Sundial House on Church Street and Ousebank on Mill Lane.

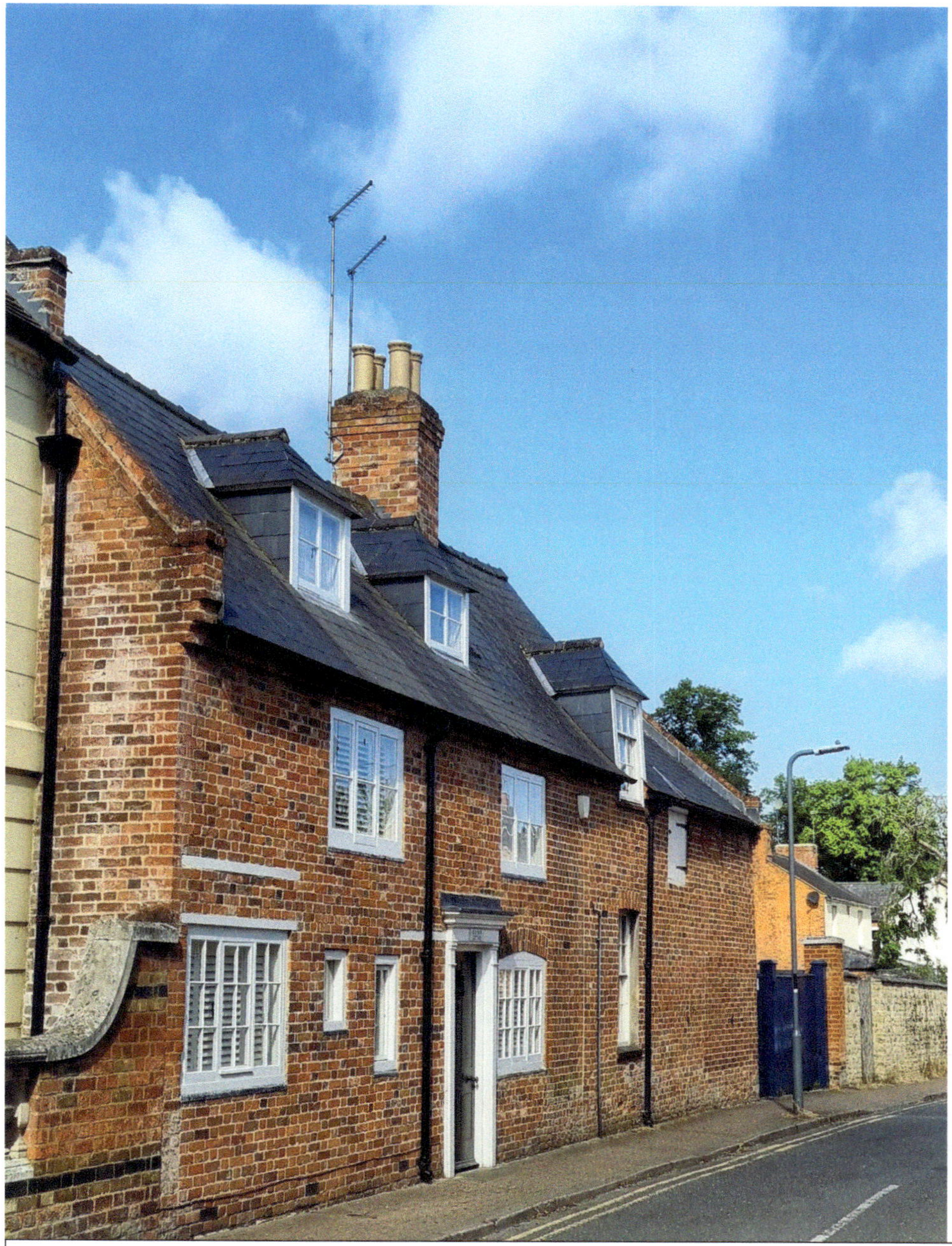

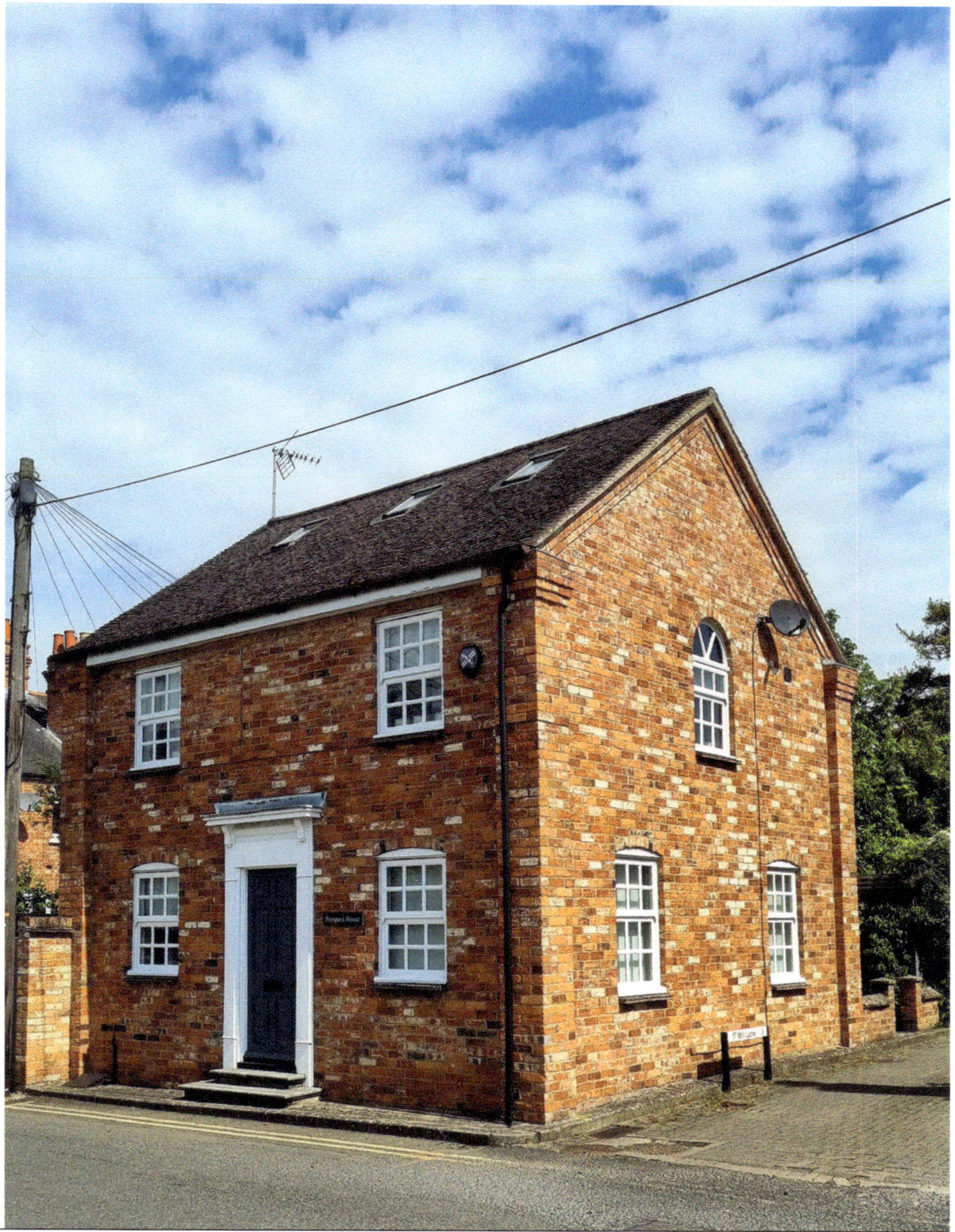

Ousebank Cottage and Prospect House on Mill Lane.

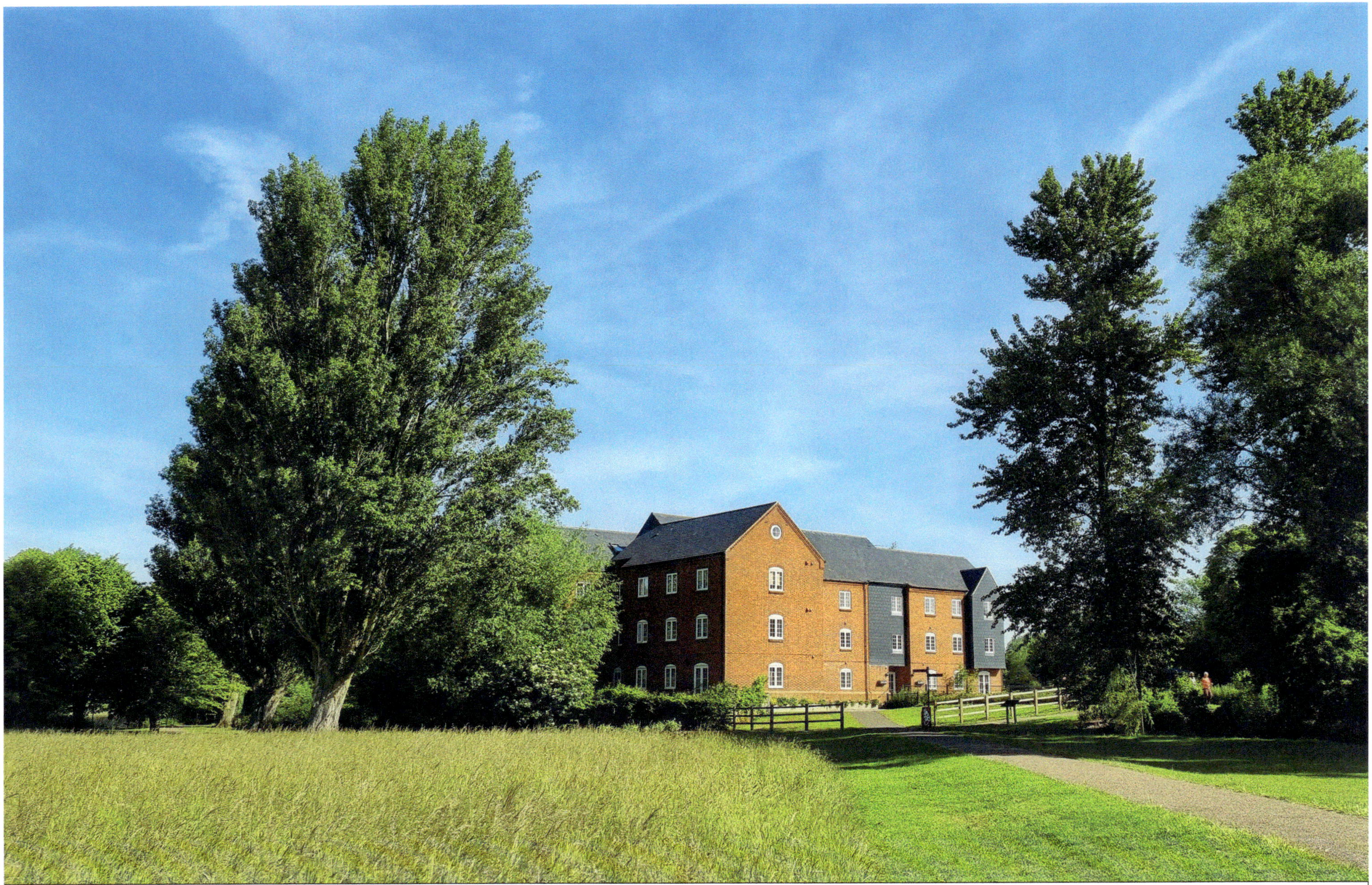

The former corn mill has been converted into flats.

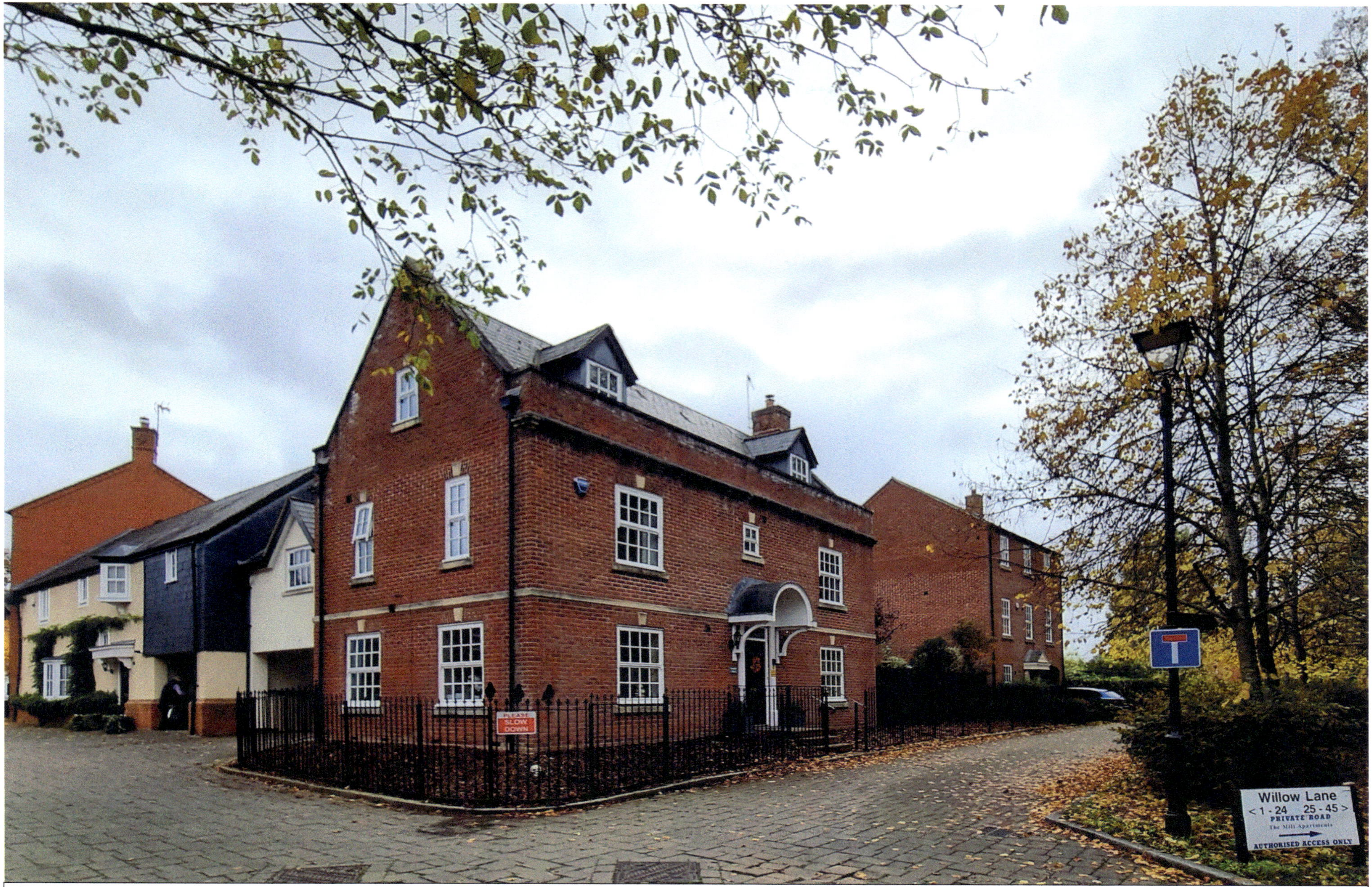

A modern development at the end of Mill Lane.

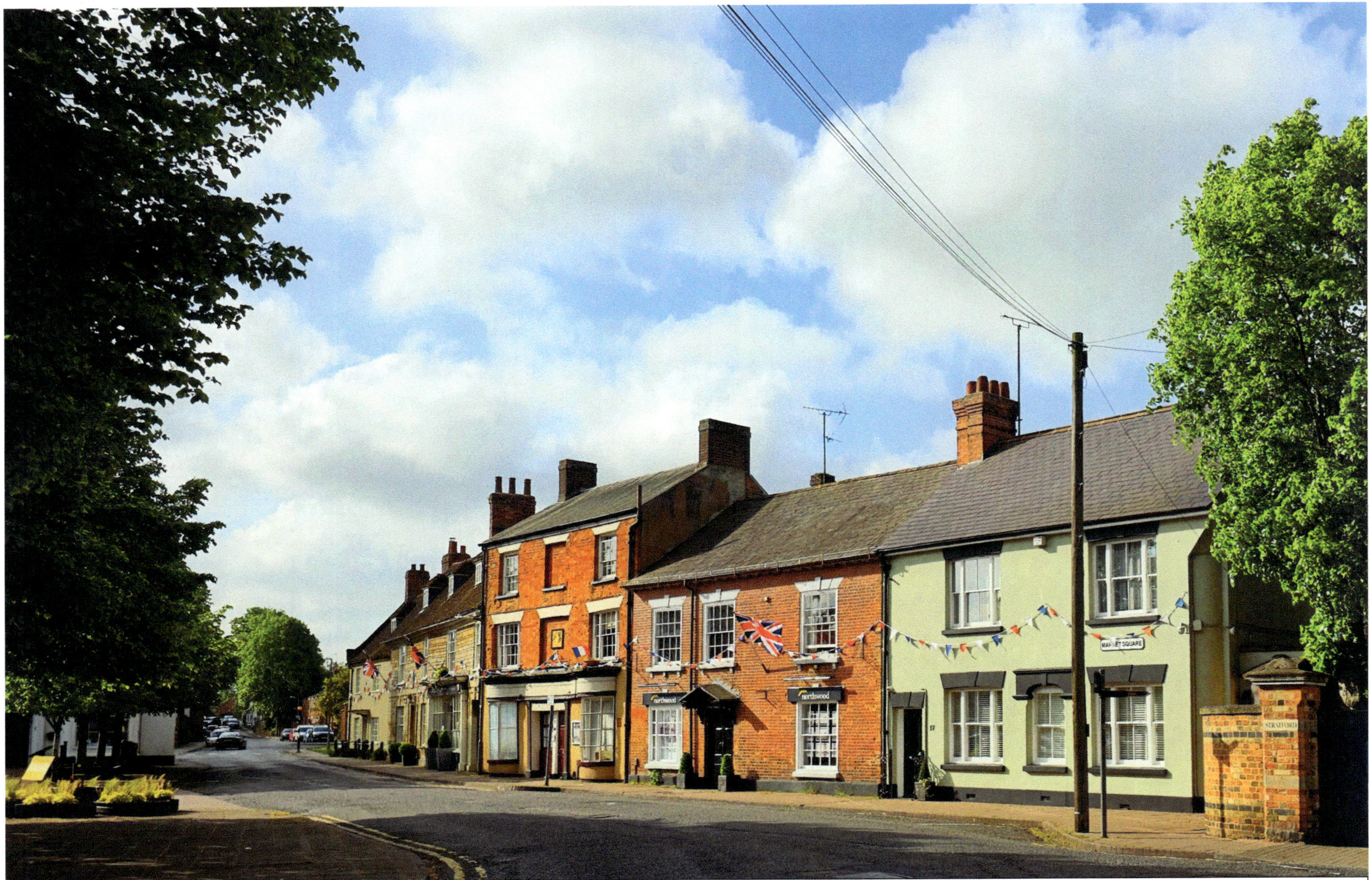

A view of the west side of the Market Square showing the former Bell, Fighting Cocks and King's Head.

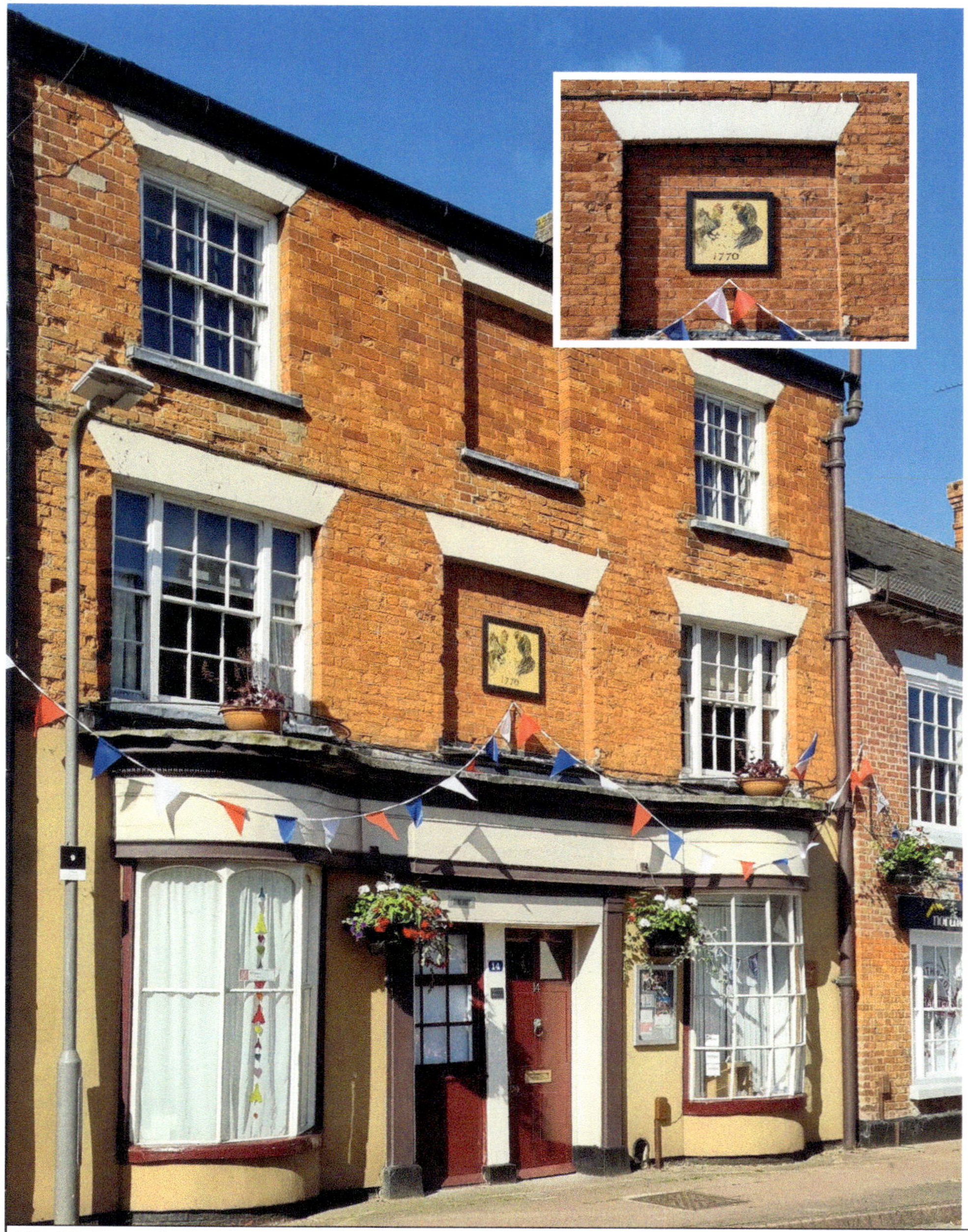

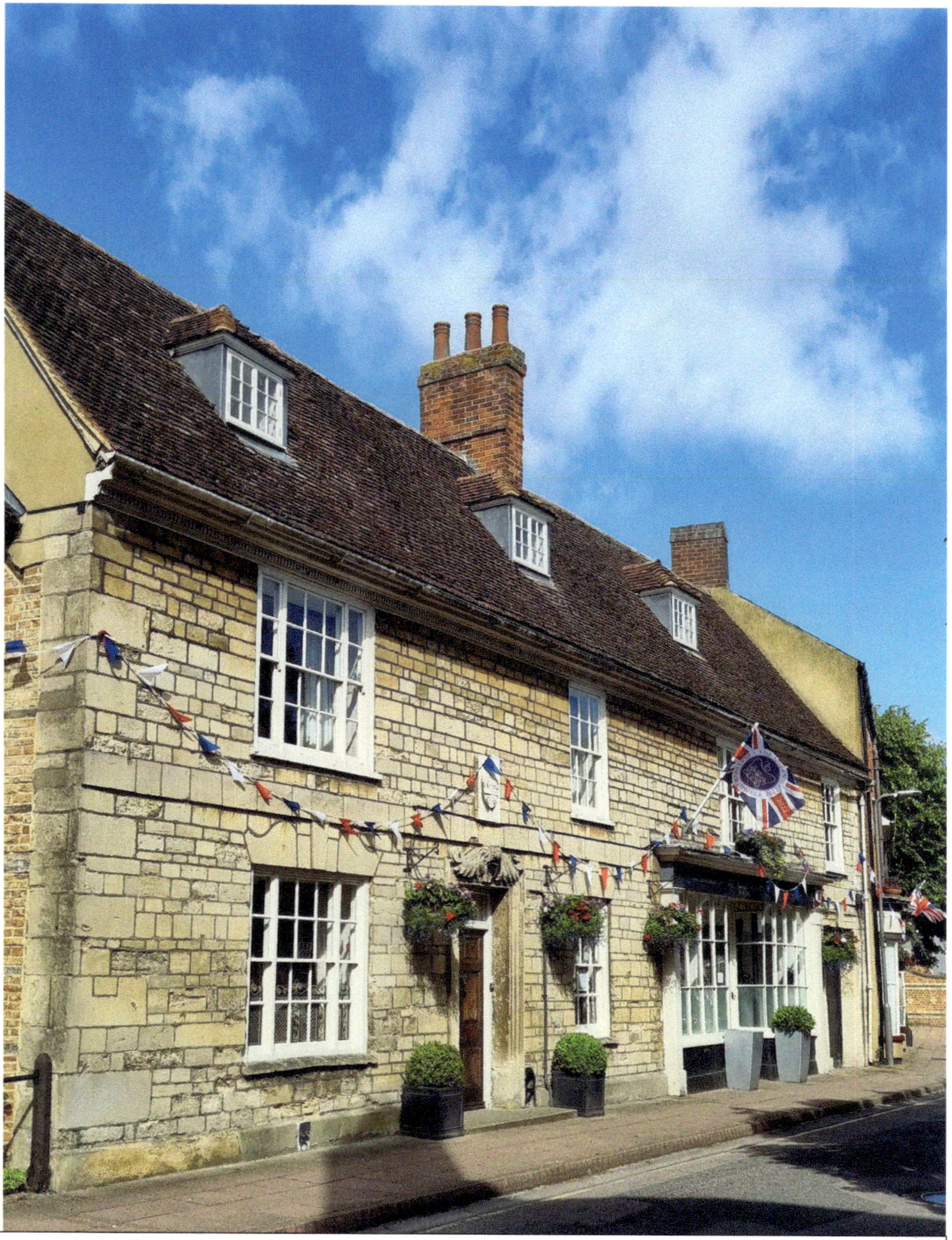

The Fighting Cocks was first licensed as an inn in 1760. It was sold in 1794. The spacious stone house on the right was occupied in the 18th century by Joseph Malpas, a London merchant.

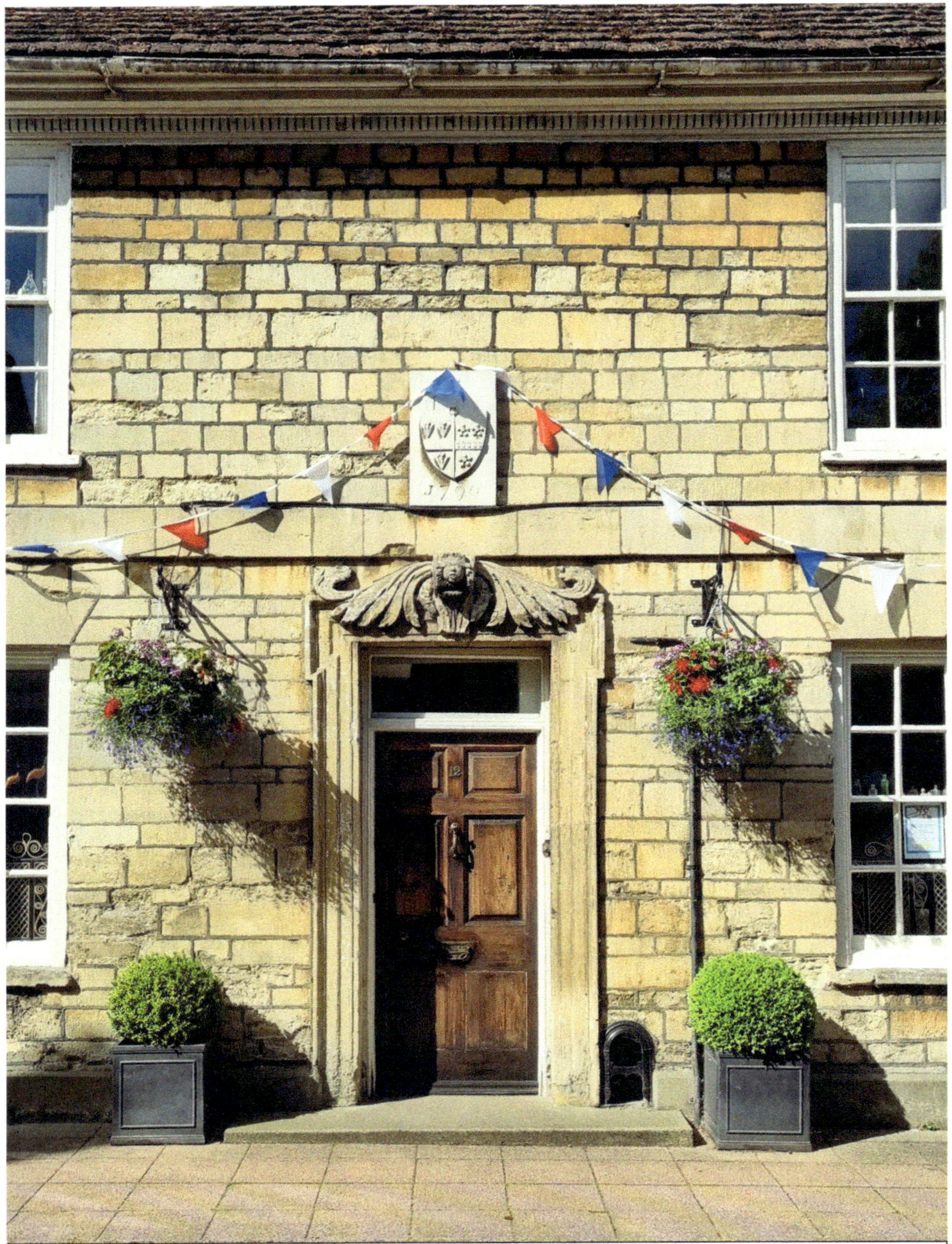

The house of Joseph Malpas, decorated with his coat of arms.

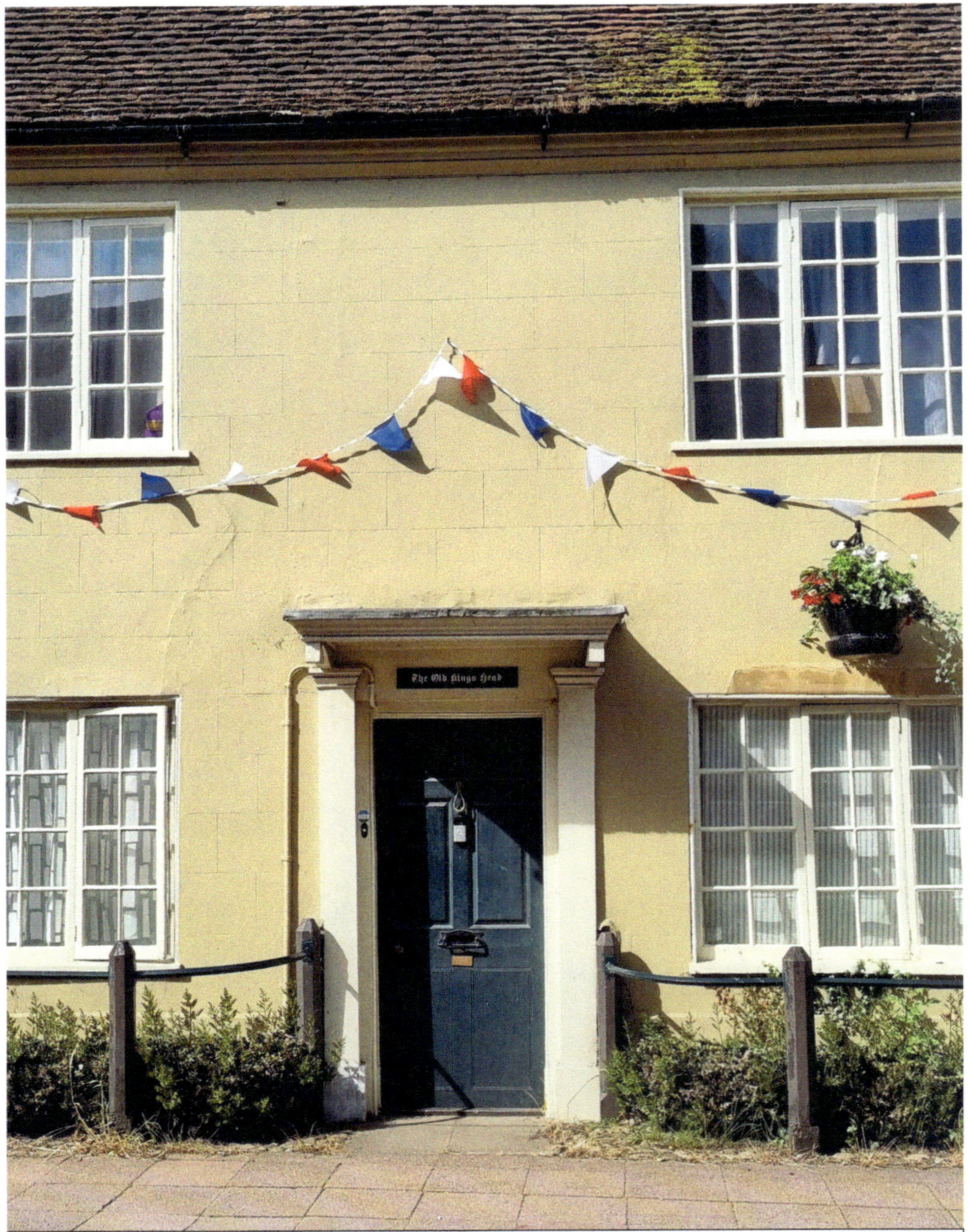

The King's Head flourished from the 17th to the 19th century.

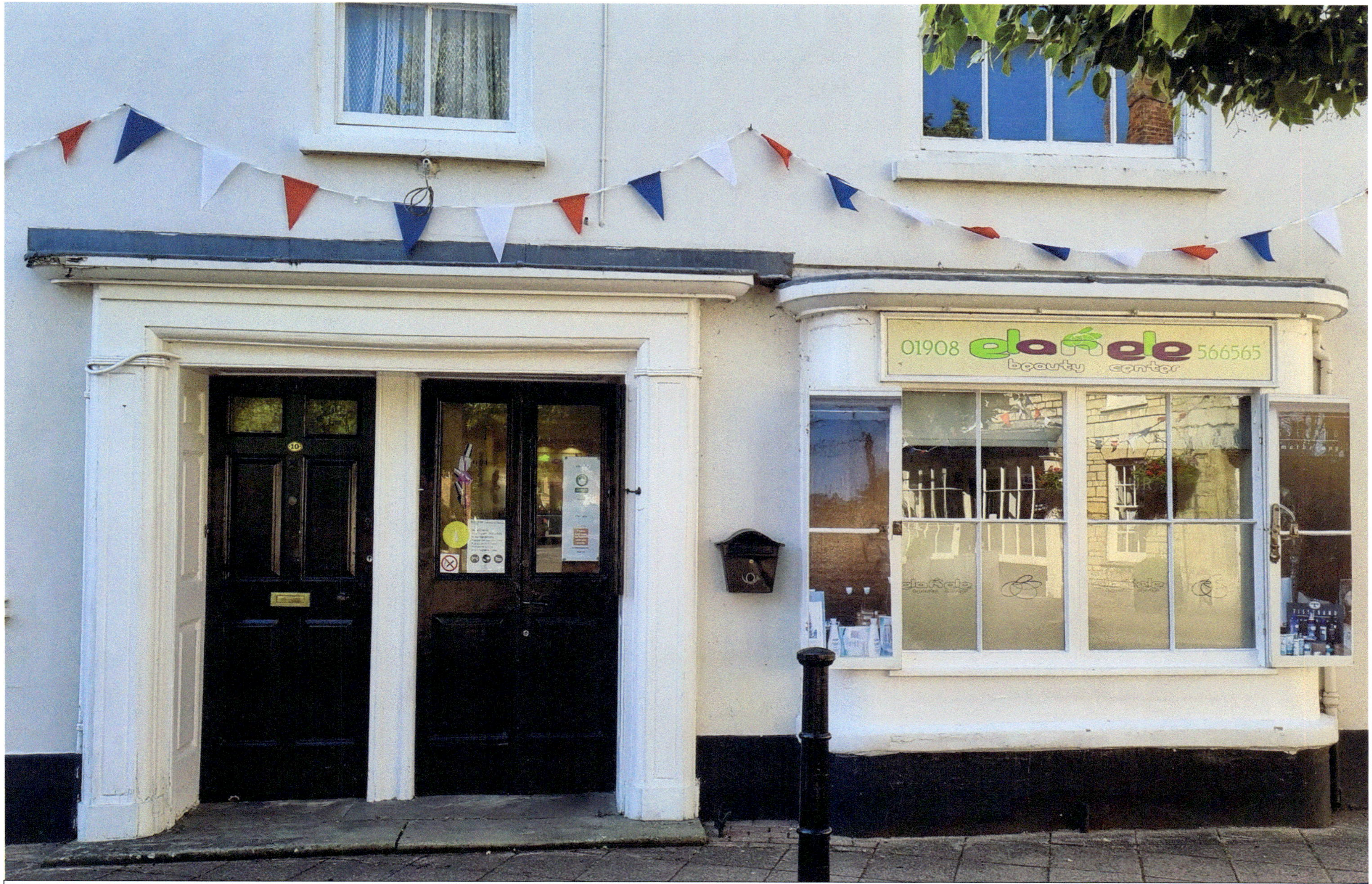

There were two Barley Mows in Stony Stratford at one time. This was one of them.

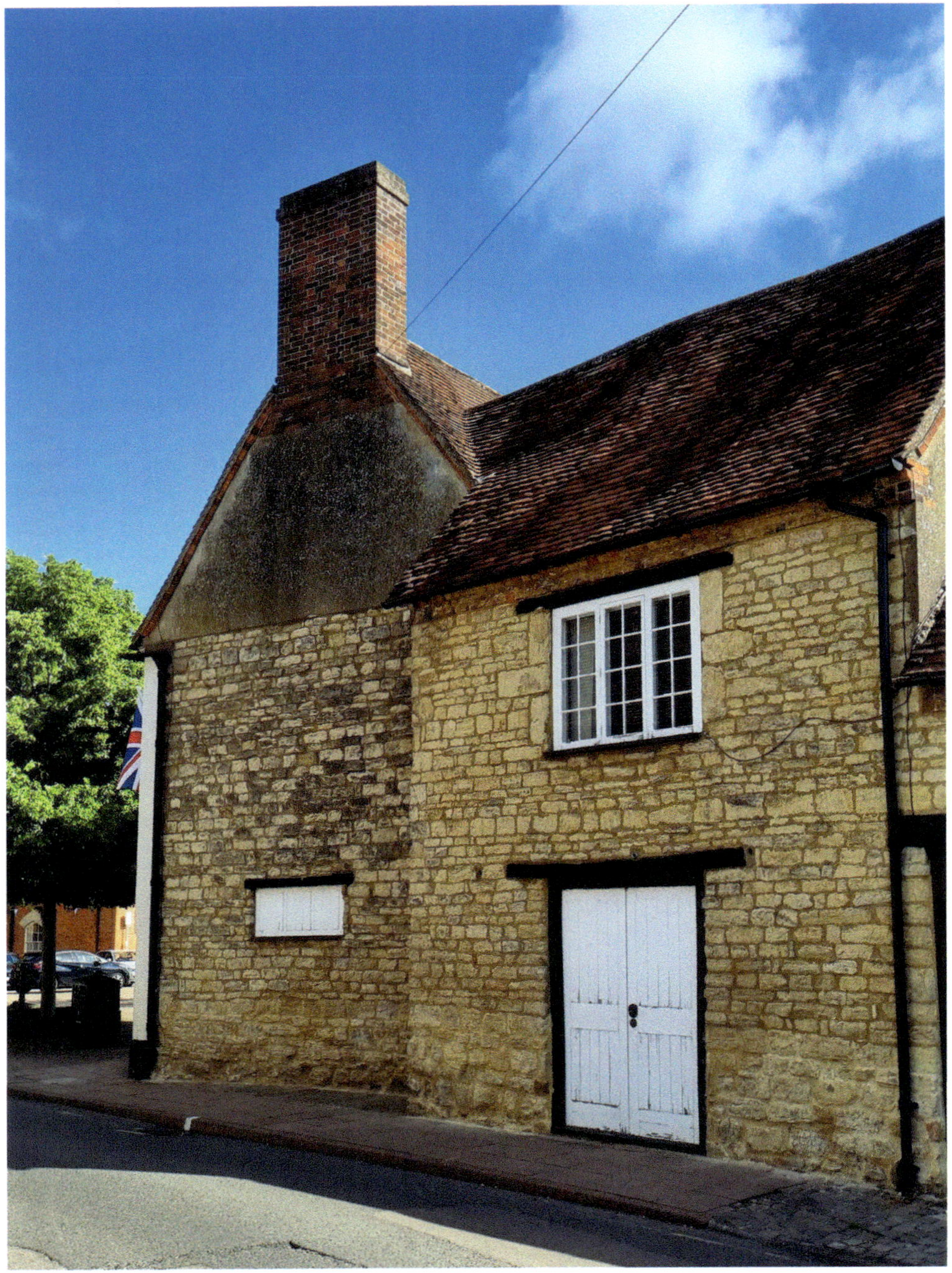

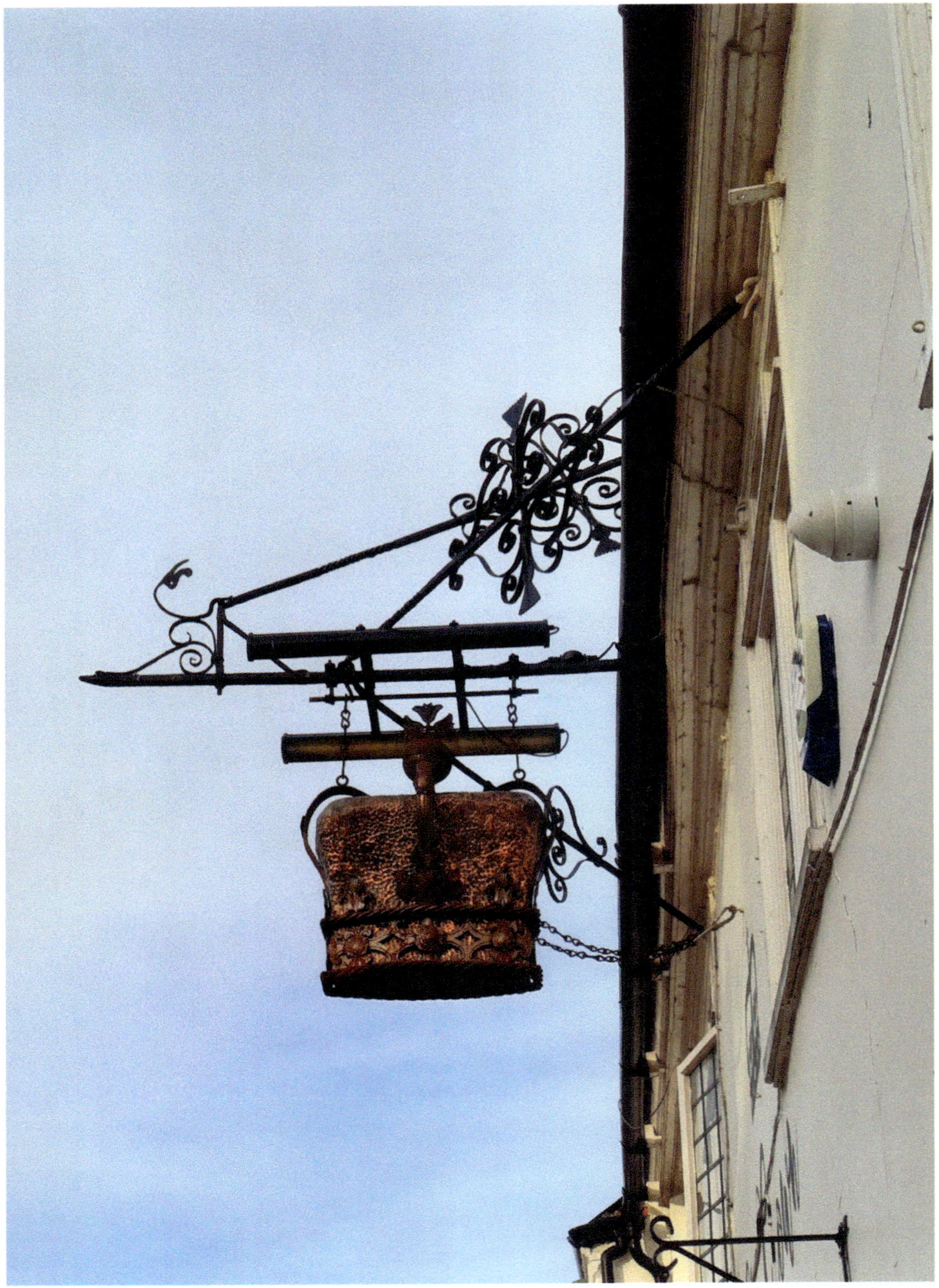

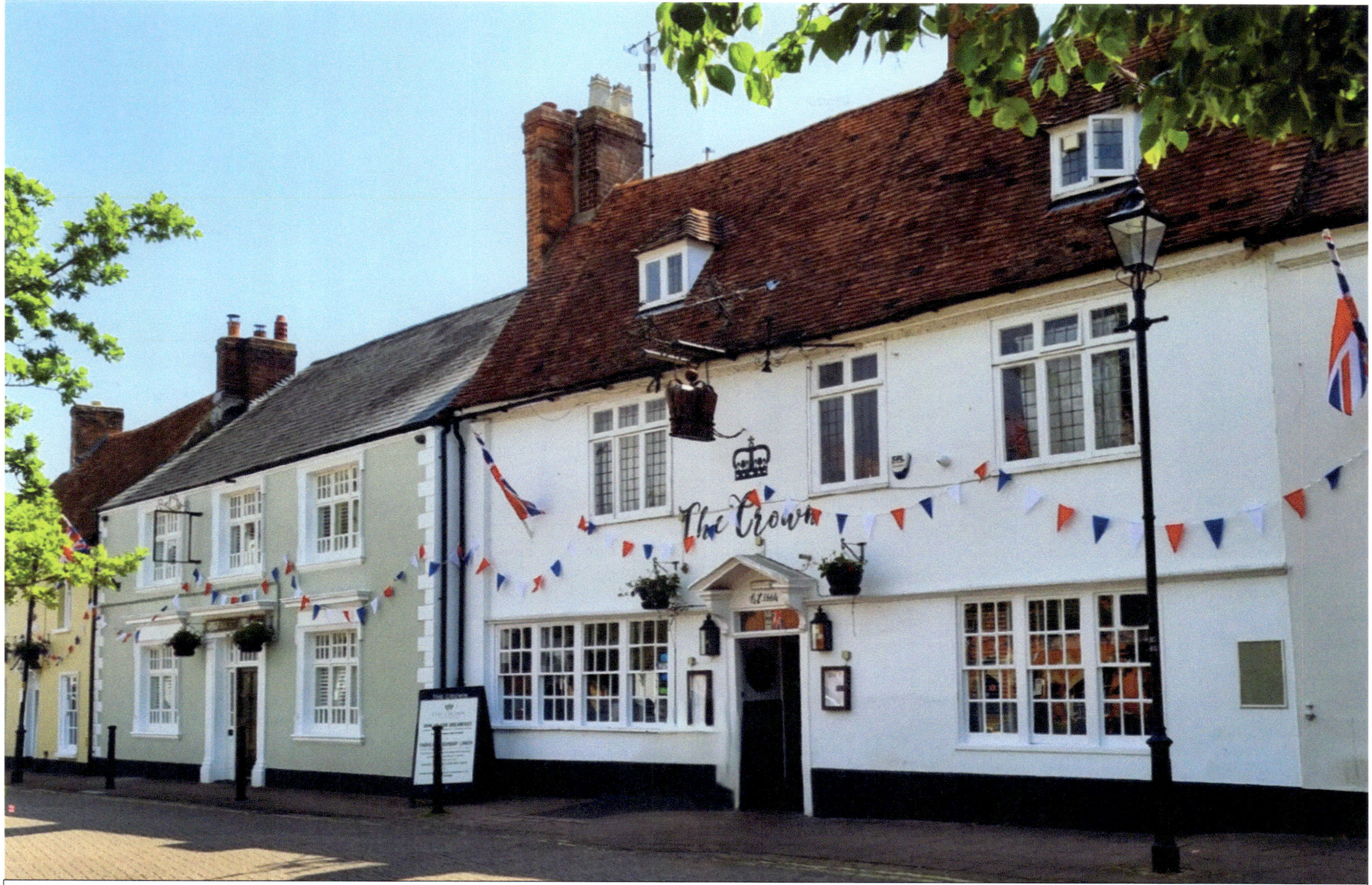

The south side of the square once offered The Plough, The Green Dragon, The White Hart, The Crown and The Barley Mow. Only The Crown is still in business.

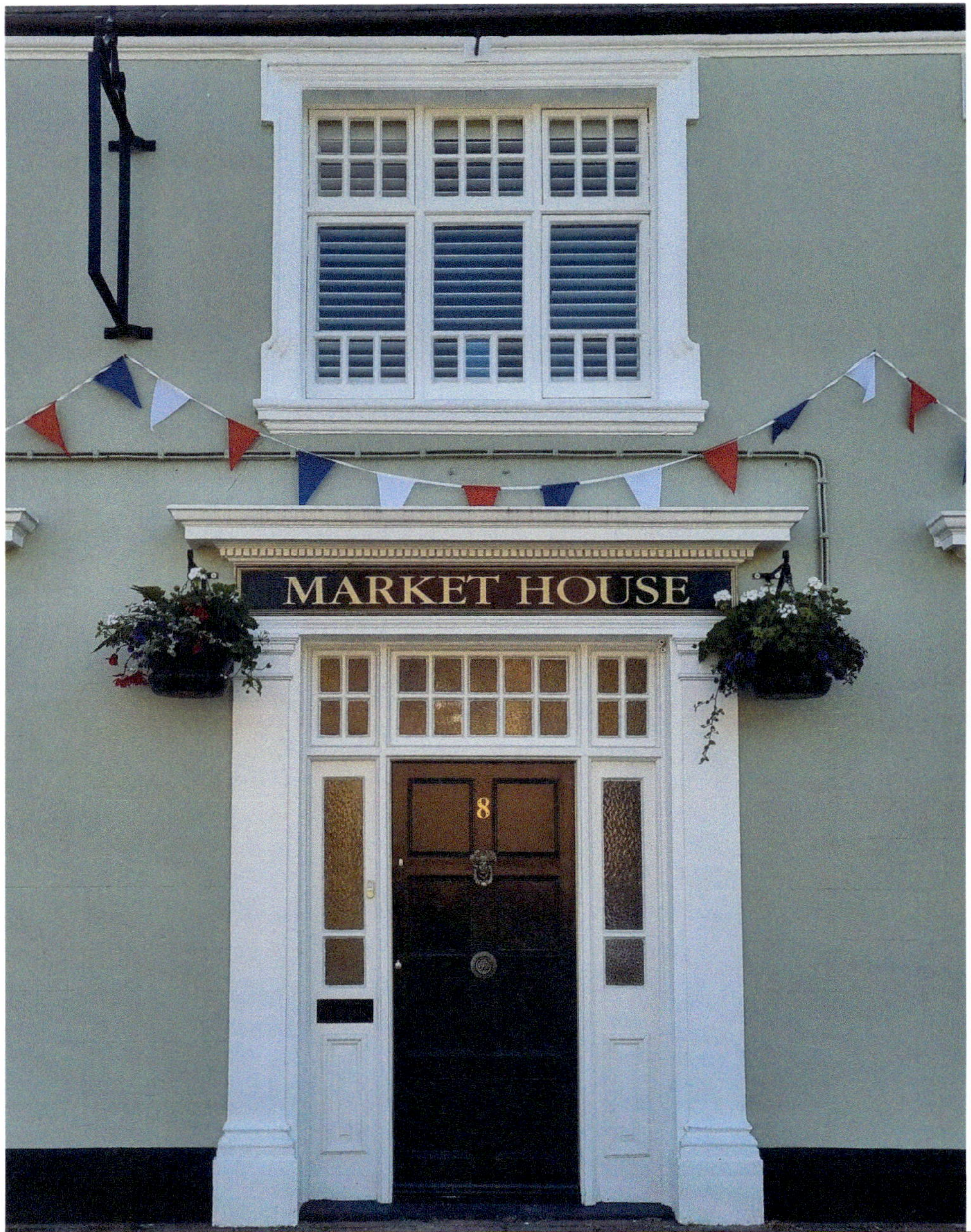

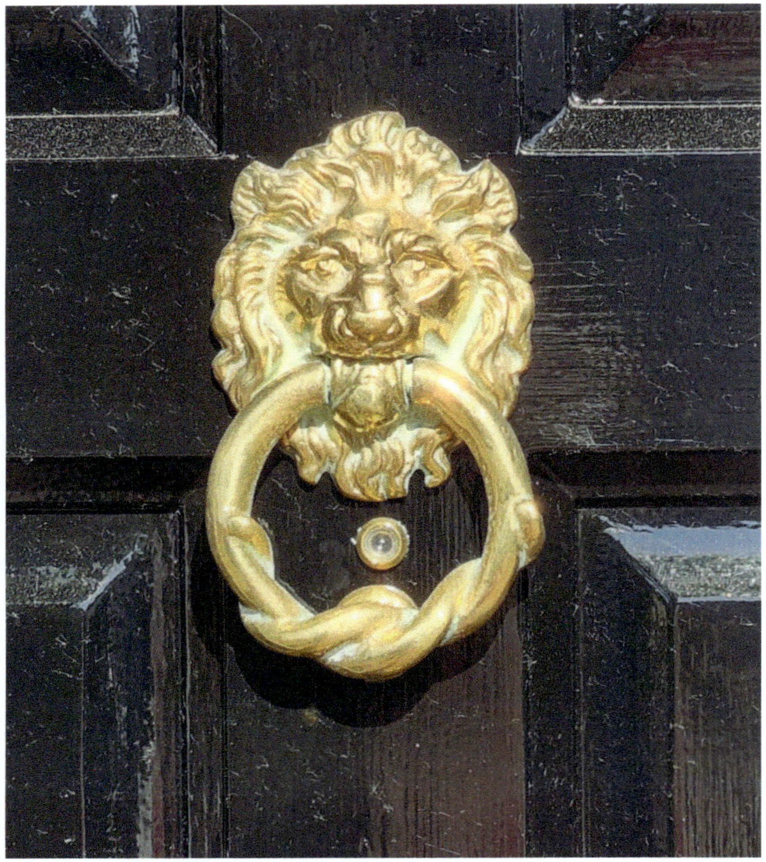

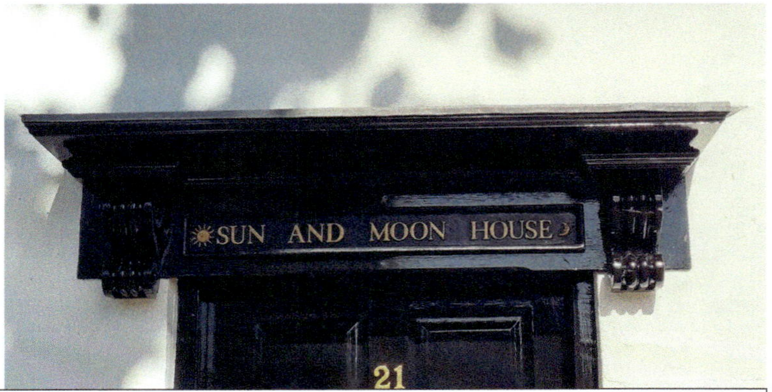

The Market House was once the White Hart. Sun and Moon house records the location of a former inn.

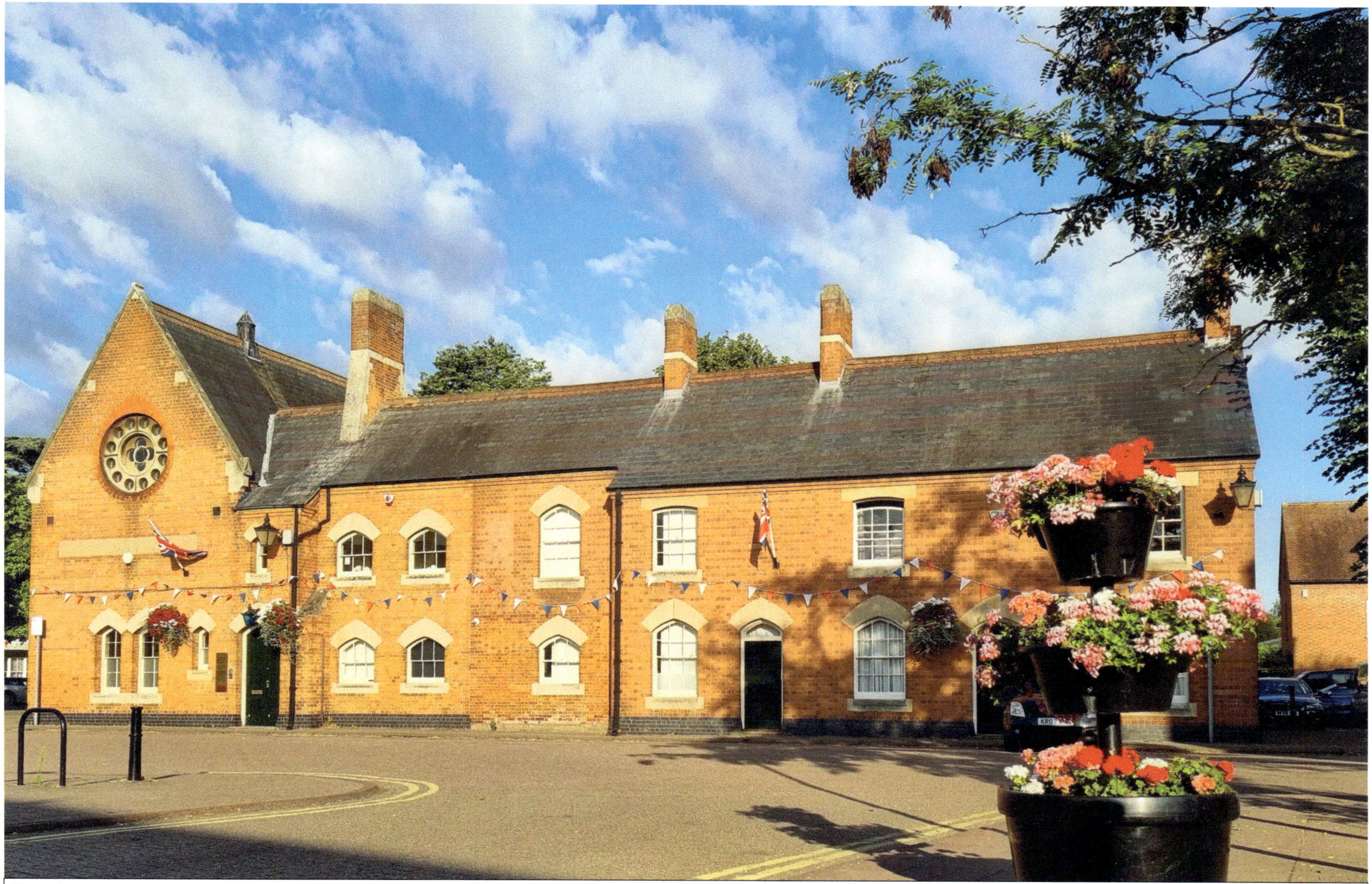

The police station and court house was built in 1864.

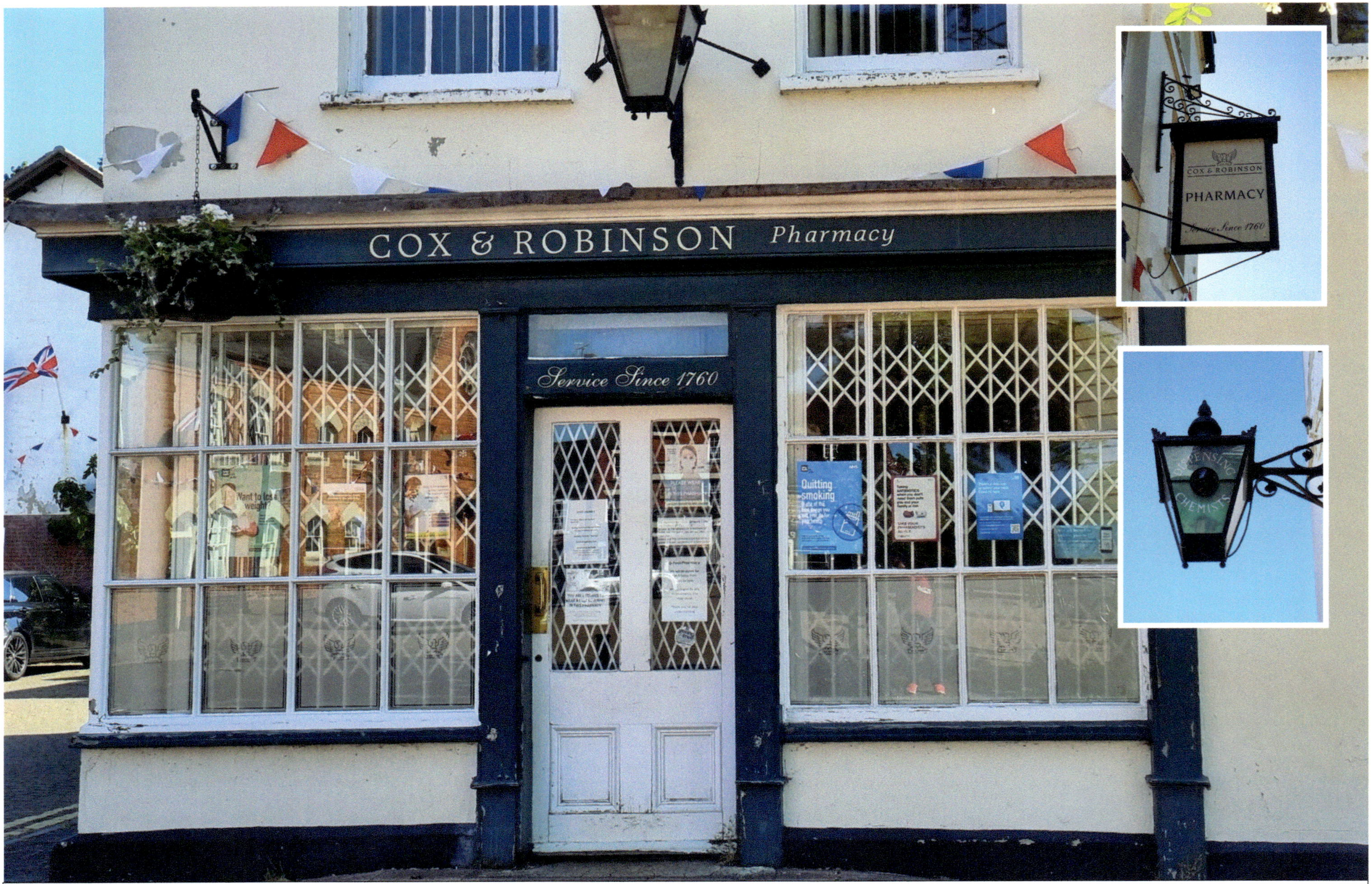

The chemists, Cox and Robinson, had premises on the High Street from the mid 18th century. In recent years the company moved to this house on the Square.

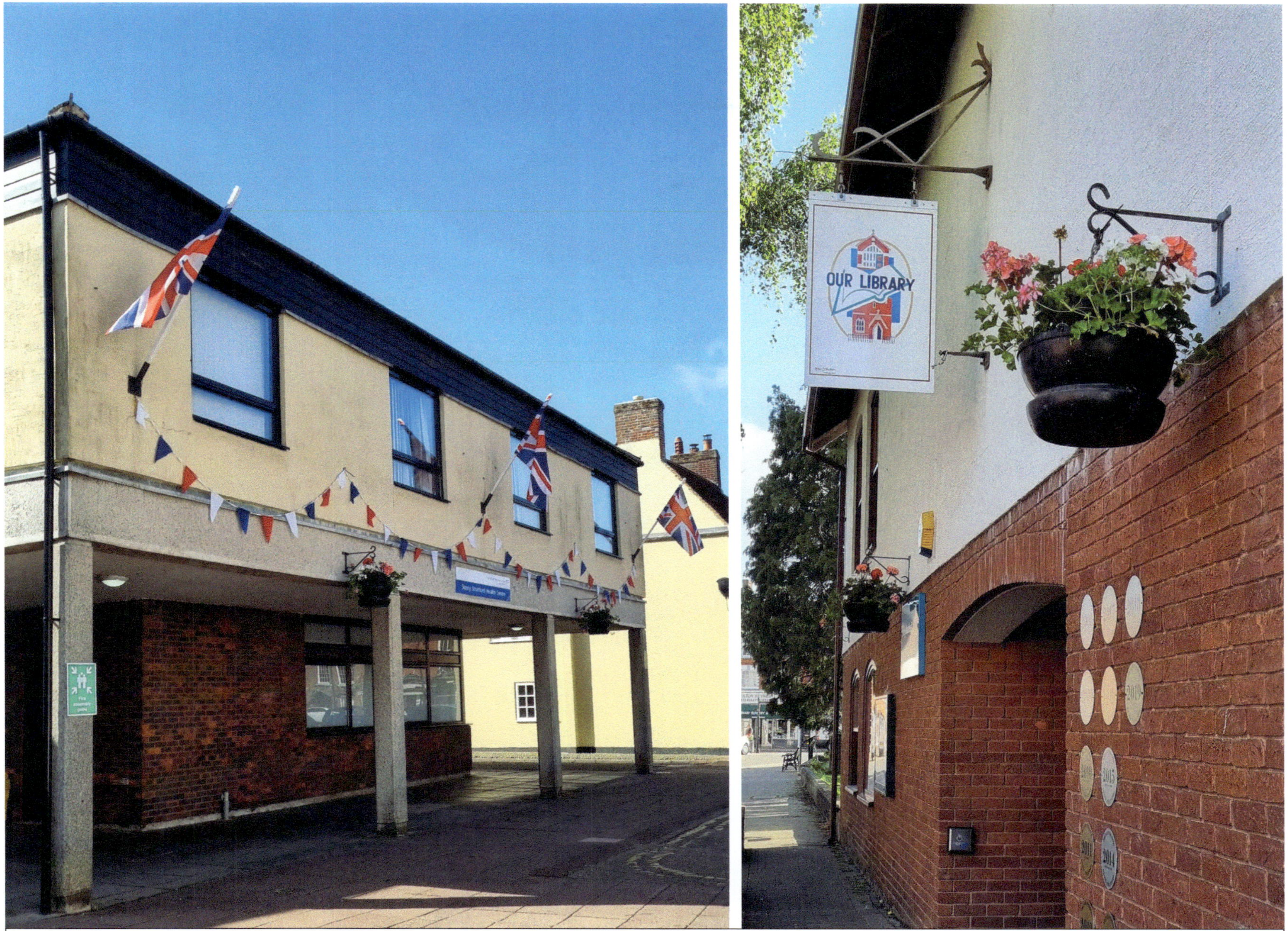

Stony Stratford's Health Centre and Branch Library.

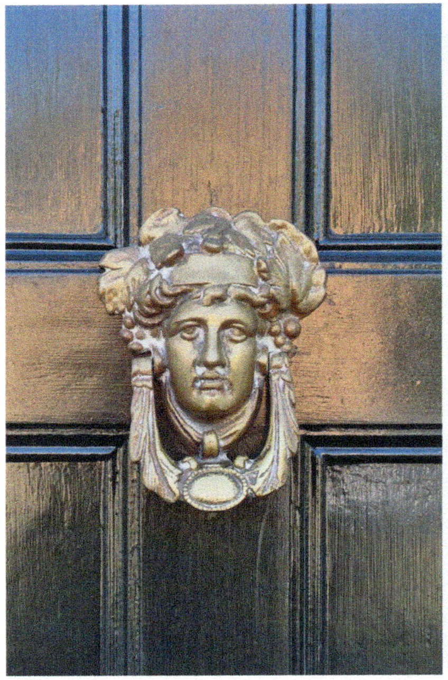
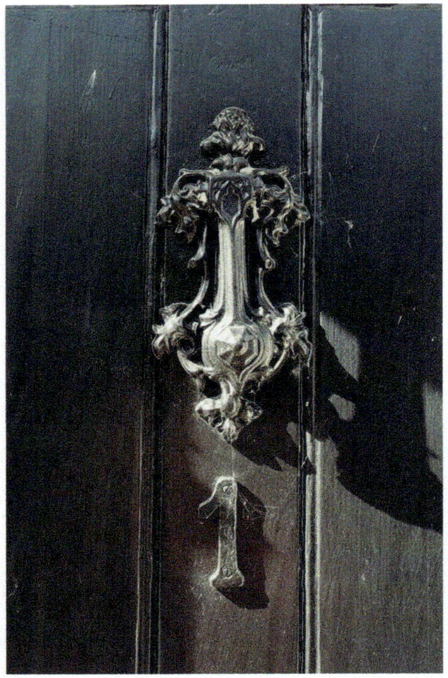
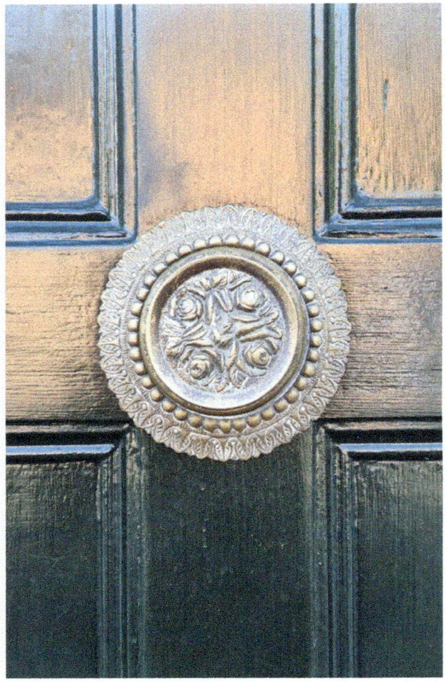
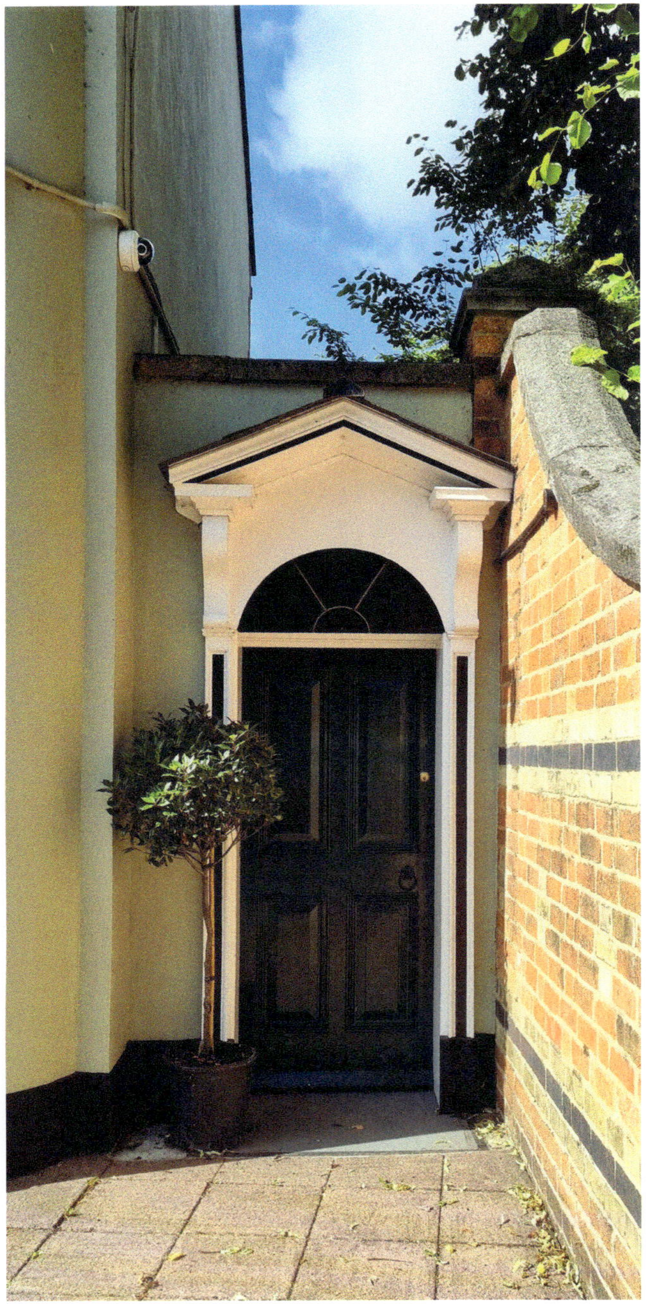
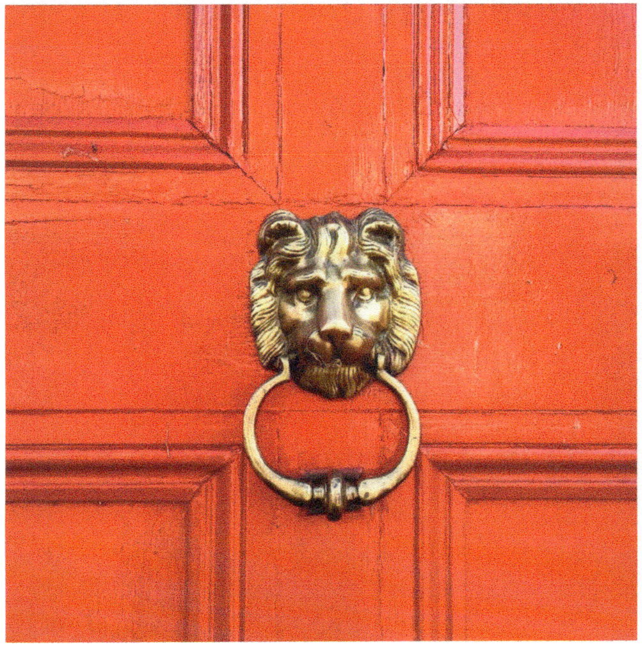
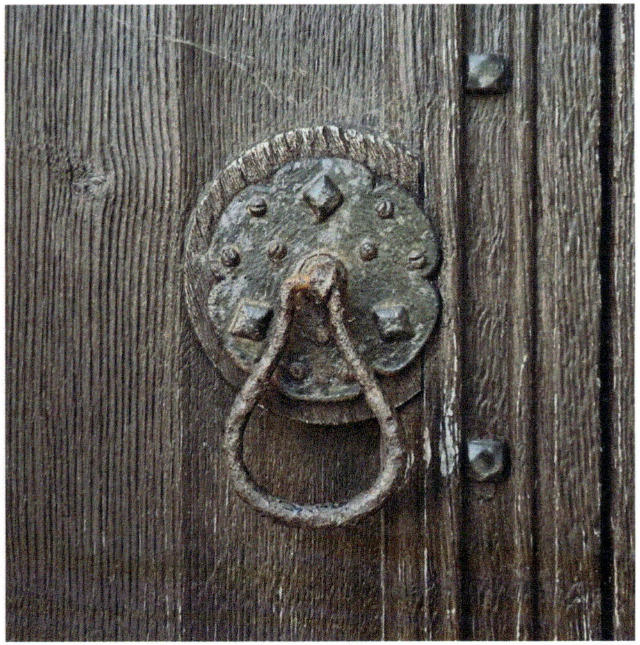

LOOK IN

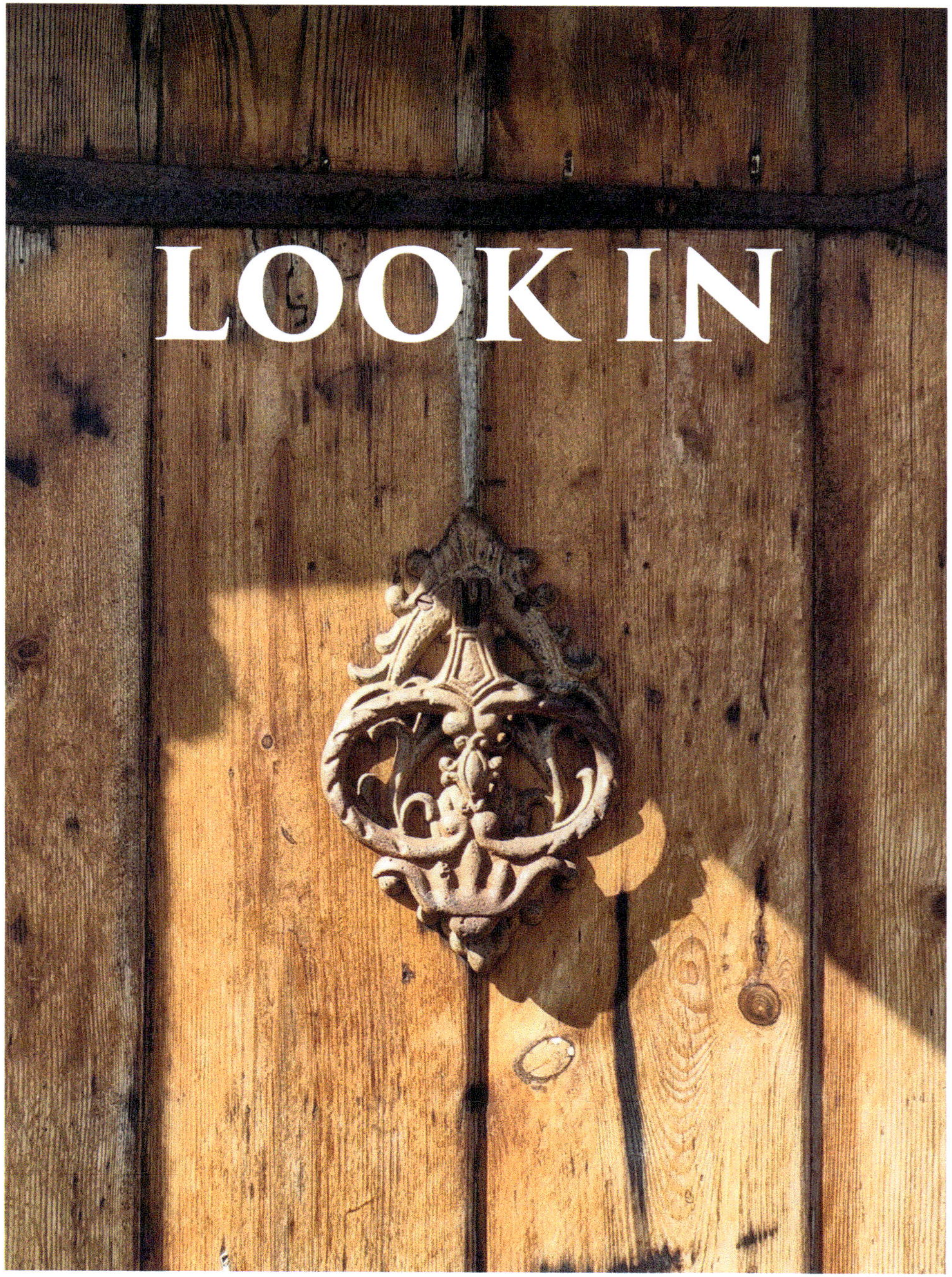

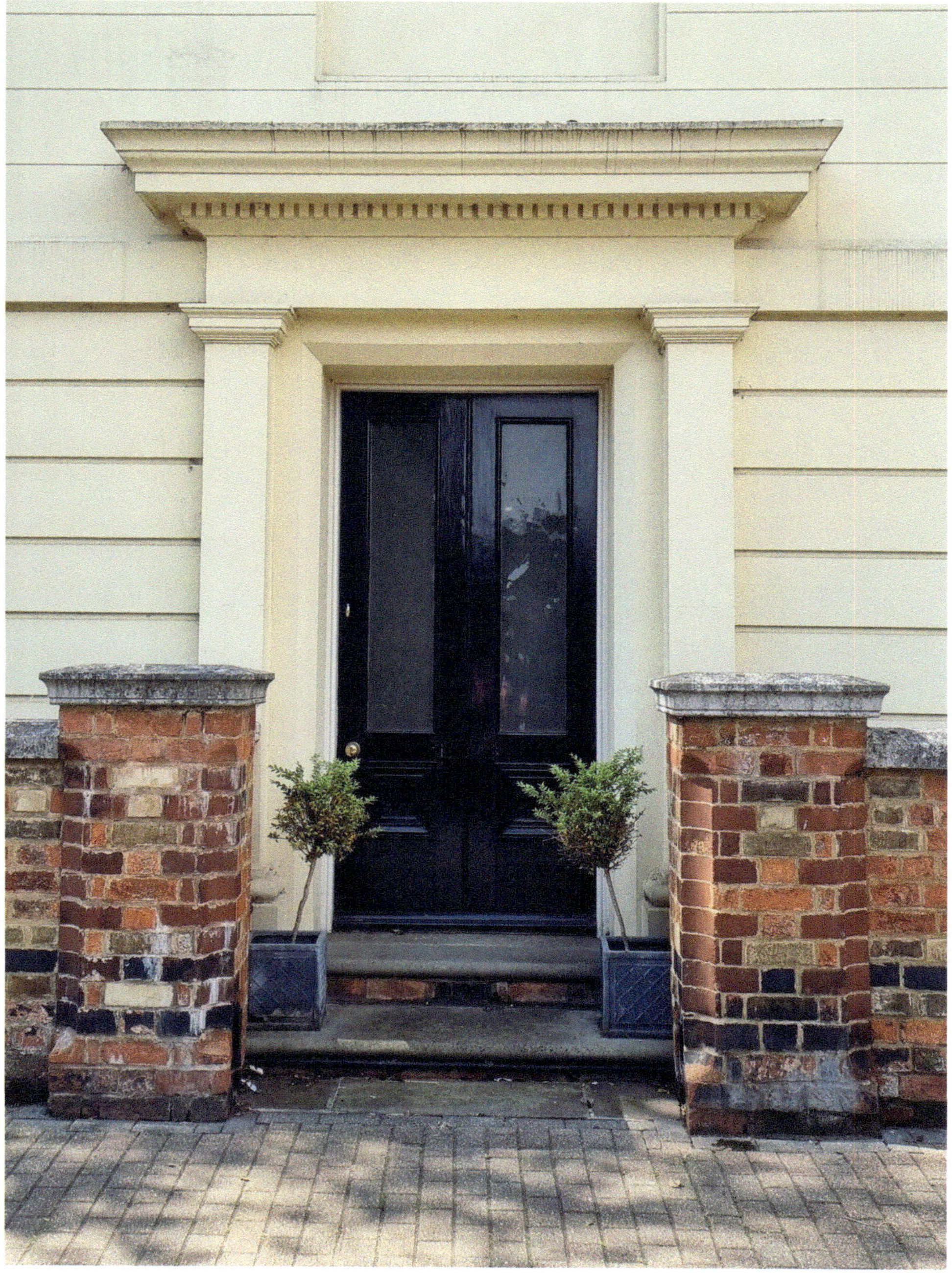

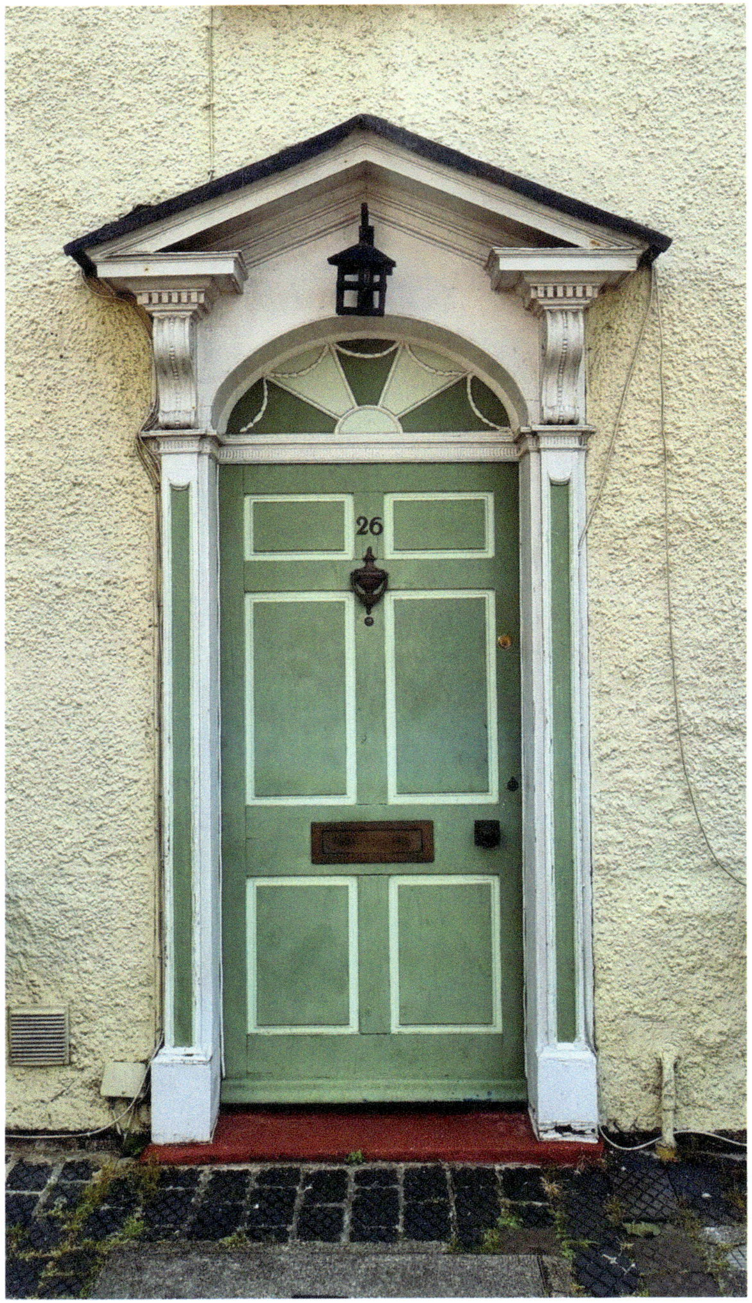
26
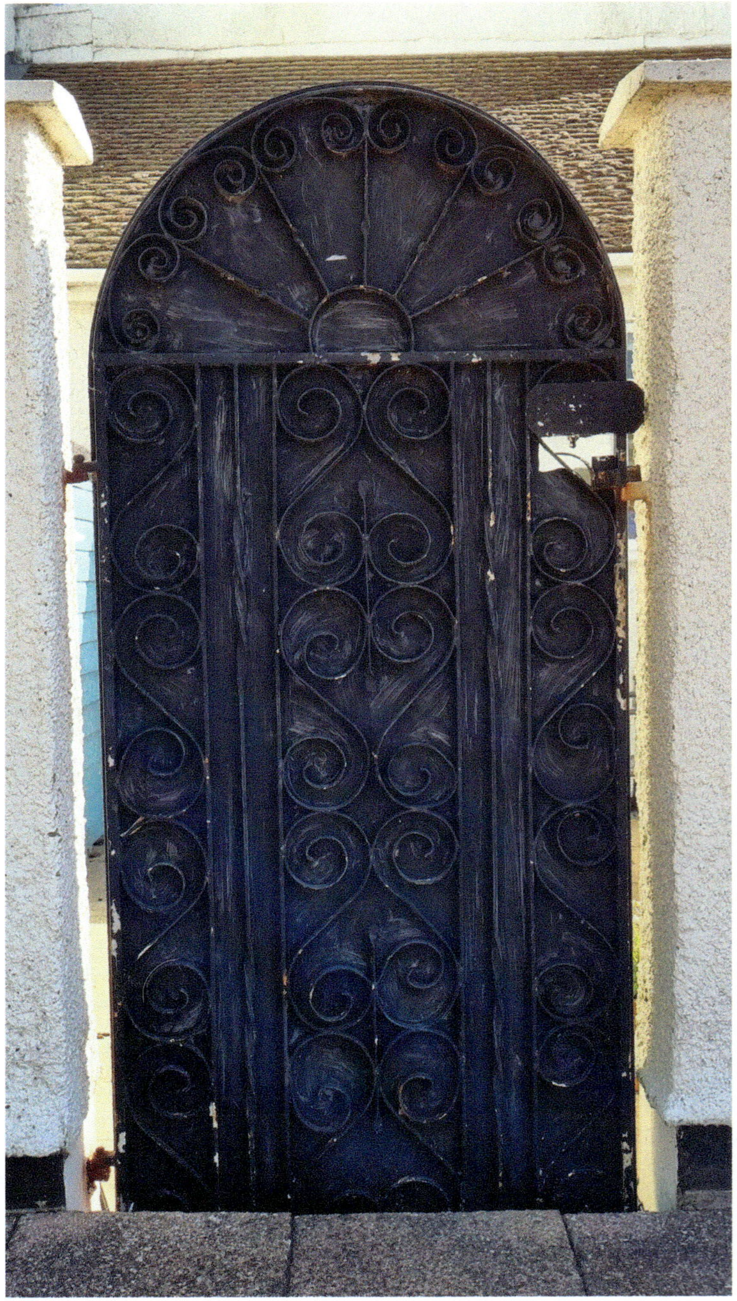
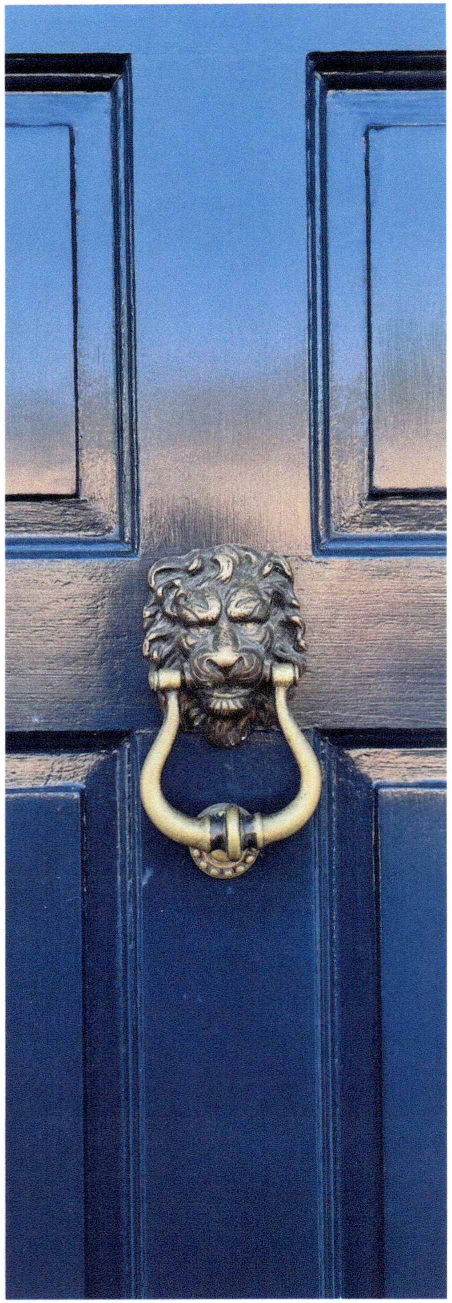

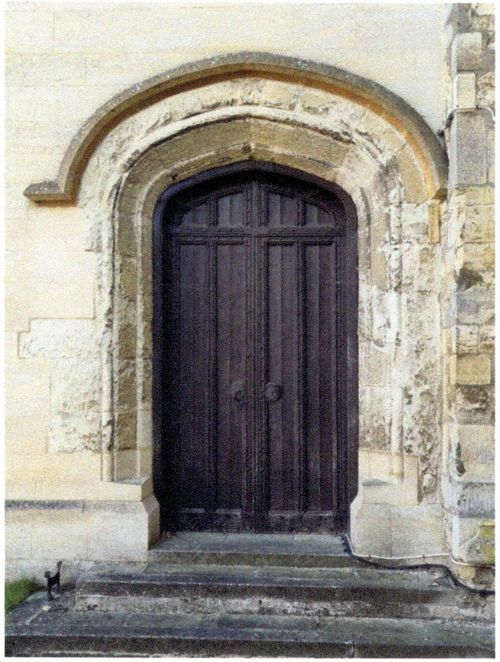

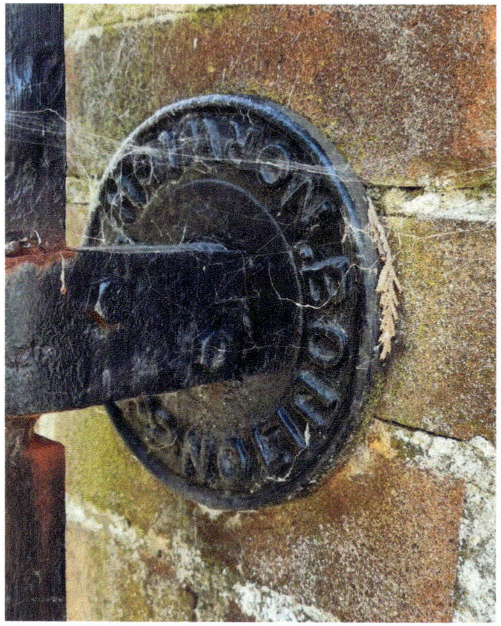

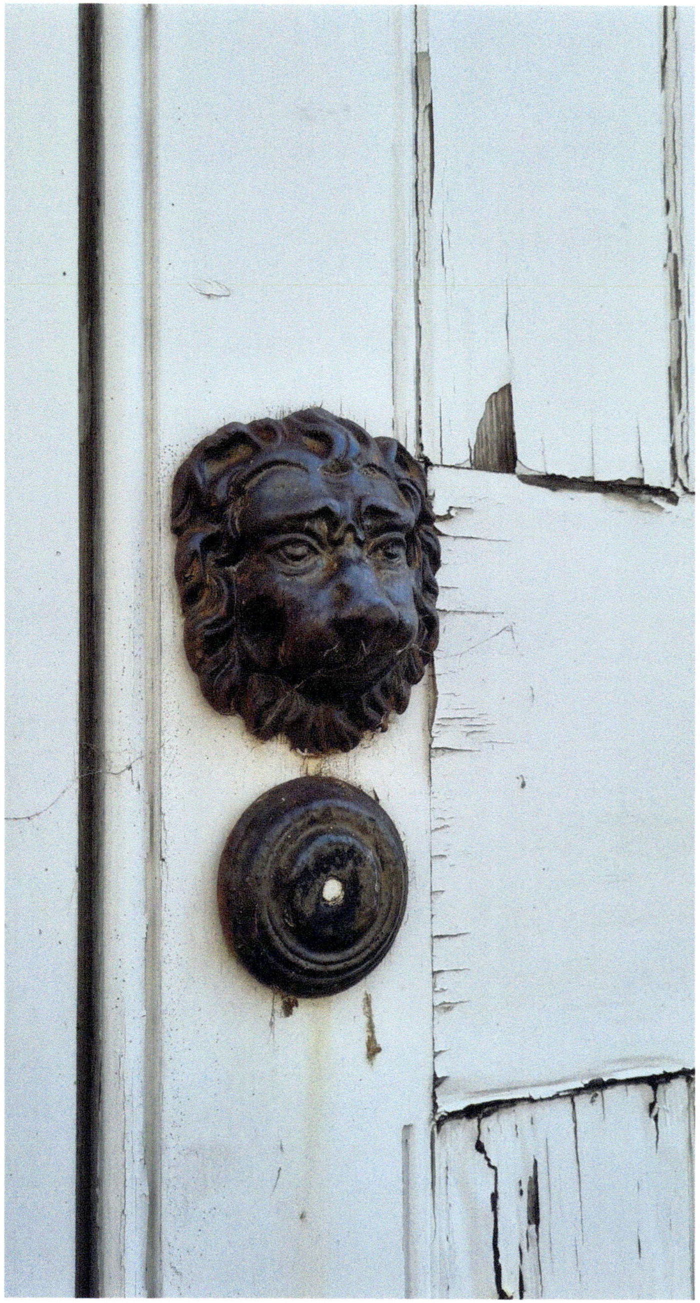

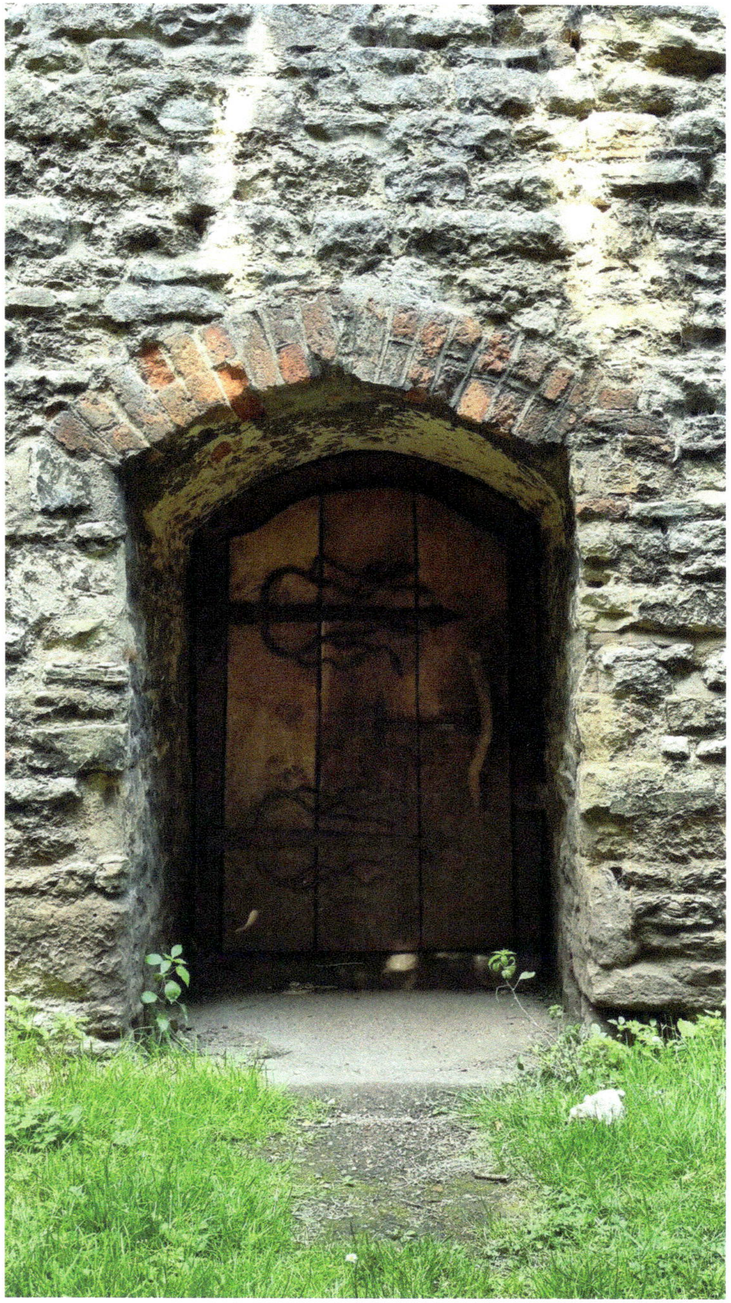

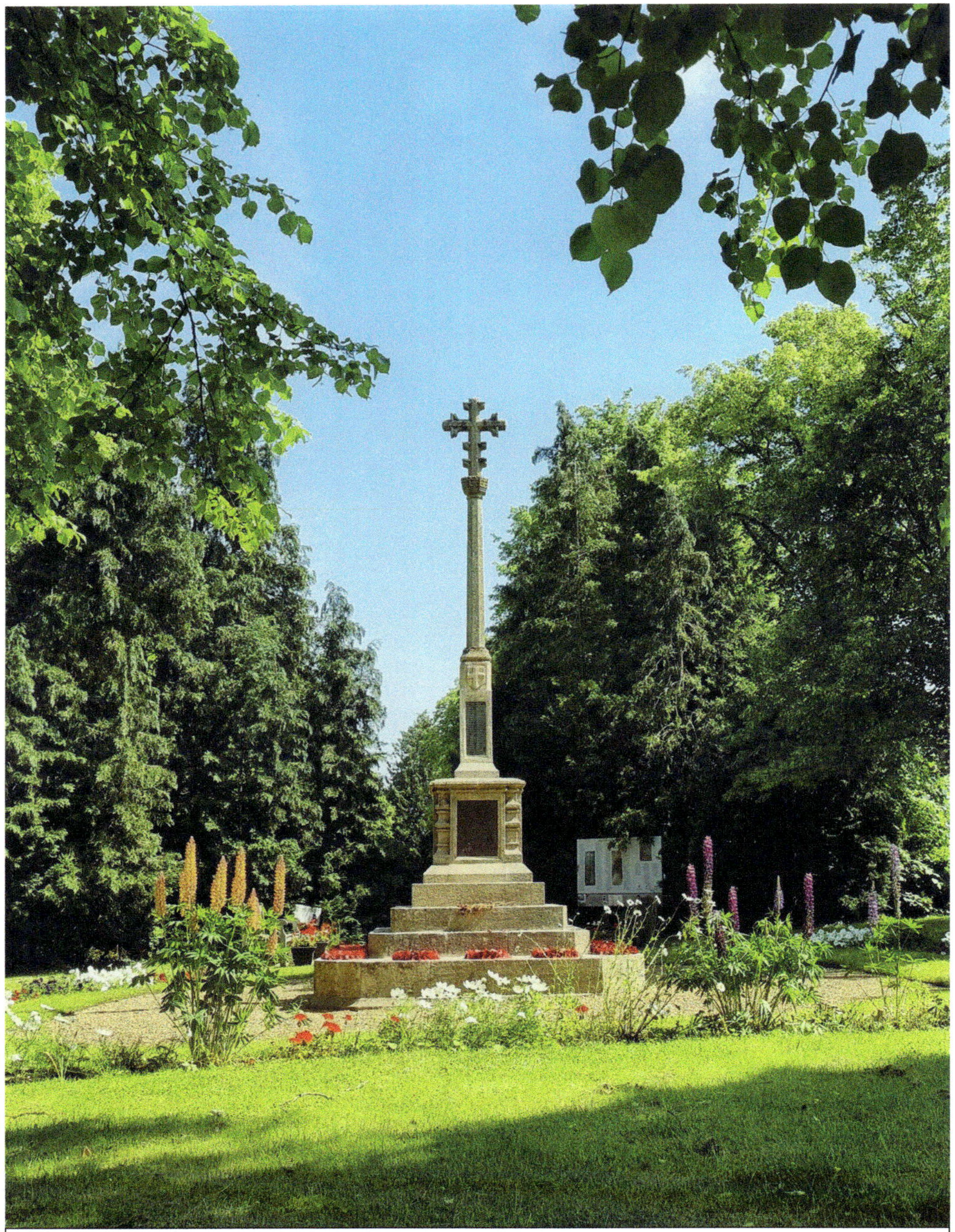

The war memorial on Horsefair Green.

Horse Fair

The south east side of the High Street was little developed, apart from a farmhouse and associated buildings, until the late 19th century. Cofferidge Close was an enclosed field and the Market Square extended south into Cow Fair and then Horse Fair. As their names suggest, these were cattle and horse markets.

Cow Fair developed as a street in the 19th century. At the time of Queen Victoria's silver jubilee in 1862, the parish decided on a more genteel name and it became Silver Street.

Horse Fair remained as part of the Calverton parish until the 20th century and old names were not changed. Horse Fair Green experienced some piecemeal development in the 18th and 19th centuries.

Two houses side by side at the west end of Horse Fair opened as alehouses in the 18th century. They were both outside the jurisdiction of the Stony Stratford authorities and this may have given them an advantage in licensing hours.

Curiously, they both adopted the same name - *The Royal Oak*. There must have been some dispute about this, because after a year or two one became the *Old Royal Oak* and the other the *New Royal Oak*. They are shown in the picture on pages 68 and 69. The smaller house closed in the 1830s, but the larger house continued to trade as the *Royal Oak* until the late 20th century.

Silver Street

Most of Silver Street is 19th century development and includes the Methodist Church and hall. There was also a small fire station on the west side, able to house a single fire engine.

LOOK AT HORSE FAIR

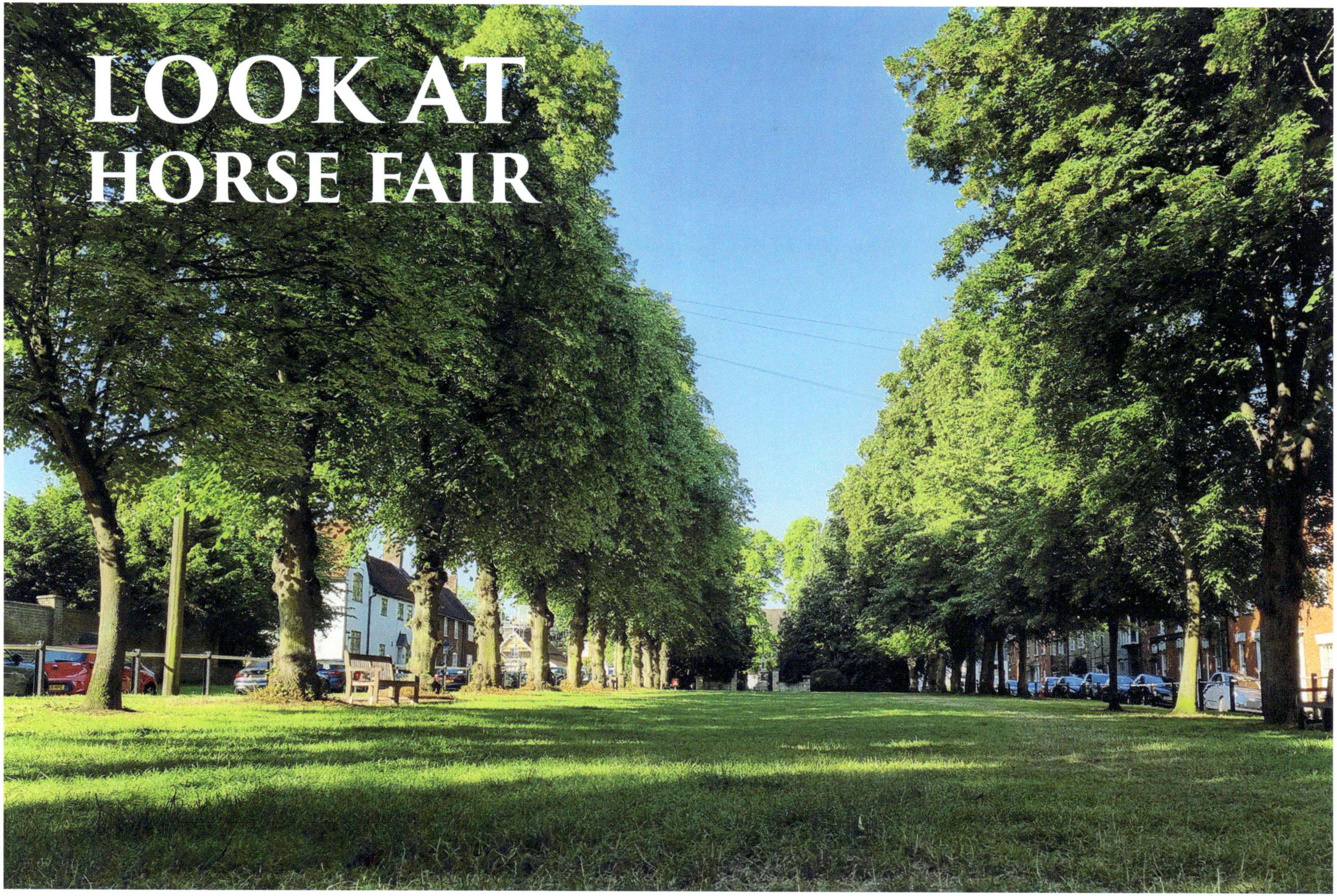

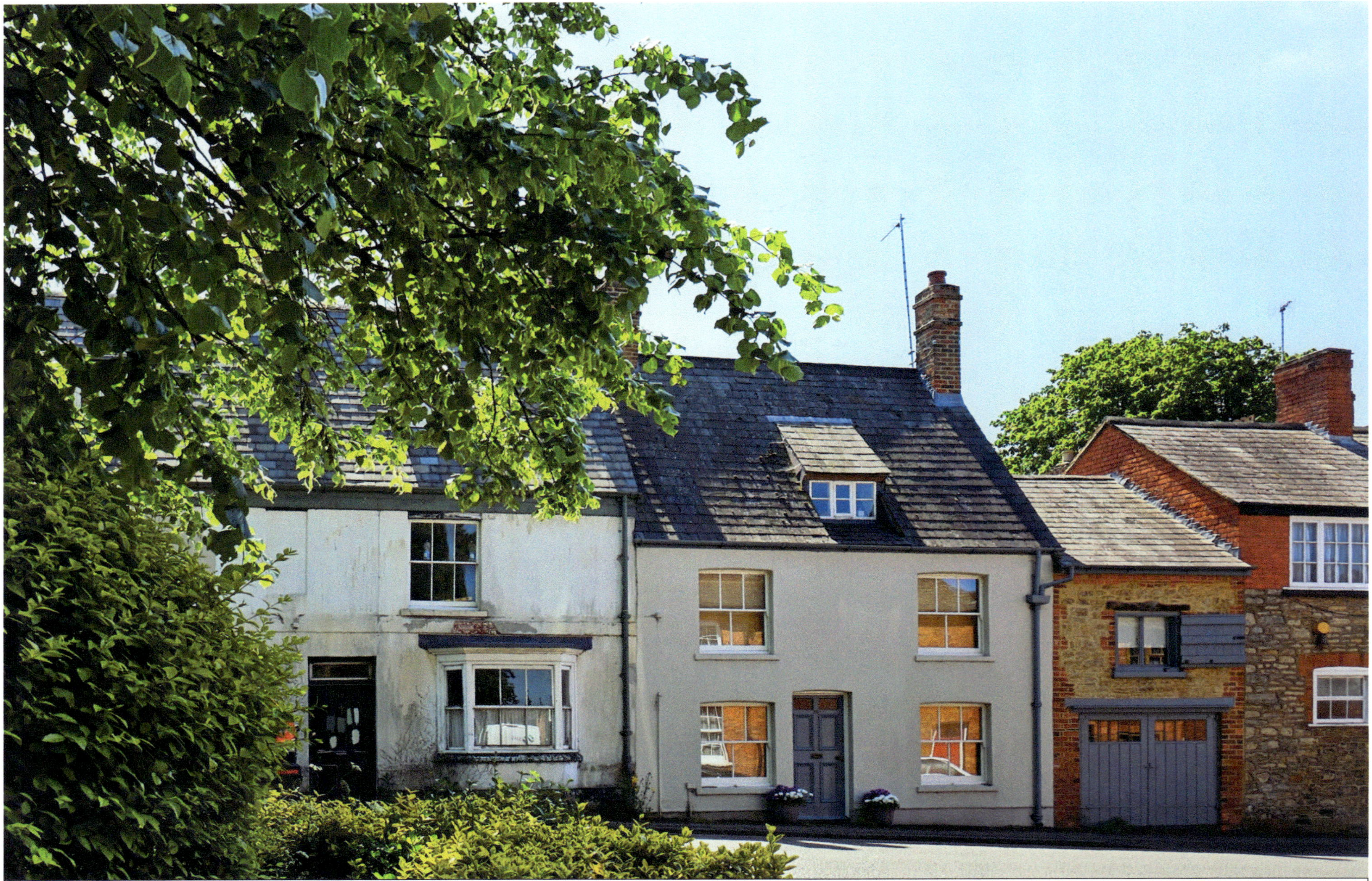

Two former public houses, side by side and both trading independently under the sign of The Royal Oak. The house on the left stayed in business until the latter part of the 20th century.

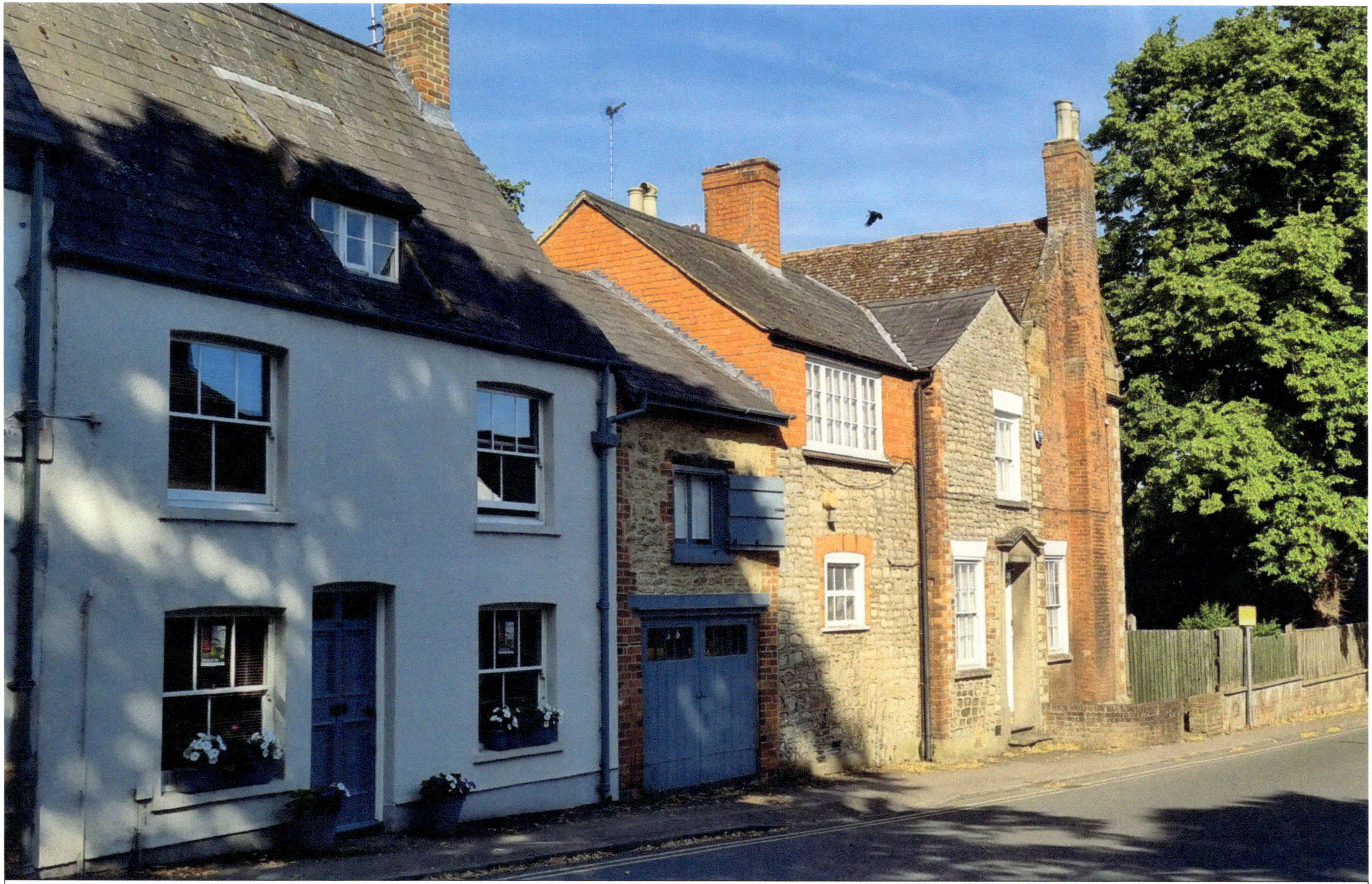

The cottage on the left was an alehouse under the sign of The Royal Oak. To the right,Burnham House, which was built in the 18th century and is more substantial than it appears from the street.

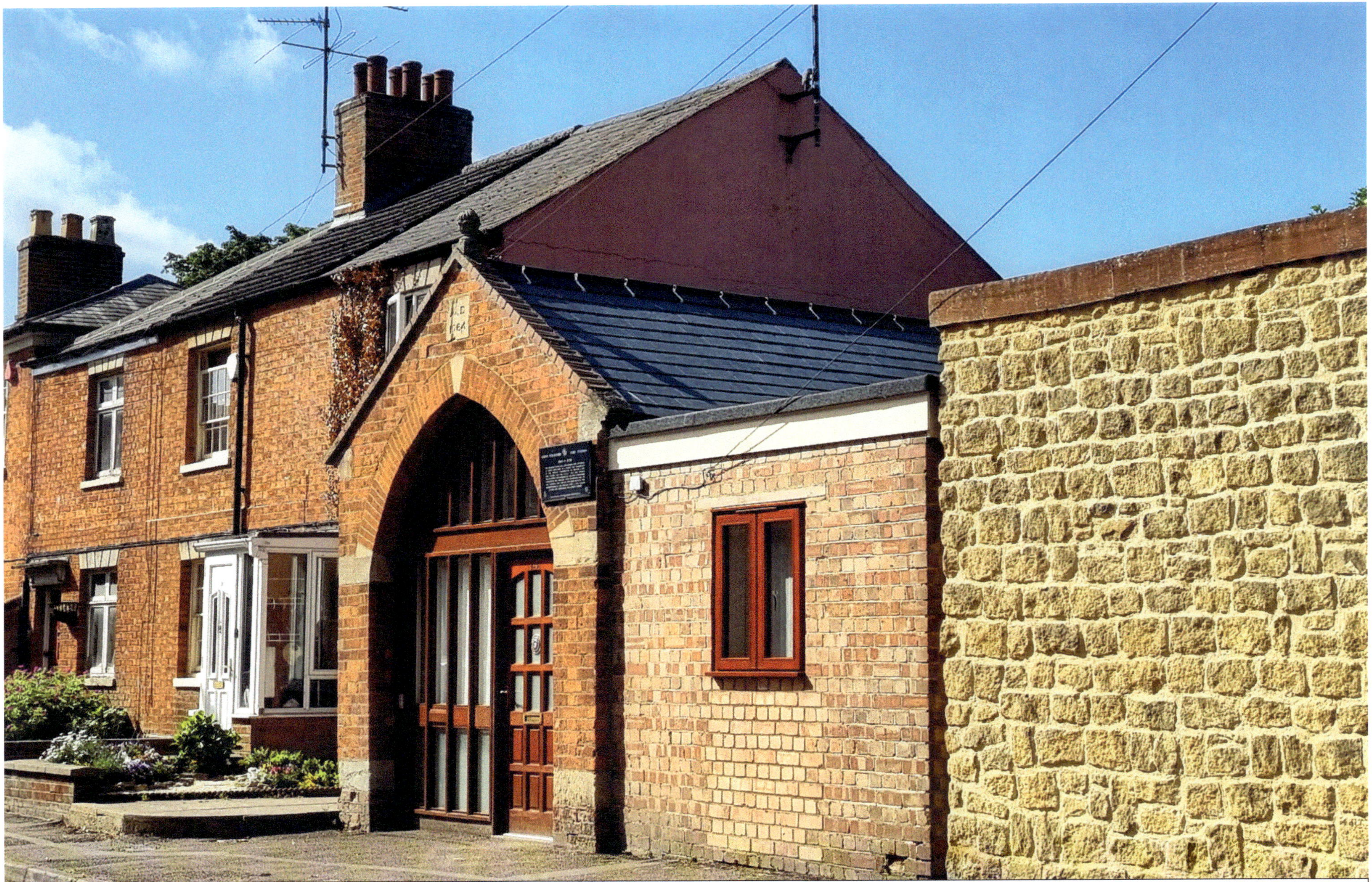

Part of Silver Street, showing the former fire station.

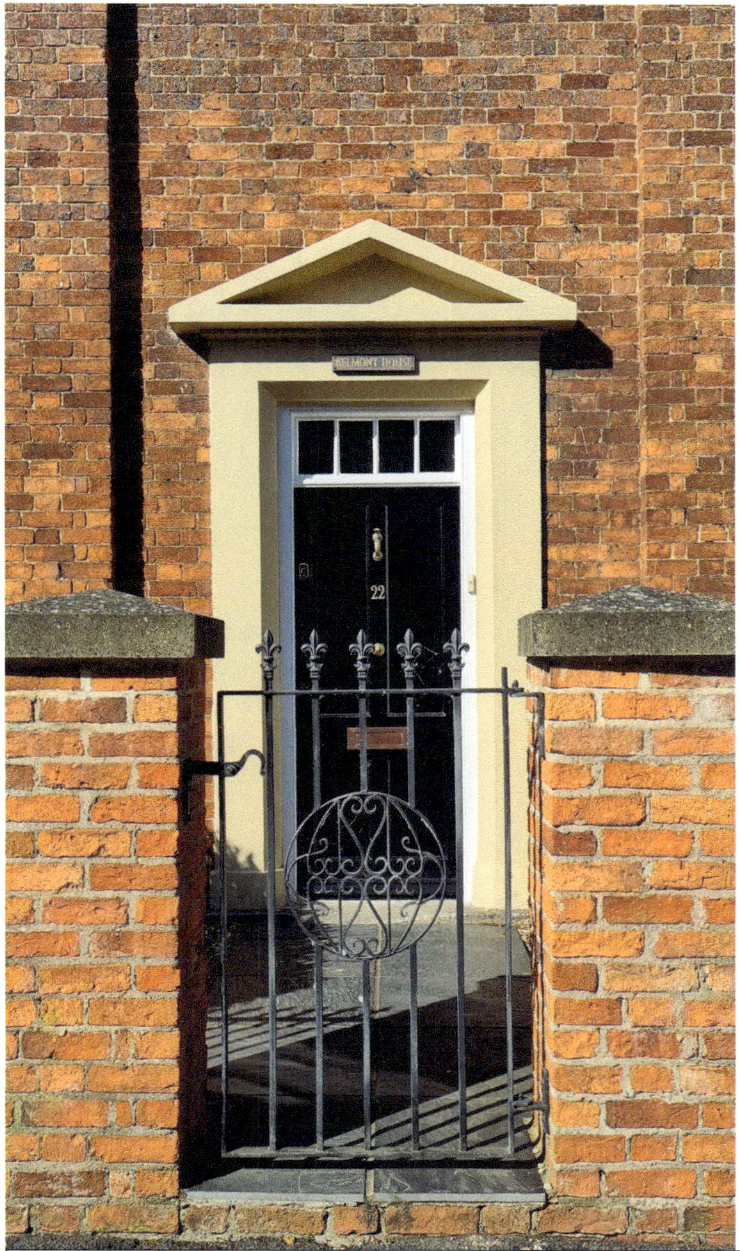

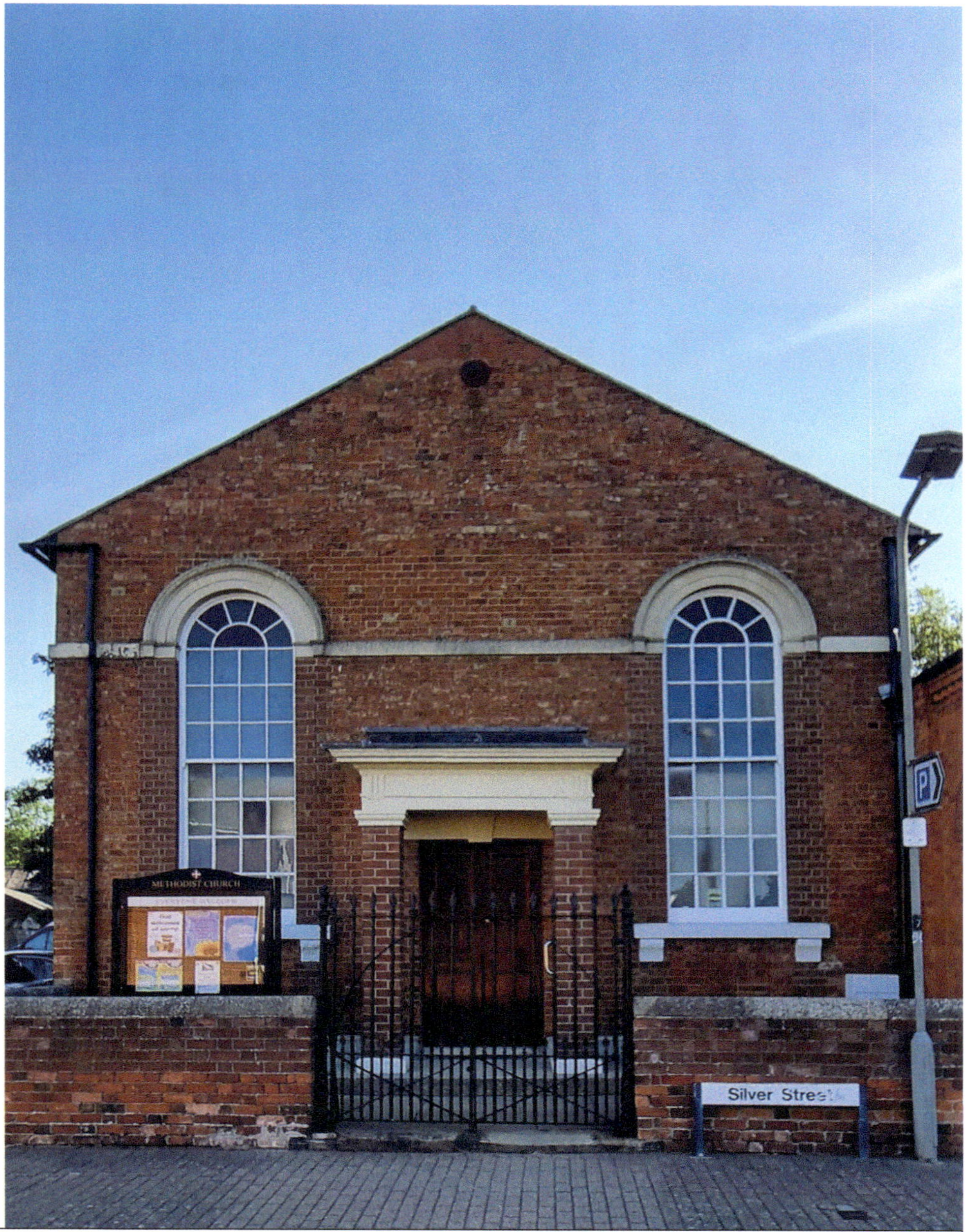

The entrance to Belmond House, a Grade II listed building. Right: The Methodist Chapel on Silver Street.

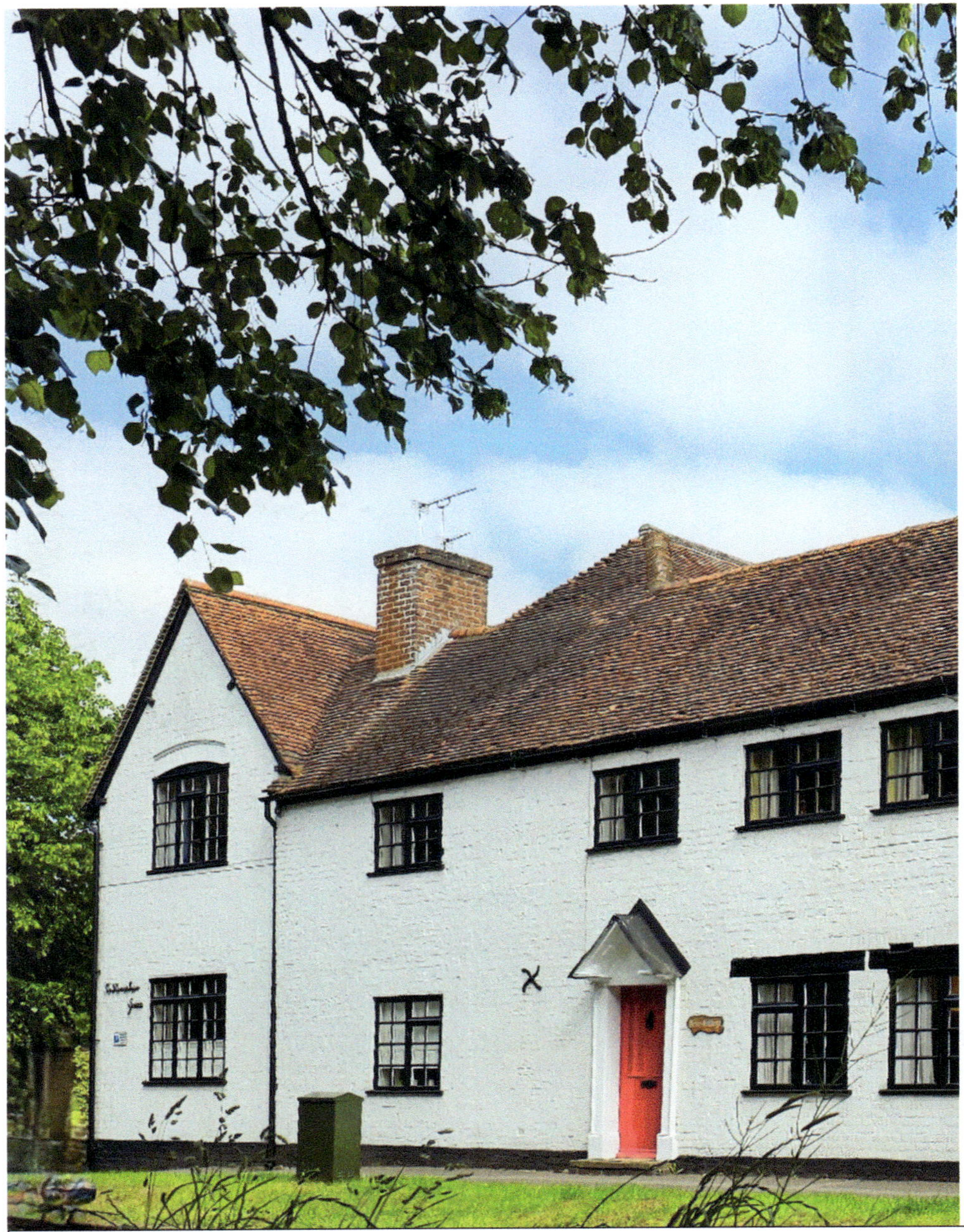

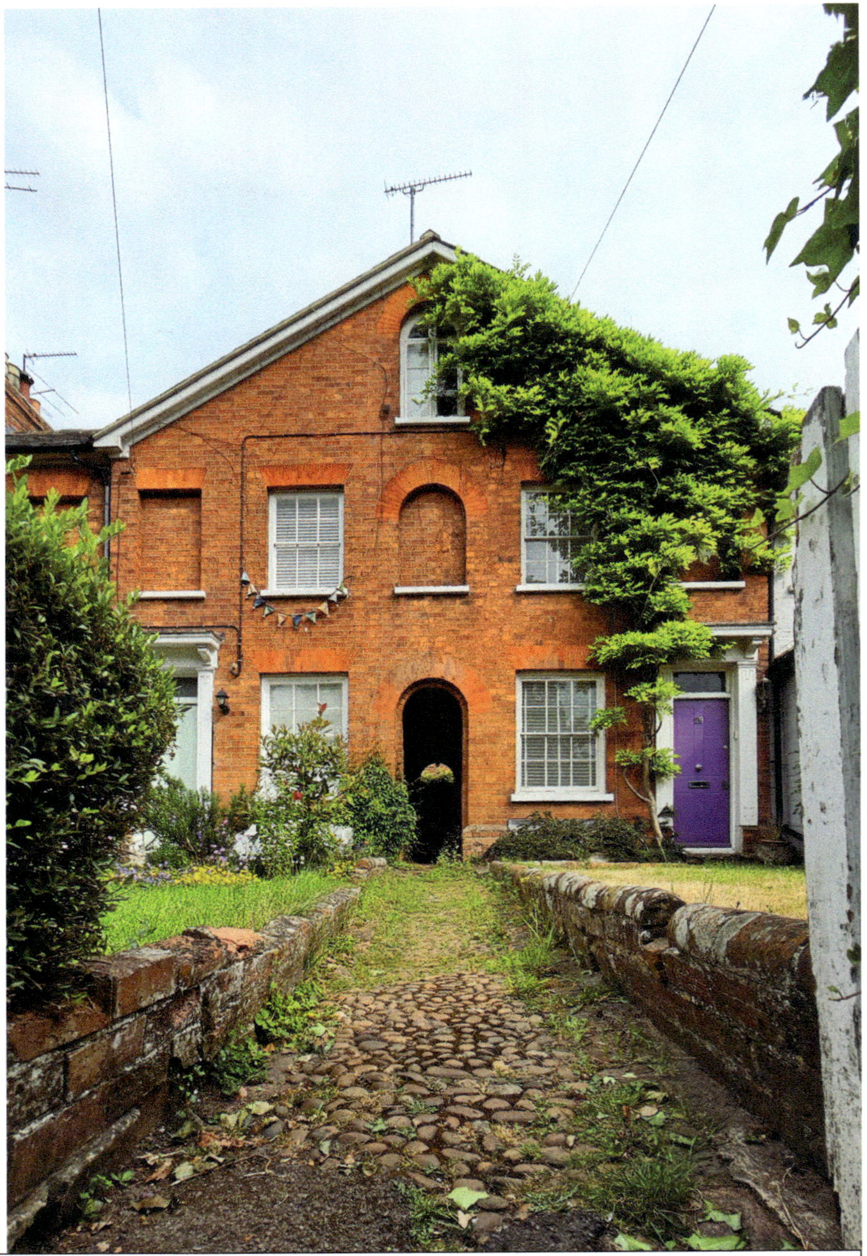

Properties on Horsefair Green. The white house was probably an 18th century farm house. The houses on the right have a common passage to the back in the centre of the building.

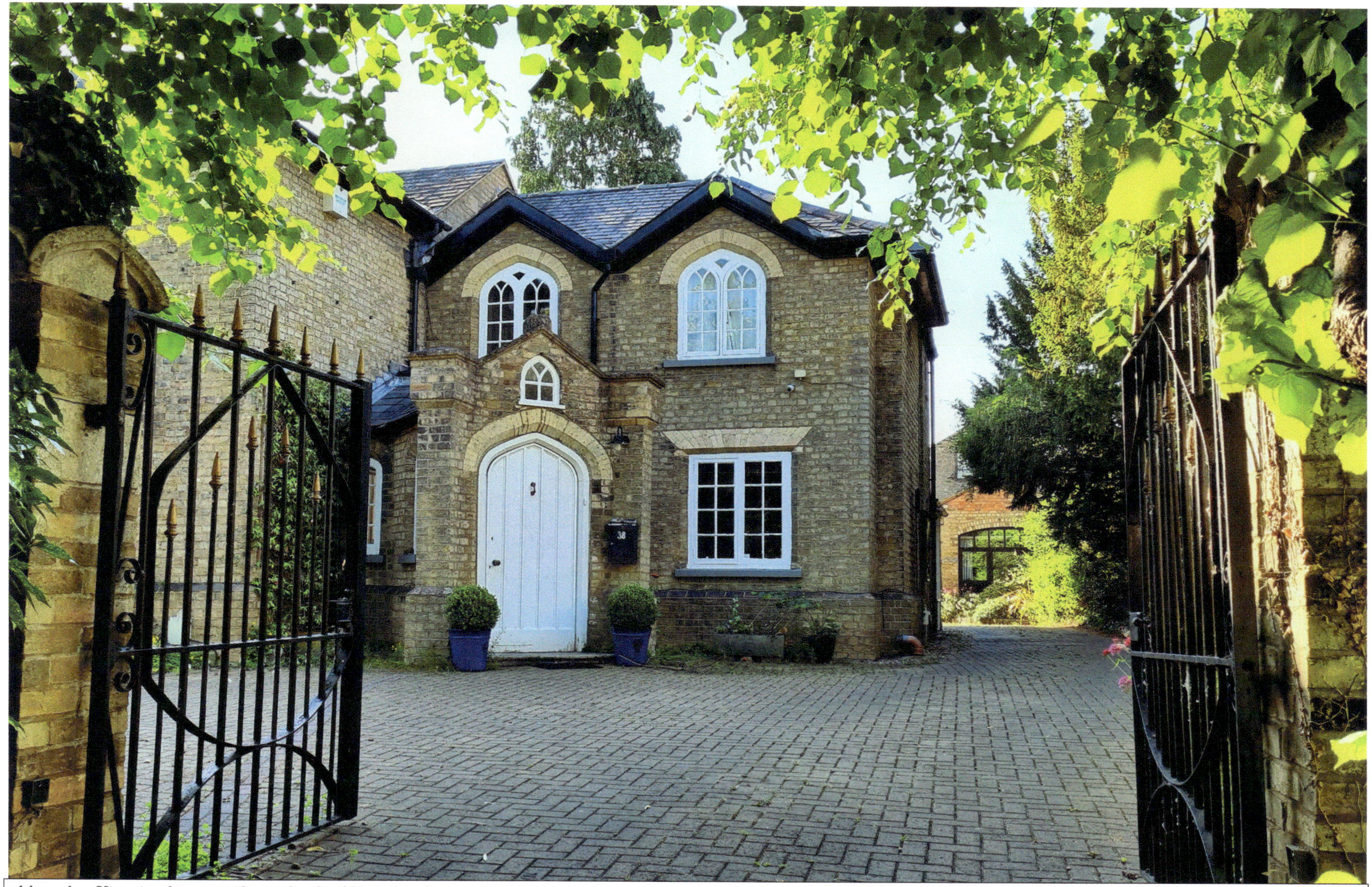

A large late Victorian house on the south side of Horsefair Green.

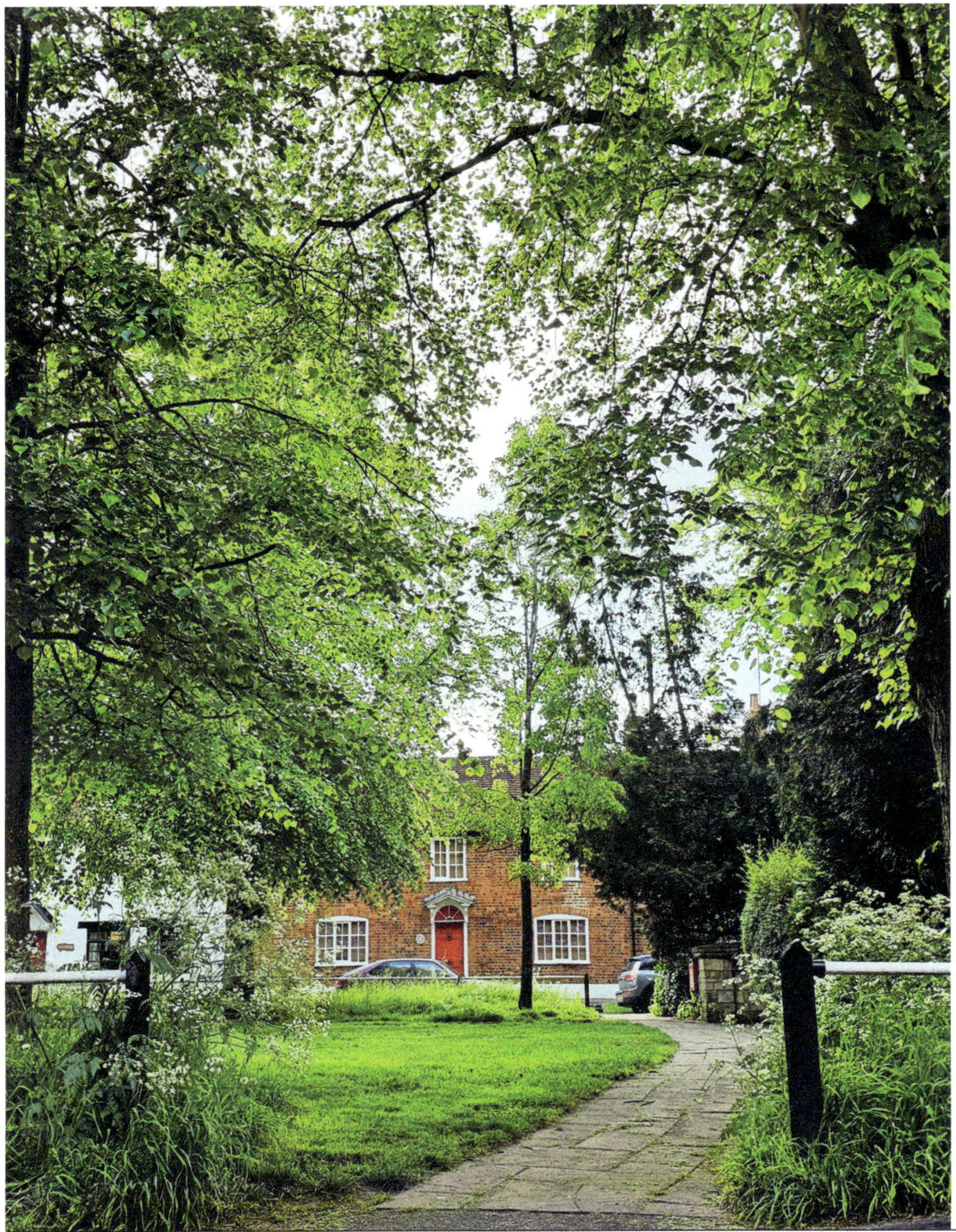

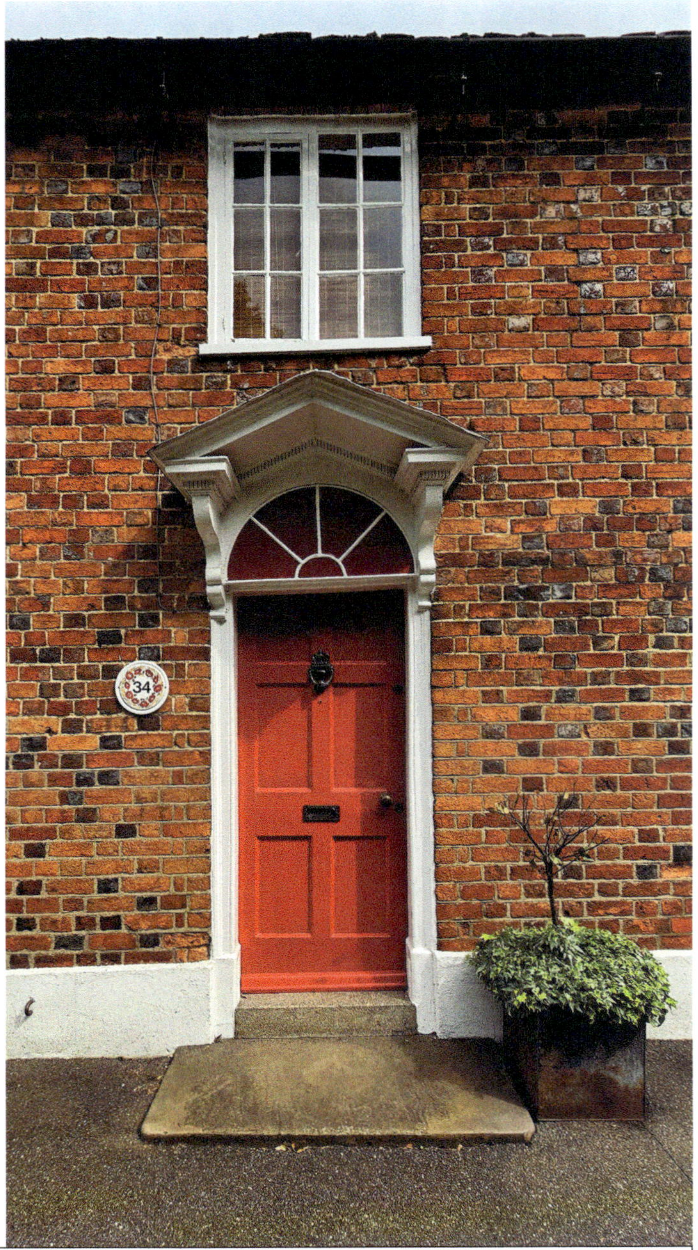

A view of the north side of Horsefair Green.

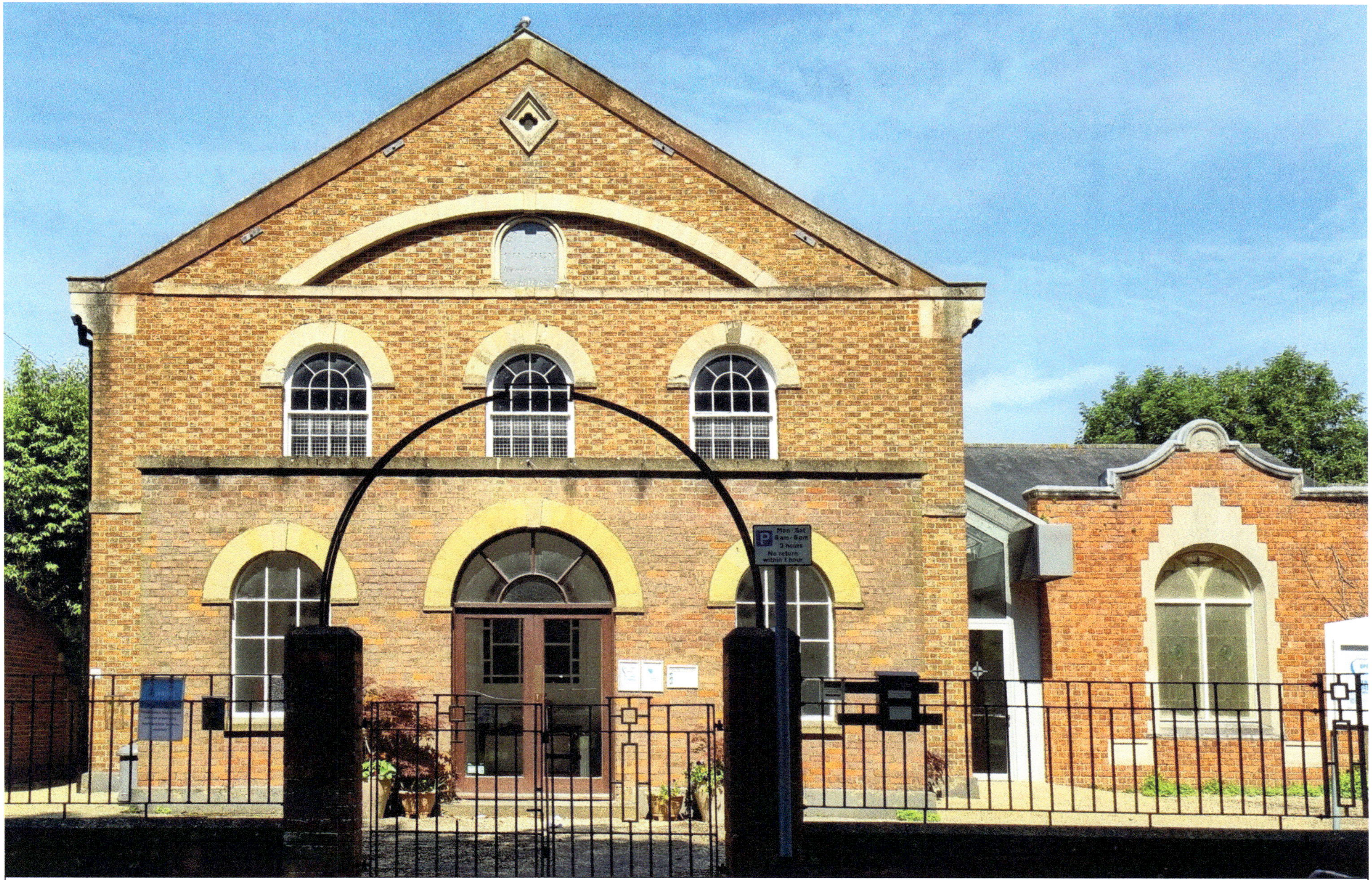

Stony Stratford Community Church, originally the Baptist Chapel.

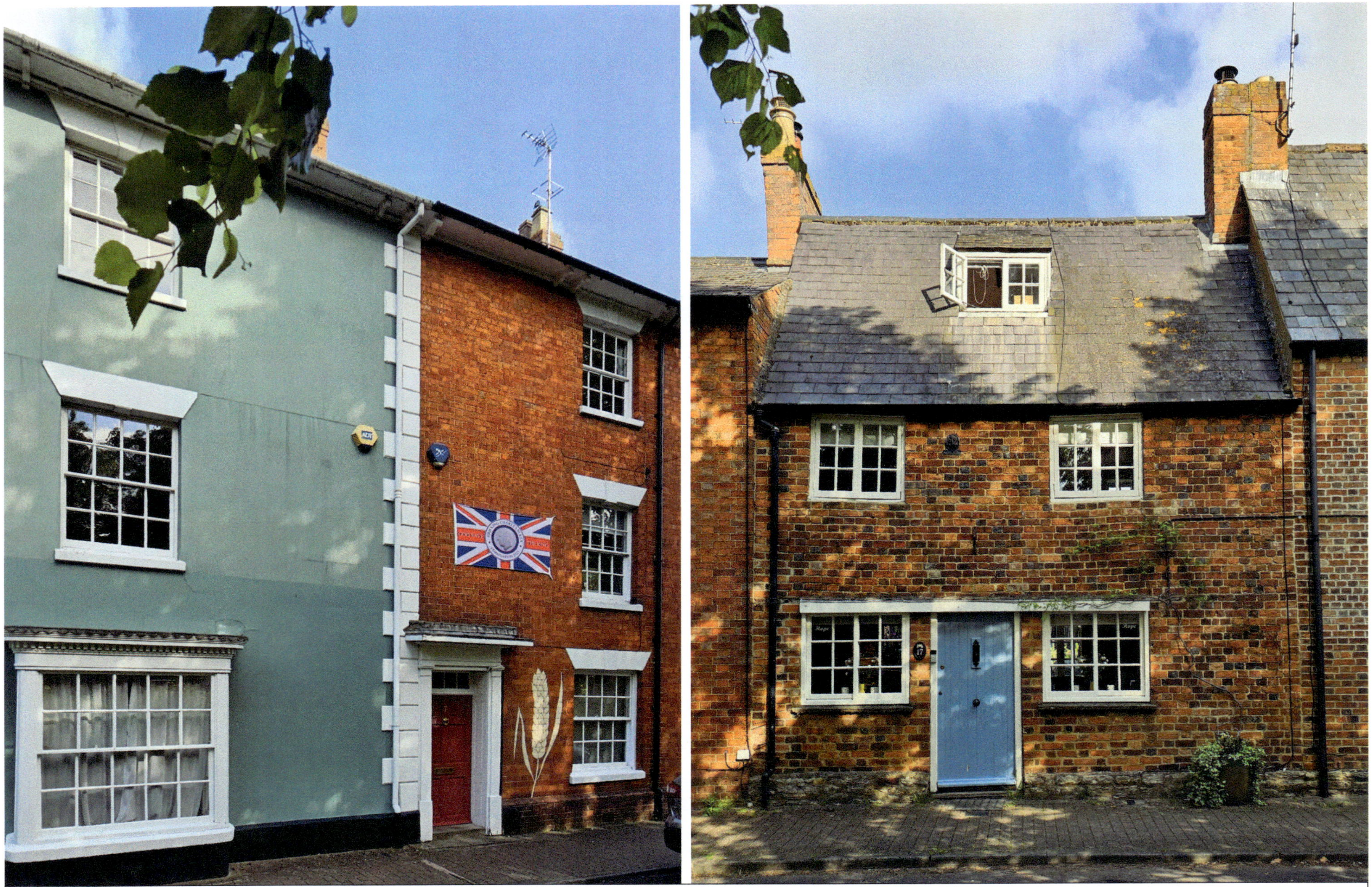

Horsefair Green properties backing on to Cofferidge Close.

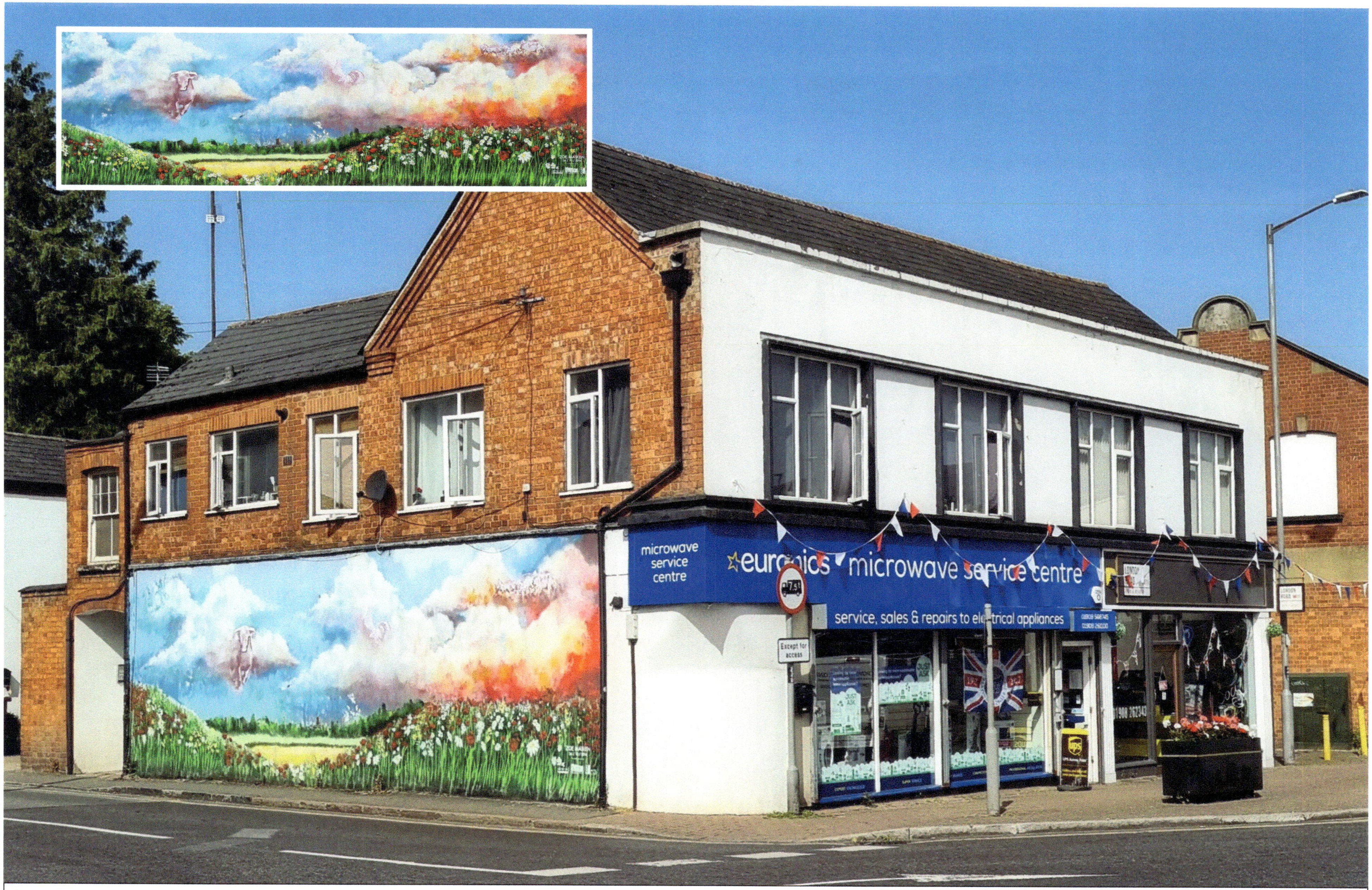

Imaginative mural painted on the side of the former Co-op by Zoe Maslin in 2016.

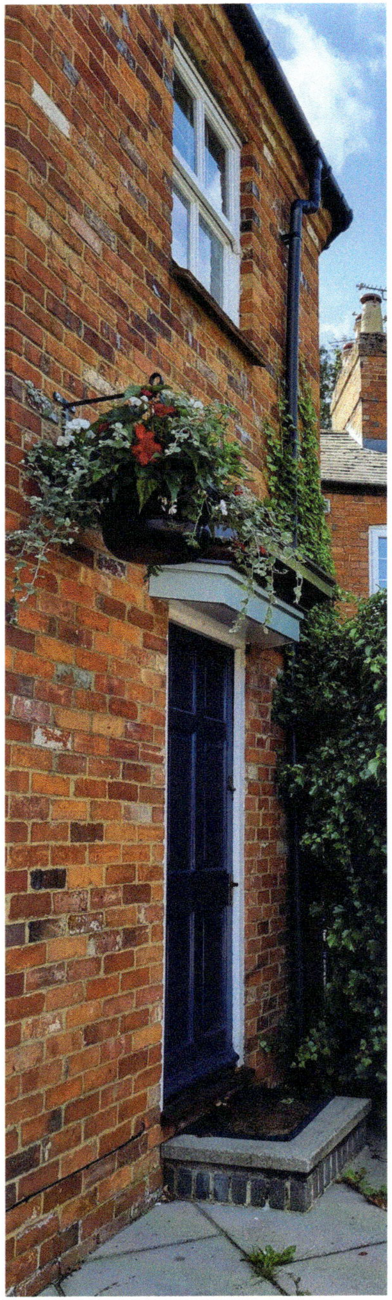

The High Street

In the 19th century, the centre of gravity of Stony Stratford moved southwards. Buildings on either side of the street to the south of St Giles, started in the 16th and 17th centuries and one side of Cofferidge Close was taken up, including three inns, known as *The Angel*, *The George* and *The White Horse*. *The Angel* disappeared under the new Cofferidge Close development, but the *George* and the *White Horse* are still in business. On the other side of the street, a new inn called the *White Swan* opened in 1823. It may have replaced an older inn. This half-timbered building is presently the *Kardamom Lounge*.

One 16th century inn, known as the *Rose and Crown* became a charity school and later a Church of England School. At the corner of the Wolverton Road, a second school opened in 1844 for children of dissenting (i.e. non-Anglican) parents. It was known as the British School. Some buildings on the east side were demolished to build almshouses. This is known as *The Retreat*.

A recent shopping development on the west side corner mirrors the semi-circular corner on the east side, this being the mid-19th century British School. The new shopping centre, featuring enclosed shops, has been named Swinfen's Yard after the distinguished Stony Stratford architect, Edward Swinfen Harris.

50 years ago this street was a major thoroughfare with two-way traffic, including heavy lorries.

Cofferidge Close

For many centuries an enclosed field, a close, stretching from the High Street to Silver Street and from Horsefair to the Market Square, lay undeveloped. It was known as Cofferer's Close or Cofferidge Close.

In the early 17th century, properties, including The George, started to spread southwards, and in the 19th century Horsefair and Silver Street were occupied. The central area of the close remained undeveloped.

A contribution of the Milton Keynes Development Corporation to Stony Stratford was to demolish buildings on the High Street and create a large shopping and parking area in the unoccupied field. It was named Cofferidge Close and was constructed in the years 1970-1976.

Among the buildings that were demolished were *The Angel Inn*, which had been open for business since 1770 and Ron Fleming's house and motorcycle business.

The George

The building dates from the first decade of the 17th century and has managed to stay in business for well over three centuries, albeit for a period in the 20th century as a coffee shop.

LOOK AT THE HIGH STREET

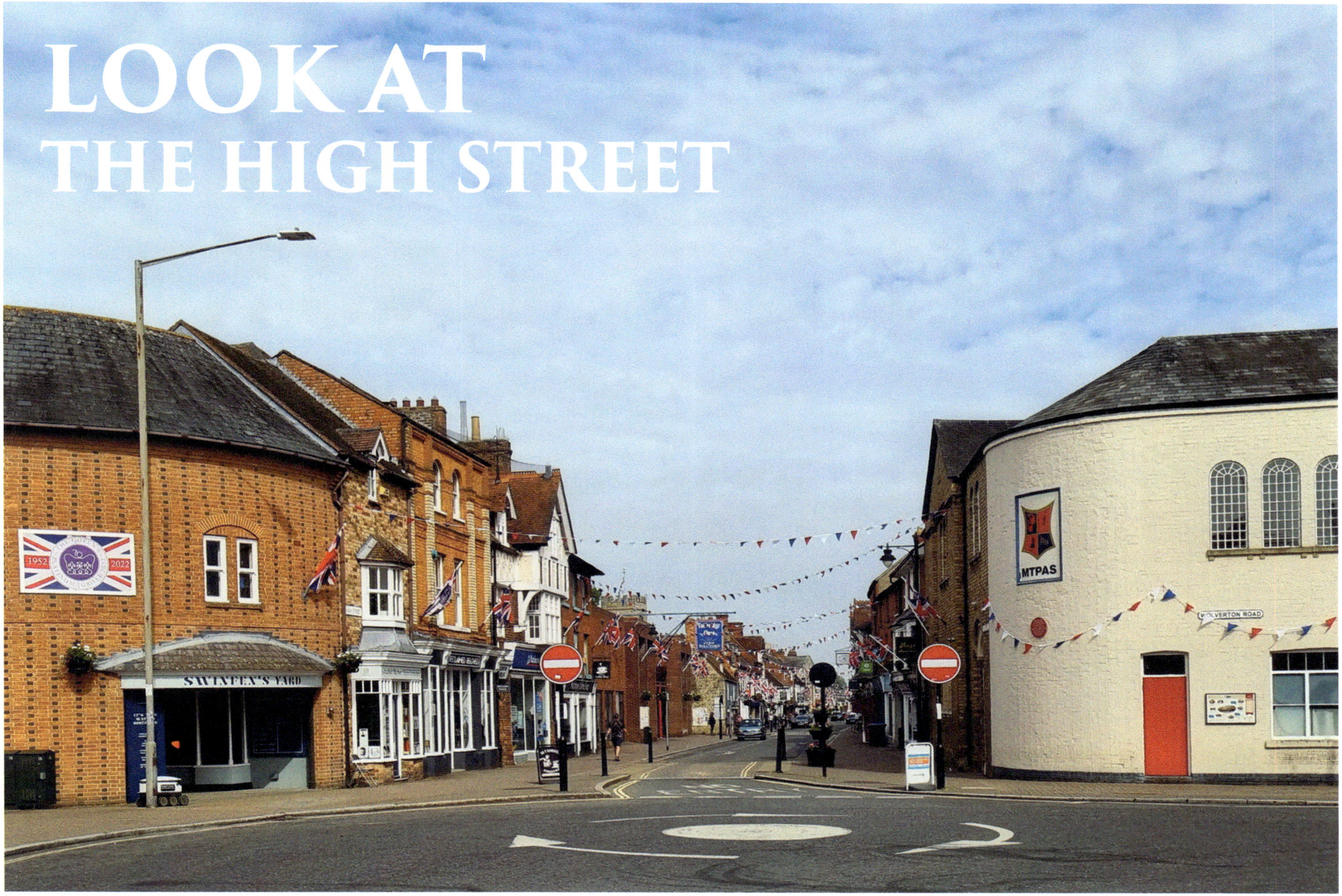

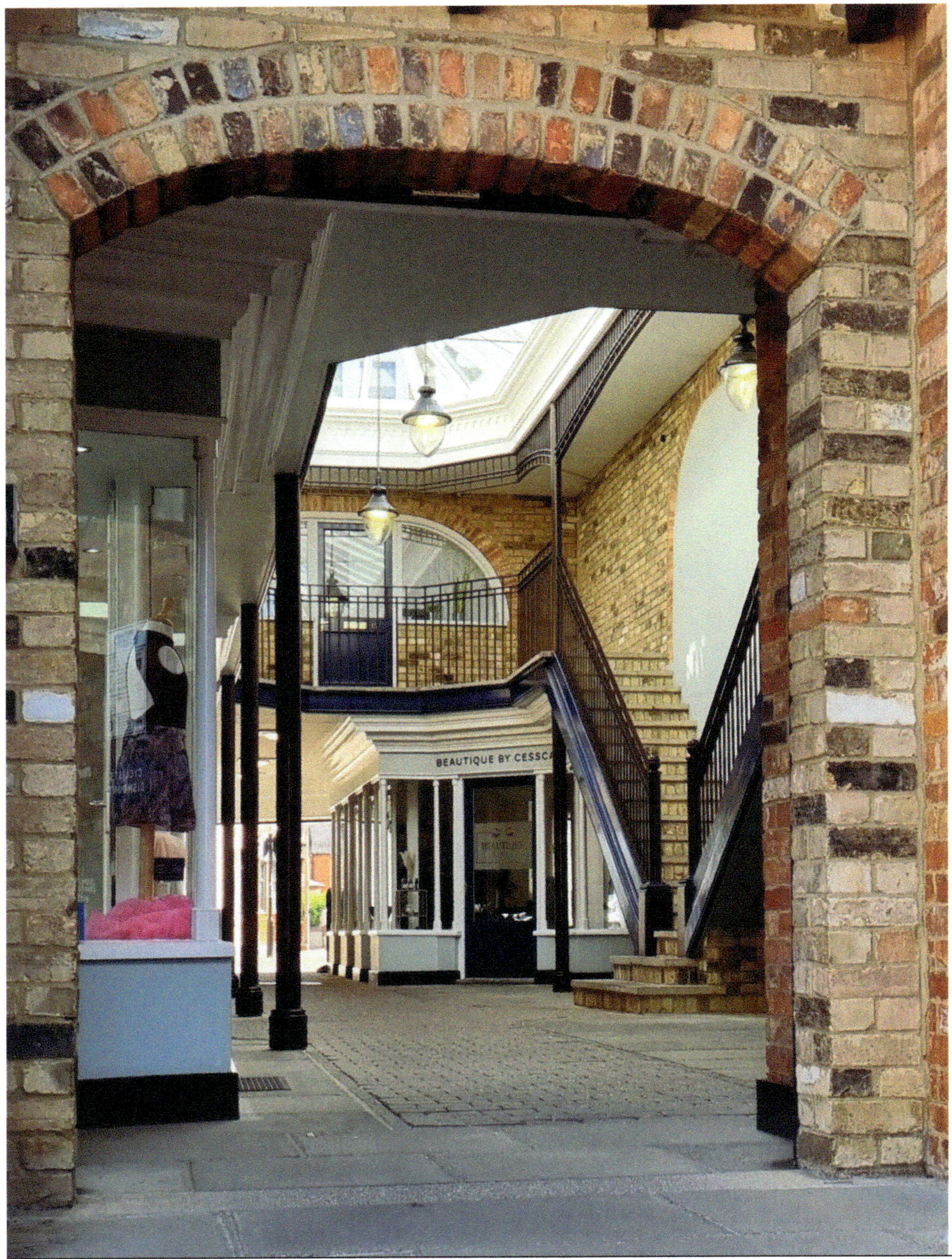

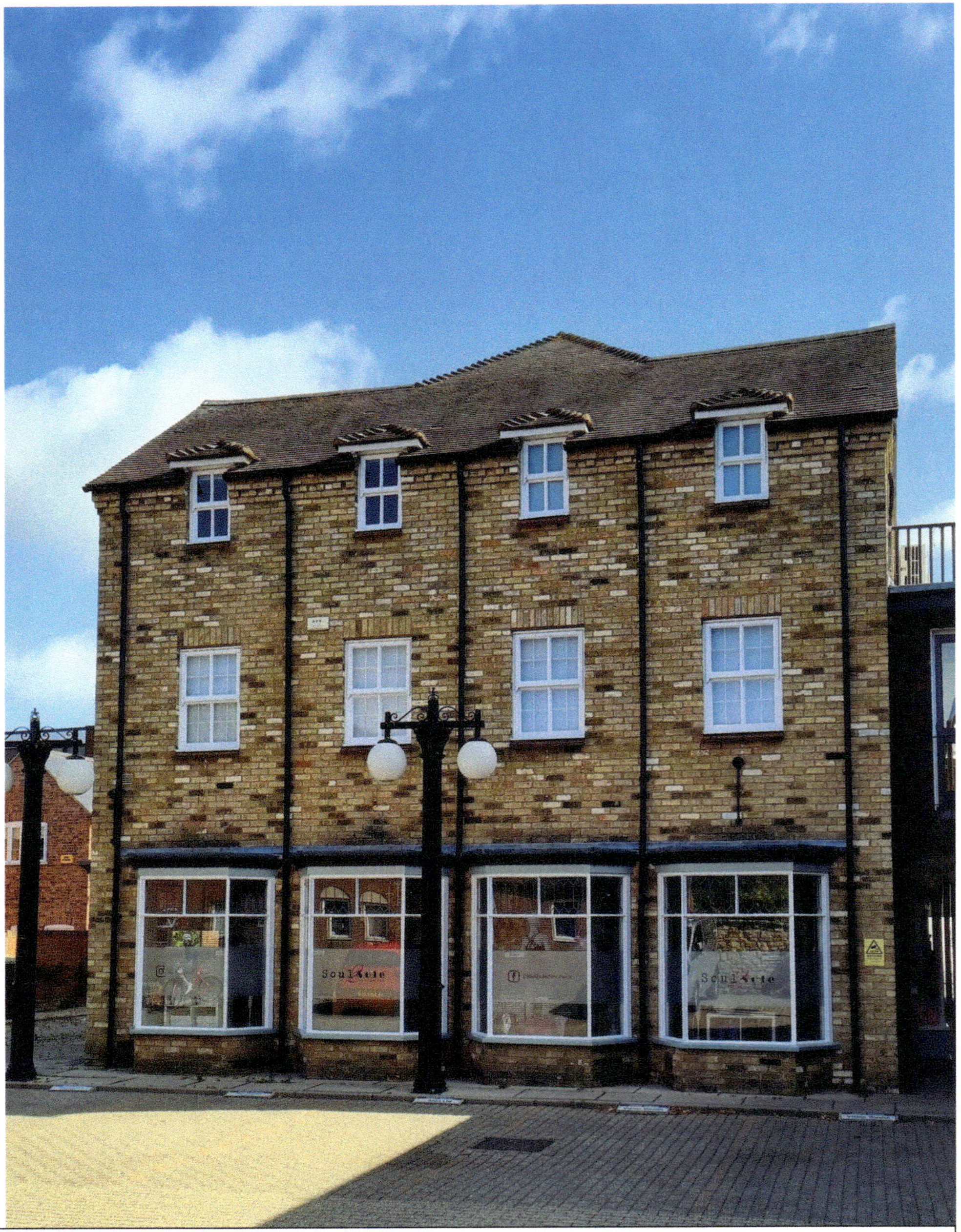

Swinfen's Yard interior and from the back.

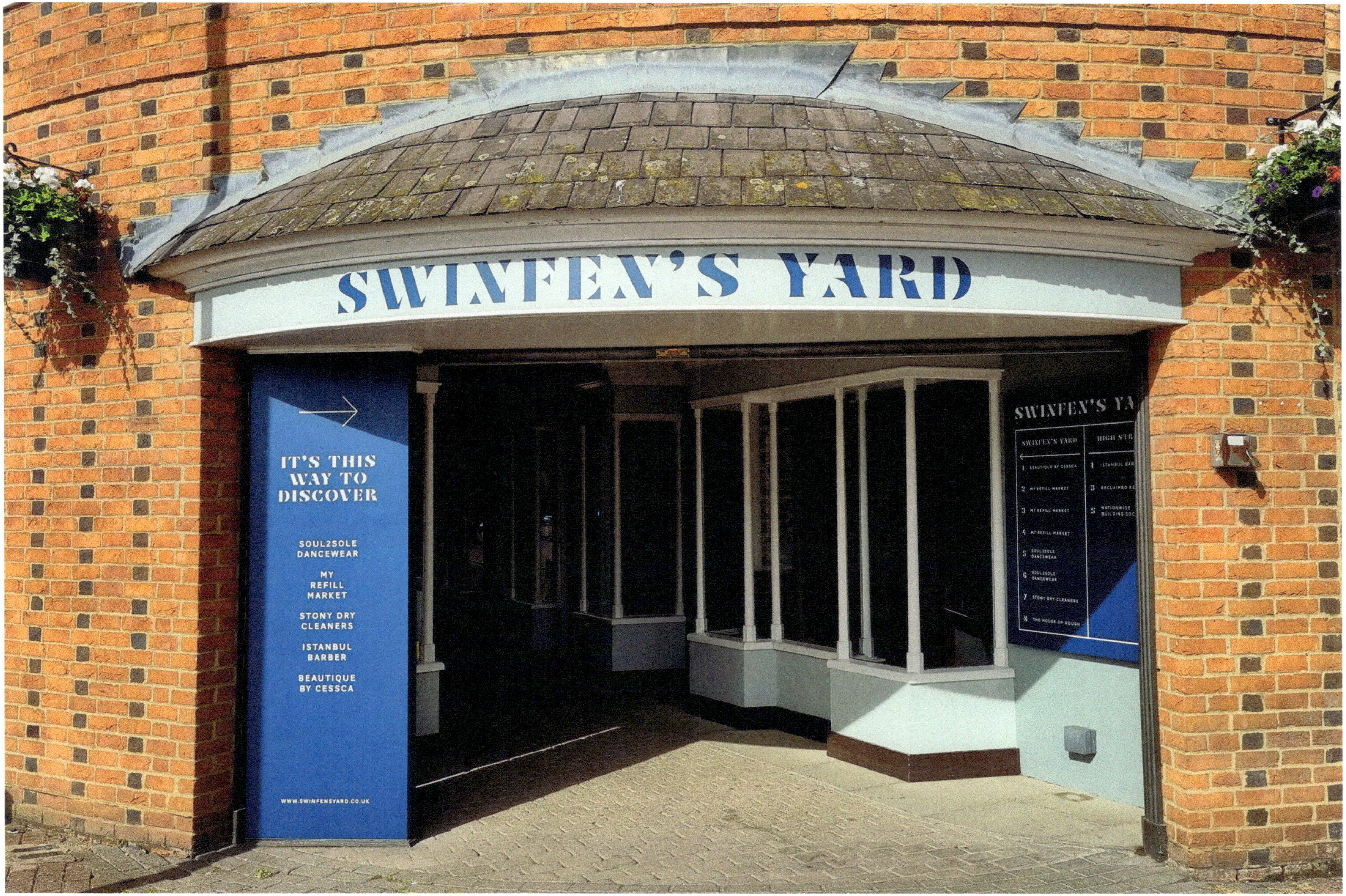
SWINFEN'S YARD
IT'S THIS WAY TO DISCOVER
SOUL2SOLE DANCEWEAR
MY REFILL MARKET
STONY DRY CLEANERS
ISTANBUL BARBER
BEAUTIQUE BY CESSCA
WWW.SWINFENSYARD.CO.UK

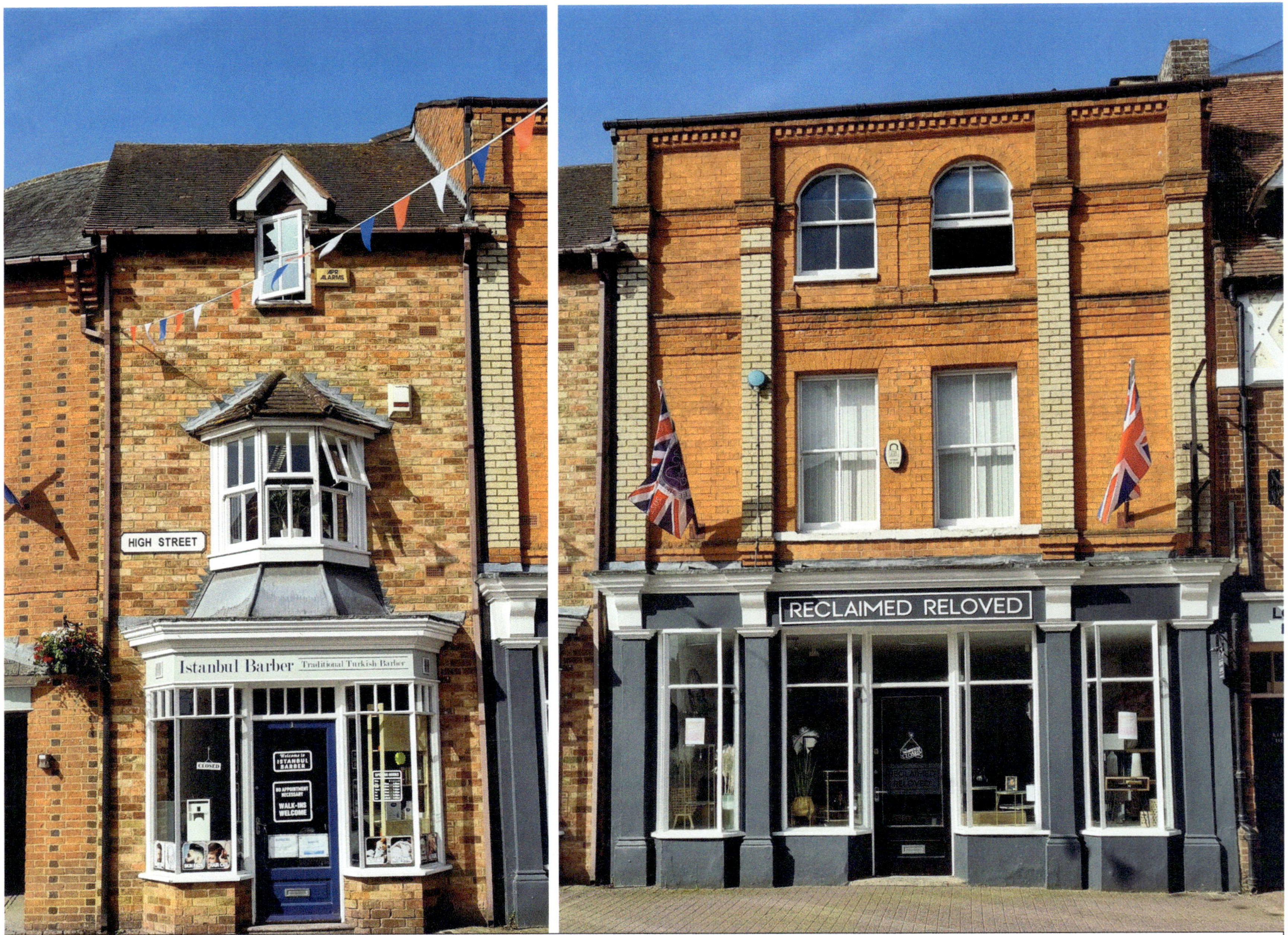

A variety of buildings on the High Street – pages 82–83 and pages 87–88.

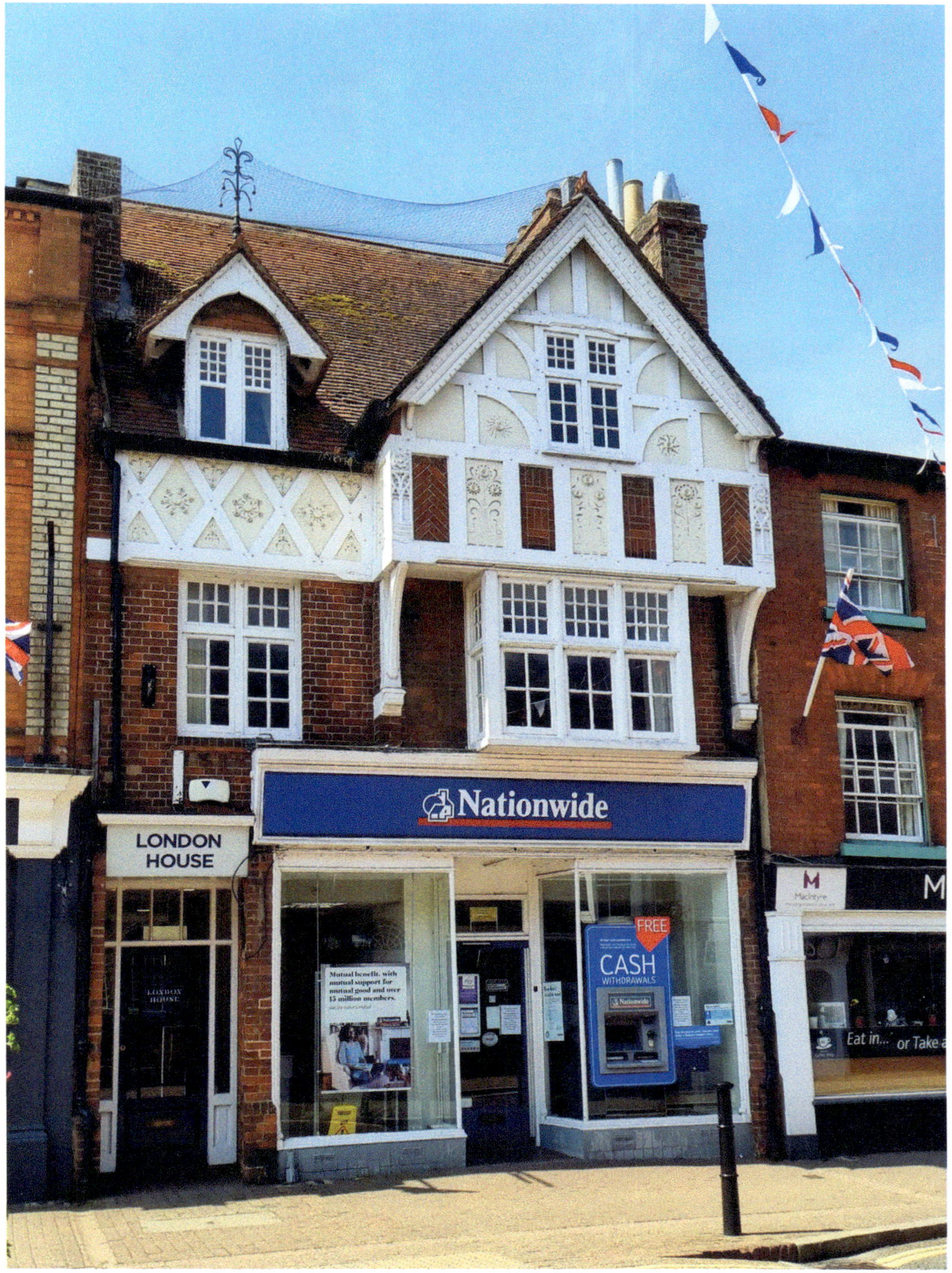
LONDON HOUSE
Nationwide
FREE
CASH
WITHDRAWALS

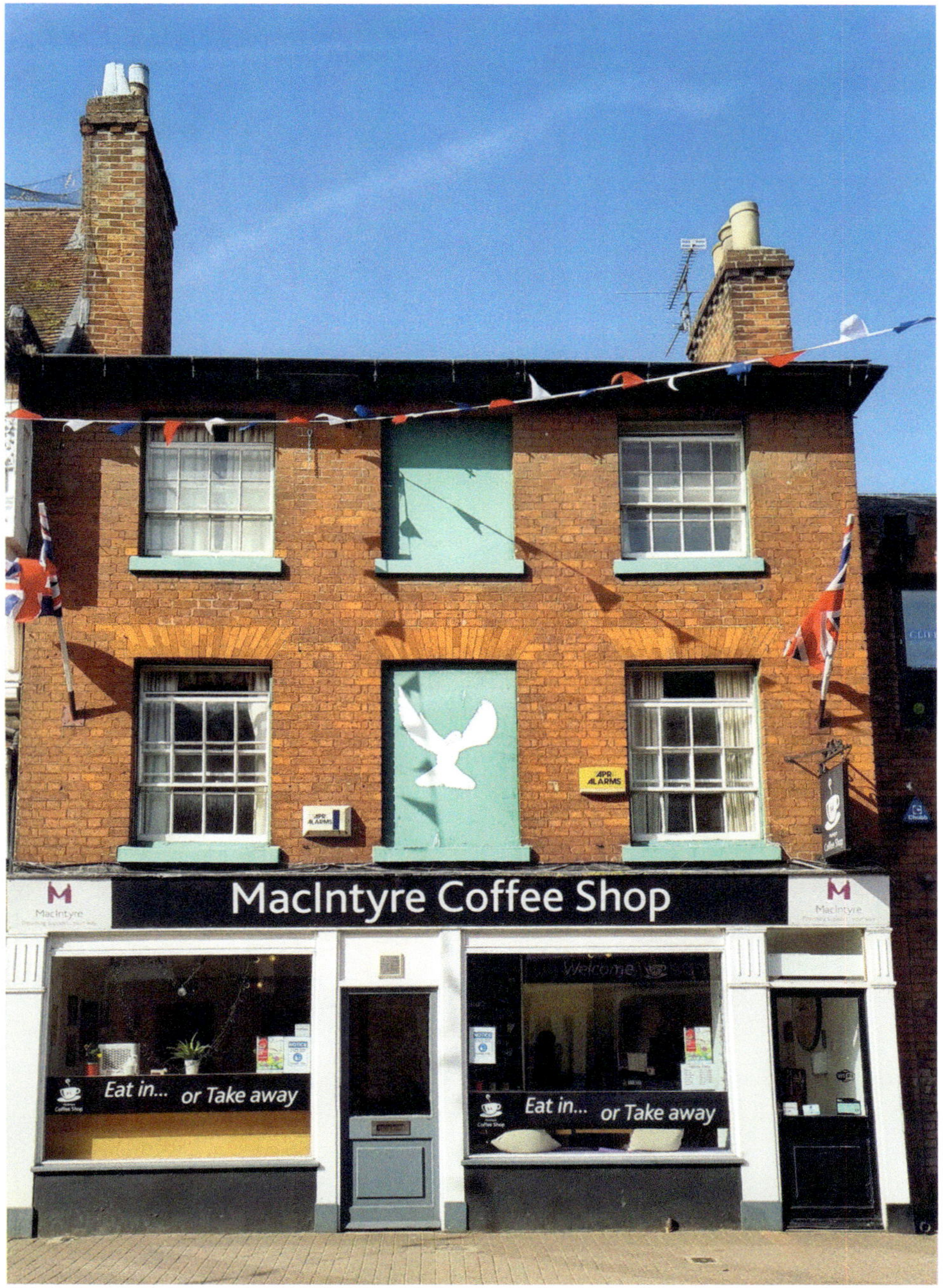
MacIntyre Coffee Shop
Eat in... or Take away
Eat in... or Take away

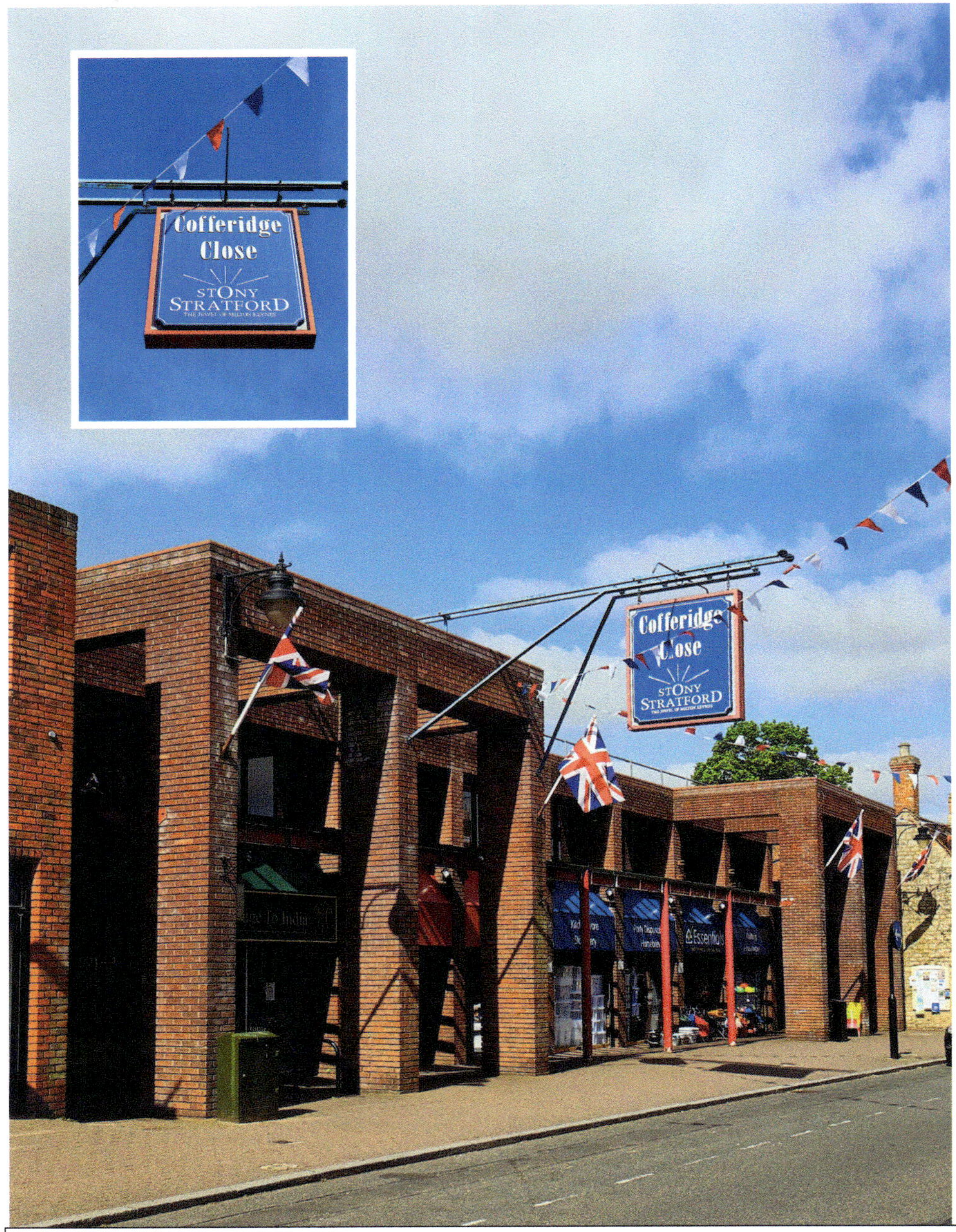

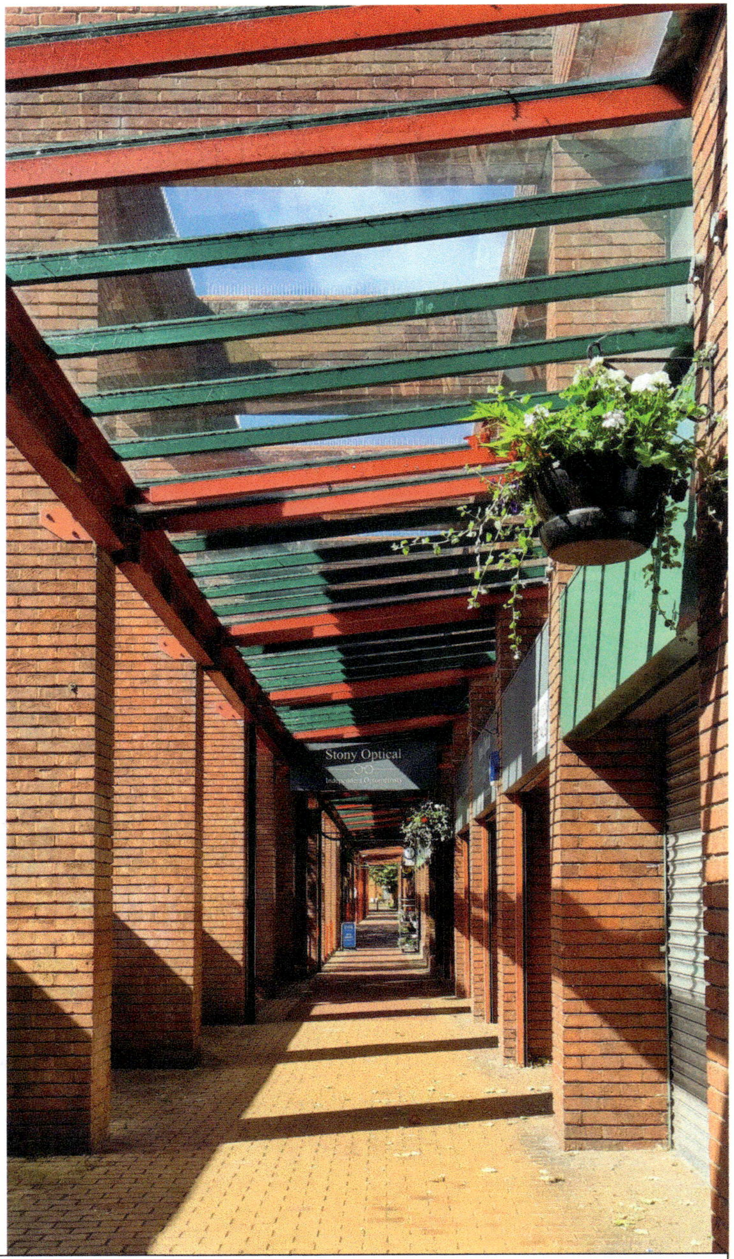

Cofferidge Close - pages 84-86.

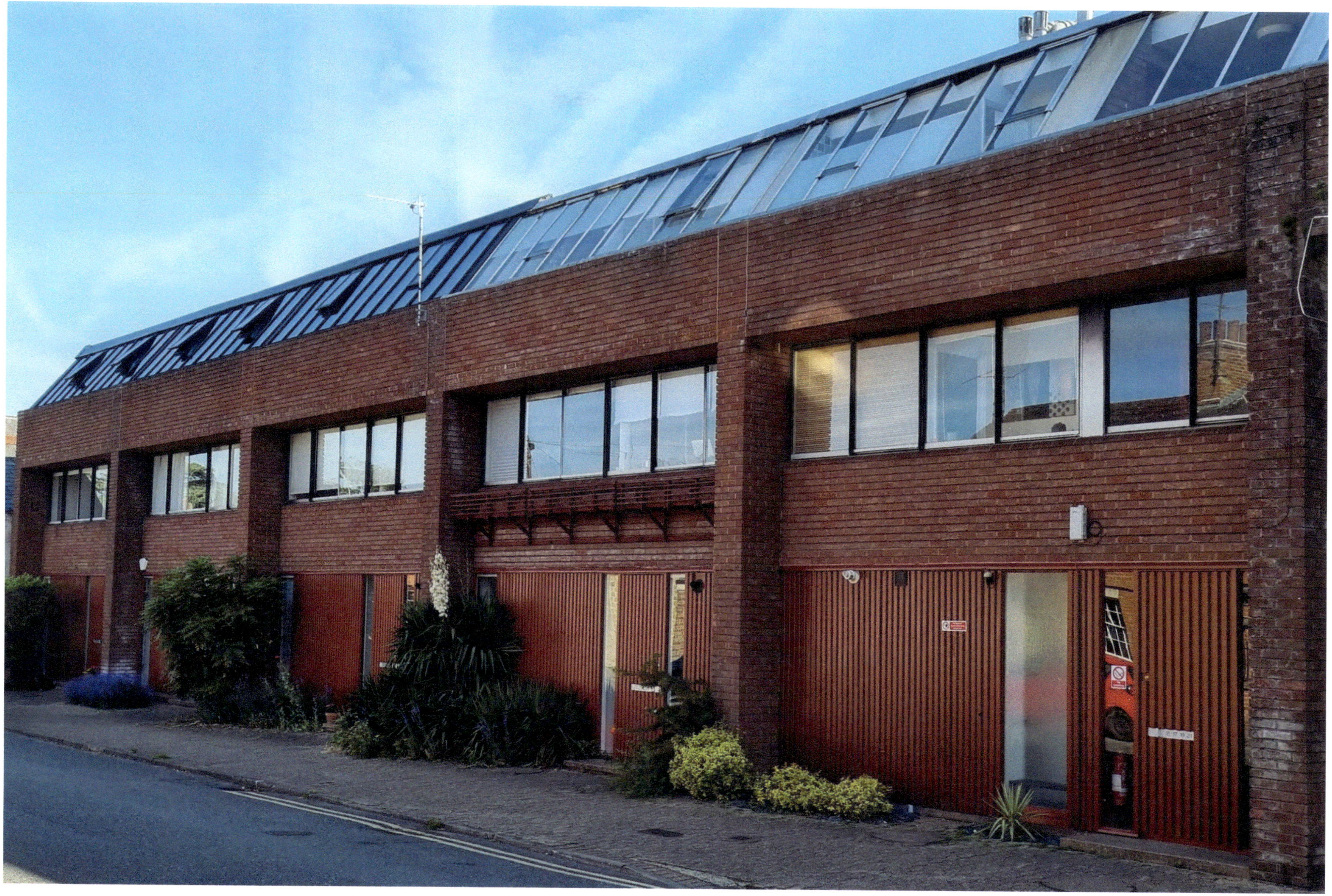

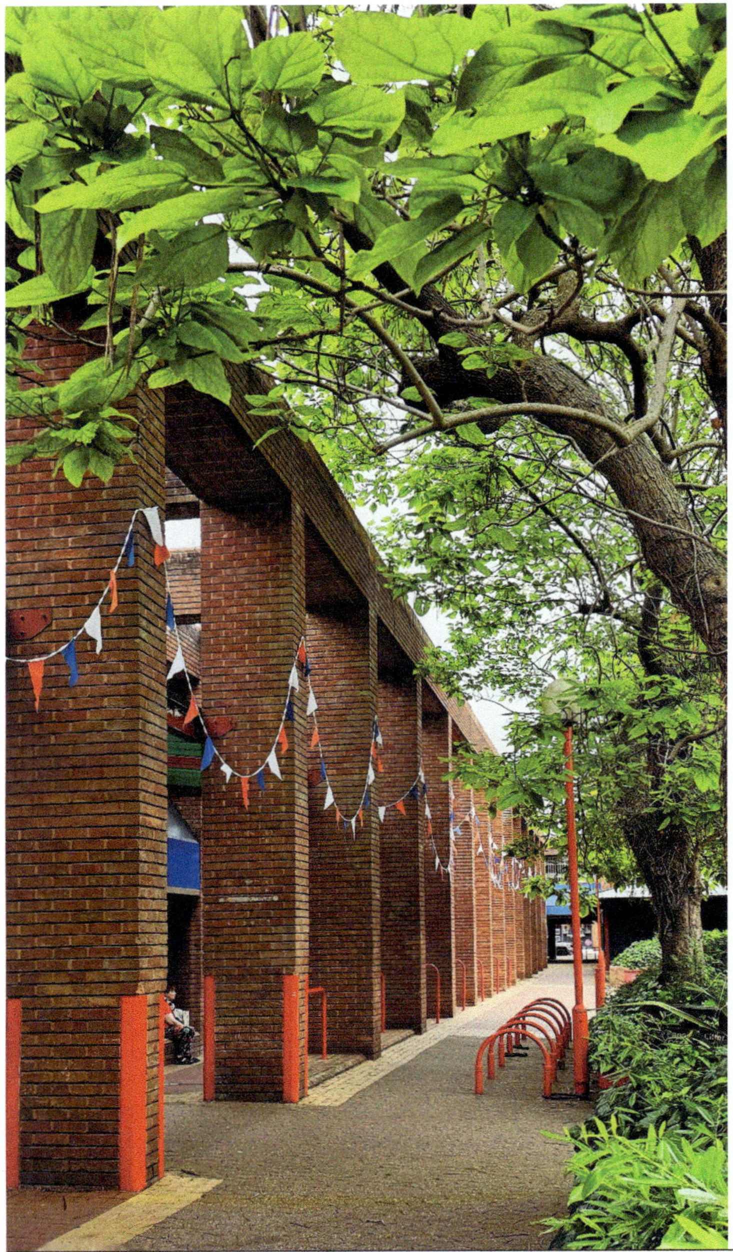

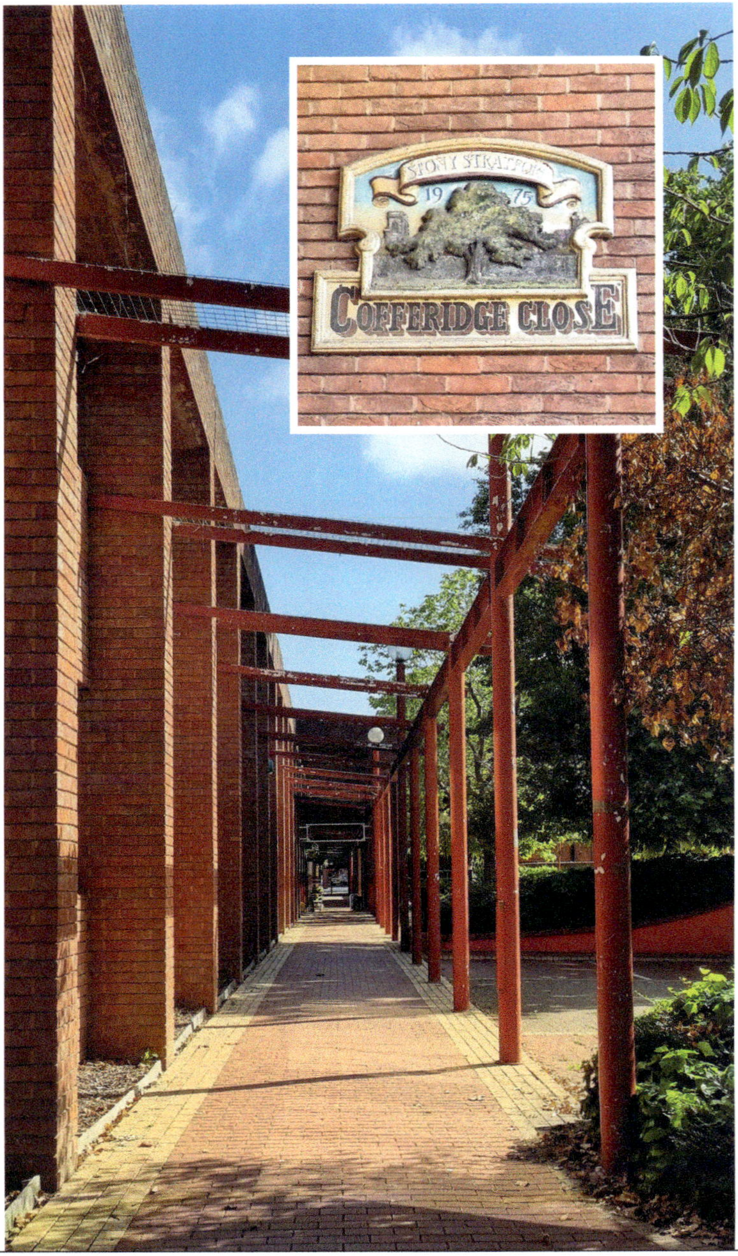

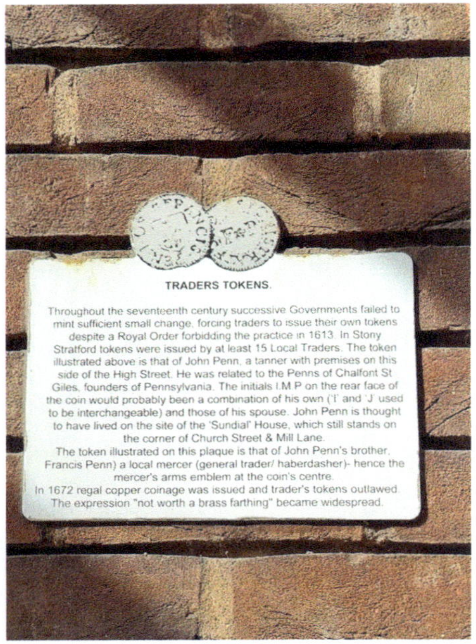

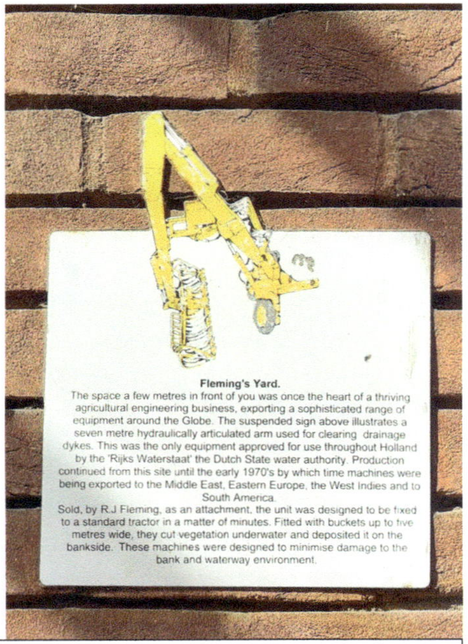

Cofferidge Close walkway and some plaques to acknowledge Stony Stratford's past.

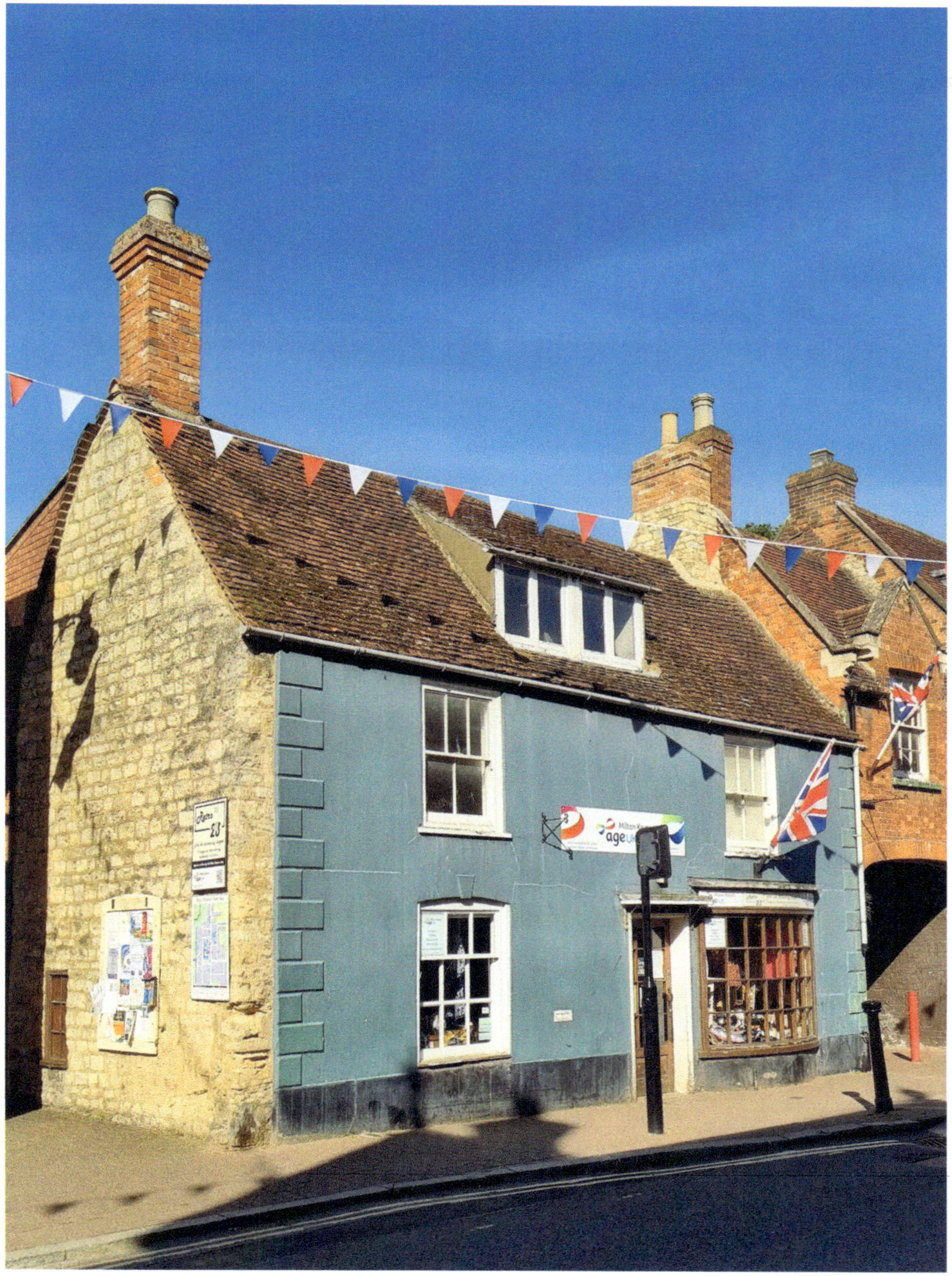

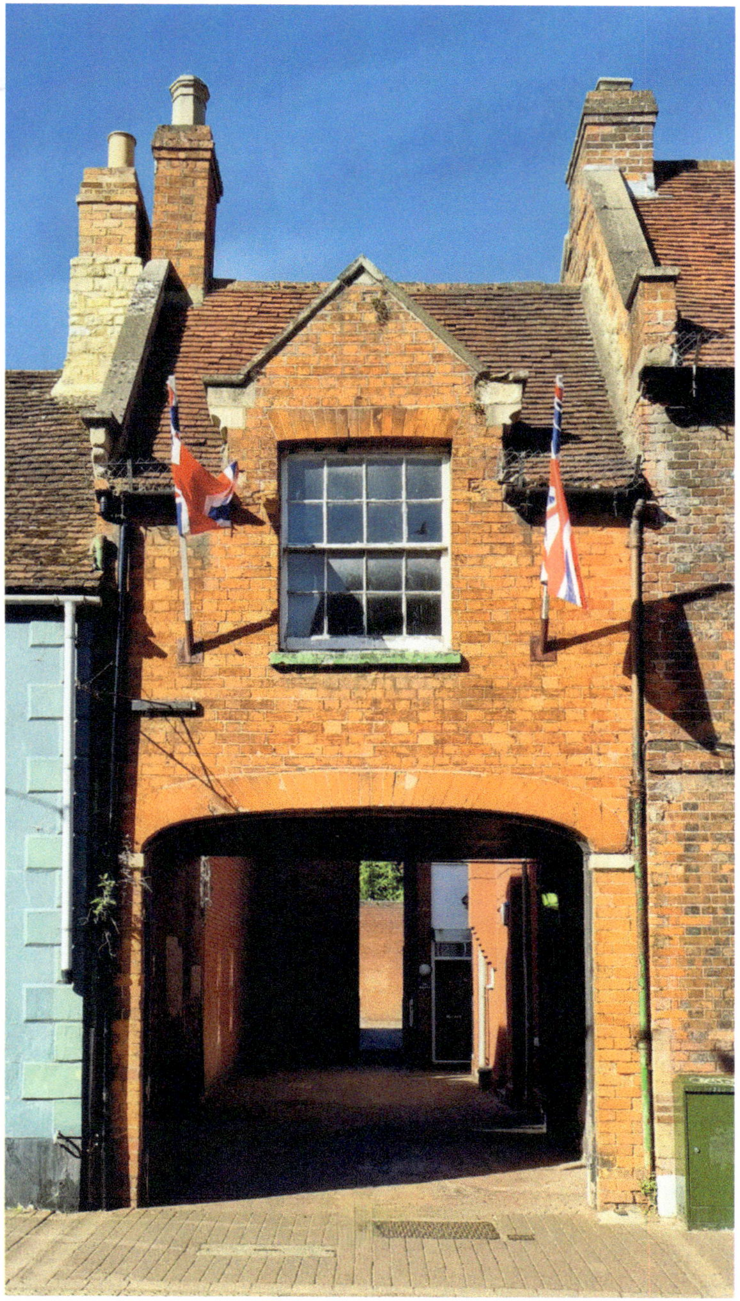

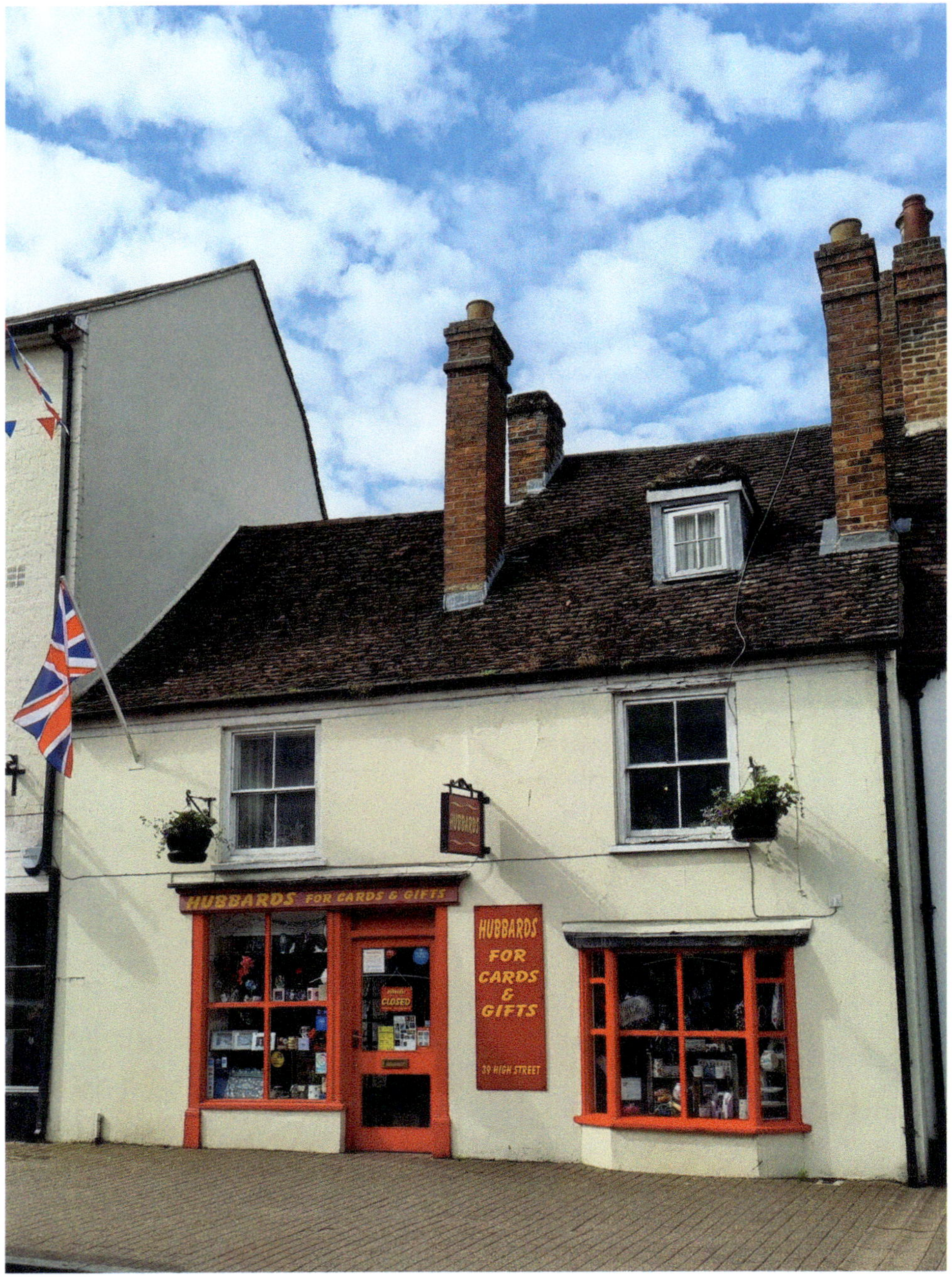
HUBBARDS FOR CARDS & GIFTS
HUBBARDS
FOR
CARDS
&
GIFTS
39 HIGH STREET
CLOSED

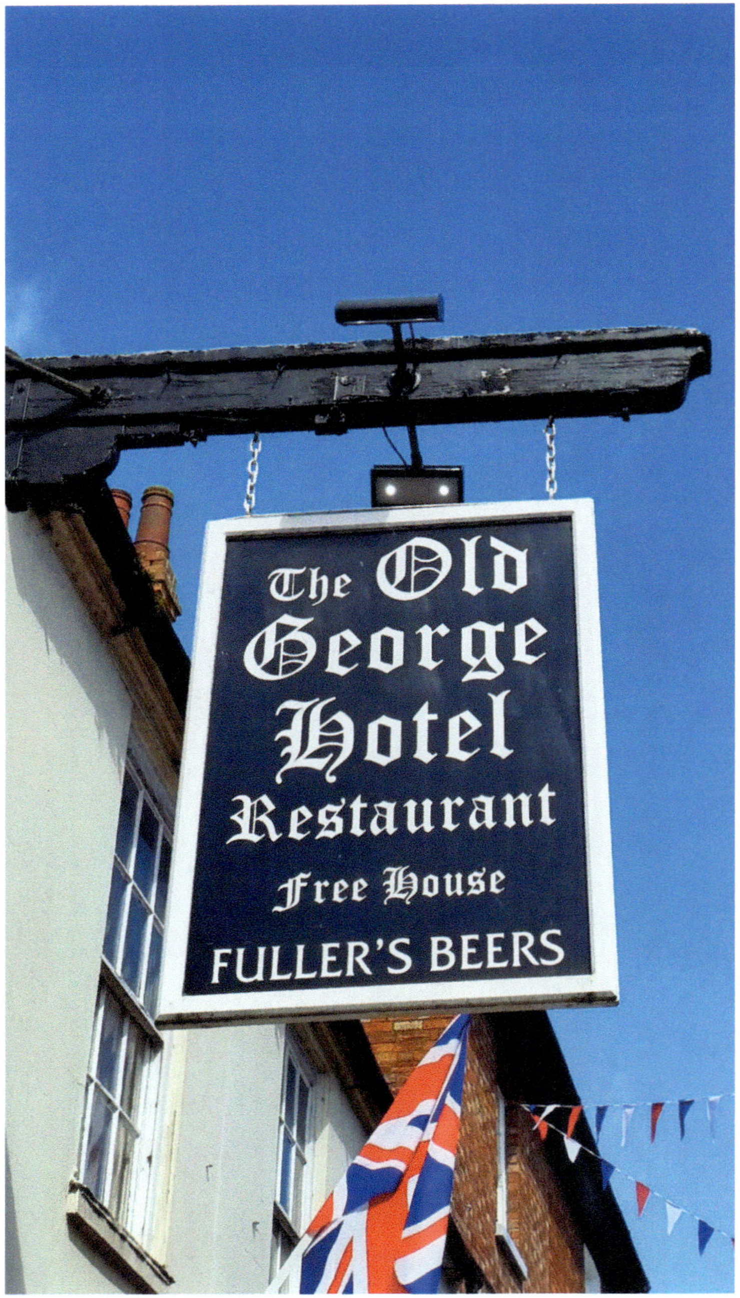
The Old
George
Hotel
Restaurant
Free House
FULLER'S BEERS

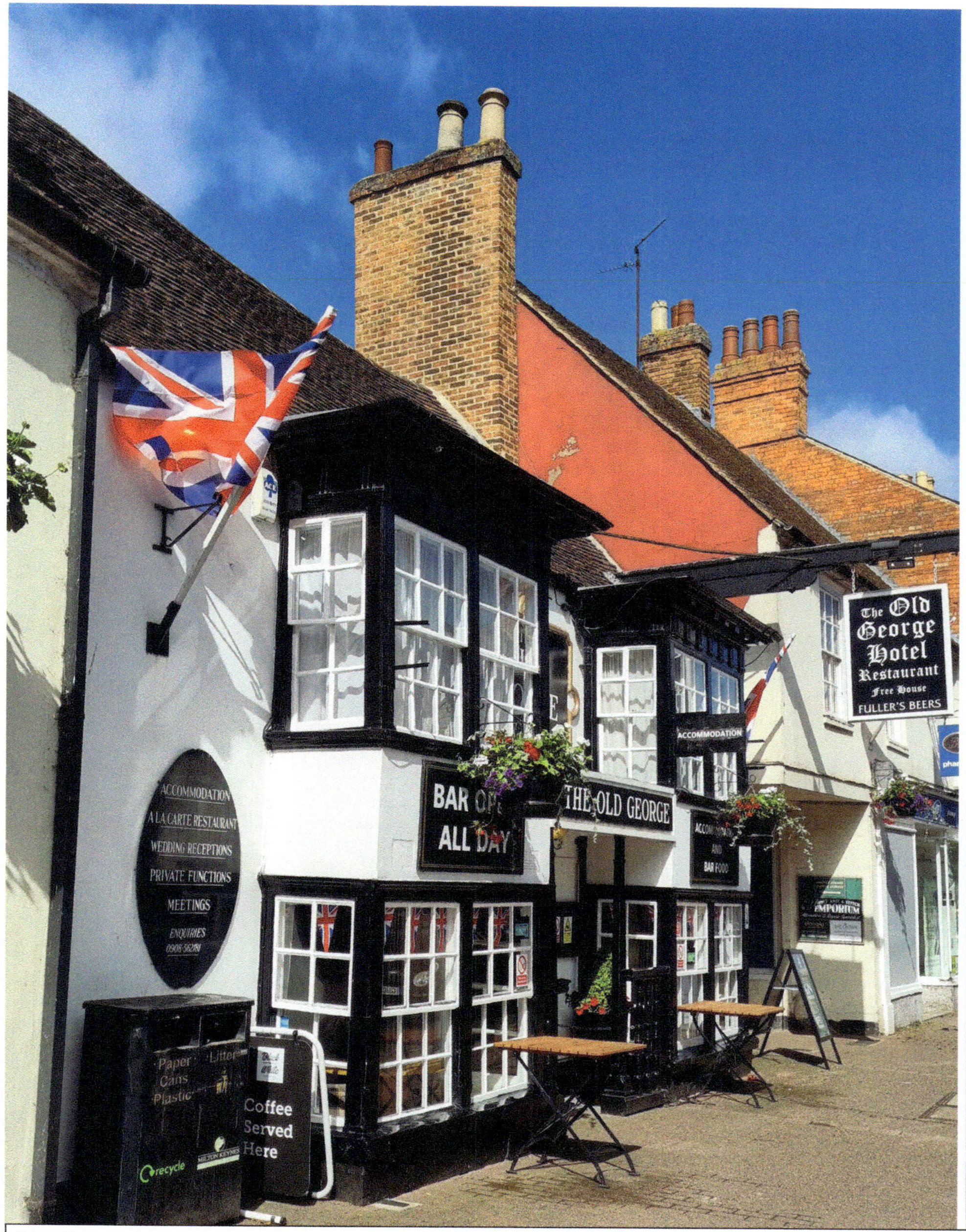

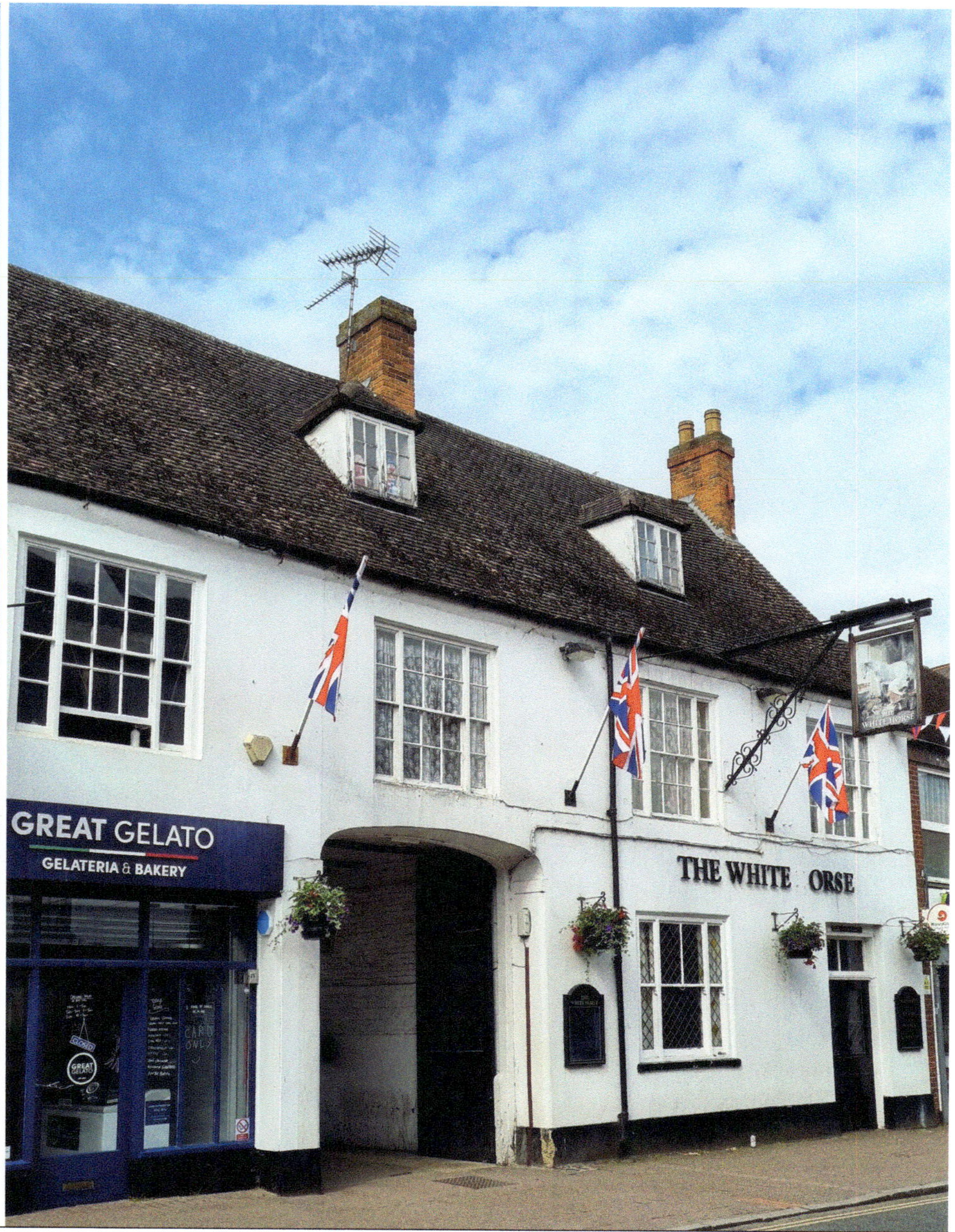

The George dates from the first decade of the 17th century. The White Horse was first licensed in 1773.

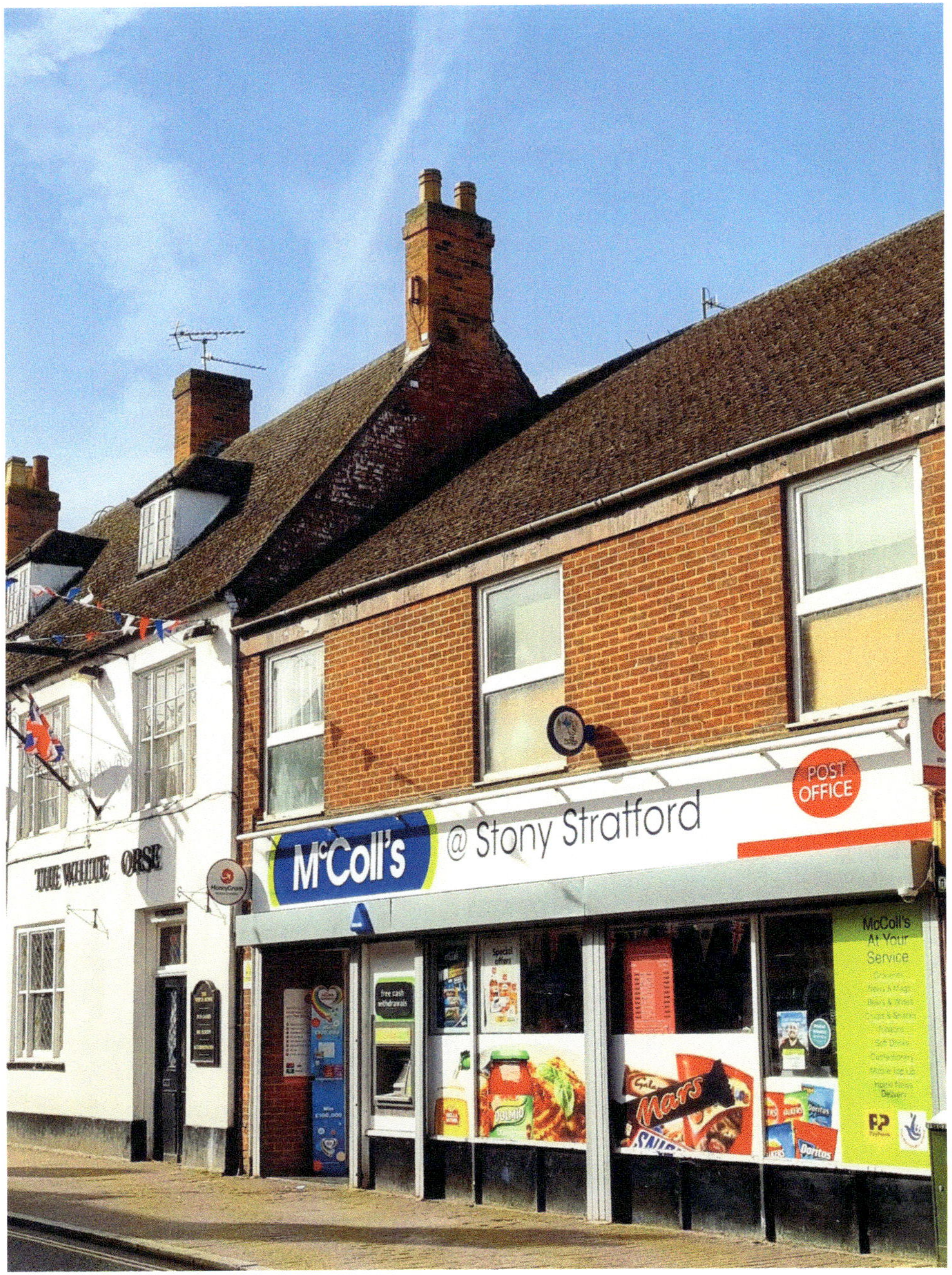

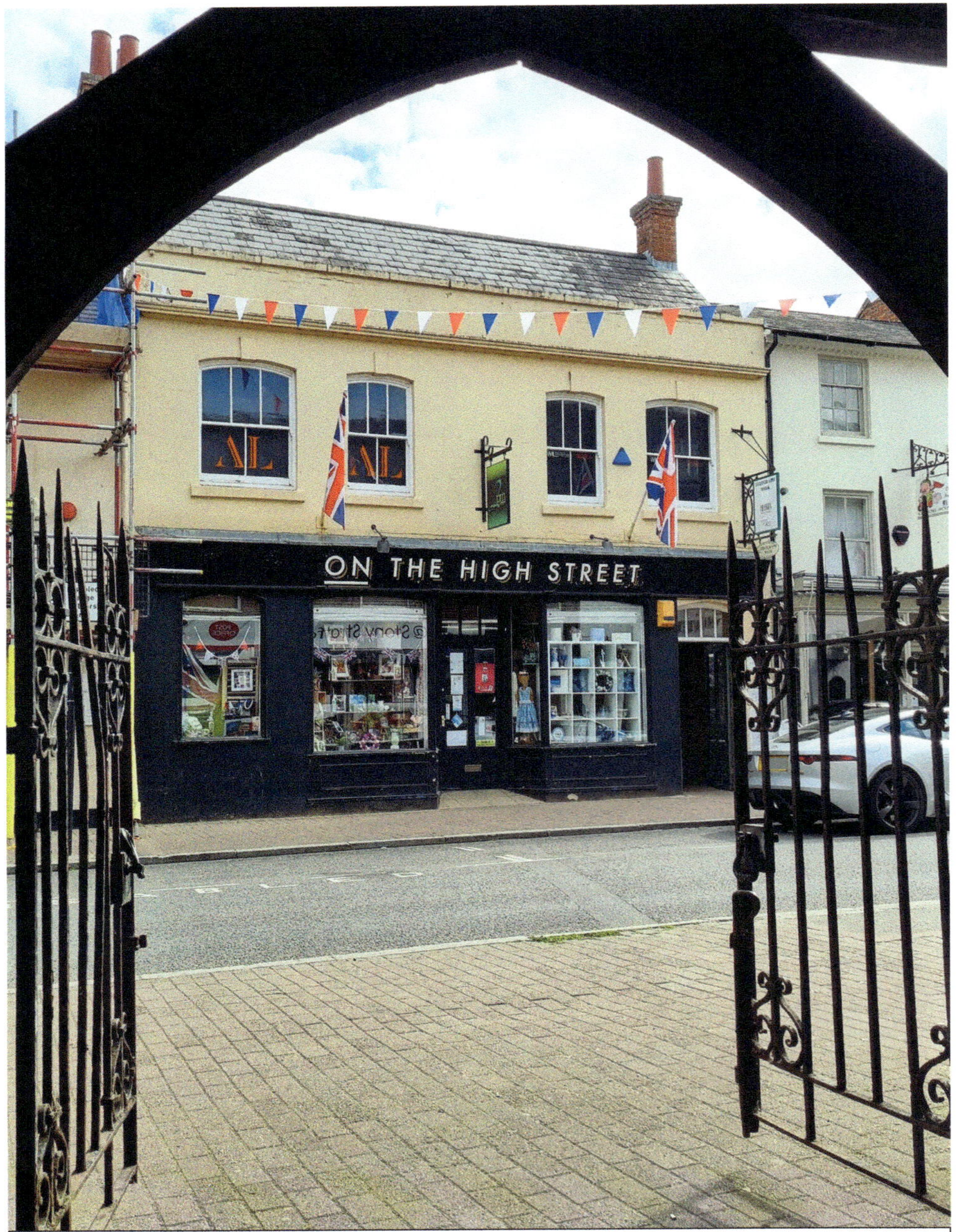

A view from the churchyard gates.

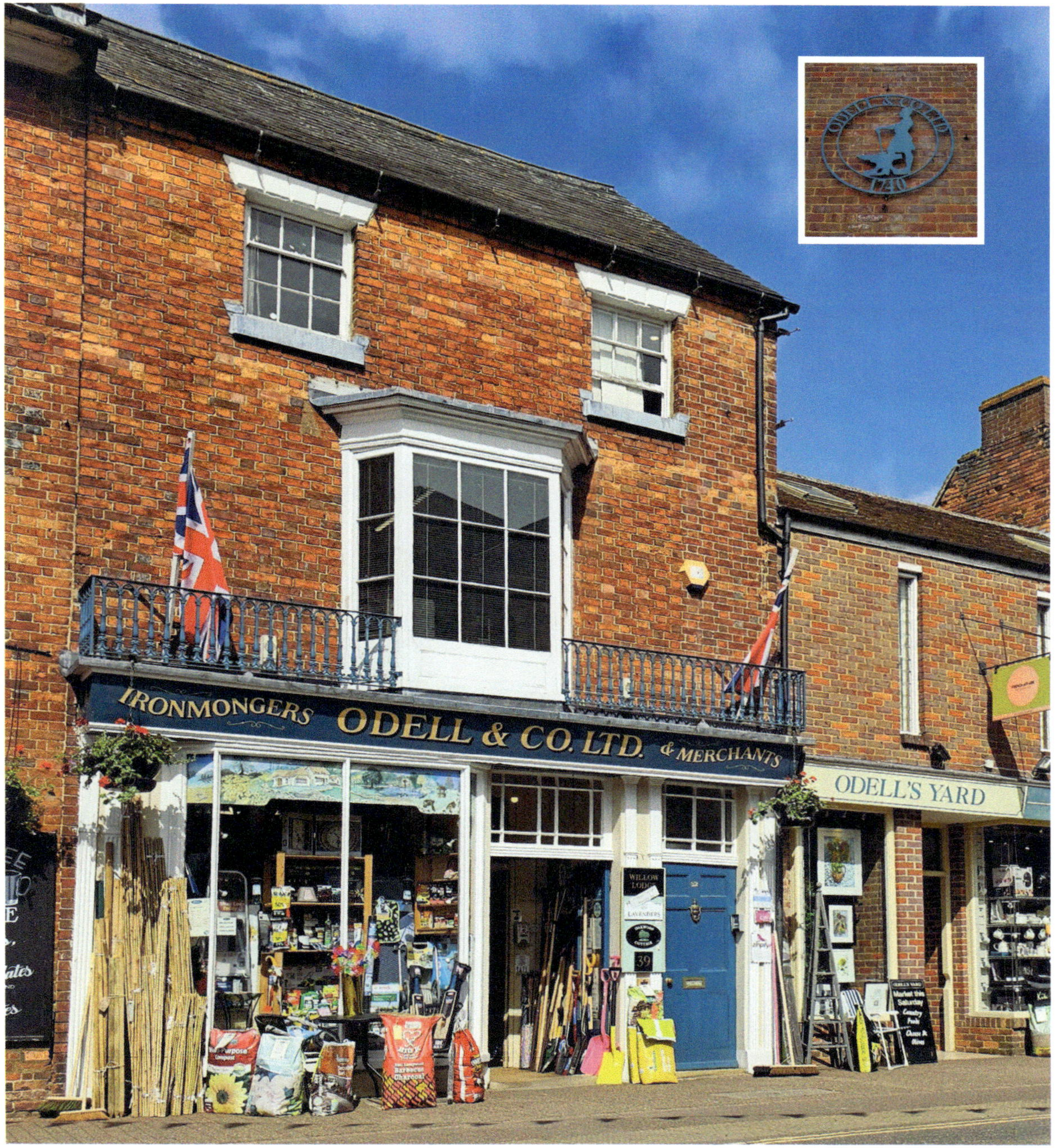

The Odell Story

Odell's have been a fixture at 60 High Street for longer than anyone can remember and indeed James Odell first set up his shop there in 1863, when he bought the business from Edwin Revill. The Revills, father and son, had been operating as blacksmiths and ironmongers since 1832, and they were involved in other enterprises, not least of which was the Revill and Thorne Brewery, which used premises at the back of the *Bull* next door.

James Odell was part of the large family of William and Sarah Odell who came from Lathbury. William Odell appears to have had farming interests in both Newport Pagnell and Cranfield. James, at any rate, was born in Kempston, Bedford, in 1835, although many of his older siblings had been born at Newport Pagnell. By this time his much older brother John had already set up as a blacksmith and ironmonger at the top of Newport Pagnell's High Street, near the church. James was able to apprentice with John before branching out on his own. The Newport shop also had a long history but closed at the end of the 20th century.

He was 27 when he came to Stony Stratford and was able to hand over a thriving business to his widow and eldest surviving son, Lionel, when he died in 1908. This tradition continued when the company passed on to the next generation. Today, Odell and Company is managed by the fourth generation of Odells.

It is a testament to the family that they have been able to maintain the business for 160 years, but it also says something about Stony Stratford that the people can stay loyal to businesses such as Odells and Cox and Robinson over the centuries.

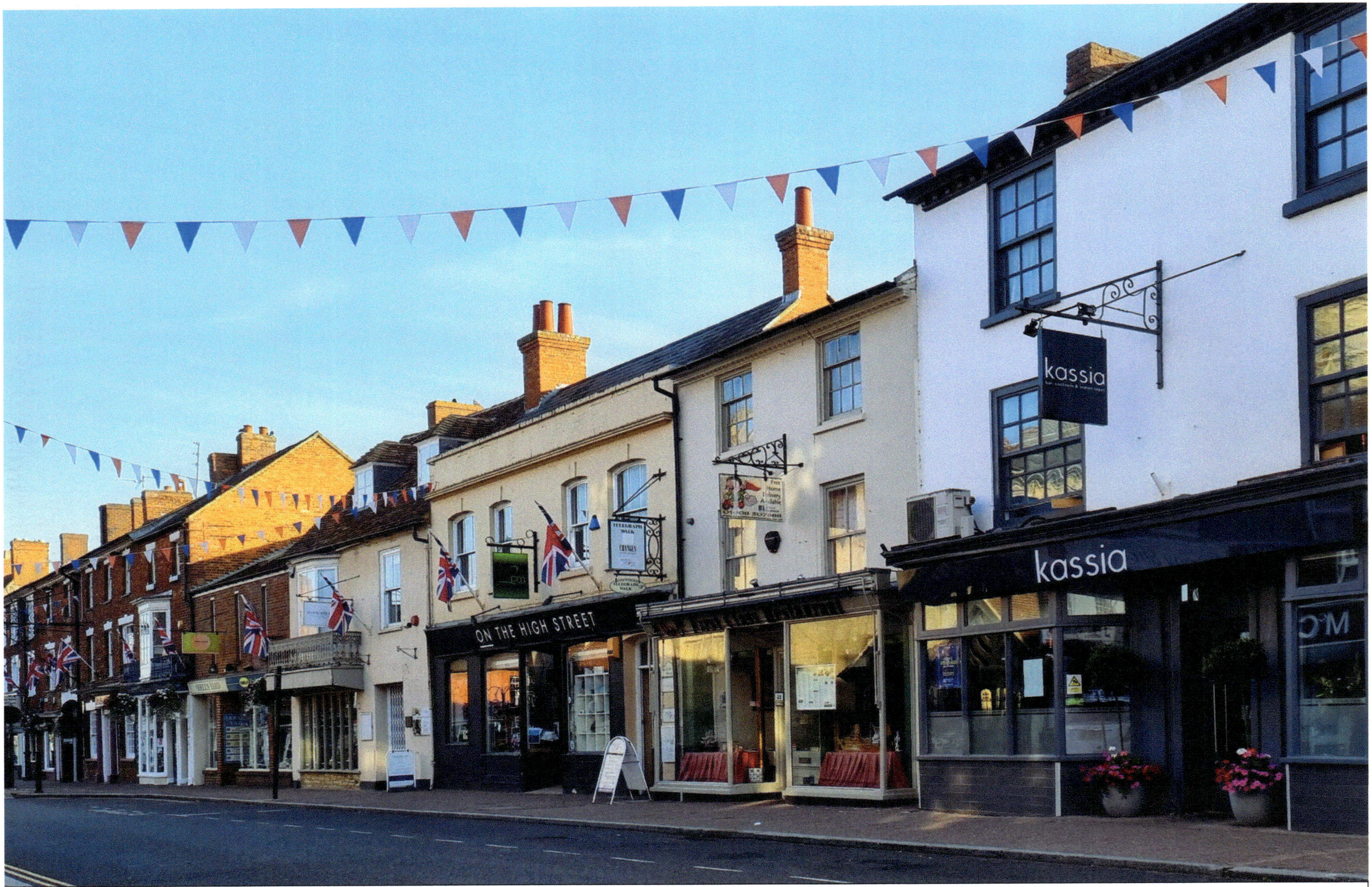

A partial view of the east side of Stony Stratford's High Street.

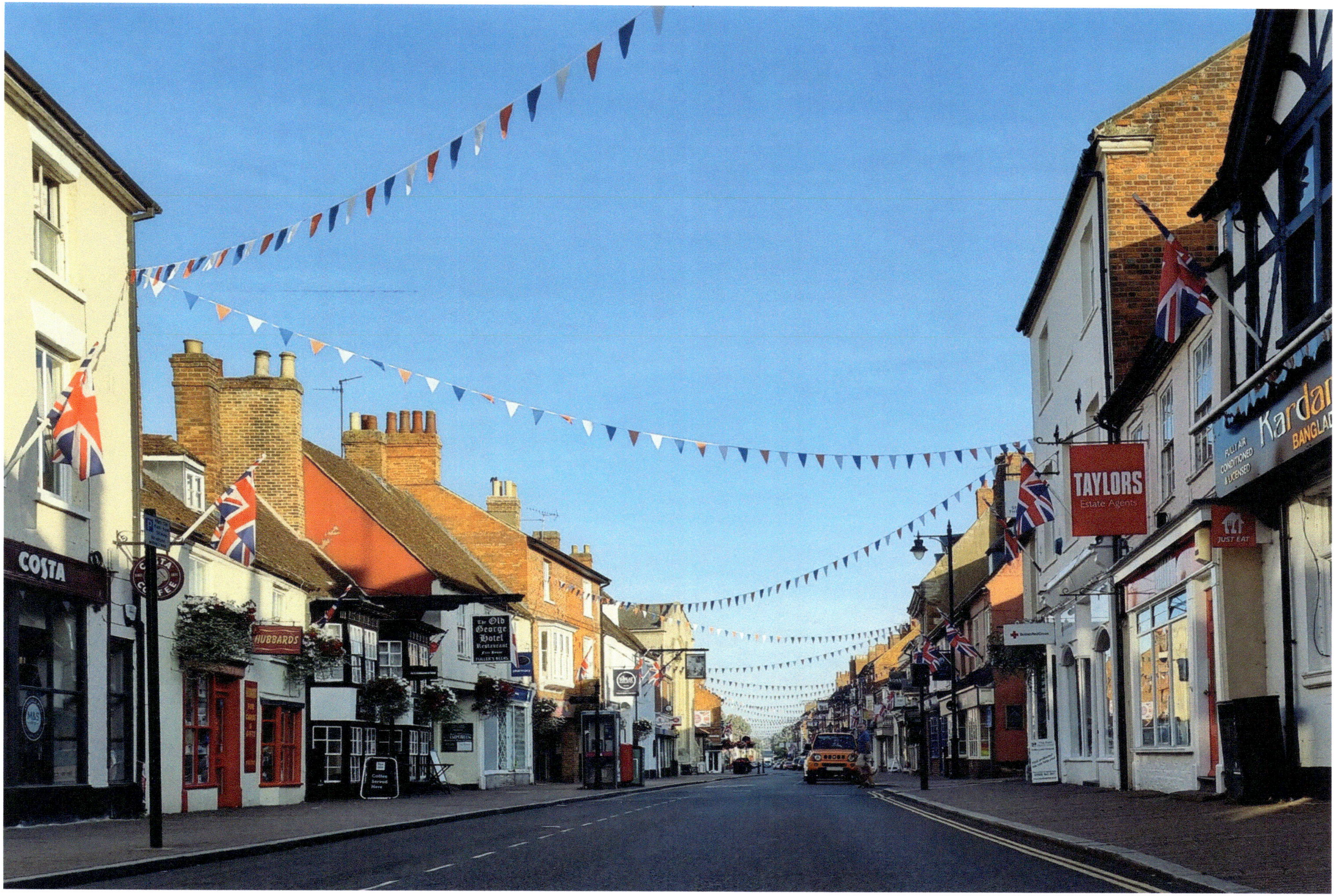
COSTA
COSTA COFFEE
HUBBARDS
The Old George Hotel Restaurant
TAYLORS
Estate Agents
FULLY AIR CONDITIONED & LICENSED
JUST EAT

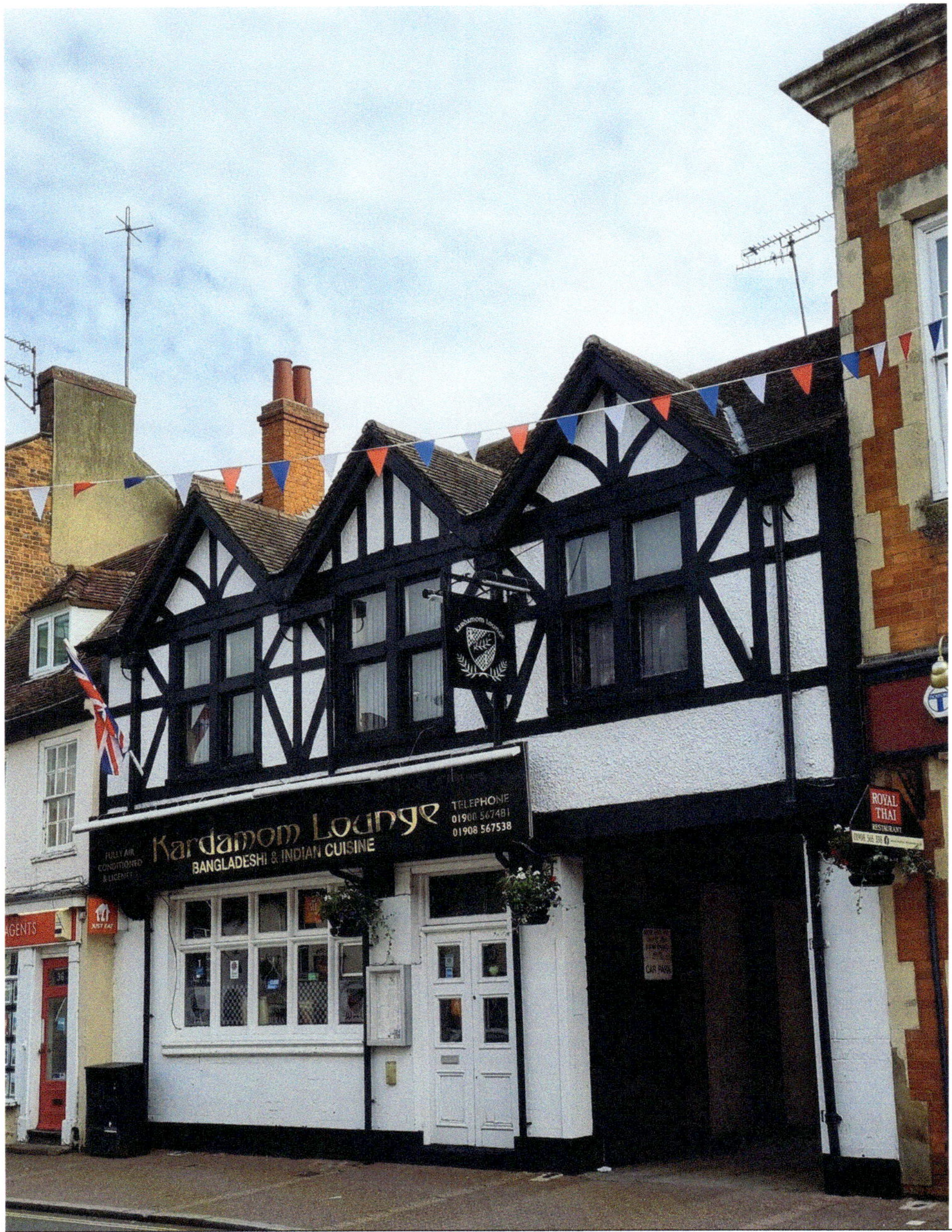

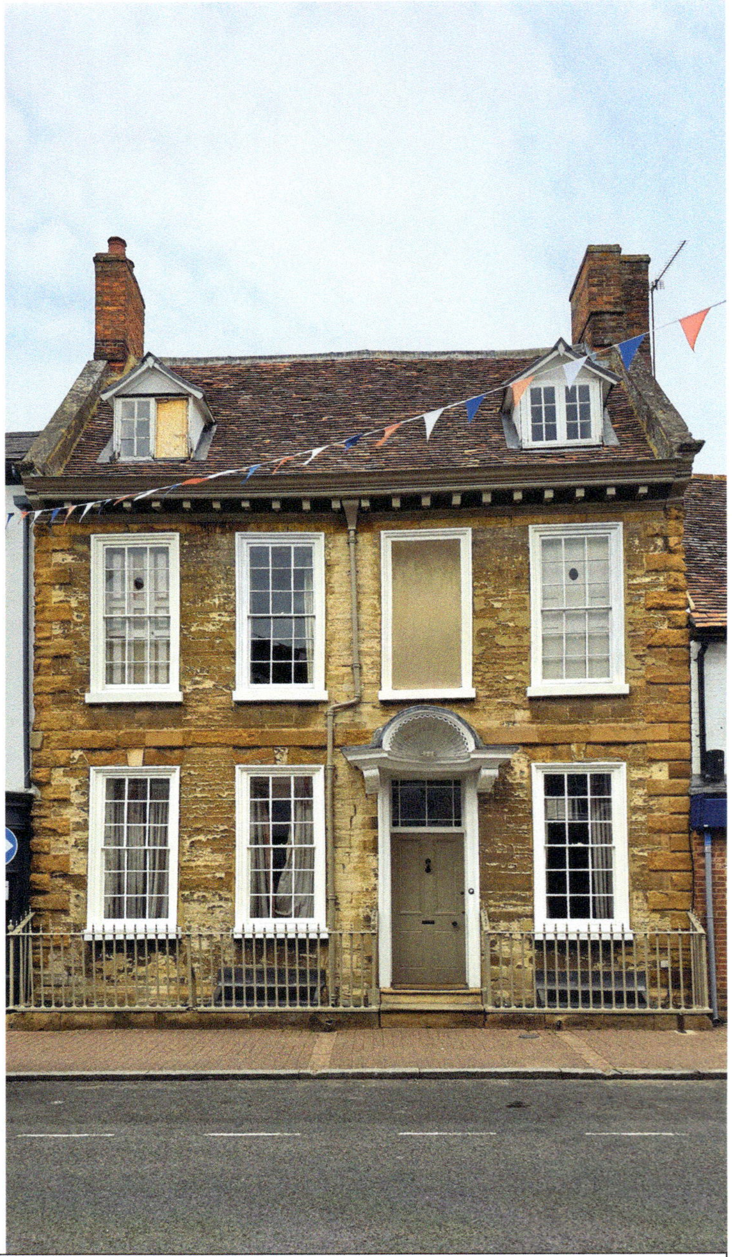

This was built in 1823 and was a public house known as The White Swan for many years. Right: 48 High Street.

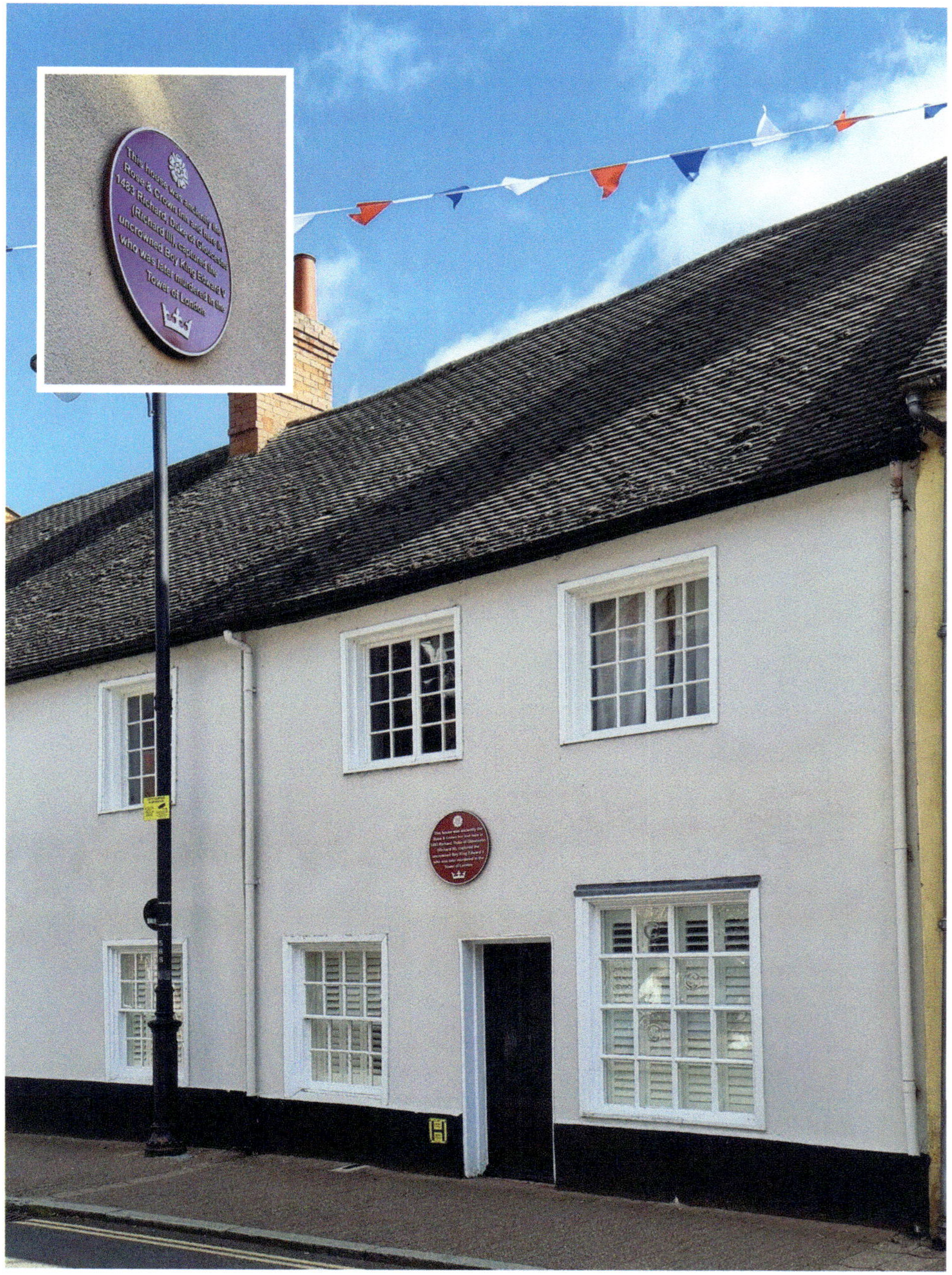

Rose and Crown

On 30 April 1483, Richard, duke of Gloucester, rode down from Northampton and took Edward, Prince of Wales into his custody. He arrested the prince's principal guardians and disbanded his retinue. He returned to Northampton that morning and from there, eventually set out to London.

Edward was placed in the Tower of London for his safety and protection and after the end of July, was never seen again. Make of that what you will. Richard was crowned as King Richard III on 6 July 1483. These are the facts.

Stony Stratford had a big role in this story and people in subsequent centuries wondered where Edward V stayed. Browne Willis, the early 18th century historian and MP, believed that it was likely to have been *The Swan*, a much larger inn north of the *Cock*. By the 19th century a view emerged that he stayed at the *Rose and Crown*, presently 26-28 High Street. People were influenced by two factors: the old medieval *Swan* had burned to the ground in the great fire of 1742, and Michael Hipwell's 1609 will had designated the proceeds from one of his properties, which he called the *Rose and Crown*, to support a charity school. A view now prevails that Edward V stayed at this building in 1483, and there is a plaque to mark this.

There are some reasons to question this version of the story. Although we know that the *Rose and Crown* was in existence in the late 16th century, there is no evidence to prove that the building was there in 1483. One might also wonder why a future king, travelling with a large retinue, would choose stay in a small inn when a much larger inn, complete with stabling and pasture for horses, was available to him in the same town.

In 1713 the *Three Swans* (re-named after a rebuild in 1687) leased 36 acres of land for arable crops and pasture, and it included an orchard. The *Rose and Crown* may have had half an acre at most. That should tell us something.

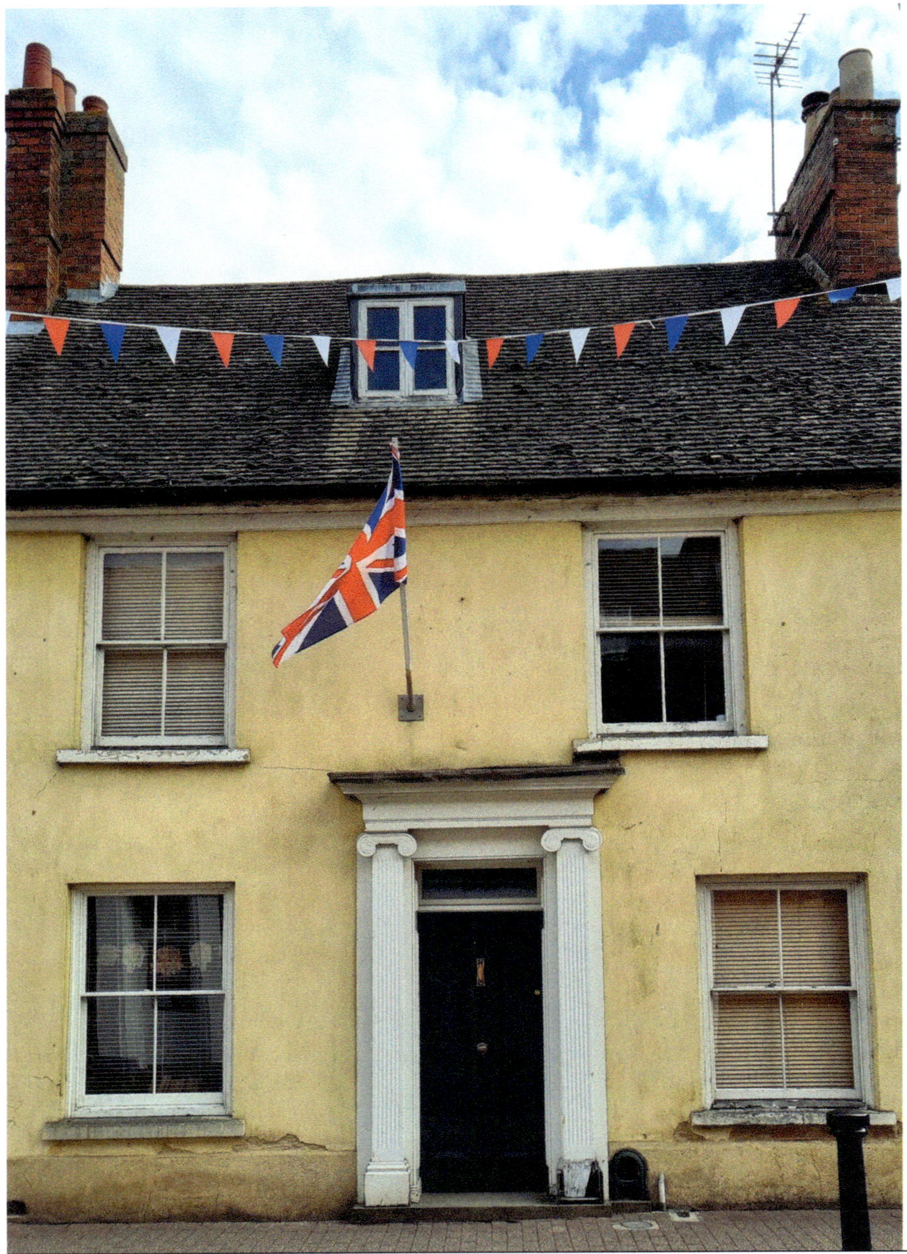

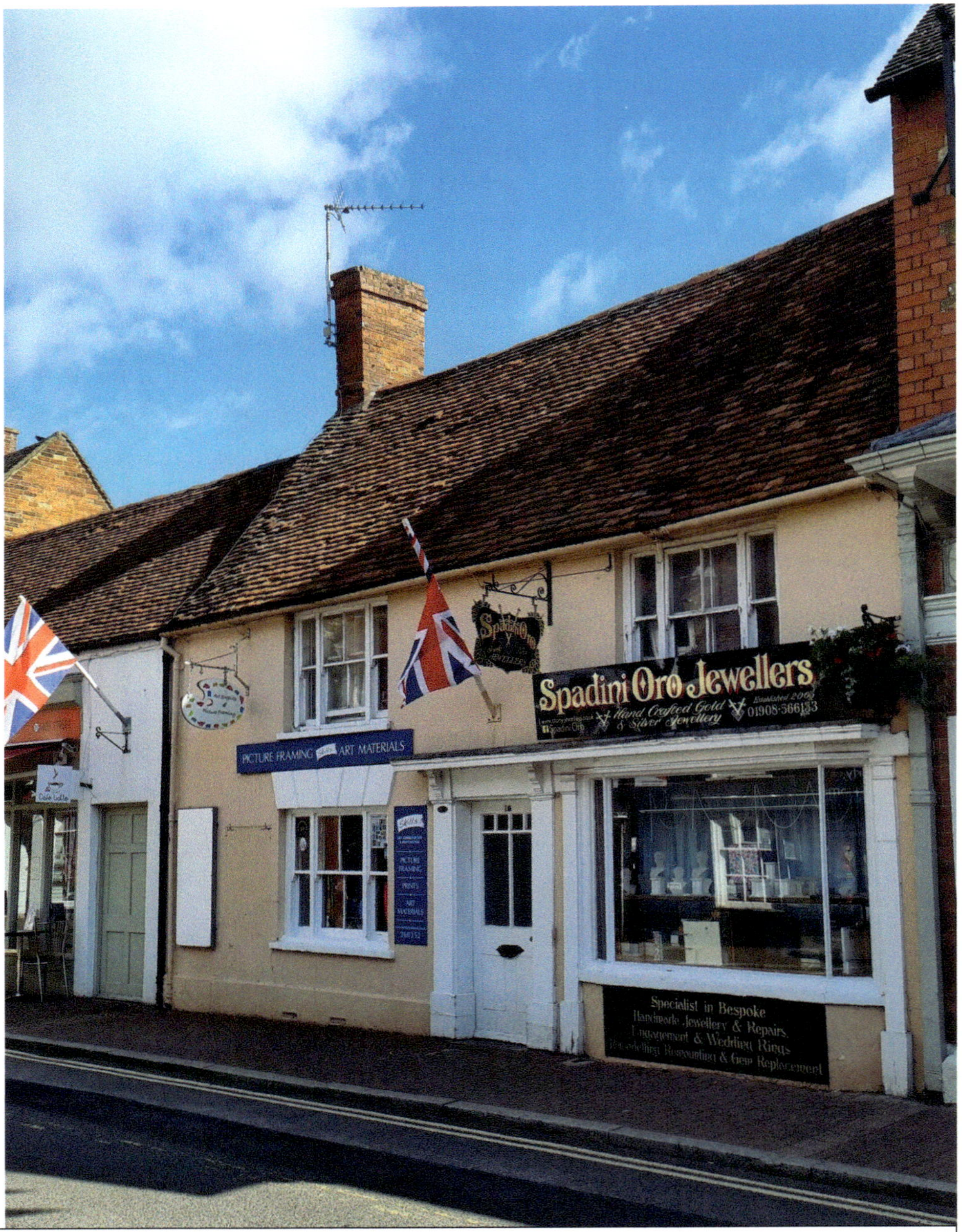

More High Street views pages 96- 99.

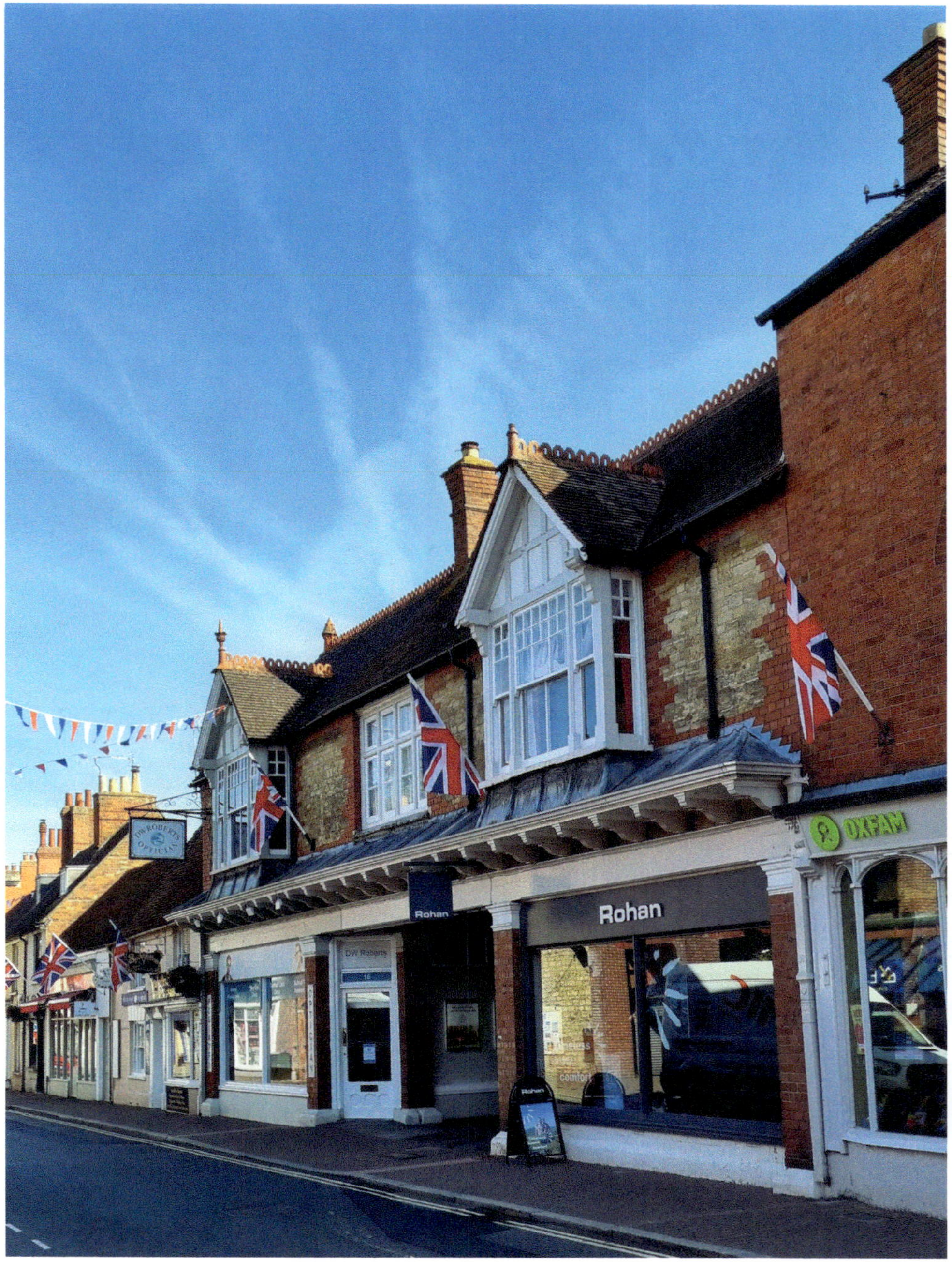
OXFAM
Rohan

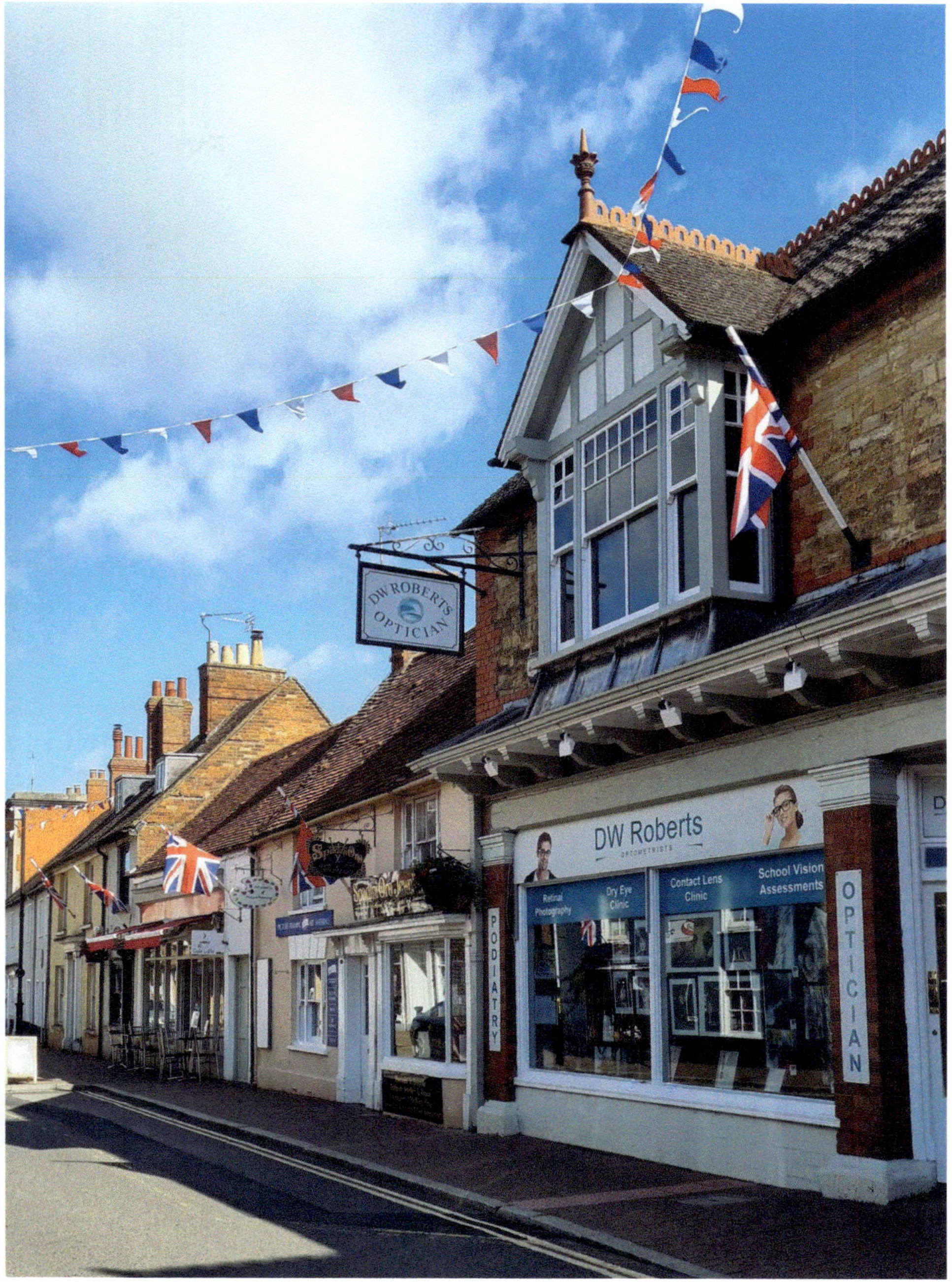
DW ROBERTS OPTICIAN
DW Roberts
Dry Eye Clinic
Contact Lens Clinic
School Vision Assessments
PODIATRY
OPTICIAN

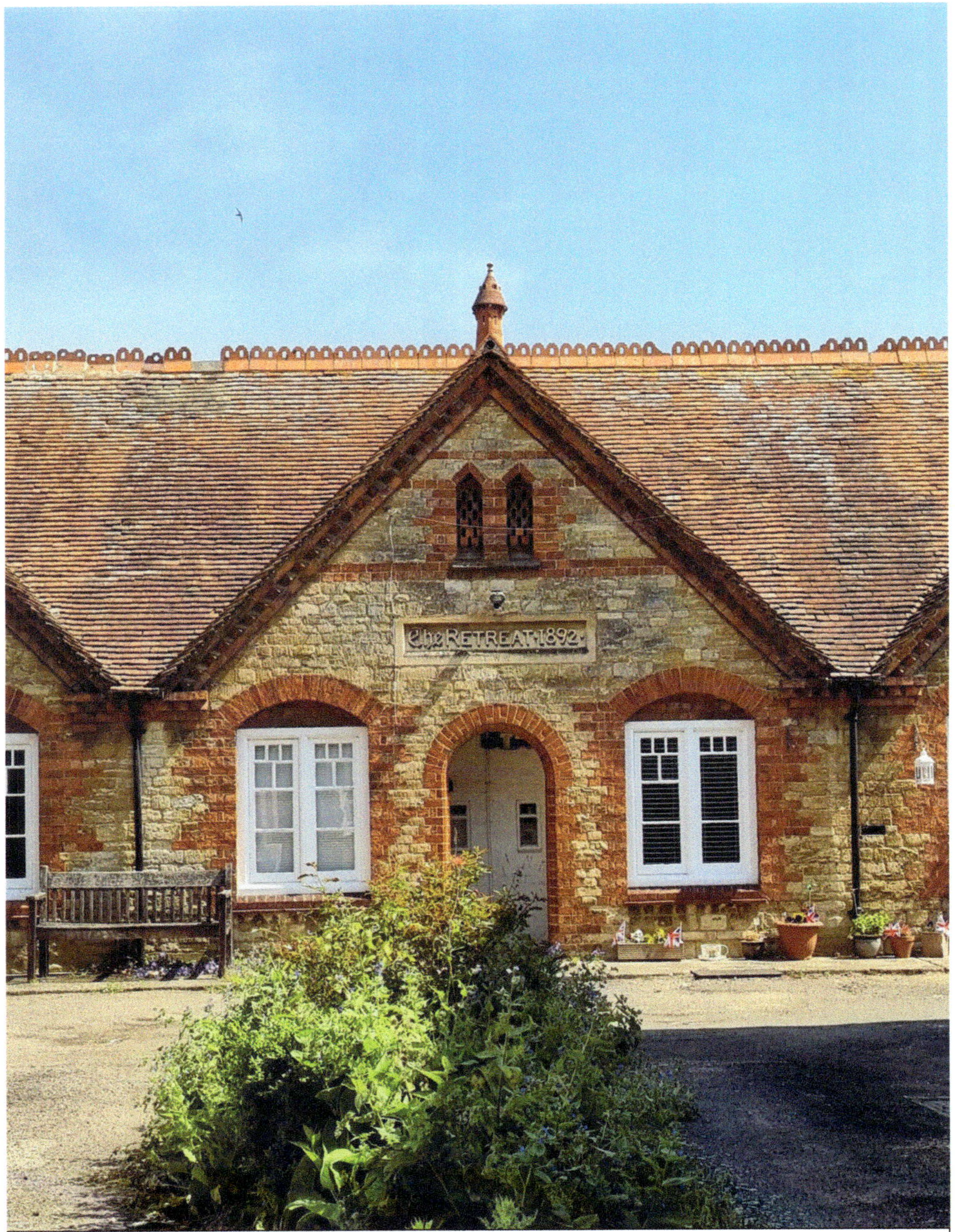

The Retreat, built as almshouses in the late 19th century.

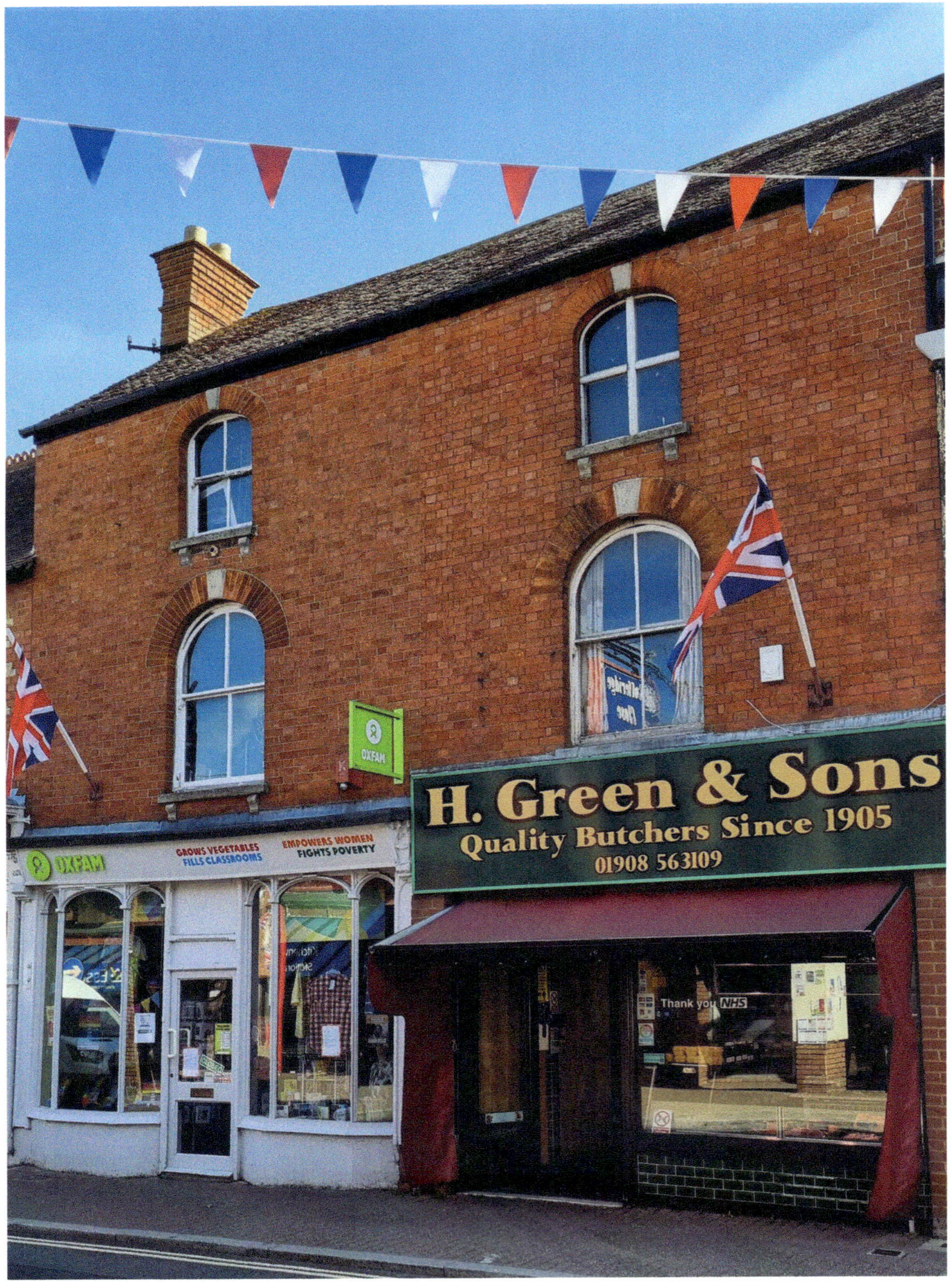

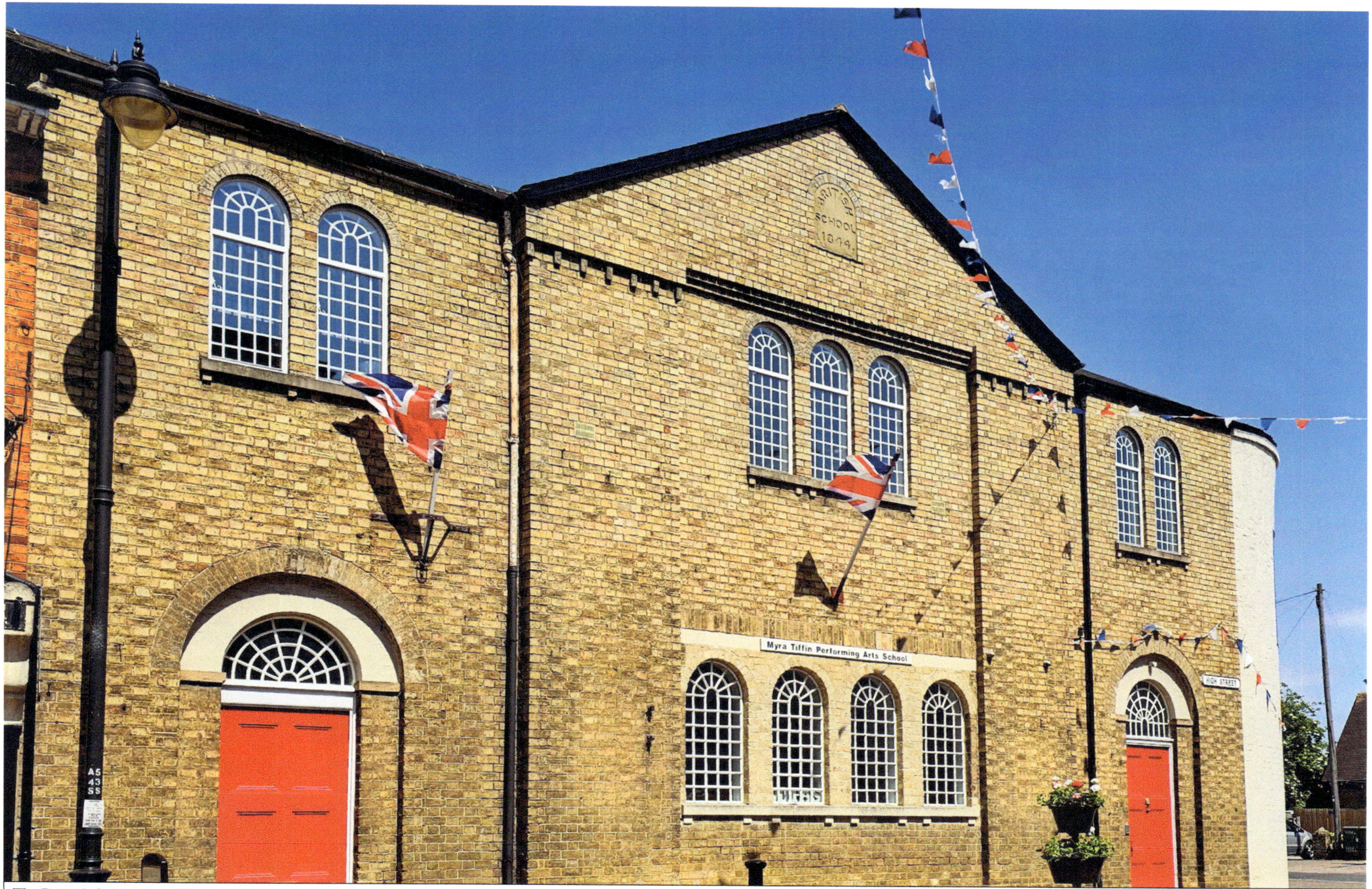

The British School, built in 1844.

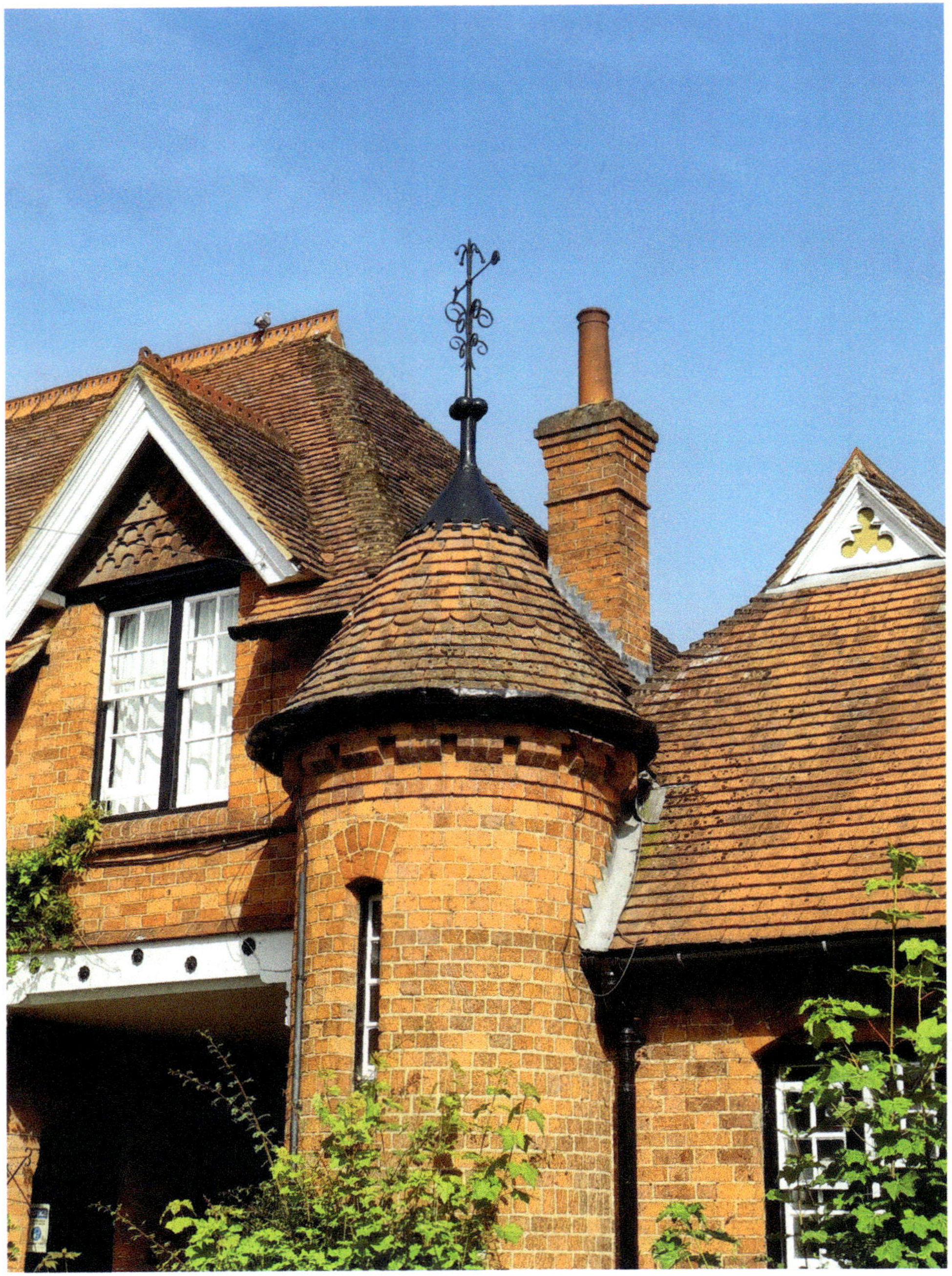

Wolverton Road

In the 1840s, William Russell developed his corner lot on the High Street. The British School was built on the corner and next to it a pub, which was originally named *The Engineer*. Later it became the *Forester's Arms* and traded under this name until a few years ago. On the corner of Back Lane (later to be known as Russell Street) the Congregationalists built a chapel, originally in 1823. In fact, in early censuses, this little stretch was known as Chapel Street.

Wolverton Road started to move eastwards, beyond the Russell Street corner, with some very substantial middle class homes, complete with stables and accommodation for servants.

Narrow streets such as King Street and Queen Street branched from the Wolverton Road. They were terraces of small cottages with no thought given to the possibility that the dwellers of these houses might own vehicles. At each corner, a public house quickly emerged. *The Duke of Edinburgh* and *The Case is Altered*. Across the road there was a third public house: *The Prince of Wales*. *The Case is Altered* closed 50 years ago and the *Duke of Edinburgh* changed its name to the *Duke of Wellington* in recent years.

Similar remarks could be made about Jubilee Terrace, a row of cottages with no street access, built around the time of Queen Victoria's Silver Jubilee year (1862) and so named.

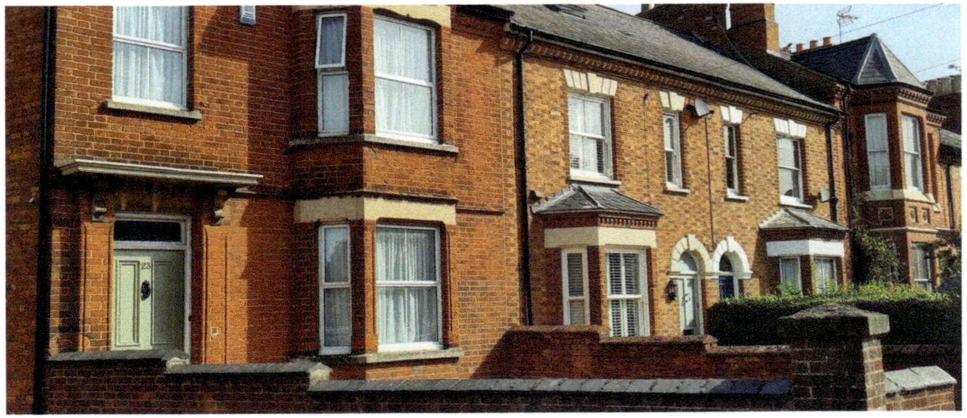

LOOK AT
THE WOLVERTON ROAD

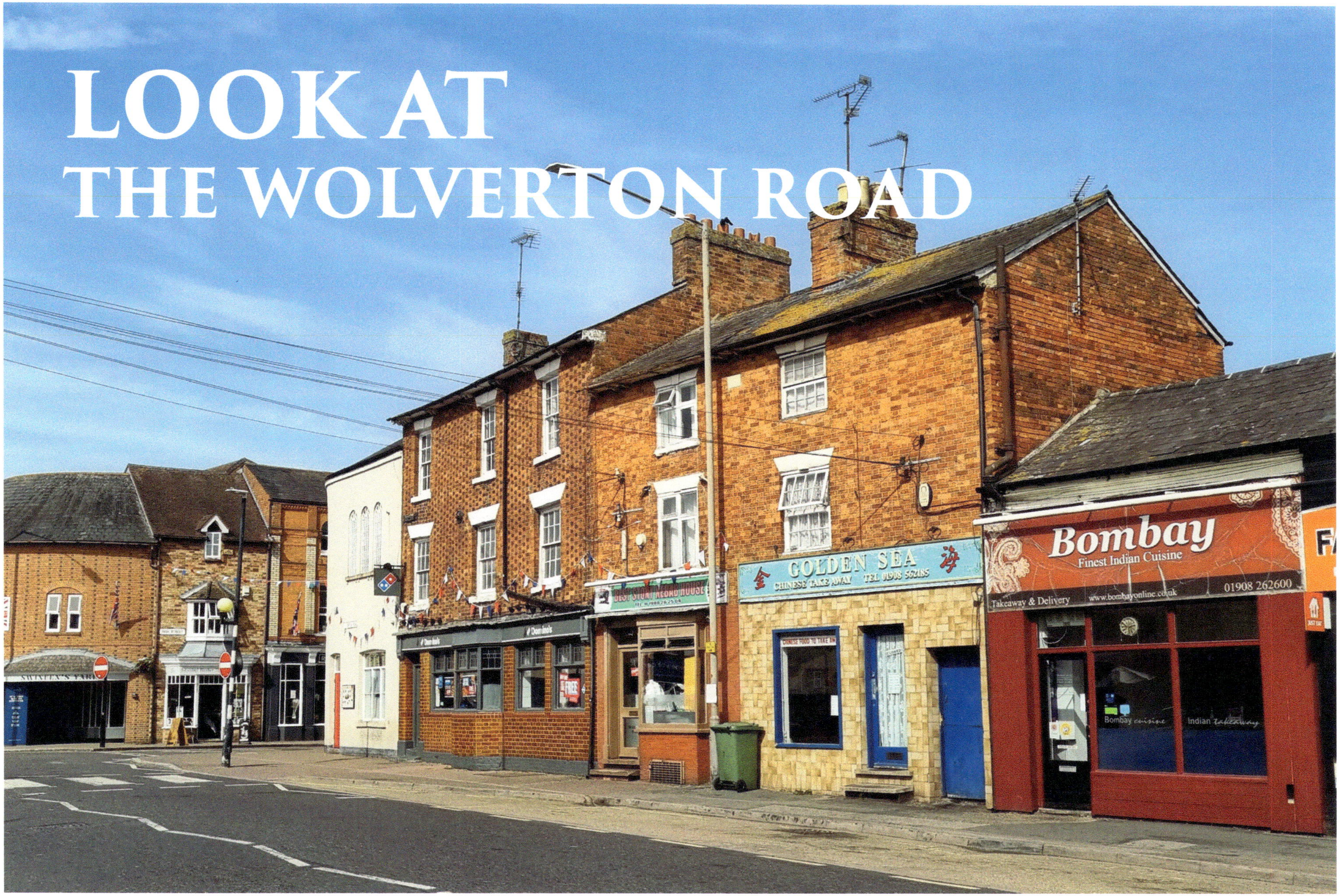

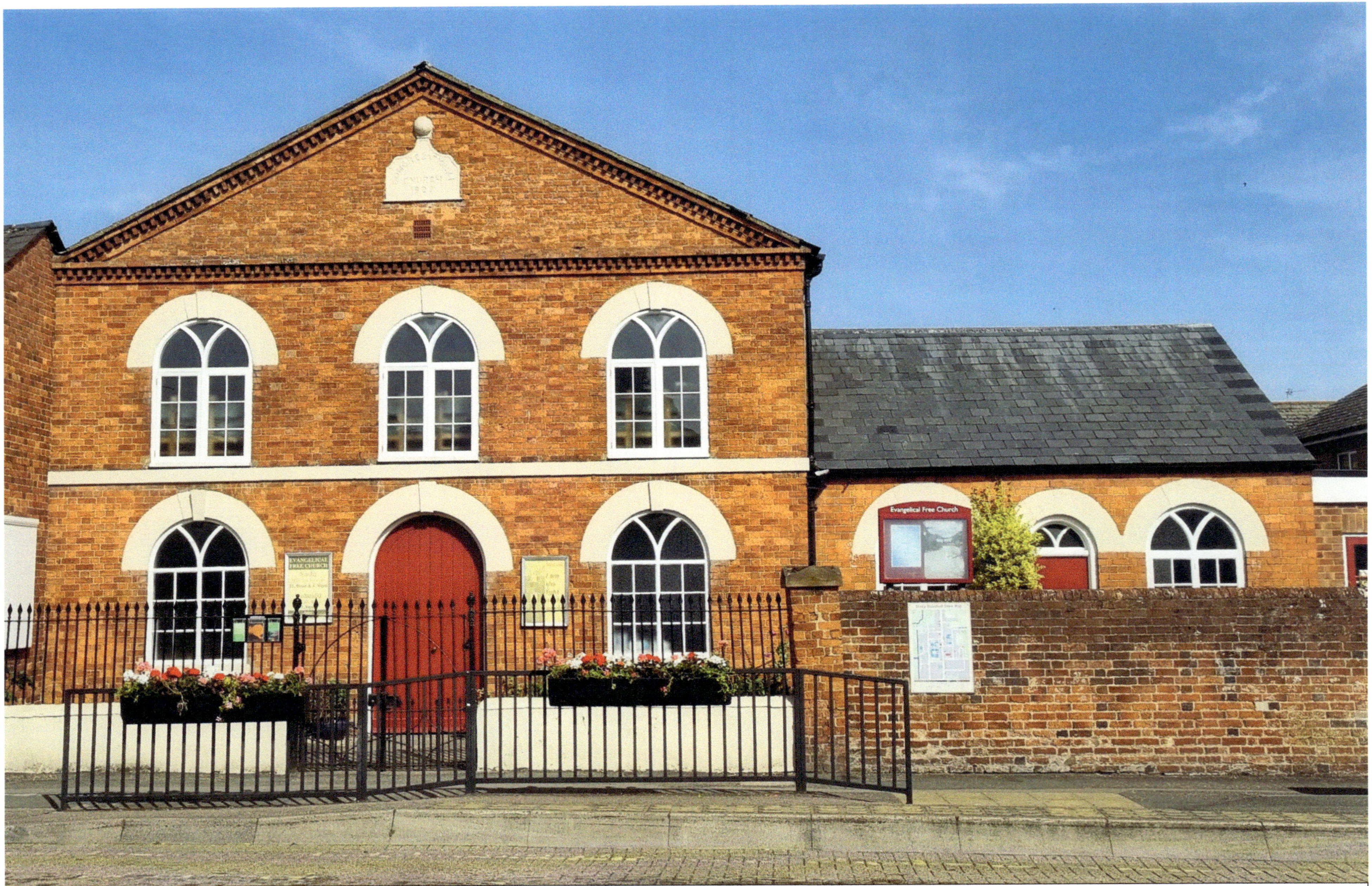

The Congregational Church was built in 1823 before any Wolverton Road development. This short street was known as Chapel Street.

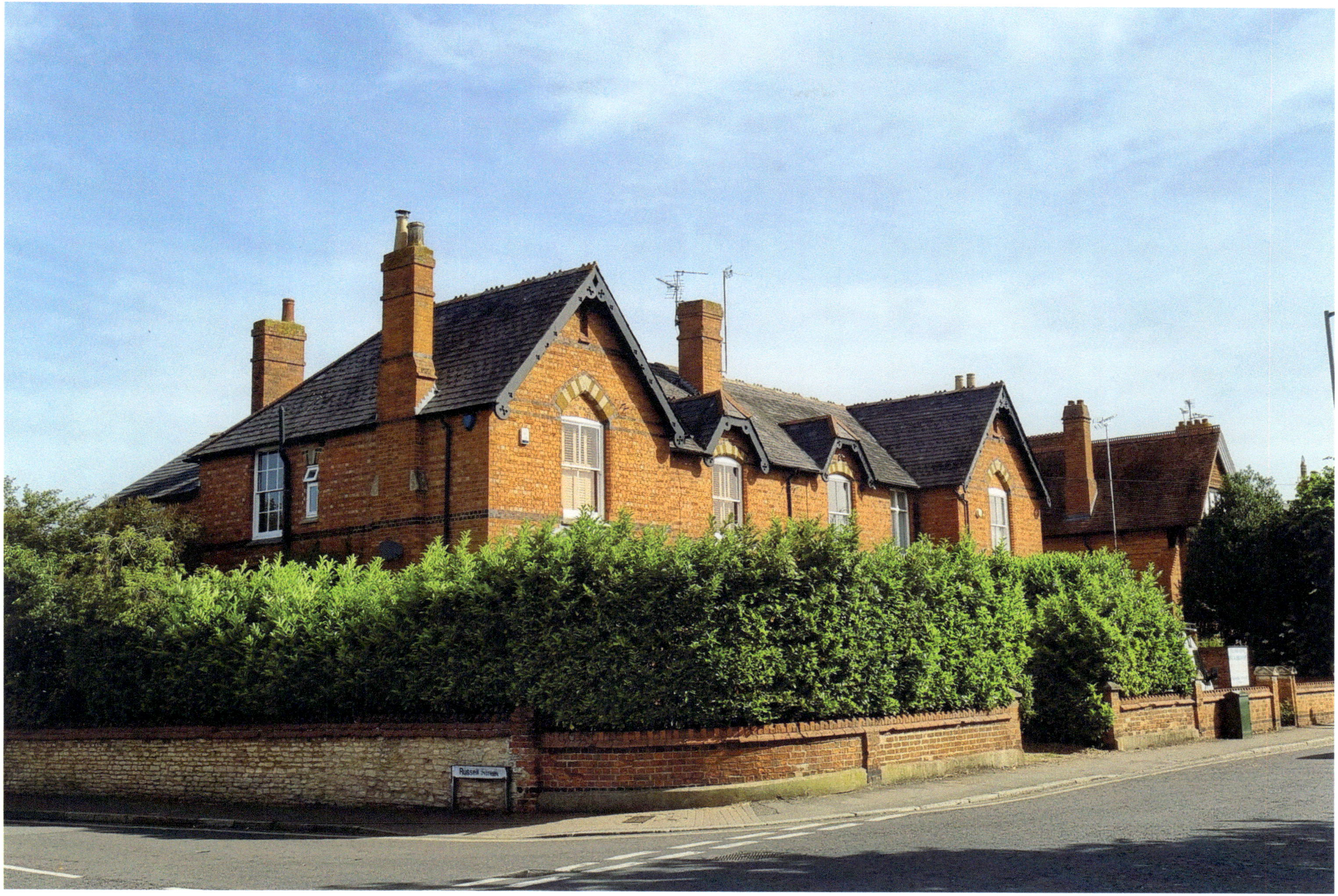
Russell

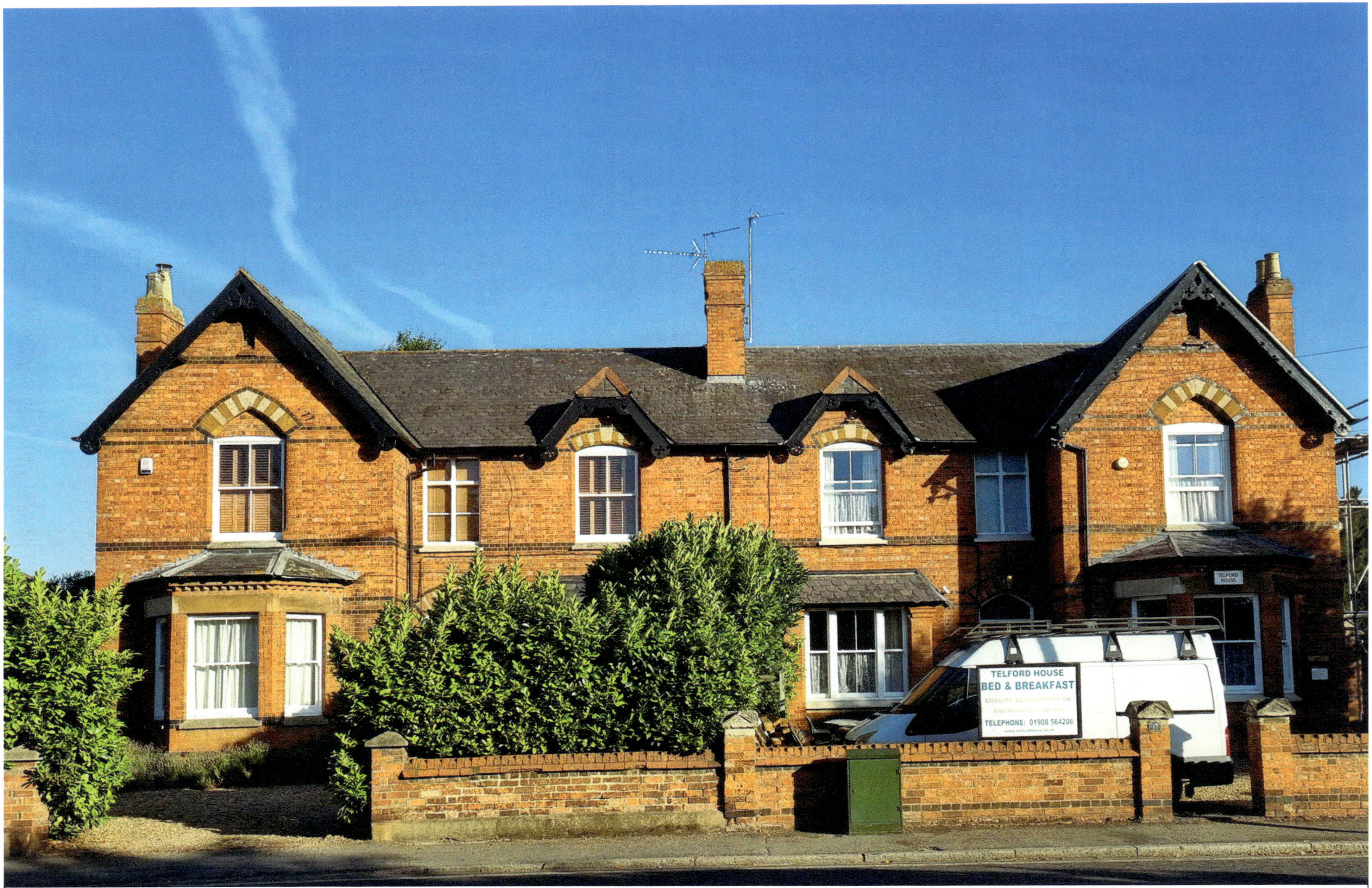

Development began with substantial villas, as shown on these pages 103 and 104.

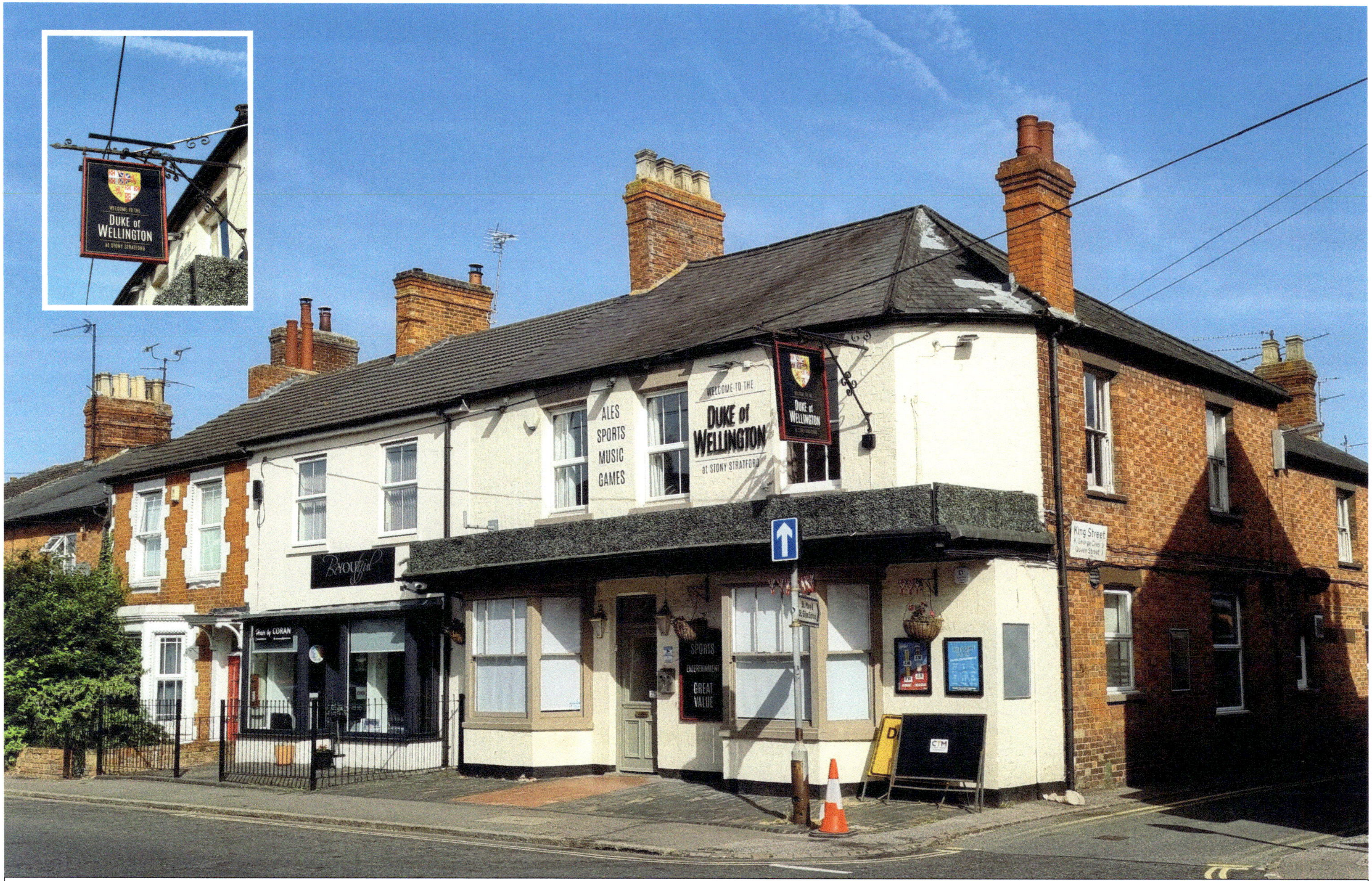

The Duke of Wellington was one of three public houses that opened on the Wolverton Road in the 1870s. It was originally called The Duke of Edinburgh.

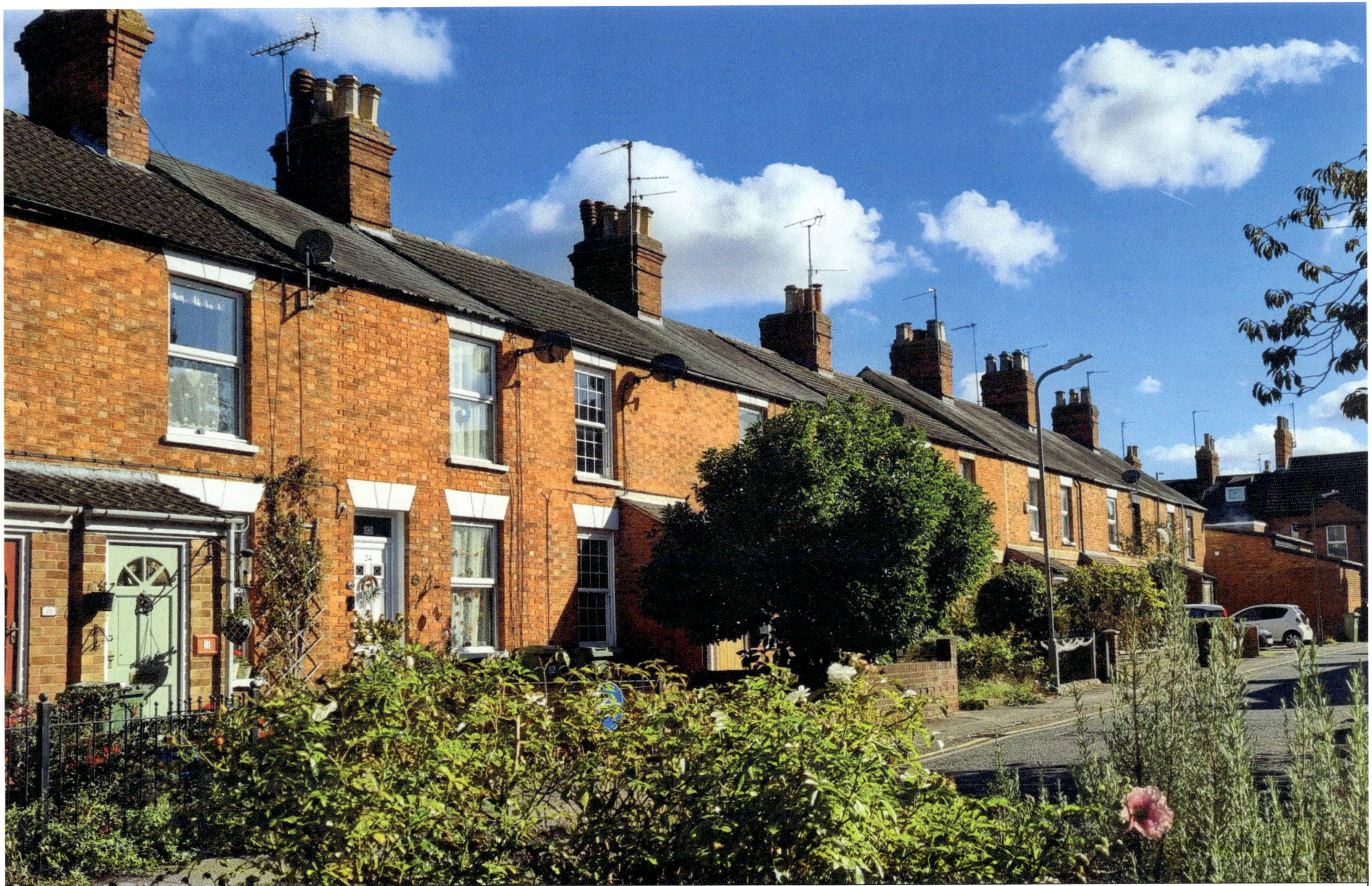

King Street. This narrow street was built many years before car ownership could be considered.

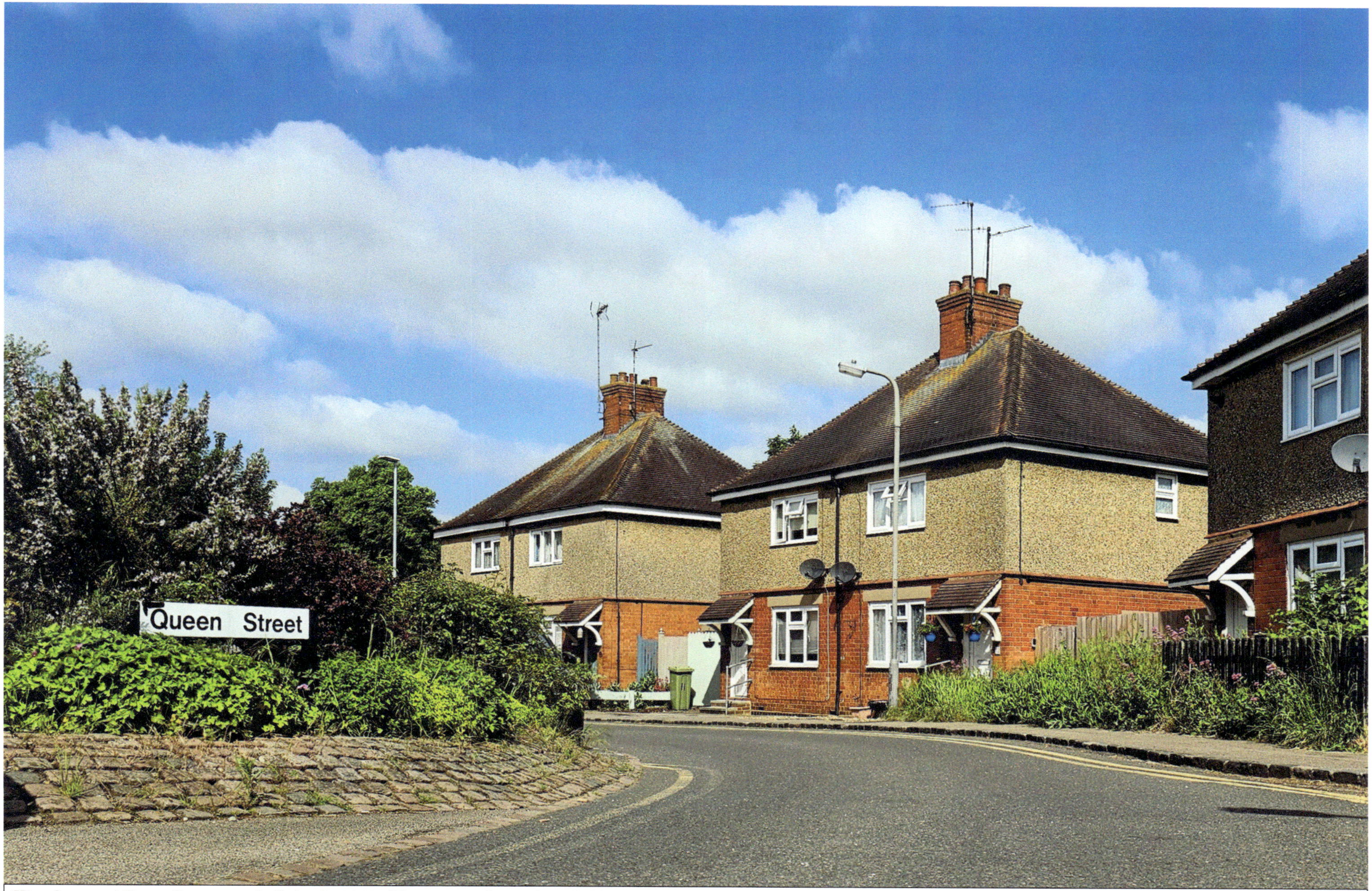

King Stret and Queen Street were built in the 1860s. The crescent of semi-detatched houses was added in the 1930s to join the two streets at the north end.

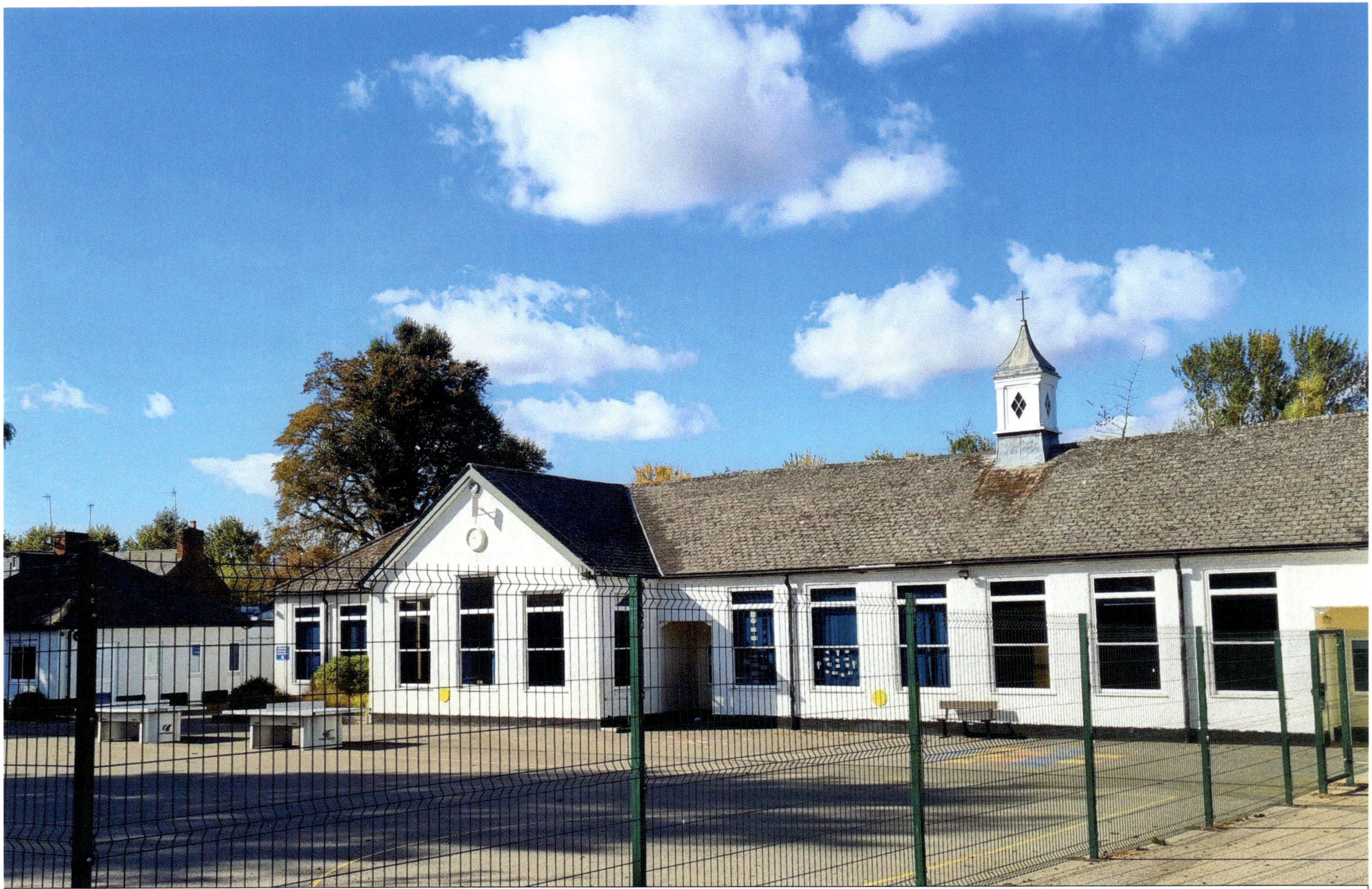

This school, at the end of King and Queen Streets was built in the 1930s to replace the old High Street schools.

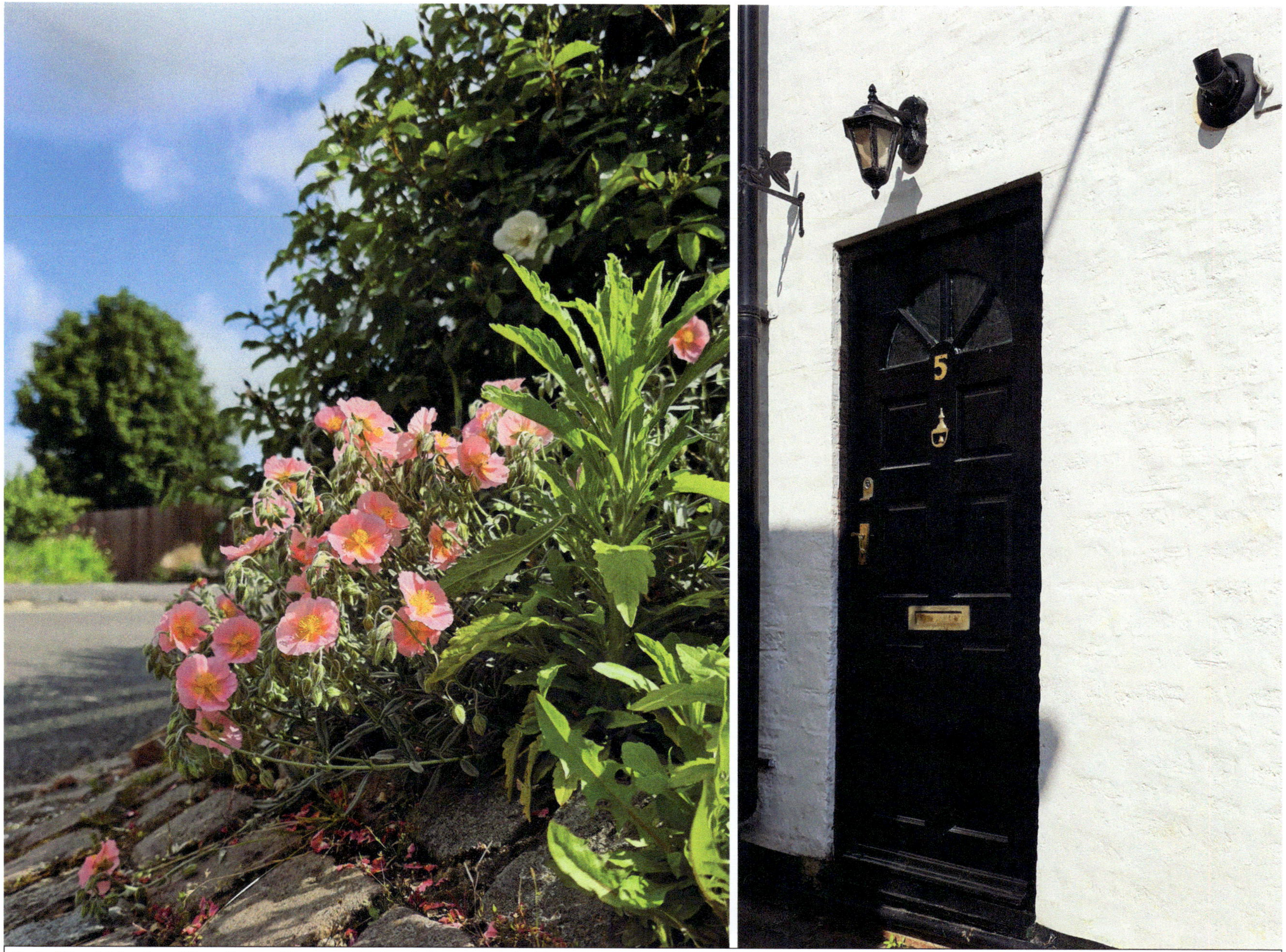

Left: Floral island on King George Crescent. Right: A door on Jubilee Terrace.

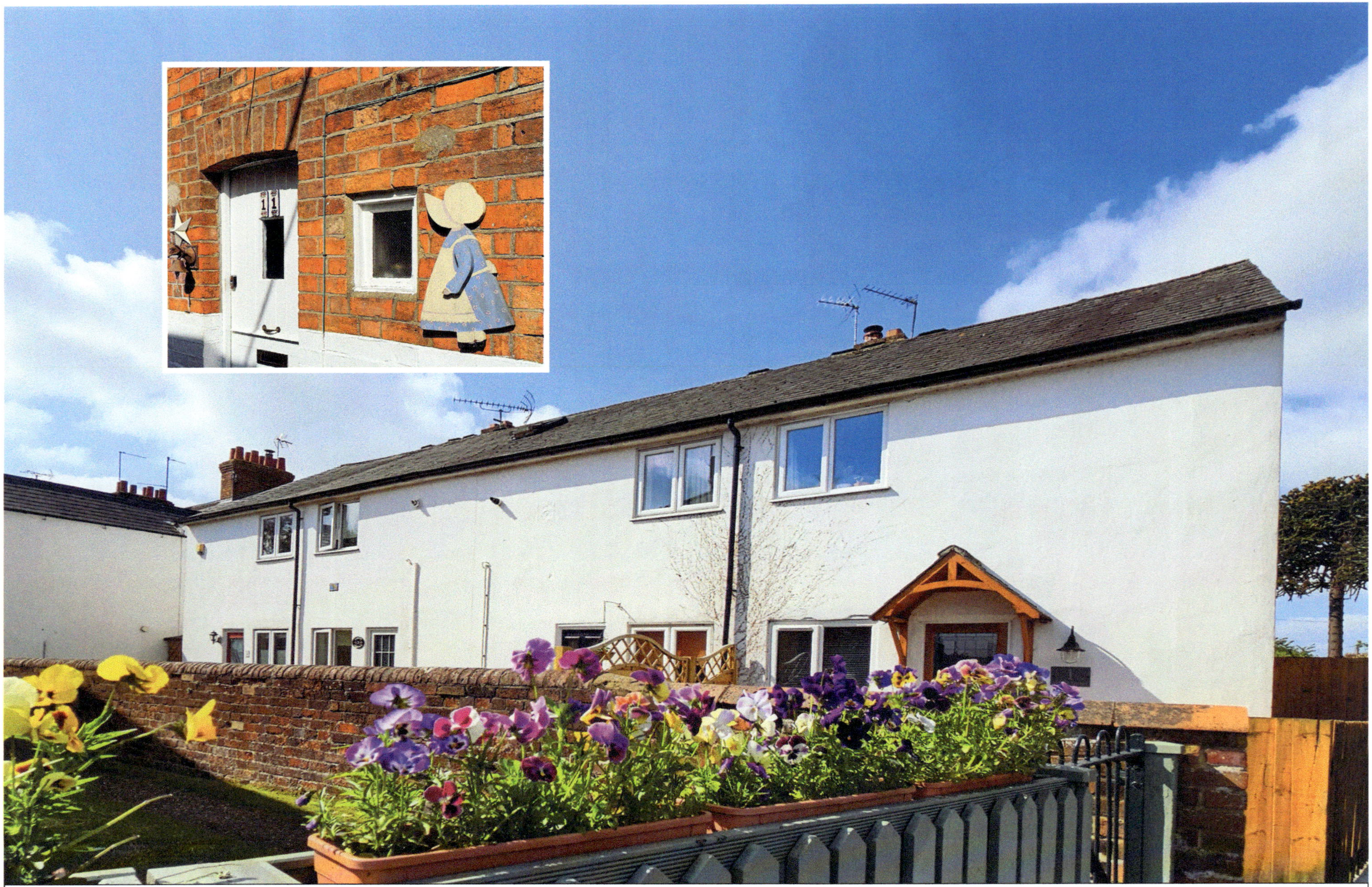

Jubilee Terrace was so-named after Queen Victoria's Silver Jubilee of 1862.

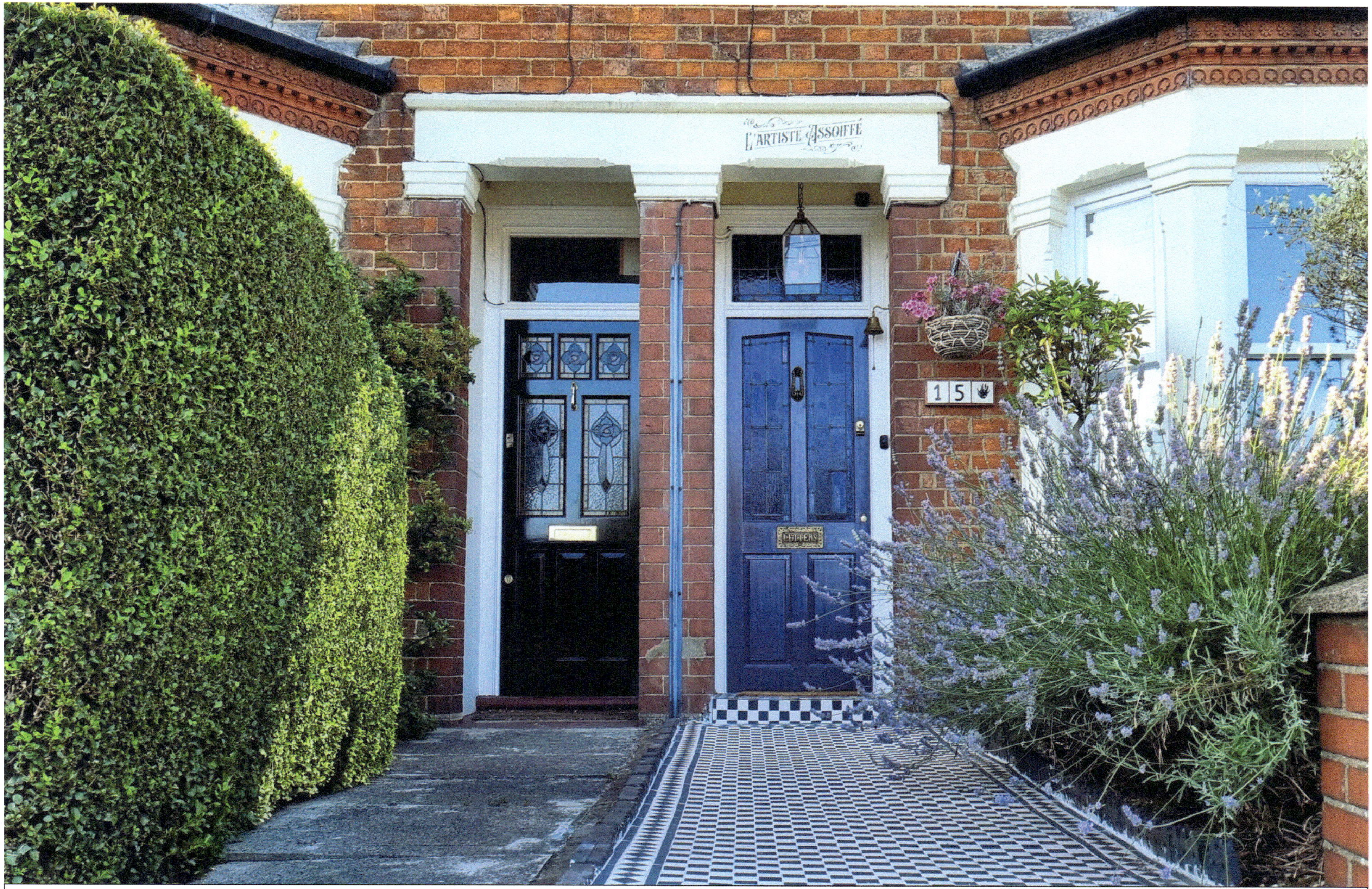

Entrances to two terraced houses on the Wolverton Road.

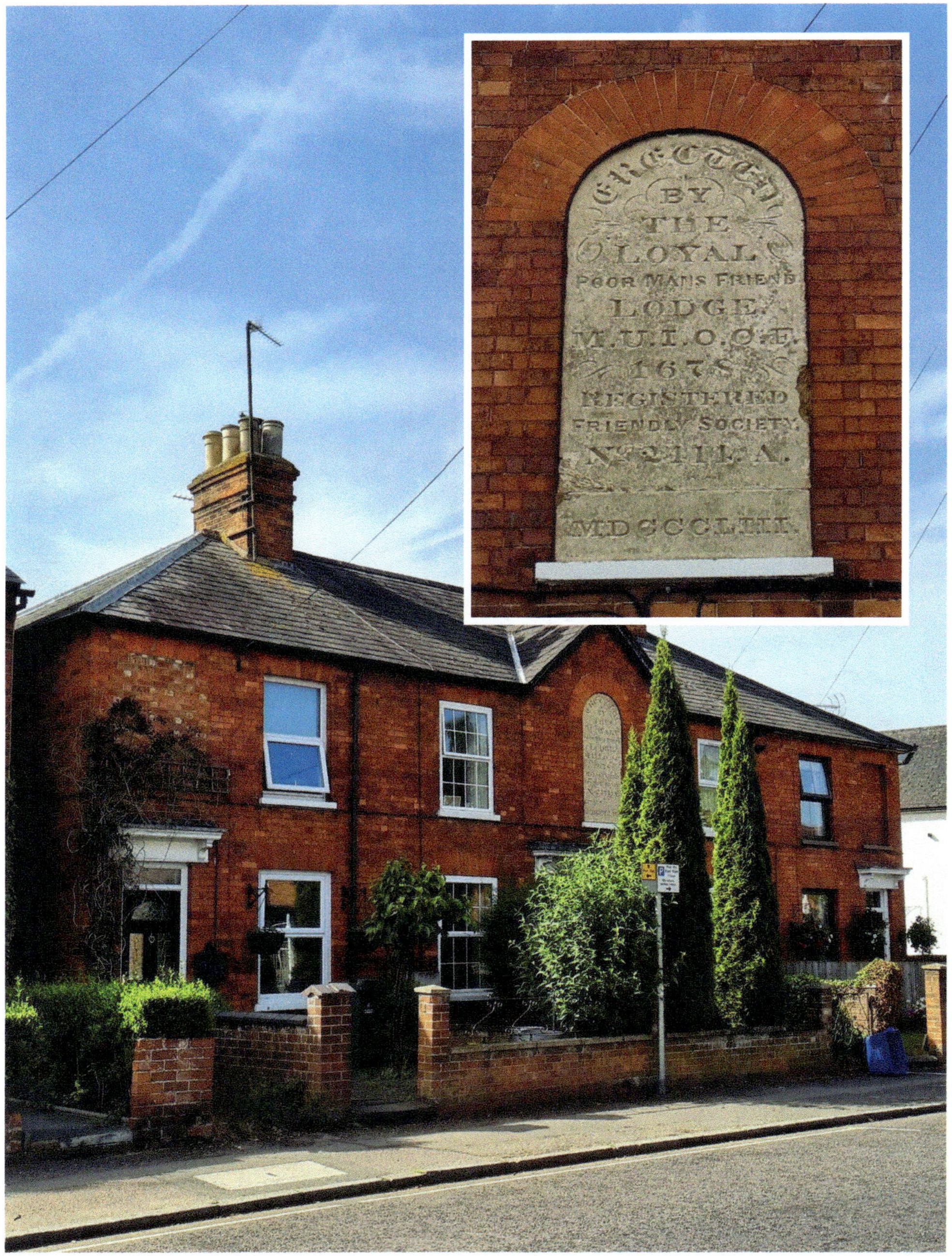
ERECTED
BY
THE
LOYAL
POOR MANS FRIEND
LODGE
M.U.I.O.O.F.
1678
REGISTERED
FRIENDLY SOCIETY
No 2111 A.
MDCCCLIII

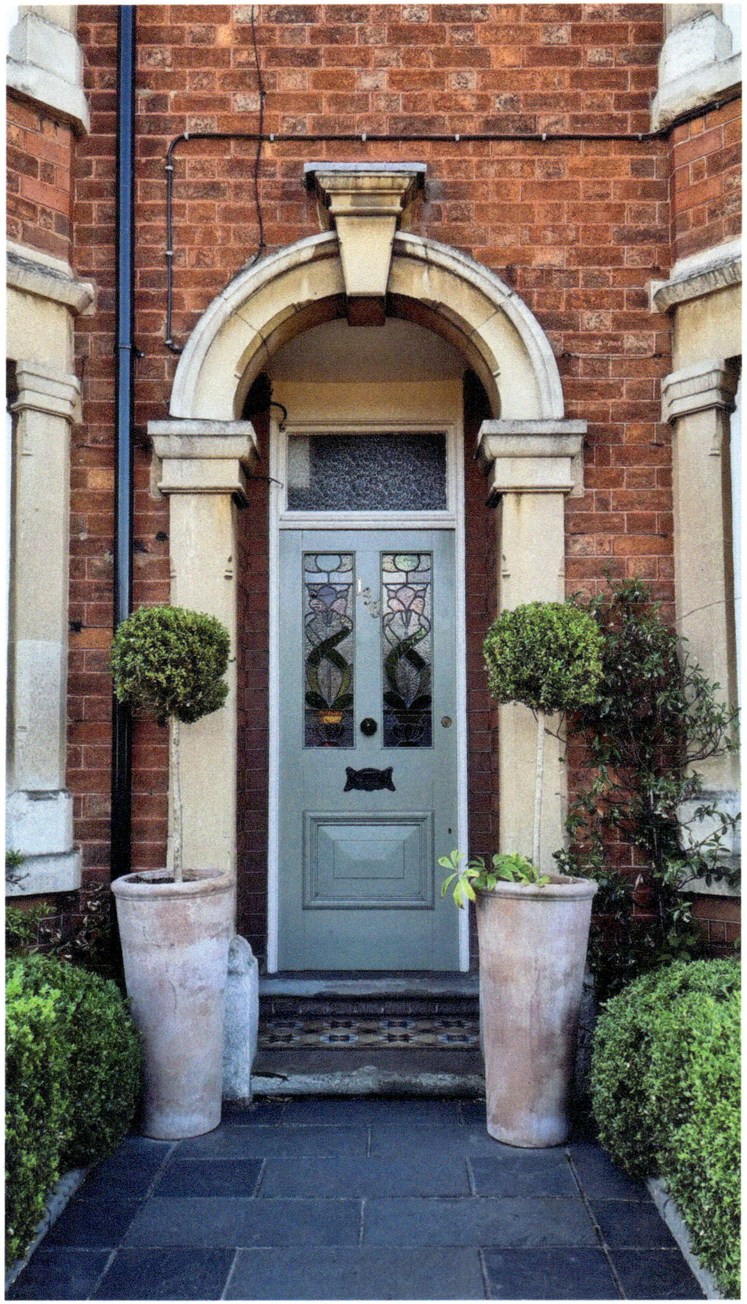

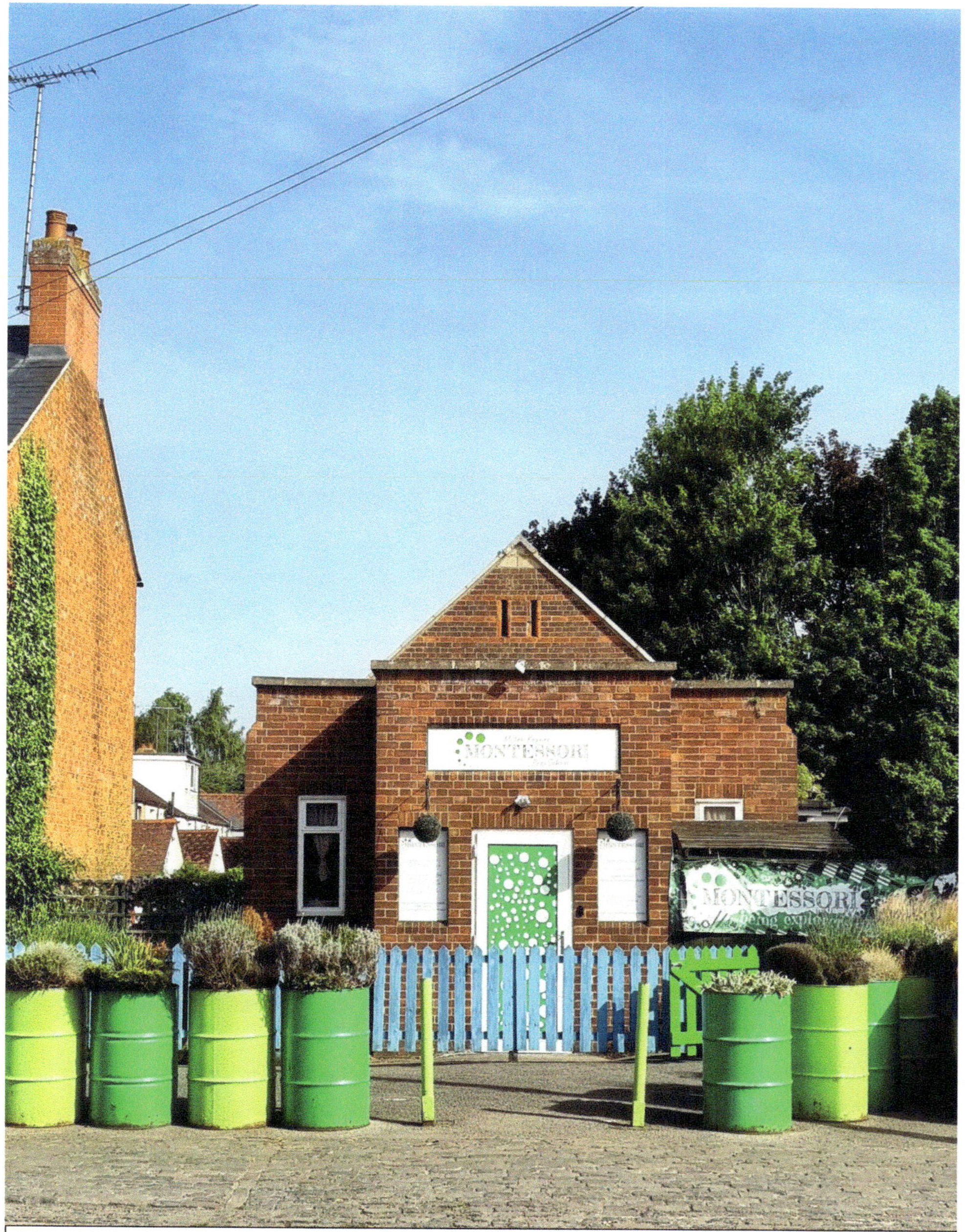

The Montessori School was a former Independent Chapel.

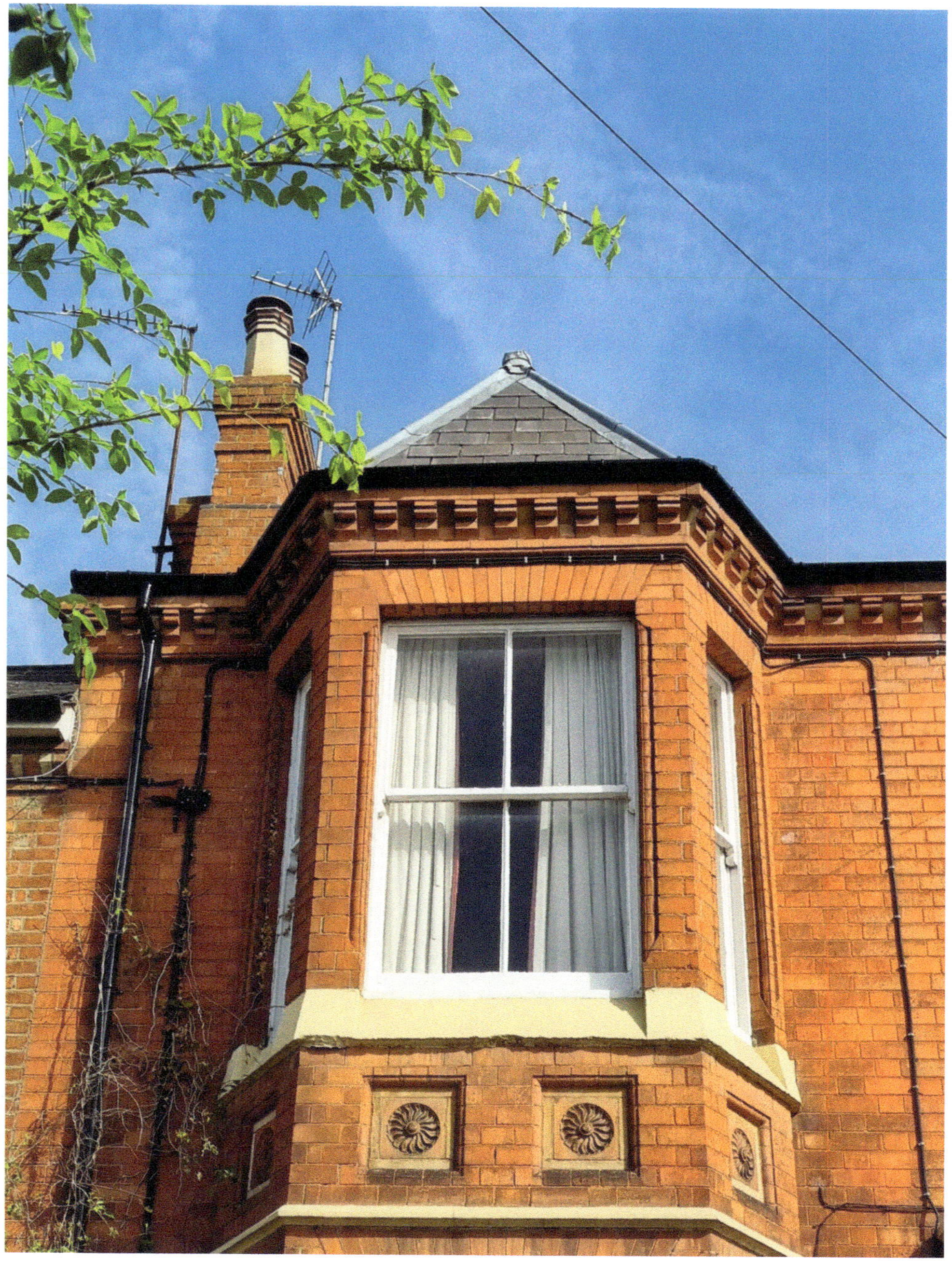

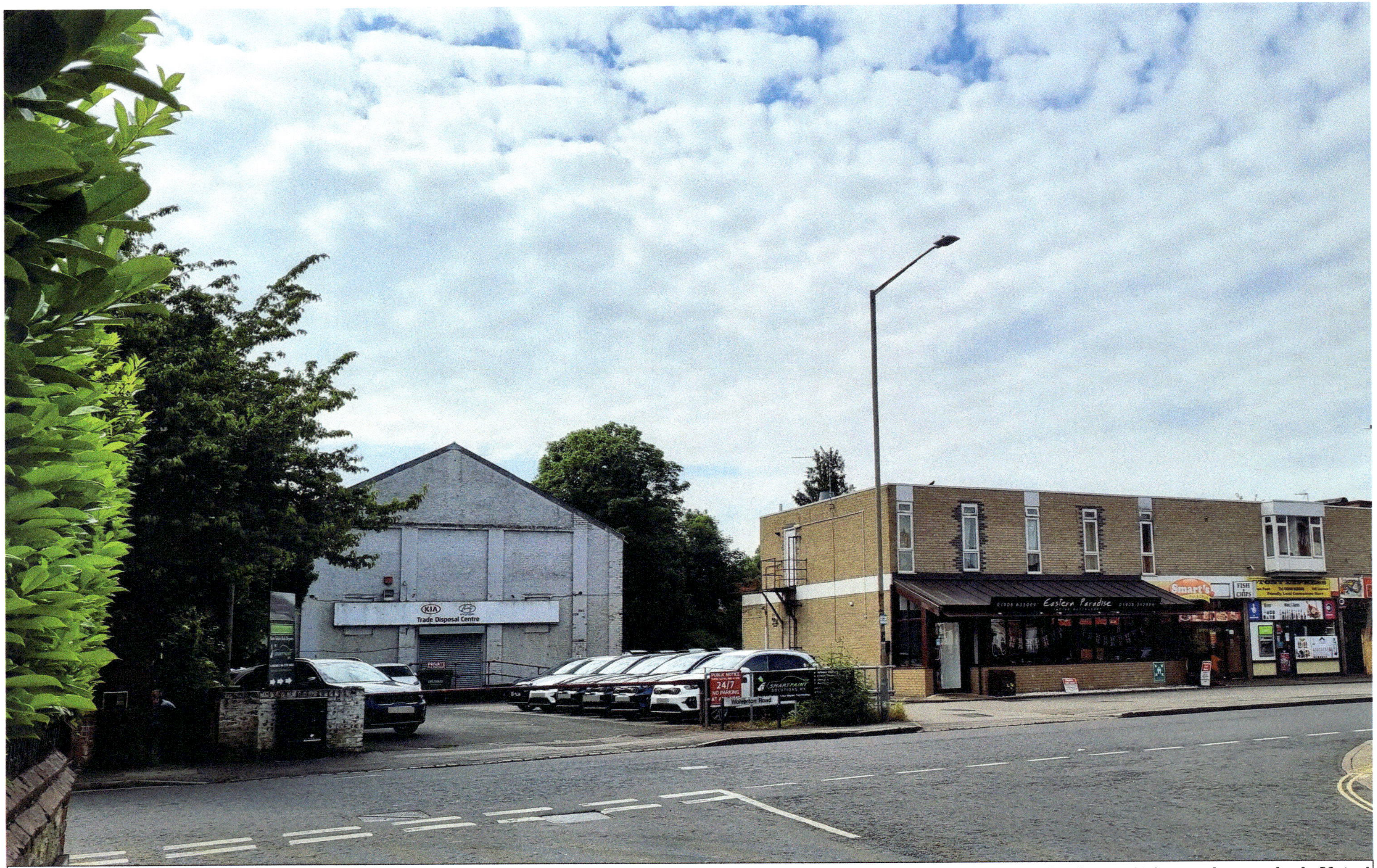

The white building on the left was built as the Scala Cinema by George Barber, who also owned the Picture Palace in Wolverton. To its right was a white house which was taken over by the United Counties bus company. The bus garage was behind it. Those buildings have been replaced by a recent development.

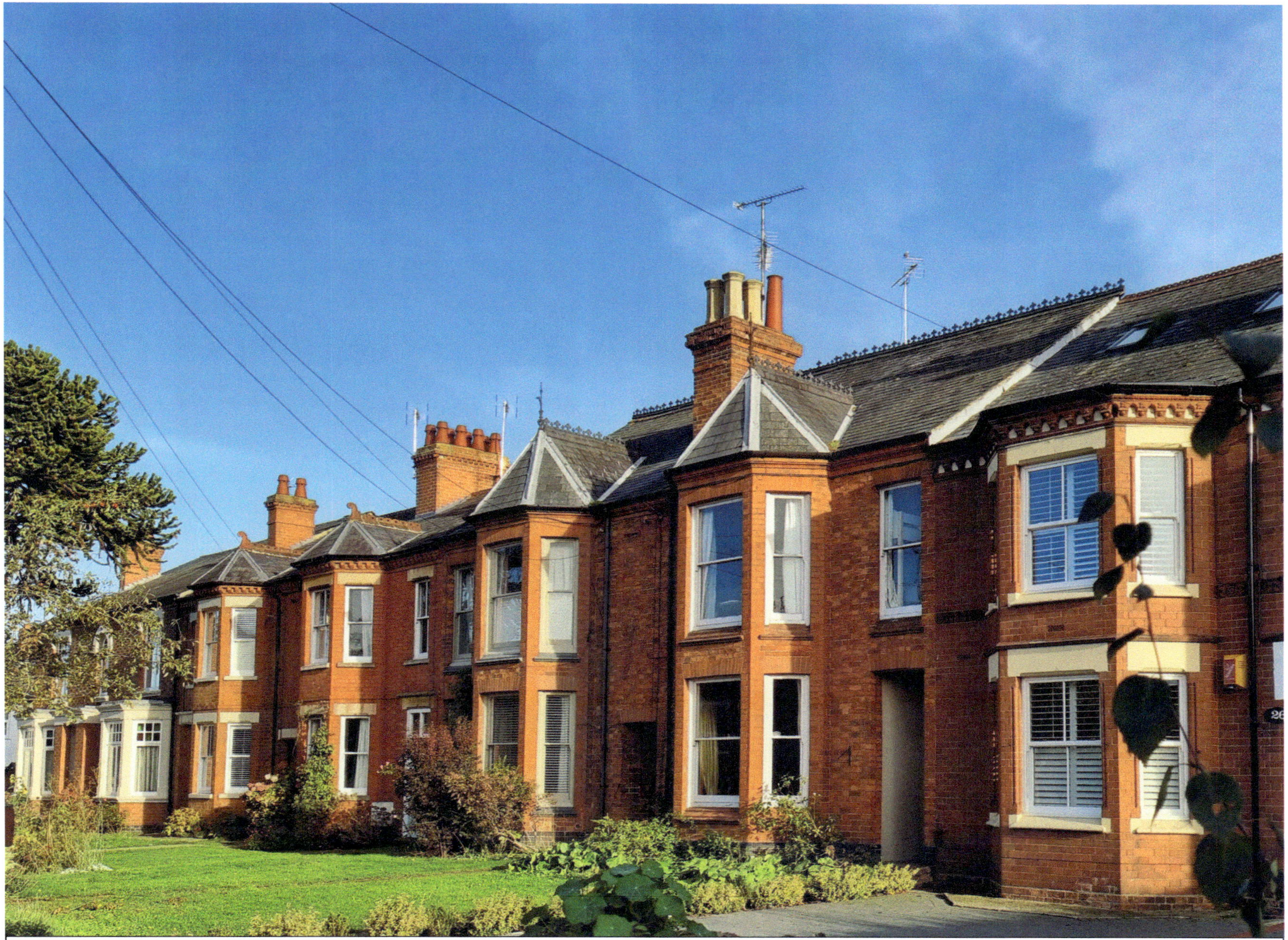

A Wolverton Road terrace.

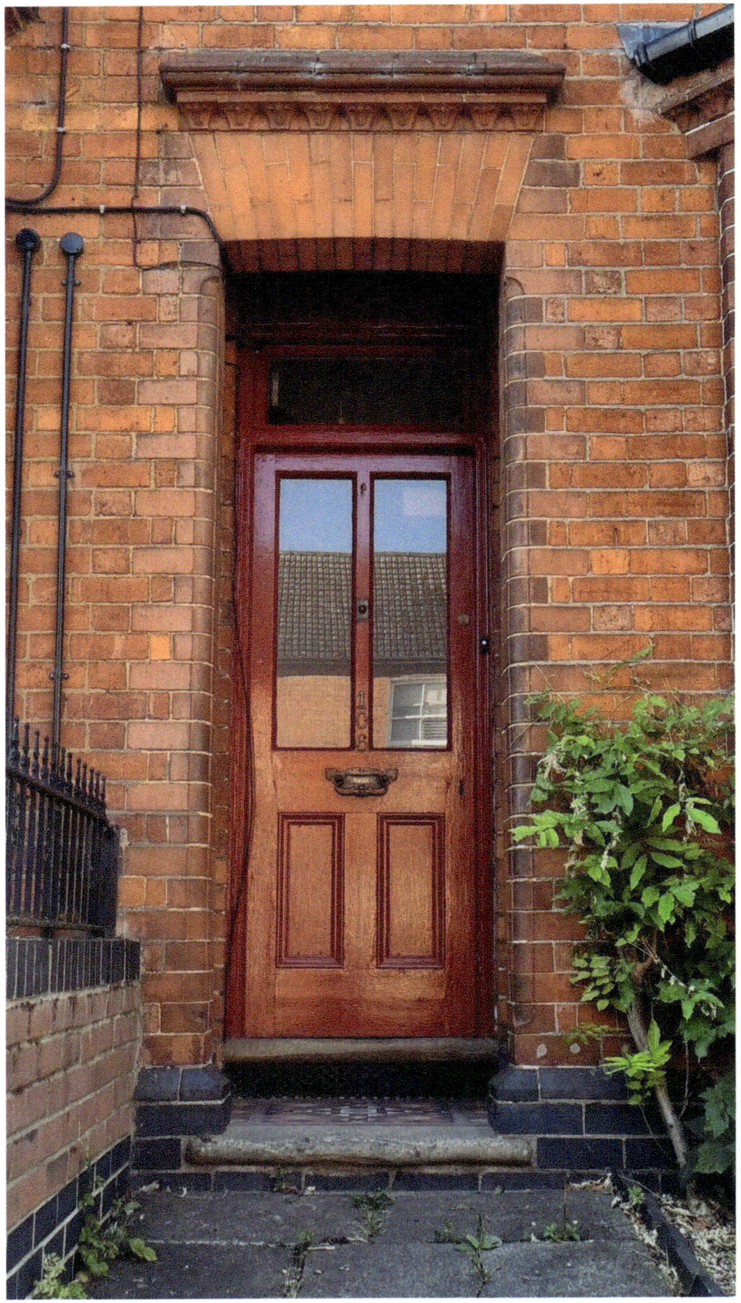

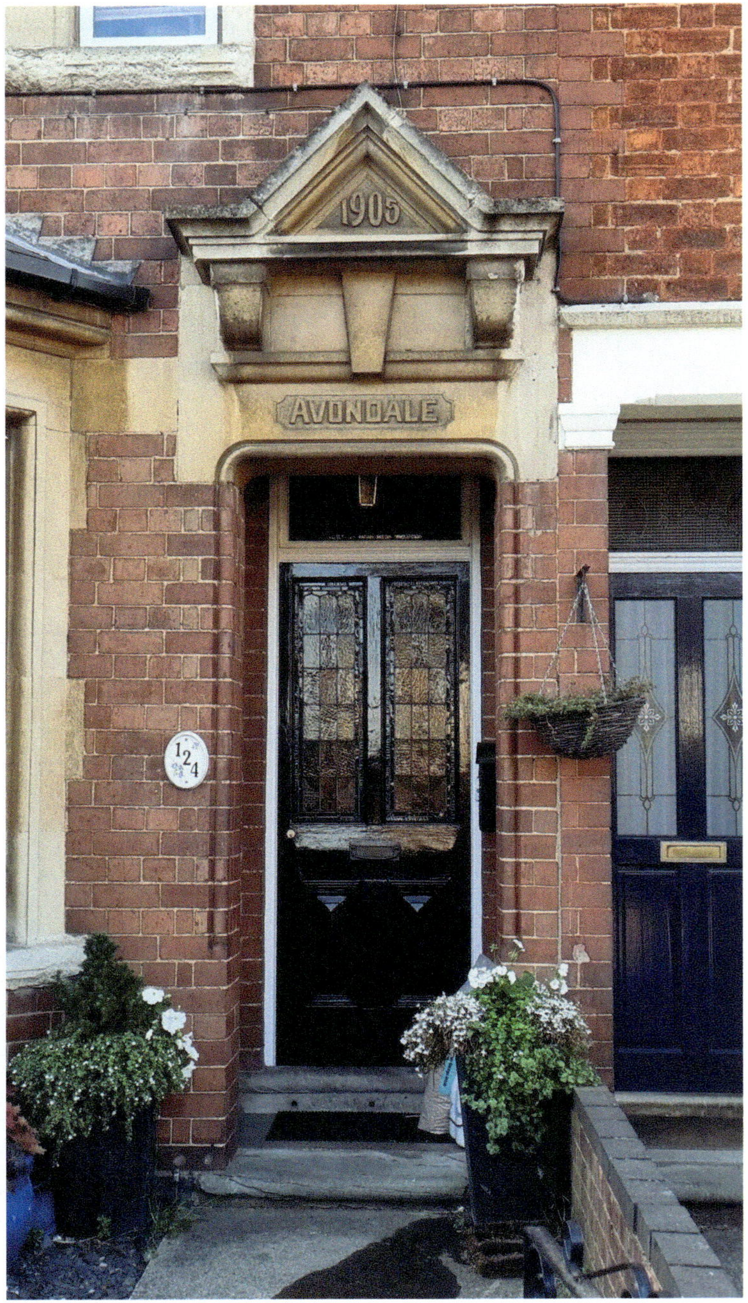
1905
AVONDALE
124

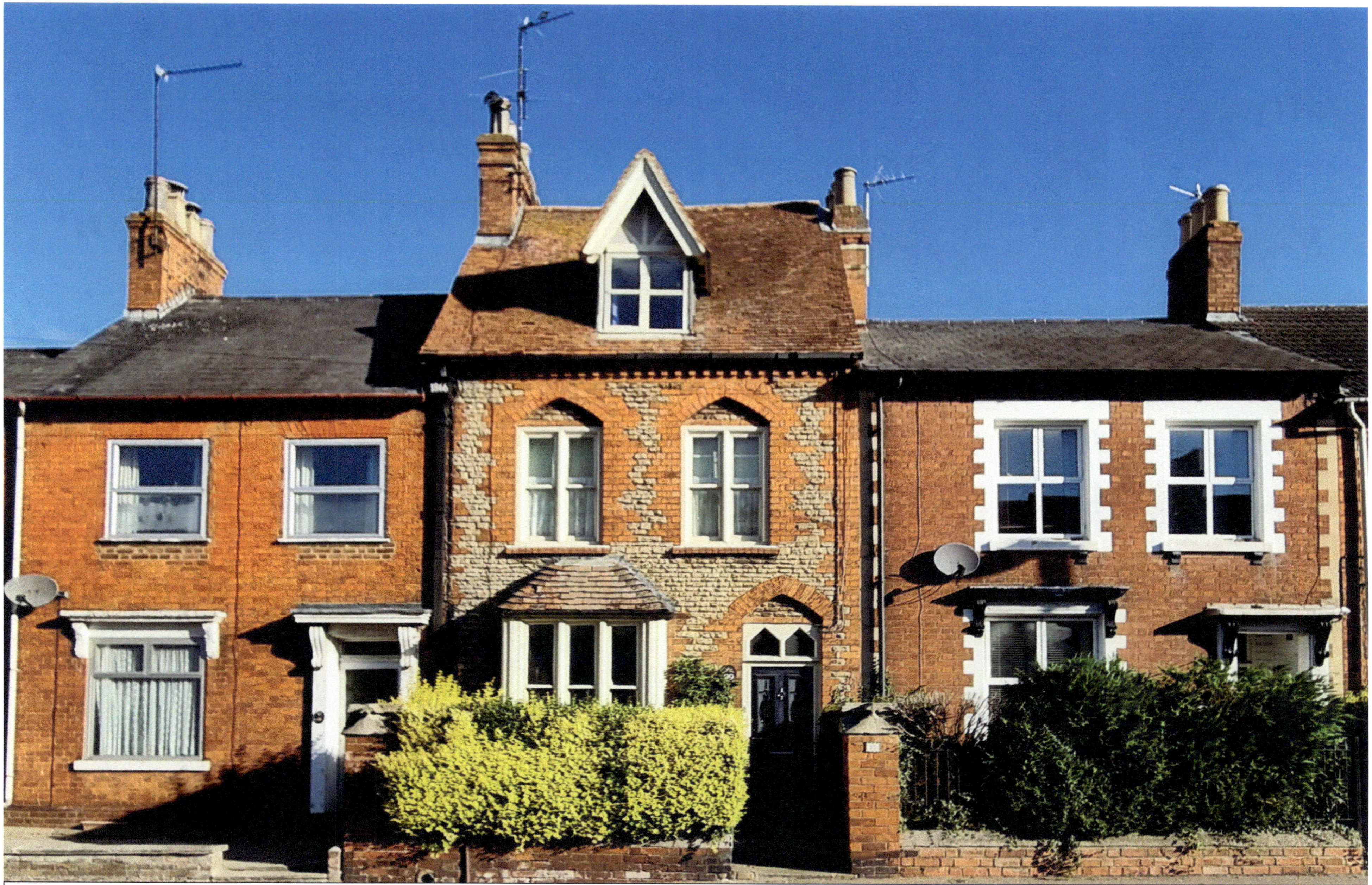

Wolverton Road houses.

RUSSELL STREET

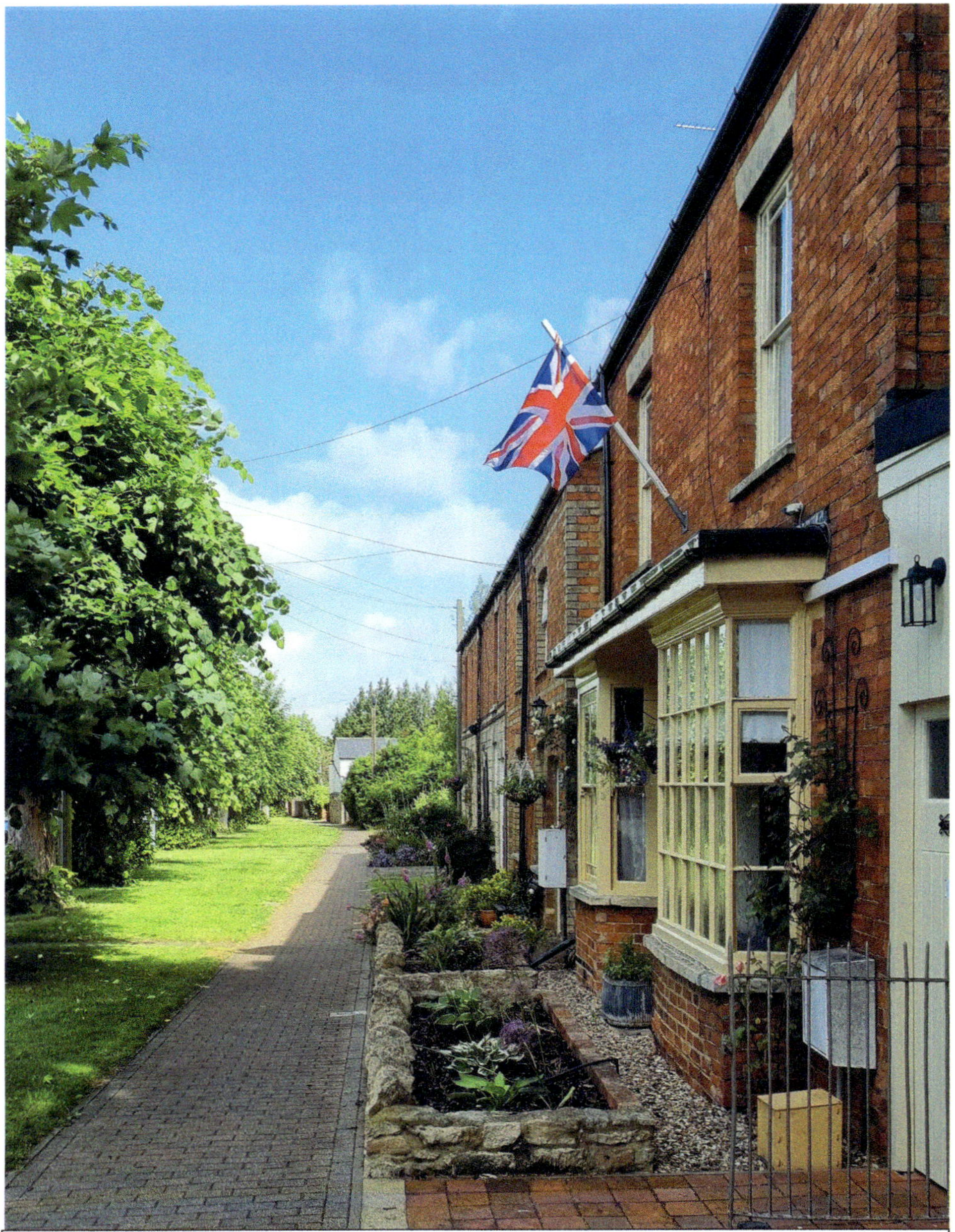

Vicarage Walk.

Traditionally known as Back Lane, this path gave rear access to the High Street properties. The first development started when William Thompson Sankey built New Street and a vicarage for his own family east of the Back Lane. The vicarage burnt down some years ago but there is a row of houses now known as Vicarage Walk, which gives a nod to what was once there.

Russell Street was named after William Russell, who owned the property on the Wolverton Road, from the High Street corner to the Congregational Chapel, although it did not bear his name until many years after his death. Properties were built at the back of High Street lots from the 1850s and census returns simply reported these residents as living on Back Lane, Back Street or Back Way.

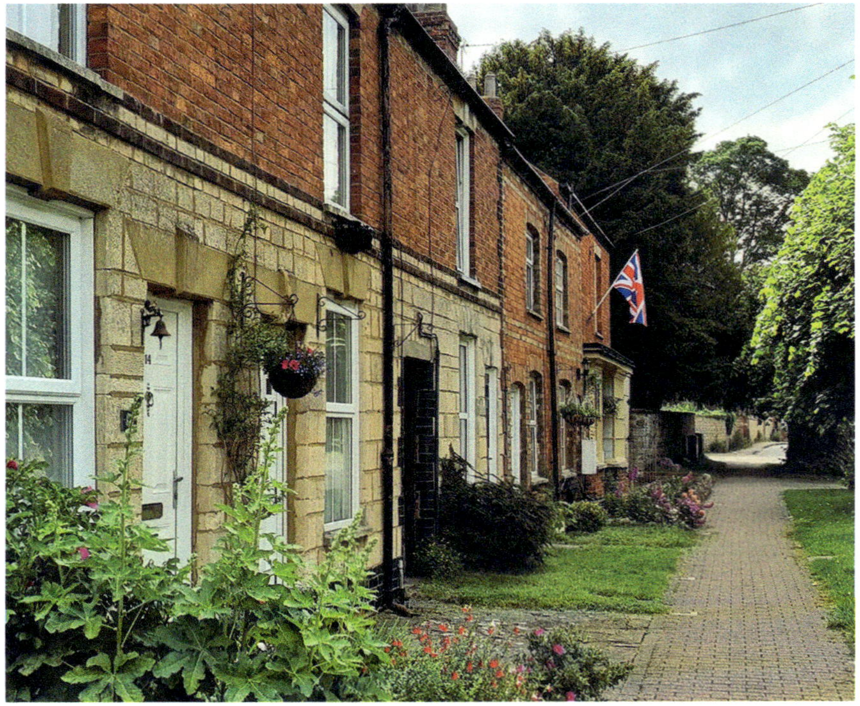

LOOK AT THE BACK OF THE HIGH STREET

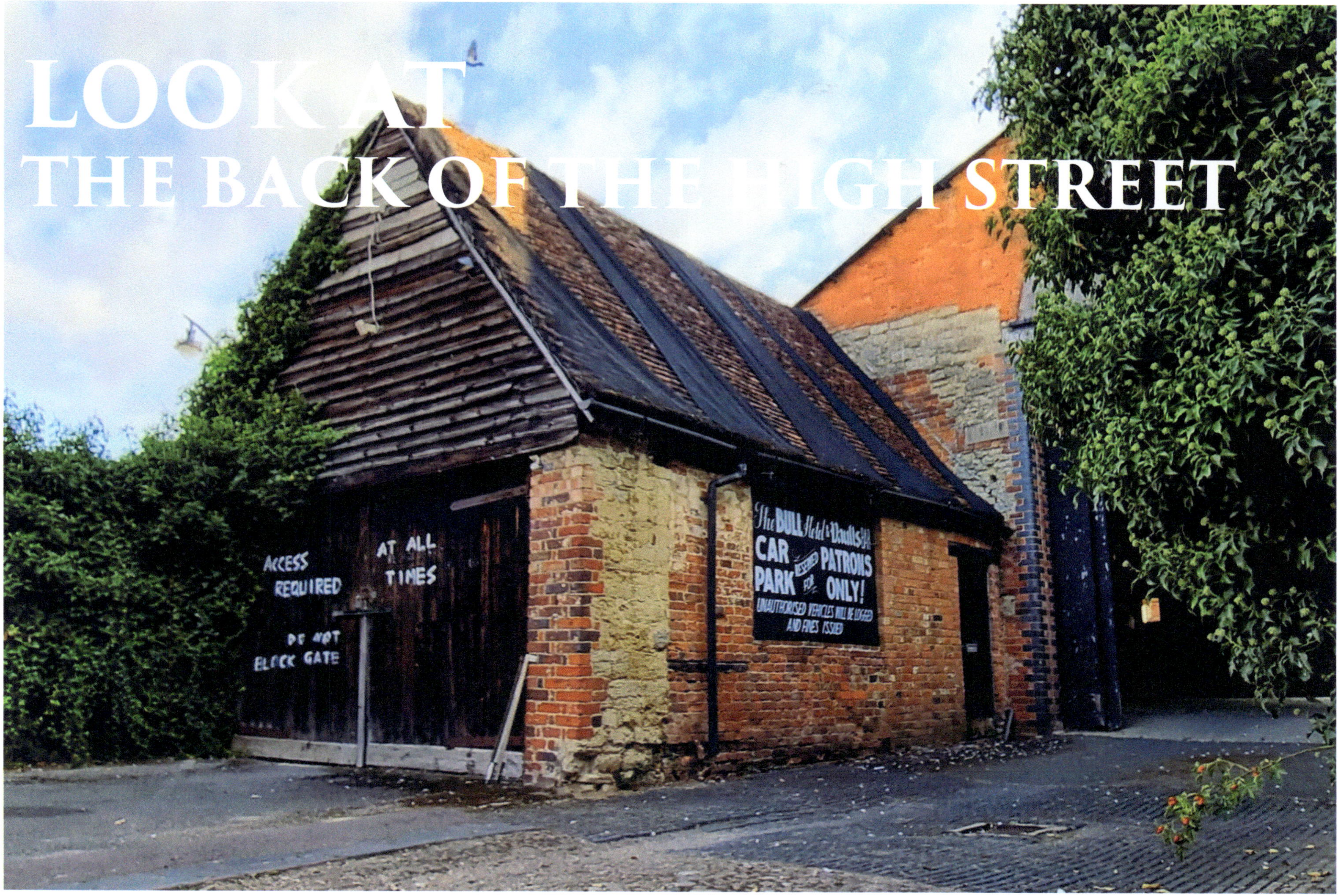

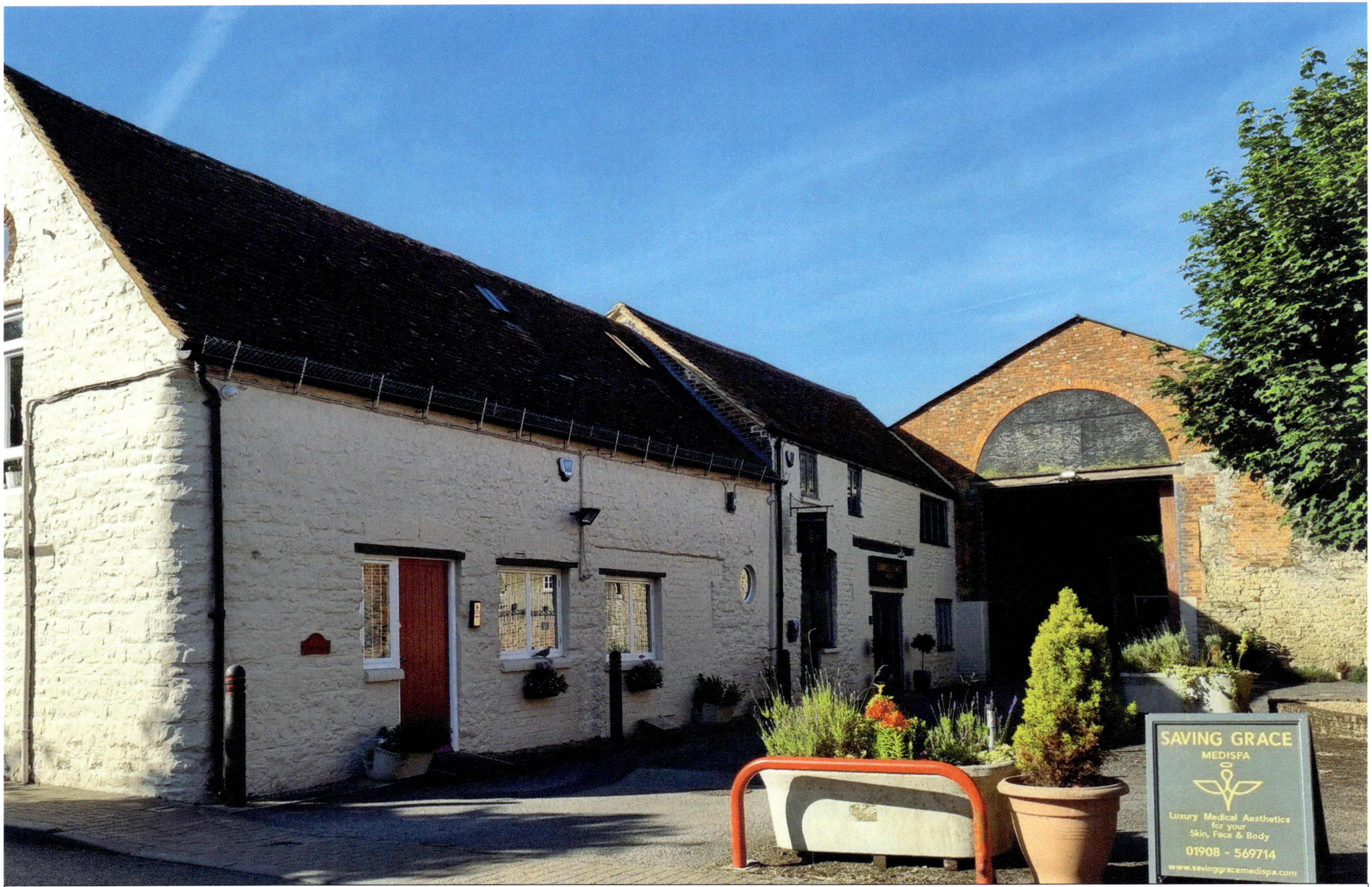

At the back of the Bull Hotel.

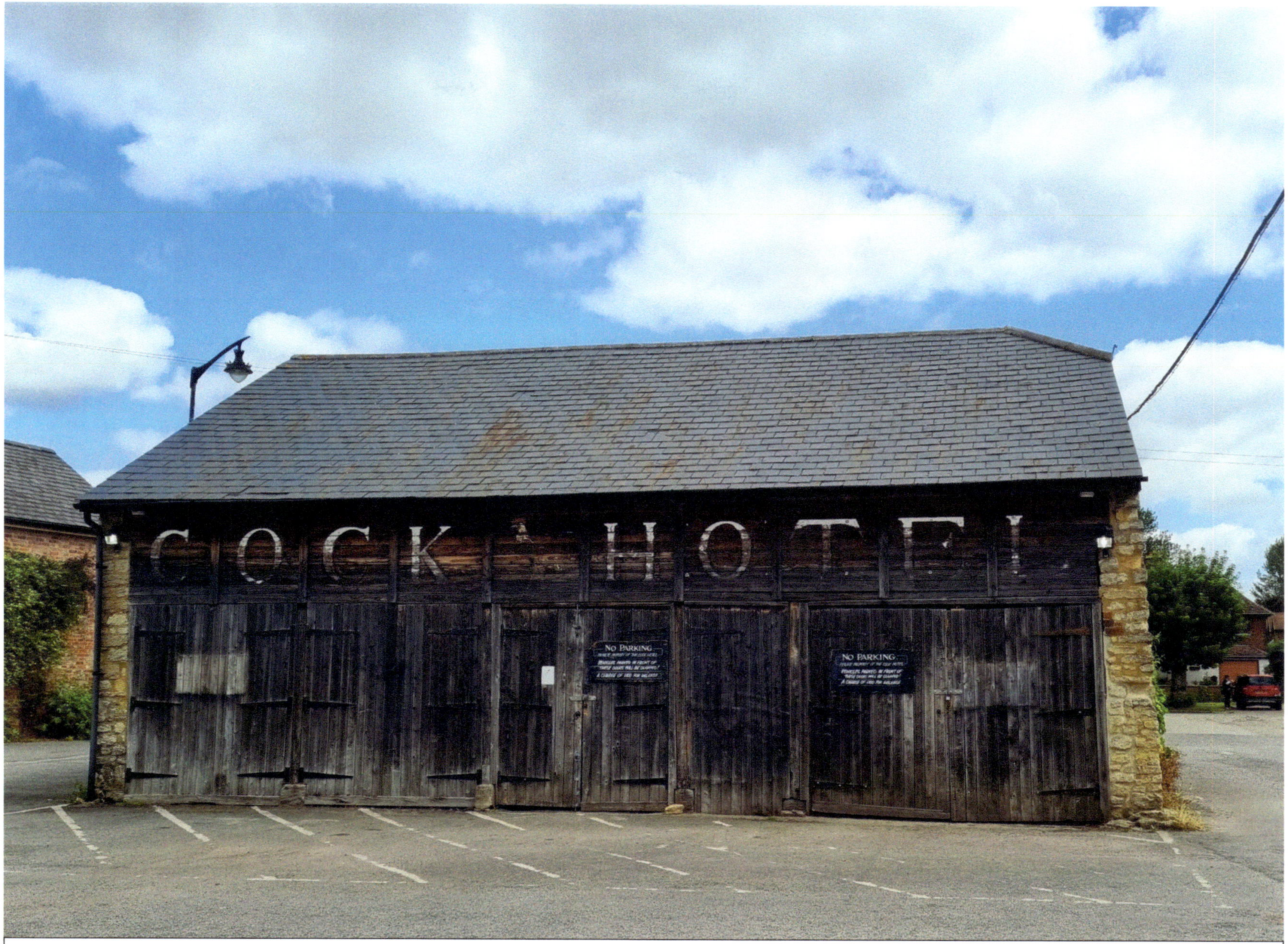

Buildings at the back of the Cock Hotel.

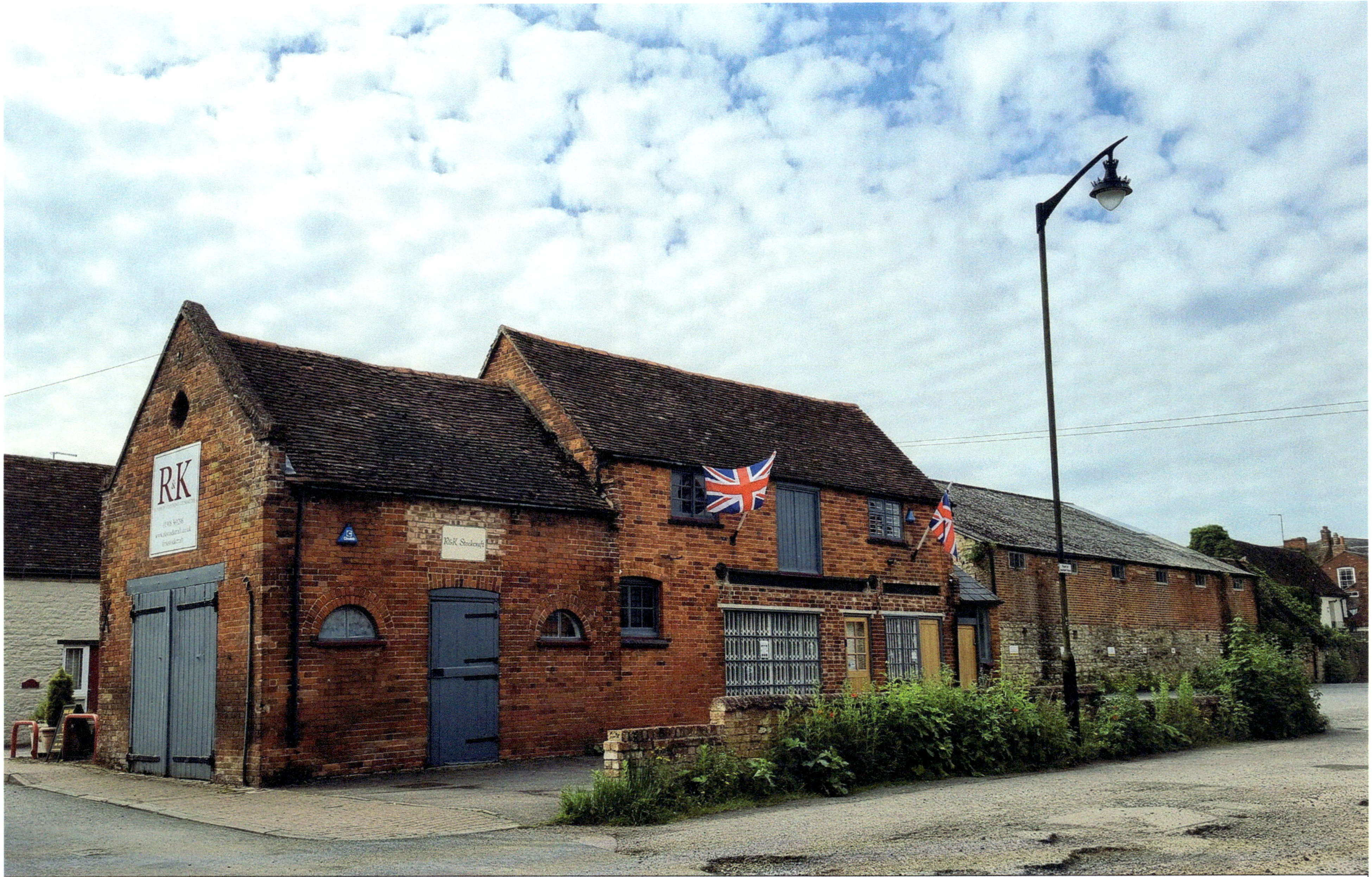

Buildings backing on to Vicarage Road.

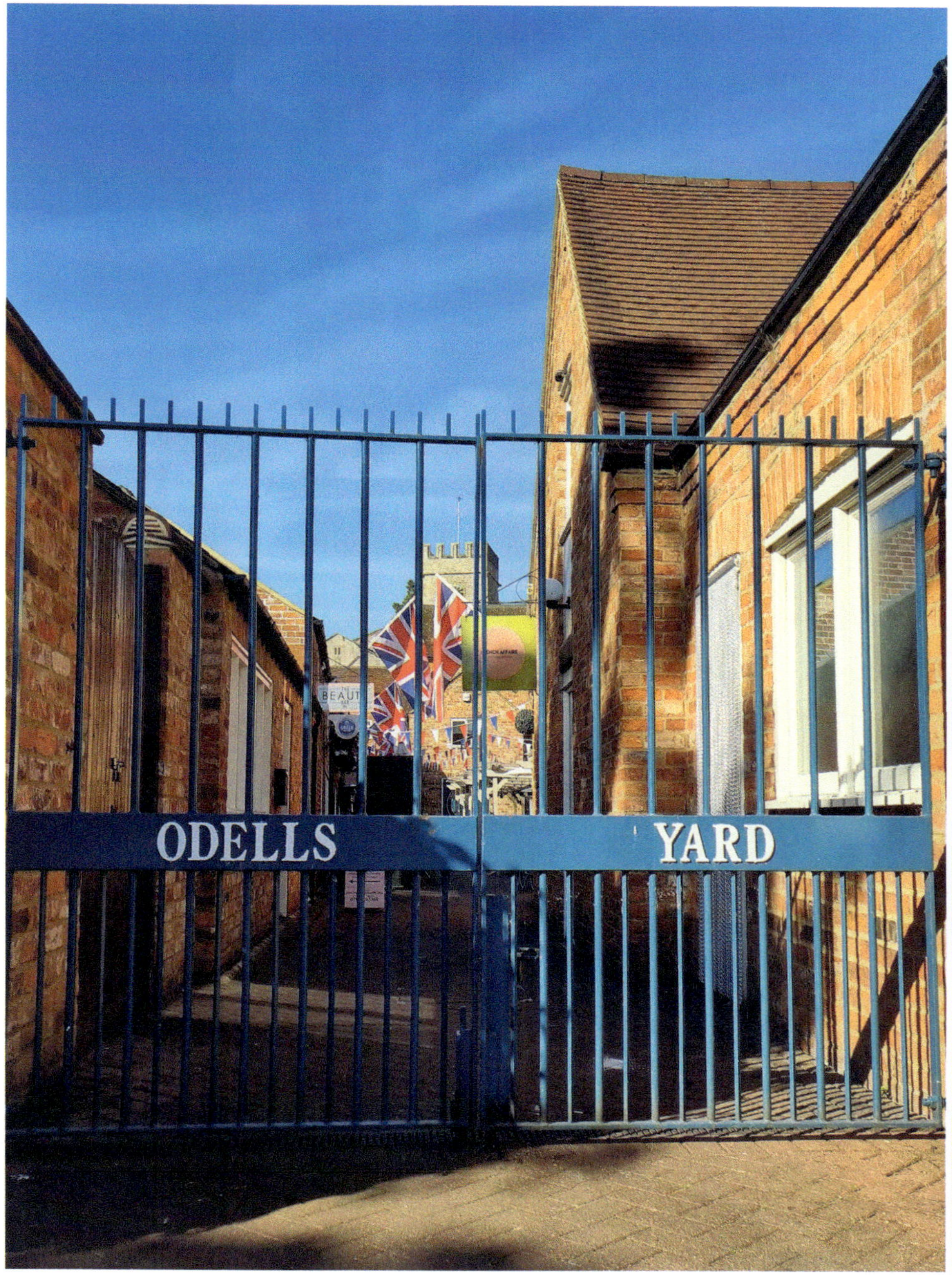
ODELLS
YARD

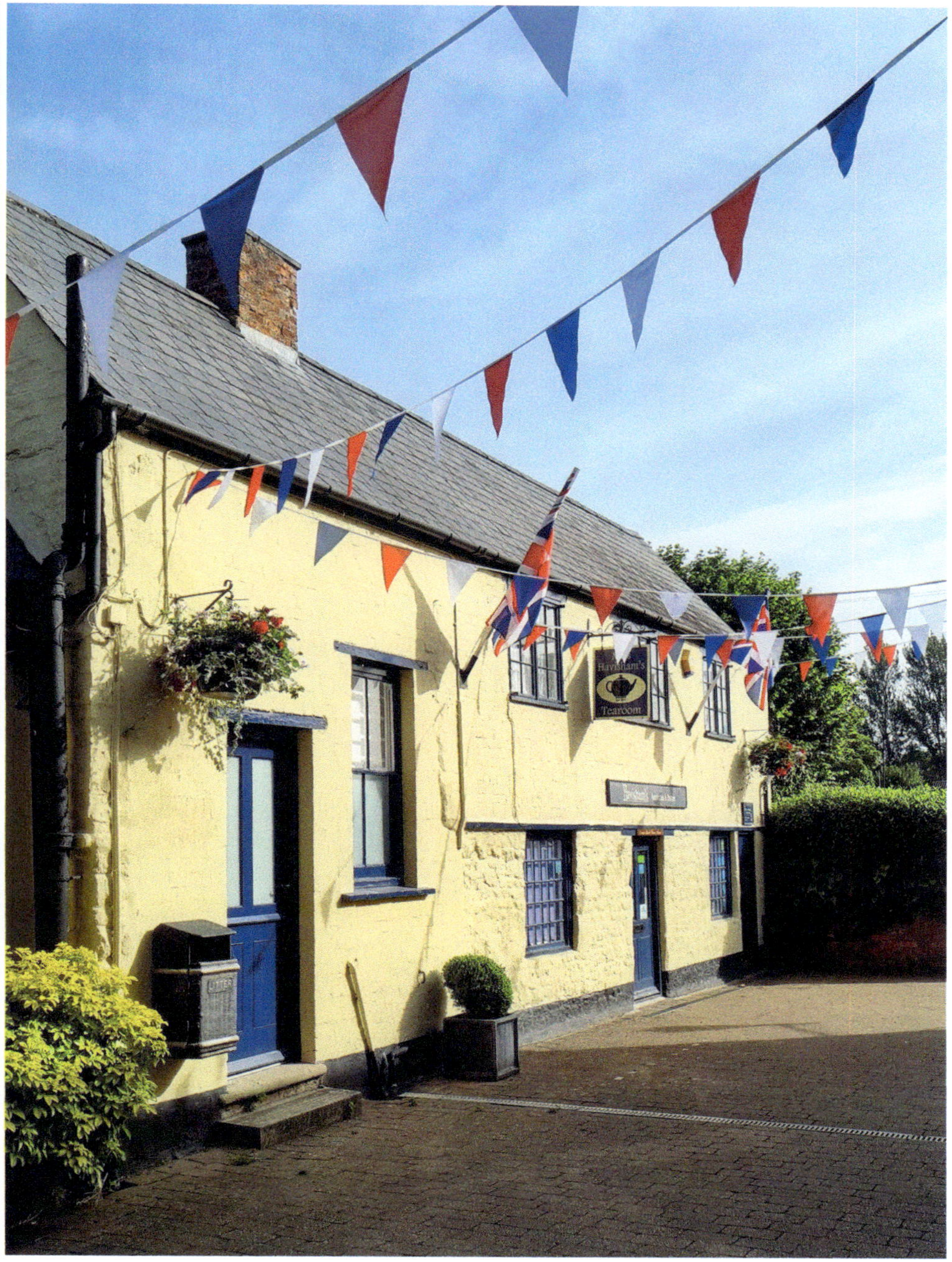

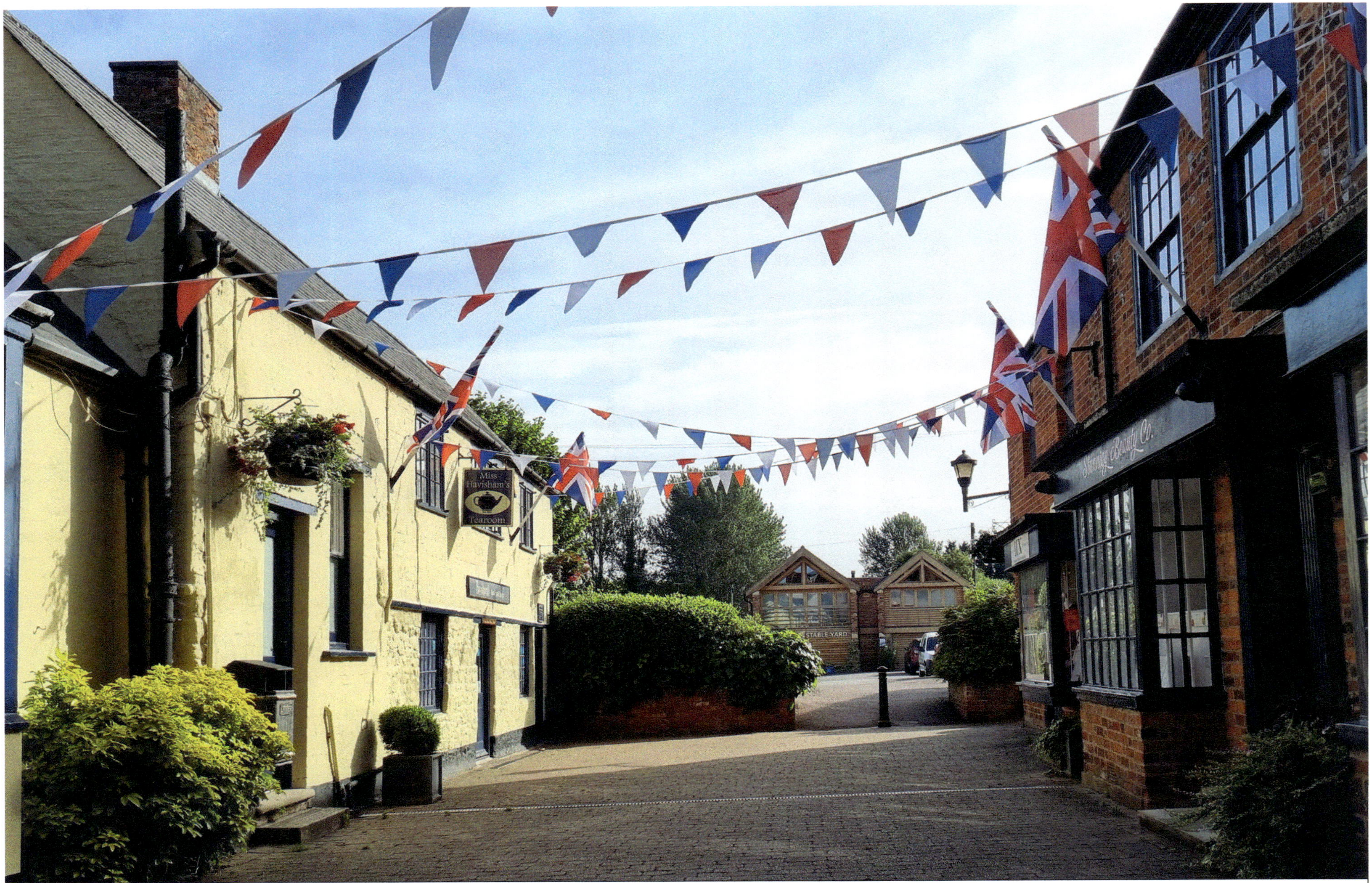

The very long lots of the medieval occupants of the High Street gave plenty of space for later development. This is Timor Court.

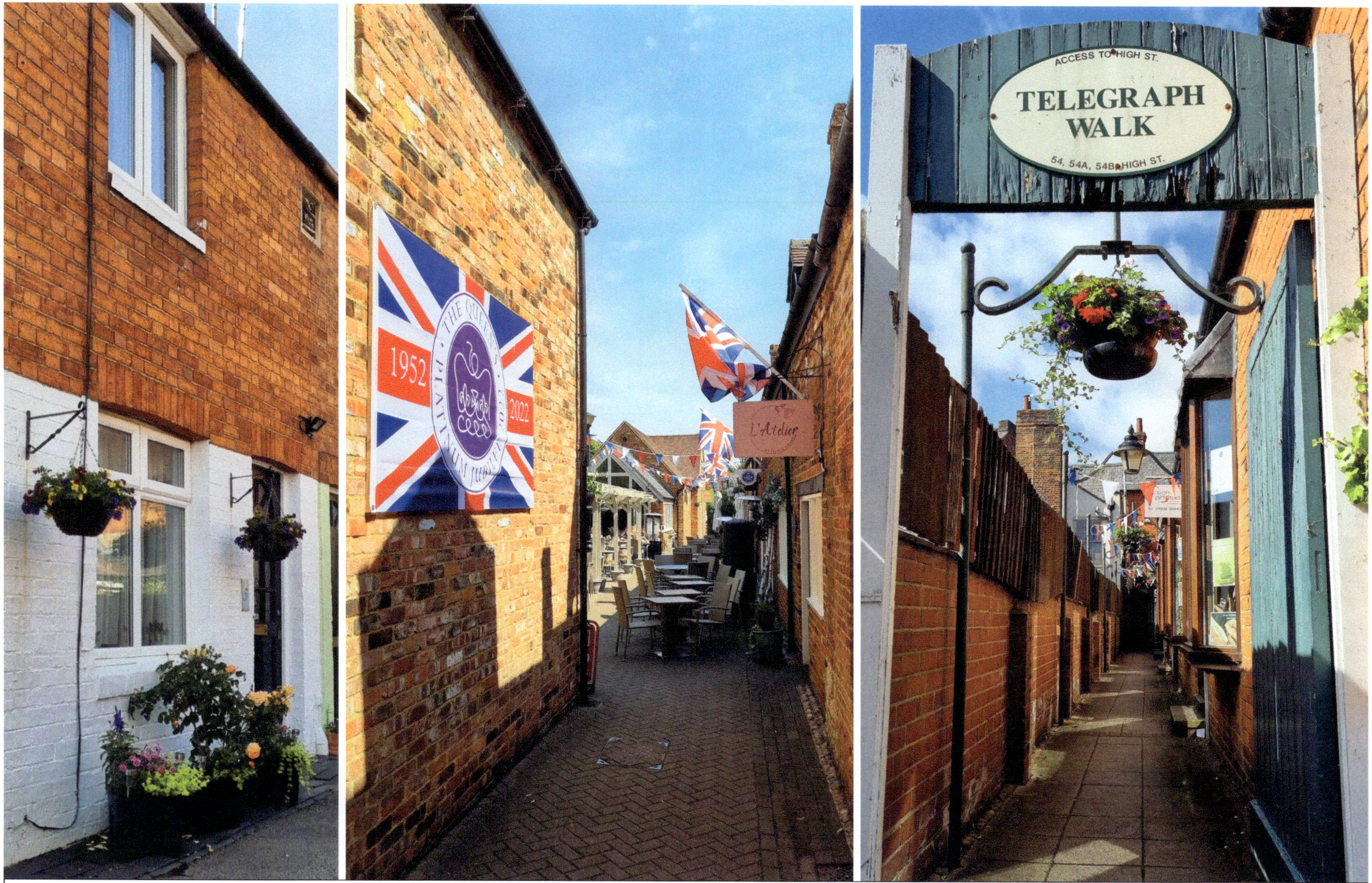

Residential and commercial developments at the back of the High Street.

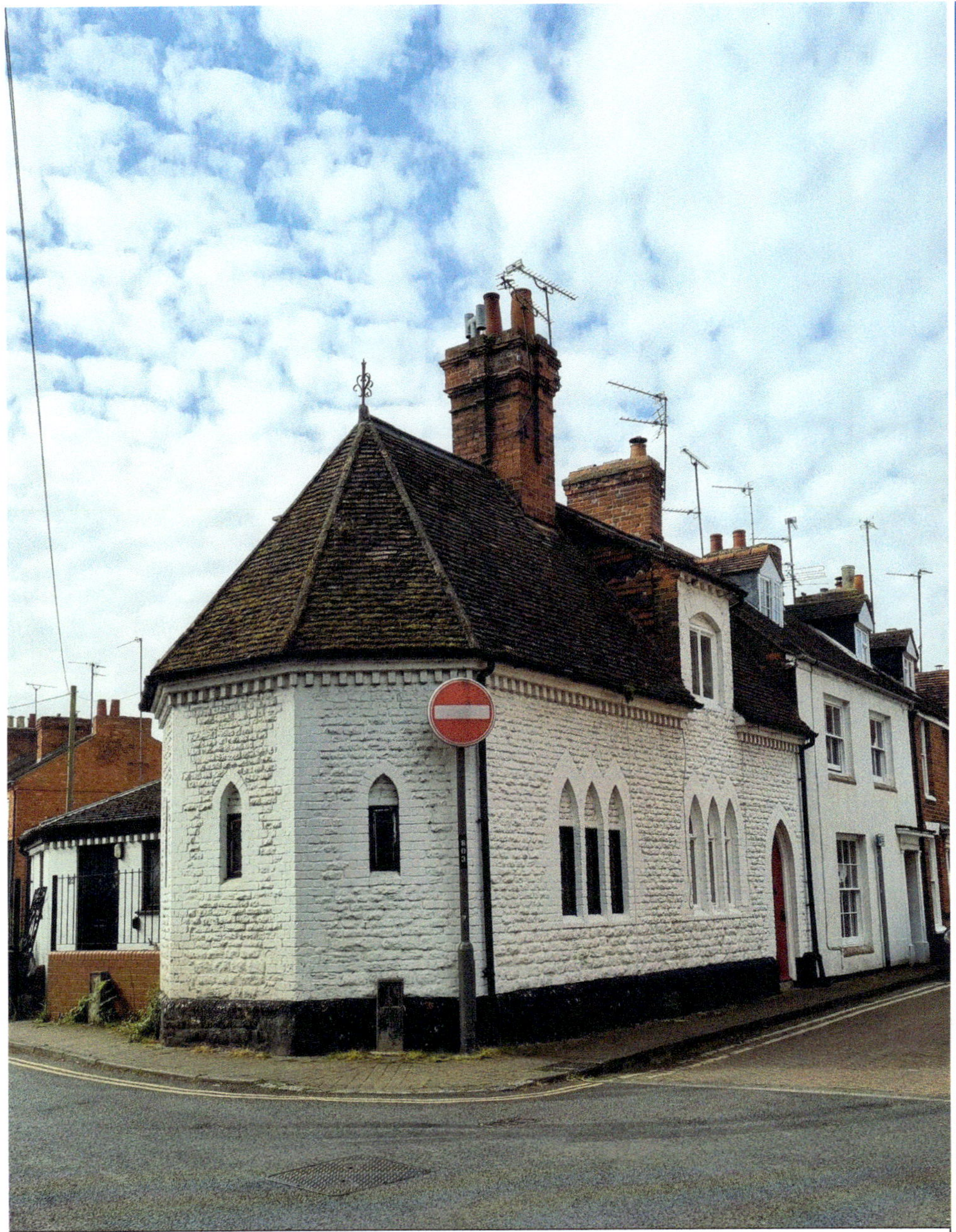

The corner of New Street and Russell Street.

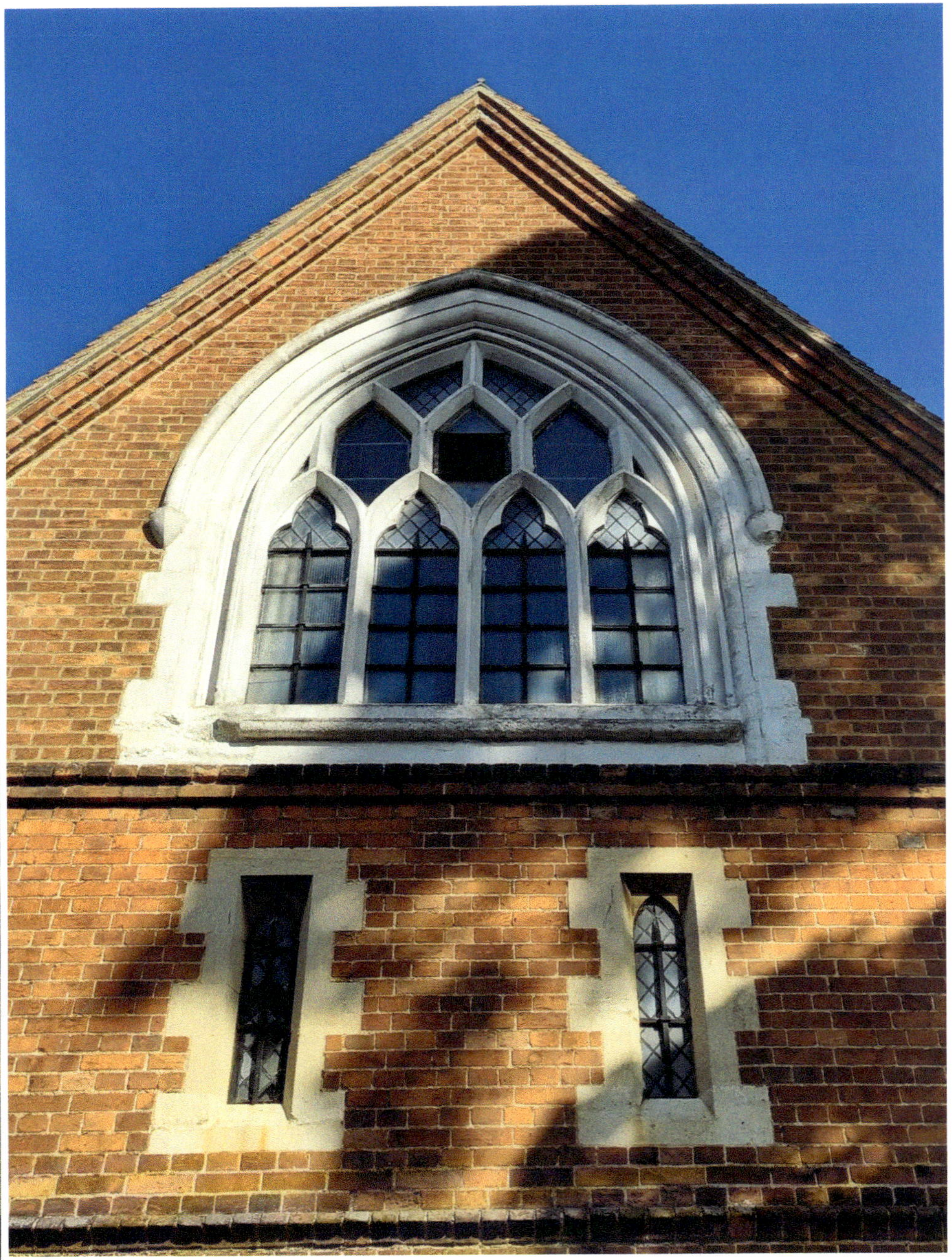

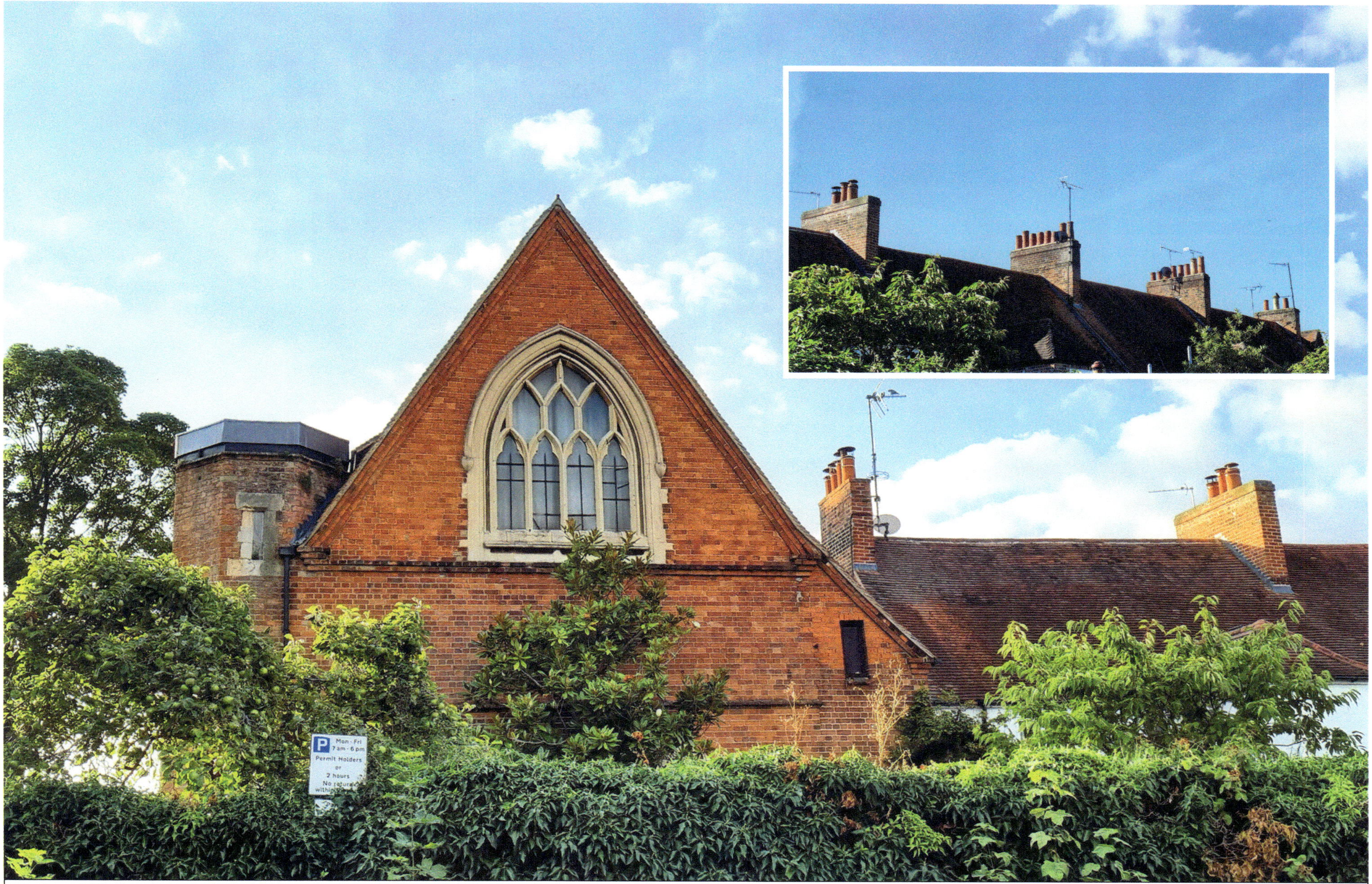

The Parish Hall at the end of New Street.

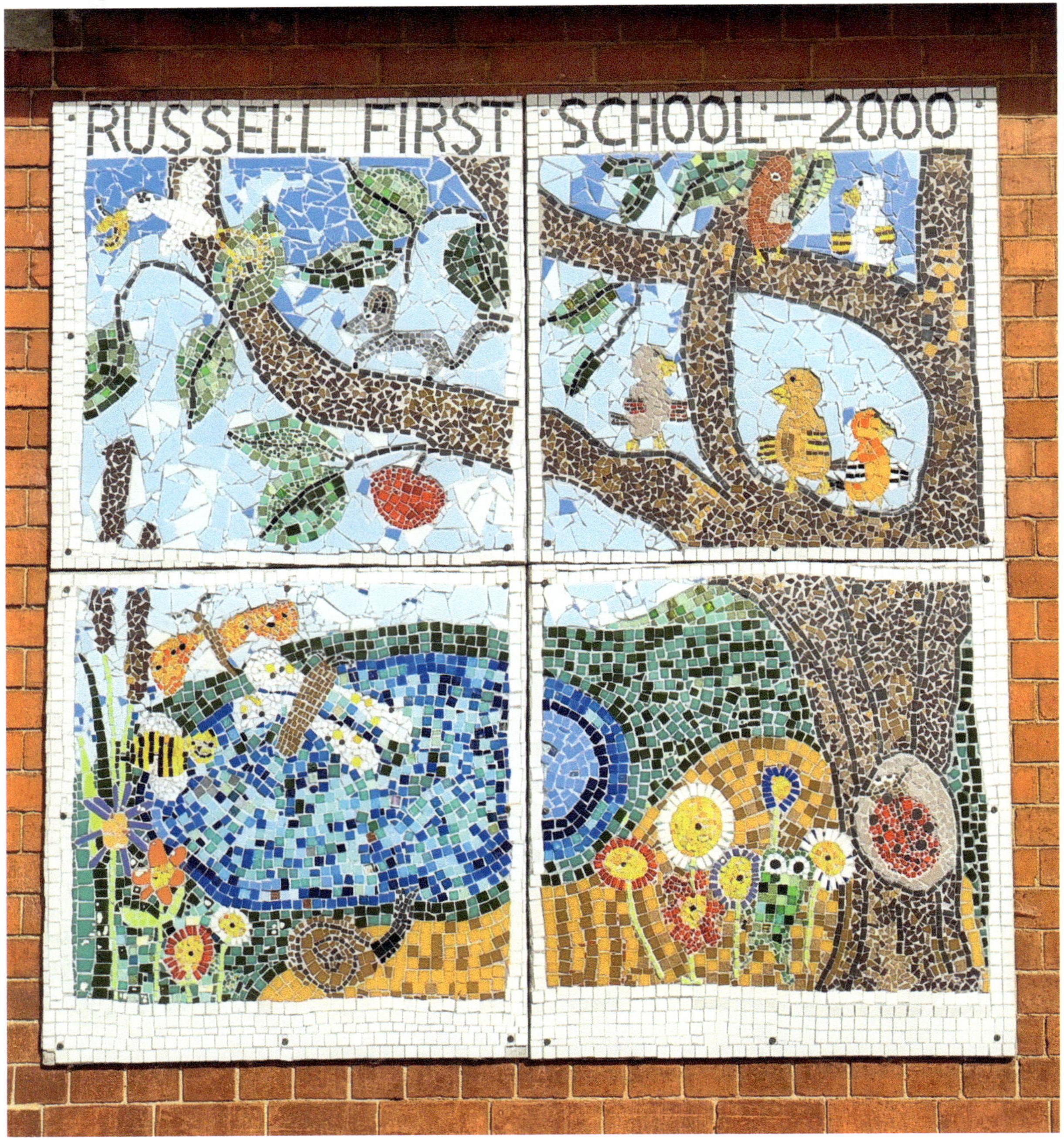
RUSSELL FIRST SCHOOL - 2000

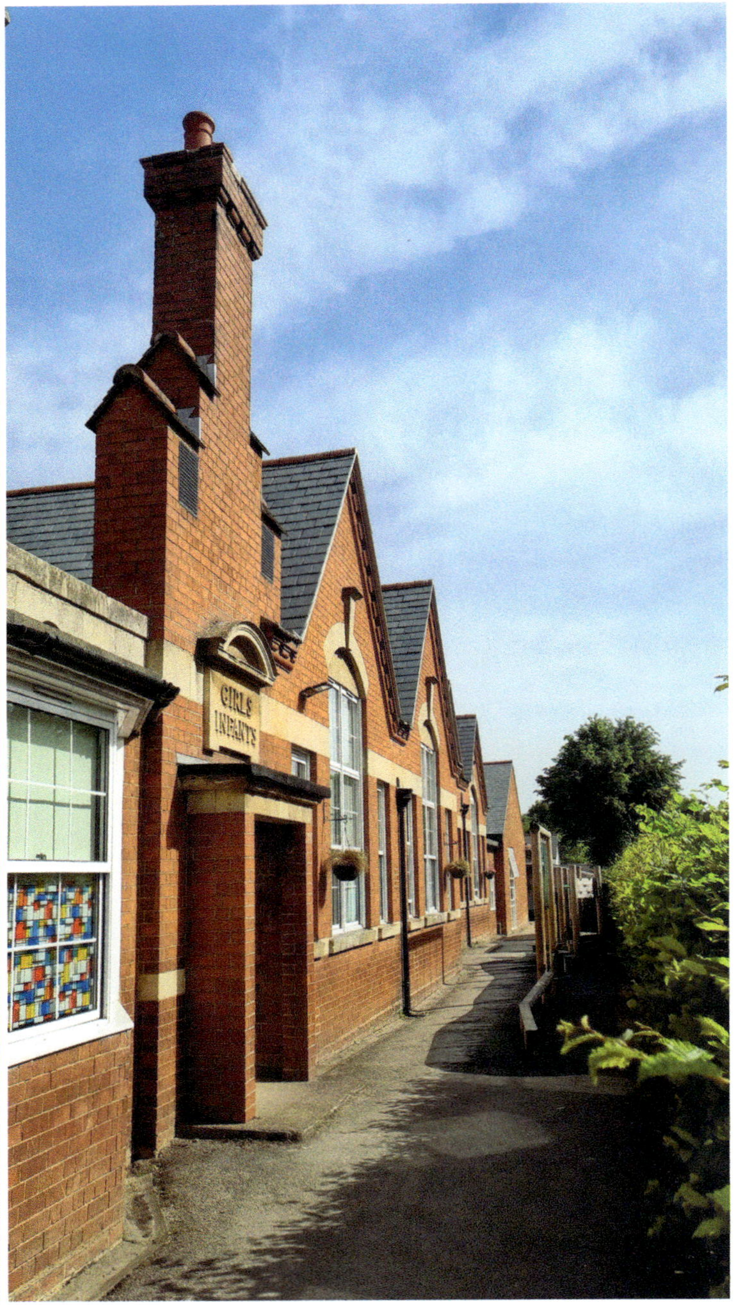
GIRLS
INFANTS

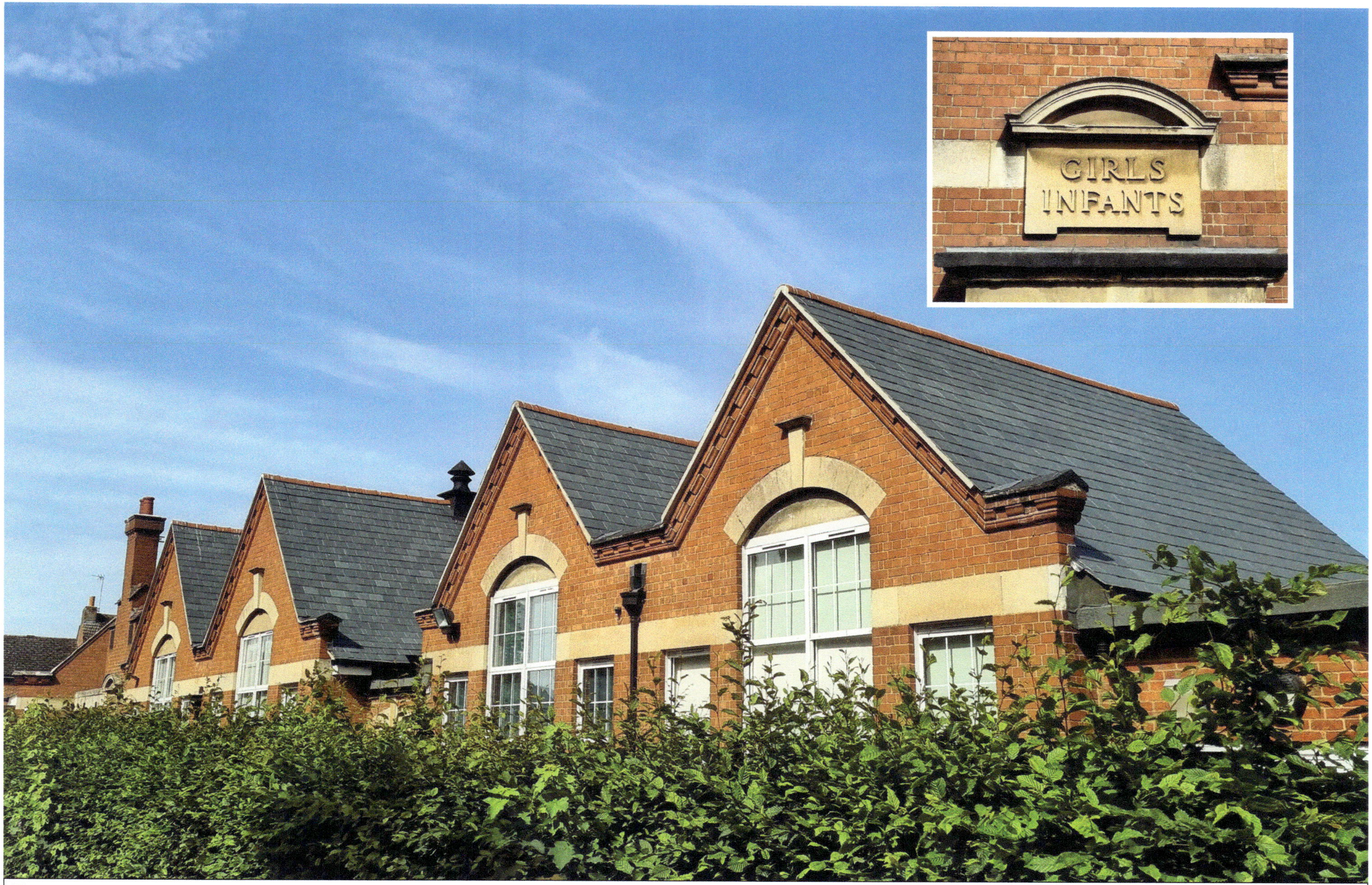

The Russell Street School, built in the early 20th century and opened in 1907.

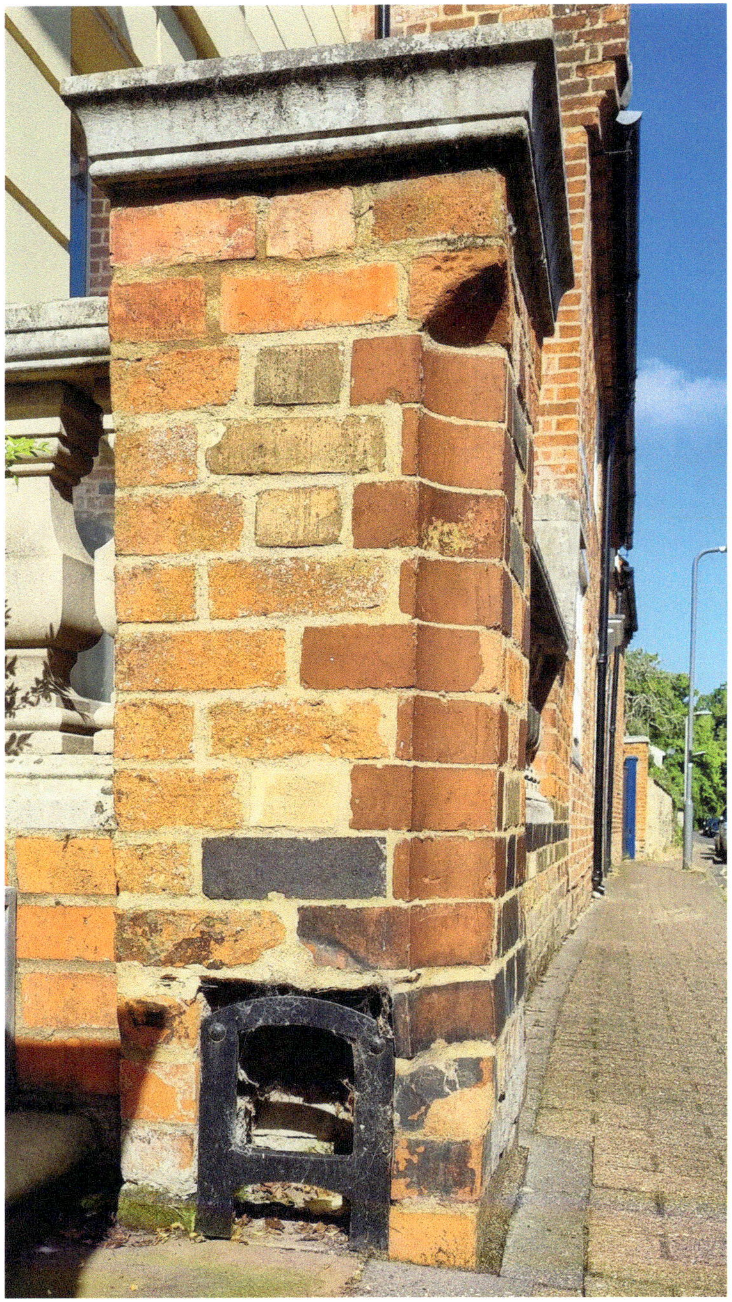
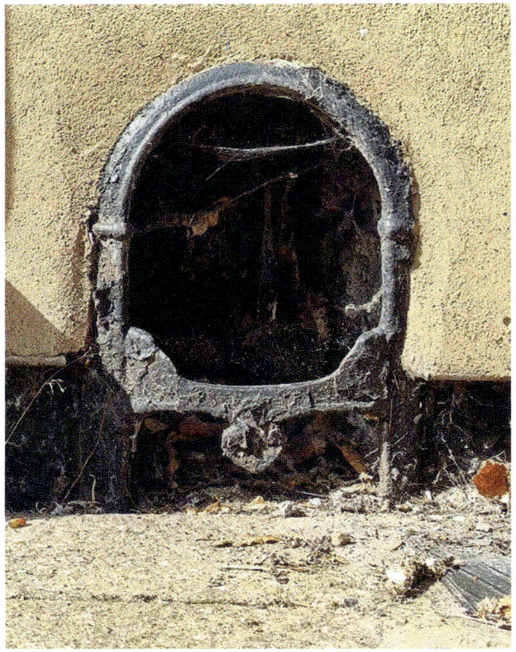
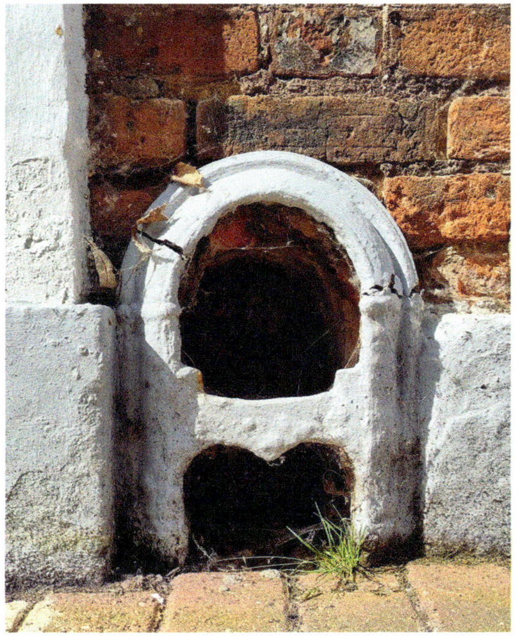
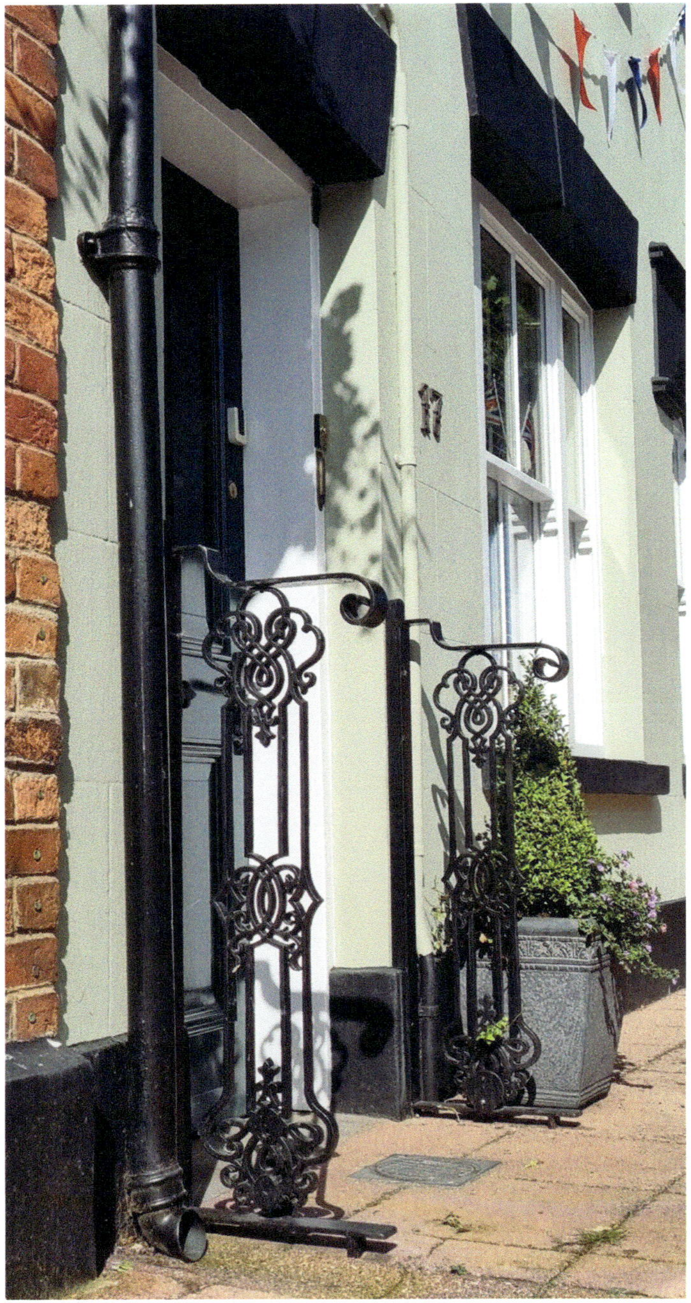

LOOK DOWN

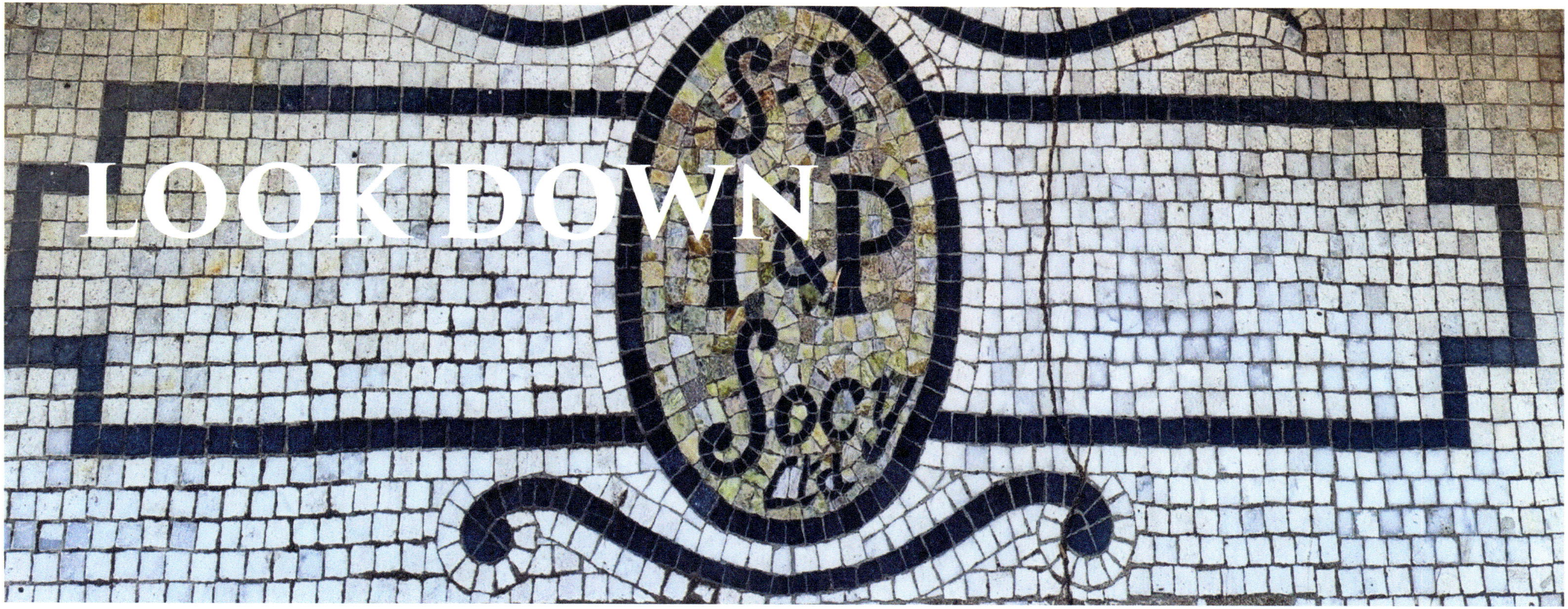

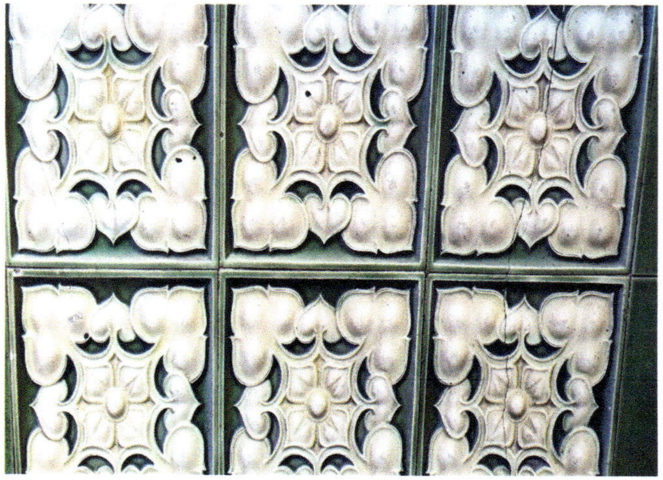

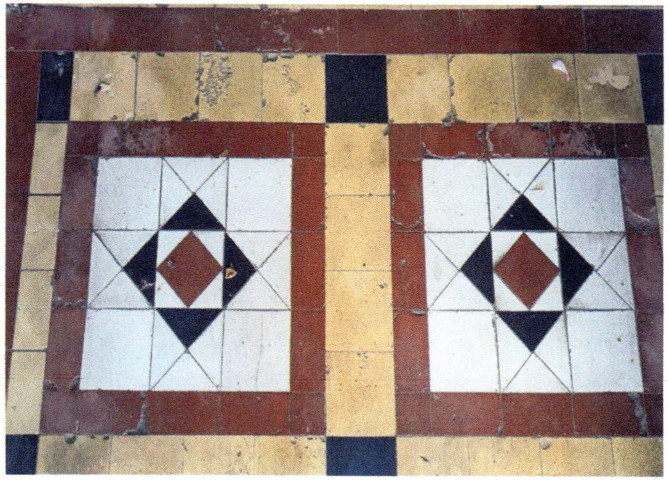

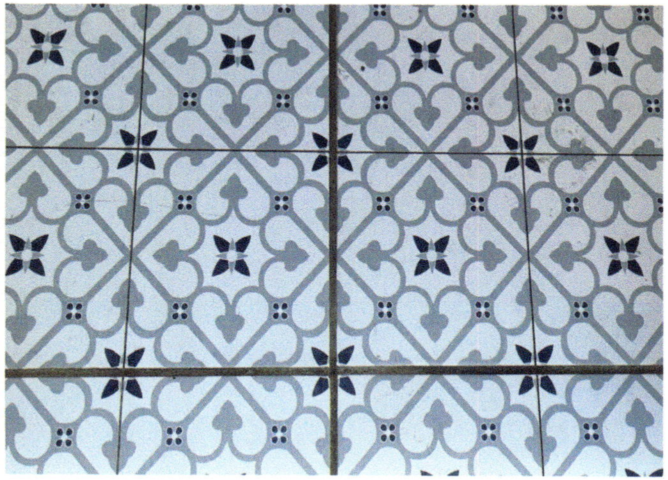

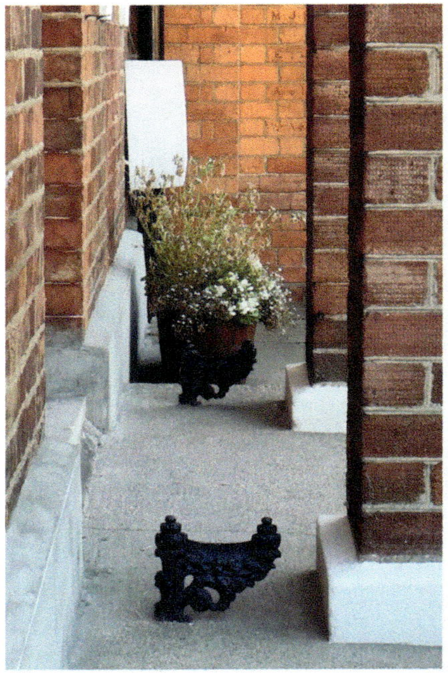
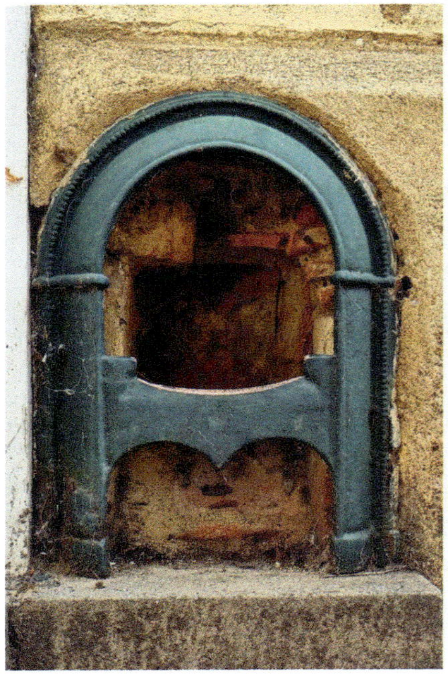
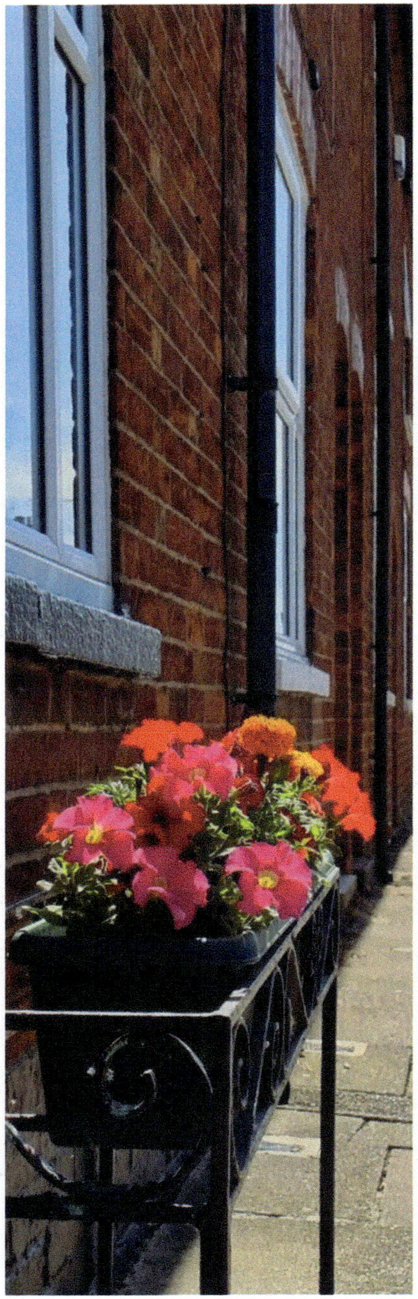
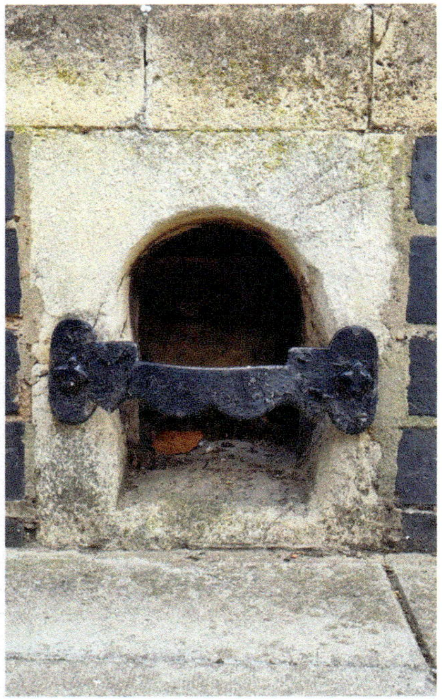
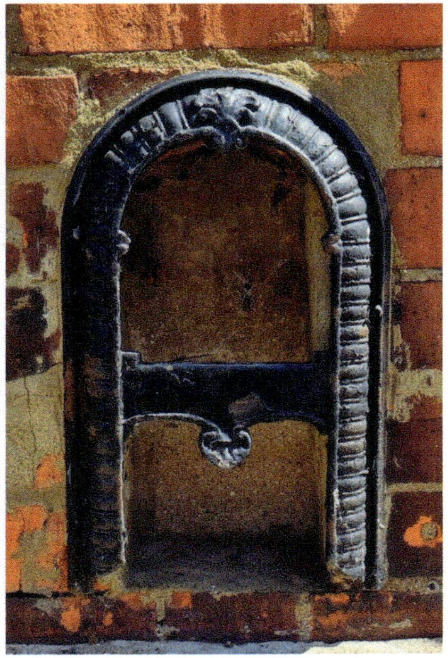
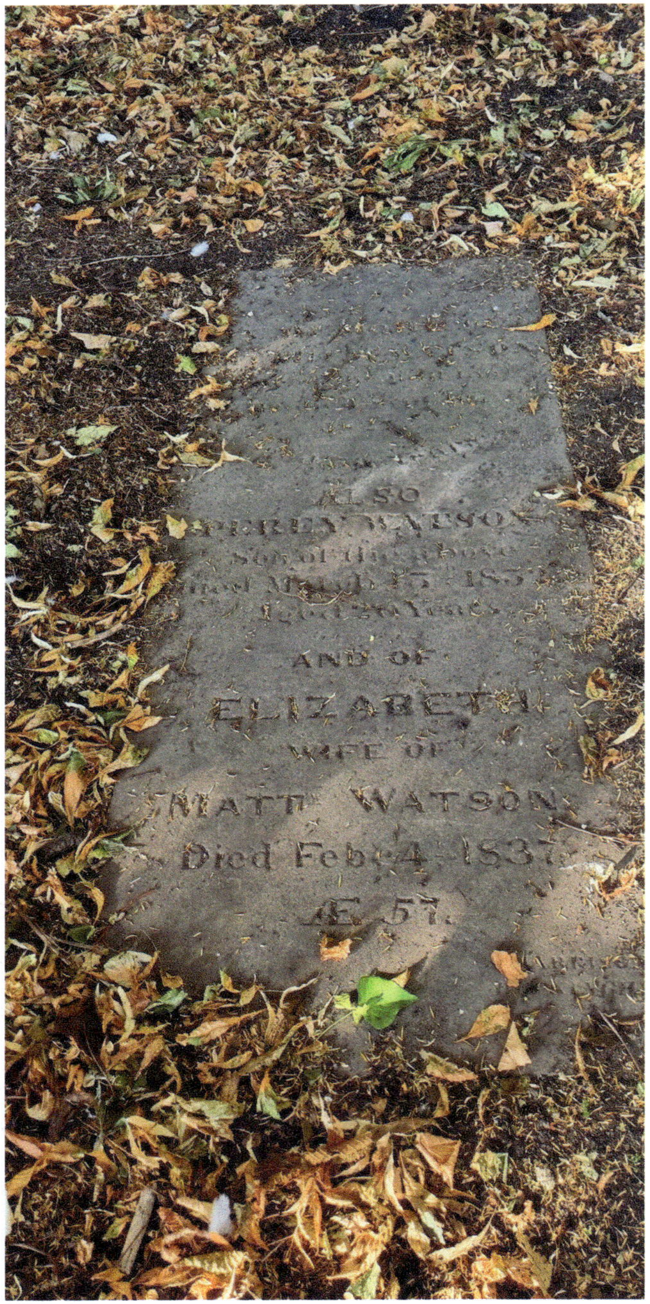
ALSO
AND OF
ELIZABETH
WIFE OF
MATT WATSON
Died Feb 4 1837
Æ 57.

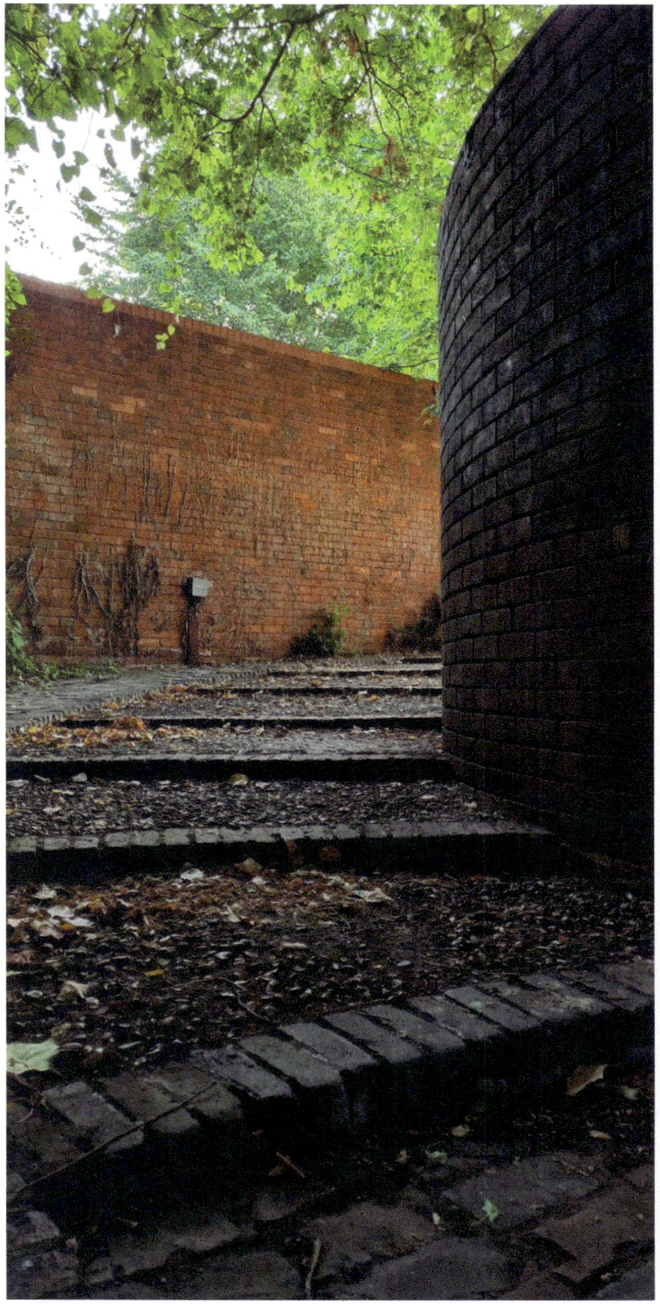
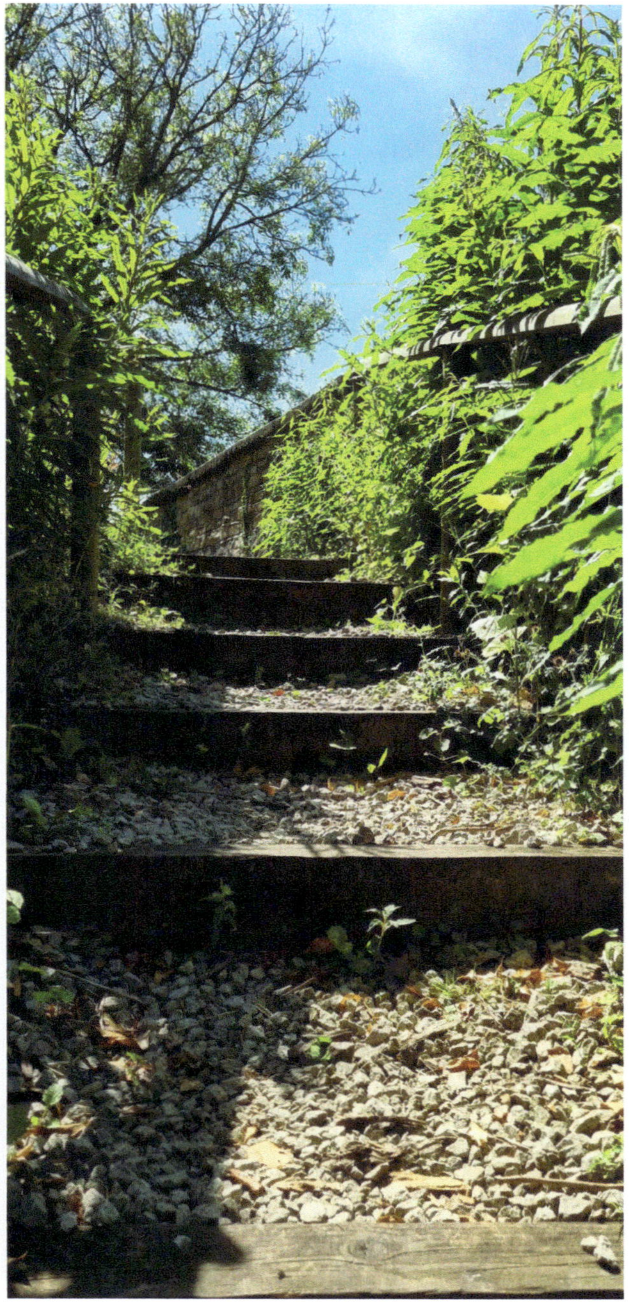
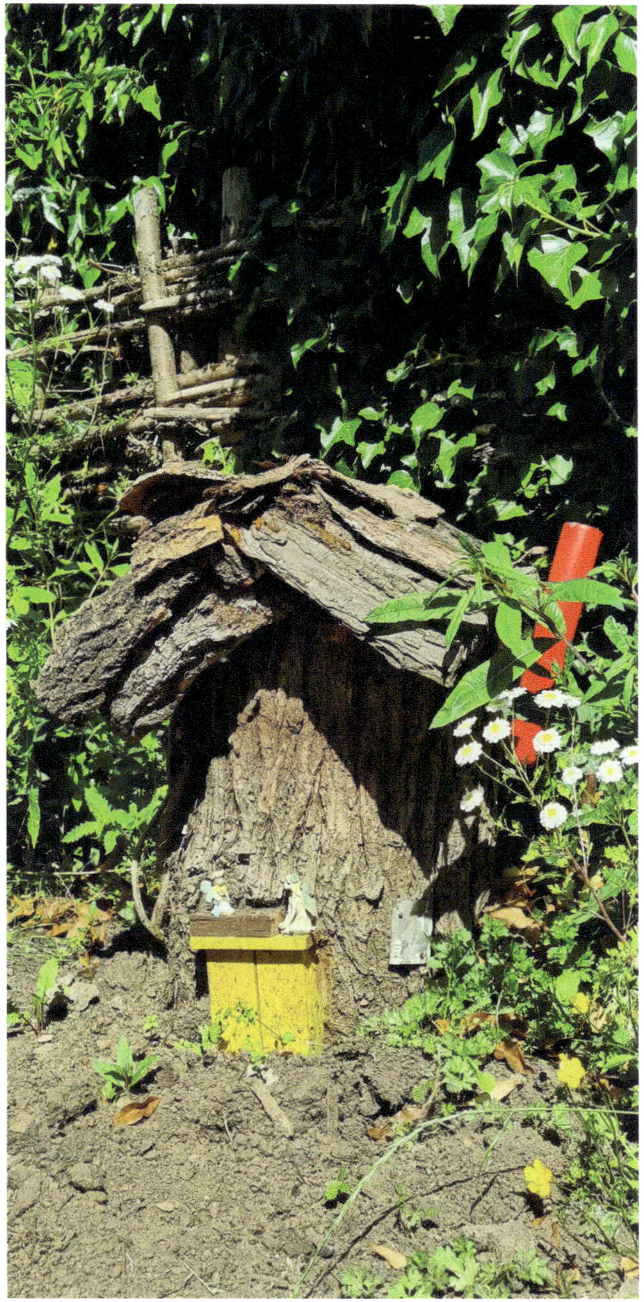

The London Road

The Watling Street was the dividing line between the Wolverton Manor on the east side and the Calverton Manor on the west side. Just over 800 years ago strips of land alongside the road began to create what we now know as Stony Stratford. After about 100 years two parishes emerged. The St Mary Magdalene parish extended from the High Street to the Back Lane (Russell Street) and ended at the corner of the Wolverton Road. The parish of St Giles held sway over the west side of the High Street to Mill Lane and Silver Street and to the south side of Cofferidge Close.

This system prevailed for many centuries and the few houses and farms on the London road were either in Wolverton or in Calverton. In fact, when development began in the late 19th century you either lived in the new parish of Wolverton St Mary or Calverton St Mary.

In the middle of the 19th century you would have discovered Debbs Farm near to Ancell Road and Brick Kiln Farm where the industrial estate of that name can be found today. On the corner of the London road and the Wolverton Road were some makeshift cottages and inn known as *The Plough*, formerly *The Sun* in the 18th centruy. On the Calverton side there was a farm and some houses on the South side of Horse Fair. Edward Hayes established his engineering works on vacant land on the Wolverton side.

The railway works at Wolverton prompted development along the Wolverton road. These new residents were technically in the Wolverton parish of Holy Trinity, but the expanding population encouraged the Vicar of Holy Trinity, William Pitt Trevelyan, to create a new church and parish, known as Wolverton St. Mary. Mostly at his own expense, he built a new church and associated buildings. Later he pioneered a second parish for Calverton, which also used the London Road church. He also engaged the services of Edward Swinfen Harris to build a new school. This building has been used as a pub since 1936.

Clarence Road branched off the London Road in the 1890s and Coronation Road in the first decade of the 20th century. Most of the development along this road took place in the 20th century.

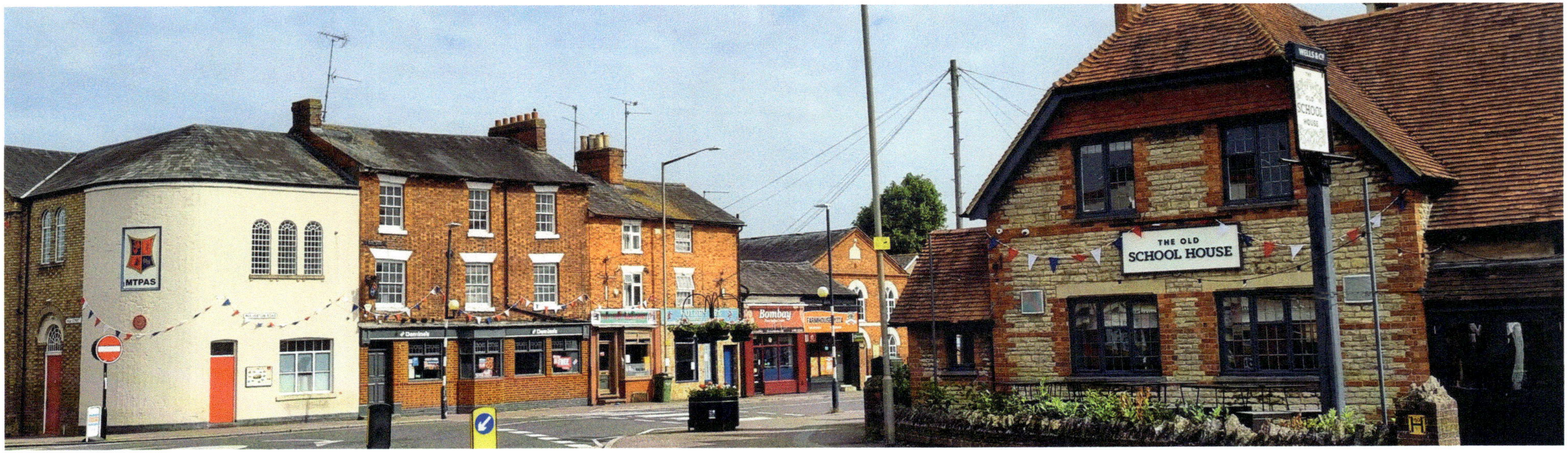

LOOK AT THE LONDON ROAD

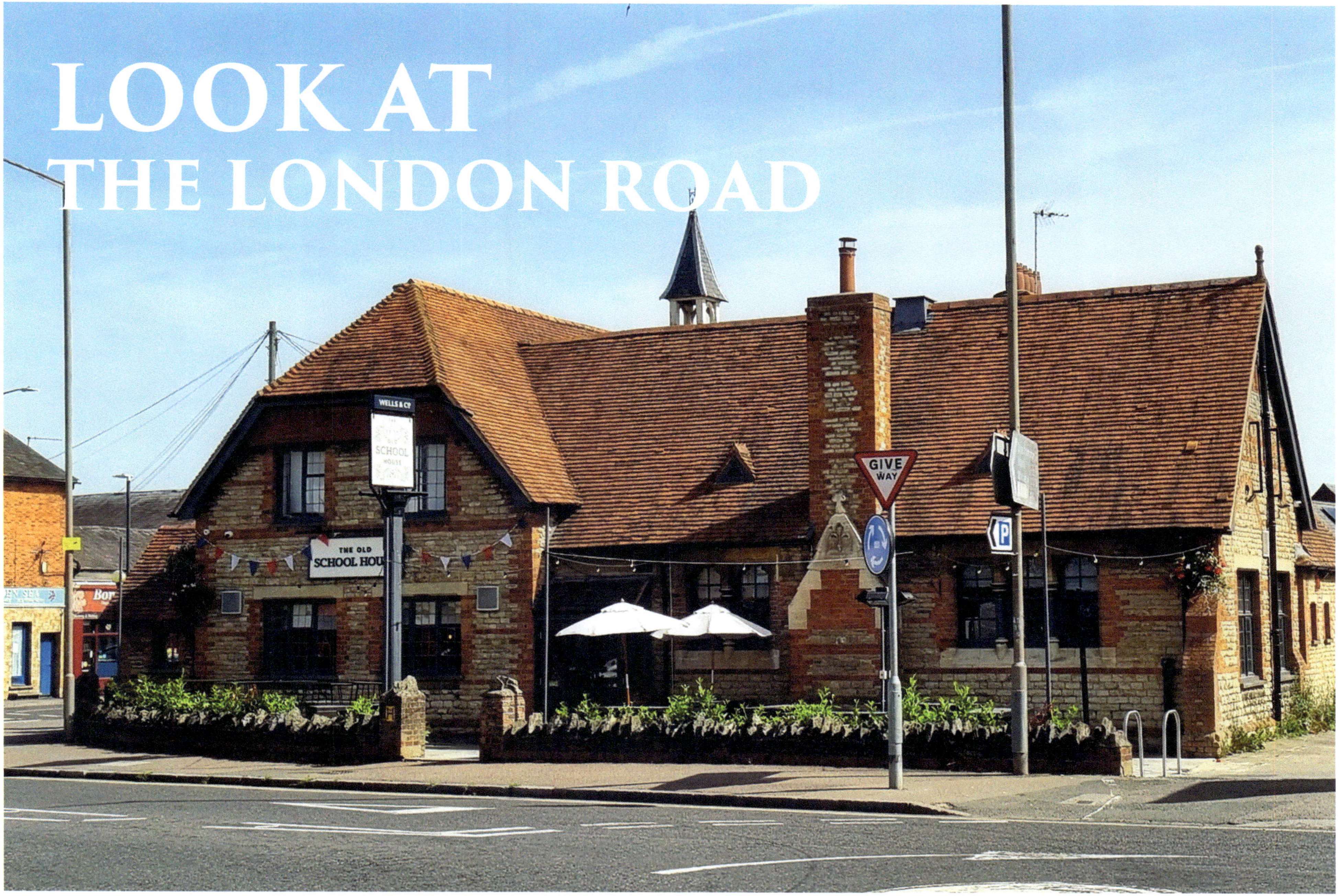

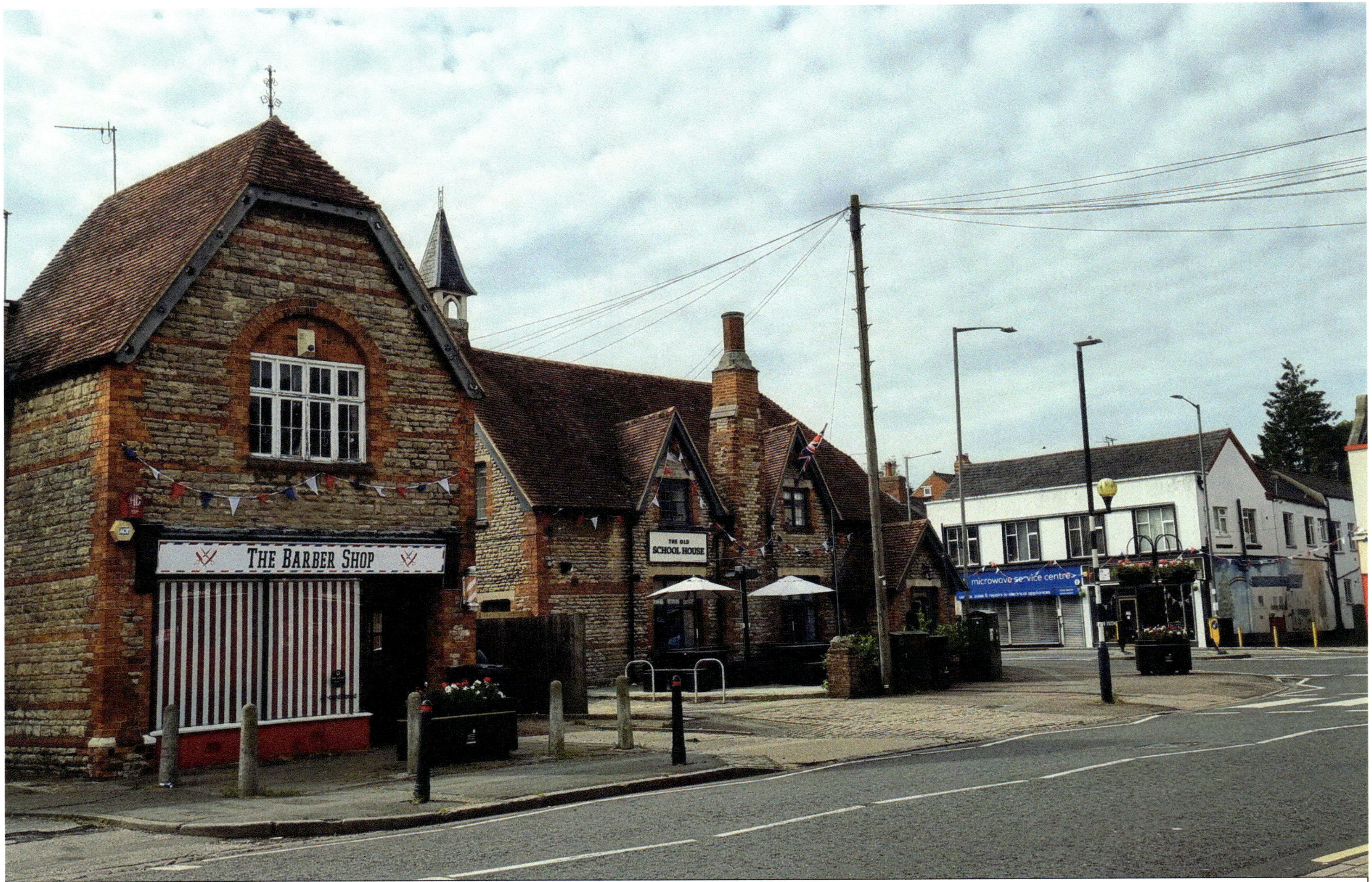

The distinctive buildings at the corner were designed as a school and a schoolteacher's house in the 19th century.

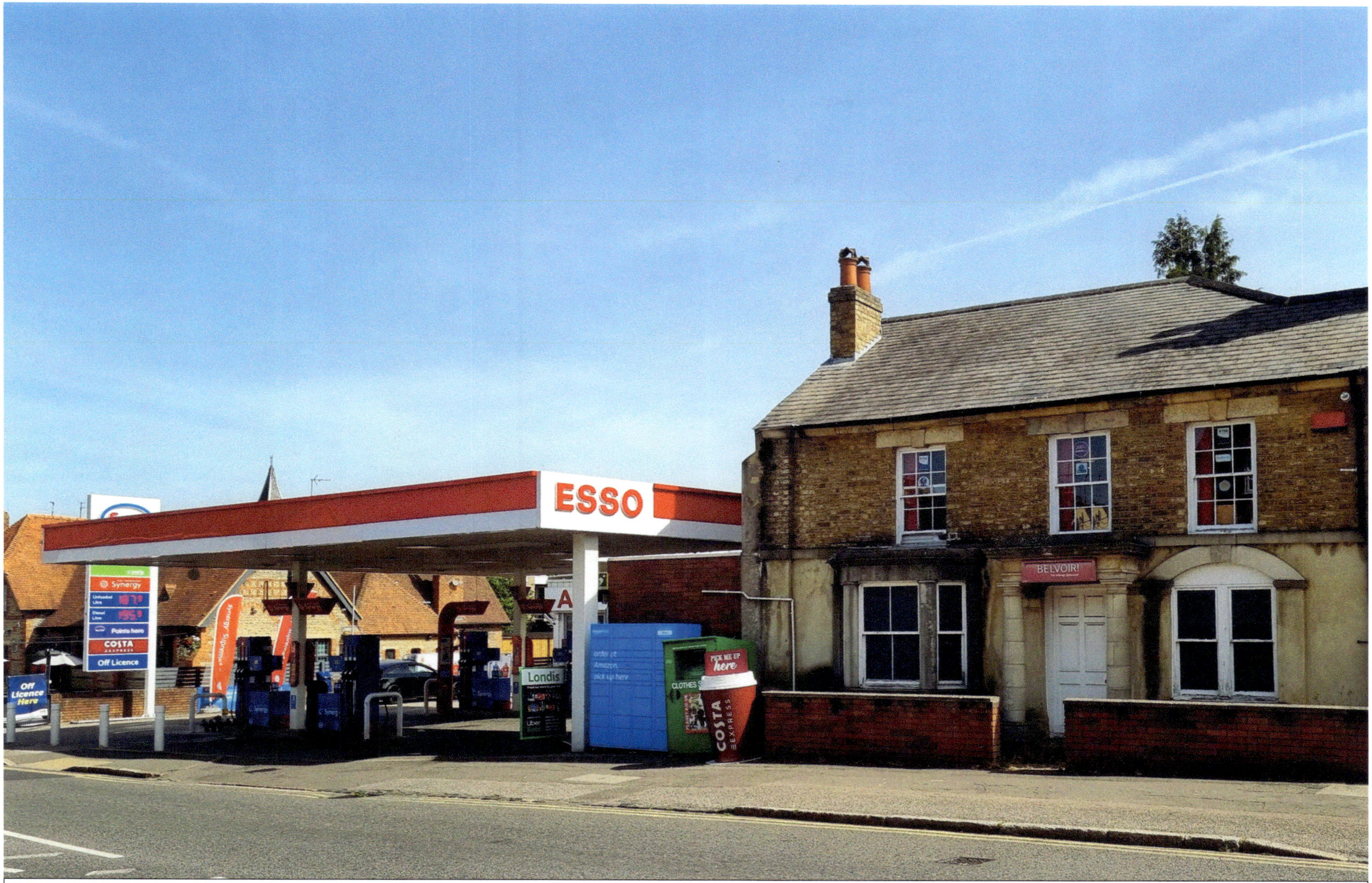

The site of the garage was occupied by an inn known as The Plough and Cave's Garage. When the Plough moved next door to the school in 1936 the pub was cleared to expand the garage.

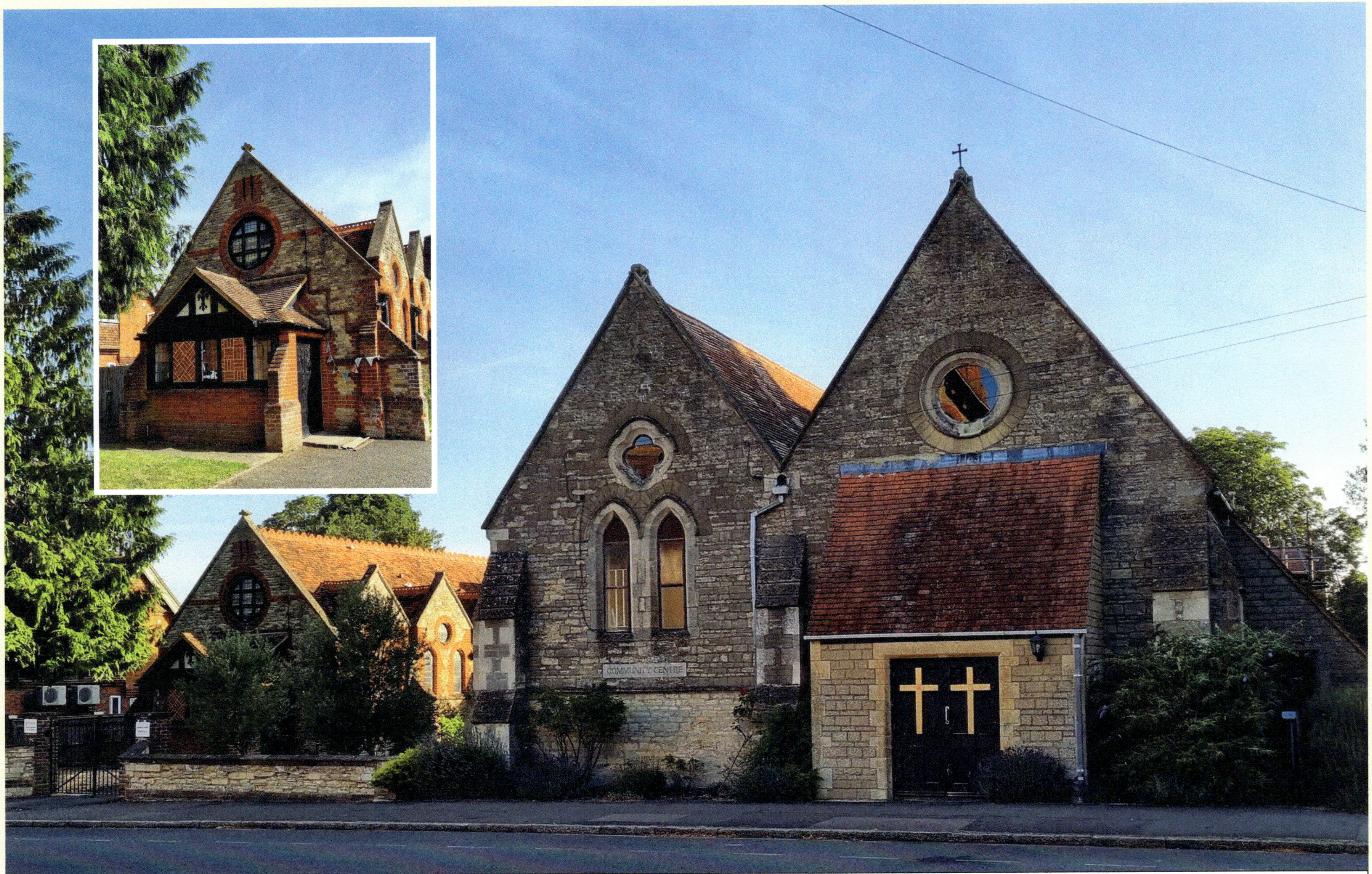

William Pitt Trevelyan, vicar of Holy Trinity at Wolverton, built the new church of St Mary's in the 1860s, largely at his own expense.

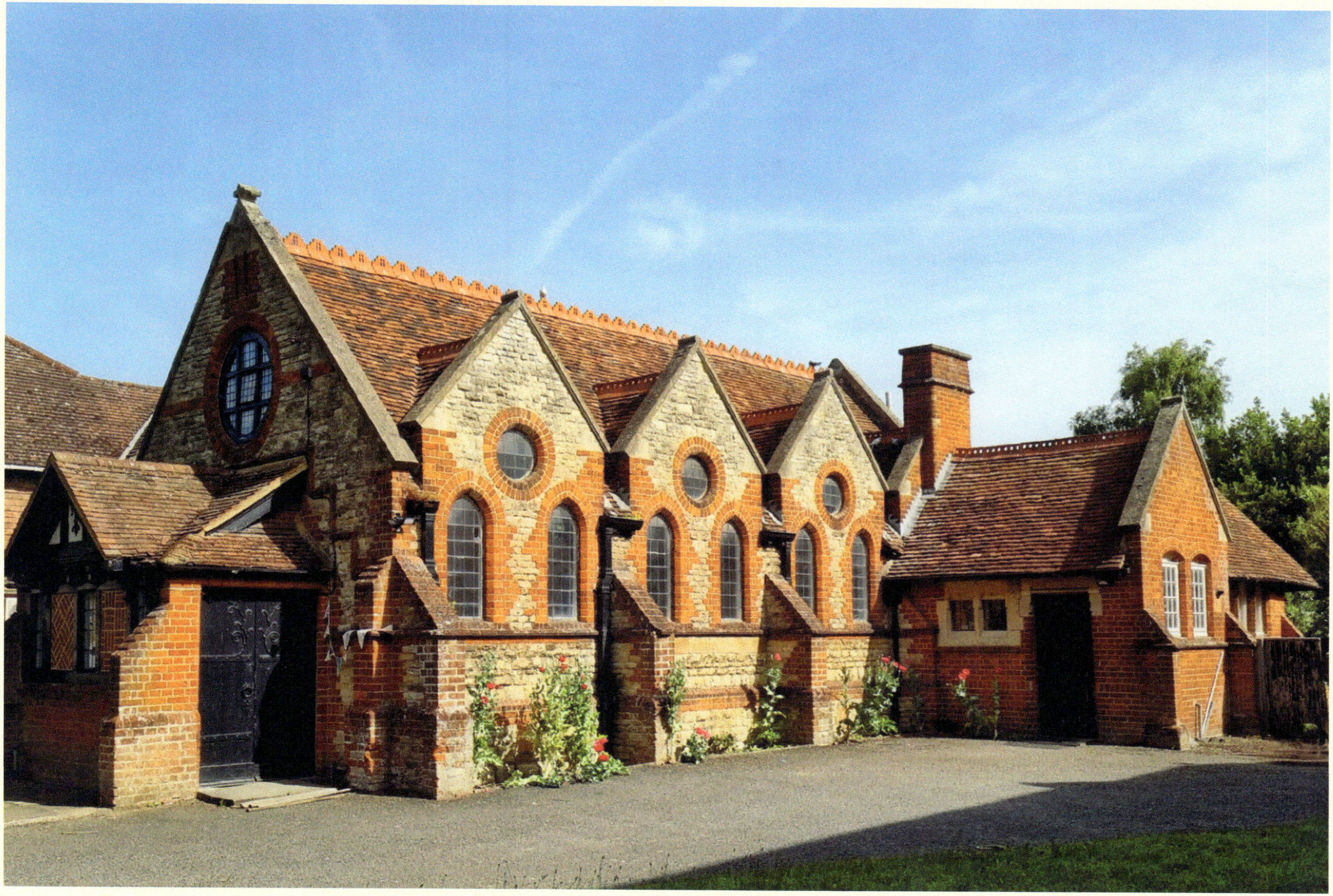

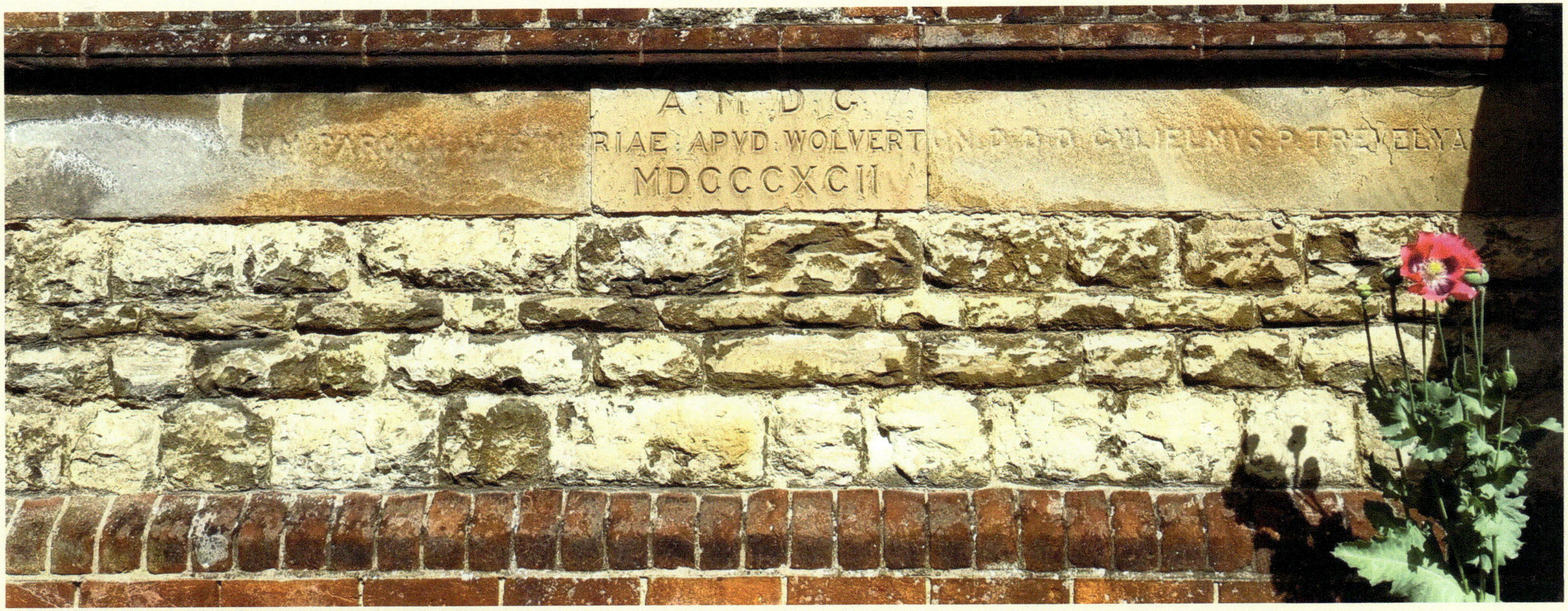

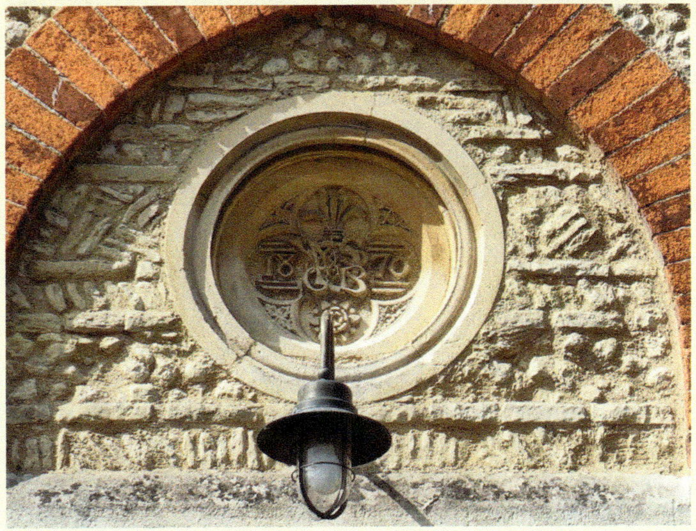

William Pitt Trevelyan

He was born to a prosperous west country family in 1812. He went to Australia as a young man and within a decade had made a good deal of money. Once financially secure, he returned to England to study at Oxford and take holy orders. He was appointed Vicar of Holy Trinity in 1859 and immediately set about using his private means to improve the community. He first built the school at Old Wolverton and then turned his attention to the west side of his parish, which was growing along the Wolverton Road. He built the new church of St Mary's on the London Road and then the school, which was converted to a pub after 1936. He opted to exchange his parish for that of Calverton, which was also growing, and in 1892 he completed his spacious house, now known as Calverton Limes. The house accommodated his family and about five servants. He died in 1905.

His building contributions to Wolverton and Stony Stratford are considerable.

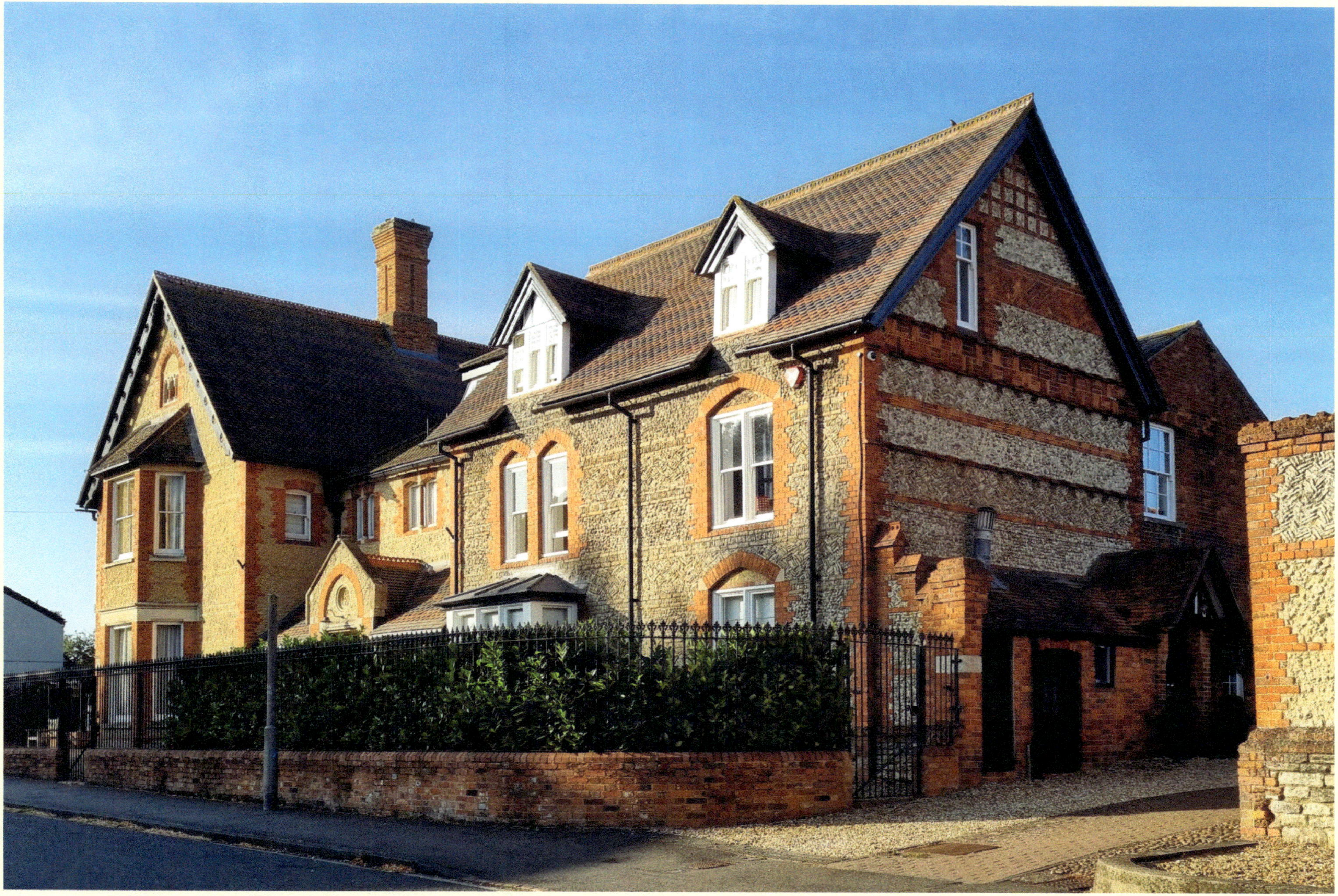

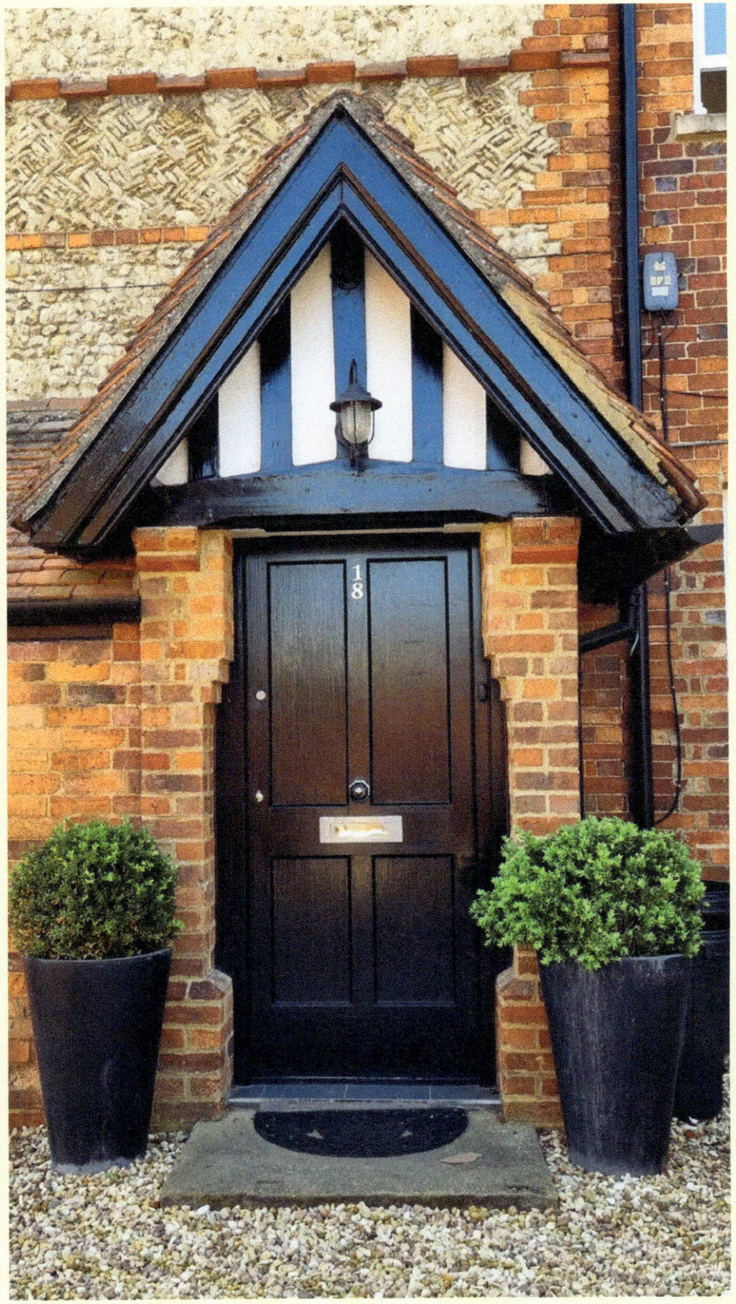
18

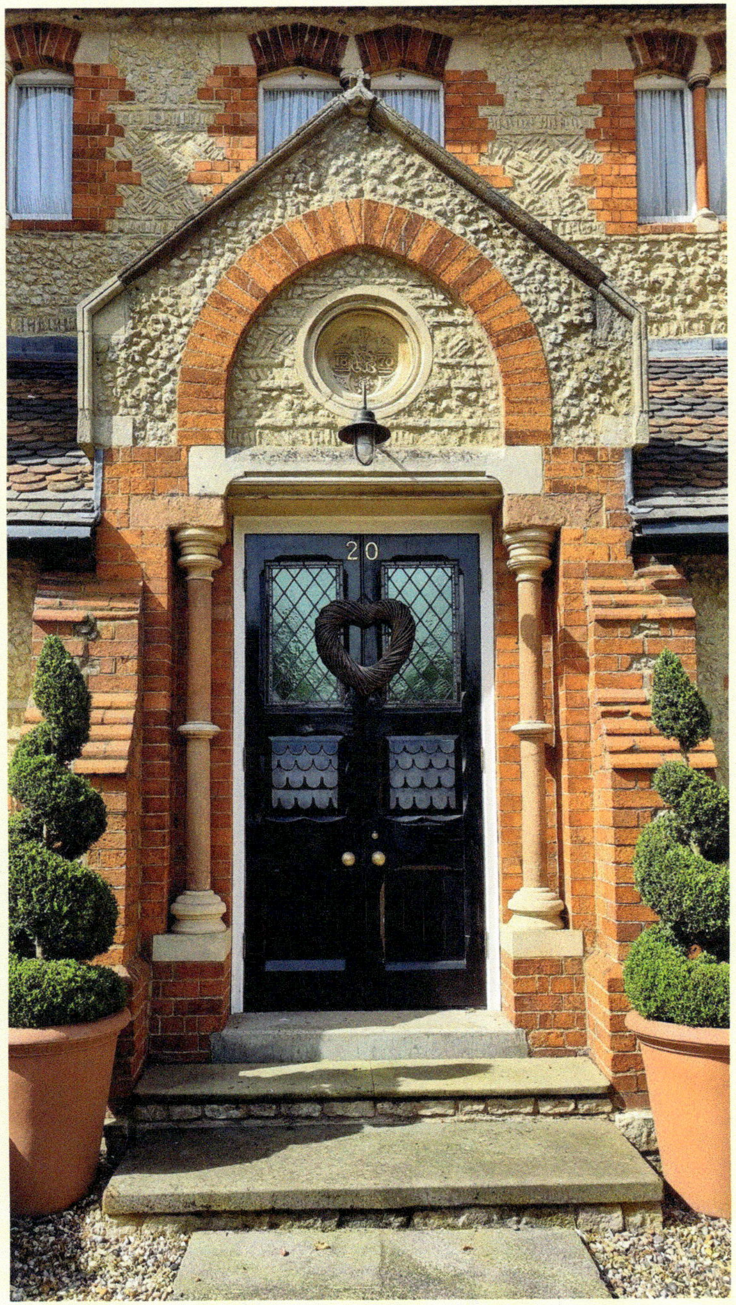
20

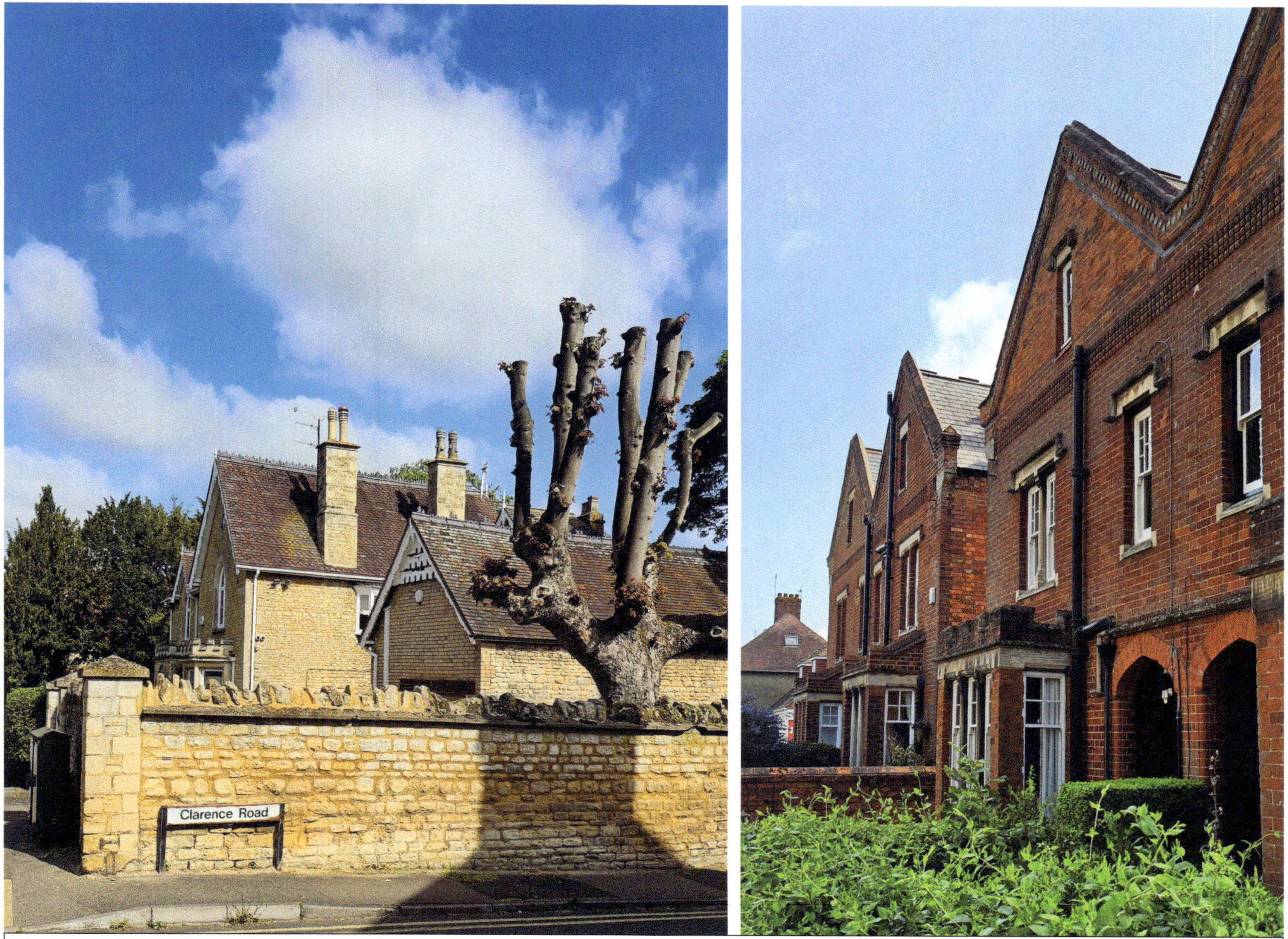

Clarence Road, created at the end of the Victorian period.

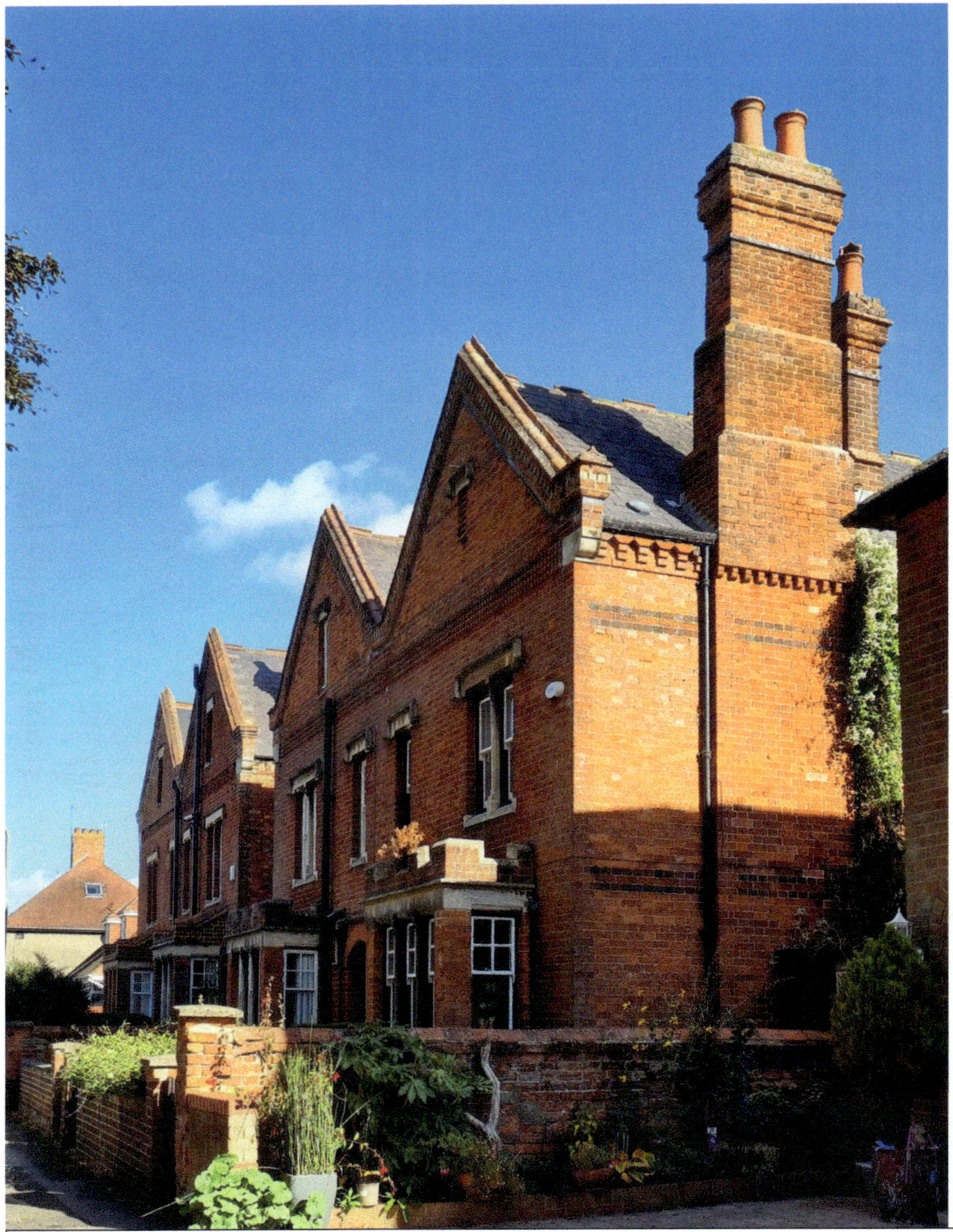

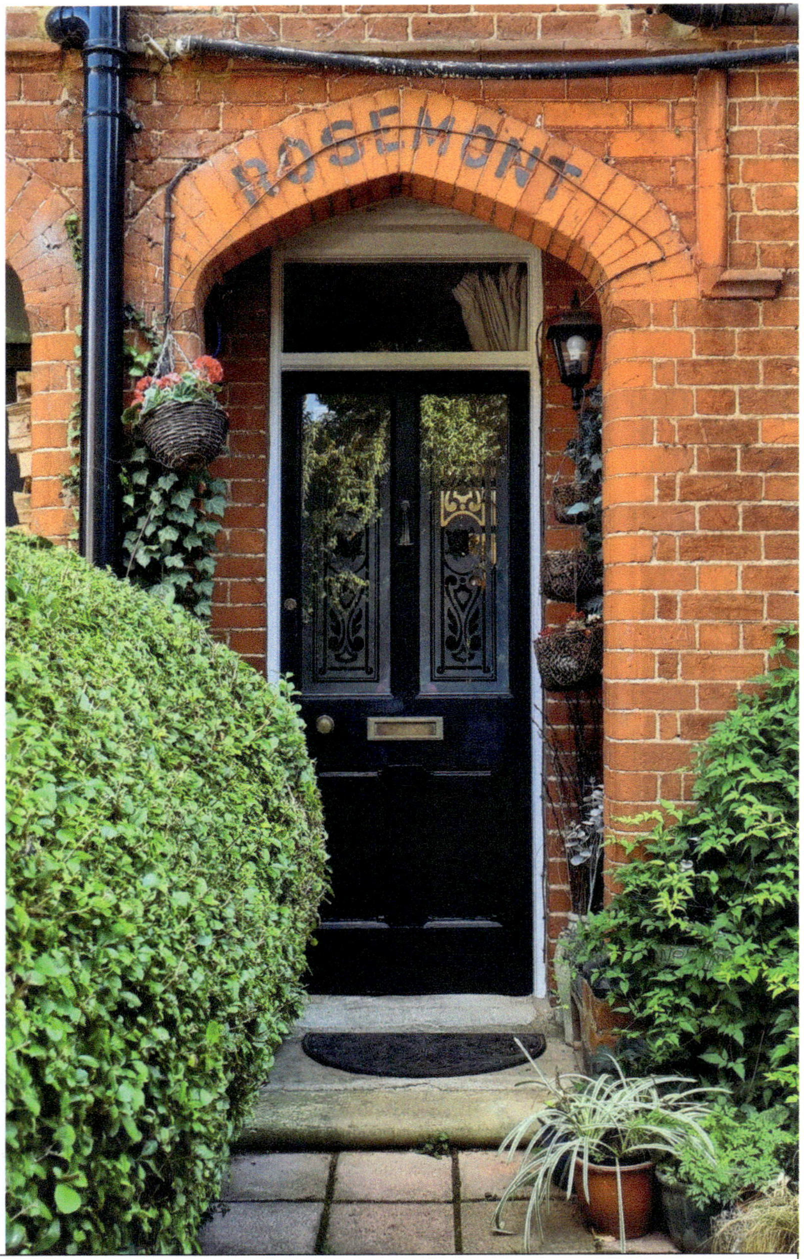

Clarence Road properties shown on pages 144 and 145.

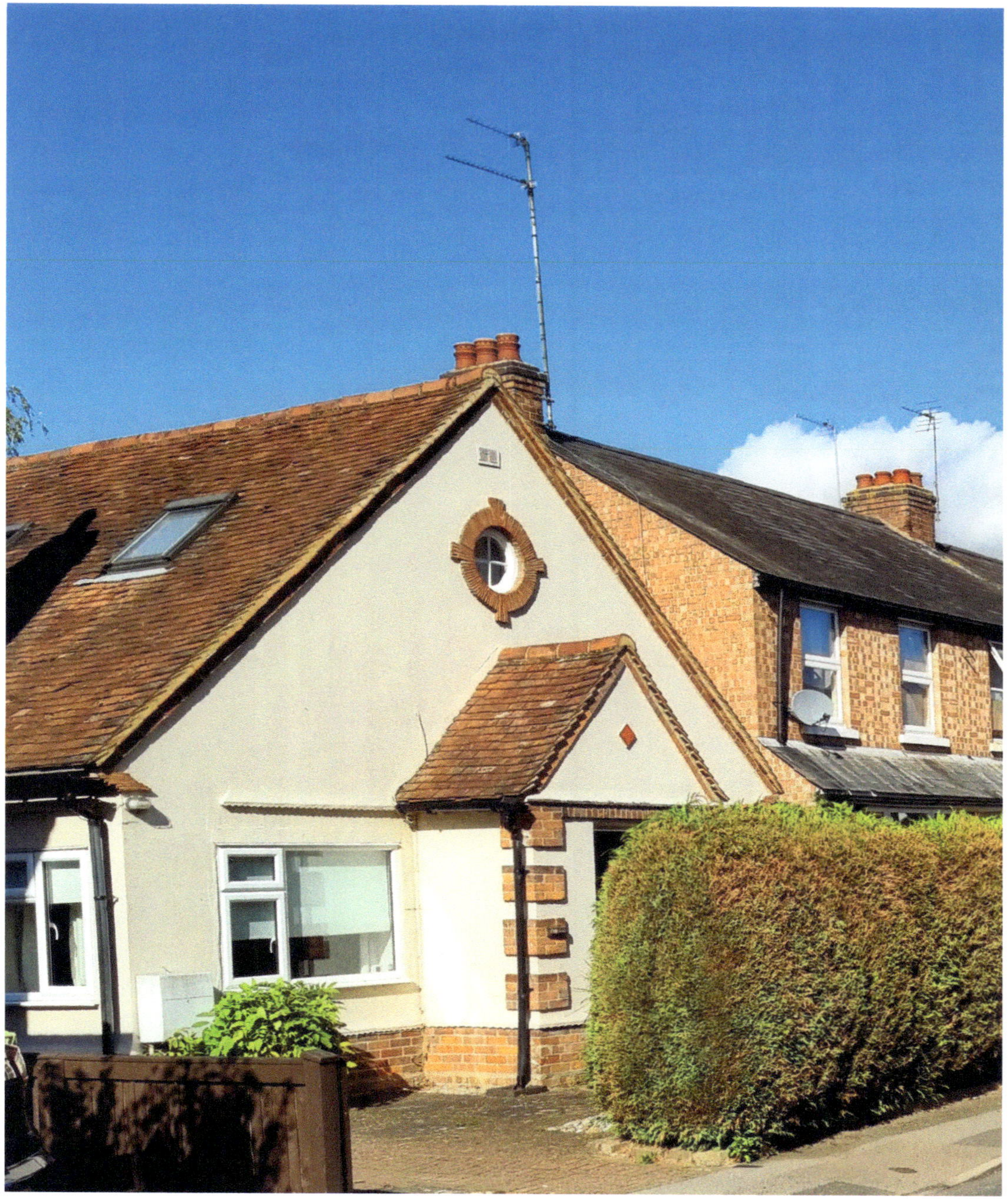

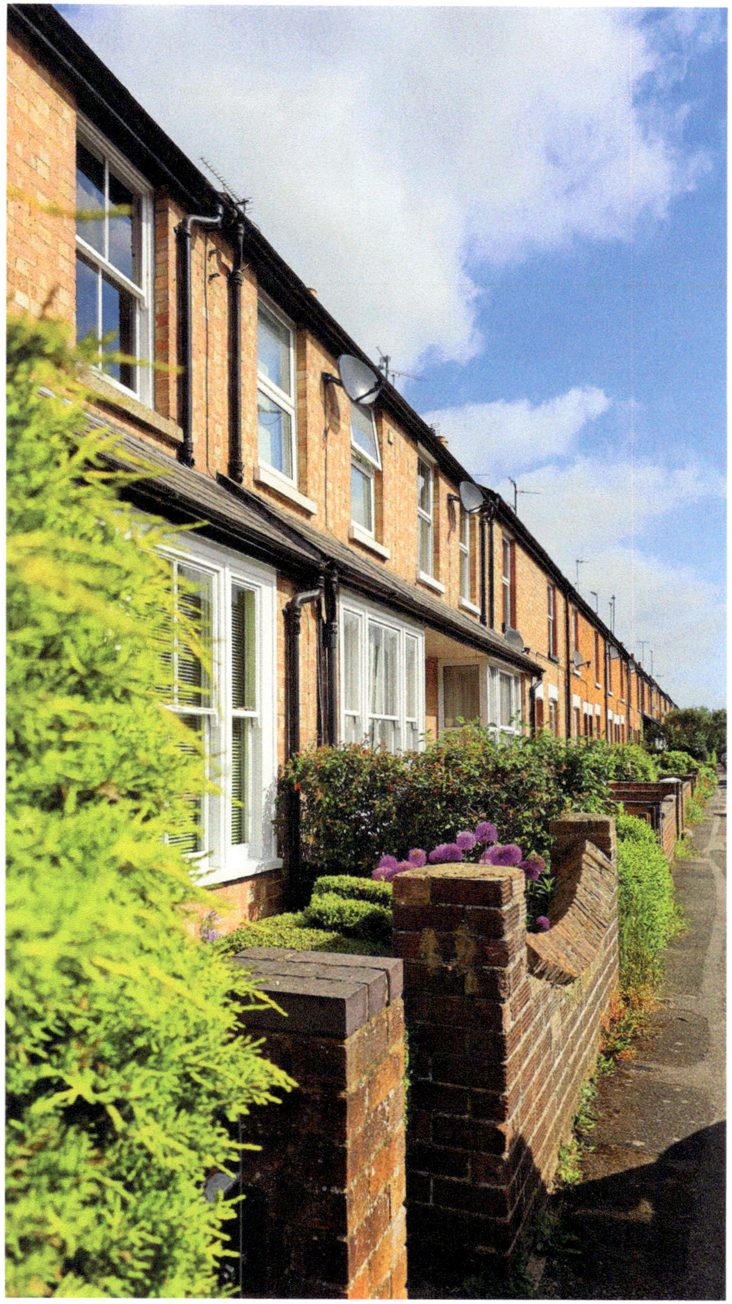

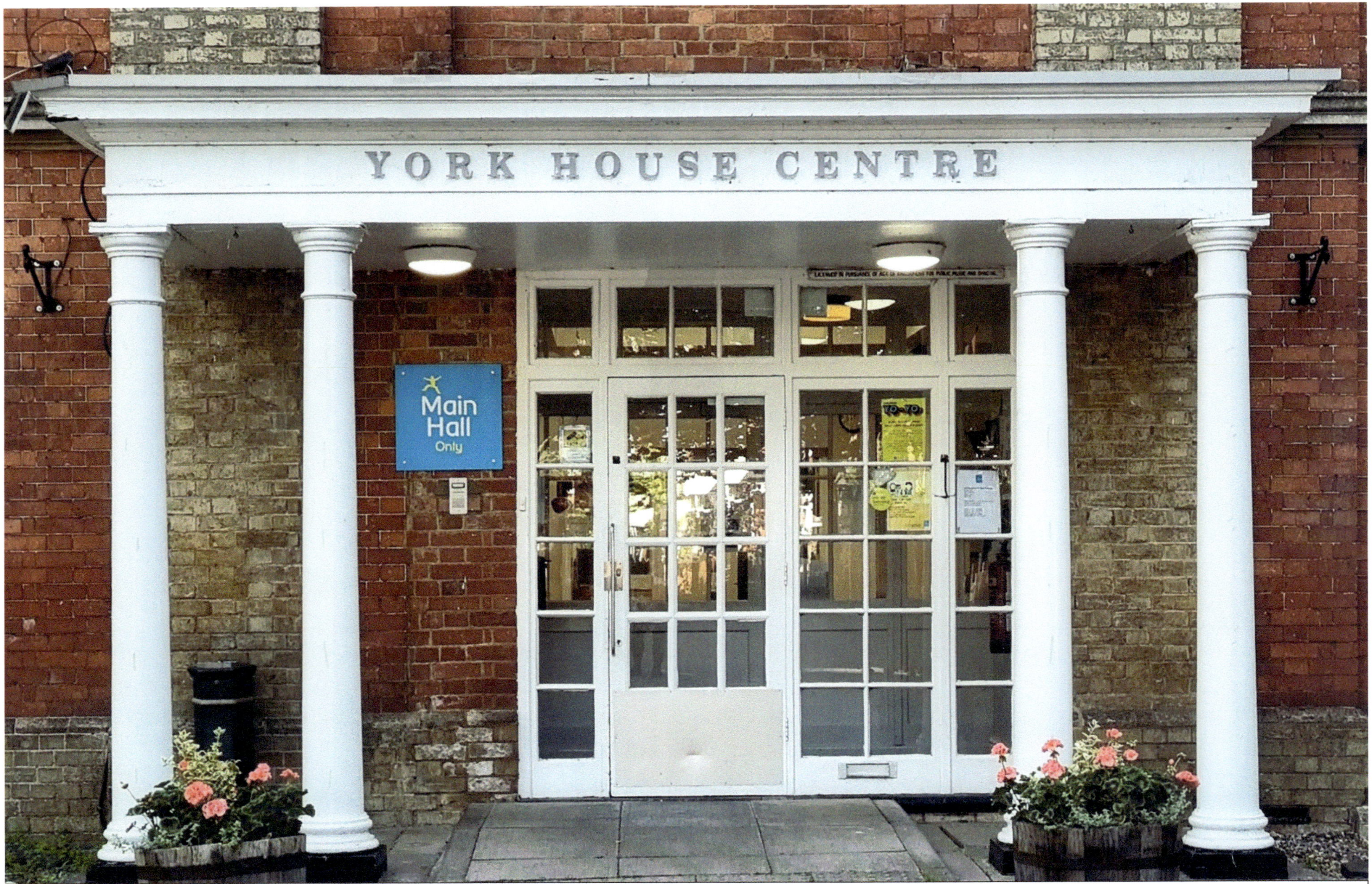

York House. For the story see page 34.

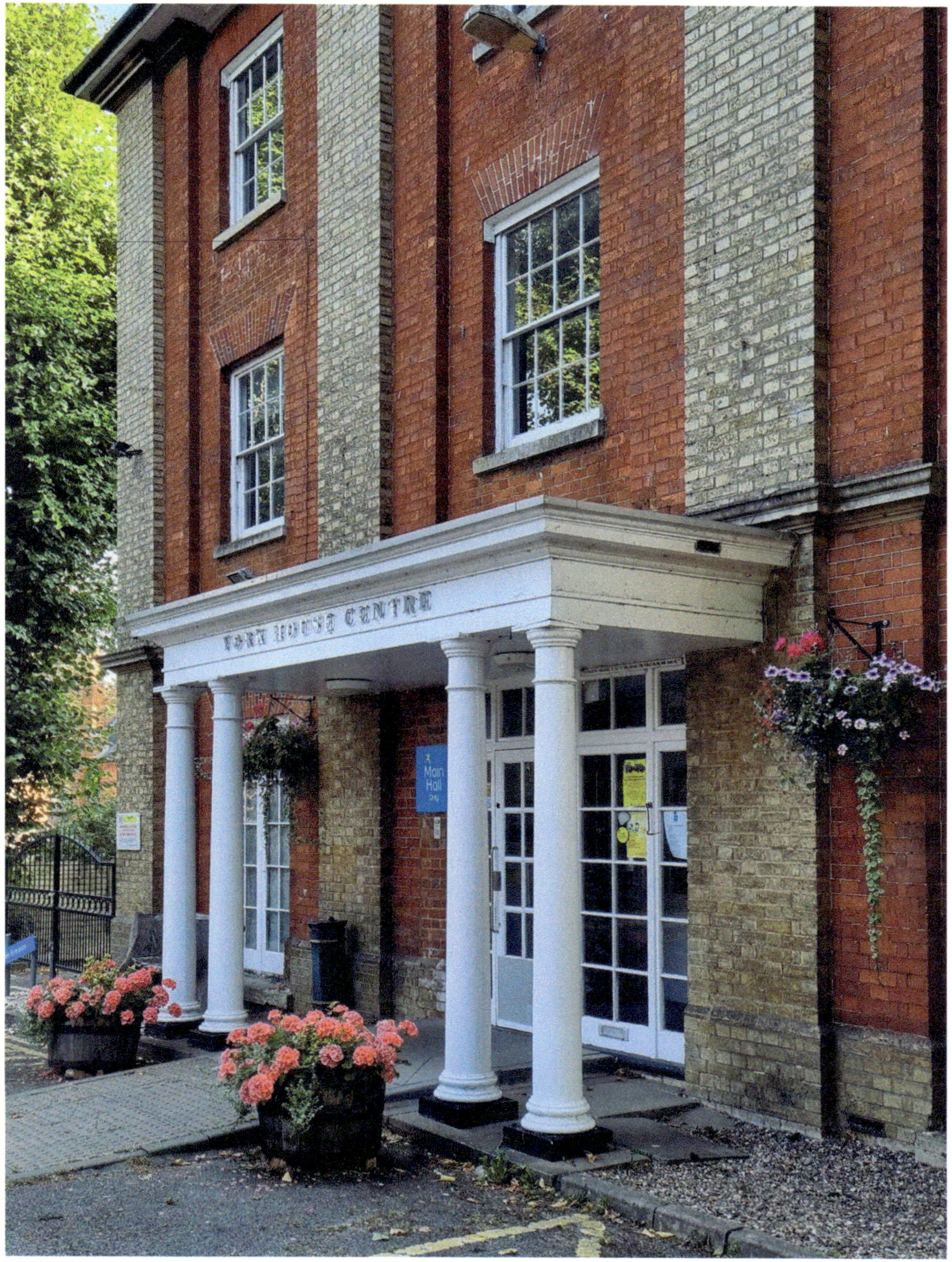
CENTRE
Main
Hall

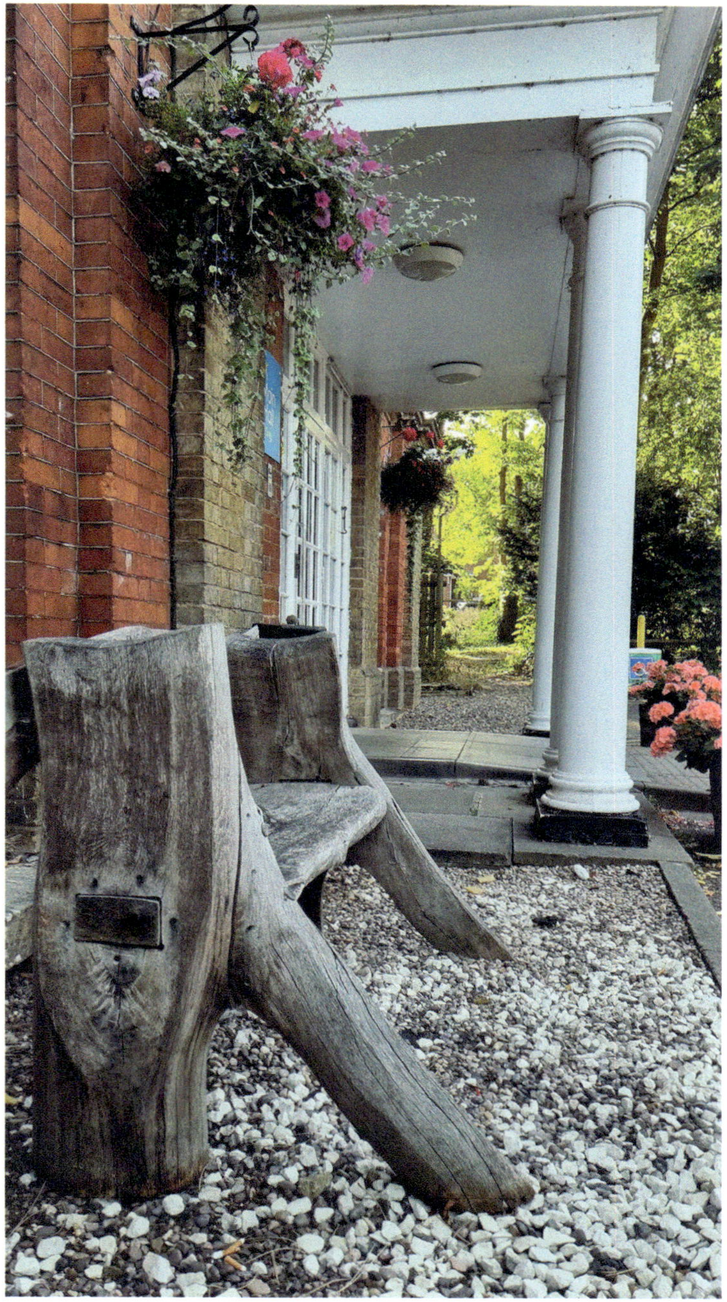

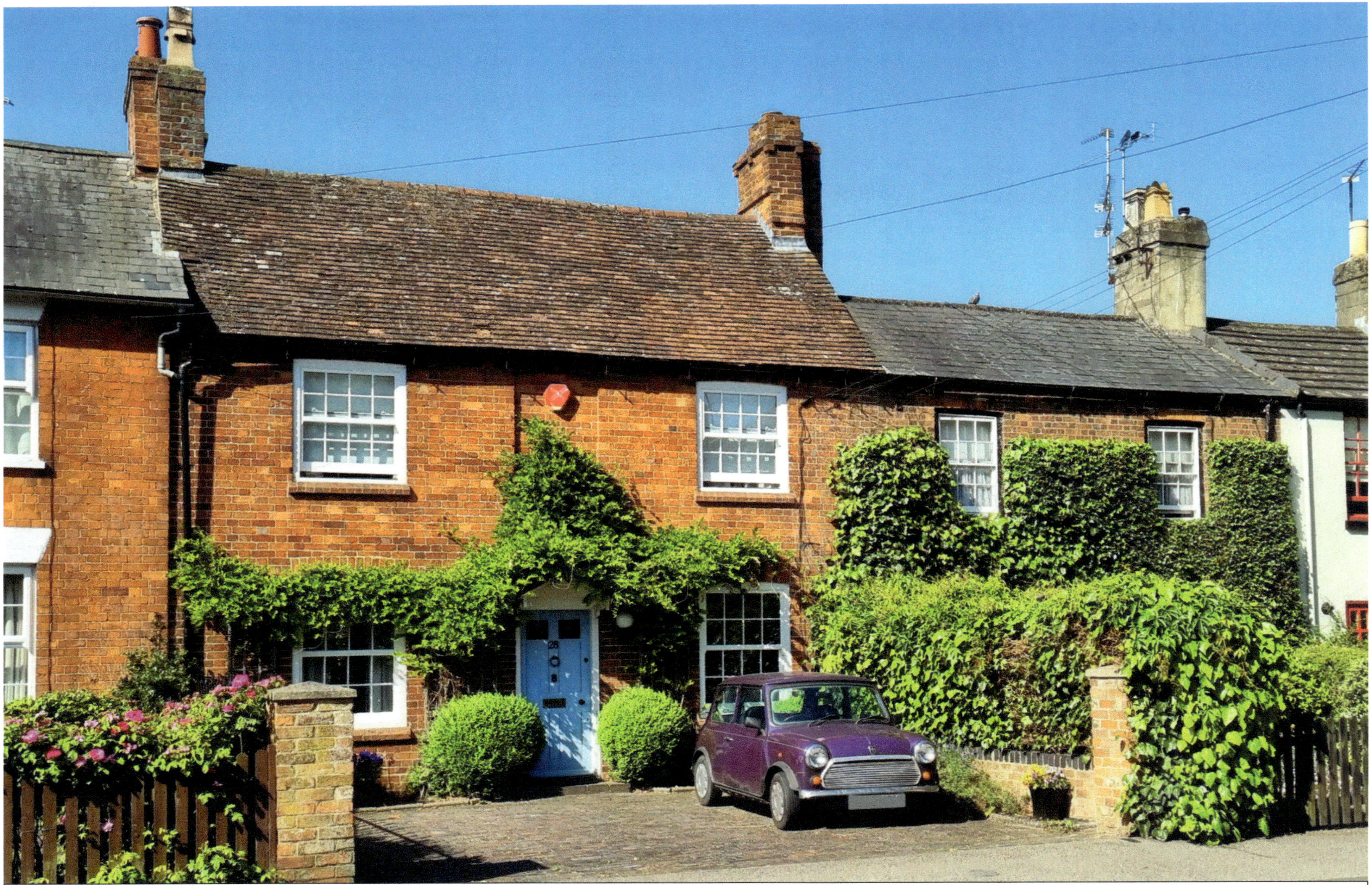

Early London Road houses.

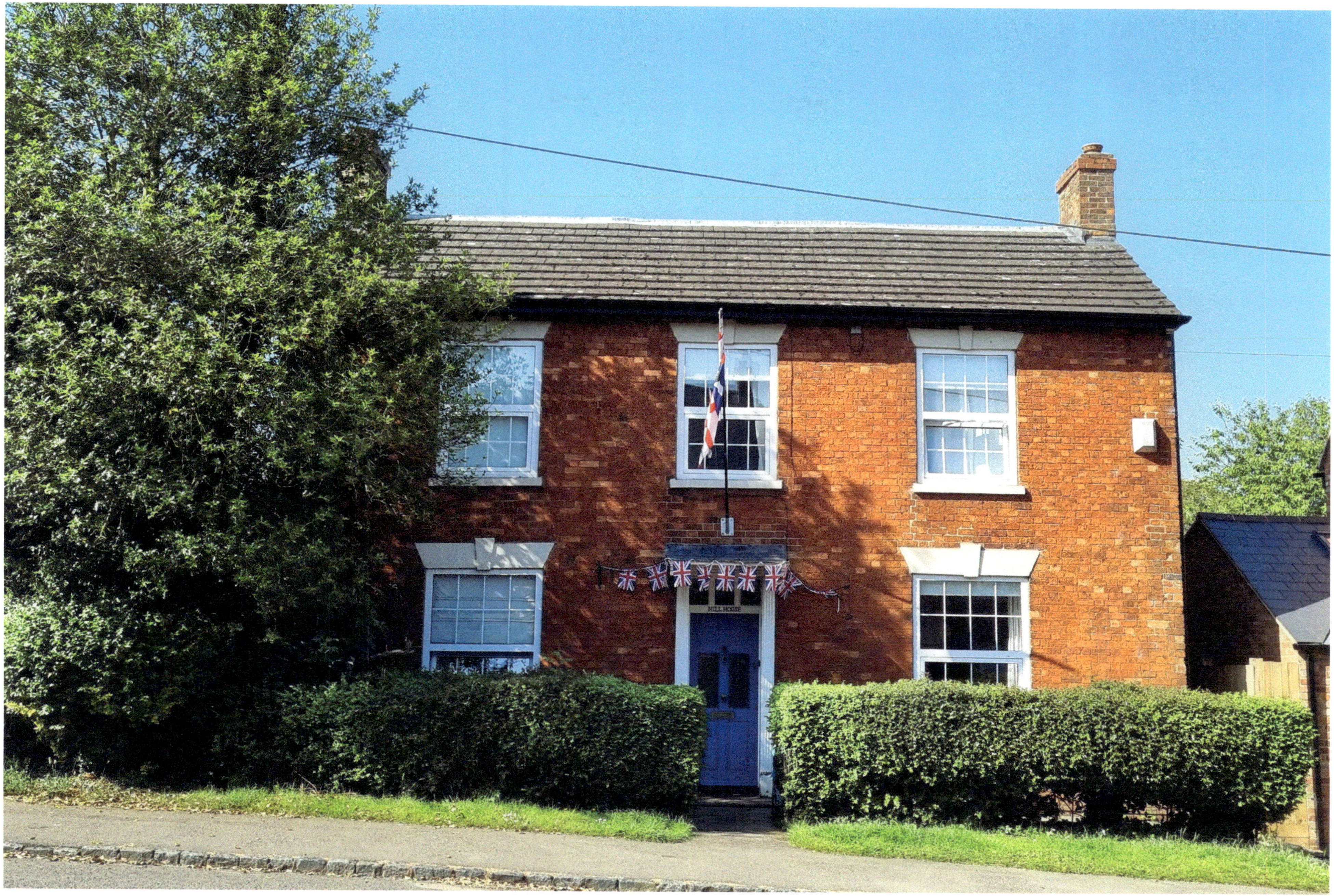
HILL HOUSE

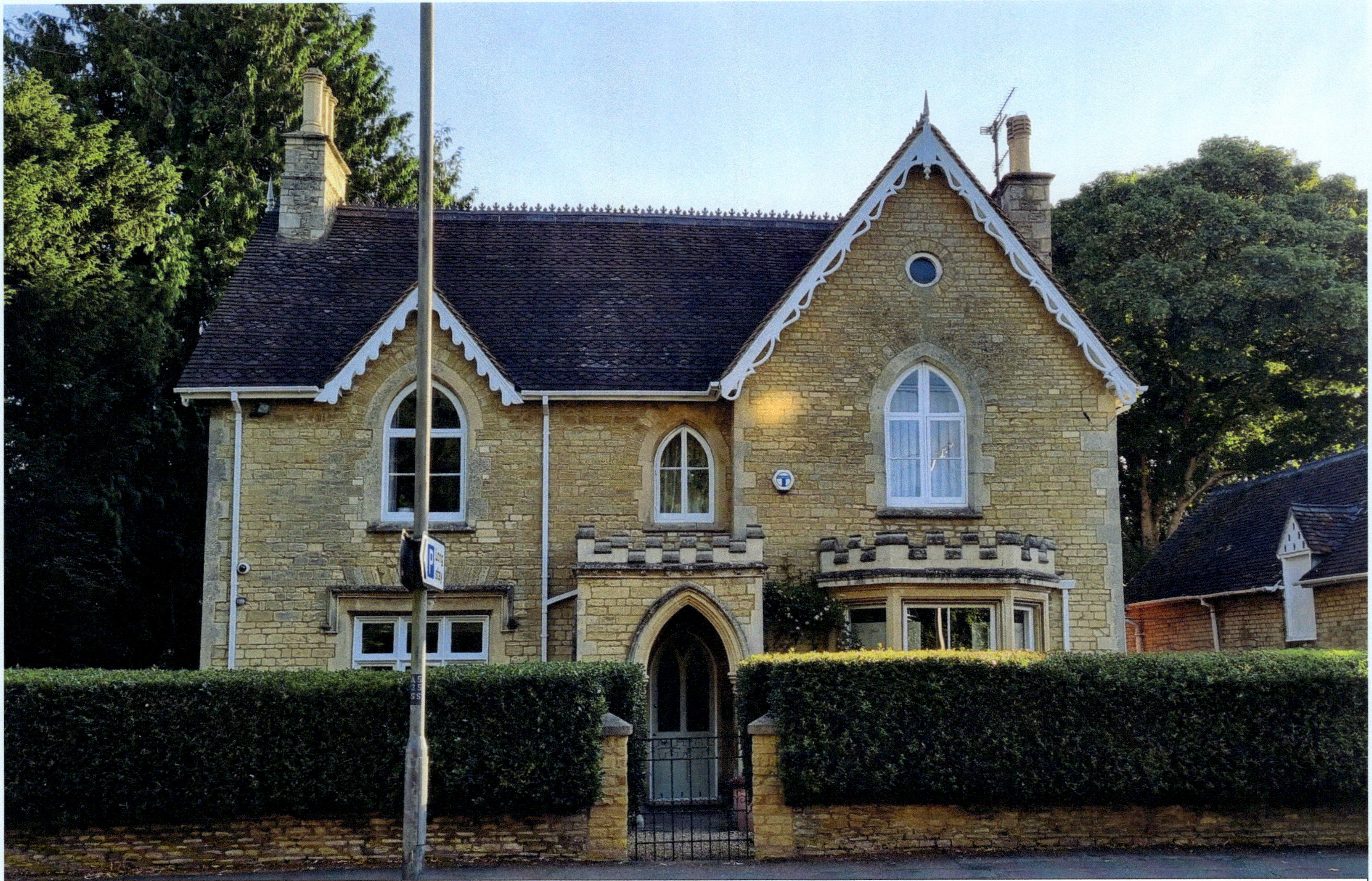

Edward Hayes, who established the Watling Engineering Works, built this house for himself and his family. Discussion of the Watling Works is found on page 151.

Edward Hayes and the Watling Works

In 1840, a young man came to Wolverton from Manchester to work in the new Wolverton Works. His name was Edward Hayes.
He was born in Manchester in 1818, where he did an apprenticeship with the Kennedy engineering firm. He would have had intelligence of the new start up at Wolverton and easily found work at the new Engine Repair shop in 1840. He was an ambitious young man and with his zeal for self improvement must have actively looked for better opportunities for himself. He married Ann Sirrett, the daughter of a Stony Stratford grocer, who had also worked as a schoolmistress. This may have prompted Hayes to temporarily take up this line of work, because he was reported in the Trade directory of 1847 as a schoolmaster at the British School.
This career was probably quite short, because in the 1851 census he describes himself as an engineer. Shortly after, if not before, he established his Watling Works on the London Road.
At first he made agricultural machinery, for which there was a demand in the 19th century. He then used the knowledge he had acquired at Wolverton to develop steam engines to power agricultural machinery. These were successful.
In the late 1860s, when the Watling Works were well established and thriving, he turned his hand to boat building. Apparently he had some knowledge of this from his apprenticeship in Manchester. Boatbuilding in the middle of the country did not strike people as a natural fit for inland Stony Stratford; nevertheless, Hayes' engineering know-how and product quality made sure of success and orders came in from many parts of the world. At one time they were building vessels up to 80 feet long.
These vessels, once finished, were transported up the High Street to the canal wharf at Old Stratford. There they were lowered into the water and comfortably delivered by canal and river to their destination.
Edward Hayes died in 1877 and his son (also Edward) took over the firm. Boat building was now the mainstay of the business. The firm continued to thrive into the first quarter of the 20th century but then seemed to lose the drive and energy of its founder. Edward Hayes junior died in 1917 and his son only lived to 1920. After this, the firm continued to 1924 when it closed down.
Hayes' commitment was not simply to making money (which he did) but also to spreading his engineering knowledge. In this sense he was also remarkable and quite early he took on apprentices, which he managed to attract from across the country. Men who went on to distinguished careers after learning the ropes at Hayes: Osborne Reynolds, Professor of Engineering at Manchester University, Sir Frederick Rebbeck, Chairman of Harland and Wolff, who had a hand in the design of the Titanic, and B J Fisher, who became Chief Engineer of the London and South Western Railway.
One of the last boats to be built was acquired by the Milton Keynes Development Museum in 2004. It can be seen at the entrance to the museum. The Watling Works are no more, but the memory of Hayes has been marked by a small sculpture park.

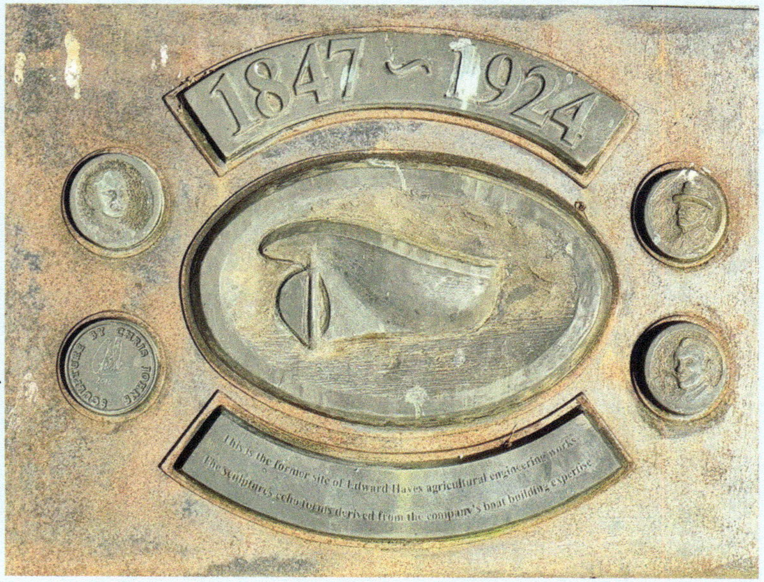

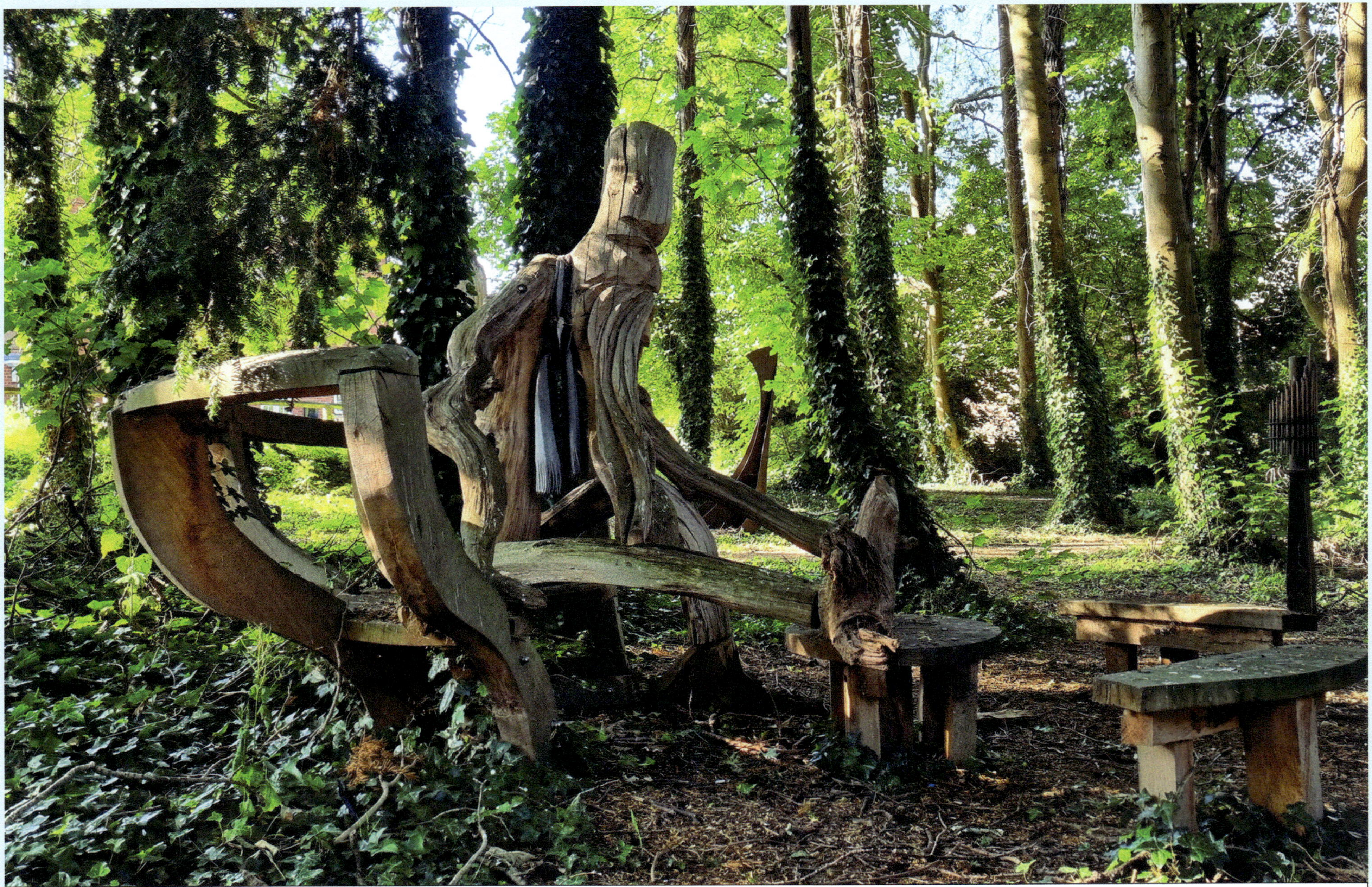

The sculptures on pages 152and 153 commemorate the Watling Engineering Works, which once occupied this site.

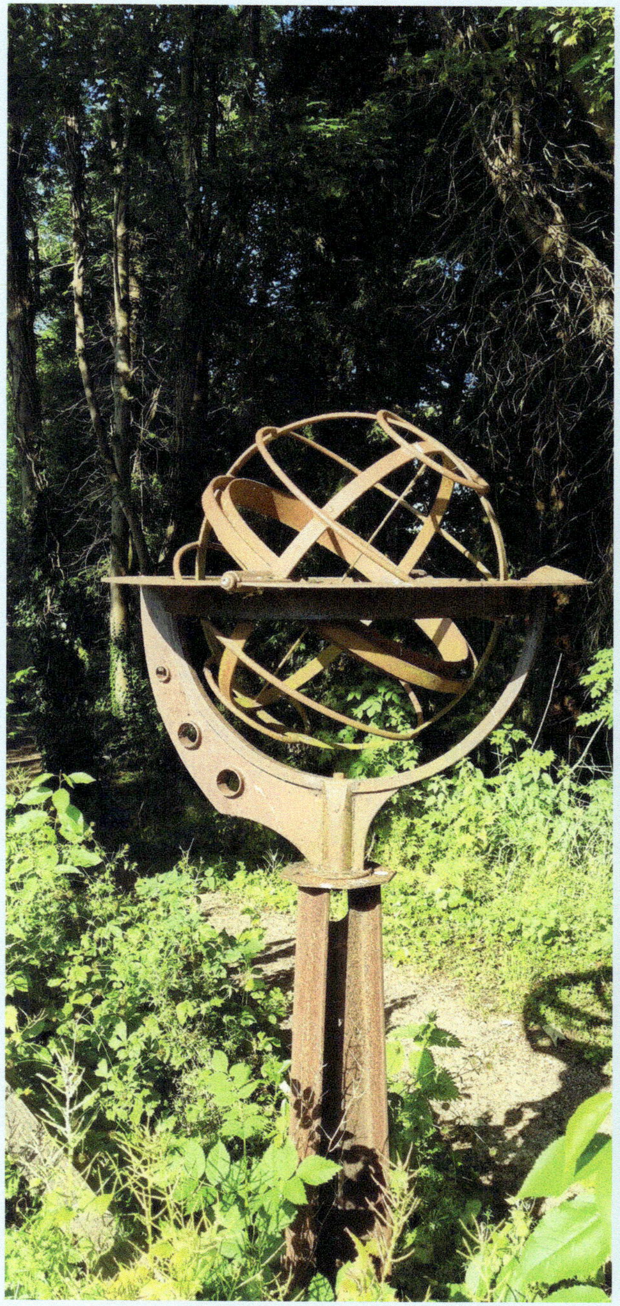
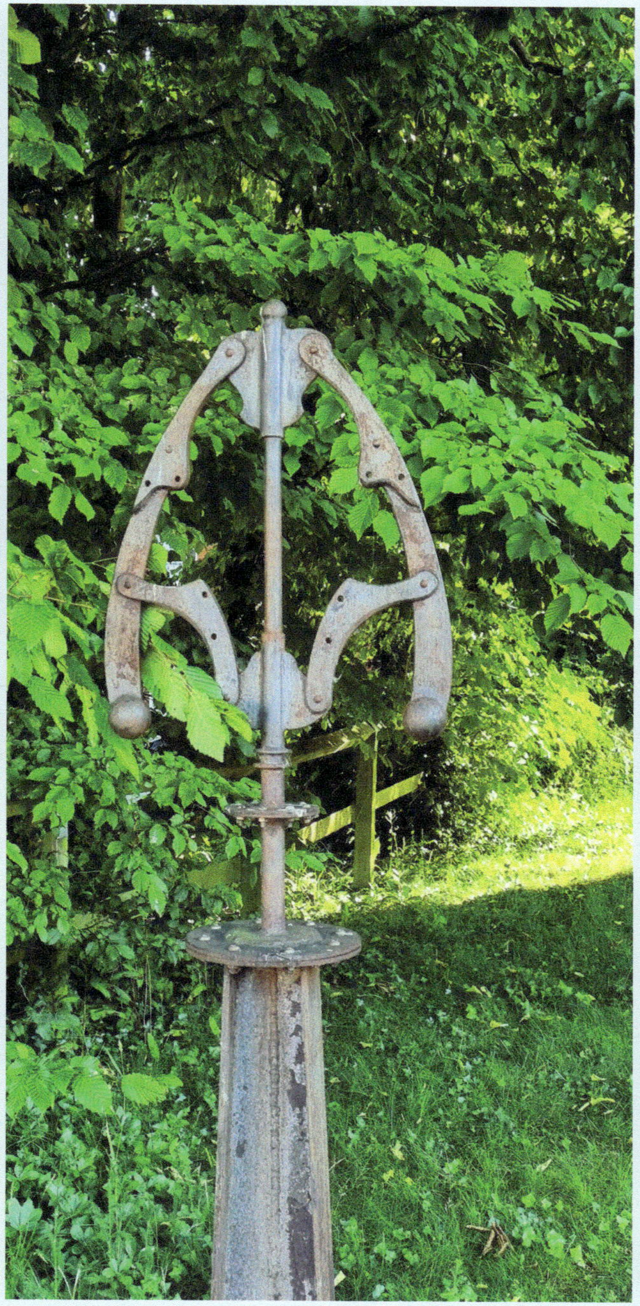
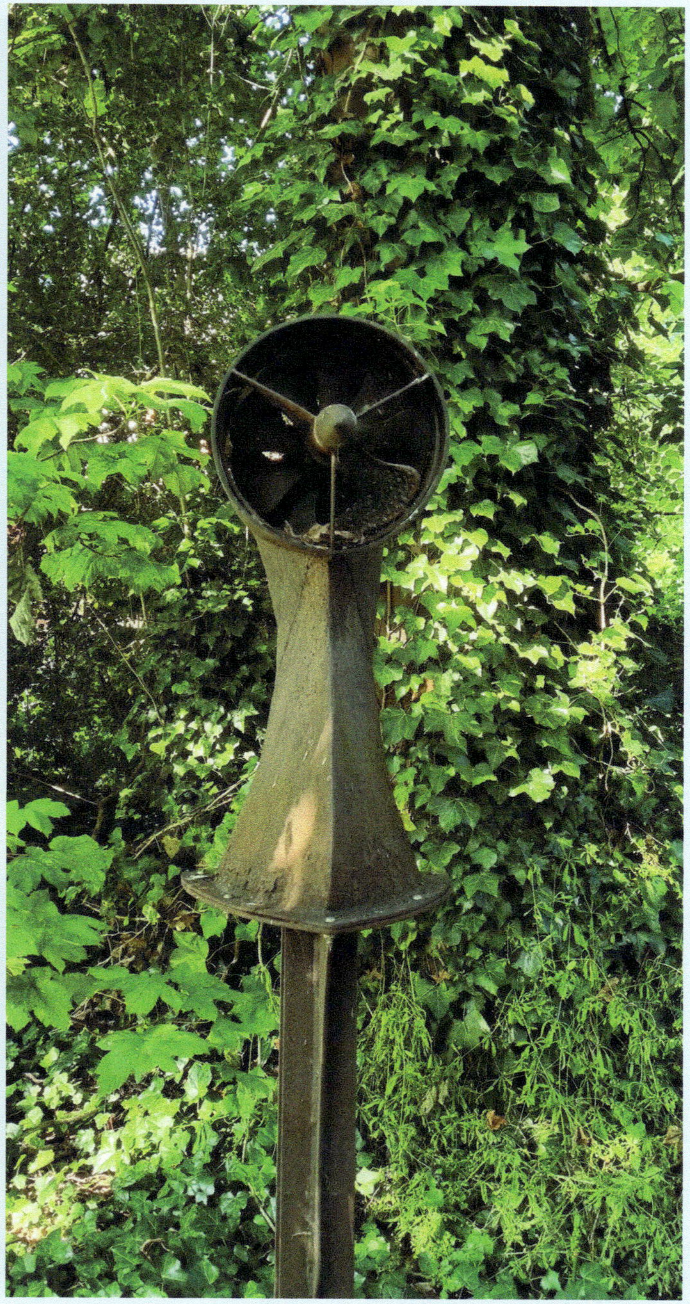

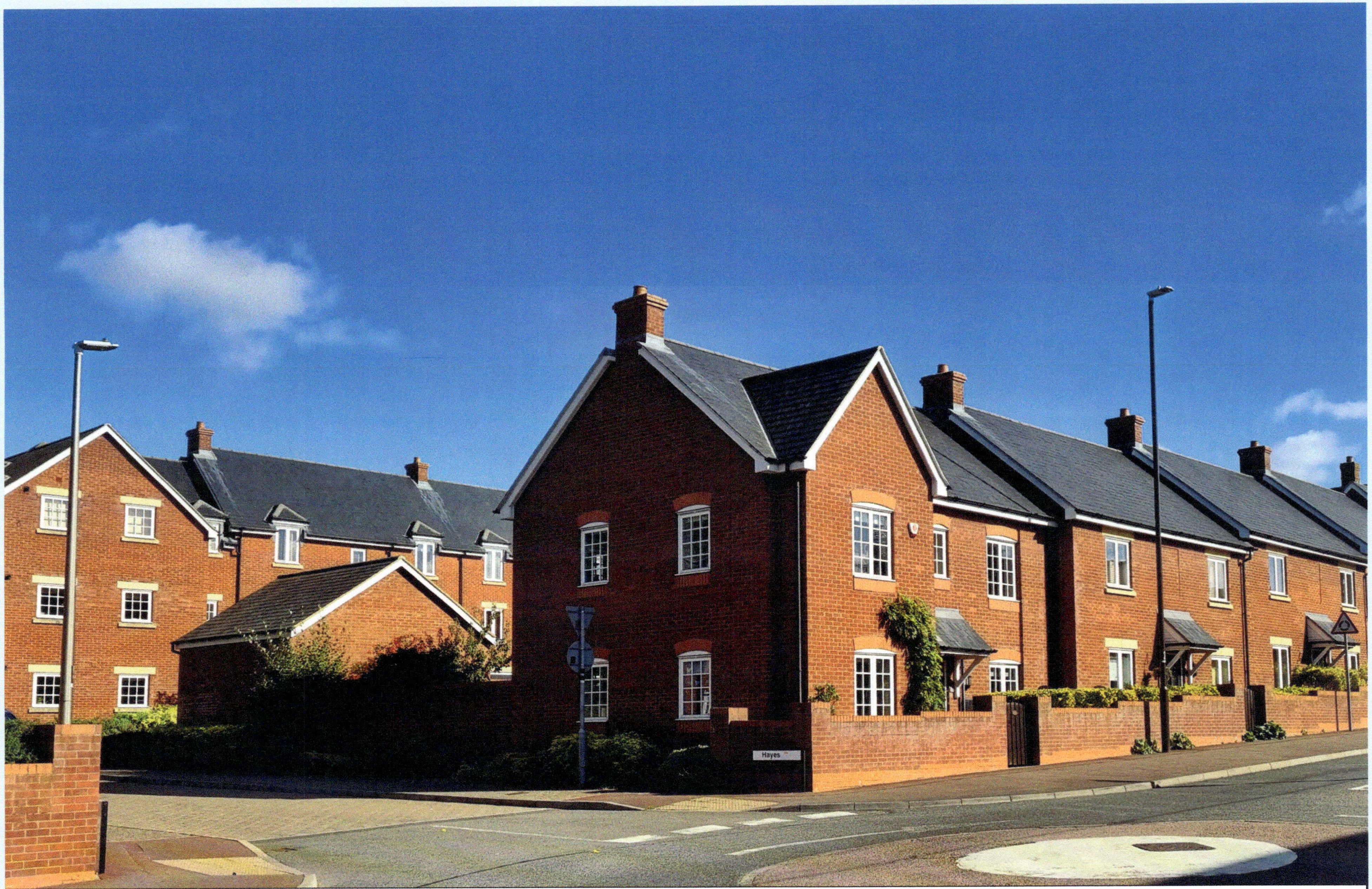

This recent housing development off the London Road has a street named after Edward Hayes.

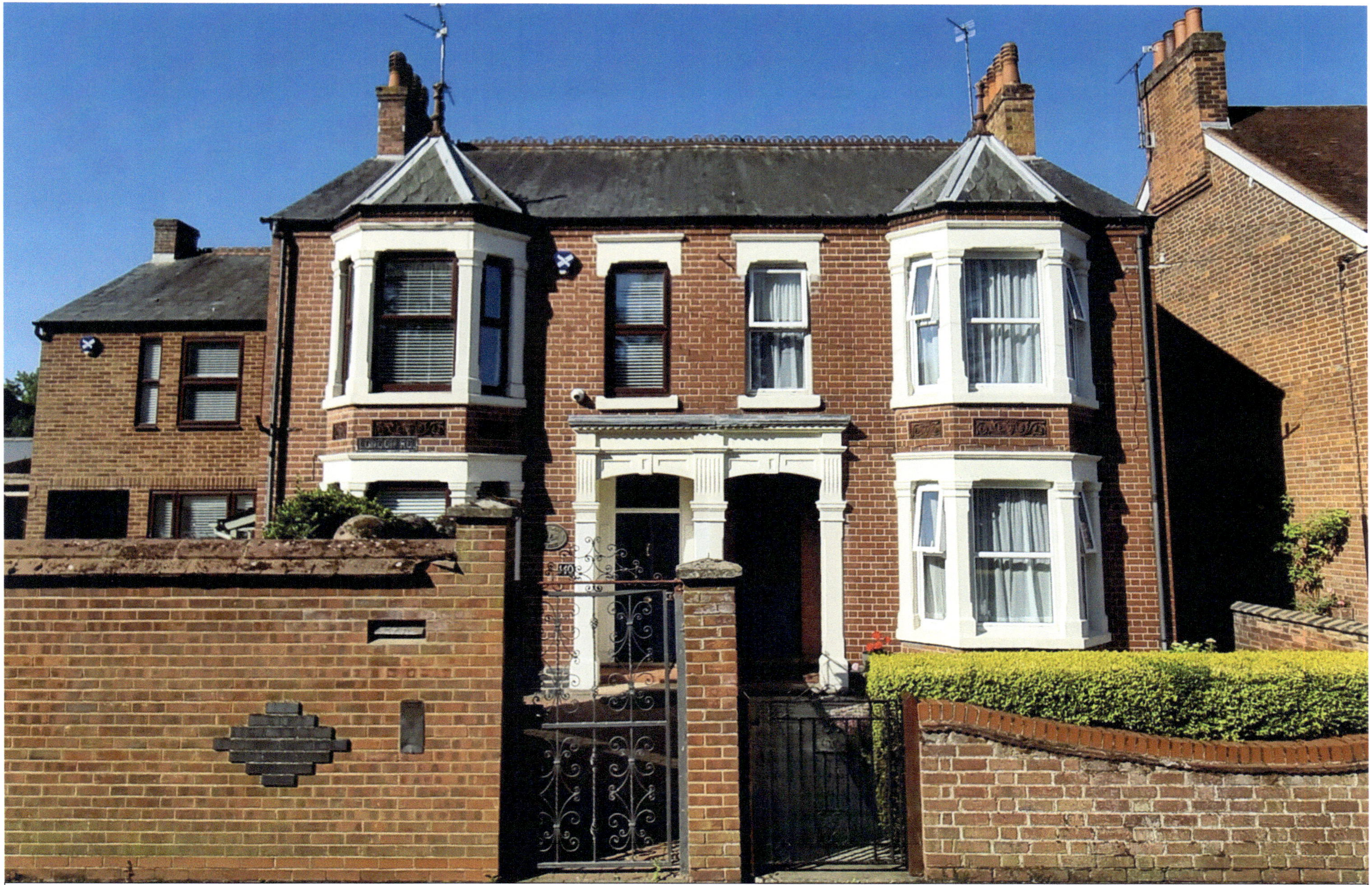

20th century houses on the London Road - pages 155 to 159.

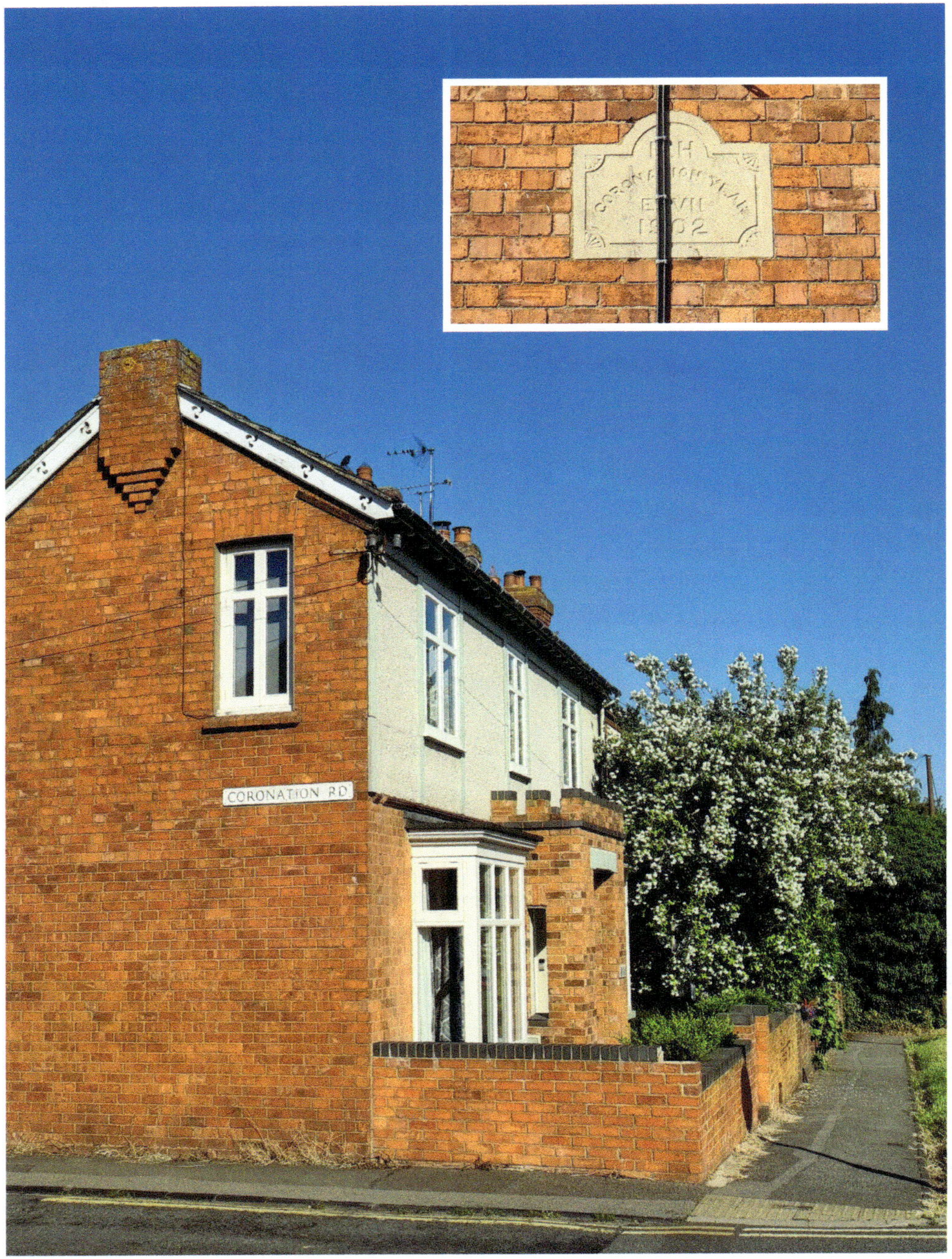
CORONATION RD

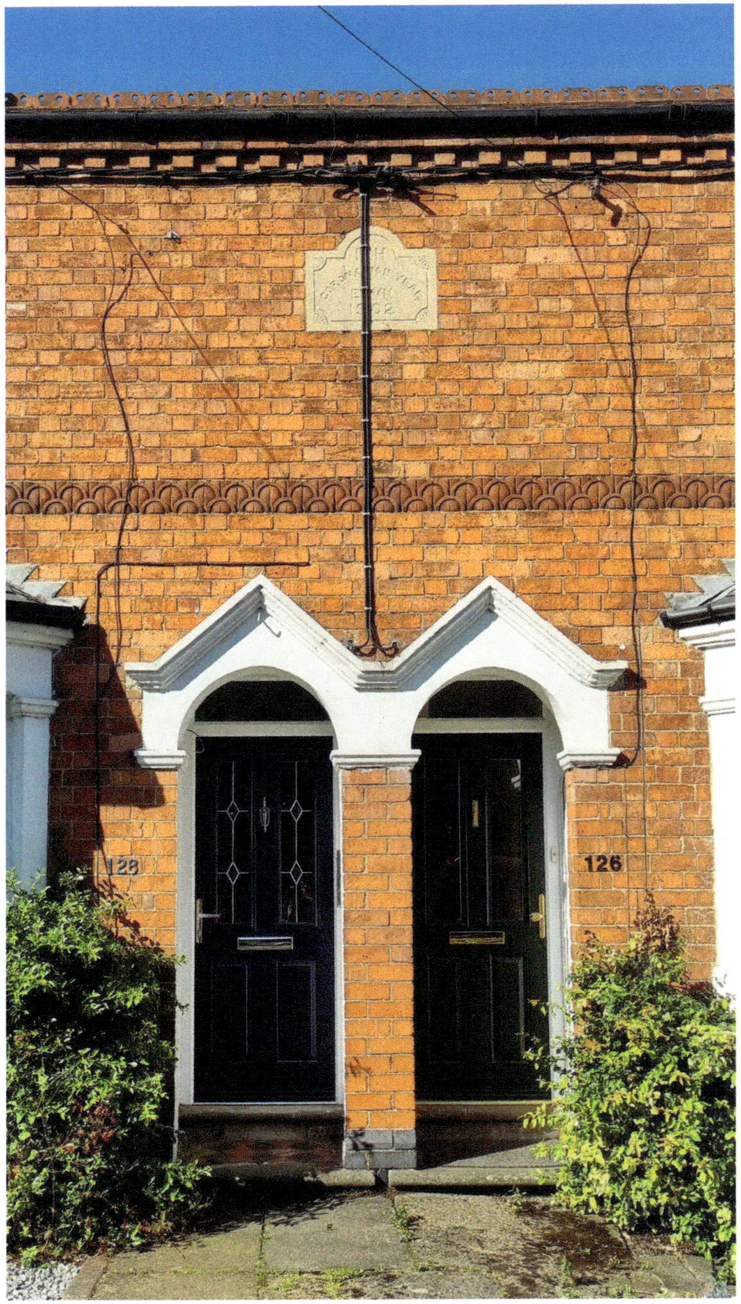
128
126

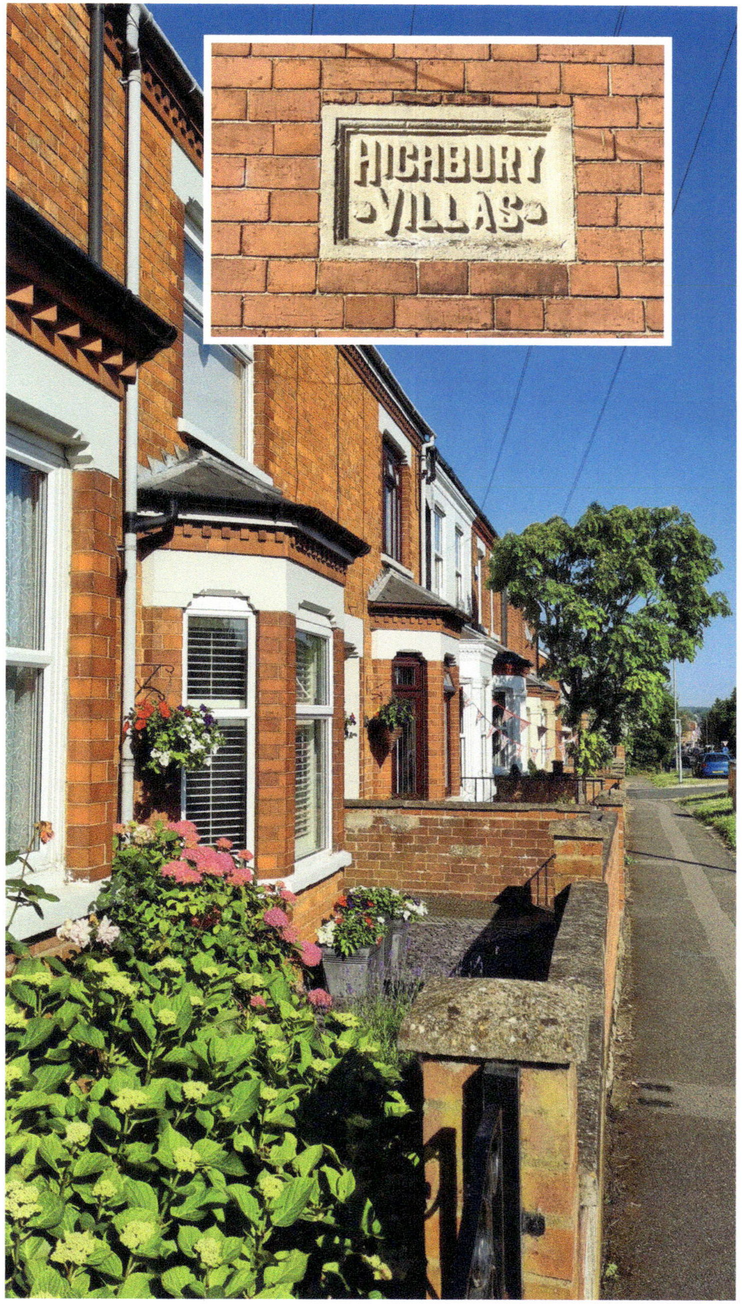
HIGHBURY
VILLAS

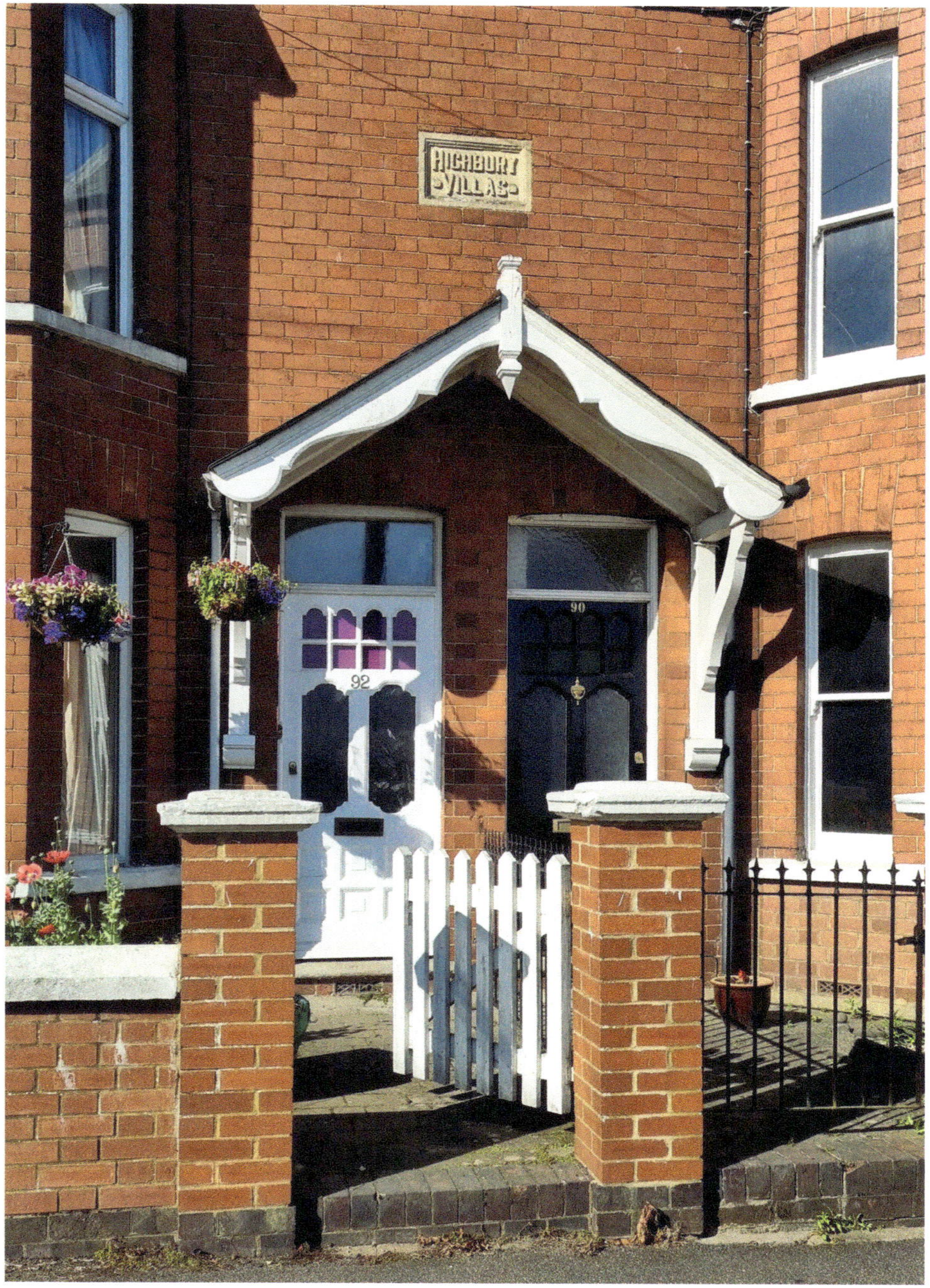
HIGHBURY
VILLAS
92
90

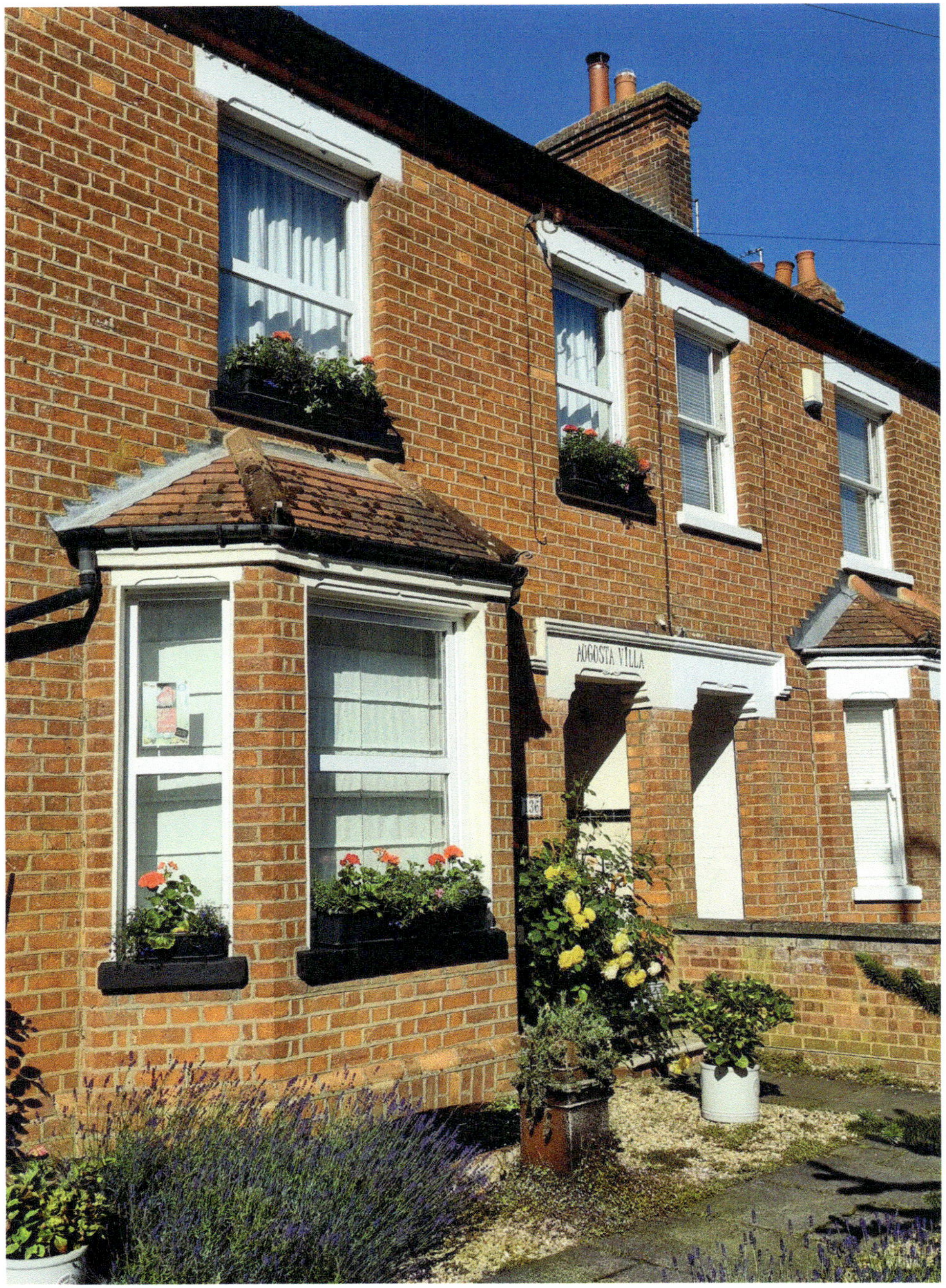
AUGUSTA VILLA

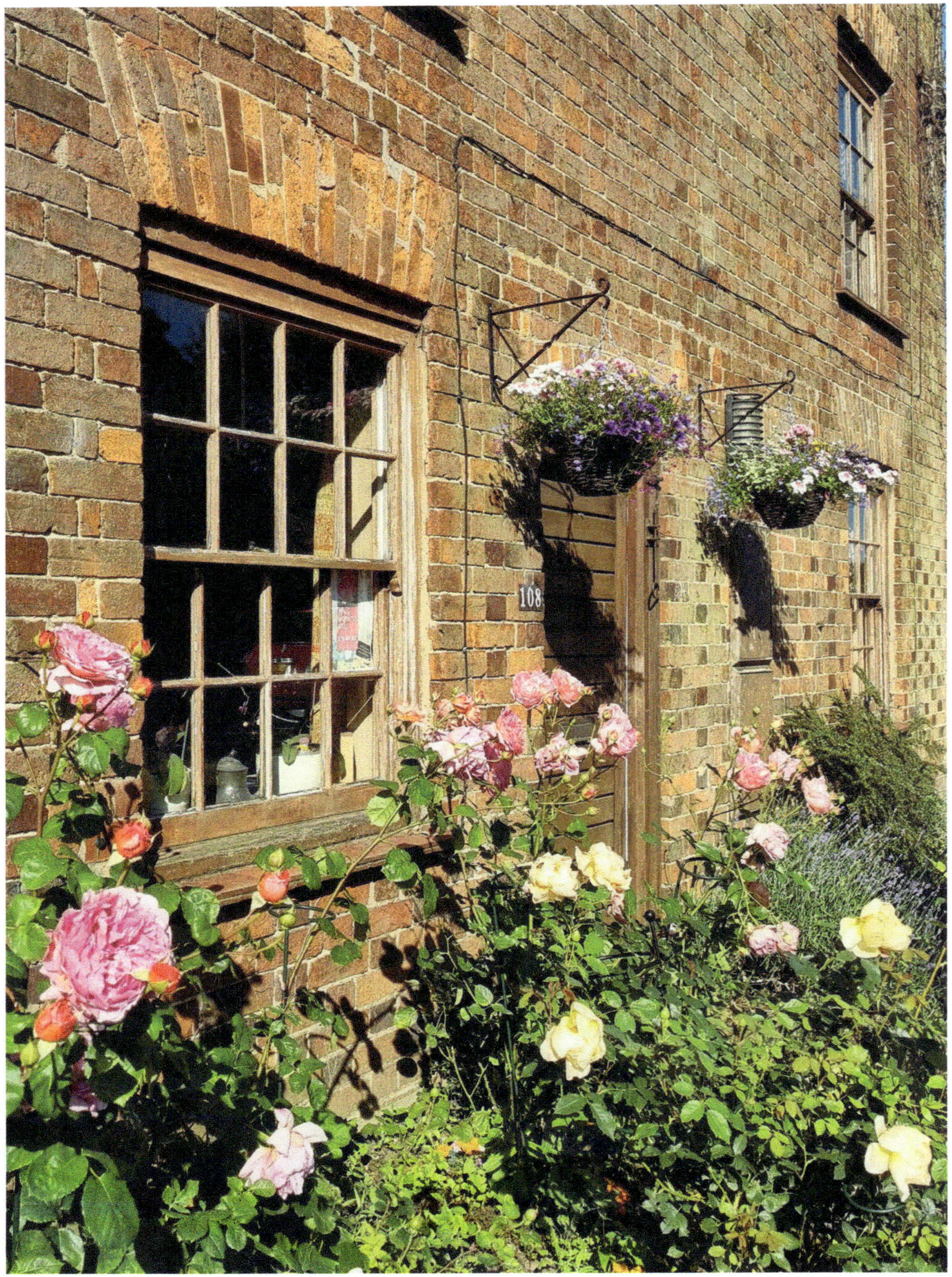
108

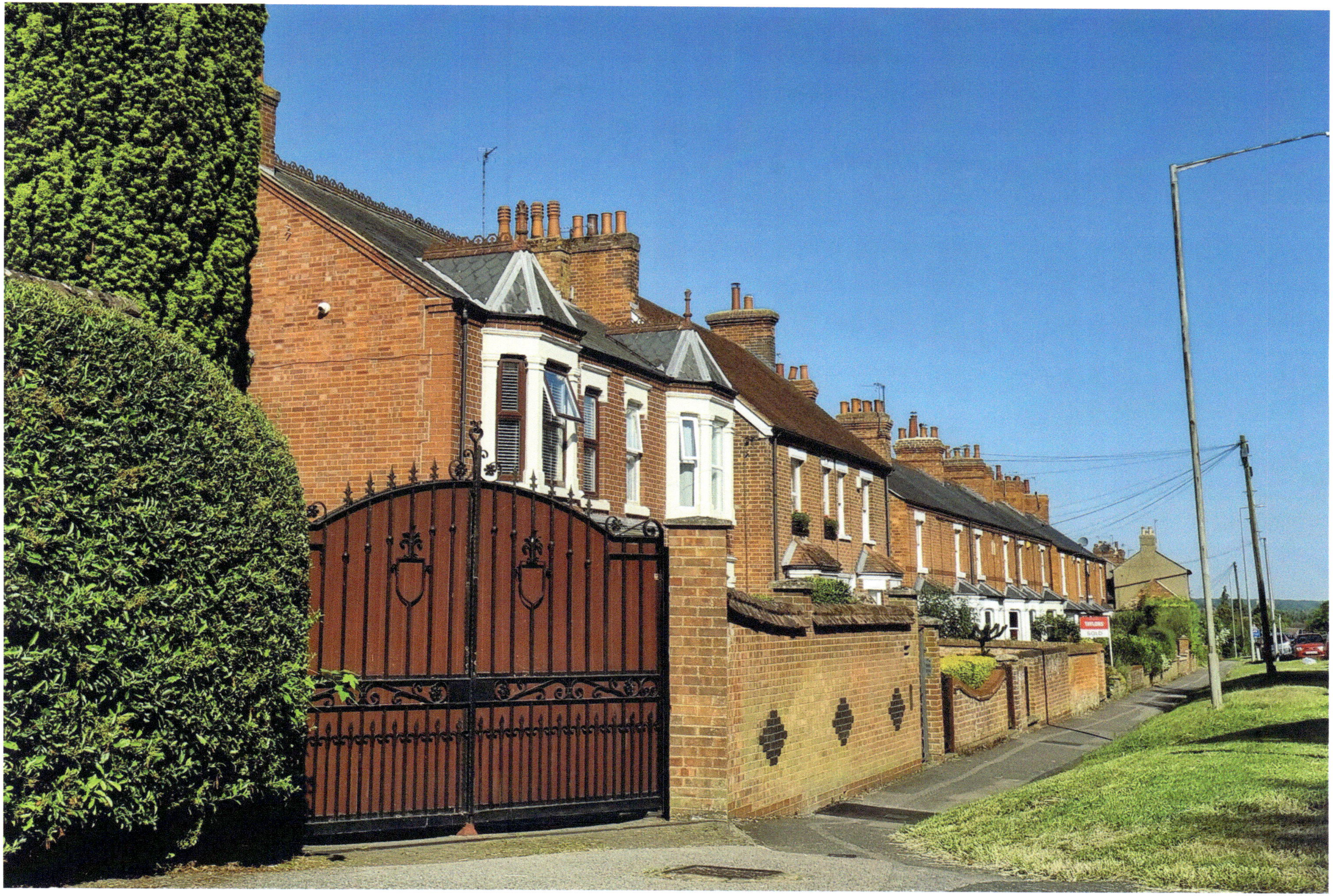

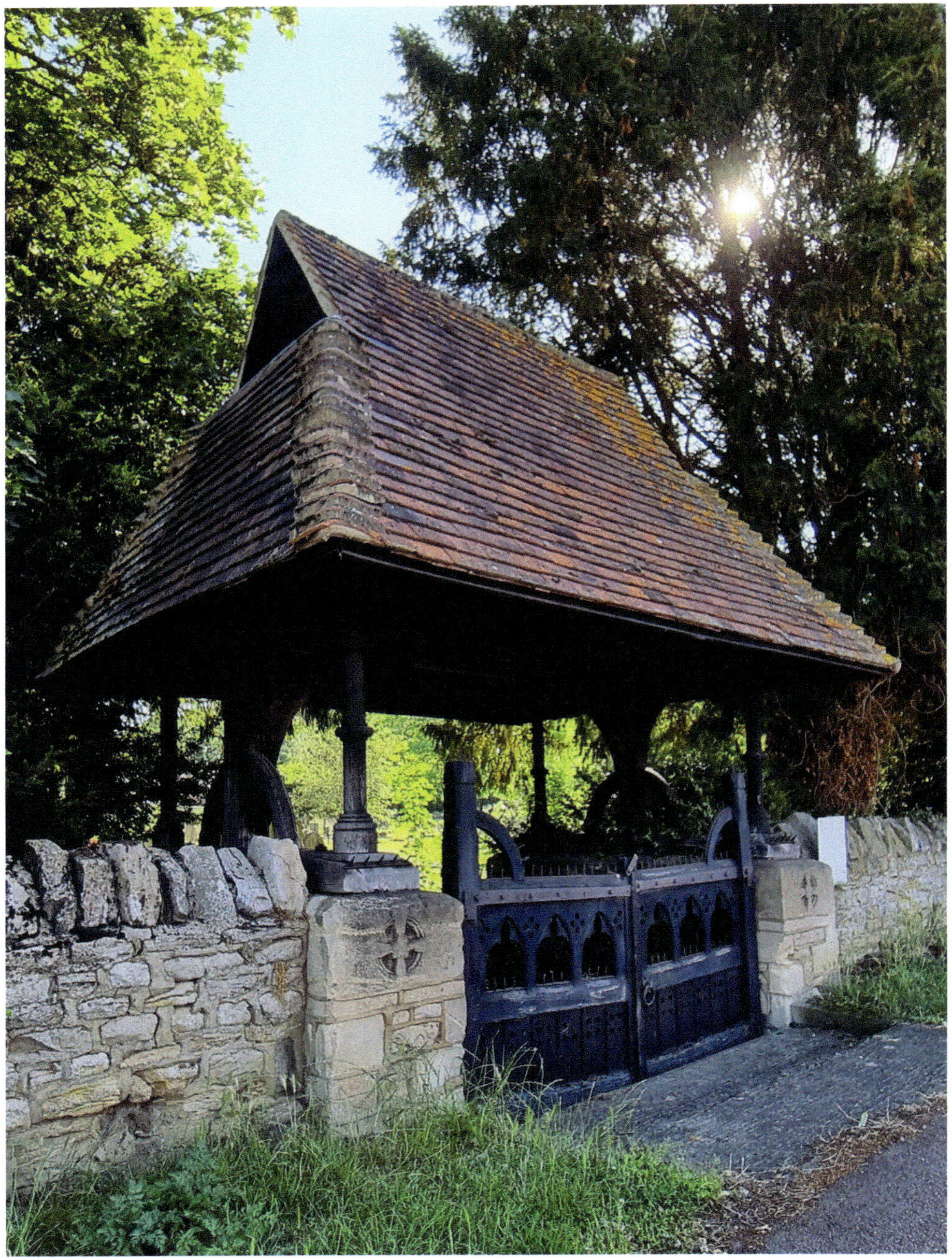

The Burial Grounds

For many centuries, the churchyards of St Mary Magdalene and St Giles were able to offer burial places for the dead of Stony Stratford, and even though the church of St Mary Magdalene was not used after 1742, bodies were still buried in that churchyard in the 19th century.

By the mid 19th century, this provision was inadequate and the Parish Council acquired 1 acre of land on the Calverton Road. A stone boundary wall enclosed the area and two chapels were built, one for Anglicans and one for Non-conformists. These chapels no exist but the original lych gate survives. This common burial ground opened in 1856.

Urban development limited expansion of the Calverton Road cemetery and in 1902, the Wolverton and Stony Stratford Parish Councils opened up a new site on the London Road. Much of this land was taken up with allotments which continued to surround the London Road Cemetery until post-Milton Keynes times when Stony Stratford expanded enormously.

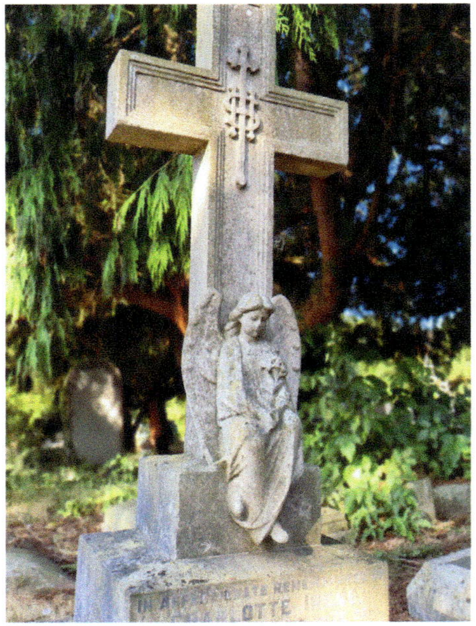

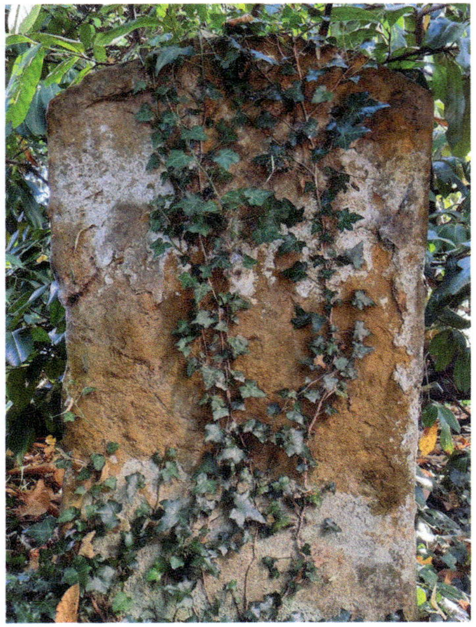

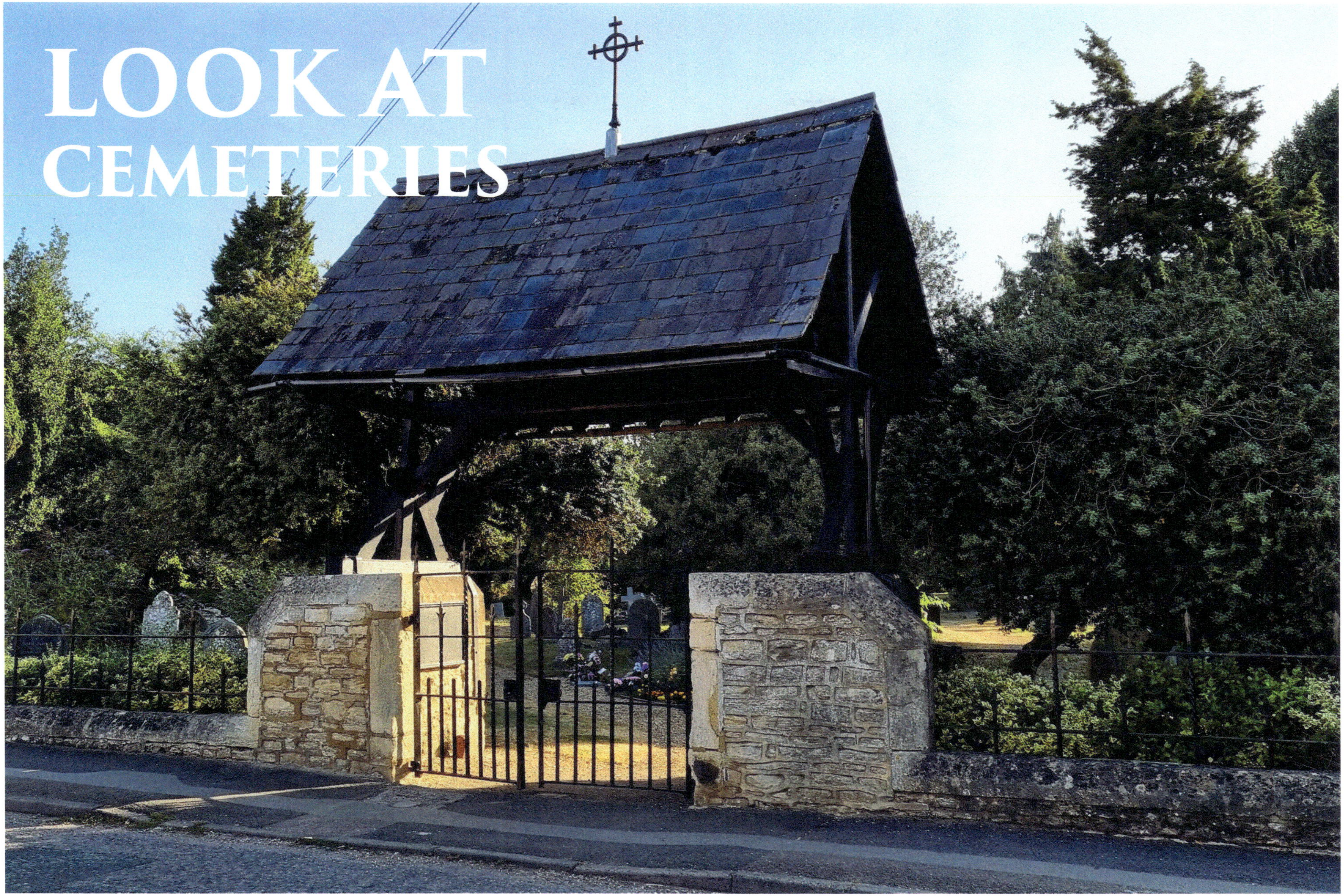

LOOK AT CEMETERIES

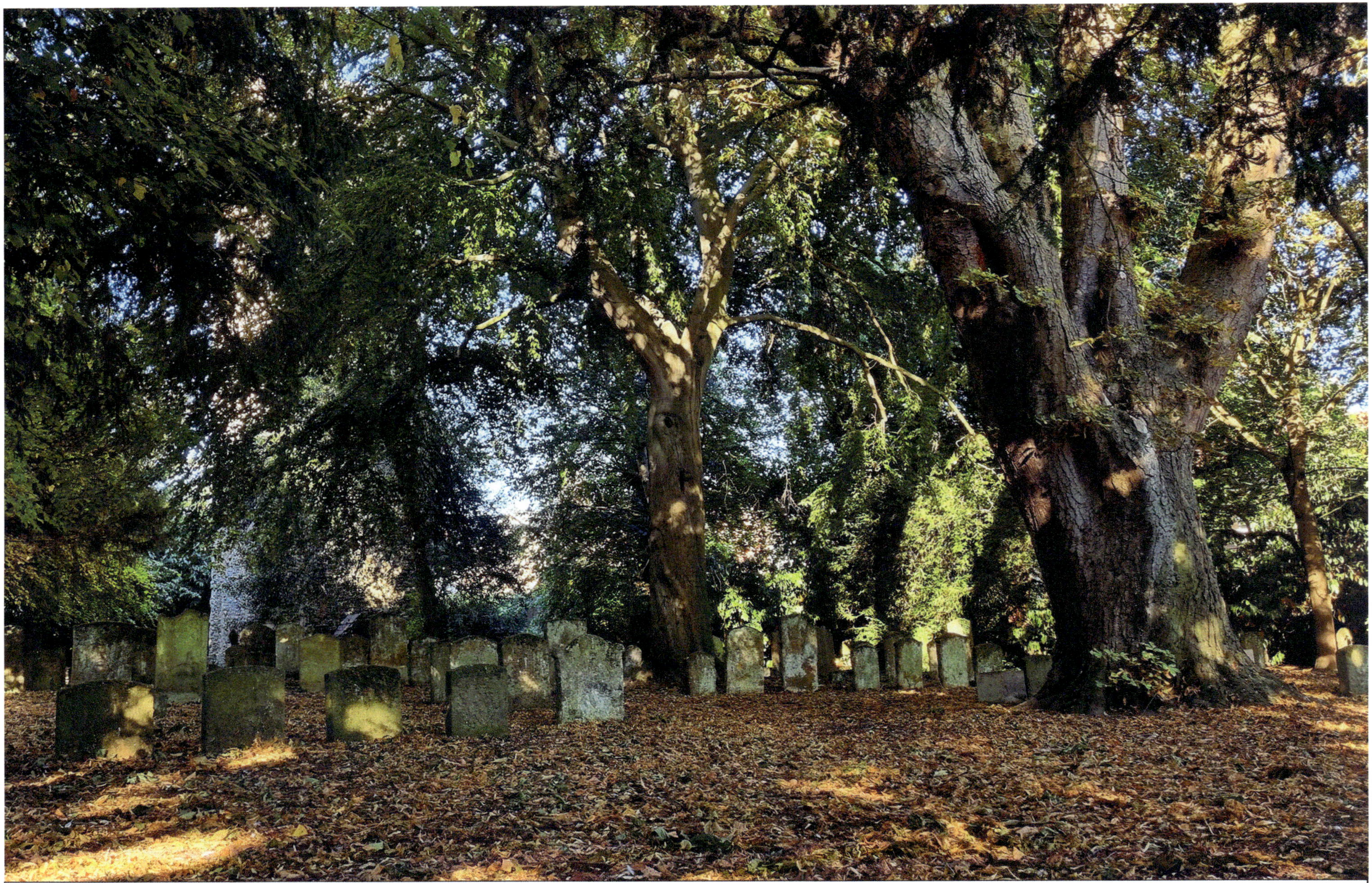

The old cemetery beside the abandoned church of St Mary Magdalene, shown on these two pages.

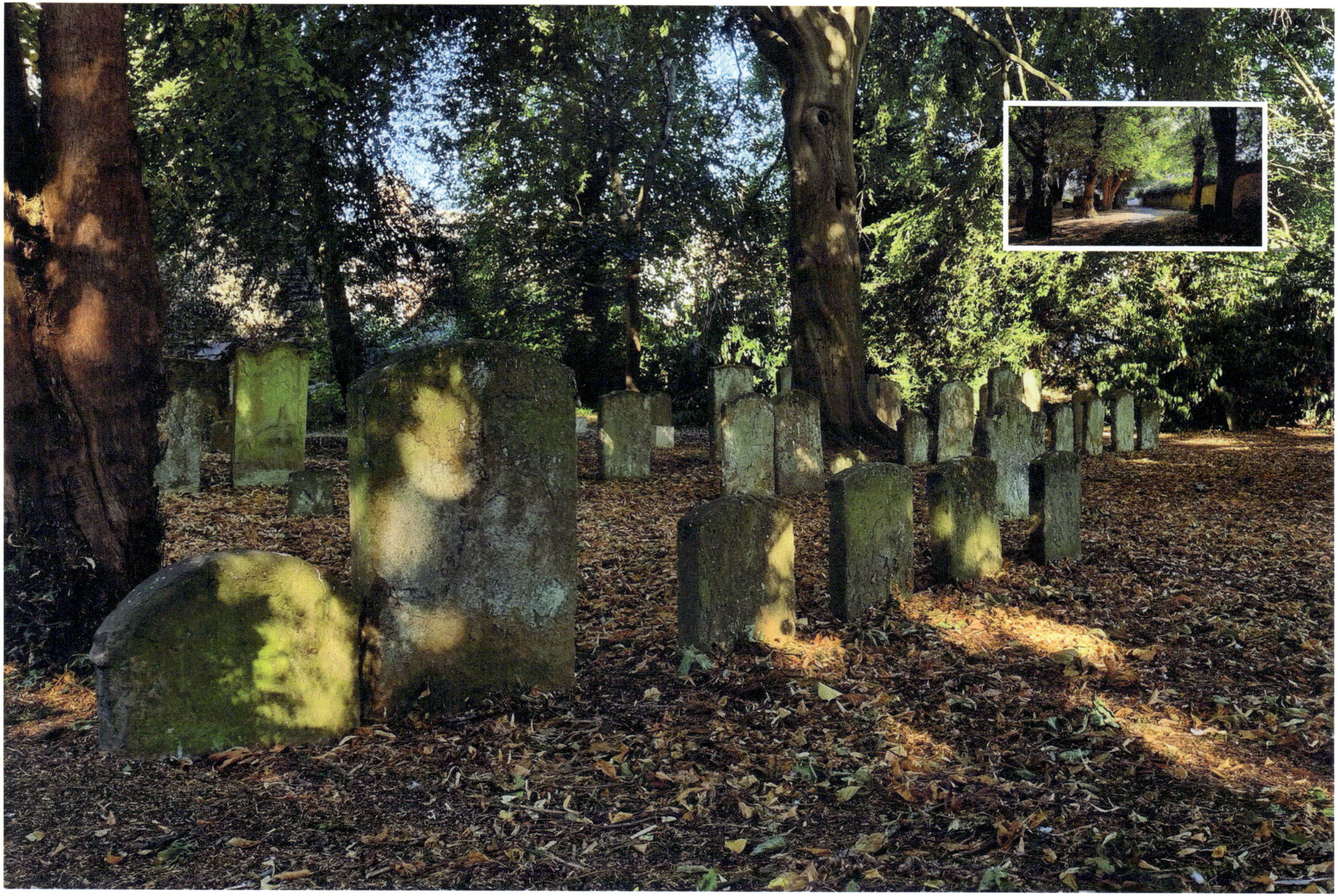

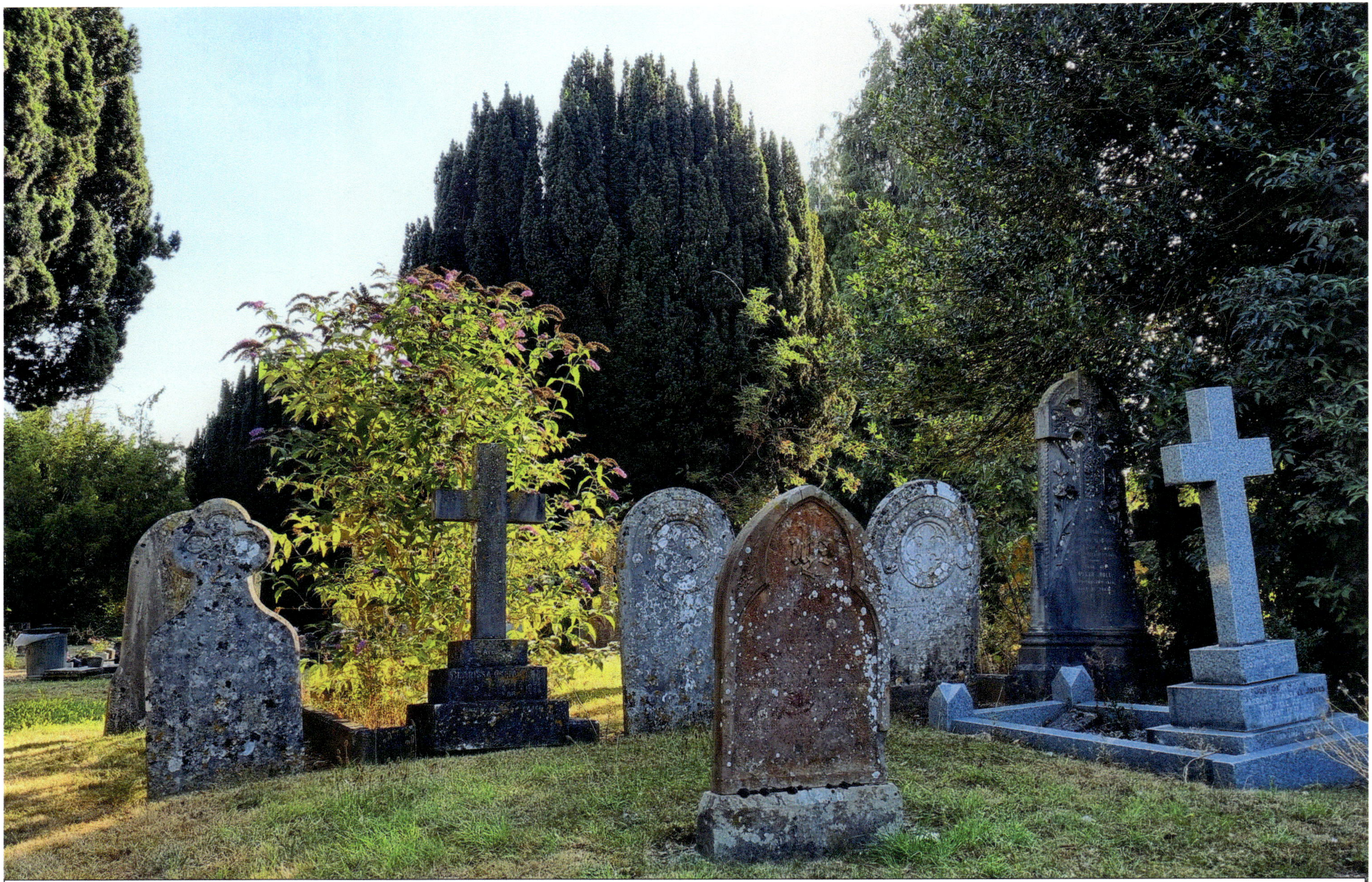

The Calverton Road cemetery was opened in 1854. Here are some images on pages 164 to 167.

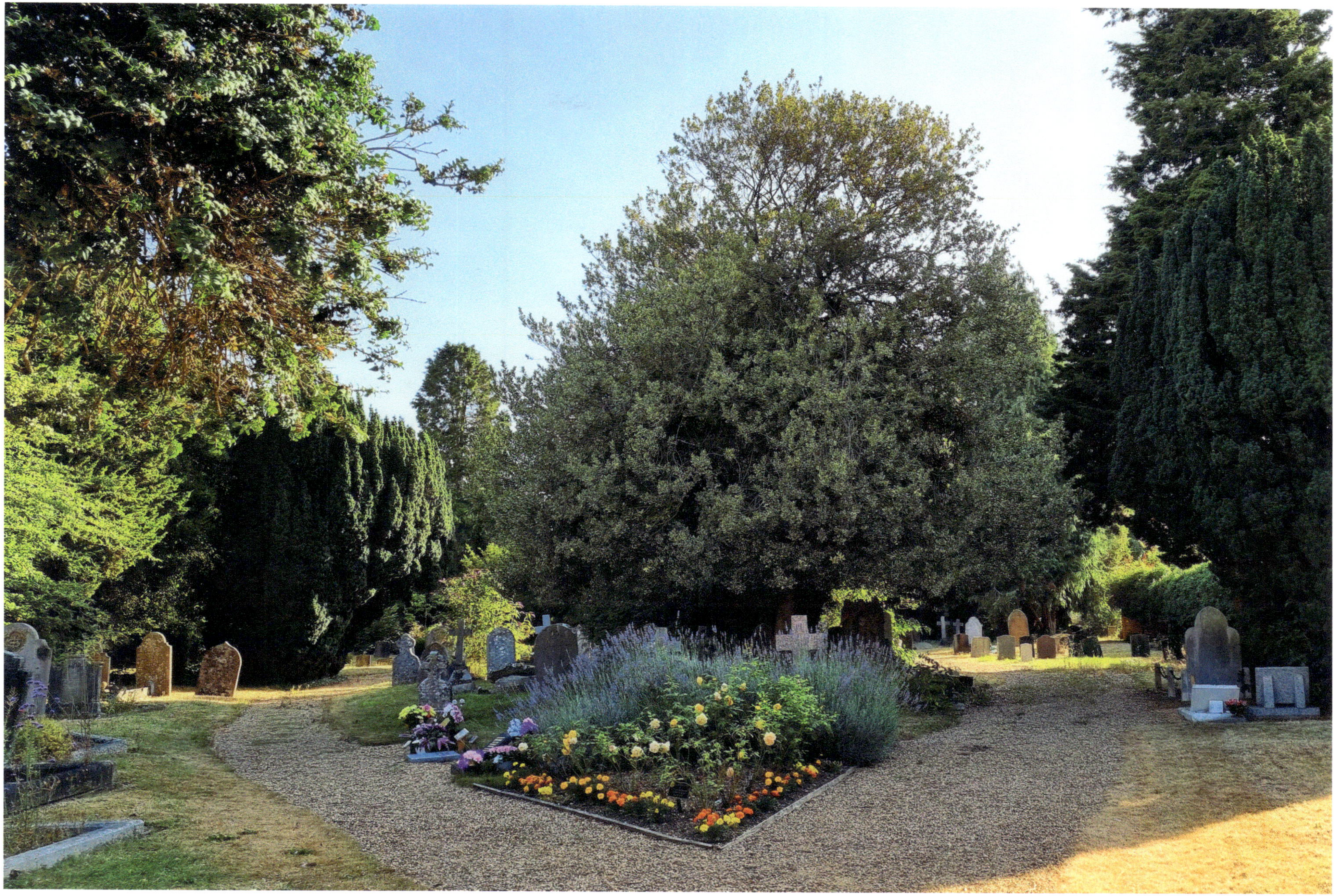

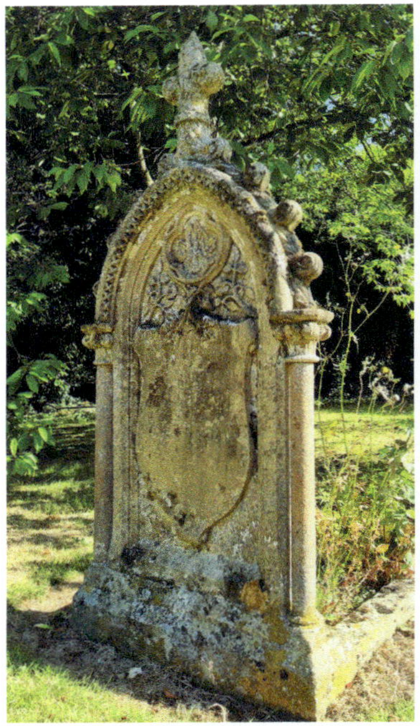
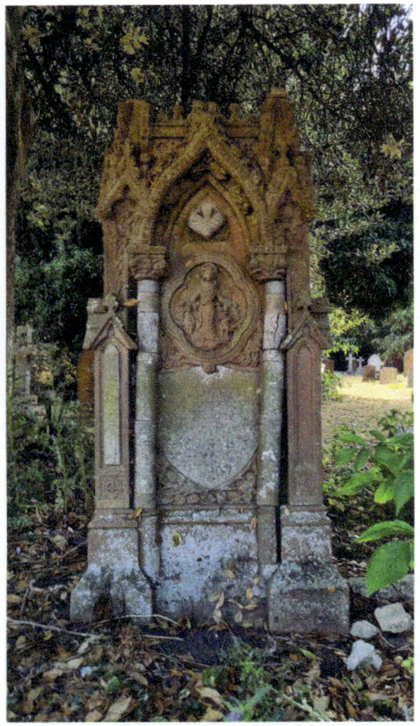
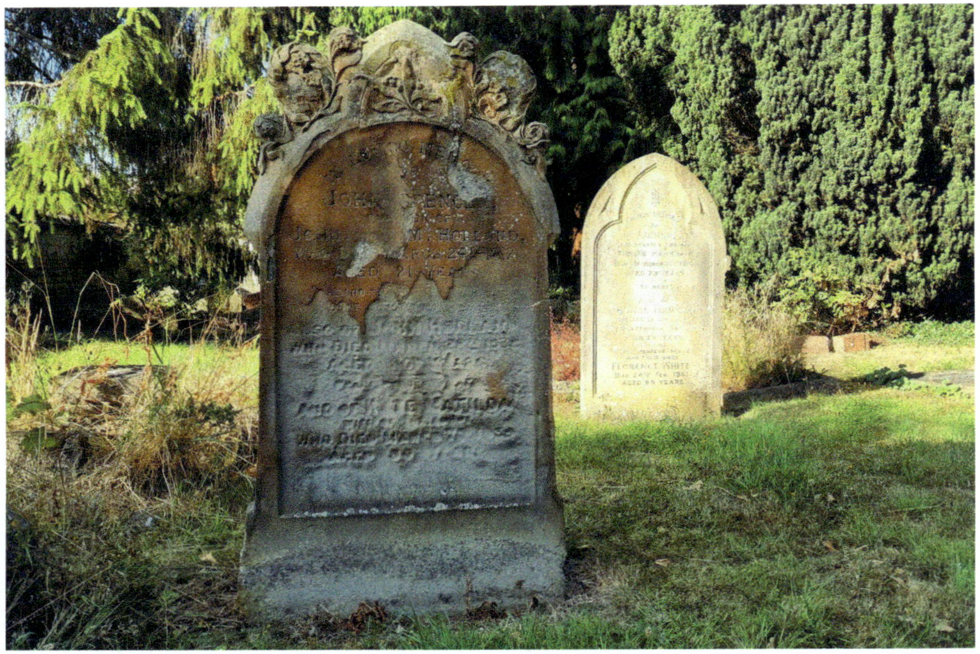
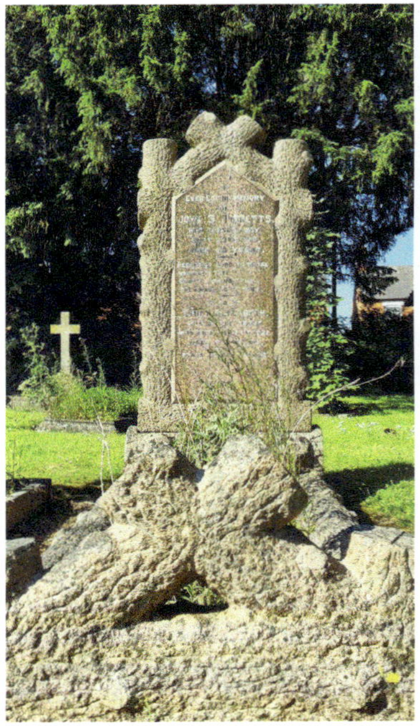
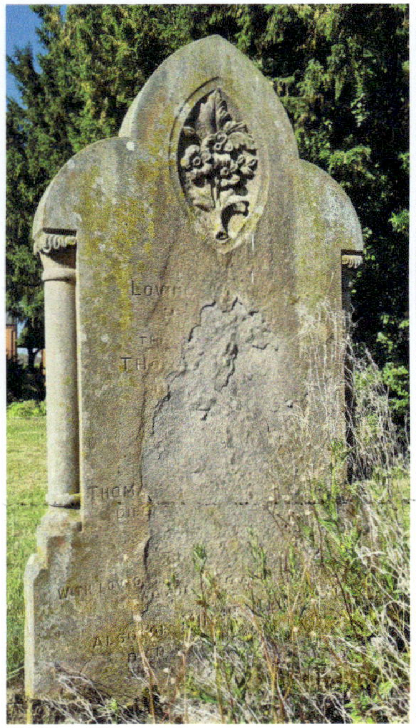
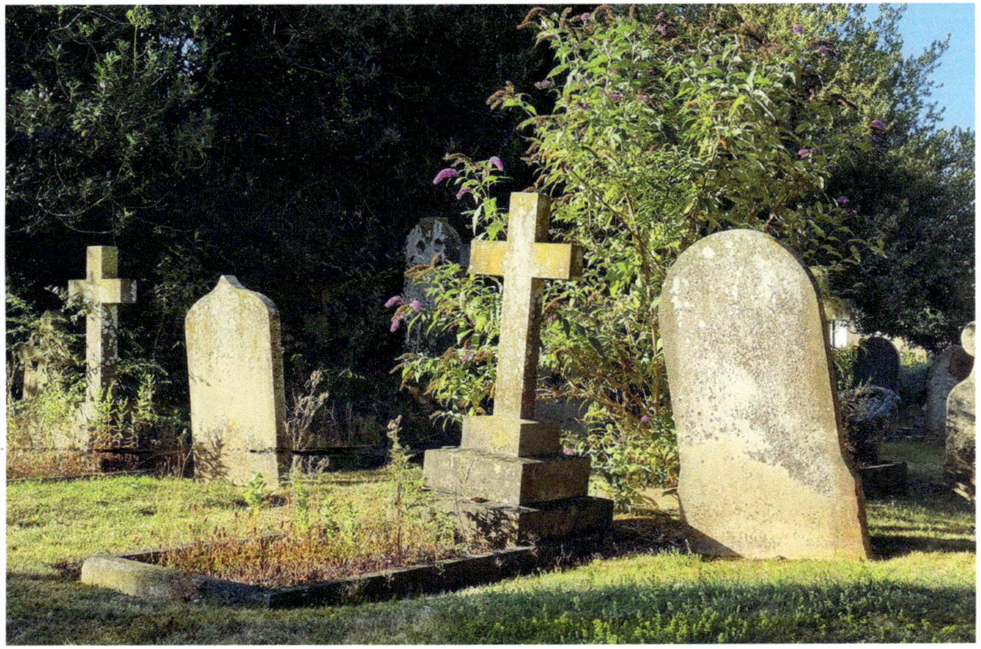

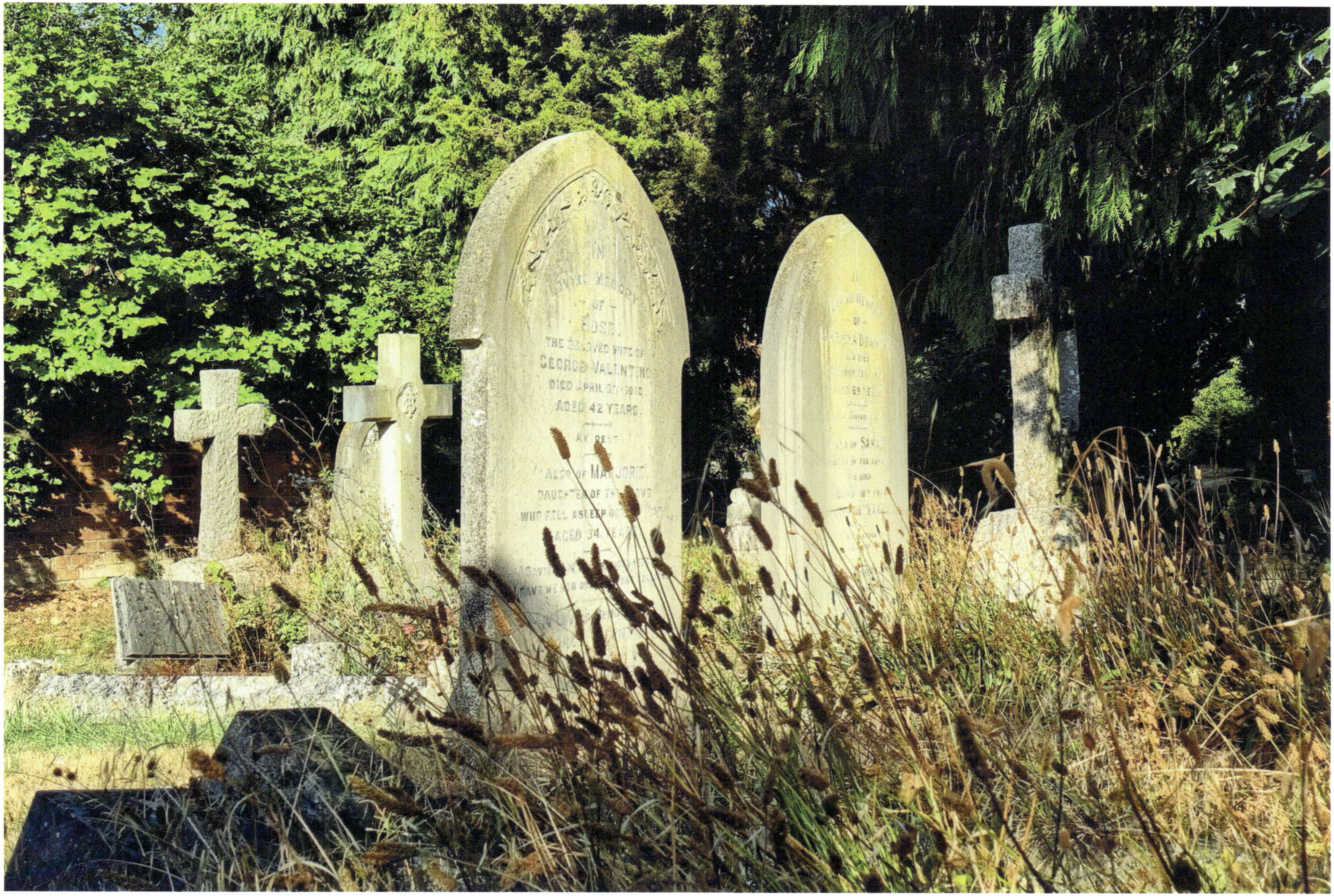
ROSE
AGED 42 YEARS

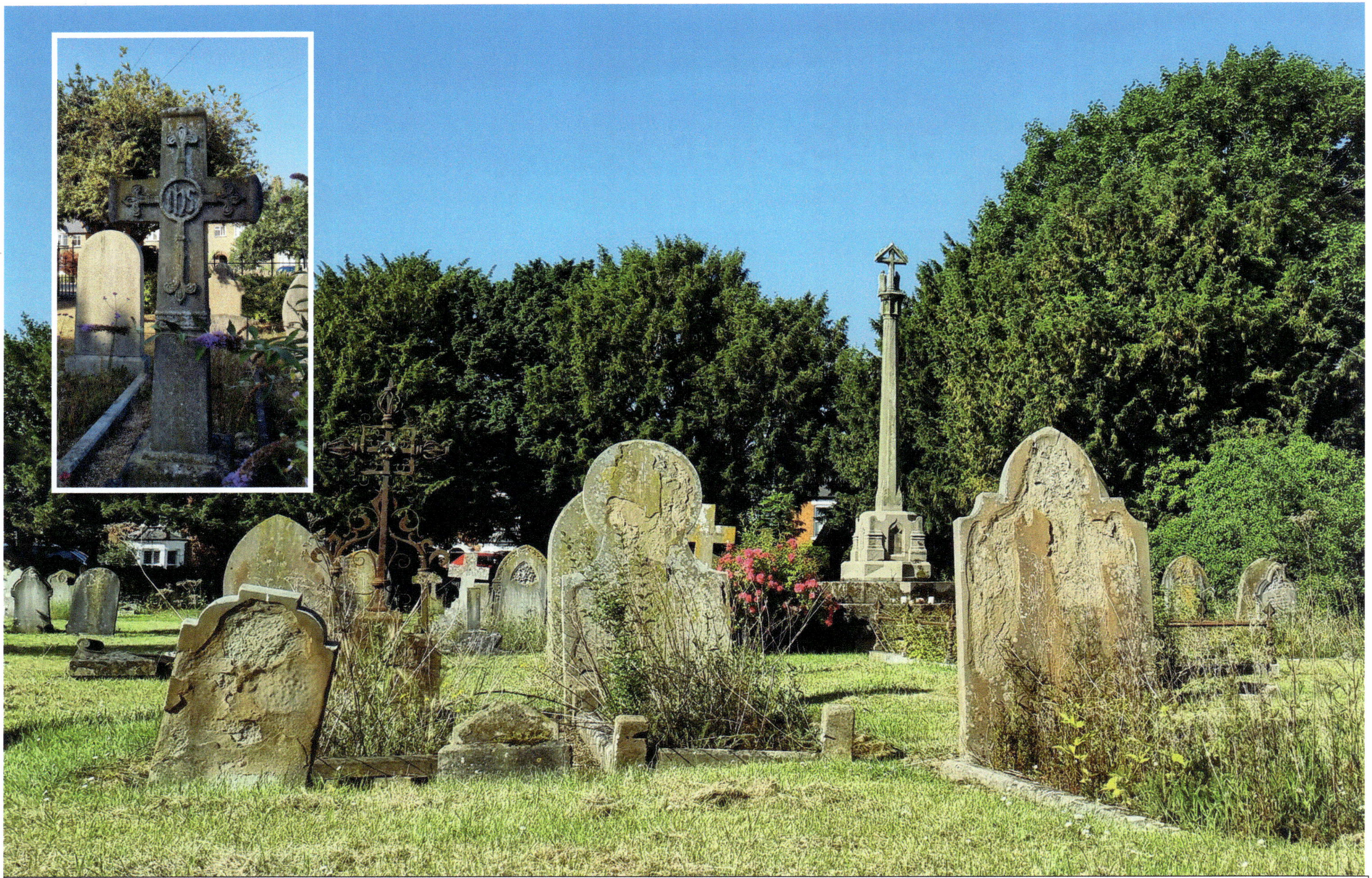

The London Road cemetery first opened in 1902. Some gravestones are shown on pages 168 to 169.

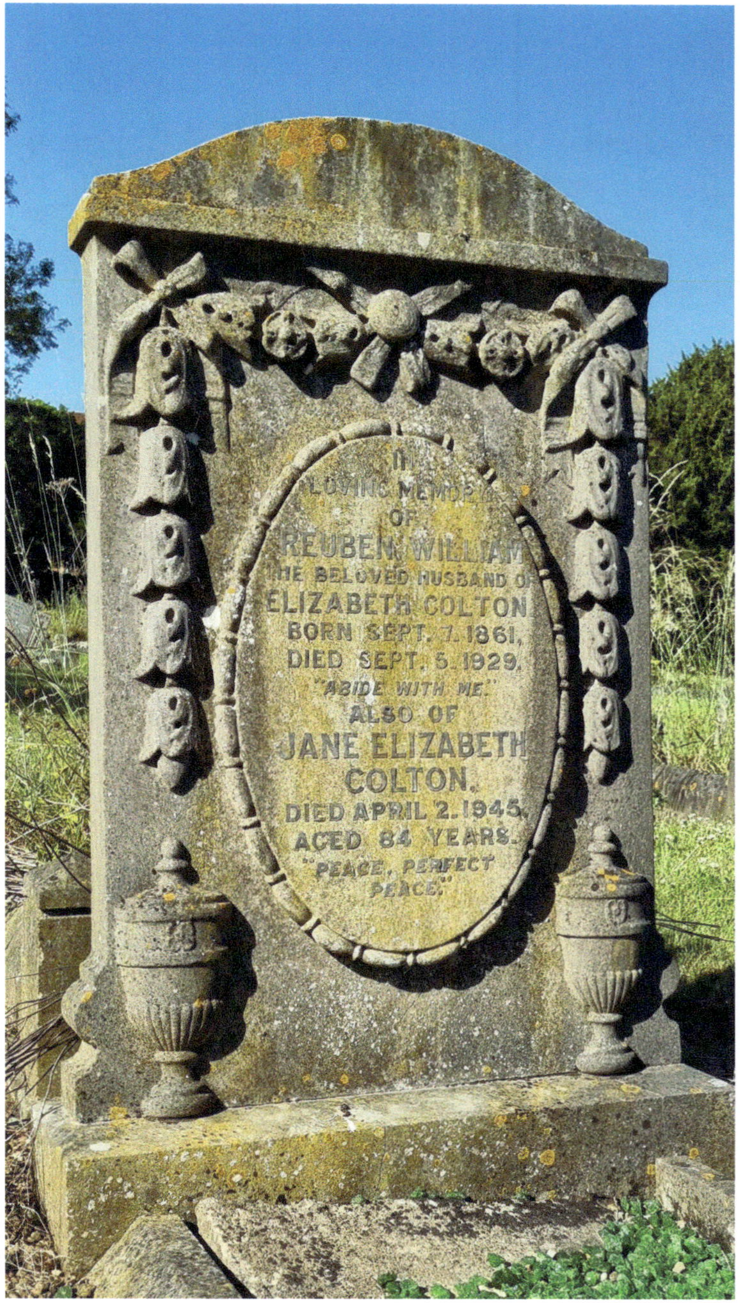
OF
REUBEN WILLIAM
THE BELOVED HUSBAND OF
ELIZABETH COLTON
BORN SEPT. 7. 1861,
DIED SEPT. 5. 1929.
"ABIDE WITH ME."
ALSO OF
JANE ELIZABETH
COLTON.
DIED APRIL 2. 1945.
AGED 84 YEARS.
"PEACE, PERFECT
PEACE."

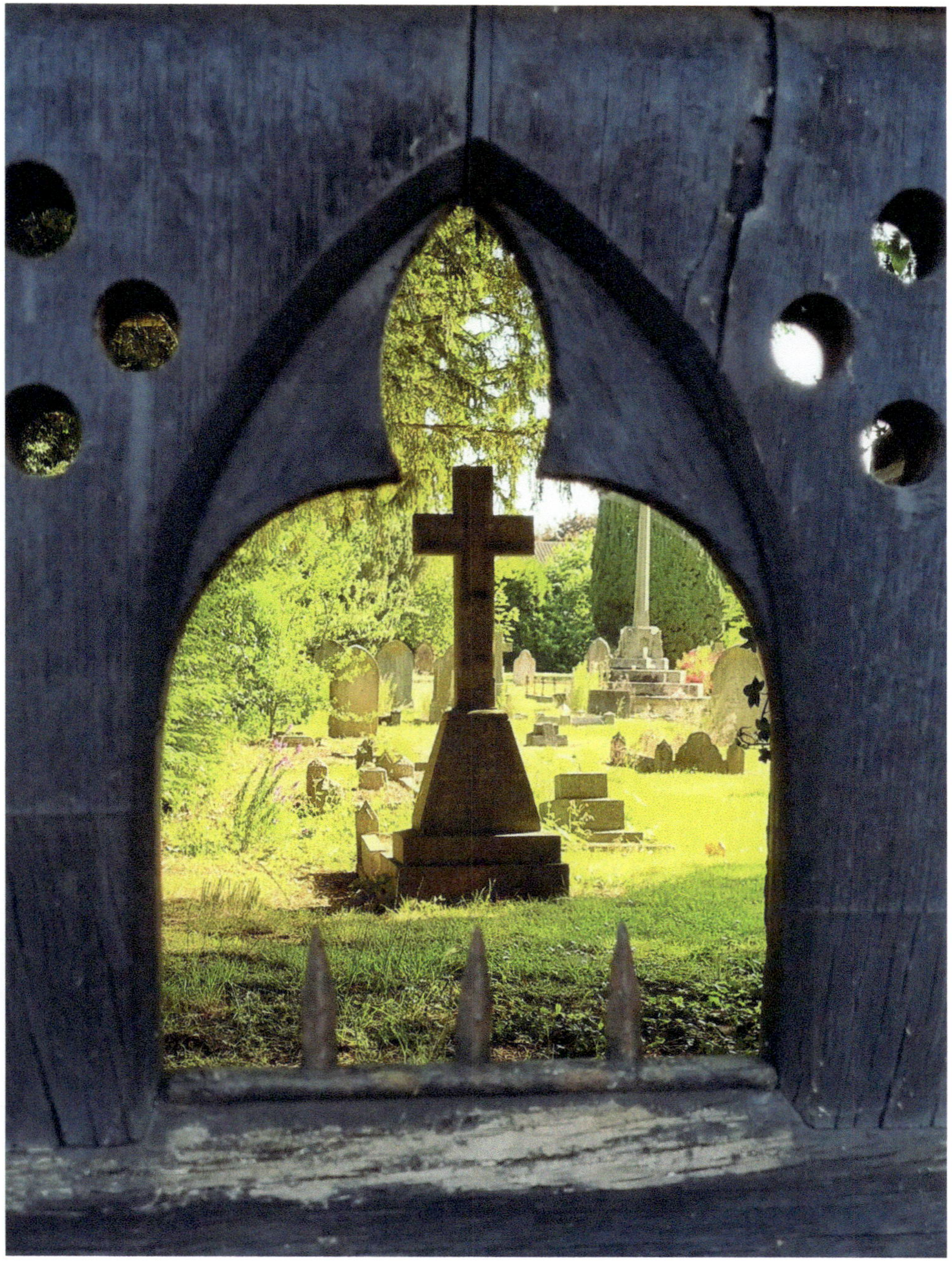

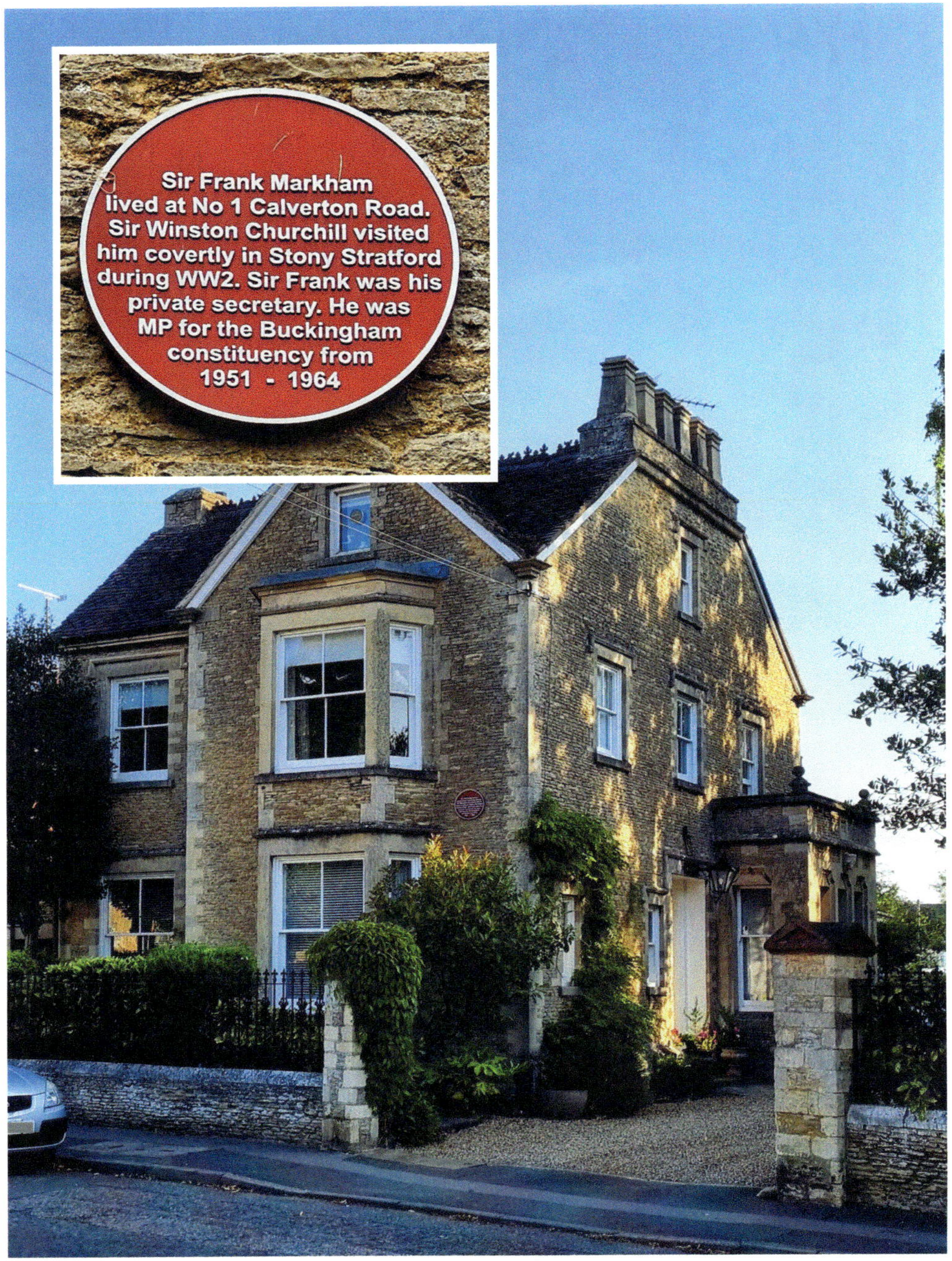

Stony Stratford Expands to Calverton

The imposing house pictured at left was once the home of Sir Frank Markham, M.P. He was born in Mill Lane and grew up on the Wolverton Road. He was commissioned as an army officer during the 1914-18 war and continued to serve until the early 1920s when he went to Oxford University. He was a Labour M.P. in the 1920s but became the Conservative candidate for Buckingham in 1950. He won the seat in 1951 and retired in 1964.

The photograph on page 172 is of Calverton House. For many years this stood in the middle of a large acreage and was the only property west of Horsefair Green. It was built in the 1850s by the Reverend Campnell Manning Christie, who came to Calverton's church in 1851. However, he was dissatisfied with the accommodation on offer and built his own 20 room house.

The house passed through several owners for about a century until in 1954 Mr. W W Dickins offered the property to Bucks County Council for use as an old people's home. They declined, and in 1959, Wolverton Urban District Council acquired the property and converted it into flats. In the Milton Keynes era the land around the house was developed as a housing estate.

In the 19th century a plot was reserved for a cemetery on the Calverton Road and two red brick terraced streets were built on either side - Park Road and Augustus Road.

After the Second World War the fields to the west of the London Road were ripe for development and some rather spacious properties were built along wide avenues. This development continued throughout the second half of the 20th century and into this century.

When the new town of Milton Keynes was conceived 50 years ago it was believed that the Calverton and Calverton Weald lands were inviolate, but the demands of the new city appear to be insatiable and the ancient village of Calverton is now only one field away from Milton Keynes development.

LOOK AT
WEST SIDE EXPANSION

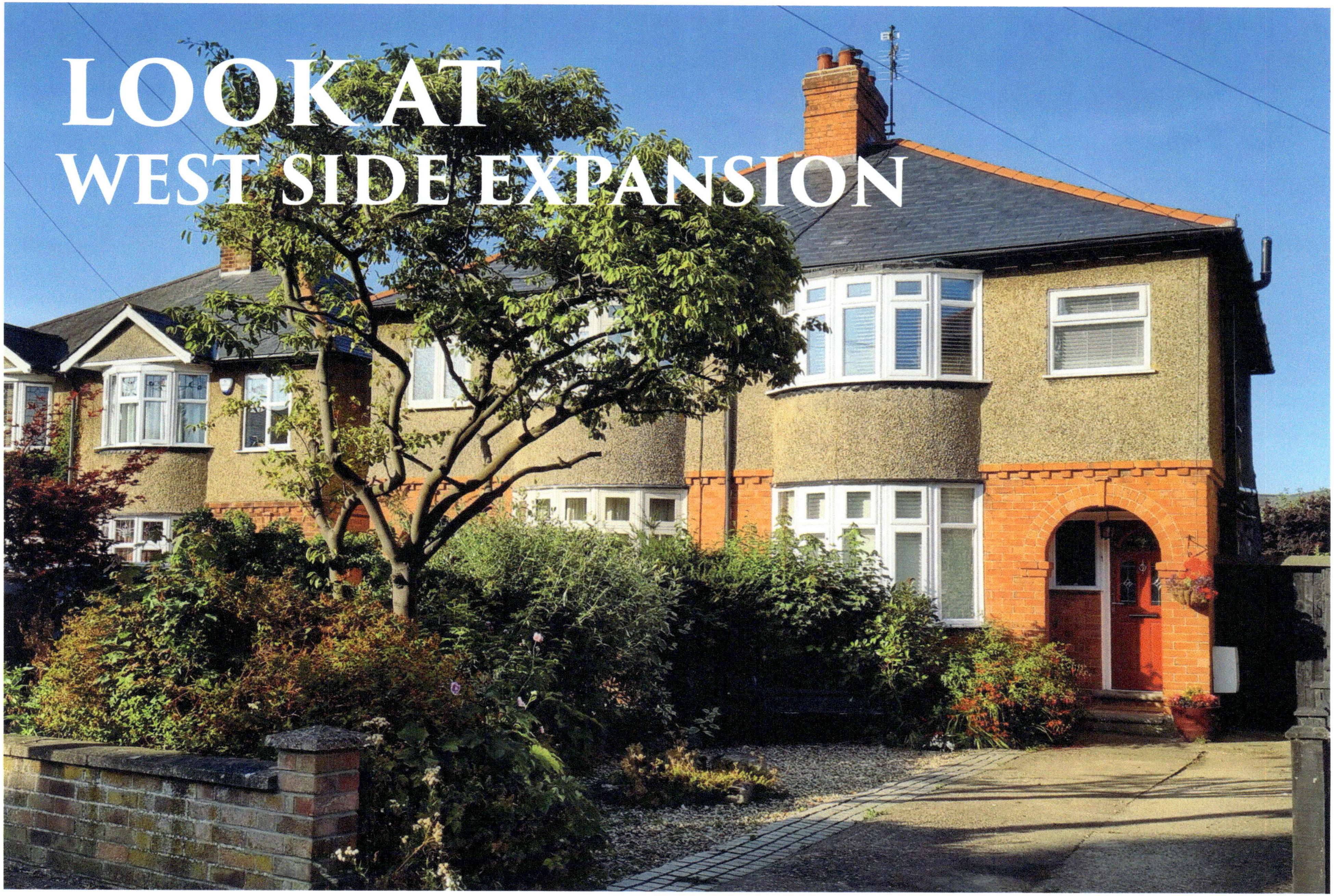

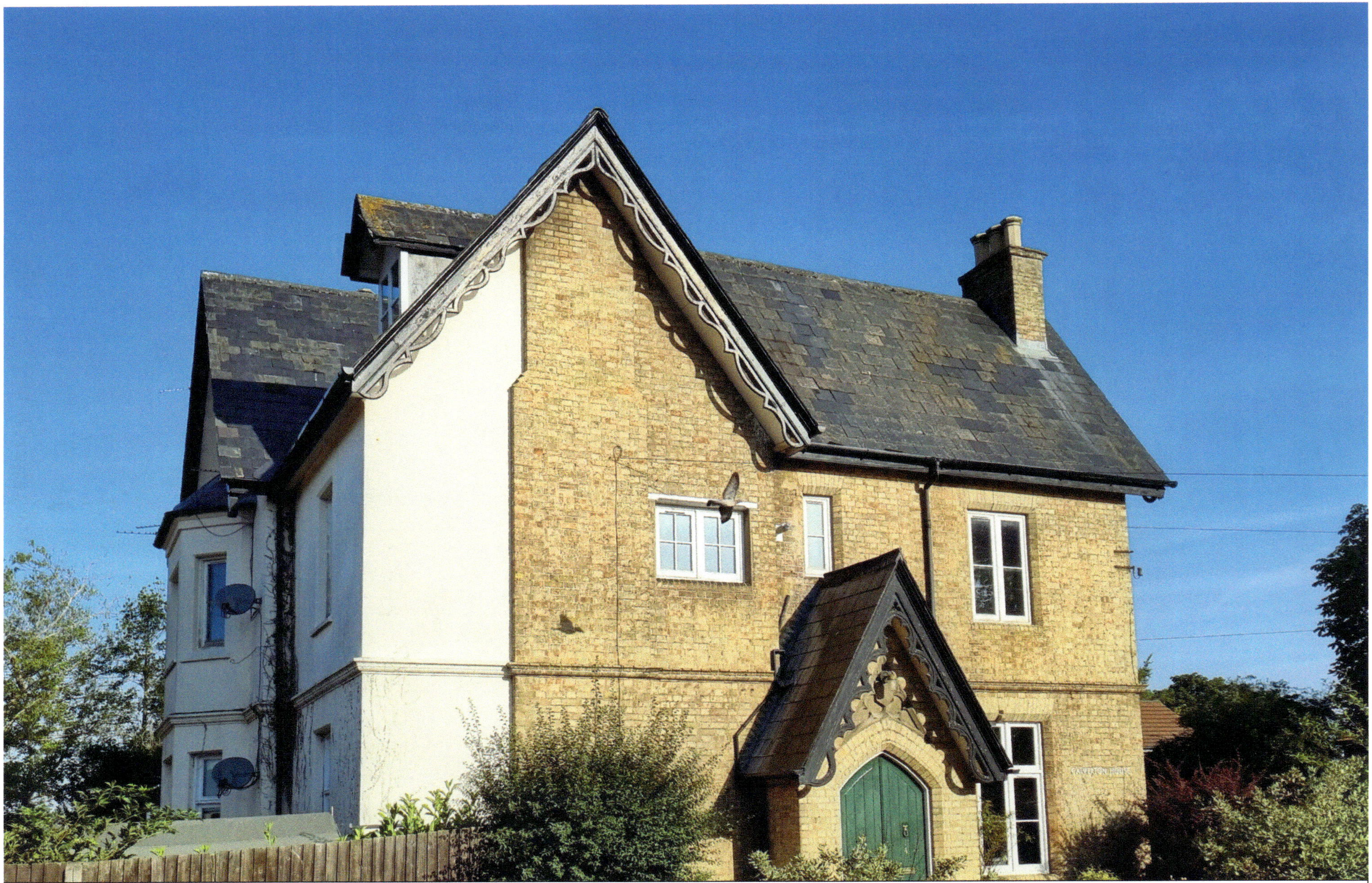

Calverton House once sat in the middle of extensive grounds. Now this land has been developed as a housing estate.

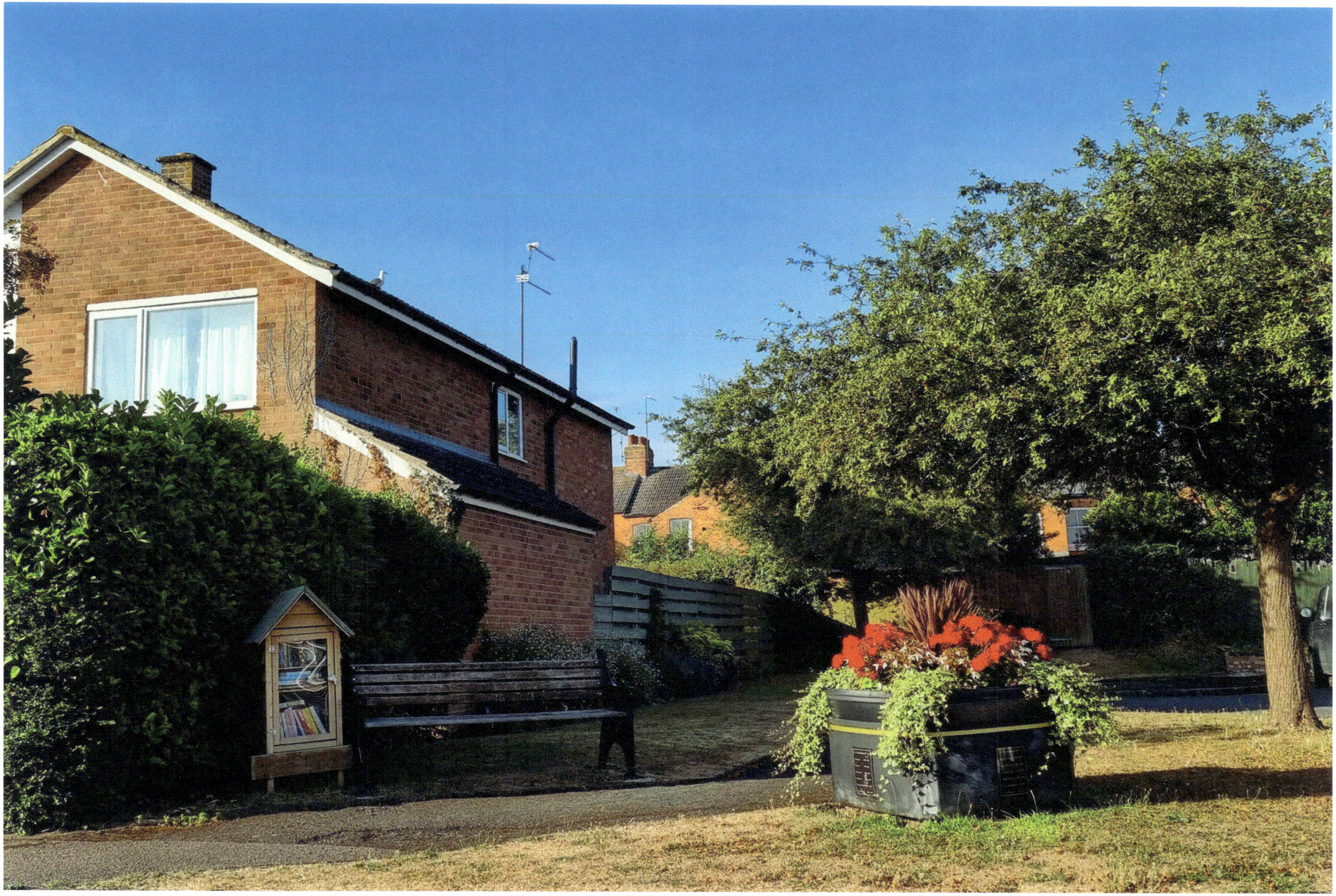

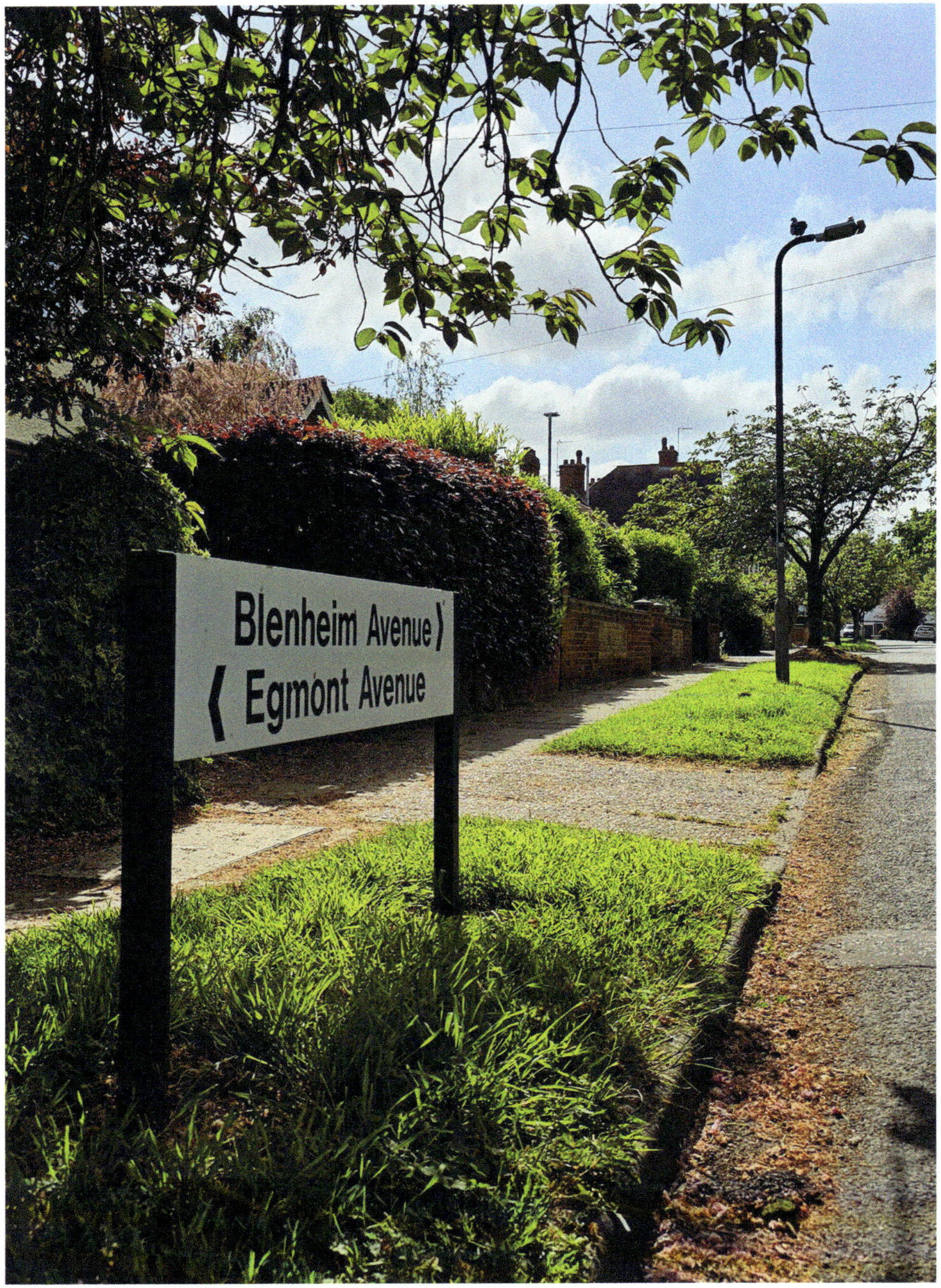
Blenheim Avenue
Egmont Avenue

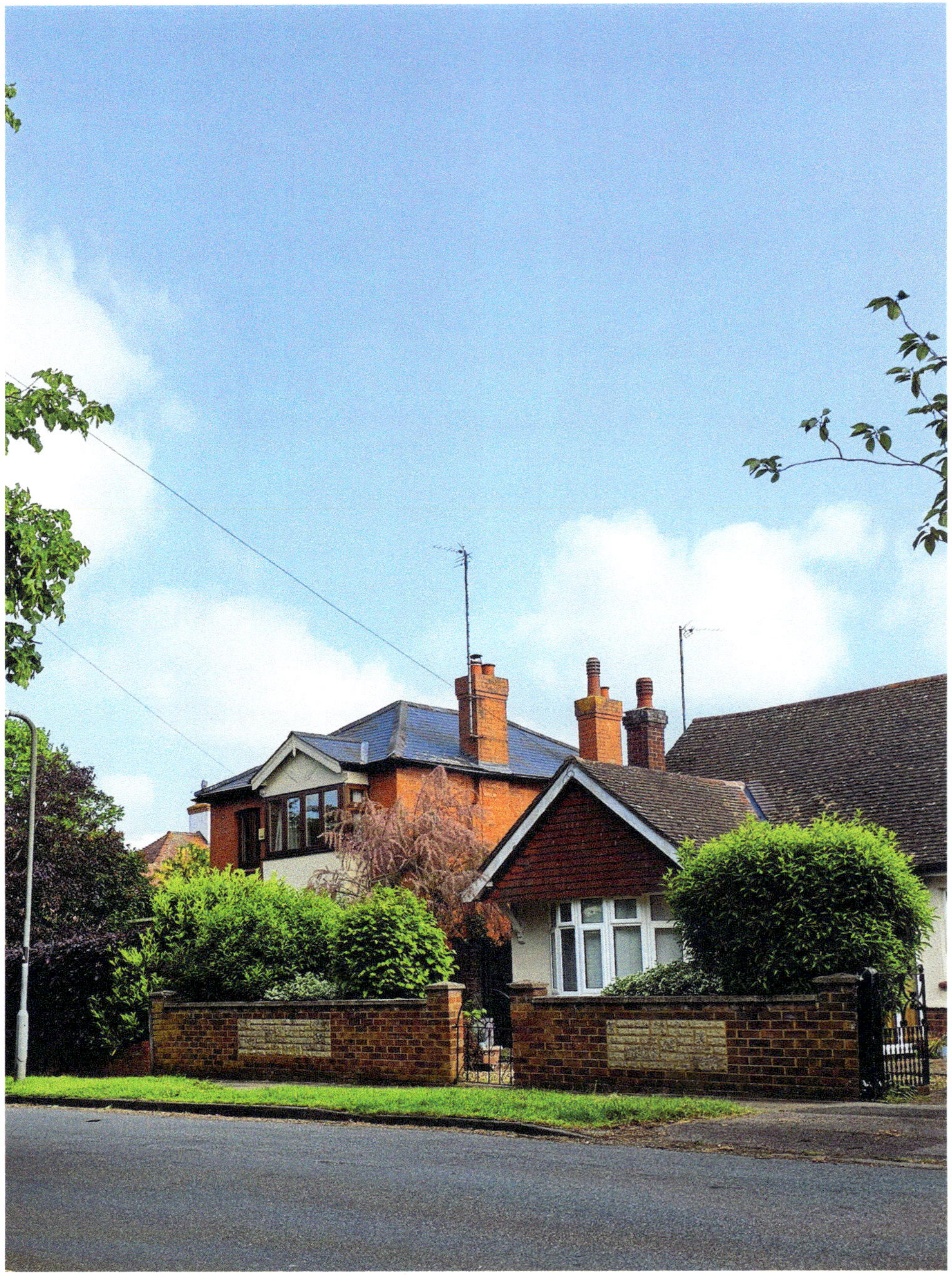

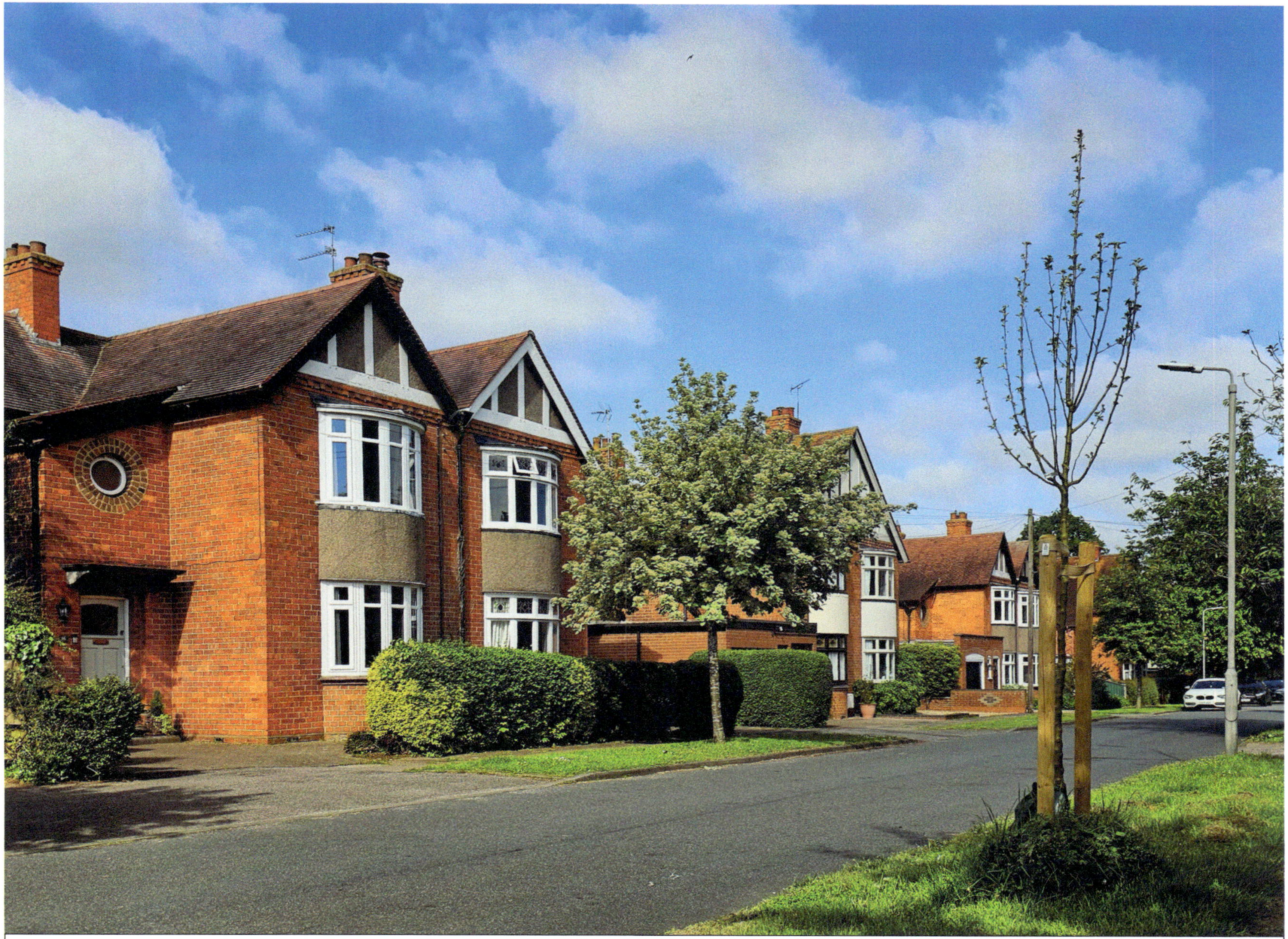

Spacious semi-detatched houses in Blenheim Avenue. This leafy development is shown on pages 174 to 178.

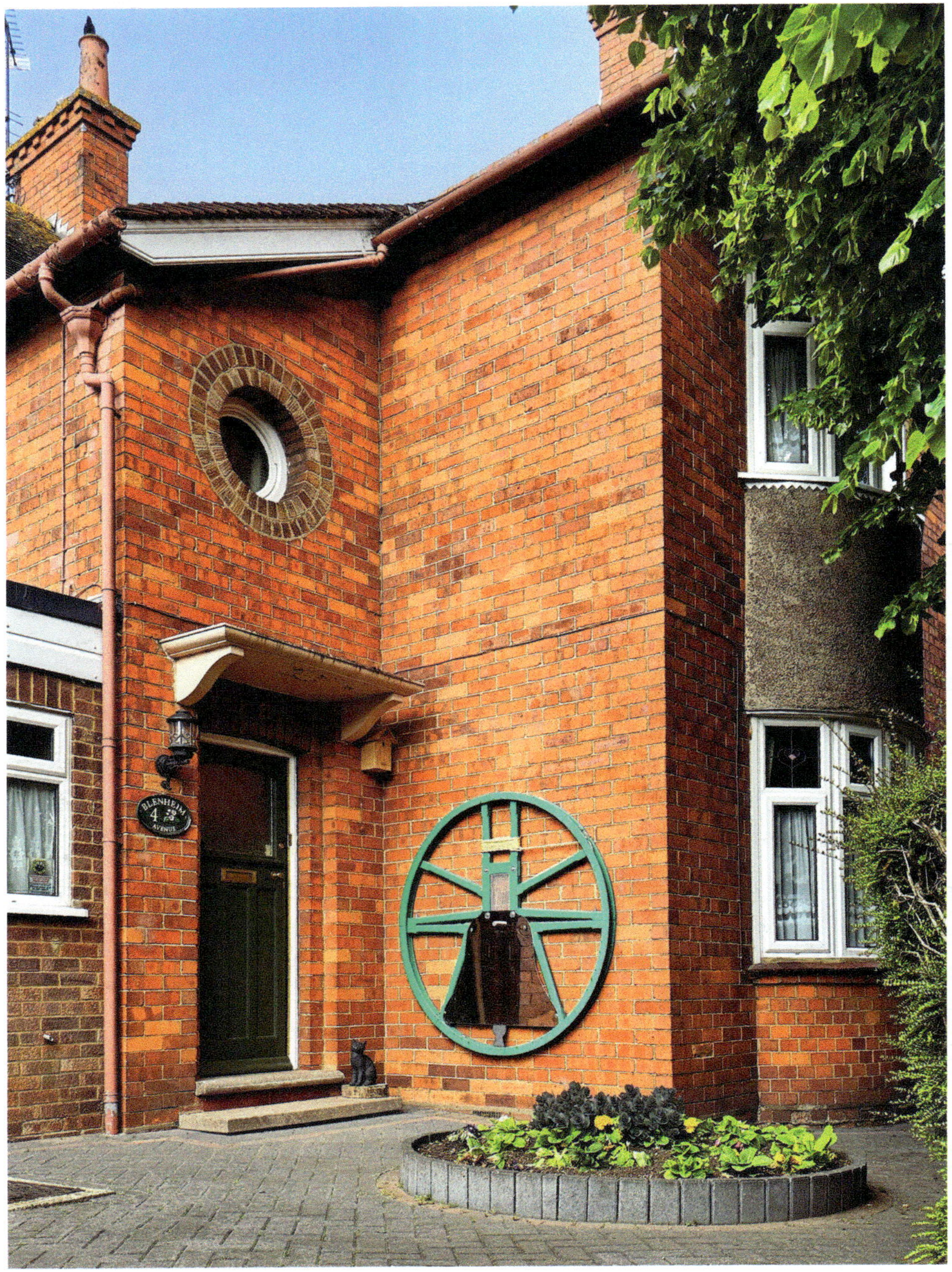
BLENHEIM
4
AVENUE

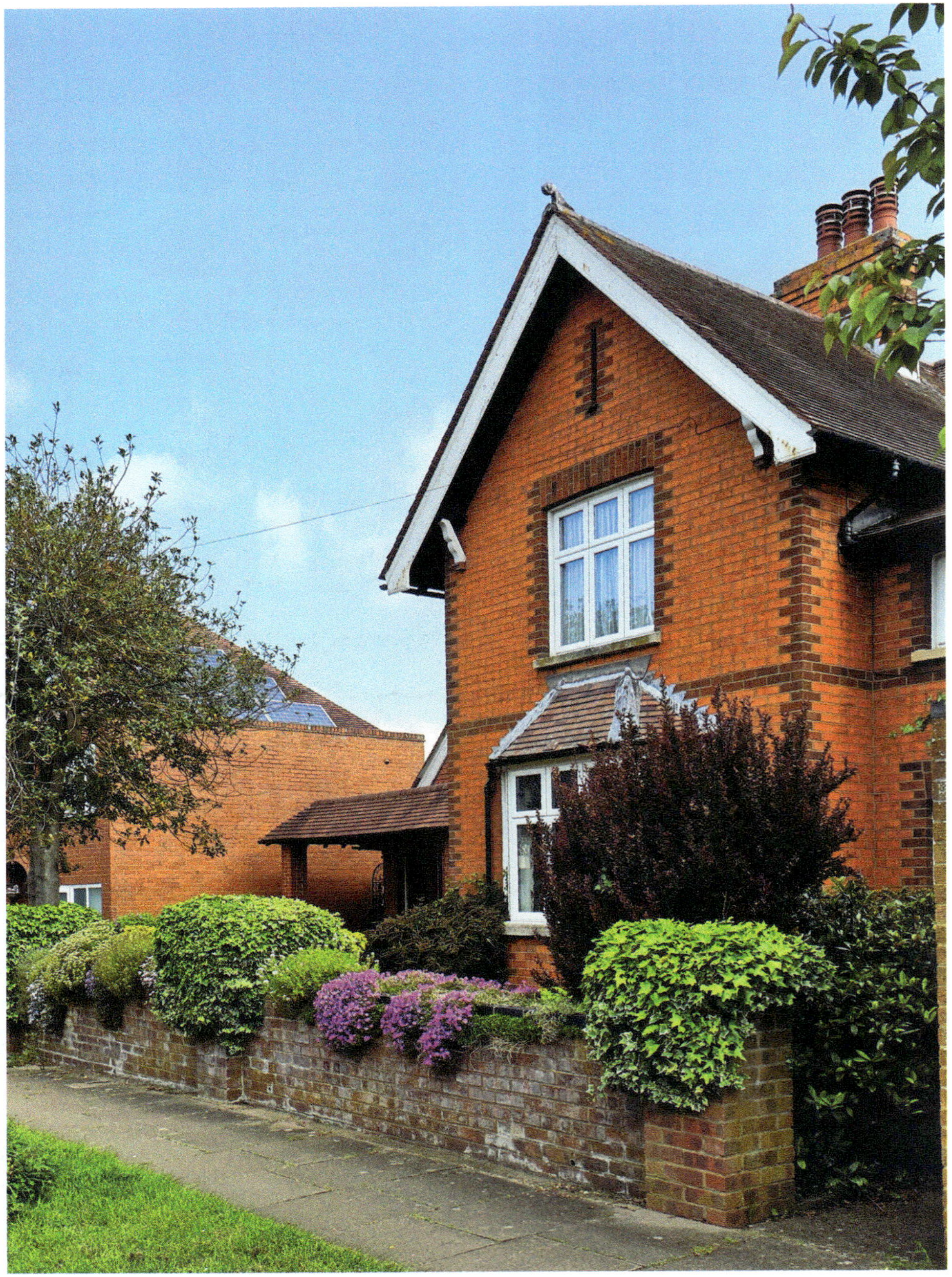

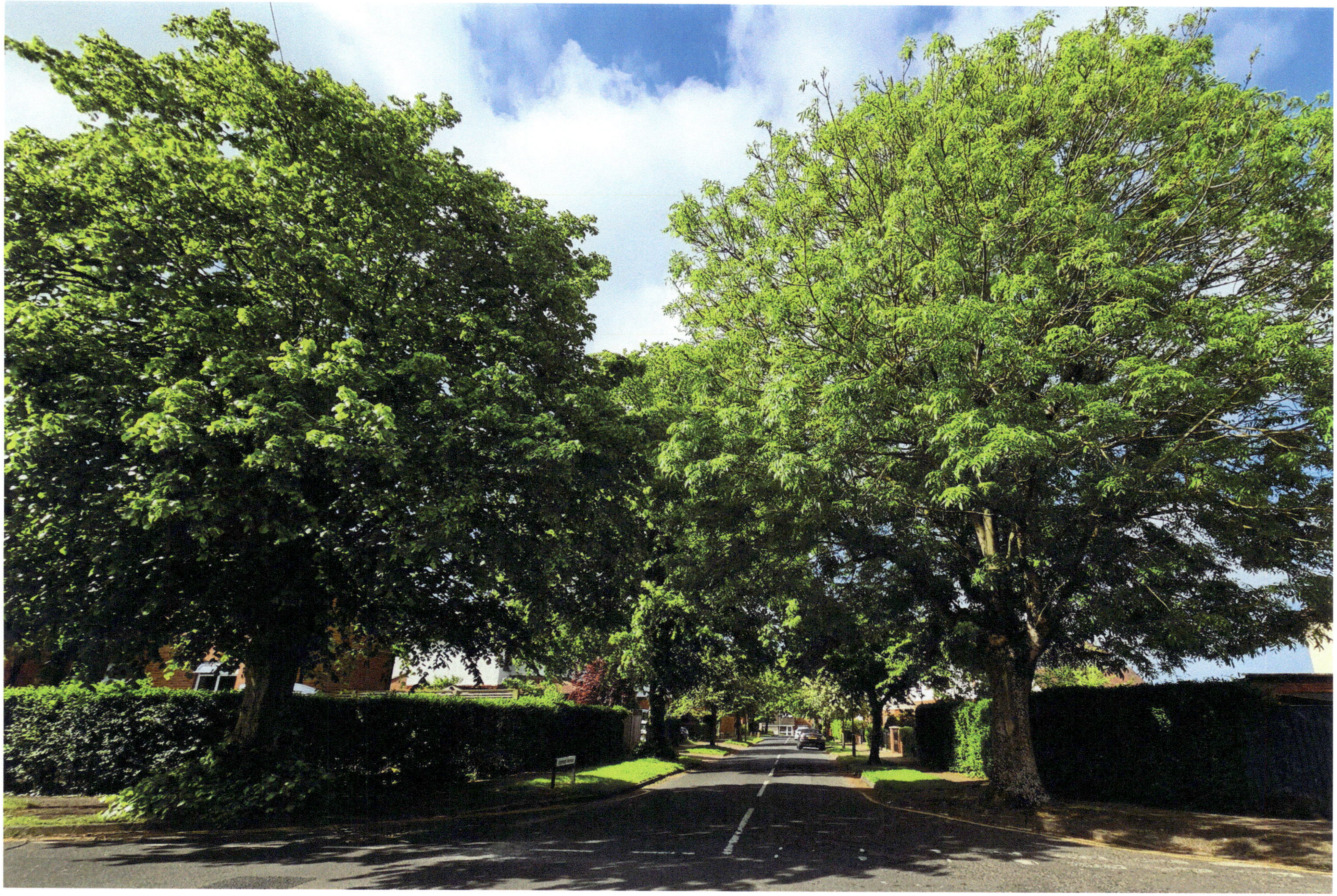

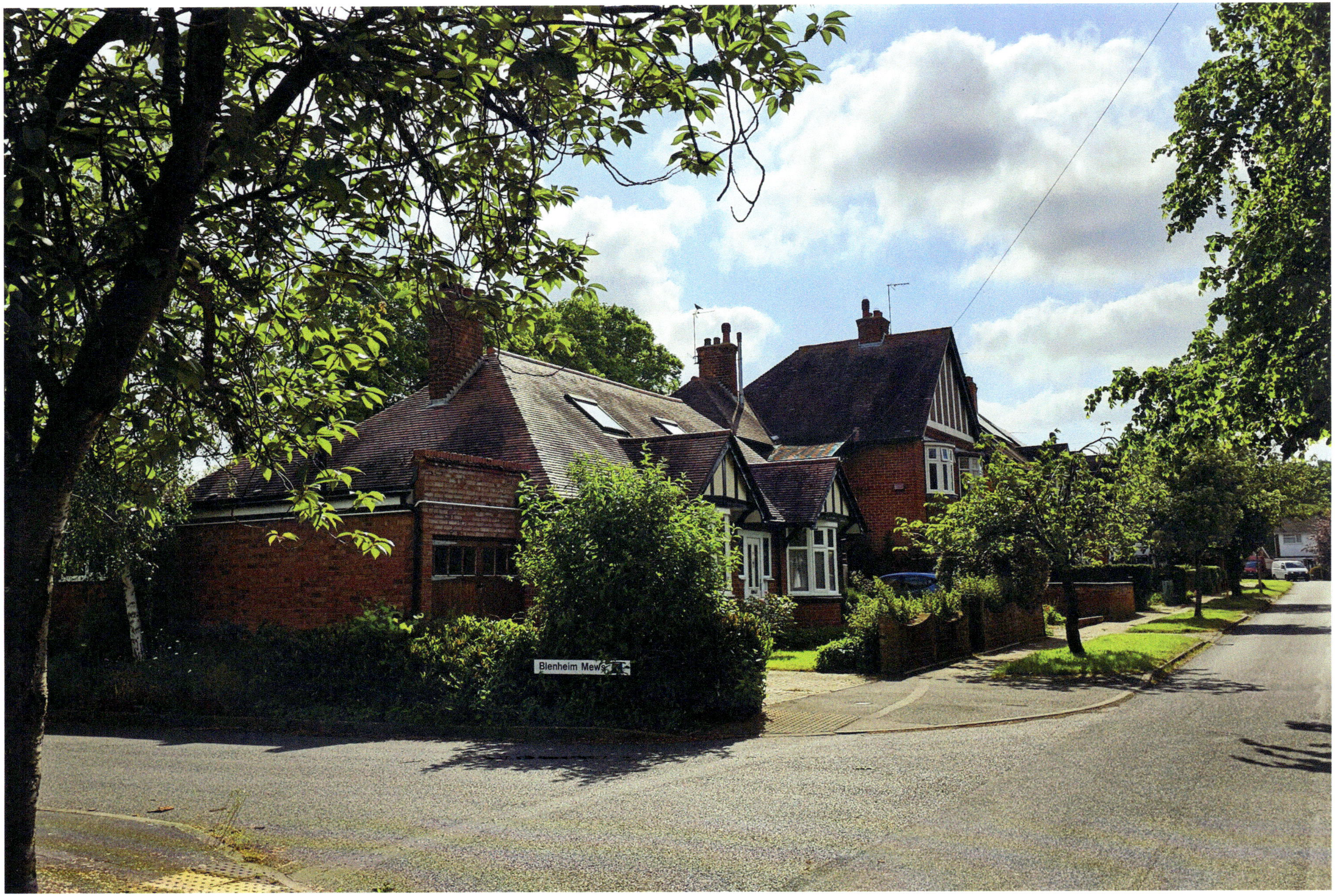
Blenheim Mews

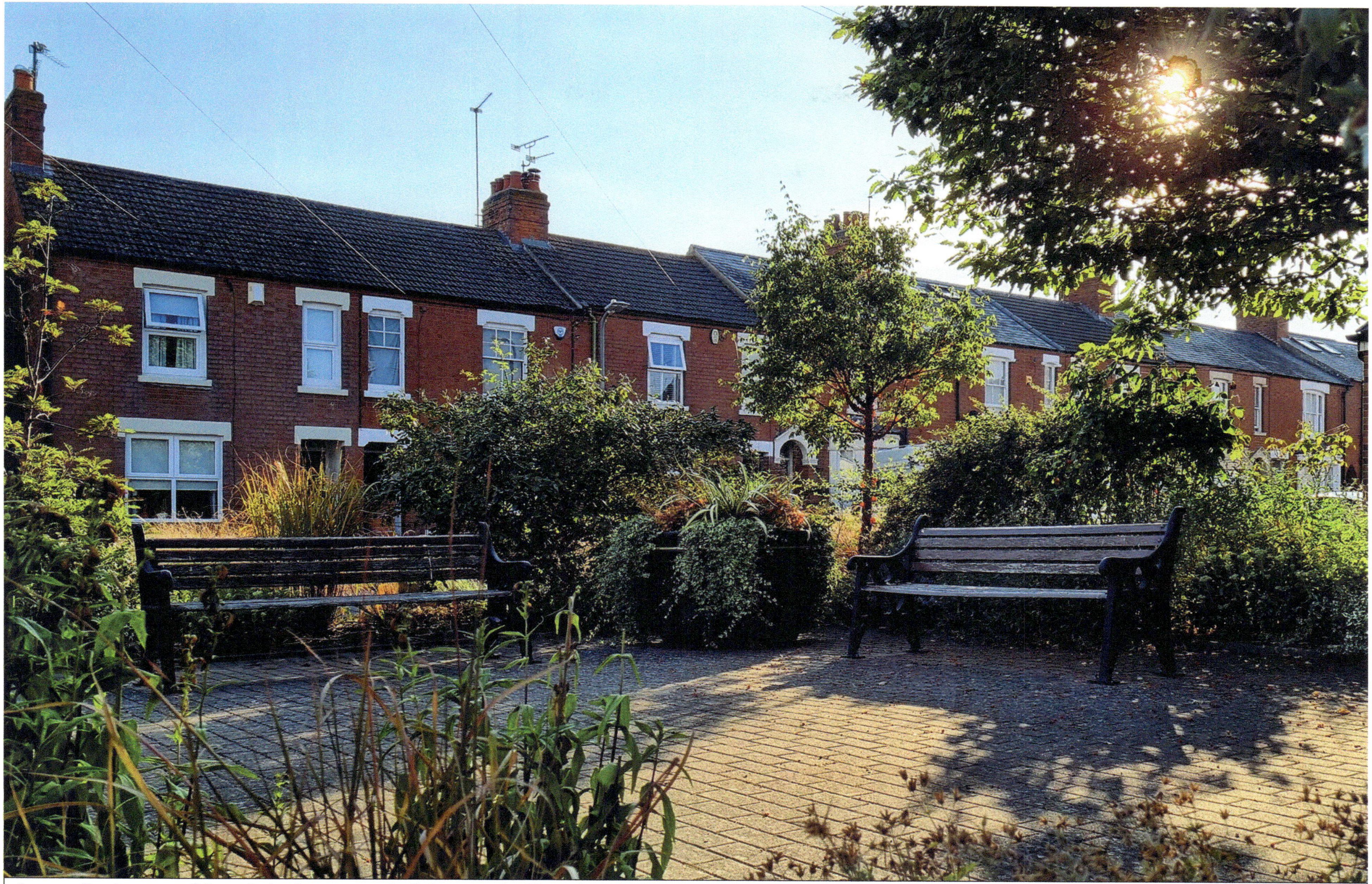

Augustus Road was one of the early developments on the Calverton side of Stony Stratford.

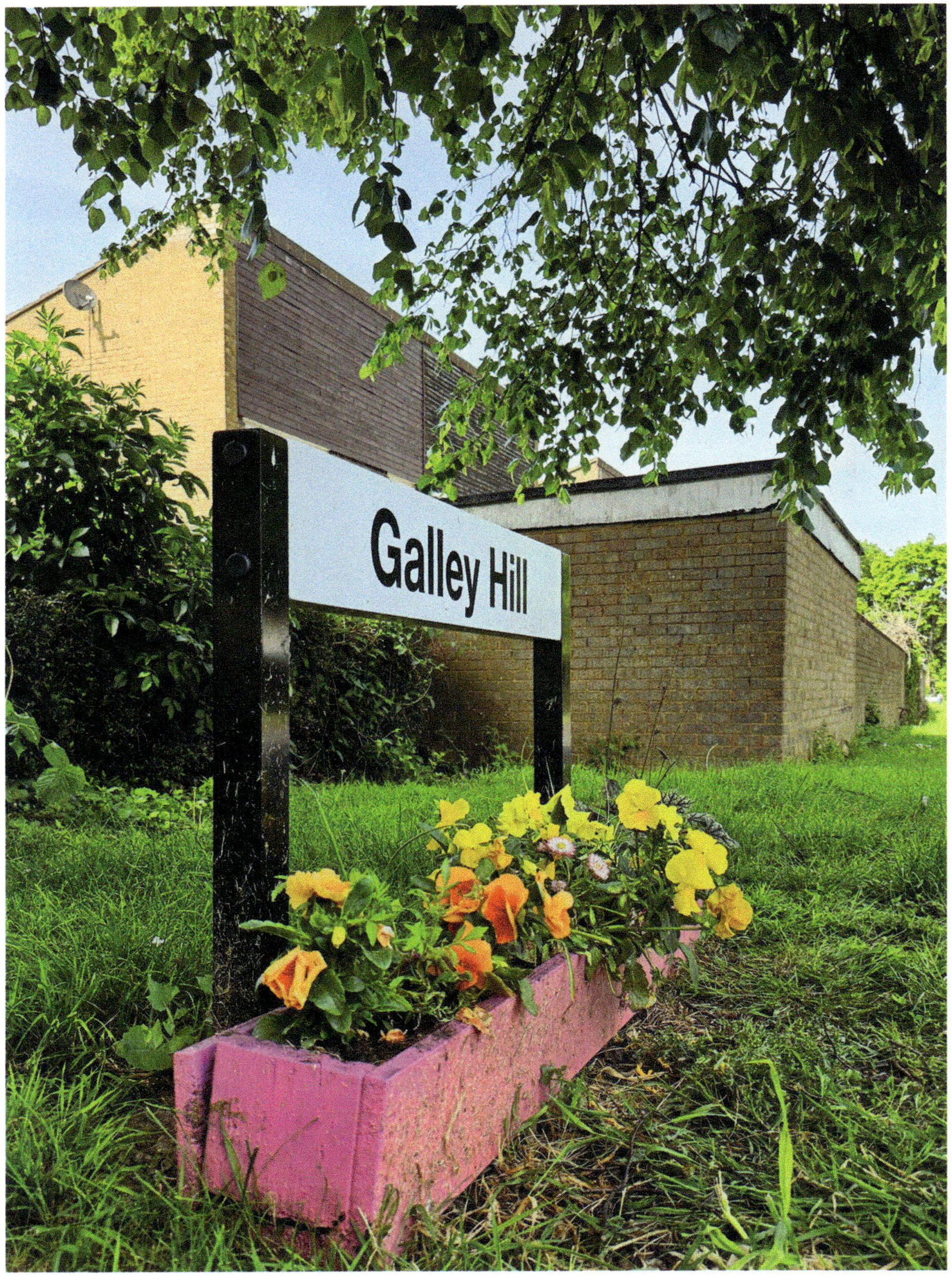

GALLEY HILL

Galley Hill has some significance for Stony Stratford and Milton Keynes, in that it was the very first housing development undertaken by the new Milton Keynes Development Corporation in 1967.

The development brought an unusual shed roof design to North Bucks. The houses were semi-detached, but no thought was given to the need for a garage. The houses were, nevertheless, quite spacious and well designed inside.

After over half a century, the landscape has matured and this now appears as a most attractive area.

Galley Hill was so named because this was the location for the gallows, should any miscreant need to be hanged. There was an ancient trackway which runs from Calverton eastward, that at one time joined Green Lane in Wolverton. In Stony Stratford it was known as Gib Lane. Gib is short for 'gibbett.'

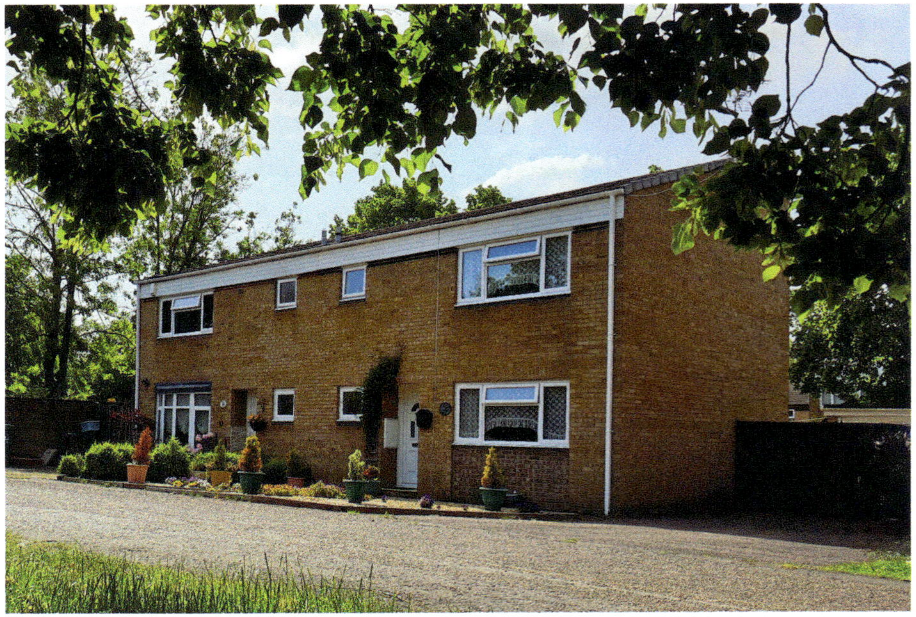

LOOK AT GALLEY HILL

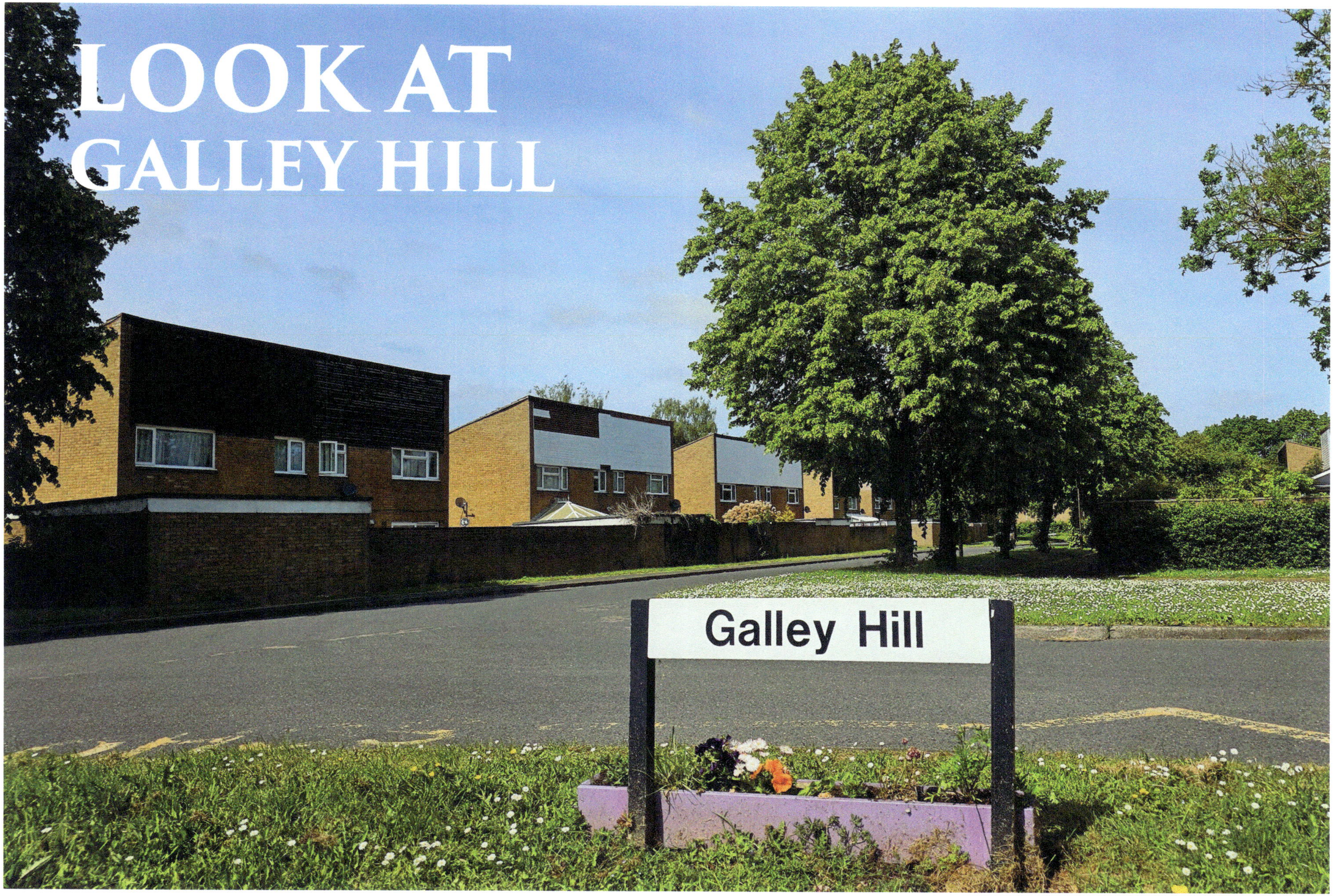

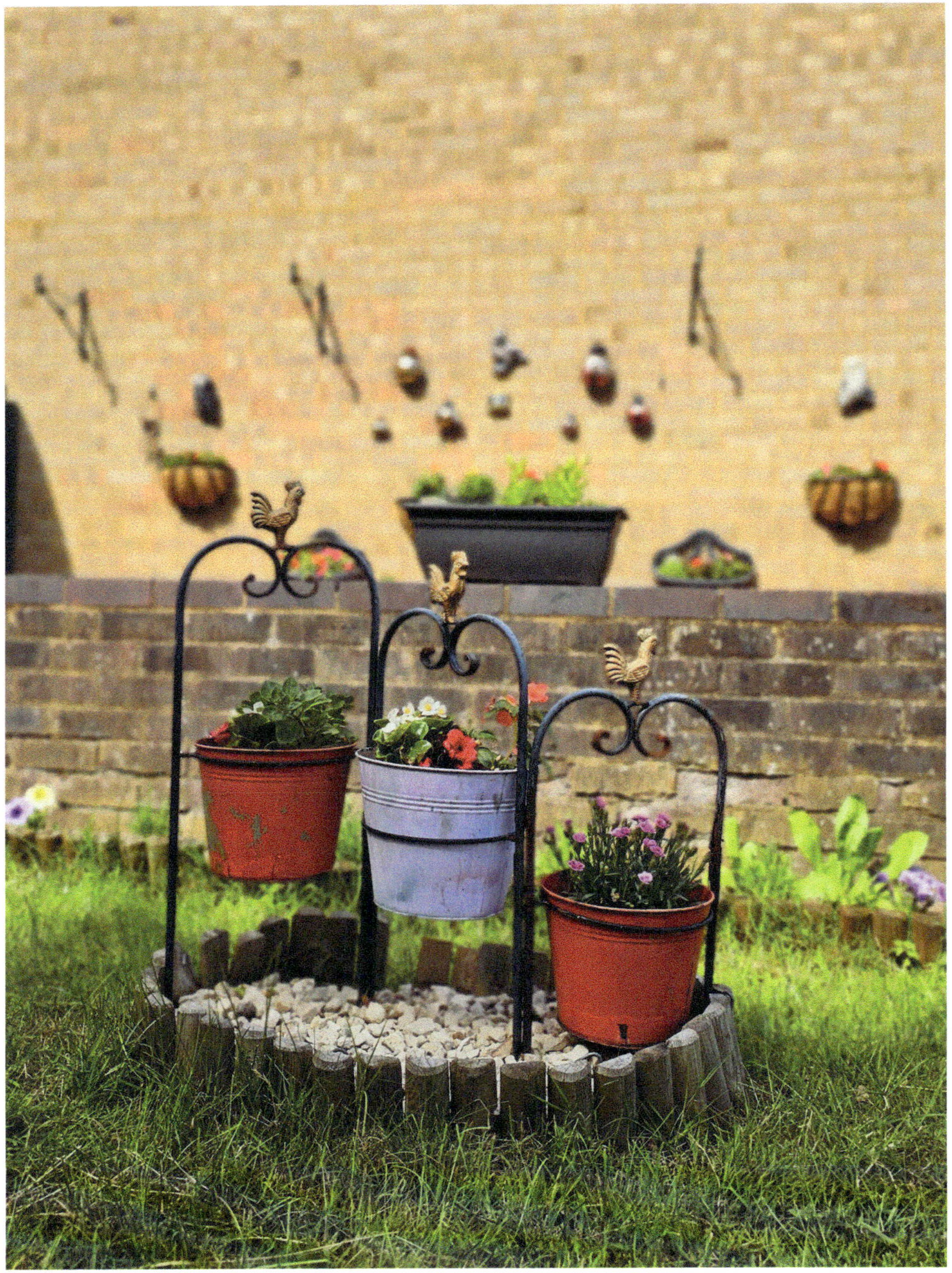

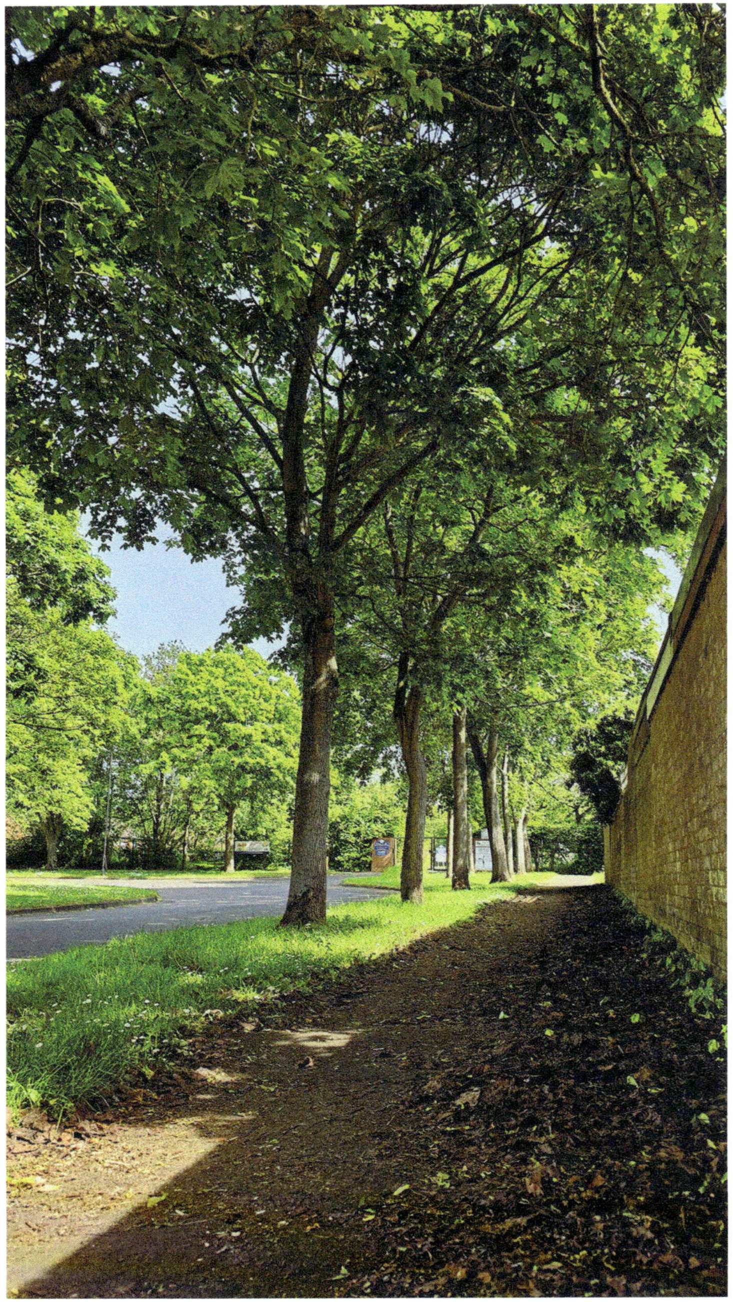

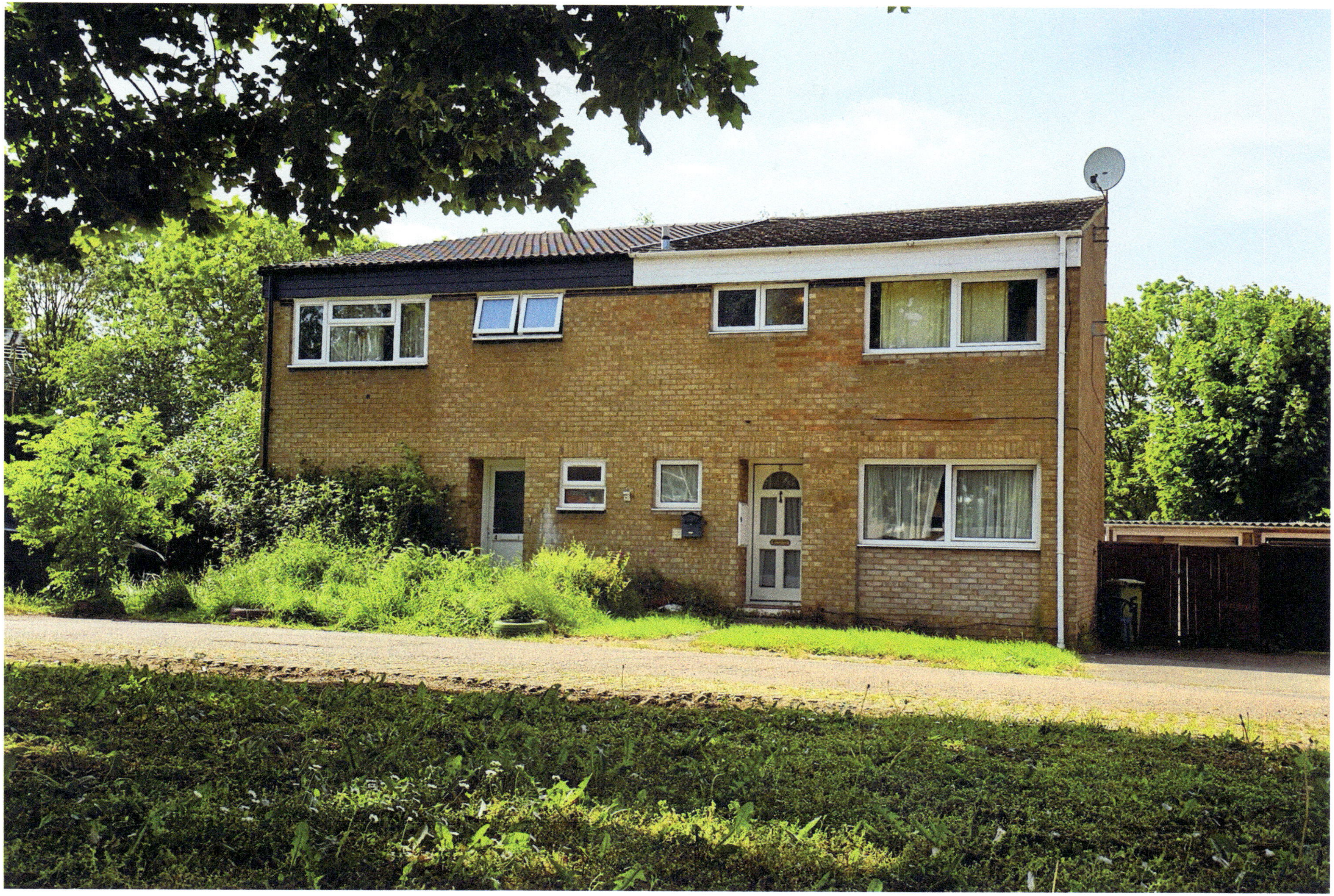

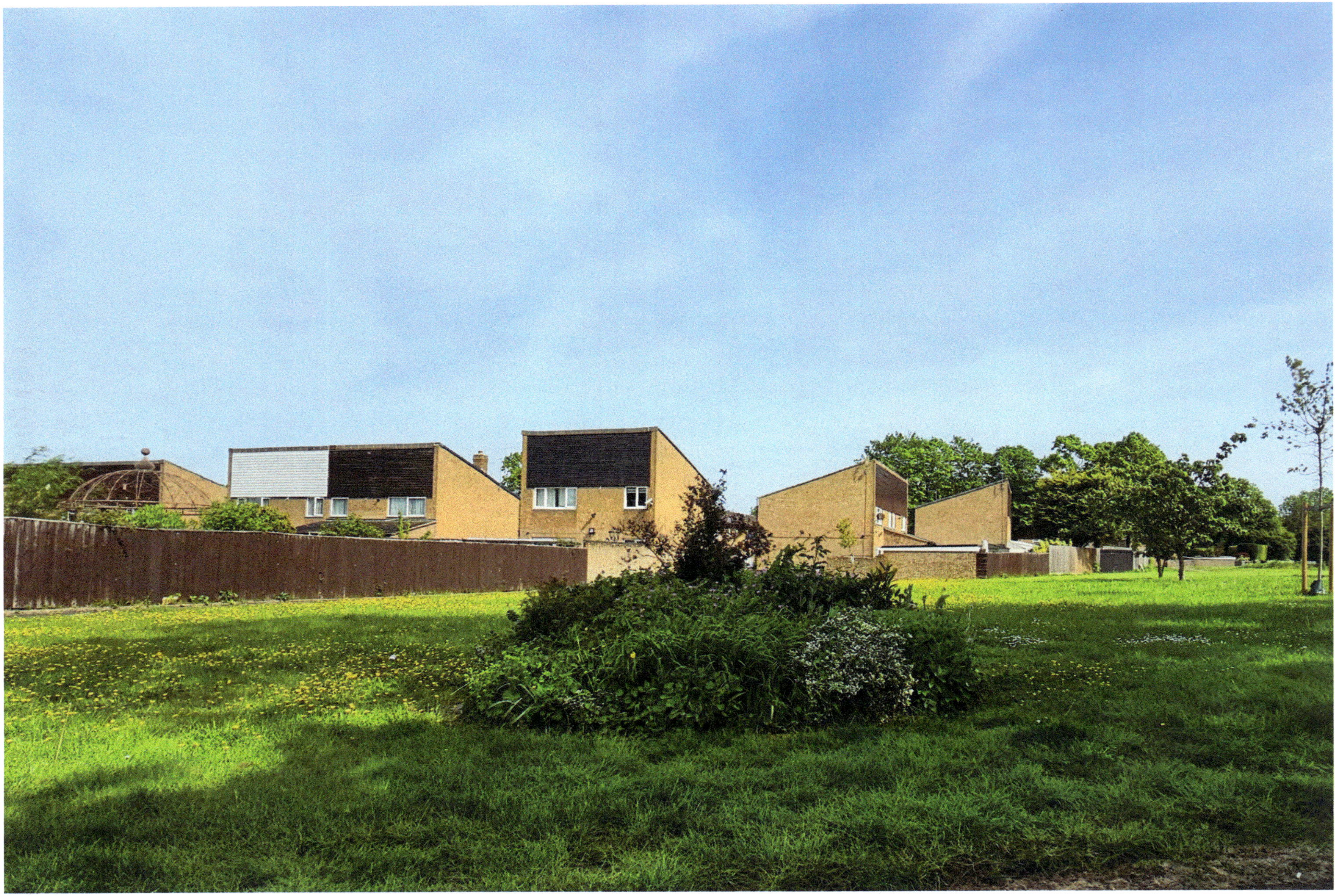

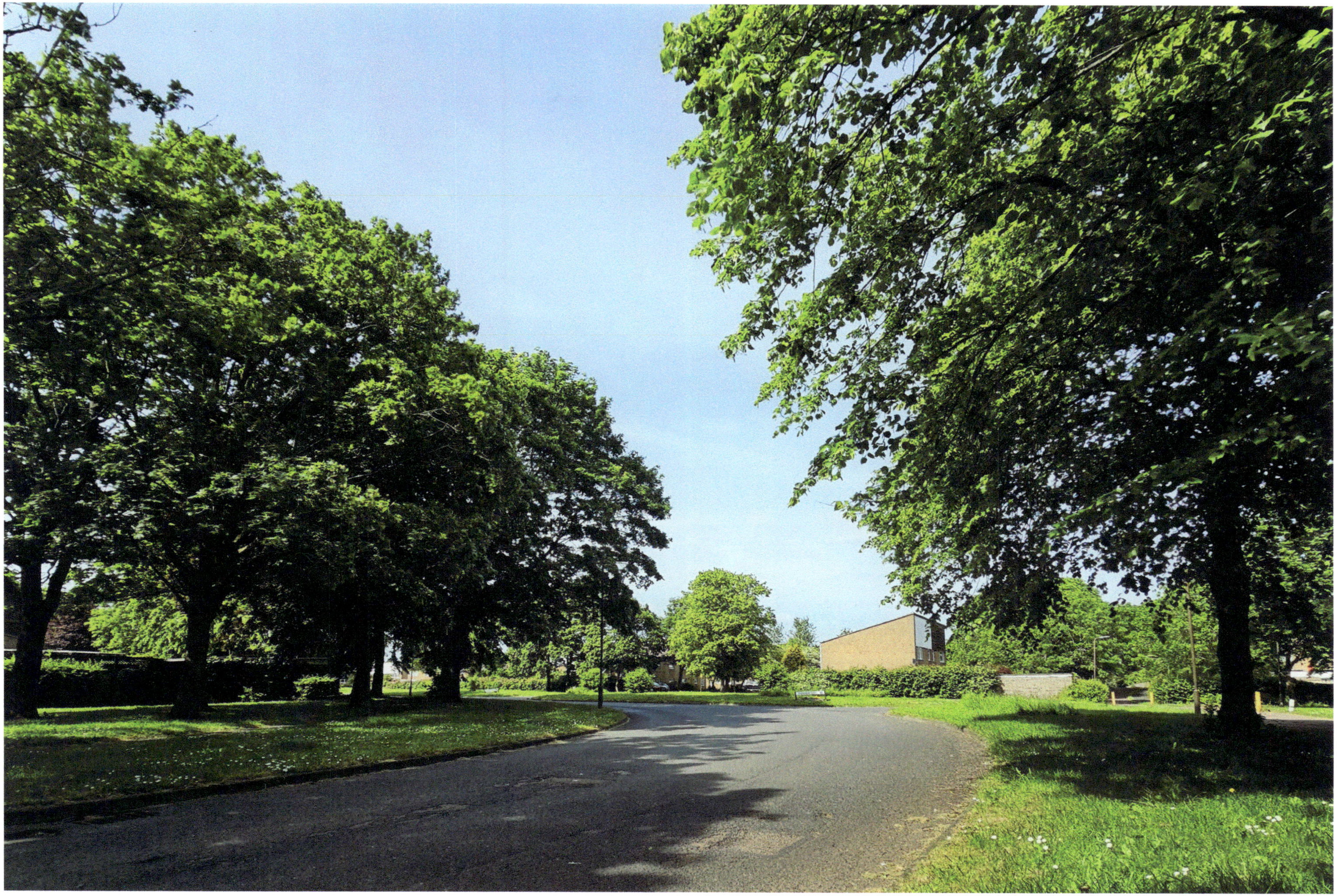

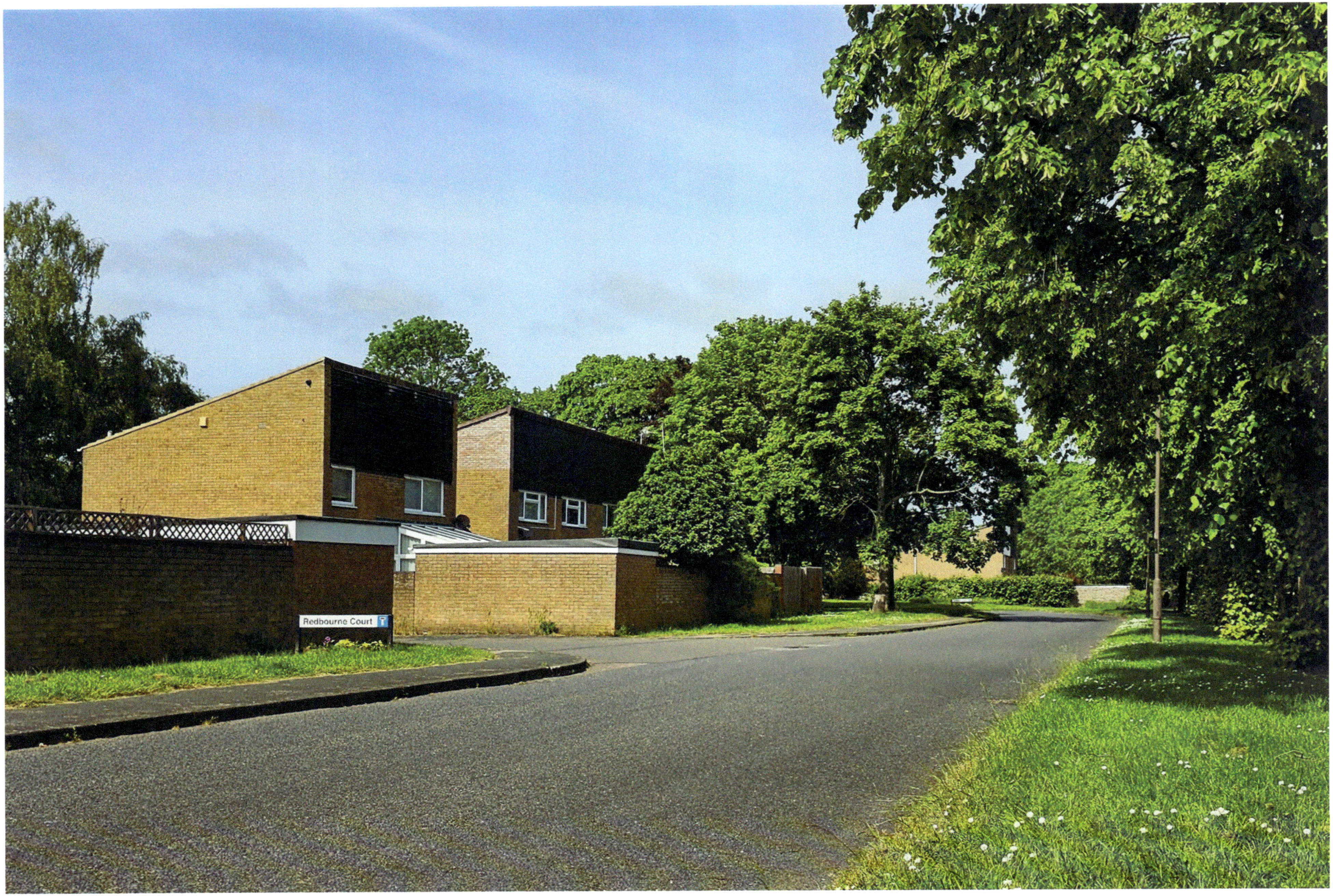
Redbourne Court

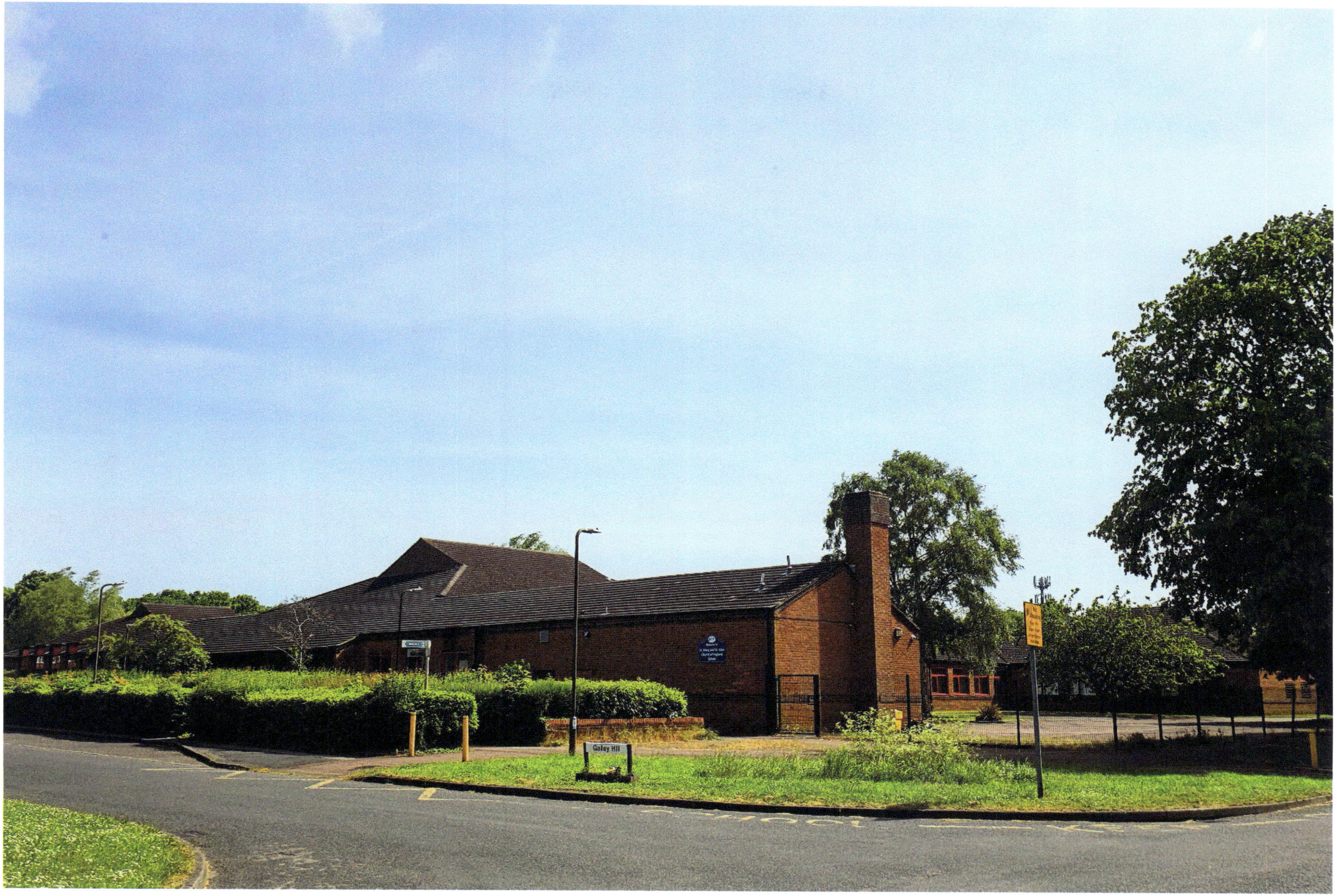
Galley Hill

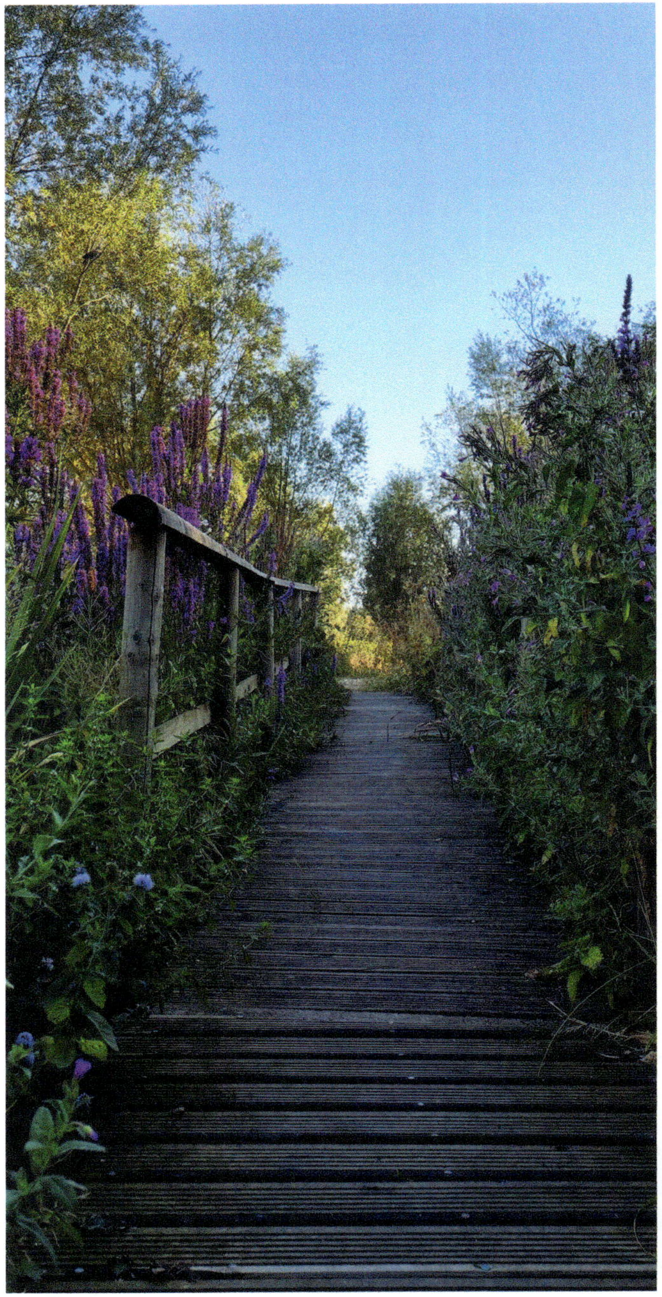

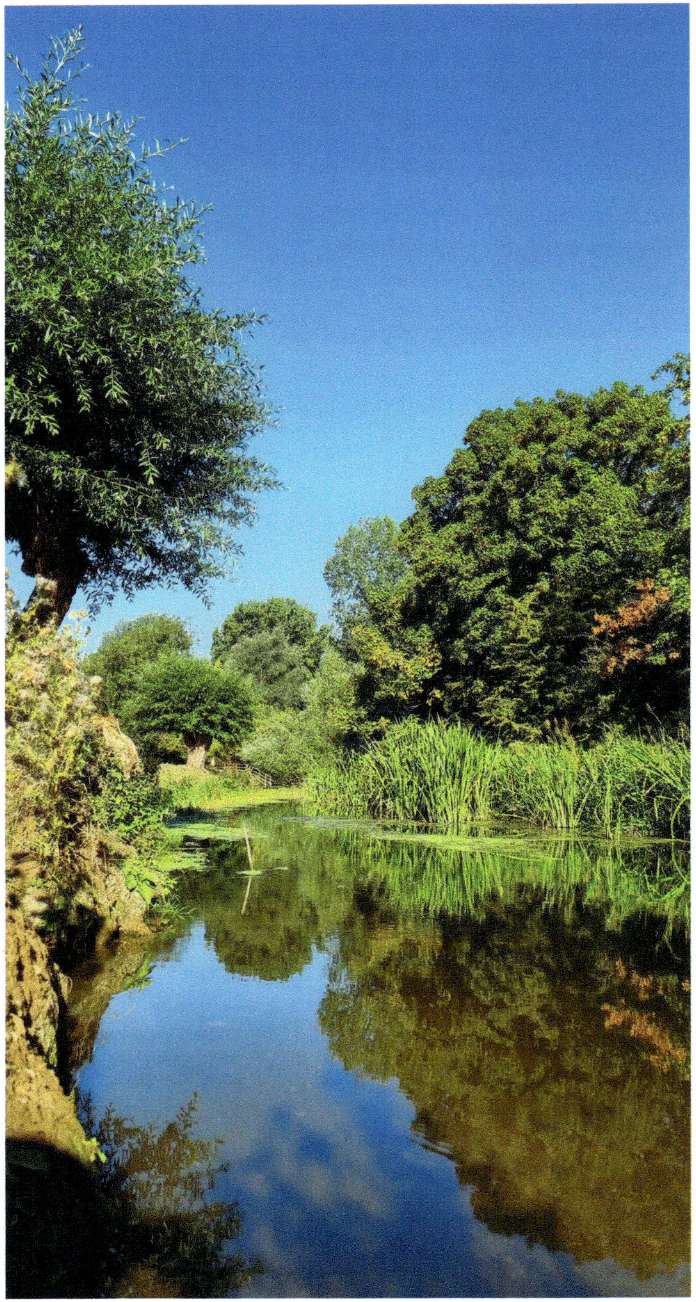

The River

The River Ouse was the ancient boundary between Buckinghamshire and Northamptonshire. It is a slow moving and tranquil river, although prone to flooding in the winter months, thus restricting any development close to the river banks. In medieval times a channel was dug to power the mill.

The river was difficult to cross, especially in winter, and a causeway was constructed, certainly in the 14th century, if not before, and various bequests were made in wills to maintain the bridge.

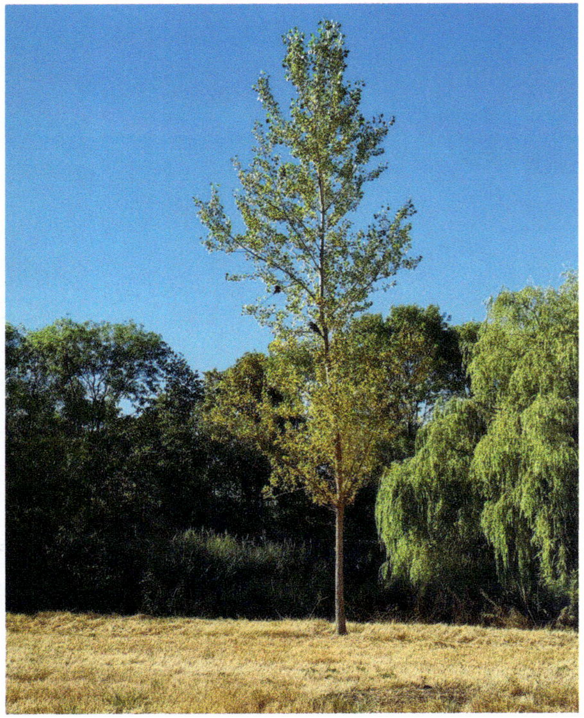

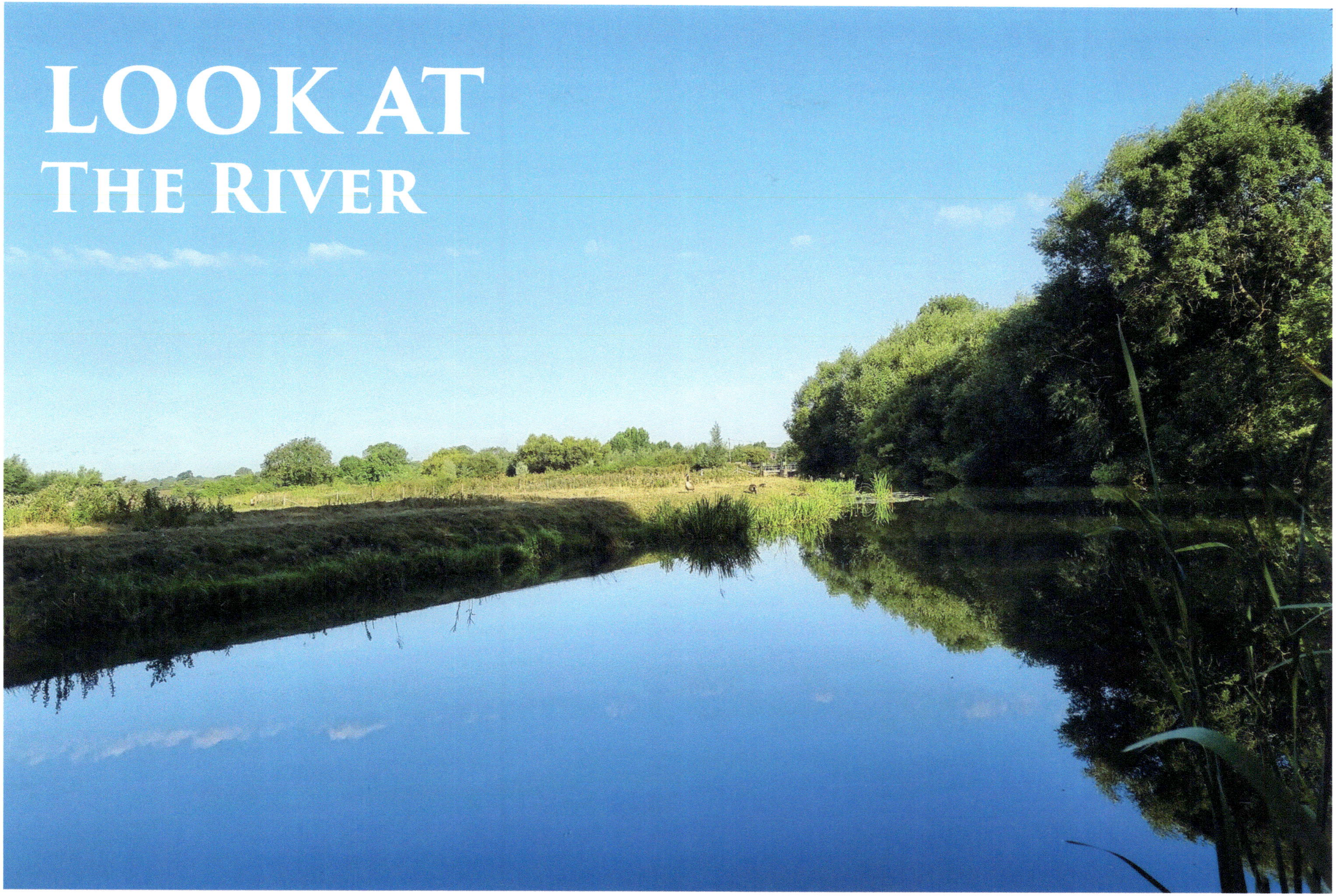

LOOK AT THE RIVER

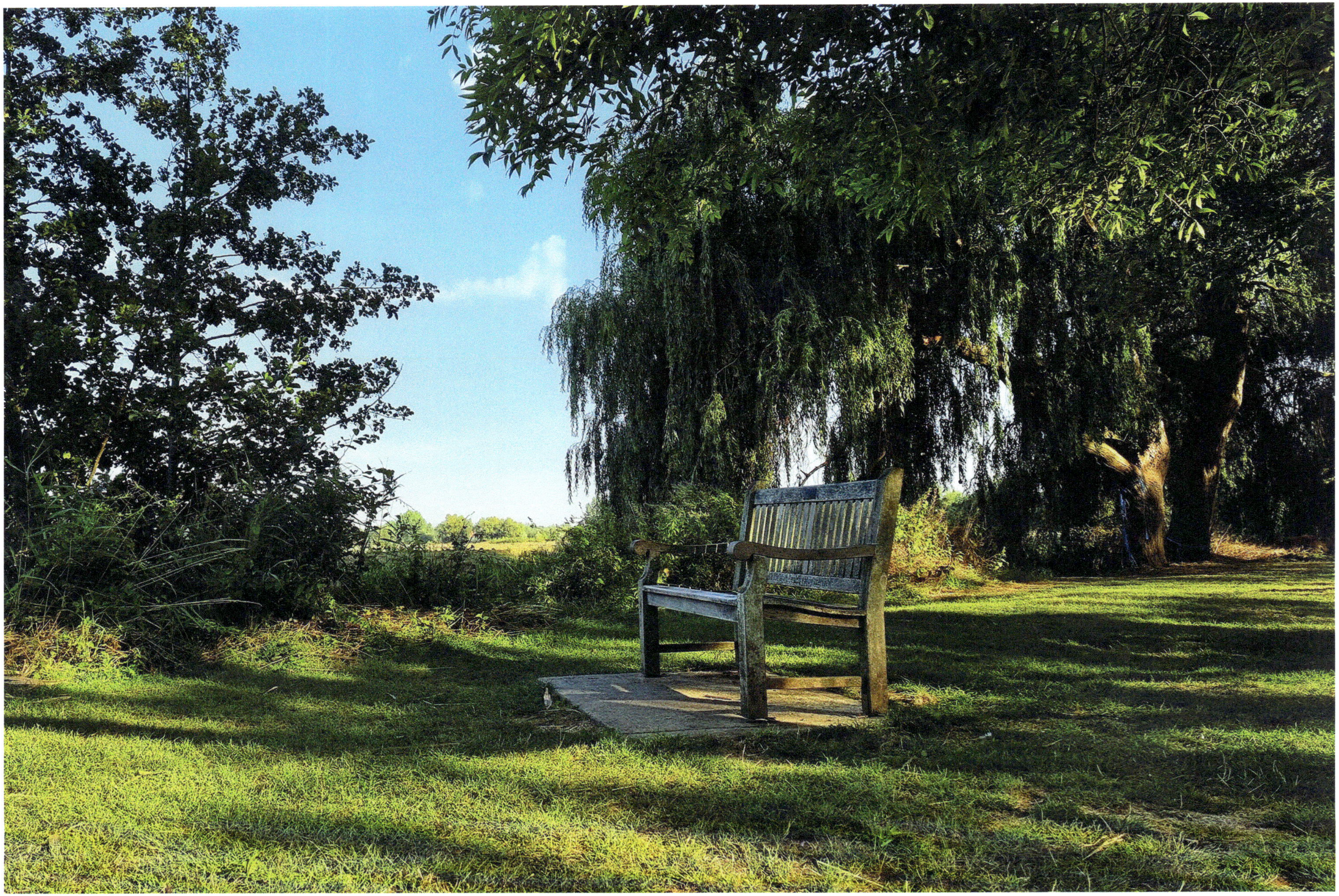

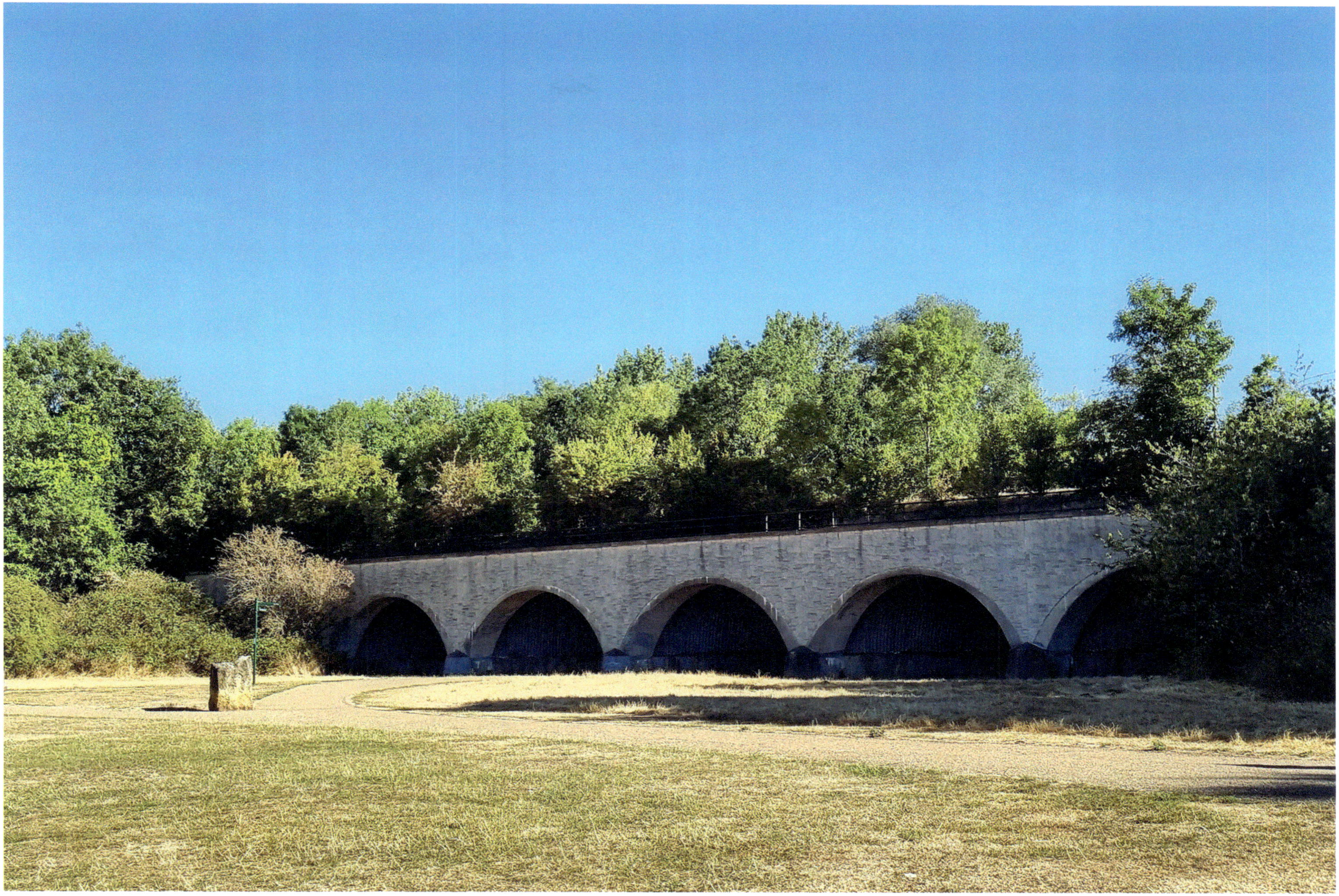

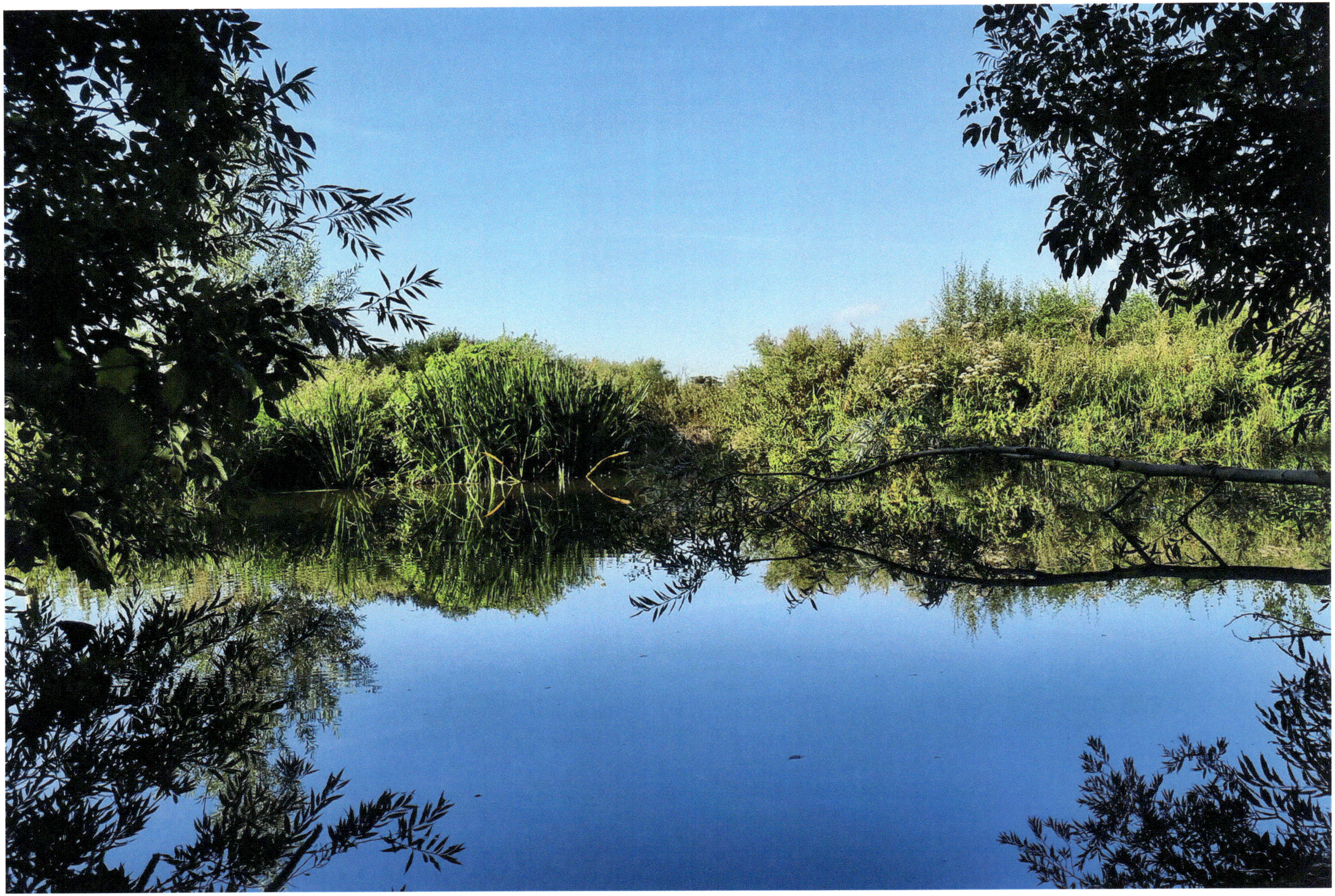

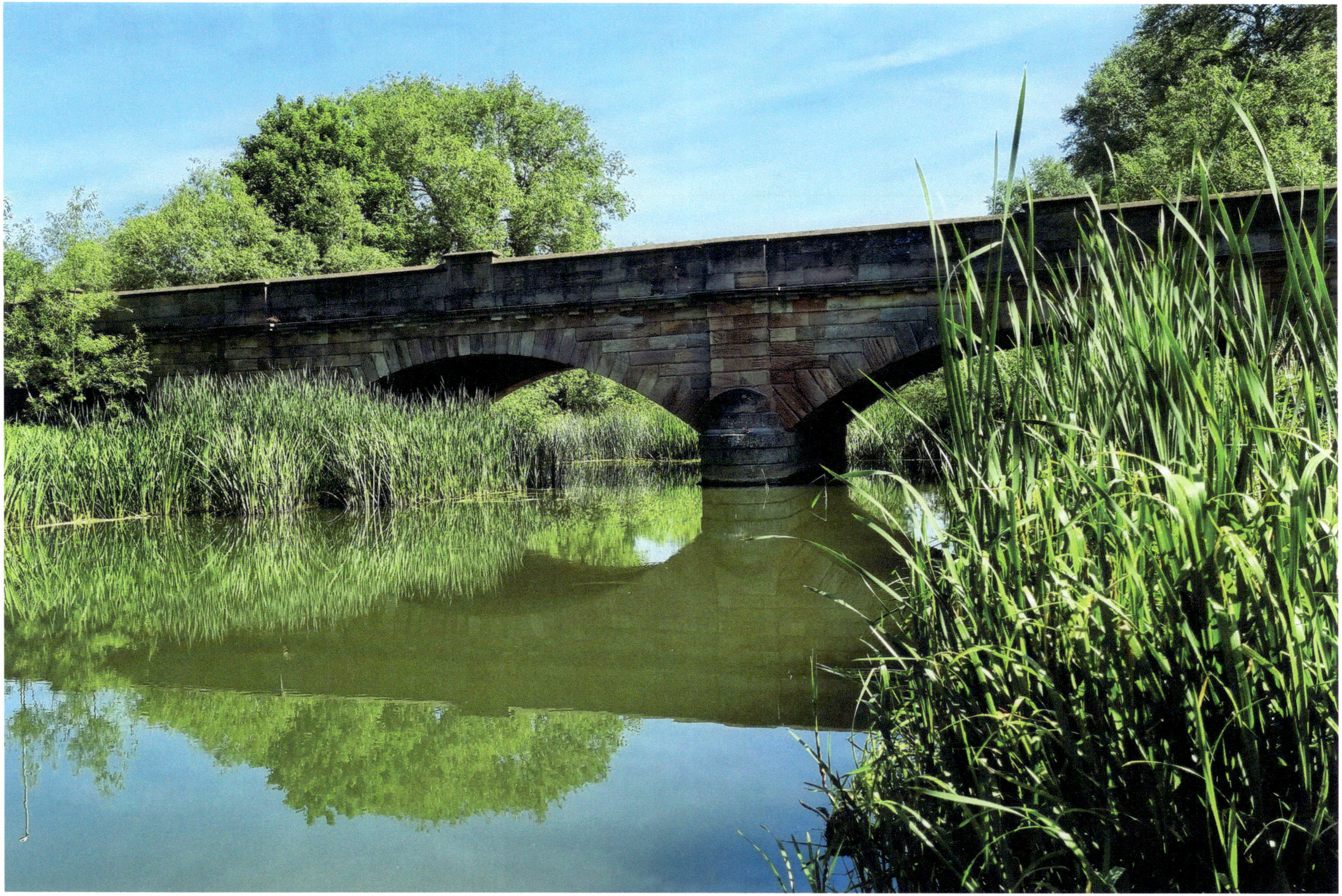

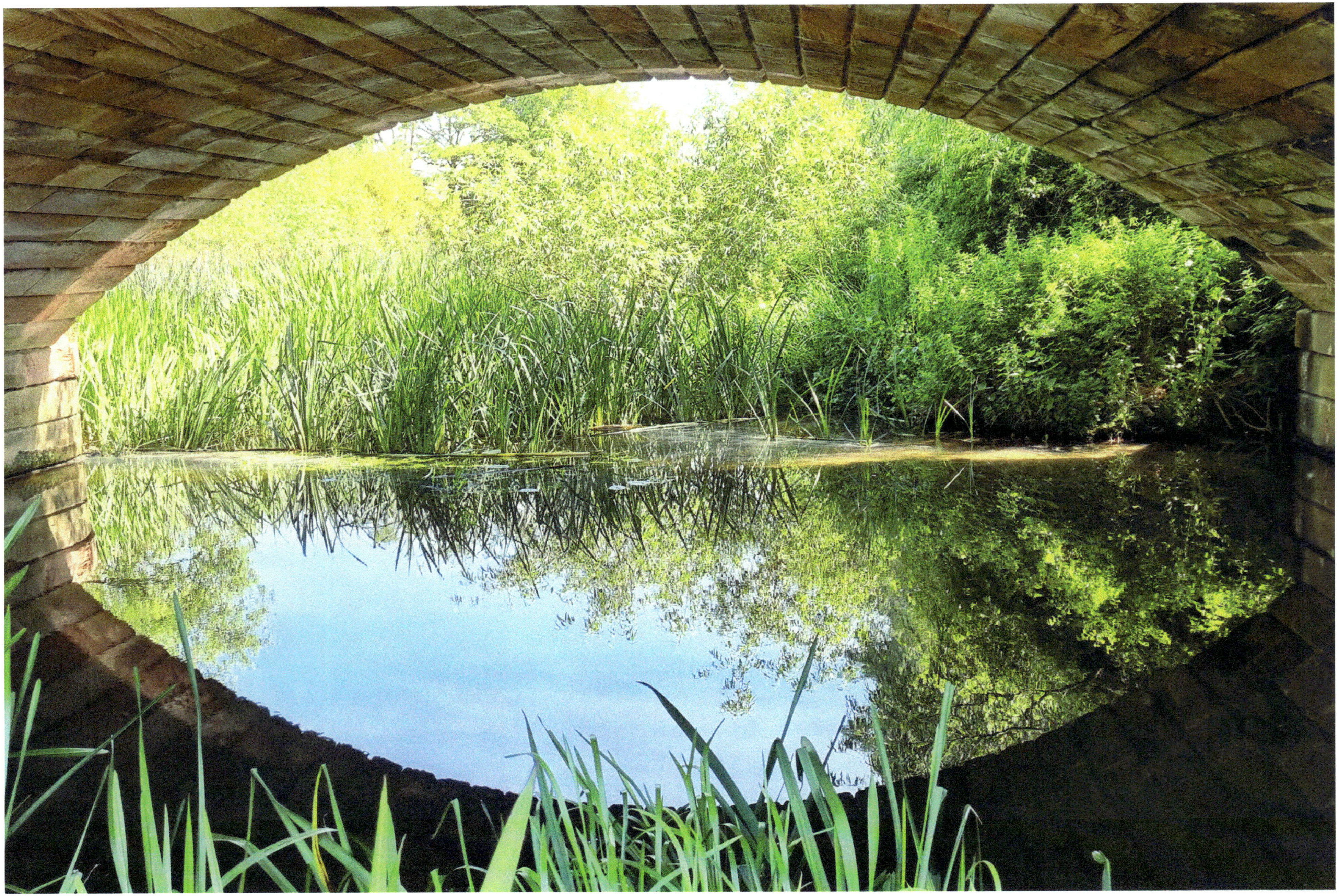

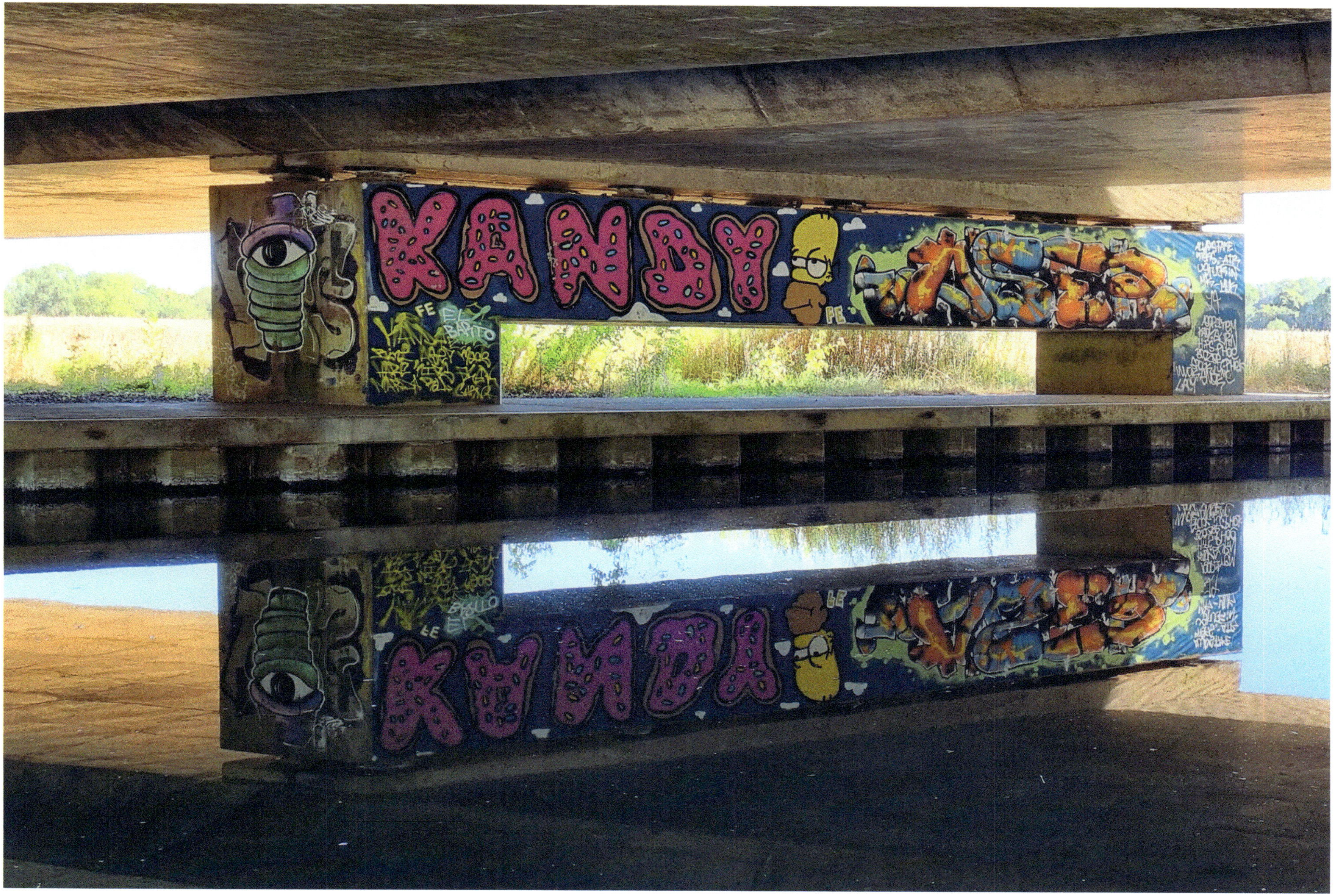
KANDY

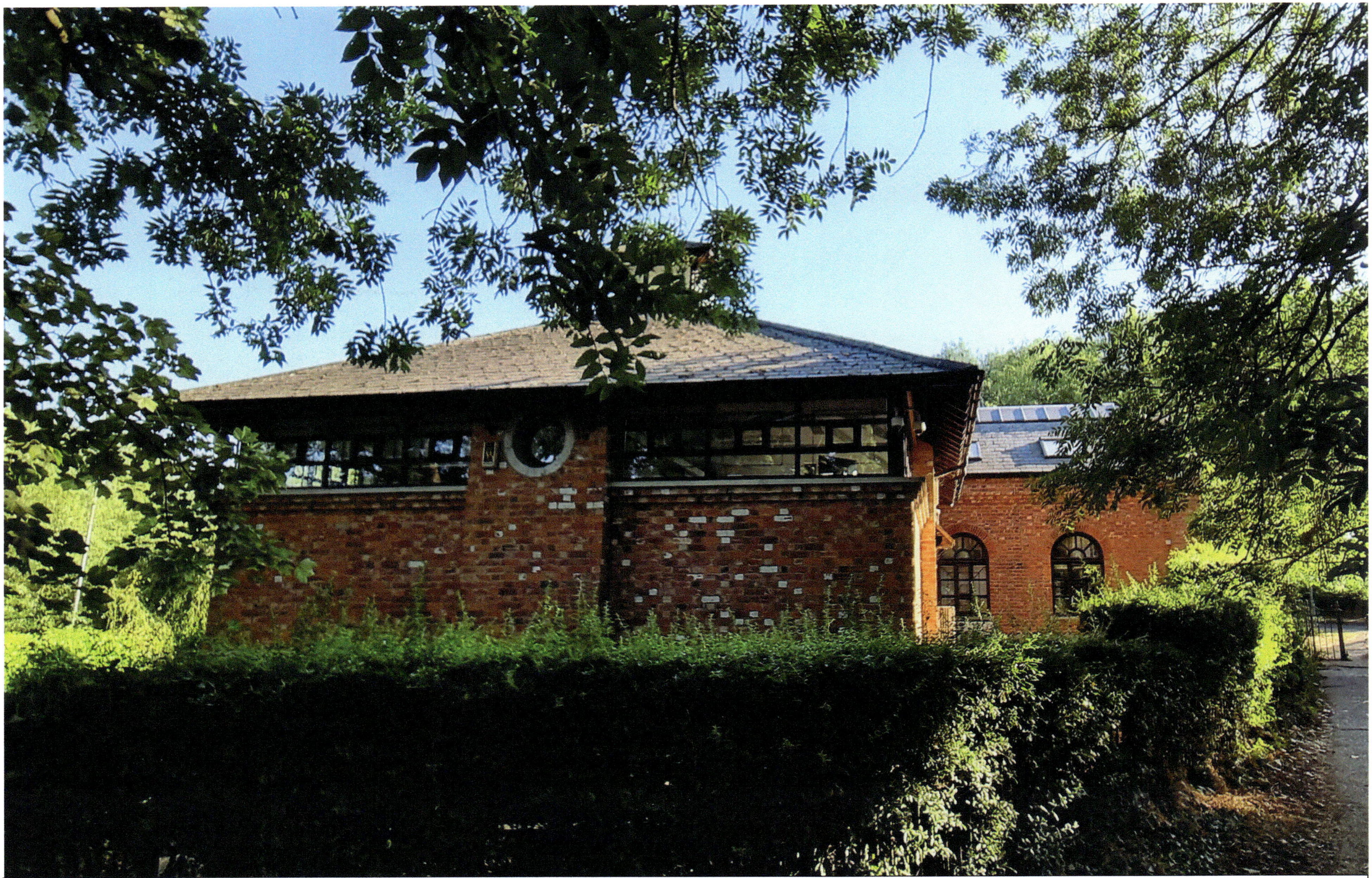

The former pumping station beside the river. It was built in 1884 to supply water to the town but fell into disuse in 1950. Since 1990 the buildings have been adapted for offices.

LOOK AT THE EDGES

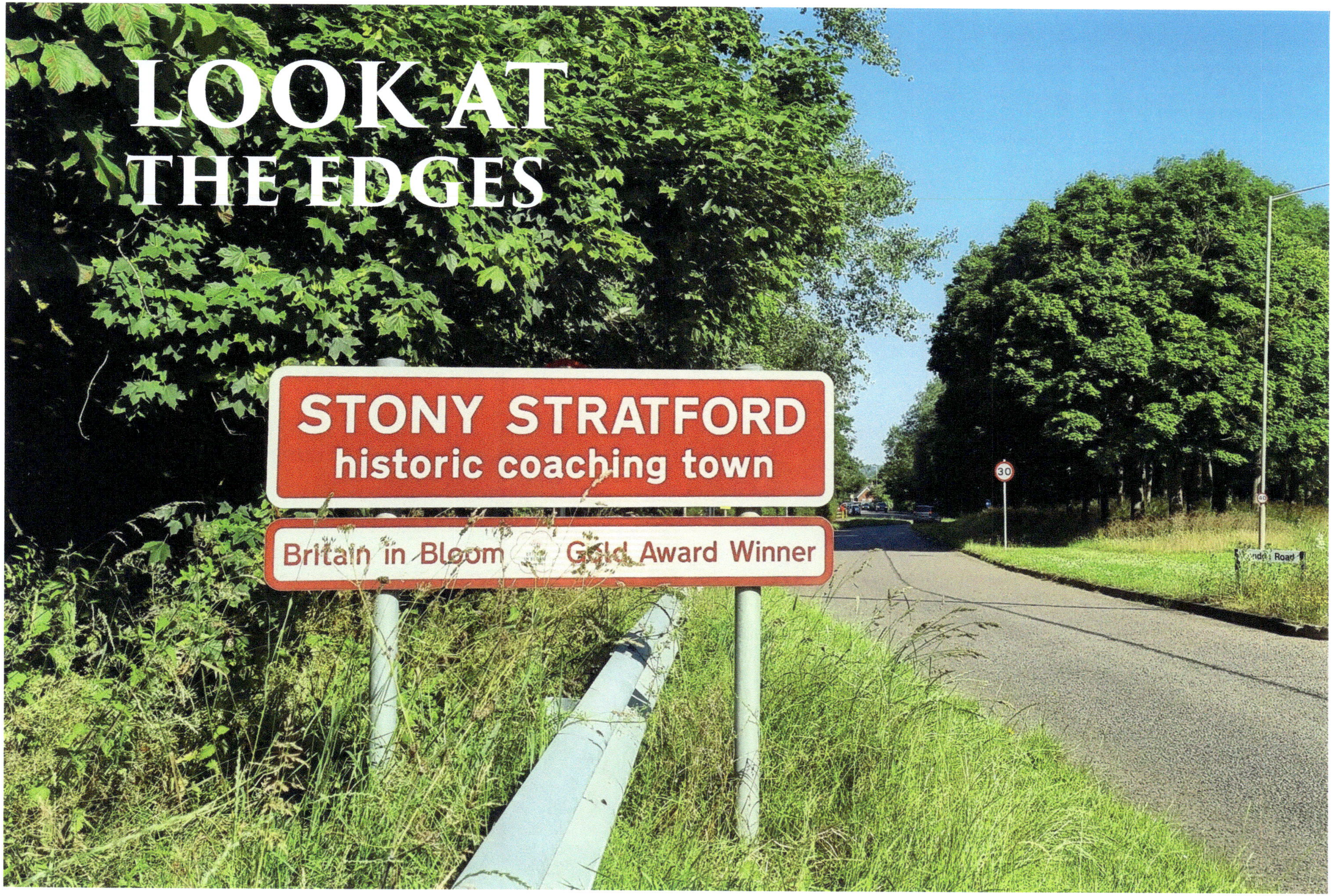

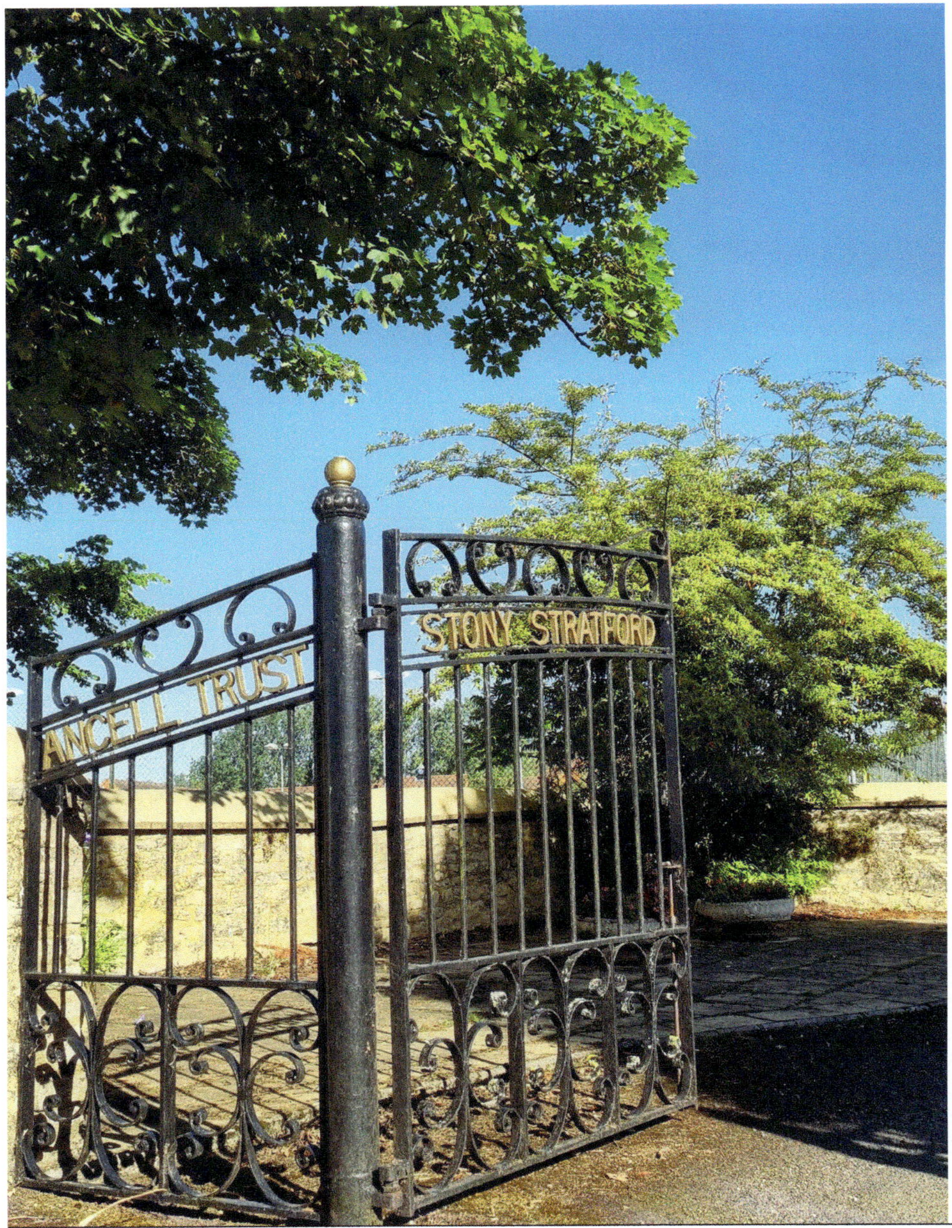

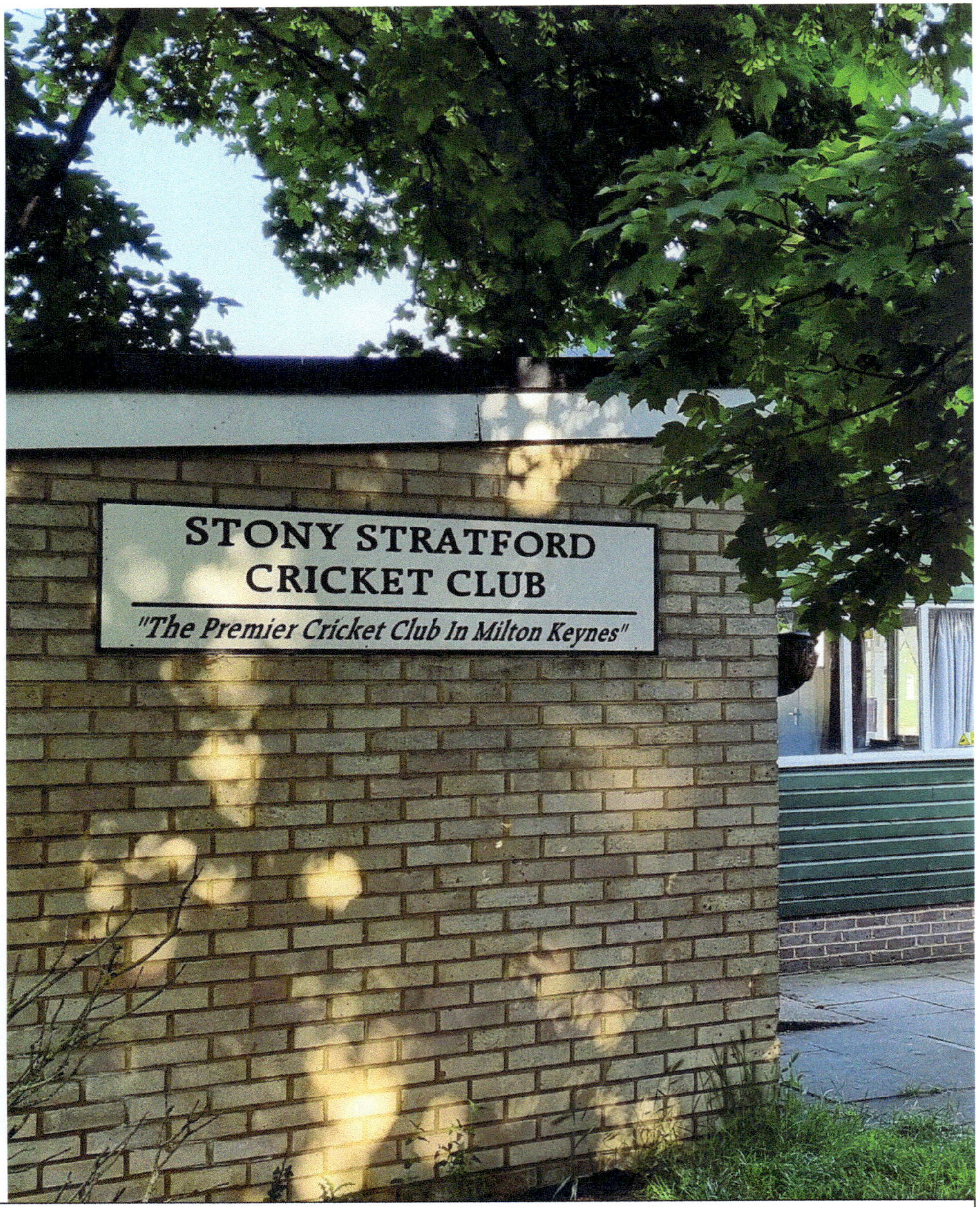

Frederick Ancell, bequeathed his estate, amounting to about £20,000, to a Trust for the benefit of the people of Stony Stratford. In 1920 the Ancell Trust purchased land for tennis courts, a bowling green and a cricket ground.

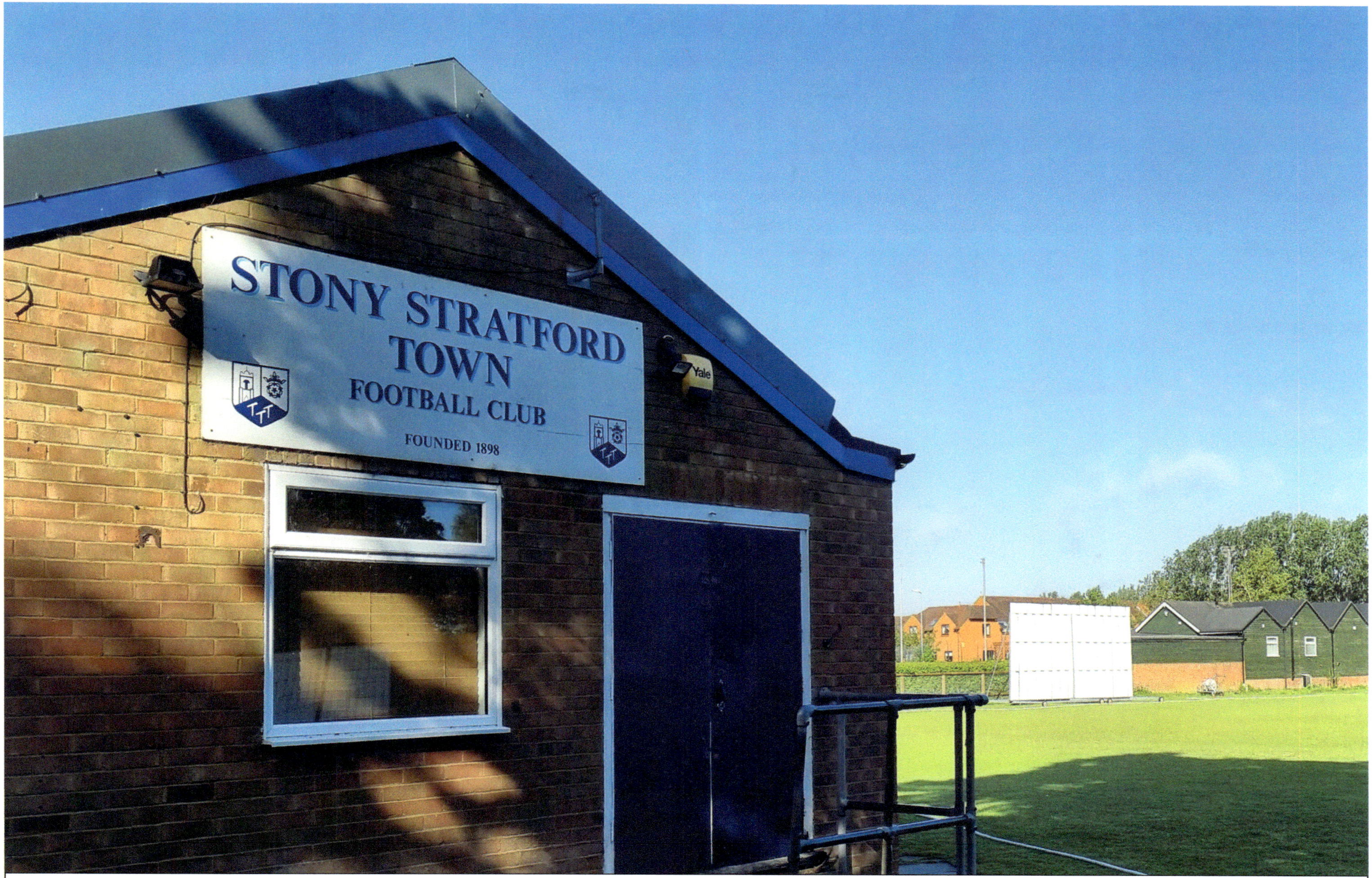

Football and Cricket were played in these fields in the 19th century. Today this formal ground is surrounded by a housing development.

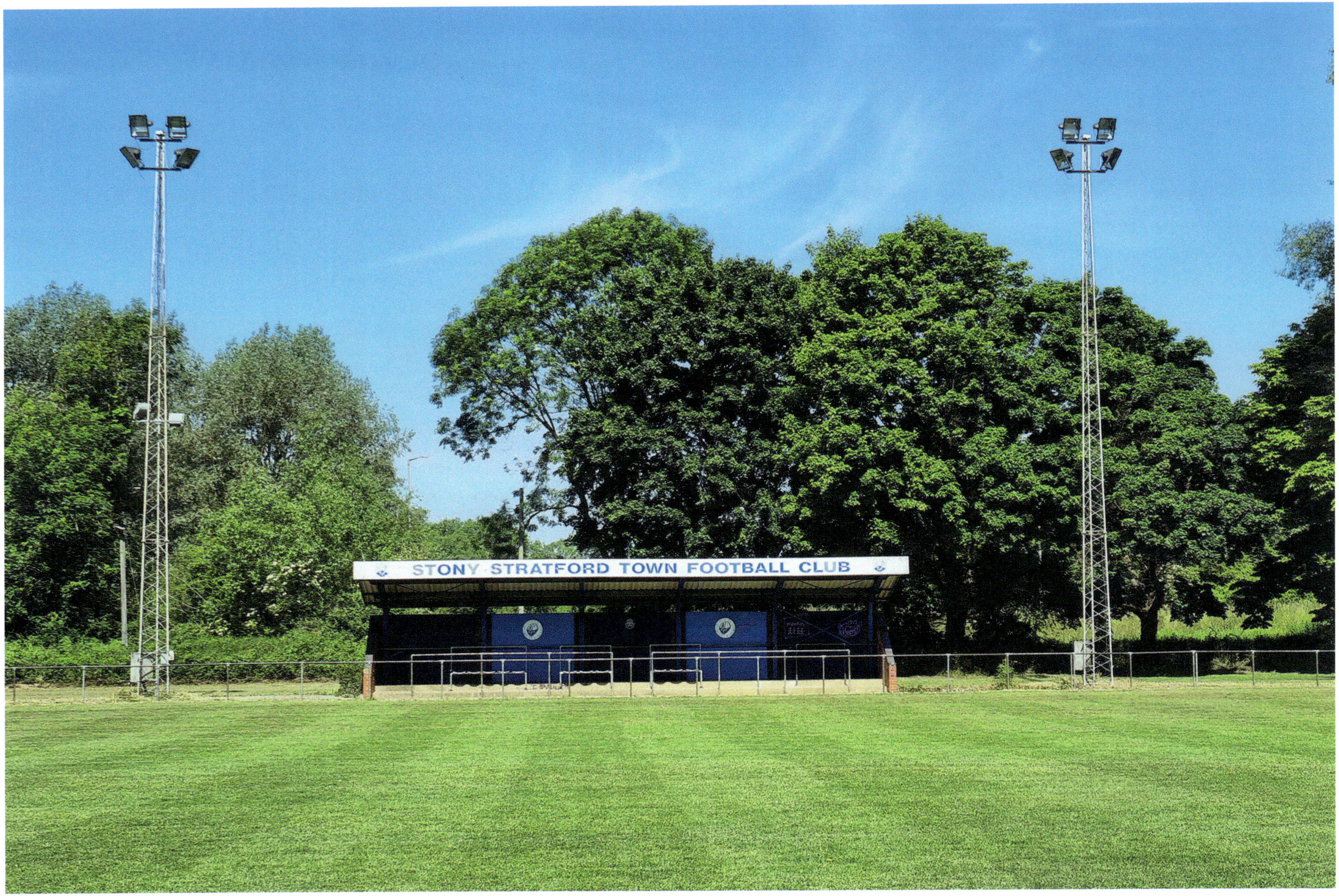
STONY STRATFORD TOWN FOOTBALL CLUB

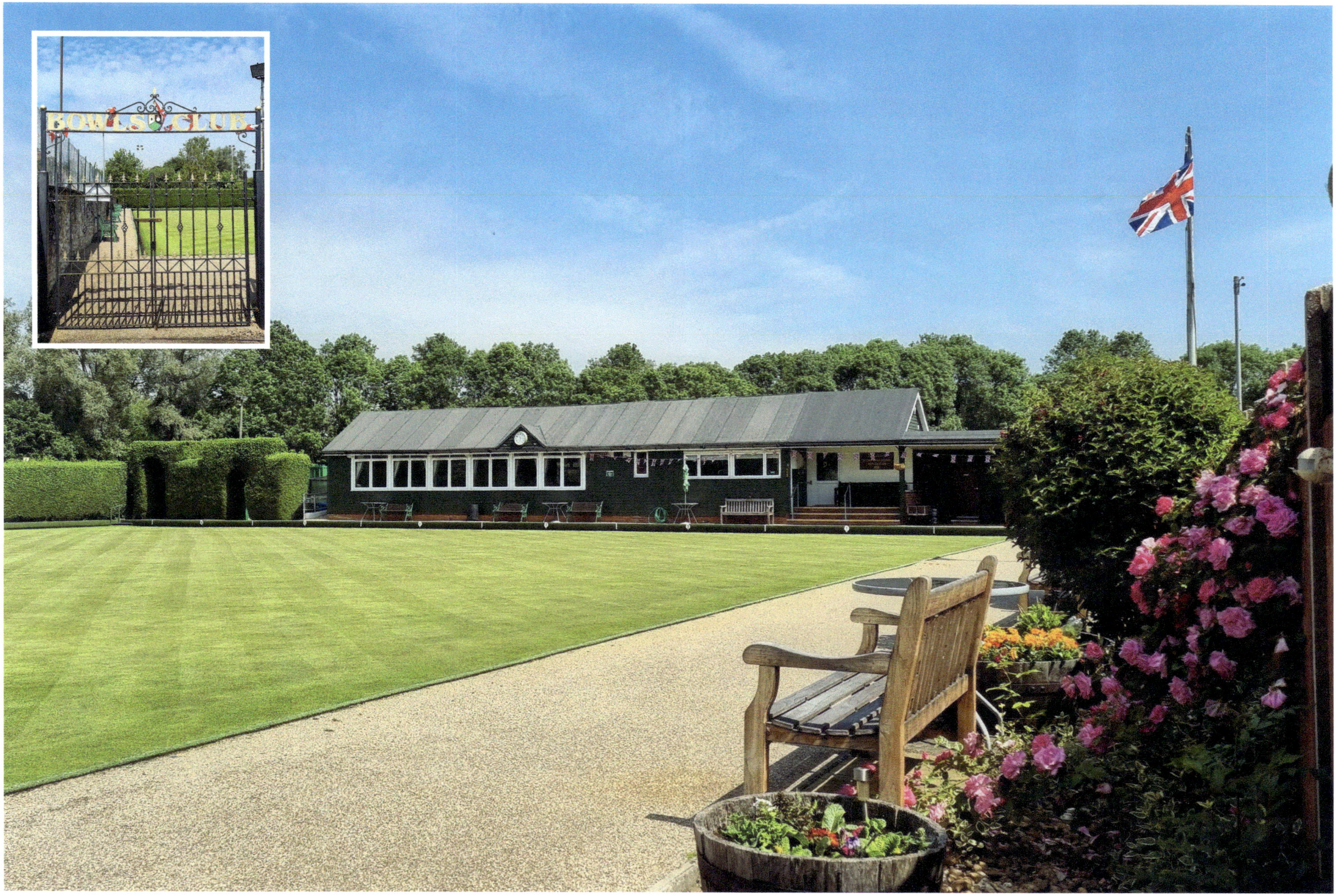
BOWLS CLUB

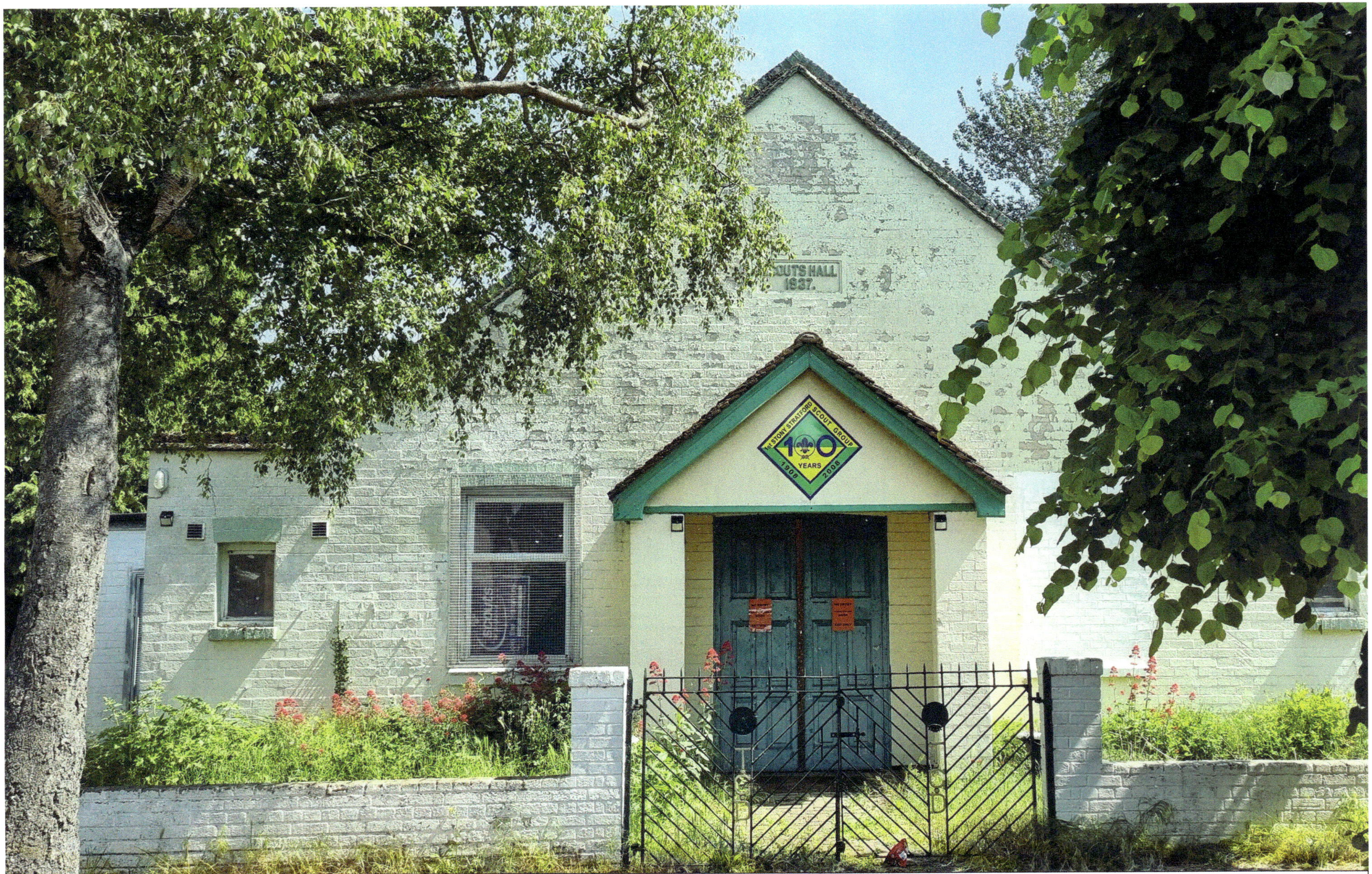

Stony Stratford's Scout Hall on Vicarage Road.

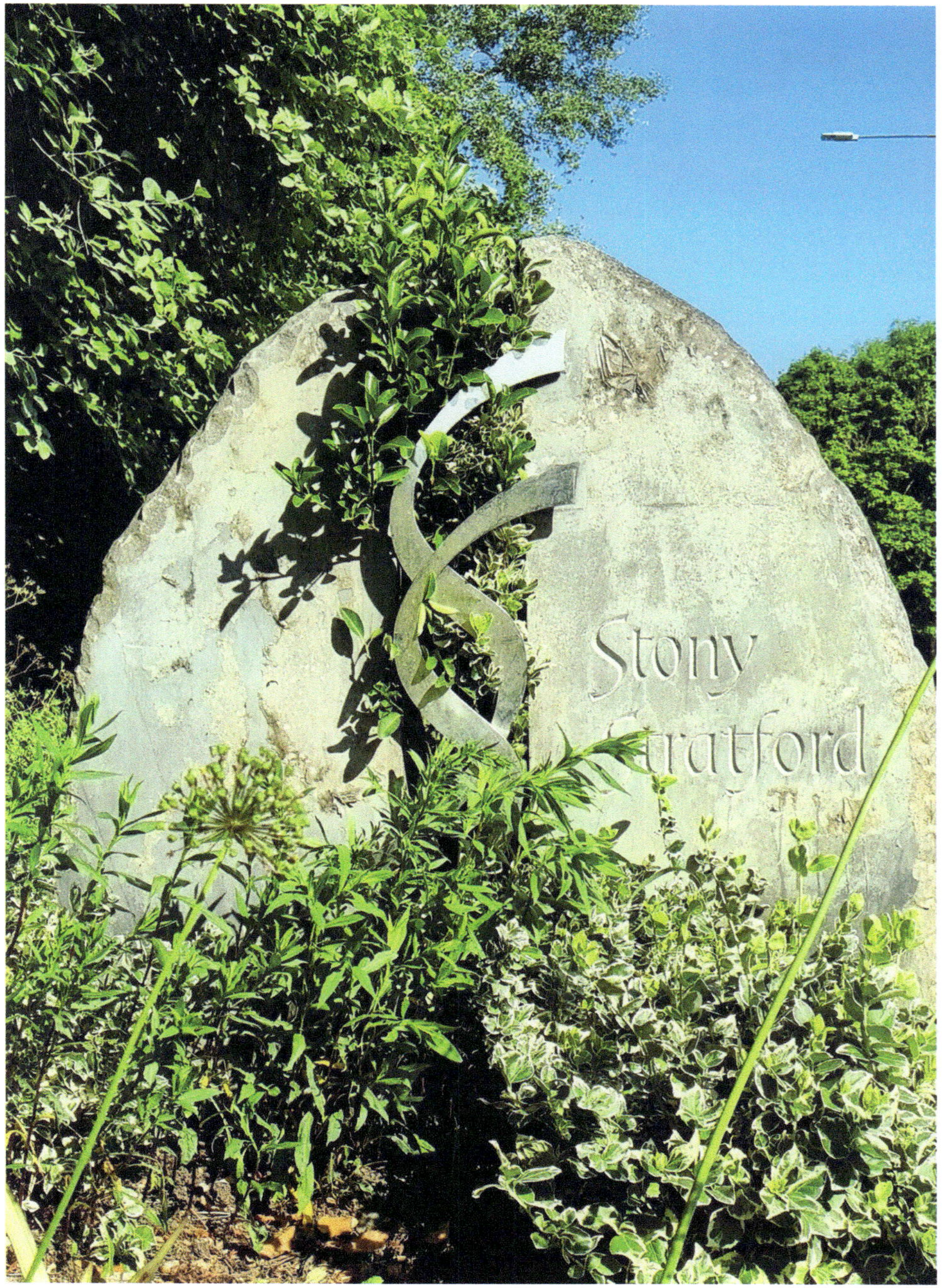
Stony

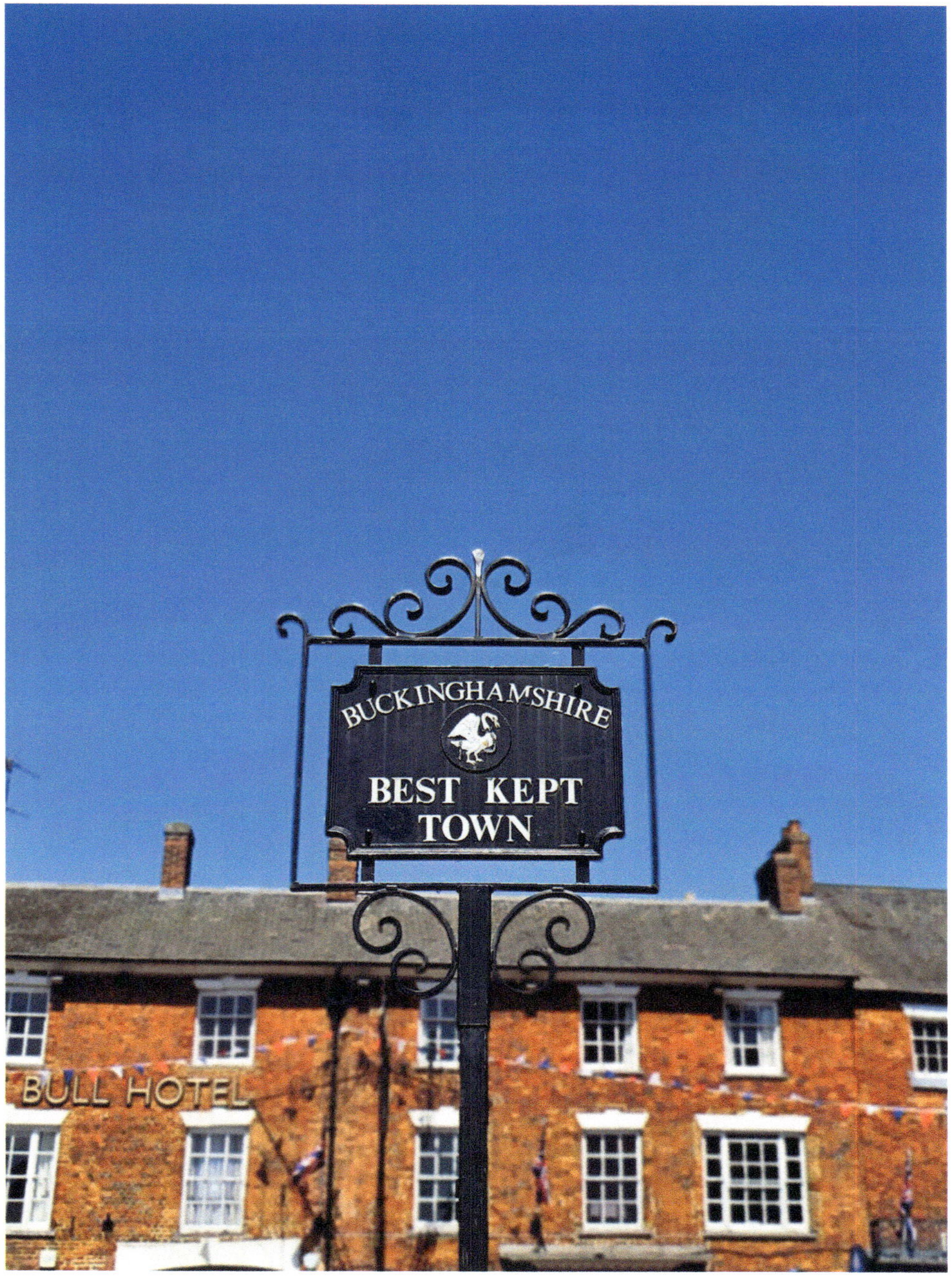
BUCKINGHAMSHIRE
BEST KEPT TOWN
BULL HOTEL

BV - #0019 - 180823 - C208 - 210/297/12 [14] - CB - 9781915166159 - Gloss Lamination